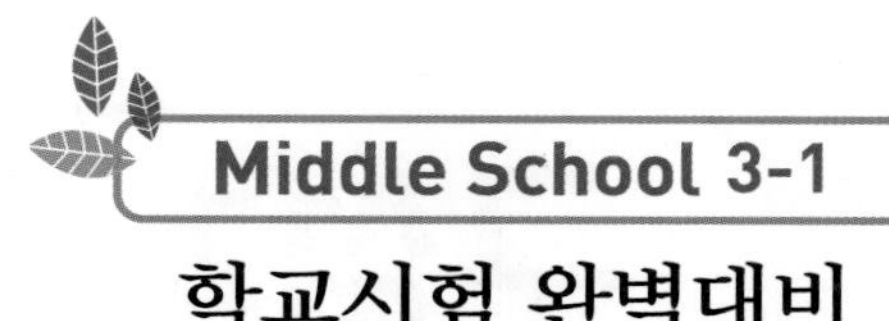

학교시험 완벽대비

적중100 plus

영어 기출문제집

중3

비상 | 김진완

Best Collection

구성과 특징

교과서의 주요 학습 내용을 중심으로 학습 영역별 특성에 맞춰 단계별로 다양한 학습 기회를 제공하여
단원별 학습능력 평가는 물론 중간 및 기말고사 시험 등에 완벽하게 대비할 수 있도록 내용을 구성

Words & Expressions

Step1 Key Words 단원별 핵심 단어 설명 및 풀이
Key Expression 단원별 핵심 숙어 및 관용어 설명
Word Power 반대 또는 비슷한 뜻 단어 배우기
English Dictionary 영어로 배우는 영어 단어

Step2 실력평가 단원별 수시평가 대비 주관식, 객관식 문제풀이

Step3 서술형 대비 학업성취도 및 수행능력평가 대비 서술형 문제풀이

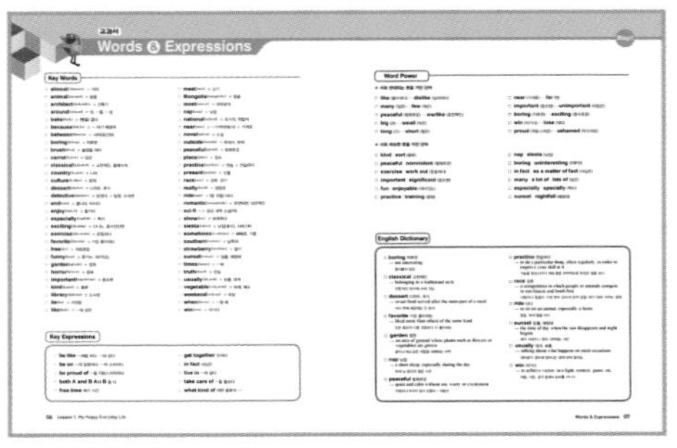

Conversation

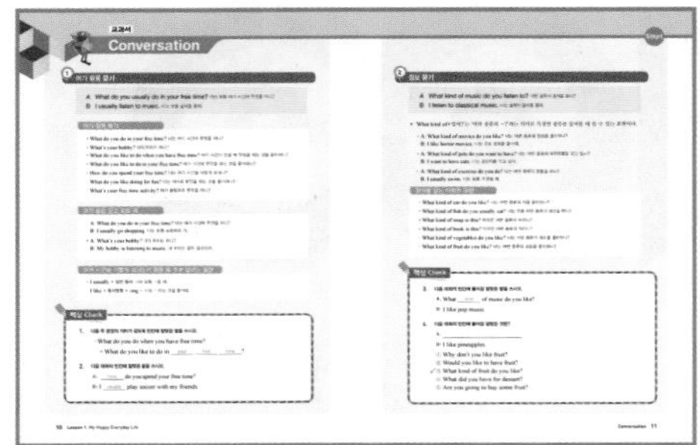

Step1 핵심 의사소통 소통에 필요한 주요 표현 방법 요약
핵심 Check 기본적인 표현 방법 및 활용능력 확인

Step2 대화문 익히기 교과서 대화문 심층 분석 및 확인

Step3 교과서 확인학습 빈칸 채우기를 통한 문장 완성 능력 확인

Step4 기본평가 시험대비 기초 학습 능력 평가

Step5 실력평가 단원별 수시평가 대비 주관식, 객관식 문제풀이

Step6 서술형 대비 학업성취도 및 수행능력평가 대비 서술형 문제풀이

Grammar

Step1 주요 문법 단원별 주요 문법 사항과 예문을 알기 쉽게 설명
핵심 Check 기본 문법사항에 대한 이해 여부 확인

Step2 기본평가 시험대비 기초 학습 능력 평가

Step3 실력평가 단원별 수시평가 대비 주관식, 객관식 문제풀이

Step4 서술형 대비 학업성취도 및 수행능력평가 대비 서술형 문제풀이

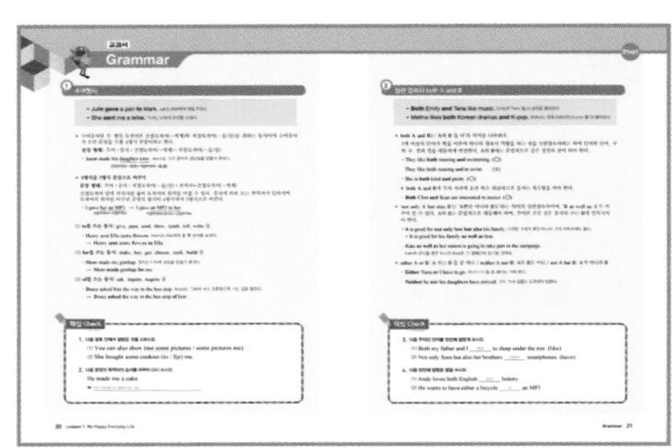

Reading

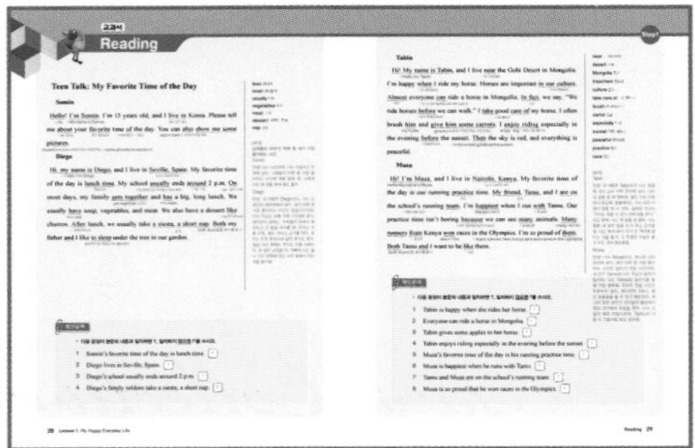

Step1 구문 분석 단원별로 제시된 문장에 대한 구문별 분석과 내용 설명
확인문제 문장에 대한 기본적인 이해와 인지능력 확인

Step2 확인학습A 빈칸 채우기를 통한 문장 완성 능력 확인

Step3 확인학습B 제시된 우리말을 영어로 완성하여 작문 능력 키우기

Step4 실력평가 단원별 수시평가 대비 주관식, 객관식 문제풀이

Step5 서술형 대비 학업성취도 및 수행능력평가 대비 서술형 문제풀이
교과서 구석구석 교과서에 나오는 기타 문장까지 완벽 학습

Composition

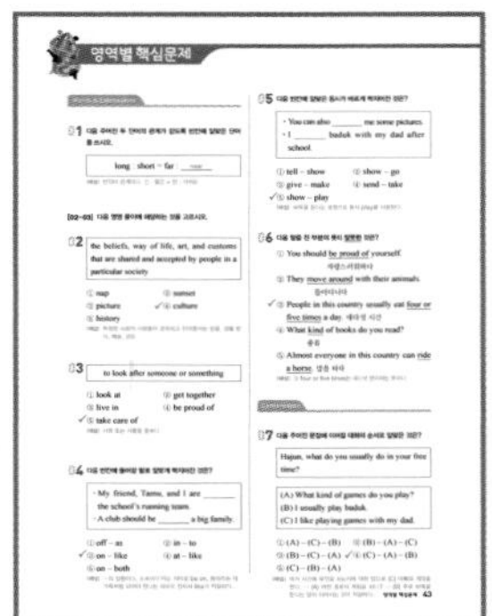

|영역별 핵심문제|

단어 및 어휘, 대화문, 문법, 독해 등 각 영역별 기출문제의 출제 유형을 분석하여 실전에 대비하고 연습할 수 있도록 문제를 배열

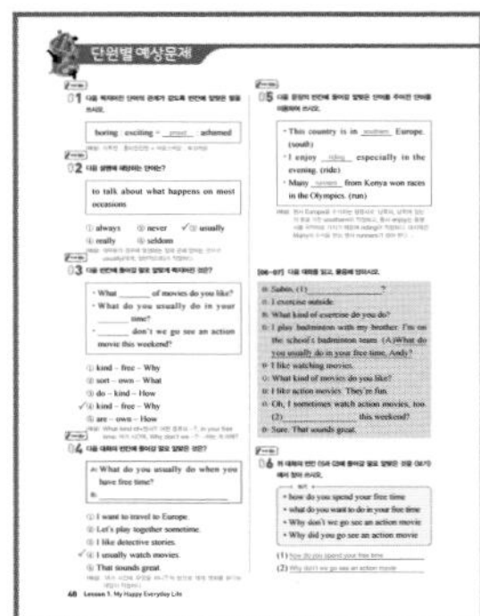

|단원별 예상문제|

기출문제를 분석한 후 새로운 시험 출제 경향을 더하여 새롭게 출제될 수 있는 문제를 포함하여 시험에 완벽하게 대비할 수 있도록 준비

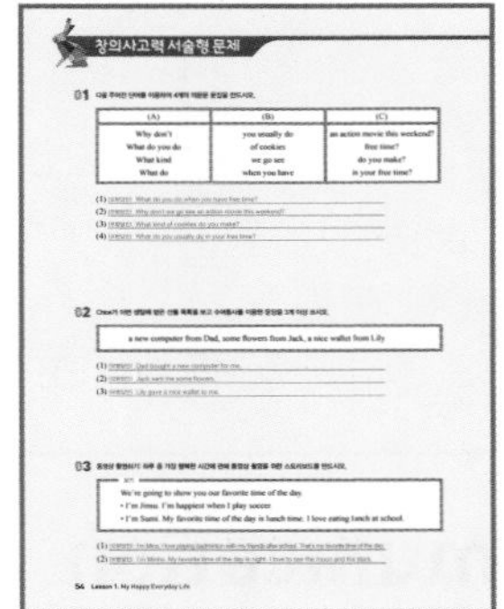

|서술형 실전 및 창의사고력 문제|

학교 시험에서 점차 늘어나는 서술형 시험에 집중 대비하고 고득점을 취득하는데 만전을 기하기 위한 학습 코너

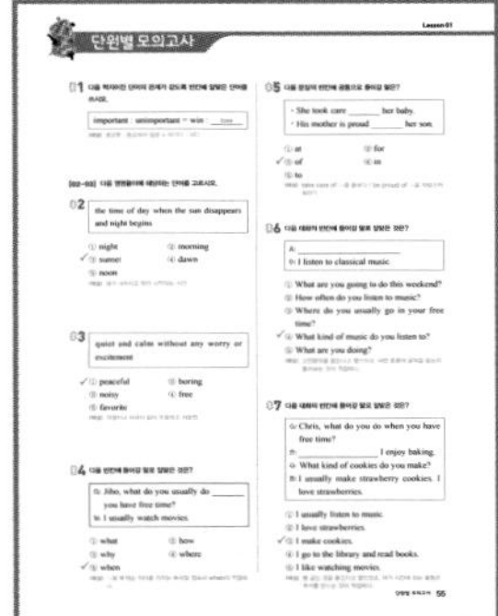

|단원별 모의고사|

영역별, 단계별 학습을 모두 마친 후 실전 연습을 위한 모의고사

교과서 파헤치기

- **단어Test1~3** 영어 단어 우리말 쓰기, 우리말을 영어 단어로 쓰기, 영영풀이에 해당하는 단어와 우리말 쓰기
- **대화문Test1~2** 대화문 빈칸 완성 및 전체 대화문 쓰기
- **본문Test1~5** 빈칸 완성, 우리말 쓰기, 문장 배열연습, 영어 작문하기 복습 등 단계별 반복 학습을 통해 교과서 지문에 대한 완벽한 습득
- **구석구석지문Test1~2** 지문 빈칸 완성 및 전문 영어로 쓰기

이책의 차례

Contents

Lesson **1**

The Art of Communication

의사소통 기능

- 화가 난 감정 표현하기
  A: How come you don't talk much with Anna these days?
  B: Well, I'm upset about an argument we had.
- 오해 지적하기
  A: I got cold feet.
  B: That's too bad. How did you get a cold?
  A: No. That's not what I meant. I meant I got scared.

언어 형식

- 관계대명사 what
  Starting a sentence with "I" can help him focus on **what** he feels.
- 관계부사
  Calli should pick a time **when** her mom is ready to listen.

교과서

Words & Expressions

Key Words

□ **actually**[ǽktʃuəli] (부) 사실은
□ **argue**[ɑ́:rgju:] (동) 말다툼하다, 언쟁하다
□ **argument**[ɑ́:rgjumənt] (명) 주장, 논쟁
□ **careless**[kɛ́ərlis] (형) 부주의한, 조심성 없는
□ **clip**[klip] (명) 동영상
□ **concentrate**[kɑ́nsəntrèit] (동) 집중하다
□ **consider**[kənsídər] (동) 배려하다, 고려하다
□ **copy**[kɑ́pi] (동) 복사하다, 모방하다
□ **demand**[dimǽnd] (명) 요구
□ **detail**[ditéil] (명) 구체적 내용, 자세한 내용
□ **direct**[dirékt] (형) 직접적인, 단도직입적인
□ **disappointed**[dìsəpɔ́intid] (형) 실망한, 낙담한
□ **diving**[dáiviŋ] (명) 다이빙, 잠수
□ **effectively**[iféktivli] (부) 효과적으로
□ **exam**[igzǽm] (명) 시험
□ **express**[ikspés] (동) 표현하다, 나타내다
□ **feeling**[fí:liŋ] (명) 감정, 느낌
□ **finish**[fíniʃ] (동) 마치다, 끝나다
□ **focus**[fóukəs] (동) 집중하다
□ **go**[gou] (동) (일의 진행이 어떻게) 되어가다, 진전되다
□ **hairstyle**[hɛ́ərstàil] (명) 머리 모양, 헤어 스타일
□ **helpful**[hélpəl] (형) 도움이 되는, 유용한
□ **hide**[haid] (동) 숨기다, 감추다
□ **instead**[instéd] (부) 그 대신에
□ **long face** 우울한 얼굴
□ **loudly**[láudi] (부) 크게, 큰 소리로
□ **mad**[mæd] (형) 화난
□ **mean**[mi:n] (형) 못된, 심술궂은 (동) 의미하다
□ **pick**[pik] (동) 선택하다, 고르다
□ **prepare**[pripɛ́ər] (동) 준비하다
□ **prevent**[privént] (동) 막다, 예방하다
□ **probably**[prɑ́bəbli] (부) 아마도
□ **quiet**[kwáiət] (형) 조용한, 소리 없는
□ **reason**[rí:zn] (명) 이유
□ **relationship**[riléiʃənʃip] (명) 관계
□ **request**[rikwést] (명) 요청
□ **scared**[skɛərd] (형) 두려워하는, 겁먹은
□ **seem**[si:m] (동) (~처럼) 보이다, ~인 듯하다
□ **simply**[símpli] (부) 단순히
□ **solve**[sɑlv] (동) 해결하다
□ **somewhere**[sʌ́mhwɛər] (부) 어딘가에
□ **text message** 문자 메세지
□ **tired**[taiərd] (형) 피곤한
□ **trouble**[trʌ́bl] (명) 고민, 문제
□ **uncomfortable**[ənkʌ́mfərtbəl] (형) 불편한
□ **unhappy**[ənhǽpi] (형) 불만스러운, 불행한
□ **upset**[ʌ́pset] (형) 화난, 기분 나쁜

Key Expressions

□ **be busy 동사ing** ~하느라 바쁘다
□ **be ready to 동사원형** ~할 준비가 되다
□ **be upset about** ~ ~에 대해서 화가 나다
□ **cut** ~ **off** ~을 중단시키다, ~을 잘라내다
□ **end up 동사ing** 결국 ~하게 되다
□ **find out** 발견하다, 알아보다
□ **first of all** 먼저, 무엇보다도
□ **focus on** ~에 집중하다
□ **free from** ~이 없는
□ **get a good grade** 좋은 성적을 얻다
□ **get cold feet** 긴장하다, 겁을 먹다
□ **go on a trip** 여행가다
□ **have a look** (한번) 보다
□ **have one's head in the clouds** 공상에 잠겨 있다
□ **hit the books** 공부하다
□ **how come** 어찌하여, 왜
□ **in class** 수업 중에
□ **in the middle of** ~의 도중에, ~의 중간에
□ **keep** ~ **in mind** ~을 명심하다, 마음에 담아 두다
□ **keep 동사ing** ~을 계속하다, 반복하다
□ **let one's hair down** 느긋하게 쉬다
□ **let the cat out of the bag** 비밀을 누설하다
□ **make a demand** 요구하다
□ **on time** 정시에, 제때에
□ **order+사람+around** ~에게 자꾸 이래라저래라 하다
□ **point the finger at** ~을 비난하다
□ **put on** 입다
□ **B rather than A** A라기보다는 B
□ **stop 동사ing** ~을 그만두다, ~하지 않게 되다
□ **stressed out** 스트레스로 지친, 스트레스가 쌓인
□ **such as** ~와 같은
□ **take a look at** ~을 보다
□ **tend to 동사원형** ~하는 경향이 있다
□ **these days** 요즘
□ **try to 동사원형** ~을 노력하다
□ **work out** 해결하다

Word Power

※ **접두사** pre-, un-

- **pre**-는 '미리, 먼저(**before**, **beforehand**)'의 의미가 있는 접두사이다.
  - □ **pre**(= **before**) + **vent** → **prevent**(막다, 예방하다)
  - □ **pre**(= **before**) + **pare** → **prepare**(준비하다)
  - □ **pre**(= **before**) + **view**(보다) → **preview**(미리 보기; (시사, 시연 등을) 보다)
  - □ **pre**(= **before**) + **caution**(주의) → **precaution**(조심, 예방책)
- **un**-은 '부정(**not**)'의 의미가 있는 접두사이다.
  - □ **un**(= **not**) + **comfortable**(편안한) → **uncomfortable**(불편한)
  - □ **un**(= **not**) + **certain**(확실한) → **uncertain**(불확실한)
  - □ **un**(= **not**) + **friendly**(친절한) → **unfriendly**(불친절한)
  - □ **un**(= **not**) + **fortunate**(운이 좋은) → **unfortunate**(불운한, 불행한)
  - □ **un**(= **not**) + **fair**(공평한) → **unfair**(불공평한)
  - □ **un**(= **not**) + **likely**(~할 것 같은) → **unlikely**(~할 것 같지 않은)

English Dictionary

□ **argument** 주장, 논쟁
→ an angry disagreement between people
사람들 간에 격심한 의견의 불일치

□ **concentrate** 집중하다
→ to give all your attention to the thing you are doing
지금 하고 있는 일에 모든 주의를 기울이다

□ **consider** 배려하다, 고려하다
→ to think about someone's feelings or reactions
어떤 사람의 감정이나 반응을 생각하다

□ **detail** 구체적 내용, 자세한 내용
→ one of many small facts or pieces of information relating to a situation
어떤 상황에 관계된 많은 사소한 사실들이나 정보 중의 하나

□ **disappointed** 실망한, 낙담한
→ unhappy because something that you hoped for or expected did not happen or because someone or something was not as good as you expected
바라거나 예상했던 것이 일어나지 않았거나, 예상했던 누군가나 어떤 것이 예상만큼 좋지 않아 행복하지 않은

□ **express** 표현하다, 나타내다
→ to tell someone about a feeling, opinion, or goal by speaking or writing about something
어떤 것에 관해 말하거나 써서 감정, 의견 또는 목표를 말하다

□ **helpful** 도움이 되는, 유용한
→ useful, or providing help
유용한 또는 도움을 제공하는

□ **hide** 숨기다, 감추다
→ to put something in a place so that no one can find or see it
아무도 어떤 것을 찾거나 볼 수 없게 그것을 어떤 장소에 놓다

□ **long face** 우울한 얼굴
→ a sad, disappointed, or serious expression on someone's face 슬프거나, 실망한 또는 심각한 누군가의 얼굴 표정

□ **mad** 화난
→ angry 화난

□ **mean** 못된, 심술궂은
→ cruel or not kind 잔인한 또는 친절하지 않은

□ **reason** 이유
→ a fact, situation, or intention that explains why something happened, why someone did something, or why something is true
왜 어떤 일이 발생했는지, 왜 누군가가 그것을 행했는지, 또는 왜 그것이 진짜인지 등에 대해 설명하는 사실이나 상황 또는 의도

□ **scared** 두려워하는, 겁먹은
→ frightened, or worried
겁먹은, 또는 걱정하는

□ **solve** 해결하다
→ to find a solution to something that is causing difficulties
어려움을 유발하는 어떤 것에 대한 해결책을 찾다

□ **unhappy** 불만스러운, 불행한
→ feeling sad or upset
슬프거나 속상한

□ **upset** 화난, 기분 나쁜
→ very sad, worried, or angry about something
무언가에 대해 매우 슬프거나, 걱정하는, 또는 화가 나는

[01~02] 다음 밑줄 친 부분과 의미가 가장 가까운 것을 고르시오.

01

Why are you so upset?

① tired ② scared ③ angry
④ serious ⑤ disappointed

02

Stop talking and concentrate on your work.

① try ② bring ③ make
④ focus ⑤ enjoy

03 중요 다음 밑줄 친 mean이 (3)의 뜻으로 사용된 것을 고르시오.

(1) to have a particular meaning
(2) to intend to do something or intend that someone else should do something
(3) cruel or not kind

① I didn't mean to upset you.
② It's a mean trick to play on a friend.
③ What I mean is that I don't feel alone anymore.
④ I've been meaning to ask you if you want to come for a meal next week.
⑤ Oh, yeah! I see what you mean.

04 다음 빈칸에 공통으로 들어갈 말을 고르시오.

• By the end of the semester I was totally stressed ________.
• I'm glad everything worked ________ fine.

① on ② in ③ out
④ off ⑤ for

05 중요 다음 주어진 표현과 이에 대한 뜻이 바르게 연결되지 않은 것을 고르시오.

① get cold feet – become too nervous and worried to do something
② have one's head in the clouds – very happy because something very good has happened
③ hit the books – study
④ let one's hair down – relax and enjoy and do not worry about behaving correctly
⑤ let the cat out of the bag – reveal something secret or private

06 다음 빈칸 (A)~(C)에 알맞은 말로 짝지어진 것을 고르시오.

• Mike is free (A)____ cares.
• We may never find (B)______ the truth about what happened.
• First (C)_____ all, clean the surface that you are going to paint.

	(A)	(B)	(C)
①	for	– out	– of
②	for	– of	– to
③	from	– out	– of
④	from	– of	– for
⑤	from	– out	– to

07 다음 빈칸에 알맞은 단어를 고르시오. (2개)

This week, let's ________ a look at some of the characteristics of successful people.

① take ② do ③ give
④ bring ⑤ have

01 다음 밑줄 친 부분의 쓰임이 자연스럽지 않은 것을 찾아 고치시오.

ⓐ I'm busy studying for the midterm exam.
ⓑ We're not ready leaving yet!
ⓒ Customers end up to spend more money than they should.

➡ ____________________

____

중요 **[02~03]** 두 문장이 같은 의미가 되도록 빈칸을 채우시오. (철자가 주어진 경우 주어진 철자로 시작할 것)

02

Sally got scared at the last moment.
= Sally got c_______ f_______ at the last moment.

03

Remember that when you come to make your decision.
= K_______ that _______ _______ when you come to make your decision.

04 다음 우리말에 맞도록 빈칸에 알맞은 말을 쓰시오. (철자가 주어진 경우 주어진 철자로 시작할 것)

(1) 그 시스템이 지역 사회에 서비스를 더 효과적으로 줄 수 있다.
➡ The system can deliver services to local communities more _______.

(2) 그녀는 Tom이 그녀의 편지에 답장을 하지 않아서 낙담했다.
➡ She was d_______ that Tom never replied to her letter.

(3) 그는 뛰어가서 덤불 뒤로 숨었다.
➡ He ran and _______ behind a bush.

(4) 왜 그토록 많은 사람이 병에 걸리는지에 대한 이유는 여전히 명확하지 않다.
➡ The r_______ why so many people caught the disease is still not clear.

05 다음 빈칸에 공통으로 들어갈 말을 쓰시오.

• It has been a _______ cold winter this year.
• He has had a _______ face ever since he failed the examination.

고난이도 **06** 다음 우리말에 맞게 주어진 단어를 바르게 배열하시오.

(1) 많은 나무들은 홍수로부터 산사태를 막는 데 도움을 줄 수 있다.
(from, trees, prevent, flood, many, landslides, to, can, help)
➡ ____________________

(2) 그녀는 당신이 당신의 문제를 해결하도록 도와줄 수 있다.
(solve, she, problem, can, your, you, help)
➡ ____________________

(3) 이 코트는 입기에 불편하다.
(this, to, uncomfortable, is, wear, coat)
➡ ____________________

(4) 그 대신에 너의 노력이 중요하다.
(your, important, instead, is, effort)
➡ ____________________

교과서

Conversation

1 화가 난 감정 표현하기

A: How come you don't talk much with Anna these days? 요즘 너는 왜 Anna와 별로 말을 하지 않니?

B: Well, I'm upset about an argument we had. 음, 나는 우리가 한 논쟁에 화가 나.

■ 'be upset about ~'은 '~에 대해서 화가 난다'라는 의미로 화가 난 감정을 나타낼 때 사용하는 표현이다. 화남을 나타내는 또 다른 표현으로는 'be angry at[with] ~', 'be mad at ~', 'be upset with[because of] ~', 등이 있다. 그 외에도 'be annoyed with ~', 'can't stand ~', 'make me mad' 등을 이용해 화가 났음을 나타낼 수 있다.

화남을 나타내는 표현

- I am upset about[with, because of] ~. (나는 ~에 대해[~에게, ~ 때문에] 화가 나.)
- I am mad at ~.
- I am angry at[with] ~.
- I am annoyed with[by] ~.
- I can't stand ~. (나는 ~을 참을 수 없어.)
- ~ make(s) me mad. (~은 나를 화나게 해.)

핵심 Check

1. 다음 우리말과 일치하도록 주어진 단어를 배열하여 문장을 쓰시오.

A: ____________________ (friend, upset, I, with, am, my)
(나는 내 친구 때문에 화가 나.)
B: What's the matter?
A: She forgot my birthday.

2. 다음 대화의 순서를 바르게 배열하시오.

(A) She tore my book.
(B) What did she do?
(C) I'm upset with my dog.

➡ ____________________

3. 다음 문장과 같은 의미가 되도록 주어진 단어를 이용하여 쓰시오.

I'm very upset because of my sisters.

➡ ____________________ (angry)

2 오해 지적하기

A: I got cold feet. 난 겁이 났어.
B: That's too bad. How did you get a cold? 그거 안 됐구나. 어떻게 감기에 걸렸니?
A: No. That's not what I meant. I meant I got scared. 아니. 그런 뜻이 아니야. 내가 겁먹었다는 뜻이야.

- That's not what I meant.는 '그런 뜻이 아니야.'라는 의미이며, 상대방이 자신의 말의 의도를 오해할 때 정정하기 위해 쓰는 표현이다. 'That's not what I meant to say.', 'I didn't mean to say that.', 'I hope there is no misunderstanding.' 등도 비슷한 표현이다.
- 오해를 지적하는 말을 하고, 이어서 'I mean[meant] ~.'을 이용해서 자신이 의도했던 바를 얘기할 수 있다.

오해 지적하기

- That's not what I meant. (내가 의미한 것은 그게 아니야.)
- I didn't mean to say that. (그 말을 하려던 것이 아니었어.)
- I'm afraid you don't understand what I'm saying. (제가 하는 말을 이해 못 하시는 것 같군요.)

핵심 Check

4. 다음 우리말과 일치하도록 빈칸에 알맞은 말을 쓰시오.

A: Let's hit the road!
B: Why do you want to hit the road?
A: ____________________ __________ let's start our trip.
(그런 뜻이 아니야. 그건 여행을 시작하자는 말이야.)

5. 다음 대화의 순서를 바르게 배열하시오.

(A) That's not what I meant to say. I mean you should eat more vegetables.
(B) You are eating too much meat.
(C) Do you think I should not eat meat?

➡ ______________________________

Conversation 교과서 대화문 익히기

Listen & Talk 1 A-1

M: Sally, ❶how come you don't talk much with Anna these days?
W: Well, ❷I'm upset about an argument we had.
M: Why are you upset?
W: She ❸kept cutting me off ❹in the middle of my sentences, so I ❺got mad. We ❻argued and I ❼stopped talking to her.
M: Oh, ❽I'm sorry to hear that.

M: Sally야, 요즘에 왜 Anna와 많이 대화를 하지 않니?
W: 음, 나는 우리가 한 논쟁 때문에 화가 나.
M: 왜 화가 난 거야?
W: 그녀가 계속해서 내가 말을 하고 있는 도중에 끊어서 화가 났어. 우리는 논쟁을 했고, 나는 그녀와 이야기를 하지 않았어.
M: 오, 그거 유감이구나.

❶ how come을 이용해서 상대방에게 이유를 물을 수 있다. 이때 그 다음에 '주어+동사'의 어순이 이어지는 것에 주의해야 한다. talk with ~: ~와 대화를 나누다 much는 '많이'의 뜻인 부사로 talk를 수식하고 있다. these days: 요즘
❷ upset: 화난, 기분 나쁜 'an argument'와 'we had' 사이에는 목적격 관계대명사 which 또는 that이 생략되어 있다.
❸ keep은 동명사를 목적어로 가지는 동사이다. cut ~ off: ~을 중단시키다, ~을 잘라내다
❹ in the middle of: ~ 도중에, ~ 중간에
❺ got 대신에 was나 felt를 대신 사용할 수 있다.
❻ argue: 말다툼하다, 언쟁하다
❼ stop 동사ing: ~을 그만두다, ~하지 않게 되다
❽ 'I'm sorry to hear that.'은 '유감이구나.'란 의미로 상대방에게 유감이나 동정을 표현할 때 사용하는 표현이다.

Check(√) True or False

(1) Sally doesn't talk to Anna these days. T ☐ F ☐
(2) The man is asking why Sally is happy. T ☐ F ☐

Listen & Talk 2 A-2

W: Did you finally ❶go diving yesterday, Nick?
M: ❷Actually, I ❸got cold feet, Mina.
W: That's too bad. How did you get a cold?
M: No, Mina. ❹That's not what I meant. ❺I meant that I got scared, so I didn't dive.

W: Nick, 어제 드디어 다이빙하러 갔니?
M: 미나야, 사실 난 겁이 났어.
W: 그거 안 됐구나. 어떻게 감기에 걸렸니?
M: 아니, 미나야. 그건 그런 뜻이 아니야. 내가 겁을 먹어서 다이빙을 안 했다는 뜻이야.

❶ go diving: 다이빙하러 가다
❷ actually: 사실은
❸ 'get cold feet' 또는 'have cold feet'은 어떤 것에 대해 긴장하거나(nervous), 걱정하거나(worried), 겁이 날 때(scared) 쓰는 표현이다.
❹ 'That's not what I meant.'는 '그런 뜻이 아니야.'라는 의미이며, 상대방이 자신의 말을 오해할 때 이를 정정하기 위해 쓰는 표현이다.
❺ meant 다음의 that은 접속사로 meant의 목적어를 이끌어 주는 역할을 하고 있으며 생략할 수 있다.

Check(√) True or False

(3) Nick caught a cold. T ☐ F ☐
(4) Nick didn't dive yesterday. T ☐ F ☐

Listen & Talk 1 A-2

W: How is your science homework ❶going?
M: Not good. ❷I'm upset about my science group.
W: ❸What's wrong?
M: The group members only speak and never listen. I don't think that we can finish the homework ❹on time.
W: That's too bad.

W: 너의 과학 숙제는 어떻게 되어 가고 있니?
M: 좋지 않아. 나는 나의 과학 그룹에 화가 나.
W: 뭐가 문제인데?
M: 그룹 구성원들이 말만 하고 전혀 듣지 않아. 나는 우리가 숙제를 제시간에 끝낼 수 있을 거라고 생각하지 않아.
W: 그것 참 안 됐구나.

❶ go: (일의 진행이 어떻게) 되어가다, 진전되다
❷ upset: 화난, 기분 나쁜 어떤 상황에 대하여 화가 났음을 말할 때 'I'm upset about+명사'로 표현할 수 있다.
❸ 'What's wrong?'은 상대방의 슬픔이나 불만족, 실망의 원인에 관해 물을 때 사용되는 표현으로 'What's the matter to you?', 'What's the problem?', 'Is there anything wrong?', 'What happened to you?' 등으로 바꿔 쓸 수 있다.
❹ on time: 정시에, 제때에

Check(√) True or False

(5) The man is pleased with his science group. T ☐ F ☐

(6) The man hopes that his science group can finish the homework on time. T ☐ F ☐

Listen & Talk 1 B

M: ❶Why the long face, Julie?
W: I ❷got angry at my sister yesterday and said some mean things to her.
M: Oh, why were you angry?
W: I was really tired and I wanted to sleep. But she ❸was talking loudly on the phone. I was really upset about that.
M: I see. And you two ❹haven't worked it out yet?
W: No, not yet. I want to say I'm sorry that I was mean to her, but I don't know ❺how.
M: ❻Why don't you write her a note or send her a text message?
W: Hmm, that's a good idea. Thanks.

M: 왜 그렇게 우울한 얼굴이니, Julie?
W: 어제 내 여동생한테 화가 나서 그녀에게 심술궂은 말을 했어.
M: 오, 왜 화가 났니?
W: 정말 피곤해서 자고 싶었어. 하지만 여동생은 전화로 큰 소리로 이야기하고 있었어. 나는 그것에 대해 정말 화가 났어.
M: 그렇구나. 그리고 너희 둘은 아직 화해하지 않았니?
W: 아니, 아직이야. 내가 여동생에게 심술궂게 굴어서 미안하다고 말하고 싶지만, 방법을 모르겠어.
M: 그녀에게 편지를 쓰거나 문자 메시지를 보내는 게 어때?
W: 음, 좋은 생각이야. 고마워.

❶ the long face: 우울한 얼굴
❷ 'get angry at'을 이용해서 화남을 나타내고 있다. 같은 의미의 표현들로 'be upset at[with, because of]', 'be mad at', 'be angry at[with]', 'be annoyed with[by]' 등이 있다.
❸ talk on the phone: 전화로 얘기하다 loudly는 동사인 talk를 수식하고 있다.
❹ work out: 해결하다 'you two haven't worked it out yet?'의 문장에서 동사는 현재완료의 '완료 용법'으로 사용되고 있다.
❺ how 다음에 'to say I'm sorry that I was mean to her'가 생략되어 있다.
❻ 'Why don't you ~?'는 '~하는 건 어때?'의 의미로 상대방에게 충고할 때 쓰는 표현이다. 'You'd better ~.', 'I advice you to ~.' 등으로 바꿔 쓸 수 있다.

Check(√) True or False

(7) Julie said some mean things to her sister yesterday. T ☐ F ☐

(8) Julie and her sister have worked it out already. T ☐ F ☐

Listen & Talk 1 Get Ready

A: Why do you ❶look so unhappy?

B: I'm upset about Roy. He always copies me.

A: ❷Don't take it so hard.

❶ look+형용사: ~하게 보이다 unhappy: 불만스러운, 불행한

❷ 'Don't take it so hard.'는 상대방의 안 좋은 상황을 위로하는 표현으로 'Don't feel so bad.'로 사용할 수 있다.

Listen & Talk 2 Get Ready

A: Don't ❶let the cat out of the bag about Clara's surprise party.

B: A cat? I don't have a cat.

A: ❷That's not what I meant. ❸Keep her party a secret.

❶ let the cat out of the bag: 비밀을 누설하다

❷ That's not what I meant.: 그건 그런 뜻이 아니야.

❸ keep이 5형식으로 사용되어 her party가 목적어, a secret이 목적격 보어이다.

Listen & Talk 2 A-1

W: Mr. Brown, I want to ❶get a good grade in English. What should I do?

M: Well, Sujin, ❷you should concentrate in class, ❸first of all. I see you often ❹have your head in the clouds.

W: Clouds? I can't see the sky from inside the classroom.

M: ❺That's not what I meant. I meant you don't ❻focus in class.

❶ get a good grade: 좋은 성적을 얻다.

❷ 충고를 할 때는 'You should ~'로 말할 수 있다. 이외에 'You'd better ~.', 'Why don't you ~?', 'What[How] about ~?', 'I advise you to ~.' 등을 이용해 충고할 수 있다. concentrate: 집중하다

❸ first of all: 먼저, 무엇보다도

❹ have one's head in the clouds: 공상에 잠겨 있다

❺ 'That's not what I meant.'는 '그런 뜻이 아니야.'라는 의미이며 상대방이 자신의 말의 의도를 오해할 때 정정하기 위해 쓰는 표현이다.

❻ focus: 집중하다 in class: 수업 중에

Listen & Talk 2 B

W: I'm so ❶stressed out about my exams, Jinsu.

M: Yeah, me, too. ❷We have two more to go.

W: After finishing my exams, ❸I want to go on a trip and just let my hair down.

M: You want to change your hair style?

W: No, that's not what I meant. I want to go somewhere and ❹feel free from all my troubles.

❶ stressed out: 스트레스로 지친, 스트레스가 쌓인

❷ two more 다음에 exams가 생략되어 있다.

❸ go on a trip: 여행가다 let one's hair down: 느긋하게 쉬다

❹ 접속사 and로 to go somewhere와 feel free from all my troubles가 병렬 관계를 이루고 있다. feel free from all my troubles 앞에 to가 생략되어 있다. free from: ~이 없는 trouble: 고민, 문제

Communication

W: Hey, Jason. You ❶seem upset. ❷Anything wrong?

M: People keep ❸telling me that I'm too direct. I'm upset about that.

W: Hmm.... ❹I kind of know what they're talking about.

M: What do you mean?

W: Well, ❺sometimes you tend to say what's on your mind too strongly.

M: Should I just keep quiet, then?

W: ❻That's not what I meant. You can ❼try to consider others' feelings.

M: I see. I'll try that.

❶ seem: ~처럼 보이다 upset: 화난, 기분 나쁜

❷ 'Anything wrong?'은 '무슨 문제 있니?'의 뜻으로 상대방의 슬픔이나 불만족, 실망의 원인에 대해 물을 때 사용되는 표현이다. 'What's wrong?', 'What's the problem?', 'Is there anything wrong?', 'What happened to you?', 'Why the long face?' 등으로 바꿔 쓸 수 있다.

❸ tell이 4형식 동사로 me가 간접목적어, that I'm too direct가 직접목적어이다. direct: 딱 부러지는, 단도직입적인

❹ kind of: 약간, 어느 정도

❺ tend to 동사원형: ~하는 경향이 있다 what's on your mind에서 what은 관계대명사로 '~하는 것'으로 해석한다. the thing(s) which[that]으로 바꿔 쓸 수 있다.

❻ That's not what I meant: 그건 그런 뜻이 아니야.

❼ try to 동사원형: ~하려고 노력하다 consider: 배려하다, 고려하다 other'=other people's

Conversation 교과서 확인학습

● 다음 우리말과 일치하도록 빈칸에 알맞은 말을 쓰시오.

Listen & Talk 1 Get Ready

A: ________ do you look so ________?

B: I'm upset ________ Roy. He always copies me.

A: Don't ________ ________ so hard.

A: 너는 왜 침울해 보이니?
B: 나는 Roy한테 화가 나. 그는 항상 나를 따라 해.
A: 너무 속상해 하지 마.

Listen & Talk 1 A-1

M: Sally, how ________ you don't talk much ________ Anna ________ ________?

W: Well, I'm ________ ________ ________ ________ we had.

M: ________ are you upset?

W: She kept ________ ________ ________ ________ the middle of my sentences, so I got ________. We argued and I stopped ________ ________ her.

M: Oh, I'm sorry to hear that.

M: Sally야, 요즘에 왜 Anna와 별로 대화를 하지 않니?
W: 음, 나는 우리가 한 논쟁 때문에 화가 나.
M: 왜 화가 난 거야?
W: 그녀가 계속해서 내가 말을 하고 있는 도중에 끊어서 화가 났어. 우리는 논쟁을 했고, 나는 그녀와 이야기를 하지 않았어.
M: 오, 그거 유감이구나.

Listen & Talk 1 A-2

W: ________ is your science homework ________?

M: Not good. ________ ________ ________ my science group.

W: What's wrong?

M: The group members only speak and never listen. ________ ________ ________ ________ we can finish the homework ________ time.

W: That's too bad.

W: 너의 과학 숙제는 어떻게 되어 가고 있니?
M: 좋지 않아. 나는 나의 과학 그룹에 화가 나.
W: 뭐가 문제인데?
M: 그룹 구성원들이 말만 하고 전혀 듣지 않아. 나는 우리가 숙제를 제시간에 끝낼 수 있을 거라고 생각하지 않아.
W: 그것 참 안 되었구나.

Listen & Talk 1 B

M: ________ the ________ face, Julie?

W: I got ________ ________ my sister yesterday and ________ ________ ________ things to her.

M: Oh, why were you angry?

W: I was really tired and I wanted ________ ________. ________ she was ________ ________ ________ ________ ________. I was really ________ about that.

M: 왜 그렇게 우울한 얼굴이니, Julie?
W: 어제 여동생한테 화가 나서 그녀에게 심술궂은 말을 했어.
M: 오, 왜 화가 났니?
W: 정말 피곤해서 자고 싶었어. 하지만 여동생은 전화로 큰 소리로 이야기하고 있었어. 나는 그것에 대해 정말 화가 났어.

M: I see. And you two ________ ________ ________ out yet?

W: No, not yet. I want to say I'm sorry ________ I was mean to her, ________ ________ ________ ________ ________.

M: ________ don't you write her a note or ________ her a text message?

W: Hmm, that's a good idea. Thanks.

해석

M: 그렇구나. 그리고 너희 둘은 아직 화해하지 않았니?
W: 아니, 아직이야. 내가 여동생에게 심술궂게 굴어서 미안하다고 말하고 싶지만, 방법을 모르겠어.
M: 그녀에게 편지를 쓰거나 문자 메시지를 보내는 게 어때?
W: 음, 좋은 생각이야. 고마워.

Listen & Talk 2 Get Ready

A: Don't ________ ________ ________ ________ ________ ________ ________ about Clara's surprise party.

B: A cat? I don't have a cat.

A: ________ ________ ________ I meant. Keep her party ________ ________.

A: Clara의 깜짝 파티에 대해 비밀을 누설하지 마.
B: 고양이? 나는 고양이가 없어.
A: 그건 그런 뜻이 아니야. 그녀의 파티를 비밀로 해.

Listen & Talk 2 A-1

W: Mr. Brown, I want to ________ a good grade ________ English. What ________ I do?

M: Well, Sujin, you should ________ in class, ________ ________ ________. I see you often ________ ________ ________ ________ ________ ________.

W: Clouds? I can't ________ ________ ________ from inside the classroom.

M: ________ ________ ________ ________ ________. I ________ you don't ________ in class.

W: Brown 선생님, 저는 영어에서 좋은 점수를 받고 싶어요. 어떻게 해야 하죠?
M: 음, 수진아, 너는 우선 수업에 집중해야 해. 난 네가 종종 공상에 잠겨 있는 것을 본단다.
W: 구름이요? 교실 안에서는 하늘을 볼 수 없어요.
M: 그건 그런 뜻이 아니야. 내 말은 네가 수업에 집중하지 않는다는 거야.

해석

Listen & Talk 2 A-2

W: Did you finally ________ ________ yesterday, Nick?

M: Actually, I ________ ________ ________, Mina.

W: That's too bad. How did you ________ ________ ________?

M: No, Mina. That's not what I meant. ________ ________ ________ I got ________, so I didn't dive.

W: Nick, 어제 드디어 다이빙하러 갔니?
M: 미나야, 사실 난 겁이 났어.
W: 그거 안됐구나. 어떻게 감기에 걸렸니?
M: 아니, 미나야. 그건 그런 뜻이 아니야. 내가 겁을 먹어서 다이빙을 안 했다는 뜻이야.

Listen & Talk 2 B

W: I'm so ________ ________ ________ my exams, Jinsu.

M: Yeah, me, too. We have ________ ________ ________ ________.

W: After ________ my exams, I want to ________ ________ ________ trip and just let my ________ ________.

M: You want to change your ________ ________?

W: No, that's not ________ ________ ________. I want to go somewhere and ________ ________________ all my troubles.

W: 진수야, 나는 시험에 대해 너무 스트레스를 받아.
M: 그래, 나도. 우리는 볼 시험이 두 개 더 있어.
W: 시험을 마친 후, 나는 여행을 가서 느긋하게 쉬고 싶어.
M: 머리 스타일을 바꾸고 싶다고?
W: 아니, 그런 뜻이 아니야. 난 어디 가서 내 모든 고민에서 벗어나고 싶어.

Communication

W: Hey, Jason. You ________ upset. Anything wrong?

M: People ________ ________ ________ ________ I'm too ________. I'm ________ about that.

W: Hmm.... I kind of know ________ ________ ________ ________.

M: What do you mean?

W: Well, sometimes you ________ ________ ________ ________ ________ your mind too ________.

M: ________ I just keep quiet, then?

W: ________ ________ ________ ________ ________. You can ________ ________ ________ others' feelings.

M: I see. I'll ________ that.

W: 안녕, Jason. 화나 보여. 무슨 문제라도 있니?
M: 사람들은 내가 너무 단도직입적이라고 계속 말해. 나는 그것에 대해 화가 나.
W: 흠…. 난 그들이 무슨 이야기를 하는지 어느 정도 알아.
M: 무슨 의미야?
W: 음, 가끔 넌 네 마음에 있는 것을 너무 강하게 말하는 경향이 있어.
M: 그럼, 그냥 조용히 있어야 하니?
W: 내 말은 그게 아니야. 너는 다른 사람의 감정을 고려하도록 노력하면 돼.
M: 알겠어. 그렇게 해 보도록 할게.

01 다음 대화의 밑줄 친 문장과 같은 의미의 문장을 고르시오.

> A: I got cold feet.
> B: That's too bad. How did you get a cold?
> A: No. <u>That's not what I meant.</u> I meant I got scared.

① That's all right.
② I mean to say that.
③ I'm afraid you don't understand what I'm saying.
④ That's not my problem.
⑤ You got it.

02 다음 대화의 순서를 바르게 배열한 것을 고르시오.

> (A) She wears my clothes without asking me first.
> (B) I'm upset about my sister.
> (C) What's wrong?

① (A) – (C) – (B) ② (B) – (A) – (C)
③ (B) – (C) – (A) ④ (C) – (A) – (B)
⑤ (C) – (B) – (A)

[03~04] 다음 대화를 읽고 물음에 답하시오.

> W: Did you finally go diving yesterday, Nick?
> M: Actually, I got cold feet, Mina.
> W: That's too bad. (A)________________________
> M: No, Mina. (B)(what, meant, that's, I, not). I meant that I got scared, so I didn't dive.

03 빈칸 (A)에 알맞은 말을 고르시오.

① How was the diving?
② Have you gotten cold feet?
③ How could you do that?
④ How did you get a cold?
⑤ Do you mean that you got scared?

04 괄호 (B) 안의 단어들을 순서대로 바르게 배열하시오.

➡ ____

01 다음 대화의 순서를 바르게 배열한 것을 고르시오.

(A) Well, Sujin, you should concentrate in class, first of all. I see you often have your head in the clouds.
(B) Clouds? I can't see the sky from inside the classroom.
(C) Mr. Brown, I want to get a good grade in English. What should I do?
(D) That's not what I meant. I meant you don't focus in class.

① (B) – (A) – (C) – (D)
② (B) – (C) – (A) – (D)
③ (C) – (A) – (B) – (D)
④ (C) – (B) – (A) – (D)
⑤ (C) – (D) – (B) – (A)

[02~04] 다음 대화를 읽고 물음에 답하시오.

W: Hey, Jason. You seem upset. (①) Anything wrong?
M: People keep telling me that I'm too direct. I'm upset about that. (②)
W: Hmm.... I kind of know what they're talking about.
M: (A)________________
W: Well, sometimes you tend to say what's on your mind too strongly. (③)
M: Should I just keep quiet, then? (④)
W: (⑤) You can try to consider others' feelings.
M: I see. I'll try that.

02 위 대화의 ①~⑤ 중 주어진 문장이 들어갈 알맞은 곳은?

That's not what I meant.

① ② ③ ④ ⑤

03 빈칸 (A)에 알맞은 말을 고르시오.

① What do you mean?
② Why are you upset?
③ Whom do you want to talk to?
④ What should I do?
⑤ Why don't you talk with them?

04 위 대화의 내용과 일치하지 <u>않는</u> 것은?

① 여자는 Jason이 가끔 말을 강하게 한다고 생각한다.
② 여자는 Jason이 다른 사람의 감정을 이해할 필요가 있다고 생각한다.
③ Jason은 사람들이 Jason에게 조용히 하라고 한 것에 대해 화가 났다.
④ 여자는 사람들이 Jason에 대해 이야기한 것을 어느 정도 이해하고 있다.
⑤ Jason은 단도직입적이라는 말을 사람들에게 들었다.

[05~06] 다음 대화를 읽고 물음에 답하시오.

A: Why do you look so (A)________?
B: (B)<u>I'm upset about Roy.</u> He always copies me.
A: Don't take it so hard.

서답형

05 빈칸 (A)에 알맞은 말을 주어진 단어를 이용해서 채우시오.

➡ ________________ (happy)

06 중요 밑줄 친 (B)와 바꿔 쓸 수 있는 것을 고르시오.

① I don't care about Roy.
② Roy never makes me angry.
③ Roy seems to be angry.
④ I don't satisfied with Roy.
⑤ I can't stand Roy.

07 다음 대화의 빈칸에 들어갈 말을 〈보기〉에서 골라 순서대로 바르게 배열한 것은?

M: Why the long face, Julie?
W: ______________________
M: ______________________
W: ______________________
M: ______________________
W: No, not yet. I want to say I'm sorry that I was mean to her, but I don't know how.
M: Why don't you write her a note or send her a text message?
W: Hmm, that's a good idea. Thanks.

보기

(A) Oh, why were you angry?
(B) I got angry at my sister yesterday and said some mean things to her.
(C) I was really tired and I wanted to sleep. But she was talking loudly on the phone. I was really upset about that.
(D) I see. And you two haven't worked it out yet?

① (B) – (A) – (C) – (D)
② (B) – (C) – (A) – (D)
③ (C) – (A) – (B) – (D)
④ (C) – (B) – (A) – (D)
⑤ (C) – (D) – (B) – (A)

[08~09] 다음 대화를 읽고 물음에 답하시오.

A: Don't let the cat out of the bag about Clara's surprise party.
B: A cat? I don't have a cat.
A: (A)__________ Keep her party a secret.

08 빈칸 (A)에 알맞은 말을 고르시오.

① I didn't hear you.
② That's not what I meant.
③ What you are saying is right.
④ I think so, too.
⑤ Don't misunderstand me.

09 According to the dialogue, what did A intend to say to B?

① A wants to go to Clara's birthday party.
② B wants to let the cat out of A's bag.
③ A wants B to bring Clara a cat.
④ A wants to keep Clara's surprise party a secret.
⑤ A wants to have a cat.

10 중요 다음 중 짝지어진 대화가 어색한 것은?

① A: I'm really angry at Jenmy.
B: What did she do?
A: She borrowed my English book, but I found some pages missing.
② A: You look so annoyed. What's wrong?
B: One of the members in the science group doesn't do any work.
③ A: I'm angry at my brother.
B: He didn't do well on the test.
④ A: What's the matter?
B: I can't stand my older sister's behavior.
⑤ A: How come you are so upset?
B: I'm angry with my best friend for forgetting my birthday.

[01~02] 다음 대화를 읽고 물음에 답하시오.

M: How come you don't talk much with Anna these days?
W: Well, (A)____________________(upset, an, we, I, argument, am, about, had)
M: Why are you upset?
W: She kept cutting me (B)_______ in the middle of my sentences, so I got mad. We argued and I stopped talking to her.
M: Oh, I'm sorry to hear that.

01 빈칸 (A)를 괄호 안에 주어진 단어를 알맞게 배열하여 채우시오.

➡ ______________________________

중요
02 빈칸 (B)에 알맞은 전치사를 쓰시오.

➡ ____________________

[03~04] 다음 대화를 읽고 물음에 답하시오.

M: You look upset, Anna. What's wrong?
W: Well, I'm upset about my sister, Elsa.
M: (A)왜 너는 그녀에게 화가 났니?
W: She keeps (B)_______(order) me around.
M: Oh, maybe you should tell her how you feel.

03 밑줄 친 (A)의 우리말을 대화에 나온 단어를 이용해 영작하시오.

➡ ______________________________

04 빈칸 (B)를 괄호 안에 주어진 단어를 이용하여 채우시오.

➡ ____________________

[05~07] 다음 대화를 읽고 물음에 답하시오.

W: I'm so stressed (A)_______ about my exams, Jinsu.
M: Yeah, me, too. We have two more to (B)_____.
W: After finishing my exams, I want to (C)_____ on a trip and just let my hair down.
M: You want to change your hair style?
W: No, (D)that's not what I meant. I want to go somewhere and feel free from all my troubles.

중요
05 빈칸 (A)에 알맞은 단어를 쓰시오.

➡ ____________________

06 빈칸 (B)와 (C)에 공통으로 들어갈 단어를 쓰시오.

➡ ____________________

고난이도
07 밑줄 친 문장 (D)와 같은 의미가 되도록 주어진 단어를 이용해 쓰시오. (say, mean, 6단어)

➡ ______________________________

08 밑줄 친 ⓐ~ⓔ 중 어법상 어색한 것을 바르게 고치시오.

W: Mr. Brown, ⓐI want to get a good grade in English. ⓑWhat should I do?
M: Well, Sujin, ⓒyou should concentrate in class, first of all. I see you often have your head in the clouds.
W: Clouds? ⓓI can't see the sky from inside the classroom.
M: ⓔThat's not that I meant. I meant you don't focus in class.

➡ ______________________________

교과서

Grammar

1 관계대명사 what

- Starting a sentence with “I” can help him focus on **what** he feels.
  “I”로 문장을 시작하는 것은 그가 자신이 느끼는 것에 초점을 맞추도록 도울 수 있어.
- That is **what** I was afraid of. 그것이 제가 우려했던 바예요.

■ 관계대명사 what은 다른 관계대명사와 다르게 선행사를 포함한 관계대명사로 ‘~하는 것’으로 해석하며, the thing(s) which[that]의 의미이다.

- Tell me **what** you think about Susie. Susie를 어떻게 생각하는지 말해 줘.
  (= Tell me the thing which[that] you think about Susie.)

■ 관계대명사 what이 이끄는 절은 명사절로 문장에서 주어, 보어, 목적어의 역할을 한다.

(1) 주어 역할

- **What** he really wanted was revenge. 그가 정말 원했던 것은 복수였다.

(2) 보어 역할

- It was **what** I should do. 그건 제가 해야 하는 것이었어요.

(3) 목적어 역할

- Do you know **what** she said? 그녀가 뭐랬는지 알아? (동사의 목적어)
- You need to pay attention to **what** you eat. 여러분은 자신이 무엇을 먹는지에 대해 신경을 쓸 필요가 있습니다. (전치사의 목적어)

■ 관계대명사 what의 관용적인 표현

- He is **what is called** a young prince. 그는 소위 귀공자다.
- You should be satisfied with **what you** have. 당신은 당신이 가지고 있는 것에 만족해야 한다.
- **What is worse**, he lost his health. 설상가상으로 그는 건강까지 잃었다.

핵심 Check

1. 다음 우리말과 일치하도록 빈칸에 알맞은 말을 쓰시오.

(1) 내가 하고 싶은 게 뭔지 아니?
➡ Do you know __________ I want to do?

(2) 나는 지난날의 내가 아니야.
➡ I am not __________ I used to be.

(3) 그녀가 말한 것은 위험한 것이었다.
➡ __________ she said was dangerous.

2 관계부사

- Calli should pick a time **when** her mom is ready to listen.
  Calli는 그녀의 엄마가 들을 준비가 되어 있는 때를 골라야 한다.
- It's a place **where** people can recharge. 그곳은 사람들이 재충전할 수 있는 곳이죠.

■ 관계부사는 두 문장을 연결하는 접속사의 역할과 부사의 역할을 동시에 한다. 관계부사 앞에 와서 수식을 받는 명사를 선행사라 하고, 그 선행사에 따라 관계부사 when(시간), where(장소), why(이유), how(방법)를 쓴다.

- There was a time **when** things were very different. 상황이 아주 달랐던 때가 있었다.
- This is the house **where** I was born. 이것이 내가 태어난 집이다.
- This is the reason **why** I'm here. 이것이 내가 여기 온 이유다.
- Scientists are studying **how** the birds find their food. 과학자들은 그 새들이 먹이를 찾는 방법을 연구하고 있다.

■ 관계부사 how는 선행사 the way와 함께 쓰지 않고 반드시 둘 중의 하나만 써야 하며 the way that이나 the way in which를 쓸 수 있다. 다른 관계부사의 경우 the time, the place, the reason과 같은 선행사가 나올 경우 선행사나 관계부사 중 하나를 생략할 수 있다.

- Do you know **the way how** the rain falls from the sky? (×)
- Do you know **the way**[또는 **how**] the rain falls from the sky? (○)
  당신은 어떻게 하늘에서 비가 떨어지는지 아는가?

■ 선행사에 따른 관계부사

	선행사	관계부사	전치사+관계대명사
때	the time	when	in/on/at which
장소	the place	where	in/on/at which
이유	the reason	why	for which
방법	the way	how	in which

■ 주의: 관계대명사는 관계사절에서 주어나 목적어의 역할을 하므로 주어나 목적어가 빠진 불완전한 절이 오지만 관계부사는 부사 역할을 하므로 완전한 절이 온다.

핵심 Check

2. 다음 괄호 안에서 알맞은 말을 고르시오.

(1) The day (when / where) I start for my journey is drawing near.
(2) I remember the house (when / where) I grew up.
(3) The reason (why / how) he did it is complicated.

Grammar 시험대비 기본평가

01 다음 빈칸에 알맞은 것을 고르시오.

This is the house ______ I was born.

① when ② where ③ why
④ how ⑤ what

02 다음 중 어법상 어색한 문장은?

① The merchant paid customs on what he had bought in China.
② What he did to me was out of all knowledge.
③ I can't remember what I ate.
④ I want to know that you think of her music.
⑤ This is what I enjoy doing.

03 다음 주어진 두 문장을 한 문장으로 바꿀 때 옳지 않은 것은?

• You have to admire the way. • He handled the situation in the way.

① You have to admire how he handled the situation.
② You have to admire the way he handled the situation.
③ You have to admire the way in which he handled the situation.
④ You have to admire the way that he handled the situation.
⑤ You have to admire the way how he handled the situation.

04 다음 우리말에 맞게 주어진 어휘를 알맞게 배열하시오.

(1) 봄은 꽃들이 피는 아름다운 때이다.
(the flowers, spring, time, bloom, is, beautiful, a, when)
➡ ________________________________

(2) 여긴 왜 오셨죠?
(you, there, reason, here, any, is, are, why)
➡ ________________________________

(3) 의사 없는 마을에서 살지 마라.
(a town, doctors, there, live, don't, are, no, in, where)
➡ ________________________________

01 다음 중 어법상 올바른 것은?

① This is the house which Anne was born.
② Let's find out the reason why he has this problem.
③ This is the park how I met Sophie.
④ Tell me the way when you solved the problem.
⑤ I remember the day where I met her first.

중요
02 다음 중 어법상 어색한 것은?

① What he says is not important.
② Lend me the book which you bought yesterday.
③ People believe that they want to believe.
④ This dress is what I wanted to buy.
⑤ You can eat what you like to eat on World Food Day.

중요
03 다음 빈칸에 알맞은 말이 바르게 짝지어진 것은?

• ___________ he was doing would be considered as theft.
• It is the hotel ________ we stayed when we traveled to Paris.

① Which – why ② That – where
③ That – when ④ What – where
⑤ What – when

서답형
04 다음 괄호 안에서 알맞은 말을 고르시오.

(1) This is the reason (how / why) I like bananas.
(2) That's the way (how / that) the system works.
(3) There are times (when / where) I feel depressed.
(4) The store doesn't sell (that / what) I am looking for.
(5) He was deprived of all (that / what) he owned.

05 다음 대화의 빈칸에 들어갈 말로 알맞은 것은?

M: What did you have for lunch yesterday?
W: Oh, _______ I had for lunch was some delicious spaghetti.

① it ② this ③ that
④ which ⑤ what

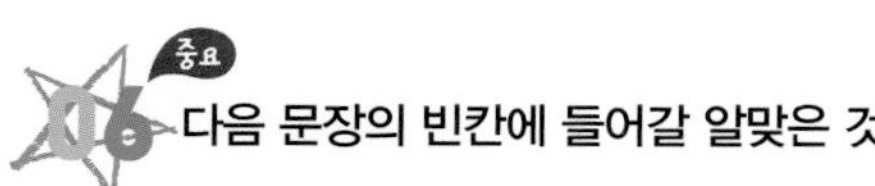

중요
06 다음 문장의 빈칸에 들어갈 알맞은 것은?

That is the place ______ my dog hides his food.

① where ② when
③ why ④ how
⑤ what

중요
07 다음 문장 중에서 어법상 틀린 것을 고르시오.

① Calli should pick a time when her mom is ready to listen.
② I will never forget the place where I met her.
③ It is the way how he proved the principle.
④ I don't know the reason why she left us.
⑤ This is the house which Sarah was born in.

08 다음 주어진 문장의 밑줄 친 what과 같은 용법으로 쓰인 것을 모두 고르시오.

Tell me what you know about Mars.

① What are you talking about?
② That's not what I meant.
③ He asked me what I wanted.
④ I guess that's what made me do it.
⑤ Please inform me what to do next.

서답형
09 주어진 어휘를 바르게 배열하여 다음 우리말을 영작하시오.

크리스마스는 우리가 가족과 함께 나누는 때이다. (Christmas, a time, we, is, share, families, with, when)

➡ ______________________________

서답형
10 다음 문장에서 어법상 틀린 부분을 찾아 바르게 고쳐 쓰시오.

The Sahara Desert is that is called "the sea of death."

➡ ______________________________

중요
11 다음 두 문장을 한 문장으로 바르게 연결한 것은?

• Every man had to gather to see the thing. • It was happening.

① Every man had to gather to see happening.
② Every man had to gather to see it was happening.
③ Every man had to gather to see which was happening.
④ Every man had to gather to see that was happening.
⑤ Every man had to gather to see what was happening.

[12~13] 다음 빈칸에 들어갈 말이 나머지와 다른 하나는? (대・소문자 무시)

12
① This is the house ______ Anne lives.
② 1921 is the year ______ Einstein received the Nobel Prize.
③ It was the day ______ we had your birthday party.
④ Do you know the time ______ TVs first appeared?
⑤ It's the month ______ Jesus was born.

중요
13
① Do you know ______ he is talking about?
② This is the bank ______ Marisol works at.
③ Let me know ______ you find out there.
④ ______ I want to do is playing computer games.
⑤ ______ you need is a good rest.

14 다음 두 문장을 한 문장으로 바르게 연결한 것을 고르시오.

- Korea is the country.
- The 1988 Olympic Games were held in the country.

① Korea is the country when the 1988 Olympic Games were held.
② Korea is the country why the 1988 Olympic Games were held.
③ Korea is the country how the 1988 Olympic Games were held.
④ Korea is the country which the 1988 Olympic Games were held.
⑤ Korea is the country in which the 1988 Olympic Games were held.

서답형

15 다음 우리말과 일치하도록 주어진 어휘에 한 단어를 추가하여 영작하시오.

- 나는 현실이 내 예상과는 아주 다르다는 것을 알았다.

(I, I, the reality, imagined, quite, had, different, found, from)

➡ ______________________________
____

중요

16 다음 중 어법상 어색한 것을 고르시오. (2개)

① I'm very sorry for that I did that night.
② What she says will sound like a request rather than a demand.
③ The birthday presents were the reason why I looked forward to my birthday.
④ May 1 is the day how workers celebrate the rights they have fought for.
⑤ This is the station where we met.

서답형

17 다음 문장에서 어법상 어색한 것을 바르게 고쳐 다시 쓰시오.

(1) He didn't let us know the way how he solved the problem.
➡ ______________________________
____

(2) Judy went to the restaurant which she had dinner with her friends.
➡ ______________________________
____

(3) Yuna remembers the day how she won the Olympic gold medal.
➡ ______________________________
____

(4) I can't believe that you're saying.
➡ ______________________________

(5) I like the bag what I bought yesterday.
➡ ______________________________

(6) I would like to do that I want when I want.
➡ ______________________________

서답형

18 다음 〈보기〉와 같이 주어진 두 문장을 한 문장으로 바꾸어 쓰시오.

보기

- I know a small restaurant.
- We can have very delicious cakes there.

→ I know a small restaurant where we can have very delicious cakes.

- 1950 is the year.
- The Korean War broke out in the year.

➡ ______________________________

Grammar 서술형 시험대비

고 난이도

01 괄호 안의 지시대로 우리말을 영어로 옮기시오.

(1) 그가 왜 여기 왔는지 아니?

➡ ____________________

(관계부사를 써서)

➡ ____________________

____

(관계대명사를 써서)

(2) 자연 재해(natural disasters)는 사람들이 살고 있는 곳에 피해를 입힌다.

➡ ____________________

(관계부사를 써서)

➡ ____________________

____

(관계대명사를 써서)

02 다음 우리말에 맞게 주어진 어휘를 이용하여 영작하시오.

(1) 그녀는 인생에서 하고 싶은 것을 할 권리가 있다. (the right, in her life, have, do, what)

➡ ____________________

____

(2) 내가 하고 싶은 것은 개를 한 마리 입양하는 것이다. (to adopt, do, want)

➡ ____________________

(3) 왜 그런 결정을 하셨는지 물어봐도 될까요? (the reason, that decision, you, may, 11 단어)

➡ ____________________

____

03 그림을 보고, 주어진 어휘를 이용하여 빈칸을 알맞게 채우시오.

(1) This is the hotel ____________________ last summer. (stay, we) (3 words)

(2) Big Ben is ____________________ to see. (I, want) (3 words)

중요

04 다음 문장의 빈칸에 알맞은 말을 쓰시오. (두 가지를 쓸 것.)

(1) I remember the café ______________ he and I first met.

(2) We don't know ______________ she solved the puzzle.

(3) I'm curious about the reason ______________ she was late for the meeting.

05 주어진 두 문장을 what을 이용하여 하나의 문장으로 쓰시오.

(1) • He politely denied the thing.
• I suggested it.
➡ ______________________

(2) • He did not listen to the thing.
• I said the thing.
➡ ______________________

(3) • The thing was proposed by him.
• It was not allowed.
➡ ______________________

(4) • Love is the thing.
• It helps mend a broken heart.
➡ ______________________

고난이도

06 주어진 두 문장을 관계부사를 이용하여 하나의 문장으로 쓰시오.

(1) • I don't know the reason.
• He hides it for the reason.
➡ ______________________

(2) • Bill didn't know the time.
• She would arrive at the time.
➡ ______________________

(3) • Avoid the area.
• The accident took place in the area.
➡ ______________________

(4) • We studied the way.
• Computers store information by the way.
➡ ______________________

(5) • Cambridge Park is a nice park.
• You can sit on the grass in the park.
➡ ______________________
____

중요

07 다음 두 문장에서 관계대명사의 사용을 비교하여 차이점을 서술하시오.

(1) He does something that really bothers me.
➡ ______________________
____

(2) He does what really bothers me.
➡ ______________________
____

08 다음 문장에서 어법상 어색한 것을 바르게 고치시오.

(1) That is the building where they built last year.
➡ ______________________

(2) Machines have changed the way how we work.
➡ ______________________
____

(3) Friday afternoon is the time which he is least busy.
➡ ______________________
____

(4) Do you remember the things what Megan brought at the mart?
➡ ______________________

(5) That I want to do is bring hope to my family.
➡ ______________________

(6) Did you understand that she said yesterday?
➡ ______________________

교과서

Reading

Speak Your Mind Effectively

Welcome to "All about Teens." I'm Dr. Carter. Today, we're going to talk about using(동명사) good communication skills to express(to부정사의 부사적 용법(목적)) ourselves more effectively(effectively의 비교급).

Let's start with(~으로 시작하다) our first clip about Brian. When he tries to talk(to부정사의 명사적 용법) to his brother, he always ends up arguing(end up ~ing: 결국 ~하게 되다) with his brother. Let's find out the reason why(관계부사(= for which)) he has this problem.

Brian: *You lost my earphones again. Why are you so careless(↔ careful)?*

Brian is starting a sentence with "you" to express(to부정사의 부사적 용법(목적)) his feelings. Instead(= Instead of starting a sentence with "you"), he should use the "I-message." Starting(동명사(주어)) with "I" can help him focus on what(관계대명사 (= the thing which)) he feels or thinks rather than(B rather than A: A라기보다는 B) point the finger at his brother.

Brian: ***I'm really upset because my favorite earphones are lost.*** ("I-message"의 예)

Next is Calli. She is trying to(try to: ~하려고 노력하다) talk to her mother, but she is busy preparing(be busy ~ing: ~하느라 바쁘다) to go to work. Let's have a look(=take a look).

effectively 효과적으로
welcome to: ~에 온 걸 환영하다
communication 의사소통
skill 기술
express 표현하다
clip 동영상
argue with ~와 말다툼을 벌이다
find out 알아내다
careless 부주의한
sentence 말, 문장
instead 대신에
focus on ~에 집중을 하다, ~에 초점을 맞추다
point the finger at ~을 비난하다

확인문제

● 다음 문장이 본문의 내용과 일치하면 T, 일치하지 않으면 F를 쓰시오.

1 When Brian tries to talk to his brother, he always ends up arguing with his brother. ☐

2 Brian is starting a sentence with "I" to express his feelings. ☐

3 Starting with "I" can help Brian focus on what he feels or thinks. ☐

4 Starting with "I" can also help Brian point the finger at his brother. ☐

5 Calli is trying to talk to her mother. ☐

6 Calli is busy preparing to go on a trip. ☐

Calli: *Hey, Mom. Could I talk to you about something?*
Can보다 정중한 표현

Calli needs to find the right time to talk to her mom. Maybe Calli's mom wanted to listen to what Calli was going to say. But she didn't have enough time to talk with her daughter. Calli should pick a time when her mom is ready to listen.

(to talk: to부정사의 형용사적 용법 / what: 관계대명사(= the thing which) / to talk: to부정사의 형용사적 용법 / be ready to: ~할 준비가 되어 있다)

Calli: ***Hey, Mom. Could I talk to you about something?***

Mom: *Sure.*

Now, let's take a look at our last clip. Anna and Julie are best friends, but Anna often hurts Julie's feelings.

(take a look at = have a look at = look at)

Anna: *Don't put your bag on my desk!*

Julie probably felt uncomfortable because Anna made a demand using the word "don't." People simply don't like taking orders. Anna should try to use words such as "can," "could," or "please." Then, what she says will sound like a request rather than a demand.

(uncomfortable: uncomfortably(×) / using: 현재분사 / taking: = to take / such as: = like / what: 관계대명사(주어) / sound like+명사: ~처럼 들리다. / B rather than A: A라기보다는 B)

Anna: ***Could you put your bag on your desk?***
'요청'처럼 들리는 질문의 예

As we saw in the video clips, a small change in the way we express ourselves can solve or even prevent communication problems. Let's keep these tips in mind!

(As: ~인 것처럼(접속사) / the way: the way how (×) / ourselves: 주어와 목적어가 같을 때 재귀대명사를 쓴다. / keep[bear] ~ in mind: ~을 명심하다)

right 알맞은
enough 충분한
pick 고르다, 선택하다
hurt 마음을 아프게[감정을 상하게] 하다
feeling 감정
probably 아마도(=perhaps)
uncomfortable 불편한, 언짢은 (↔comfortable 편안한)
demand 요구, 강요
take orders 명령을 받다
request 요청
change 변화
solve 해결하다
prevent 예방하다
tip 조언

확인문제

● 다음 문장이 본문의 내용과 일치하면 T, 일치하지 않으면 F를 쓰시오.

1 Calli needs to find the right time to talk to her mom. ☐
2 Calli's mom didn't want to listen to what Calli was going to say. ☐
3 Calli's mom didn't have enough time to talk with her daughter. ☐
4 Anna and Julie aren't on good terms with each other. ☐
5 Anna should try to use words such as "can," "could," or "please." ☐
6 A small change in the way we express ourselves can't solve communication problems. ☐

Reading 교과서 확인학습 A

• 우리말을 참고하여 빈칸에 알맞은 말을 쓰시오.

1 Speak Your Mind _______

2 _______ _______ "All about Teens."

3 _______ Dr. Carter.

4 Today, we're going to talk about _______ _______ _______ _______ to express ourselves more effectively.

5 Let's start with _______ _______ _______ about Brian.

6 When he tries to talk to his brother, he always _______ _______ _______ with his brother.

7 Let's find out _______ _______ _______ he has this problem.

8 **Brian:** ***You lost my earphones again. Why are you so _______?***

9 Brian is starting a sentence with "you" _______ _______ _______ _______.

10 _______, he should use the "_______."

11 Starting with "I" can help him _______ _______ what he feels or thinks _______ _______ point the finger at his brother.

12 **Brian:** _______ ***really*** _______ ***because my favorite earphones*** _______ _______.

13 _______ is Calli.

14 She is trying to talk to her mother, but she _______ _______ _______ to go to work.

15 Let's _______ _______ _______.

1 당신의 마음을 효과적으로 말하라!

2 '십 대들의 모든 것'에 오신 걸 환영합니다.

3 저는 Carter 박사입니다.

4 오늘 우리는 자신을 더 효과적으로 표현하기 위해 적절한 의사소통 기술을 사용하는 것에 대해 이야기해 보겠습니다.

5 Brian에 대한 첫 번째 동영상으로 시작해 보죠.

6 Brian이 남동생과 이야기하려고 할 때, 그는 결국 동생과 항상 말다툼을 하게 돼요.

7 그에게 이런 문제가 있는 이유를 알아봅시다.

8 Brian: "너 또 내 이어폰 잃어버렸지. 너는 왜 그렇게 조심성이 없니?"

9 Brian은 그의 감정을 표현하기 위해 '너'로 문장을 시작하고 있군요.

10 대신에 그는 '나 메시지'를 써야 해요.

11 '나'로 시작하는 것은 그가 남동생을 비난하기보다는 자신이 느끼거나 생각하는 것에 집중하도록 도울 수 있답니다.

12 Brian: "내가 가장 좋아하는 이어폰이 없어져서 난 정말 속상해."

13 다음은 Calli입니다.

14 그녀는 어머니와 이야기하려고 하지만, 어머니는 출근 준비로 바쁘시군요.

15 한번 보시죠.

16 **Calli: *Hey, Mom.* _______ _______ *talk to you about something?***

17 Calli needs to find _______ _______ _______ to talk to her mom.

18 Maybe Calli's mom wanted to listen to _______ Calli was going to say.

19 But she didn't have _______ _______ to talk with her daughter.

20 Calli should _______ _______ _______ when her mom _______ _______ _______ _______.

21 **Calli: *Hey, Mom.* _______ _______ *talk to you about something?***

22 **Mom: _______.**

23 Now, let's _______ _______ _______ _______ our last clip.

24 Anna and Julie are best friends, but Anna often _______ Julie's feelings.

25 **Anna: _______ _______ *your bag on my desk!***

26 Julie probably _______ _______ because Anna made a demand using the word "don't."

27 People simply don't like _______ _______.

28 Anna should try to use words _______ _______ "can," "could," or "please."

29 Then, _______ she says will sound like a _______ rather than a _______.

30 **Anna: _______ _______ *put your bag on your desk?***

31 As we saw in the video clips, _______ _______ _______ in the way we express ourselves can solve or even _______ _______ _______.

32 Let's _______ these tips _______ _______!

16 Calli: "저기, 엄마. 엄마랑 뭔가에 대해 이야기 좀 할 수 있을까요?"

16 Calli는 어머니와 이야기를 나눌 적절한 때를 찾아야 해요.

16 Calli의 어머니도 아마 Calli가 말하려고 했던 것을 듣고 싶어 하셨을 거예요.

16 그러나 어머니에게는 딸과 이야기할 시간이 충분하지 않았어요.

20 Calli는 어머니가 들으실 준비가 된 때를 골라야 해요.

21 Calli: "저기, 엄마. 엄마랑 뭔가에 대해 이야기 좀 할 수 있을까요?"

22 Mom: "물론이지."

23 이제 마지막 동영상을 봅시다.

24 Anna와 Julie는 가장 친한 친구 사이이지만, Anna가 종종 Julie의 마음을 상하게 합니다.

25 Anna: "네 가방을 내 책상에 놓지 마!"

26 Anna가 don't라는 단어를 써서 요구했기 때문에 Julie는 아마 불편하게 느꼈을 거예요.

27 사람들은 명령 받는 것을 전혀 좋아하지 않아요.

28 Anna는 can, could 또는 please와 같은 말을 사용하도록 노력해야 해요.

29 그러면 그녀가 하는 말이 요구보다는 요청처럼 들릴 거예요.

30 Anna: "네 가방은 네 책상에 놔 두겠니?"

31 우리가 동영상에서 본 것처럼, 우리 자신을 표현하는 방식을 조금만 바꾸어도 의사소통의 문제를 해결하거나 심지어 막을 수도 있답니다.

32 이 조언들을 명심합시다!

Reading 교과서 확인학습 B

• 우리말을 참고하여 본문을 영작하시오.

1 당신의 마음을 효과적으로 말하라!

➡ ______________________________

2 '십 대들의 모든 것'에 오신 걸 환영합니다.

➡ ______________________________

3 저는 Carter 박사입니다.

➡ ______________________________

4 오늘 우리는 자신을 더 효과적으로 표현하기 위해 적절한 의사소통 기술을 사용하는 것에 대해 이야기해 보겠습니다.

➡ ______________________________

5 Brian에 대한 첫 번째 동영상으로 시작해 보죠.

➡ ______________________________

6 Brian이 남동생과 이야기하려고 할 때, 그는 결국 동생과 항상 말다툼을 하게 돼요.

➡ ______________________________

7 그에게 이런 문제가 있는 이유를 알아봅시다.

➡ ______________________________

8 Brian: "너 또 내 이어폰 잃어버렸지. 너는 왜 그렇게 조심성이 없니?"

➡ ______________________________

9 Brian은 그의 감정을 표현하기 위해 '너'로 문장을 시작하고 있군요.

➡ ______________________________

10 대신에 그는 '나 메시지'를 써야 해요.

➡ ______________________________

11 '나'로 시작하는 것은 그가 남동생을 비난하기보다는 자신이 느끼거나 생각하는 것에 집중하도록 도울 수 있답니다.

➡ ______________________________

12 Brian: "내가 가장 좋아하는 이어폰이 없어져서 난 정말 속상해."

➡ ______________________________

13 다음은 Calli입니다.

➡ ______________________________

14 그녀는 어머니와 이야기하려고 하지만, 어머니는 출근 준비로 바쁘시군요.

➡ ______________________________

15 한번 보시죠.

➡ ______________________________

16 Calli: "저기, 엄마. 엄마랑 뭔가에 대해 이야기 좀 할 수 있을까요?"
➡ ______

17 Calli는 어머니와 이야기를 나눌 적절한 때를 찾아야 해요.
➡ ______

18 Calli의 어머니도 아마 Calli가 말하려고 했던 것을 듣고 싶어 하셨을 거예요.
➡ ______

19 그러나 어머니에게는 딸과 이야기할 시간이 충분하지 않았어요.
➡ ______

20 Calli는 어머니가 들으실 준비가 된 때를 골라야 해요.
➡ ______

21 Calli: "저기, 엄마. 엄마랑 뭔가에 대해 이야기 좀 할 수 있을까요?"
➡ ______

22 Mom: "물론이지."
➡ ______

23 이제 마지막 동영상을 봅시다.
➡ ______

24 Anna와 Julie는 가장 친한 친구 사이이지만, Anna가 종종 Julie의 마음을 상하게 합니다.
➡ ______

25 Anna: "네 가방을 내 책상에 놓지 마!"
➡ ______

26 Anna가 don't라는 단어를 써서 요구했기 때문에 Julie는 아마 불편하게 느꼈을 거예요.
➡ ______

27 사람들은 명령 받는 것을 전혀 좋아하지 않아요.
➡ ______

28 Anna는 can, could 또는 please와 같은 말을 사용하도록 노력해야 해요.
➡ ______

29 그러면 그녀가 하는 말이 요구보다는 요청처럼 들릴 거예요.
➡ ______

30 Anna: "네 가방은 네 책상에 놔두겠니?"
➡ ______

31 우리가 동영상에서 본 것처럼, 우리 자신을 표현하는 방식을 조금만 바꾸어도 의사소통의 문제를 해결하거나 심지어 막을 수도 있답니다.
➡ ______
______

32 이 조언들을 명심합시다!
➡ ______

Reading 시험대비 실력평가

[01~03] 다음 글을 읽고 물음에 답하시오.

Welcome to "All about Teens." I'm Dr. Carter. ⓐToday, we're going to talk about using good communication skills to express us more effectively.

Let's start with our first clip about Brian. When he tries ⓑto talk to his brother, he always ends up arguing with his brother. Let's find out the reason why he has this problem.

서답형

01 위 글의 밑줄 친 ⓐ에서 어법상 틀린 부분을 찾아 고치시오.

➡ ______________________

02 위 글의 밑줄 친 ⓑto talk와 to부정사의 용법이 같은 것을 모두 고르시오.

① He decided to talk to her.
② She hurried to talk about the news.
③ I have nothing to talk about.
④ It's necessary to talk to your doctor.
⑤ We were happy to talk over a cup of coffee.

중요

03 위 글을 읽고 알 수 없는 것을 고르시오.

① the name of the program
② the name of the MC
③ the topic of the program
④ the subject of the first clip
⑤ the reason of the argument between Brian and his brother

[04~06] 다음 글을 읽고 물음에 답하시오.

Next is Calli. ①She is trying to talk to her mother, but (A)그녀는 출근 준비를 하느라고 바쁘십니다. Let's have a look.

Calli: *Hey, Mom. Could ②I talk to you about something?*

Calli needs to find the right time to talk to ③her mom. ___ⓐ___ Calli's mom wanted to listen to what Calli was going to say. But ④she didn't have enough time to talk with her daughter. Calli should pick a time when ⑤her mom is ready to listen.

Calli: *Hey, Mom. Could I talk to you about something?*

Mom: *Sure.*

04 위 글의 빈칸 ⓐ에 들어갈 가장 알맞은 말을 고르시오.

① Consequently ② Exactly
③ Particularly ④ Maybe
⑤ Especially

중요

05 밑줄 친 ①~⑤ 중에서 가리키는 대상이 나머지 넷과 다른 것은?

① ② ③ ④ ⑤

06 위 글의 밑줄 친 (A)의 우리말에 맞게 주어진 어휘를 이용하여 8 단어로 영작하시오.

go to work

➡ ______________________

[07~09] 다음 글을 읽고 물음에 답하시오.

Let's start with our first clip about Brian. When he tries to talk to his brother, he always ends up arguing with his brother. Let's find out (A)the reason why he has this problem.

Brian: *You lost my earphones again. Why are you so careless?*

Brian is (B)<u>starting</u> a sentence with "you" to express his feelings. Instead, he should use the "I-message." (C)<u>Starting</u> with "I" can help him focus ___ⓐ___ what he feels or thinks rather than point the finger ___ⓑ___ his brother.

Brian: *I'm really upset because my favorite earphones are lost.*

07 위 글의 빈칸 ⓐ와 ⓑ에 들어갈 전치사가 바르게 짝지어진 것은?

ⓐ ⓑ
① on – at
② for – to
③ in – to
④ for – at
⑤ on – from

서답형

08 다음 빈칸 (a)와 (b)에 알맞은 단어를 넣어 위 글의 밑줄 친 (A)에 대한 설명을 완성하시오.

Because Brian is starting a sentence with "you" to express (a)_______ _______ and points the finger at his brother, he always ends up arguing with (b)_______ _______.

서답형

09 아래 <보기>에서 위 글의 밑줄 친 (B)<u>starting</u>, (C)<u>Starting</u>과 문법적 쓰임이 같은 것을 각각 <u>모두</u> 고르시오.

보기
① Would you mind <u>opening</u> the door?
② I saw him <u>playing</u> the piano.
③ <u>Smiling</u> babies are the cutest in the world.
④ Her job is <u>designing</u> a building.
⑤ She sat <u>reading</u> a book.

➡ (B)와 같은 것: __________
(C)와 같은 것: __________

[10~12] 다음 글을 읽고 물음에 답하시오.

Now, let's take a look at our (A)[last / latest] clip. Anna and Julie are best friends, but Anna often hurts Julie's feelings.

Anna: *Don't put your bag on my desk!*

Julie probably felt (B)[uncomfortable / uncomfortably] because Anna made a demand using the word "don't." People simply don't like ___ⓐ___. Anna should try to use words such as "can," "could," or "please." Then, what she says will sound like a request rather than a demand.

Anna: *Could you put your bag on your desk?*

As we saw in the video clips, a small change in the way we express ourselves can solve or even (C)[prevent / protect] communication problems. Let's keep these tips in mind!

10 위 글의 빈칸 ⓐ에 들어갈 알맞은 말을 고르시오.

① asking advice
② taking orders
③ giving advice
④ taking turns
⑤ giving orders

11 위 글의 괄호 (A)~(C)에서 문맥이나 어법상 알맞은 낱말을 골라 쓰시오.

➡ (A)________ (B)________ (C)________

12 위 글에 어울리는 속담으로 가장 알맞은 것을 고르시오.

① Better late than never.
② A friend in need is a friend indeed.
③ One good turn deserves another.
④ Birds of a feather flock together.
⑤ A bird in the hand is worth two in the bush.

[13~15] 다음 글을 읽고 물음에 답하시오.

ⓐAs we saw in the video clips, ⓑa small change in the way how we express ourselves can solve or even prevent communication problems. ⓒLet's keep these tips in mind!

13 위 글의 밑줄 친 ⓐAs와 같은 의미로 쓰인 것을 고르시오.

① Her anger grew as she talked.
② As the poet says, a little learning is a dangerous thing.
③ He came up as I was speaking.
④ She works as a computer programmer.
⑤ As he is honest, he is trusted by everyone.

서답형
14 위 글의 밑줄 친 ⓑ에서 어법상 틀린 부분을 찾아 고치시오.

➡ ______________________

서답형
15 위 글의 밑줄 친 ⓒ를 다음과 같이 바꿔 쓸 때 빈칸에 들어갈 알맞은 단어를 쓰시오.

➡ Let's _______ these tips in mind!

[16~18] 다음 글을 읽고 물음에 답하시오.

Brian: *You lost my earphones again. Why are you so careless?*

Brian is starting a sentence with "___ⓐ___" to express his feelings. Instead, he should use the "I-message." Starting with "___ⓑ___" can help him focus on what ⓒhe feels or thinks rather than ⓓpoint the finger at his brother.

Brian: *I'm really upset because my favorite earphones are lost.*

서답형
16 Fill in the blanks ⓐ and ⓑ with suitable words.

➡ ⓐ____________ ⓑ____________

서답형
17 위 글의 밑줄 친 ⓒhe가 가리키는 것을 본문에서 찾아 쓰시오.

➡ ______________________

18 위 글의 밑줄 친 ⓓpoint the finger at과 바꿔 쓸 수 있는 단어를 모두 고르시오.

① insist ② criticize
③ blame ④ describe
⑤ suggest

[19~21] 다음 글을 읽고 물음에 답하시오.

Now, let's take a look at our last clip. Anna and Julie are best friends, but Anna often hurts Julie's feelings.

Anna: *Don't put your bag on my desk!*

Julie probably felt uncomfortable because Anna made a demand using the word "ⓐ___." People simply don't like taking ⓑorders. Anna should try to use words such as "can," "could," or "please." ⓒThen, what she says will sound like a demand rather than a request.

Anna: *Could you put your bag on your desk?*

서답형
19 Fill in the blank ⓐ with a suitable word.

➡ ____________________

20 위 글의 밑줄 친 ⓑorder와 같은 의미로 쓰인 것을 고르시오.

① The names are listed in alphabetical order.
② The house had been kept in good order.
③ The police are trying to restore public order.
④ Dogs can be trained to obey the order.
⑤ I would like to place an order for ten copies of this book.

서답형
21 위 글의 밑줄 친 ⓒ에서 흐름상 어색한 부분을 찾아 고치시오. (두 군데)

➡ ____________________

[22~24] 다음 글을 읽고 물음에 답하시오.

Next is Calli. She is trying to talk to her mother, but she is busy preparing to go to work. Let's have a look.

Calli needs to find the ⓐright time ⓑto talk to her mom. Maybe Calli's mom wanted to listen to what Calli was going to say. But she didn't have enough time to talk with her daughter. Calli should pick a time when her mom is ready to listen.

22 위 글의 밑줄 친 ⓐright와 같은 의미로 쓰인 것을 고르시오.

① Keep on the right side of the road.
② Was he right to leave her?
③ Lee was standing right behind her.
④ Everyone has a right to a fair trial.
⑤ I was waiting for the right moment to ask him.

중요
23 위 글의 밑줄 친 ⓑto talk와 to부정사의 용법이 같은 것을 모두 고르시오.

① I am happy to hear that.
② He worked hard only to fail.
③ There is no one to do it.
④ We expect her to pass the exam.
⑤ Do you have anything to eat?

서답형
24 위의 그림 A와 B에서 Calli는 그녀의 엄마에게 같은 말을 물어보고 있는데, 엄마의 반응이 다른 이유를 우리말로 쓰시오.

➡ 그림 A: ____________________

____

➡ 그림 B: ____________________

____

[01~03] 다음 글을 읽고 물음에 답하시오.

Welcome to "All about Teens." I'm Dr. Carter. Today, we're going to talk about using good communication skills (A)to express ourselves more effectively.

Let's start with our first clip about Brian. When he tries to talk to his brother, (B)그는 결국 남동생과 항상 말다툼을 하게 됩니다. Let's find out the reason ___ⓐ___ he has this problem.

01 Fill in the blank ⓐ with a suitable word.

➡ ________________

02 중요 위 글의 밑줄 친 (A)를 다음과 같이 바꿔 쓸 때 빈칸에 들어갈 알맞은 단어를 쓰시오.

➡ (1) ________ to express ourselves more effectively

(2) ________ to express ourselves more effectively

(3) ________ we can[may] express ourselves more effectively

(4) ________ we ________ express ourselves more effectively

03 위 글의 밑줄 친 (B)의 우리말에 맞게 주어진 어휘를 이용하여 8 단어로 영작하시오.

end up

➡ ________________

[04~06] 다음 글을 읽고 물음에 답하시오.

Next is Calli. She is trying to talk to her mother, but she is busy ___ⓐ___ to go to work. Let's have a look.

Calli: *Hey, Mom. Could I talk to you about something?*

Calli needs to find the right time to talk to her mom. Maybe Calli's mom wanted to listen to ⓑwhat Calli was going to say. But she didn't have enough time to talk with her daughter. Calli should pick a time when her mom is ready to listen.

Calli: *Hey, Mom. Could I talk to you about something?*

Mom: *Sure.*

04 중요 위 글의 빈칸 ⓐ에 prepare를 알맞은 형태로 쓰시오.

➡ ________________

05 위 글의 밑줄 친 ⓑwhat을 선행사와 관계대명사로 바꿔 쓰시오.

➡ ________________

06 고난이도 위 글을 읽고 Calli가 엄마와 대화할 때의 문제점과 효과적인 의사소통 방법을 다음과 같이 정리하고자 한다. 빈칸 (A)와 (B)에 들어갈 알맞은 단어를 본문에서 찾아 쓰시오.

- 문제점: Calli didn't (A)________ ________ ________ ________ to talk to her mom.
- 효과적인 의사소통 방법: Calli should pick a time when her mom (B)________ ________ ________ ________.

[07~09] 다음 글을 읽고 물음에 답하시오.

Brian: *You lost my earphones again. Why are you so careless?*

Brian is starting a sentence with "you" to express his feelings. ⓐInstead, he should use ⓑthe "I-message." Starting with "I" can help him ⓒpoint the finger at his brother rather than focus on what he feels or thinks.

Brian: *I'm really upset because my favorite earphones are lost.*

고난이도

07 위 글의 밑줄 친 ⓐInstead를 Instead of로 시작하여 고칠 때, 빈칸에 들어갈 알맞은 말을 쓰시오.

➡ Instead of ________ ________ ________ with "you" to express his feelings

08 위 글의 밑줄 친 ⓑthe "I-message"를 사용하는 방법을 30자 내외의 우리말로 설명하시오.

➡ ____

____

09 위 글의 밑줄 친 ⓒ에서 흐름상 어색한 부분을 찾아 고치시오.

➡ ____

____

____

[10~14] 다음 글을 읽고 물음에 답하시오.

ⓐNow, let's take a look at our last clip. Anna and Julie are best friends, but Anna often hurts Julie's feelings.

Anna: ⓑ*Don't put your bag on my desk!*

Julie probably felt uncomfortable because Anna made a demand using the word "don't." People simply don't like taking orders. Anna should try to use words such as "can," "could," or "please." Then, what she says will sound like ⓒa request rather than a demand.

Anna: (A)________________________

As we saw in the video clips, ⓓa small change in the way we express ourselves can solve or even prevent communication problems. Let's keep these tips in mind!

10 위 글의 밑줄 친 ⓐ를 다음과 같이 바꿔 쓸 때 빈칸에 들어갈 알맞은 단어를 쓰시오.

➡ Now, let's ________ a look at our last clip.
= Now, let's ________ ________ our last clip.

중요

11 위 글의 빈칸 (A)에, 밑줄 친 ⓑ의 어감이 '요청하는 말'처럼 들리도록 바꿔 쓰시오.

➡ ____

____

12 위 글의 밑줄 친 ⓒ를 다음과 같이 바꿔 쓸 때 빈칸에 들어갈 알맞은 단어를 쓰시오.

➡ rather[more] a ________ than a ________
= not so much a ________ as a ________
= less a ________ than a ________

13 위 글의 밑줄 친 ⓓ에 해당하는 것을 본문에서 찾아 쓰시오.

➡ ____

중요

14 위 글에서 Anna가 사용하지 말아야 할 단어와 사용하려고 노력해야 하는 단어들을 각각 쓰시오.

➡ 사용하지 말아야 할 단어: ________
사용하려고 노력해야 하는 단어들: ________, ________ or ________

교과서

구석구석

Wrap Up 1-2

1. **M:** You look upset, Anna. What's wrong?
~하게 보이다 = What's the problem? = Is there anything wrong? = What happened?
W: Well, I'm upset about my sister, Elsa.
~에 대해서 화가 난다
M: Why are you upset about her?
W: She keeps ordering me around.
keep 동사ing: ~을 계속하다, 반복하다 order+사람+around: ~에게 자꾸 이래라저래라 하다
M: Oh, maybe you should tell her how you feel.
'you should+동사원형 ~. ~해야 한다'는 상대방에게 충고할 때 쓰는 표현. tell은 4형식 동사로 간접목적어(her)와 직접목적어(how you feel)를 취하고 있다.
2. **W:** Hey, Mike! How come you didn't come to my birthday party yesterday?
How come을 이용해 이유를 물어볼 수 있다.
M: Sorry. I really had to hit the books yesterday.
hit the books: 공부하다
W: Why did you hit your books? Were you angry about something?
M: Oh no, that's not what I meant. I had to study yesterday because I had an exam this morning.
That's not what I meant (to say).: 그런 뜻이 아니야. 상대방이 자신의 말의 의도를 오해할 때 정정하기 위해 쓰는 표현.

구문해설 • upset: 화가 난, 기분 나쁜 • be angry about: ~에 대해서 화가 나다

해석

1. M: 너 화나 보여, Anna. 무슨 일 있니?
W: 음, 난 내 여동생 Elsa에 대해 화가 나.
M: 왜 Elsa 때문에 화가 났니?
W: 그녀는 계속 나한테 이래라저래라 해.
M: 오, 어쩌면 네가 어떻게 느끼는지 그녀에게 말해야 할지도 몰라.
2. W: 안녕, Mike! 너는 왜 어제 내 생일 파티에 안 왔니?
M: 미안해. 나는 어제 정말 'hit the books(열심히 공부하다)' 해야 했어.
W: 왜 책을 쳤니? 너 뭔가에 화가 났니?
M: 아 아니, 그런 뜻이 아니야. 나는 오늘 아침에 시험이 있어서 어제 공부를 해야 했어.

Read and Think B

Which tip was the most helpful to you, and why?
의문형용사 / 뒤에 was it the most helpful 생략
Using the "I-message" was the most helpful. I often have an argument with my sister, and now I understand the reason.
동명사로 주어 / 동명사가 주어일 경우 단수 취급 / 뒤에 why I often have an argument with my sister 생략

구문해설 • argument: 논쟁, 말다툼

어떤 조언이 너에게 가장 도움이 되었니, 그리고 이유는?
"나 메세지"를 사용하는 것이 가장 도움이 되었어. 나는 자주 내 여동생과 논쟁을 벌이곤 했는데, 이제 그 이유를 이해해.

After You Read A. Read and Write

By using good communication skills,
동명사
we can express ourselves more effectively.
us(×)

ⓐ Use the "I-message."
You can focus on what you feel or think rather than point the finger at others.
B rather than A: A라기보다는 B
ⓑ Pick the right time.
Others will listen to you when they have enough time to talk with you.
to부정사의 형용사적 용법
ⓒ Make a request.
Use words such as "can," "could," or "please."
= like

구문해설 • focus on: ~에 집중하다, 초점을 맞추다 • point the finger at: …을 비난[책망]하다 • pick: 고르다, 선택하다 • request: 요청 • such as: ~와 같은

좋은 대화 기술을 사용함으로써, 우리는 스스로를 더 효과적으로 표현할 수 있다.
ⓐ "나 메세지"를 사용하라.
남을 비난하기보다 당신이 느끼거나 생각하는 것에 조점을 맞출 수 있다.
ⓑ 올바른 시간을 선택하라.
다른 사람들은 그들이 당신과 이야기할 충분한 시간이 있을 때 당신의 말을 들을 것이다.
ⓒ 요청을 하라.
"can," "could," 또는 "please"와 같은 말을 사용하라.

영역별 핵심문제

Words & Expressions

01 주어진 단어 중 접두사 'pre-'를 이용해 만들어지지 않은 단어를 고르시오.

① precaution ② preview
③ prepare ④ premium
⑤ prevent

02 다음 빈칸에 공통으로 들어갈 말을 쓰시오.

• ________ this lesson in mind.
• She told him to do the dishes, so he couldn't ________ watching TV.

03 다음 빈칸에 들어갈 말을 〈보기〉에서 찾아 쓰시오.

보기
about at in off on up

(1) Don't cut me ________ when I'm talking.
(2) He focused ________ taking pictures.
(3) I'm ________ the middle of doing something quite important.

04 다음 영영풀이가 나타내는 말을 고르시오.

cruel or not kind

① clever ② mean
③ different ④ hard
⑤ wild

Conversation

[05~07] 다음 대화를 읽고 물음에 답하시오.

M: Sally, (A)________ come you don't talk much with Anna these days?
W: Well, I'm upset about an argument we had.
M: Why are you upset?
W: She kept cutting me off in the middle of my sentences, so I got mad. We argued and I stopped talking to her.
M: Oh, I'm sorry to hear that.

05 빈칸 (A)에 알맞은 말을 고르시오.

① what ② why ③ which
④ how ⑤ how long

06 위 대화에서 다음 영영풀이에 해당하는 단어를 찾아 쓰시오.

an angry disagreement between people

➡ ____________________

07 위 대화의 내용과 일치하는 것을 모두 고르시오.

① Sally는 Anna의 말을 중간에 끊었다.
② Sally는 Anna와 요즘 말을 하고 있지 않다.
③ 남자는 Sally와 Anna가 싸운 것에 대해 안타까워하고 있다.
④ 남자는 Sally가 왜 Anna와 사이가 안 좋은지 알고 있었다.
⑤ Sally는 Anna가 한 행동에 대해 즐거워했다.

[08~10] 다음 대화를 읽고 물음에 답하시오.

W: Mr. Brown, I want to get a good grade in English. (①)
M: (②) Well, Sujin, you should concentrate in class, (A)____________. I see you often have your head in the clouds. (③)
W: Clouds? (④) I can't see the sky from inside the classroom. (⑤)
M: (B)____________________ I meant you don't focus in class.

08 ①~⑤ 중 주어진 문장이 들어갈 곳은?

What should I do?

① ② ③ ④ ⑤

09 빈칸 (A)에 알맞은 말을 고르시오.

① instead ② in advance
③ exactly ④ however
⑤ first of all

10 빈칸 (B)에 들어갈 내용으로 적절하지 않은 것을 고르시오.

① You got me wrong.
② I didn't mean to say that.
③ You misunderstood me.
④ That's exactly what I meant.
⑤ That's not what I meant.

[11~12] 다음 대화를 읽고 물음에 답하시오.

M: You look upset, Anna. What's wrong?
W: Well, I'm upset (A)_______ my sister, Elsa.
M: Why are you upset (B)_______ her?
W: She keeps ordering me around.
M: Oh, maybe (C)________________________.

11 빈칸 (A)와 (B)에 공통으로 들어갈 수 있는 말을 모두 고르시오.

① about ② in ③ for
④ of ⑤ with

12 빈칸 (C)에 알맞은 말을 고르시오.

① I advise you to keep your promise
② you had better follow the order
③ you should have written the letter
④ you should tell her how you feel
⑤ you can see her ordering

[13~14] 다음 대화를 읽고 물음에 답하시오.

W: 나는 시험에 대해 너무 스트레스를 받는다, Jinsu.
M: Yeah, me, too. We have two more to go.
W: After finishing my exams, I want to go on a trip and just (A)____________.
M: You want to change your hair style?
W: No, that's not what I meant. I want to go somewhere and feel free from all my troubles.

13 밑줄 친 우리말과 일치하도록 주어진 단어를 이용해 문장을 만드시오. (7 words)

➡ __________________________________
(stress, so, exams)

14 빈칸 (A)에 들어갈 말을 고르시오.

① let my hair down
② keep my hair on
③ pull my hair out
④ make my hair grow
⑤ keep my hair long

Grammar

15 다음 두 문장의 뜻이 같도록 빈칸에 들어갈 알맞은 말은?

I went to the hospital where my boyfriend works.
= I went to the hospital ________ my boyfriend works.

① which ② in which
③ which in ④ for which
⑤ on which

16 다음 중 밑줄 친 부분이 어법상 어색한 것을 고르시오.

① I didn't read the book that you gave to me the other day.
② What is the reason for which she was absent from school?
③ I like that she bought for me.
④ You'd better change the way that you study English.
⑤ You may bring what you want to sell on Sale Day.

17 다음 밑줄 친 부분의 쓰임이 〈보기〉와 같은 것은?

보기
Sandwich is also the name of the town where he lived.

① I wonder where they will take us to.
② Where do you stand on this question?
③ Where there is a will, there is a way.
④ The where and the when of the accident is important.
⑤ Do you know the hotel where they stayed for the night?

18 다음 두 문장의 의미가 같도록 빈칸에 알맞은 말을 3단어로 쓰시오.

(1) The thing that she said on the phone made her mom angry.
= ________ on the phone made her mom angry.
(2) The teacher always finds out something that I've missed.
= The teacher always finds out ________.
(3) Gimbap is the food that I ate for breakfast.
= Gimbap is ________ for breakfast.

19 두 문장을 관계부사를 사용하여 한 문장으로 썼을 때, 빈칸의 문장을 쓰시오.

(1) This is the day.
+ ________________
→ This is the day when my parents got married.
(2) Let me show you the way.
+ ________________
→ Let me show you how I make gimchi.

20 다음 두 문장과 같은 의미의 한 문장으로 바꿔 쓰시오.

• The house has a small garden.
• Anne lives in the house.

(1) ________________
(2) ________________
(3) ________________

다음 ⓐ~ⓖ 중 어법상 옳은 것을 모두 고르시오.

ⓐ What I didn't know was how hard it was going to be.
ⓑ Living in a small and quiet town is that I wanted.
ⓒ I need your advice about something that I want to do for him.
ⓓ I'm searching for a nice restaurant which I can have dinner with her.
ⓔ He remembers the spring when hills and valleys were full of wildflowers.
ⓕ I don't know the reason for which she changed her mind.
ⓖ If you don't like the way how I drive, then you can drive.

➡ ____________________

Reading

[22~24] 다음 글을 읽고 물음에 답하시오.

Welcome to "All about Teens." I'm Dr. Carter. Today, we're going to talk about ⓐusing good communication skills to express ourselves more effectively.
Let's start with our first clip about Brian. ⓑ When he tries to talk to his brother, he always ends up arguing with his brother. Let's find out the reason ⓒwhy he has this problem.

22 위 글의 밑줄 친 ⓐusing과 문법적 쓰임이 같은 것을 모두 고르시오.

① Do you know that boy playing the piano?
② Barking dogs seldom bite.
③ Her dream is being a scientist.
④ Traveling by car is exciting.
⑤ His father was reading a newspaper.

23 위 글의 밑줄 친 ⓑ를 다음과 같이 바꿔 쓸 때 빈칸에 들어갈 알맞은 말을 쓰시오.

➡ ________ he tries to talk to his brother, he ends up arguing with his brother.

24 위 글의 밑줄 친 ⓒwhy를 전치사를 사용하여 두 단어로 고치시오.

➡ ____________________

[25~26] 다음 글을 읽고 물음에 답하시오.

Next is Calli. She is trying to talk to her mother, but she is busy preparing to go to work. (①) Let's have a look.
(②) Calli needs to find the right time to talk to her mom. (③) But she didn't have enough time to talk with her daughter. (④) Calli should pick a time when her mom is ready to listen. (⑤)

25 위 글의 흐름으로 보아, 주어진 문장이 들어가기에 가장 적절한 곳은?

Maybe Calli's mom wanted to listen to what Calli was going to say.

① ② ③ ④ ⑤

26 According to the passage, which is NOT true?

① Calli is trying to talk to her mother.
② Calli needs to find the right time to talk to her mom.
③ Maybe Calli's mom wanted to listen to what Calli was going to say.
④ Calli didn't have enough time to talk with her mom.
⑤ Calli should pick a time when her mom is ready to listen.

[27~29] 다음 글을 읽고 물음에 답하시오.

Now, let's take a look at our last clip. Anna and Julie are best friends, but Anna often hurts Julie's feelings.

Anna: *Don't put your bag on my desk!*

Julie ⓐprobably felt uncomfortable because Anna made a demand using the word "don't." People simply don't like taking orders. Anna should try to use words such as "can," "could," or "please." Then, ⓑ그녀가 말하는 것이 요구라기보다는 요청처럼 들릴 것입니다.

Anna: *Could you put your bag on your desk?*

27 위 글의 밑줄 친 ⓐprobably와 바꿔 쓸 수 있는 말을 쓰시오.

➡ ____________________

28 위 글의 밑줄 친 ⓑ의 우리말에 맞게 한 단어를 보충하여, 주어진 어휘를 알맞게 배열하시오.

sound / a demand / will / rather than / says / a request / she / like

➡ ____________________

____

29 위 글을 읽고 Anna가 Julie와 대화할 때의 문제점과 효과적인 의사소통 방법을 다음과 같이 정리하고자 한다. 빈칸 (A)와 (B)에 들어갈 알맞은 단어를 본문에서 찾아 쓰시오.

- 문제점: Anna (A)________ ________ ________ using the word "don't."
- 효과적인 의사소통 방법: Anna should make what she says sound like less a demand than a request by using words such as (B)"________" "________" or "________".

[30~32] 다음 글을 읽고 물음에 답하시오.

Next is Calli. She is trying to talk to her mother, but (A)she is busy preparing to go to work. Let's have a look.

Calli: *Hey, Mom. Could I talk to you about something?*

Calli needs to find the right time to talk to her mom. Maybe Calli's mom wanted to listen to what Calli was going to say. But she didn't have enough time to talk with her daughter. Calli should pick a time ___ⓐ___ her mom is ready to listen.

Calli: *Hey, Mom. Could I talk to you about something?*

Mom: *Sure.*

30 위 글의 빈칸 ⓐ에 들어갈 알맞은 말을 고르시오.

① where ② when
③ why ④ how
⑤ which

31 위 글의 밑줄 친 (A)she가 가리키는 것을 본문에서 찾아 쓰시오.

➡ ____________________

32 Which question CANNOT be answered after reading the passage?

① Does Calli's mom always have enough time to talk with her daughter?
② When is it difficult for Calli to talk to her mom?
③ What does Calli need to find in order to talk to her mom?
④ Is it likely that Calli's mom wants to listen to what Calli is going to say?
⑤ How often can Calli talk with her mom?

단원별 예상문제

출제율 90%

01 다음 괄호 안의 단어를 문맥에 맞게 고쳐 쓰시오.

A: I feel __________(comfortable) about the food.
B: What's the problem?

출제율 95%

02 밑줄 친 단어들의 영영풀이에 해당하지 않은 것을 고르시오.

- People express their sorrow by crying.
- You are clever enough to solve the problem.
- Are you disappointed at losing the race?
- The book was really helpful for the exam.

① to find a solution to something that is causing difficulties
② a fact, situation, or intention that explains why something happened, why someone did something, or why something is true
③ useful, or providing help
④ to tell someone about a feeling, opinion, or goal by speaking or writing about it
⑤ unhappy because something that you hoped for or expected did not happen or because someone or something was not as good as you expected

출제율 90%

03 다음 빈칸에 공통으로 들어갈 말을 쓰시오.

- Sally _______ cold feet at the last moment and called off the wedding.
- I _______ a good grade in the piano festival last Saturday.

출제율 90%

04 다음 빈칸에 들어갈 말을 고르시오.

You are not in a position to ________ demands right now.

① have ② let ③ find
④ come ⑤ make

[05~07] 다음 대화를 읽고 물음에 답하시오.

W: (A)________________________________
M: Not good. 나는 과학 그룹에 화가 나.
W: What's wrong?
M: The group members only speak and never listen. I (B)__________ we can finish the homework on time.
W: That's too bad.

출제율 100%

05 빈칸 (A)에 알맞은 말을 고르시오.

① How is your science homework going?
② How was your grade of science test?
③ When are you going to do your science homework?
④ Why are you mad at your science group?
⑤ How come you finished your science homework?

출제율 90%

06 빈칸 (B)에 알맞은 말을 고르시오.

① think that
② think what
③ don't think that
④ don't think how
⑤ don't think whether

밑줄 친 우리말과 일치하도록 주어진 단어를 이용해 문장을 만드시오.

➡ ________________________________
(upset)

[08~10] 다음 대화를 읽고 물음에 답하시오.

M: Why the long face, Julie?
W: I got angry at my sister yesterday and said some (A)mean things to her. (①)
M: Oh, why were you angry?
W: I was really tired and I wanted to sleep. (②) But she was talking loudly on the phone. I was really upset about that.
M: I see. (③)
W: No, not yet. (④) I want to say I'm sorry that I was mean to her, but I don't know how.
M: (⑤) Why don't you write her a note or send her a text message?
W: Hmm, that's a good idea. Thanks.

출제율 95%

08 ①~⑤ 중 주어진 문장이 들어갈 곳은?

And you two haven't worked it out yet?

① ② ③ ④ ⑤

출제율 95%

09 밑줄 친 (A)와 같은 의미로 쓰인 것은?

① Are there any means of contacting her?
② What does this mean?
③ Don't be so mean to your sister.
④ You mean we start all again?
⑤ This word means something different in French.

출제율 100%

10 위 대화의 내용과 일치하지 않는 것은?

① Julie was tired yesterday, so she wanted to sleep.
② Julie was upset, so she talked to her sister loudly.
③ Julie is depressed because of what she did to her sister.
④ Julie will be likely to send her sister a text message.
⑤ Julie wants to tell her sister that she's sorry.

출제율 95%

11 다음 빈칸에 알맞은 말을 쓰시오.

________ you will watch on Movie Day is a famous animation.

출제율 95%

12 다음 빈칸에 알맞은 말이 순서대로 짝지어진 것은?

• ________ you're saying is hard to believe.
• Do you know the reason ________ Clare didn't come to the party?

① What – how
② That – how
③ What – why
④ That – why
⑤ Which – how

출제율 95%

13 다음 중 어법상 적절한 문장은?

① Calli's mom wanted to listen to that Calli was going to say.
② That I want for breakfast is just a glass of juice.
③ The painting is which you saw in the house.
④ The ideas are not what I thought.
⑤ I'd rather talk about the things what are happening.

출제율 100%

14 다음 중 어법상 바르지 않은 것은?

① A small change in the way we express ourselves can solve or even prevent communication problems.
② He took her to the TV station which their new drama was in production.
③ What my dad planted in the garden is an apple tree.
④ I can't imagine what happened last night.
⑤ I remember the time when she was very disappointed with me because I told a lie to her.

출제율 90%

15 다음 우리말을 주어진 어휘를 이용하여 주어진 단어 수대로 영작하시오.

(1) 그 보고서는 내가 알고 싶어하는 것을 보여 주었다. (the report, show, want, 8 단어)
➡ ____________________

(2) 그는 자기가 한 것에 대하여 자랑스러워했다. (proud, do, of, 7 단어)
➡ ____________________

(3) 이 망원경은 다른 것들이 할 수 없는 일들을 할 수 있습니다. (this telescope, others, 7 단어)
➡ ____________________

(4) 7월은 여름의 열기가 본격적으로 시작되는 달이다. (the summer heat, actually, the month, begin, 10 단어)
➡ ____________________
____

(5) 우리는 시간이 정지해 버린 것 같은 어느 마을에서 머물렀다. (a village, stay, has stood, still, in, 10 단어)
➡ ____________________

(6) 인터넷은 사람들이 쇼핑하는 방법을 바꾸고 있다. (the Internet, is changing, people, 8 단어)
➡ ____________________

[16~18] 다음 글을 읽고 물음에 답하시오.

Among my relationships, I have the worst ⓐ one with my mom. I remember the time when she got angry because I didn't keep a promise with her. I also remember the time when she was very disappointed with me because I told a lie to her. I want to make my relationship better with her. So, I will keep my promises. Also I will try to be honest with her. I hope ⓑ my effort will help me work things out with my mom.

출제율 95%

16 위 글의 밑줄 친 ⓐ와 ⓑ가 가리키는 것을 각각 본문에서 찾아 쓰시오.

➡ ____________________
____

출제율 90%

17 글쓴이가 자신의 엄마를 (1) 화나게 만든 경우와 (2) 실망시킨 경우를 우리말로 쓰시오.

➡ (1) 화나게 만든 경우: ____________________
(2) 실망시킨 경우: ____________________

출제율 95%

18 본문의 내용과 일치하도록 다음 빈칸에 알맞은 단어를 쓰시오.

The writer wants to make the relationship with Mom _______.

[19~20] 다음 글을 읽고 물음에 답하시오.

> By using (A)<u>good communication skills</u>, we can express ourselves more effectively.
> ⓐ Use the "I-message."
> You can focus on what you feel or think rather than point the finger at others.
> ⓑ Pick the right time.
> Others will listen to you when they have enough time to talk with you.
> ⓒ Make a request.
> Use words such as "can," "could," or "please."

출제율 90%

19 When will others listen to you? Answer in English in a full sentence.

➡ ____________________
____

출제율 95%

20 위 글의 밑줄 친 (A)<u>good communication skills</u>에 해당하는 것 3가지를 본문에서 찾아 쓰시오.

➡ (1) ____________________
(2) ____________________
(3) ____________________

[21~23] 다음 글을 읽고 물음에 답하시오.

> **Brian:** *You lost my earphones again. Why are you so careless?*
> Brian is starting a sentence with "you" ⓐ<u>to express</u> his feelings. Instead, he should use the "I-message." Starting with "I" can help him ⓑ <u>그의 남동생을 비난하기보다는 자신이 느끼거나 생각하는 것에 집중하도록.</u>
> **Brian:** *I'm really upset because my favorite earphones are lost.*

출제율 90%

21 to부정사의 세 가지 용법 중, 위 글의 밑줄 친 ⓐ<u>to express</u>와 용법이 <u>다른</u> 것의 개수를 아래 〈보기〉에서 고르시오.

보기
① She went to the store <u>to buy</u> some fruit.
② I don't know how <u>to make</u> it.
③ I'm pleased <u>to meet</u> you.
④ He grew up <u>to be</u> a doctor.
⑤ He must be rich <u>to buy</u> such an expensive car.

① 1개 ② 2개 ③ 3개 ④ 4개 ⑤ 5개

출제율 95%

22 위 글의 밑줄 친 ⓑ의 우리말에 맞게 주어진 어구를 알맞게 배열하시오.

at his brother / what / on / rather than / he feels or thinks / focus / point the finger

➡ ____________________
____

출제율 100%

23 According to the passage, which is NOT true?

① Brian is starting a sentence with "you."
② Brian wants to express his feelings.
③ Brian should use the "I-message."
④ Starting with "I" can help him focus on what he feels or thinks.
⑤ Starting with "I" can also help him point the finger at his brother.

서술형 실전문제

01 대화의 흐름상 빈칸에 들어갈 말을 주어진 단어를 이용해 문장을 완성하시오.

A: Guess what I'm trying to say.
B: Are you saying "It's hot"?
A: No. ________________ This means "It's delicious" in Italy.

➡ ________________ (what, that, 5 단어)
________________ (that, mean, 6 단어)
________________ (misunderstand, 3 단어)

[02~03] 다음 대화를 읽고 물음에 답하시오.

M: ⓐSally, how come you don't talk much with Anna these days?
W: ⓑWell, I'm upset about an argument we had.
M: ⓒWhy are you upset?
W: 그녀가 계속해서 내가 말을 하고 있는 도중에 끊어서, 내가 화가 났어. ⓓWe argued and I stopped to talk to her.
M: ⓔOh, I'm sorry to hear that.

02 밑줄 친 우리말을 주어진 단어를 이용해 영작하시오.

➡ ________________________________
____
(mad, cut, in, off, so, get, keep)

03 ⓐ~ⓔ 중 흐름이나 어법상 어색한 것을 고르고 바르게 고치시오.

➡ ________________________________

04 다음 〈보기〉에 주어진 어휘와 what을 이용하여 빈칸을 채워 문맥에 맞게 문장을 완성하시오.

보기
want to wear, want to explain, remember

(1) ________________ is that he got a lot of trouble in the dark.
(2) You can put on ________________ on No Uniform Day.
(3) I couldn't understand ________________ to the people.

05 다음 우리말을 괄호 안의 지시대로 영작하시오.

(1) 나는 Jane이 우는 이유를 모르겠다.
➡ ________________________________
(관계부사를 써서)
➡ ________________________________
(관계대명사를 써서)

(2) 스마트폰이 사람들이 사는 방식을 바꾸어 왔다.
➡ ________________________________
(선행사를 써서)
➡ ________________________________
(관계부사를 써서)
➡ ________________________________
(that을 써서)

06 다음 두 문장을 관계부사를 이용하여 한 문장으로 쓰시오.

(1) • Do you remember the library?
• We studied together there.
➡ ______________________________

(2) • Do you know the date?
• Jake will get married on the date.
➡ ______________________________

07 다음 중 생략할 수 있는 두 단어를 쓰시오.

(1) This is the place where we spent so many years.
➡ ______________________________

(2) I know the reason why she didn't stay there.
➡ ______________________________

[08~10] 다음 글을 읽고 물음에 답하시오.

Brian: *You lost my earphones again. Why are you so careless?*

Brian is starting a sentence with "you" to express his feelings. Instead, he should use the "I-message." Starting with "I" can help him focus on __ⓐ__ he feels or thinks ⓑrather than point the finger at his brother.

Brian: *I'm really upset because my favorite earphones are lost.*

08 Fill in the blank ⓐ with a suitable word.

➡ ______________________________

09 위 글의 밑줄 친 ⓑ를 instead of로 바꿀 때, 빈칸에 들어갈 알맞은 말을 쓰시오.

➡ instead of ________ the finger at his brother

10 위 글을 읽고 Brian이 동생과 대화할 때의 문제점과 Brian에게 효과적인 의사소통 방법을 다음과 같이 정리하고자 한다. 빈칸 (A)와 (B)에 들어갈 알맞은 단어를 본문에서 찾아 쓰시오.

• 문제점: Brian is starting a sentence with "(A)________" to express his feelings.
• 효과적인 의사소통 방법: He should use the "I-message." Then, he can focus on (B)________ ________ ________ ________ ________ rather than point the finger at his brother.

[11~13] 다음 글을 읽고 물음에 답하시오.

Welcome to "All about Teens." I'm Dr. Carter. Today, we're going to talk about using good communication skills to express ourselves more effectively.

Let's start with (A)our first clip about Brian. When he tries to talk to his brother, he always ends up __ⓐ__ with his brother. Let's find out the reason why he has (B)this problem.

11 위 글의 빈칸 ⓐ에 argue를 알맞은 형태로 쓰시오.

➡ ______________________________

12 다음 빈칸 (a)와 (b)에 알맞은 단어를 넣어 밑줄 친 (A)에 대한 소개를 완성하시오.

This clip shows (a)________ ________ why Brian's attempt to talk to (b)________ ________ always ends up with argument between his brother and him.

13 위 글의 밑줄 친 (B)의 내용을 우리말로 쓰시오.

➡ ______________________________
____

창의사고력 서술형 문제

01 다음 주어진 표현과 이에 대한 뜻을 보고 아래 대화의 빈칸을 완성하시오.

put something on ice – be postponed

A: Our project is put on ice.
B: I didn't put anything on ice.
A: ____.

02 (A)와 (B)에 주어진 것 중 각각 하나씩과 관계부사를 이용하여 어법에 맞게 3 문장 이상 쓰시오.

(A) know the reason / my grandparents' house / show me / Saturday
(B) she left early / go to school / this copy machine / my first birthday party

(1) ____
(2) ____
(3) ____
(4) ____

03 다음 내용을 바탕으로 소중한 사람과의 관계를 회복하기 위한 행동 계획서를 쓰시오.

Q1 With whom do you have the worst relationship?
A1 I have the worst relationship with my mom.
Q1 Write two things that made her angry or disappointed.
A2 (1) There was a time when my mom got angry because I didn't keep a promise with her. (2) There was also a time when my mom was very disappointed with me because I told a lie to her.
Q3 What are you going to do to make the relationship better?
A3 (1) I will keep my promises. (2) I will try to be honest with her.

Among my relationships, I have the (A)______________ one with my mom. I remember the time when she (B)______________ because I didn't keep a promise with her. I also remember the time when she was very (C)______________ with me because I told a lie to her. I want to make my relationship better with her. So, I will (D)__________________. Also I will try (E)___________________. I hope my effort will help me work things out with my mom.

단원별 모의고사

01 두 문장이 같은 의미가 되도록 빈칸을 채우시오. (철자가 주어진 경우 주어진 철자로 시작할 것)

> If he is late, don't blame me.
> = If he is late, don't p________ ________ ________ at me.

02 다음 밑줄 친 부분의 쓰임이 자연스럽지 않은 것을 찾아 고치시오. (1개)

> ⓐ The doctor advised him to stop smoking.
> ⓑ If you keep to work, you'll pass the test.
> ⓒ The gym tends to get very busy at around six o'clock.
> ⓓ I try to avoid unnecessary arguments.

➡ ______________________________

03 빈칸 (A)~(C)에 들어갈 말로 알맞은 것끼리 짝지어진 것을 고르시오.

> • Don't let her (A)_______ you around.
> • They didn't (B)_______ on studying.
> • We've (C)_______ out our difficulties.

(A) (B) (C)
① have – interest – got
② have – concentrate – worked
③ order – interest – worked
④ order – encourage – got
⑤ order – concentrate – worked

04 다음 짝지어진 단어의 관계가 같도록 빈칸에 알맞은 말을 쓰시오.

> honest : dishonest = certain : ________

[05~06] 다음 대화를 읽고 물음에 답하시오.

> W: Did you finally go diving yesterday, Nick?
> M: Actually, I (A)________ cold feet, Mina.
> W: That's too bad. How did you get a cold?
> M: No, Mina. That's not what I meant. I meant that I (B)________ scared, so I didn't dive.

다음 빈칸 (A)와 (B)에 공통으로 들어갈 말을 쓰시오.

➡ ____________________

06 위 대화를 읽고 답할 수 없는 질문을 모두 고르시오.

① Did Nick dive yesterday?
② What does "get cold feet" mean?
③ How come Nick was scared of diving?
④ Why didn't Nick dive?
⑤ Where did Nick go diving?

[07~08] 다음 대화를 읽고 물음에 답하시오.

> W: How is your science homework (A)going?
> M: Not good. I'm upset about my science group.
> W: What's wrong?
> M: The group members only speak and never listen. I don't think that we can finish the homework on time.
> W: That's too bad.

07 밑줄 친 (A)와 같은 의미로 쓰인 것은?

① Where did Sue go?
② When the program is going on, the director sits in the control room.
③ We're planning to go to Arizona this winter.
④ Are you ready to go for lunch yet?
⑤ They'll be going from London to Paris by train.

08 위 대화의 내용과 일치하지 않는 것은?

① The man is worried that the science homework will not be finished on time.
② The members of his science group don't listen but speak.
③ The man is annoyed by the science group members.
④ The woman feels sorry for the man.
⑤ The science homework is individual work.

[09~11] 다음 대화를 읽고 물음에 답하시오.

W: Hey, Mike! (①) How come you didn't come to my birthday party yesterday? (②)
M: Sorry. I really had to hit the books yesterday. (③)
W: (④) Were you angry about something?
M: Oh no, that's not what I meant. (⑤) I had to study yesterday (A)_______ I had an exam this morning.

09 ①~⑤ 중 주어진 문장이 들어갈 곳은?

Why did you hit your books?

① ② ③ ④ ⑤

10 빈칸 (A)에 알맞은 말을 고르시오.

① when ② although ③ but
④ however ⑤ because

11 According to the dialogue, what does "to hit the books" means?

➡ ____________________

[12~14] 다음 대화를 읽고 물음에 답하시오.

A: People keep telling me that I talk too much. (①)
B: Well, sometimes you tend (A)[talking / to talk] about too (B)[much / many] details. (②)
A: (③) Should I just keep (C)[quiet / loud], then?
B: That's not what I meant. (④) You can try (D)[talking / to talk] about only the important details. (⑤)

12 ①~⑤ 중 주어진 문장이 들어갈 곳은?

I'm upset about that.

① ② ③ ④ ⑤

13 위 대화의 괄호 (A)~(D)에서 적절한 것을 골라 쓰시오.

➡ (A)_______ (B)_______
(C)_______ (D)_______

14 위 대화에서 다음 영영풀이에 해당하는 단어를 찾아 쓰시오.

one of many small facts or pieces of information relating to a situation

➡ ________________

15 다음 중 어법상 어색한 것을 고르시오.

① I remember the time when my mom got angry because I didn't keep a promise with her.
② Tell me the reason which you were upset.
③ What I like most is listen to the music.
④ I can't remember where I put my smart phone.
⑤ Let me see what you brought.

16 다음 빈칸에 공통으로 알맞은 말을 쓰시오.

• He finally told me the reason ________ he was so excited.
• This is ________ I refuse to go.

17 다음 문장에서 어법상 어색한 것을 바르게 고치시오.

(1) We have the freedom to wear that we want.
➡ ______________________

(2) This smart phone is not the thing what I want to have.
➡ ______________________

(3) Tell me the way how I can make a delicious pizza.
➡ ______________________

(4) 1939 is the year which World War Ⅱ broke out.
➡ ______________________

18 다음 문장의 빈칸에 들어갈 말이 다른 하나를 고르시오.

① I don't understand ________ they're talking about.
② I lost ________ you had bought me.
③ That's exactly ________ I am doing again.
④ I want you to buy ________ you really want.
⑤ I believe ________ you need to listen carefully to your inner voice.

19 〈보기〉와 같이 두 문장을 한 문장으로 바꿔 쓰시오.

보기
• I can't forget the moment.
• I rode my bike for the first time then.
→ I can't forget the moment when I rode my bike for the first time.

(1) • I know a restaurant.
• We can have delicious *samgyupsal* there.
➡ ______________________

(2) • Winter is the season.
• Leaves fall in the season.
➡ ______________________

[20~21] 다음 글을 읽고 물음에 답하시오.

Welcome to "All about Teens." I'm Dr. Carter. Today, we're going to talk about using good communication skills ⓐto express ourselves more effectively.

Let's start with our first clip about Brian. When he tries to talk to his brother, he always ends up arguing with his brother. Let's find out the reason why he has this problem.

20 위 글의 밑줄 친 ⓐto express와 to부정사의 용법이 같은 것을 모두 고르시오.

① She stood up to go out.
② I think it important to use your time well.
③ I need a pencil to write with.
④ I used a computer to draw it.
⑤ I asked Jane to drive slowly.

21 주어진 영영풀이에 해당하는 단어를 본문에서 찾아 쓰시오.

a short video recording that you can see on a website

➡ ____________________

[22~23] 다음 글을 읽고 물음에 답하시오.

Now, let's take a look at our last clip. Anna and Julie are best friends, but Anna often hurts Julie's feelings.

Anna: *Don't put your bag on my desk!*

Julie probably felt uncomfortable because Anna made a demand ⓐusing the word "don't." People simply don't like taking orders. Anna should try to use words such as "can," "could," or "please." Then, what she says will sound like a request rather than a demand.

Anna: *Could you put your bag on your desk?*

22 아래 〈보기〉에서 위 글의 밑줄 친 ⓐusing과 문법적 쓰임이 다른 것의 개수를 고르시오.

보기

① I won't give up playing baseball.
② He is watching TV now.
③ Skiing there is exciting.
④ The man working in the garden is my father.
⑤ His hobby is fishing in the river.

① 1개 ② 2개 ③ 3개 ④ 4개 ⑤ 5개

23 According to the passage, which is NOT true?

① Anna and Julie are best friends.
② Julie often hurts Anna's feelings.
③ People don't like taking orders.
④ Anna should try to use words such as "can," "could," or "please."
⑤ There is a way that Anna can make what she says sound like a request rather than a demand.

[24~25] 다음 글을 읽고 물음에 답하시오.

Next is Calli. She is trying to talk to her mother, but she is busy preparing to go to work. Let's have a look.

Calli: *Hey, Mom. Could I talk to you about something?*

Calli needs to find the right time to talk to her mom. Maybe Calli's mom wanted to listen to what Calli was going to say. But she didn't have enough time to talk with her daughter. ⓐ Calli는 어머니가 들으실 준비가 된 때를 골라야 합니다.

Calli: *Hey, Mom. Could I talk to you about something?*

Mom: *Sure.*

24 위 글의 밑줄 친 ⓐ의 우리말에 맞게 주어진 어휘를 이용하여 12 단어로 영작하시오.

pick, when, ready, to

➡ ____________________
____

25 다음 문장에서 위 글의 내용과 다른 부분을 찾아서 고치시오. (3 군데)

Calli had no time to talk to her mom, because she was busy preparing to go to school.

➡ ____________________

Lesson 2

Wonderful Nature

의사소통 기능

- 기대하는 일 표현하기
  A: What's your summer plan?
  B: My family is going to China. I can't wait to visit the Rainbow Mountains.
- 알고 있는 정보 말하기
  A: What are the white things in the picture?
  B: They are snow rollers. I've heard that they are made by strong wind and sticky snow.

언어 형식

- to부정사의 의미상의 주어
  Iceland is the best place **for many location scouts** to visit.
- 현재완료진행형
  I**'ve been visiting** the forest to study animals for 20 years.

교과서

Words & Expressions

Key Words

- □ **actually** [ǽktʃuəli] 부 실제로
- □ **adventure** [ədvéntʃər] 명 모험
- □ **alive** [əláiv] 형 생기 넘치는, 살아 있는
- □ **amazing** [əméiziŋ] 형 놀라운, 멋진
- □ **anywhere else** 다른 곳
- □ **aurora** [ɔ́:rɔ:rə] 명 오로라
- □ **award** [əwɔ́:rd] 명 상
- □ **canvas** [kǽnvəs] 명 도화지, 캔버스
- □ **cave** [keiv] 명 동굴
- □ **chance** [tʃæns] 명 기회
- □ **cliff** [klif] 명 절벽
- □ **clothing** [klóuðiŋ] 명 의류, 옷
- □ **colorist** [kʌ́lərist] 명 색채화가
- □ **combination** [kɑ̀mbənéiʃən] 명 조합
- □ **community center** 지역 문화 회관
- □ **competition** [kɑ̀mpətíʃən] 명 대회
- □ **countless** [káuntlis] 형 많은, 셀 수 없는
- □ **develop** [divéləp] 동 만들다, 발전하다
- □ **ecologist** [ikɑ́lədʒist] 명 생태학자
- □ **environment** [inváiəiərənmənt] 명 환경
- □ **field** [fi:ld] 명 분야, 영역
- □ **glacier** [gléiʃər] 명 빙하
- □ **glow** [glou] 동 빛나다
- □ **harsh** [hɑ:rʃ] 형 (날씨 · 생활 환경이) 혹독한, 가혹한
- □ **honor** [ɑ́nər] 동 영광으로 생각하다
- □ **improve** [imprú:v] 동 개선하다, 향상시키다
- □ **insight** [ínsàit] 명 통찰력
- □ **inspire** [inspáiər] 동 영감을 주다, 고무하다, 격려하다
- □ **investigate** [invéstəgèit] 동 조사하다
- □ **jack-in-the-box** 열면 인형 등이 튀어나오는 상자, (각종) 기계 장치
- □ **lemur** [lí:mər] 명 (마다가스카르산) 여우원숭이
- □ **level** [lévəl] 명 (건물 · 땅의) 층
- □ **location** [loukéiʃən] 명 위치, 장소
- □ **Maldives** [mǽldaivz] 명 몰디브 공화국
- □ **miracle** [mírəkl] 명 놀라운 일, 기적
- □ **mixed** [mikst] 형 섞인, 혼합한
- □ **Mongolia** [maŋgóuliə] 명 몽골
- □ **mountain range** 산맥
- □ **palm tree** 야자나무
- □ **peak** [pi:k] 동 절정[최대한도]에 이르다
- □ **period** [pí:əriəd] 명 기간
- □ **personal** [pə́rsənl] 형 개인적인
- □ **pyramid** [pírəmìd] 명 피라미드
- □ **rainfall** [réinfɔ̀l] 명 강우
- □ **recent** [rí:snt] 형 최근의
- □ **reef** [ri:f] 명 암초
- □ **research** [risə́:rtʃ] 동 조사하다, 연구하다
- □ **scout** [skaut] 명 정찰
- □ **set** [set] (해 · 달 등이) 지다
- □ **shape** [ʃeip] 명 모양, 형태
- □ **shoot** [ʃu:t] 동 촬영하다
- □ **shooting star** 유성, 별똥별
- □ **snow roller** (기상학) 두루마리 눈
- □ **spiky** [spáiki] 형 끝이 뾰족한
- □ **sticky** [stíki] 형 끈적거리는, 달라붙는
- □ **survive** [sərváiv] 동 살아남다, 생존하다
- □ **travel** [trǽvəl] 동 이동하다
- □ **unique** [ju:ní:k] 형 독특한, 특별한
- □ **unusual** [ənjú:ʒuəl] 형 특이한, 흔치 않은
- □ **view** [vju:] 명 풍경, 전망
- □ **weather report** 일기 예보
- □ **yellow dust** 황사

Key Expressions

- □ **be caused by** ~ ~에 기인하다
- □ **be filled with** ~로 가득차다
- □ **be made by** ~ ~에 의해 만들어지다
- □ **be[get] inspired by** ~에 의해 영감을 받다
- □ **come back from** ~ ~에서 돌아오다
- □ **come true** 실현되다, 사실이 되다
- □ **cut down** 자르다
- □ **due to** 명사 ~ 때문에
- □ **find out** 발견하다, 알아보다
- □ **get in shape** 좋은 몸 상태를 유지하다
- □ **hundreds of** ~ 수백의 ~, 수많은 ~
- □ **in the middle of the night** 한밤중에
- □ **keep** ~ **on one's toes** ~에게 정신을 바짝 차리게 하다
- □ **make plans (for)** (~의) 계획을 세우다
- □ **millions of** 수백만의
- □ **run up (to** 장소) (~에) 달려가다
- □ **seem**+형용사 ~처럼 보이다
- □ **stand in for** ~을 대신하다
- □ **turn out** (일 · 진행 · 결과가 특정 방식으로) 되다
- □ **walk along** 산책하다

Word Power

※ **접두어** in-

in-은 '안에(**in**)'의 의미가 있는 접두어이다.

□ **in**(= **in**) + **sight**(시야) → 안을 들여다보는 시야 → **insight**(통찰력)
□ **in**(= **in**) + **come**(오다) → 안으로 들어오는 것 → **income**(소득)
□ **in**(= **in**) + **side**(면, 지역) → **inside**(내부, 안쪽)
□ **in**(= **in**) + **door**(문) → **indoor**(실내의)

※ **a-로 시작하는 형용사는 주로 서술적 용법으로 쓰인다.**

□ **a** + **live**(살아 있는, 생방송의) → **alive**(생기 넘치는, 살아 있는)
□ **a** + **lone**(단 하나의, 혼자의) → **alone**(혼자, 홀로)
□ **a** + **like**(같은, 동등한) → **alike**(비슷한, 동등한)
□ **a** + **sleep**(자다) → **asleep**(잠이 든, 자는)
□ **a** + **wake**(깨다, 일어나다) → **awake**(깨어 있는, 잠자지 않는)

English Dictionary

□ **adventure** 모험
→ an exciting experience in which dangerous or unusual things happen
위험하고 흔치 않은 일이 발생하는 신나는 경험

□ **cave** 동굴
→ a large hole in the side of a hill or under the ground
언덕의 한쪽 면이나 땅 밑에 있는 큰 구멍

□ **cliff** 절벽
→ the steep side of an area of high land
높은 땅이 있는 지역의 가파른 면

□ **combination** 조합
→ something that combines several things
몇몇 개의 것들을 결합시킨 것

□ **countless** 많은, 셀 수 없는
→ very many, especially more than you think is reasonable
매우 많은, 특히 당신이 생각하기에 합당한 것보다 더 많은

□ **ecologist** 생태학자
→ a scientist who studies the environment and the way that plants, animals, and humans live together and affect each other
환경과 식물, 동물, 인간이 함께 살면서 서로에게 영향을 미치는 방법에 대해 연구하는 과학자

□ **glacier** 빙하
→ a very large mass of ice that moves very slowly
매우 느리게 움직이는 아주 큰 얼음 덩어리

□ **glow** 빛나다
→ to shine with a soft light
부드러운 빛으로 빛나다

□ **harsh** (날씨 · 생활 환경이) 혹독한
→ difficult to live in and very uncomfortable
살기에 힘들고 매우 불편한

□ **inspire** 영감을 주다, 고무하다, 격려하다
→ to encourage someone by making them feel confident and eager to do something
어떤 사람을 자신감 있게 그리고 어떤 것을 하고 싶게 만듦으로써 북돋우다

□ **mixed** 섞인, 혼합한
→ consisting of several different types of things or people 몇 개의 다른 종류의 사물이나 사람으로 구성된

□ **peak** 절정[최대한도]에 이르다
→ to reach the highest point or level
가장 높은 지점이나 수준에 이르다

□ **period** 기간
→ a particular length of time with a beginning and an end 처음과 끝을 가진 특정한 시간의 길이

□ **rainbow** 무지개
→ a large curve of different colors that can appear in the sky when there is both sun and rain
태양과 비 둘 다 있을 때 하늘에 나타날 수 있는 여러 가지의 색깔을 가진 큰 곡선

□ **research** 조사하다, 연구하다
→ to study a subject in detail, especially in order to discover new facts or test new ideas
특히 새로운 사실을 발견하거나 새로운 생각을 검사하기 위해 자세히 어떤 대상을 연구하다

□ **shooting star** 유성, 별똥별
→ a piece of rock or metal from space that burns brightly as it falls towards the Earth
지구로 떨어질 때 밝은 빛을 내며 타는 우주로부터 온 돌이나 금속 조각

□ **unique** 독특한, 특별한
→ very special, unusual, or good
매우 특별한, 흔하지 않은, 혹은 좋은

□ **unusual** 특이한, 흔치 않은
→ different from what is usual or normal
보통의 평범한 것과는 다른

[01~02] 다음 빈칸에 알맞은 단어를 고르시오.

01

Because of the ________ weather conditions, the marathon was postponed for two weeks.

① harsh ② soft
③ sticky ④ moderate
⑤ mild

02

Oil production ______ in the early 1980s.

① peaked ② acquired
③ became ④ determined
⑤ fought

중요 **03** 다음 빈칸에 들어갈 말이 나머지와 다른 하나를 고르시오. (대 • 소문자 무시)

① I know the mayor really well. _____ fact, I had dinner with her last week.
② The phone rang ______ the middle of the night.
③ The movie was inspired _______ real events.
④ During the dangerous scenes, a stunt woman stood _____ for Goldie Hawn.
⑤ I really want to get ______ shape before summer.

중요 **04** 다음 밑줄 친 부분의 의미로 알맞지 않은 것은?

① I haven't had a <u>chance</u> to look at it yet. (기회)
② Keith has a degree in engineering, but couldn't find a job in his <u>field</u>. (분야)
③ Our problems were due to a <u>combination</u> of bad management and lack of experience. (조합, 결합)
④ If I'm going out for a meal, I prefer to <u>try</u> something different. (노력하다)
⑤ They forgot that Picasso was a brilliant <u>colorist</u>. (색채화가)

05 다음 빈칸에 공통으로 들어갈 말을 고르시오.

• We need someone who can _______ the team. • They think his music _________s and moves people.

① investigate ② bring ③ set
④ increase ⑤ inspire

중요 **06** 다음 빈칸 (A)와 (B)에 알맞은 말로 짝지어진 것을 고르시오.

• However, the parents and teachers (A)_______ out a problem with the race. • Did you (B)_________ plans for your summer vacation?

(A) (B)
① found – call ② found – make
③ made – call ④ made – make
⑤ made – have

01 두 문장이 같은 의미가 되도록 빈칸을 채우시오.

Every time I wash my car, it rains the next day.
= ________ I wash my car, it rains the next day.

02 빈칸에 적절한 말을 주어진 단어를 이용하여 채우시오.

The research provides new ________ into the way we process language. (sight)

03 다음 밑줄 친 부분의 쓰임이 자연스럽지 않은 것을 찾아 고치시오.

ⓐ Sorry, but I need to be lone right now.
ⓑ Are all your grandparents still alive?
ⓒ I think my mother and I are very much alike in some ways.

➡ ____________________

[04~05] 다음 빈칸에 공통으로 들어갈 말을 쓰시오.

04

• When did you ________ back from the States?
• This is the land where dreams ________ true.

05

• I just need a car to get me from my house ________ the station.
• This project will not continue next year due ________ a lack of funds.

고난이도

06 다음 우리말에 맞도록 빈칸에 알맞은 말을 쓰시오.

(1) 오로라의 색깔들은 공기의 조건에 따라 달라집니다.
➡ An ________ colors depend on the conditions of the air.

(2) 기후 변화는 다양한 인간 활동에 의해서 야기된다.
➡ Climate change ________ ________ ________ various human activities.

(3) 몇몇 생태학자들은 많은 다양한 방식으로 생명을 연구한다.
➡ Some ________ study life in many different ways.

(4) 누가 그녀를 대신해 줄 수 있는가?
➡ Who could possibly ________ ________ ________ her?

07 다음 빈칸을 <보기>에 있는 어휘를 이용하여 채우시오.

보기
cut fill keep turn

(1) They do random checks to ________ workers on their toes.
(2) It was a difficult time, but eventually things ________ out all right.
(3) People ________ down too many trees, destroying the habitats of wildlife.
(4) The air was ________ with the scent of roses.

교과서

Conversation

1 기대하는 일 표현하기

A: What's your summer plan? 여름 계획은 무엇이니?
B: My family is going to China. I can't wait to visit the Rainbow Mountains.
나의 가족은 중국에 갈 거야. 나는 레인보우 산맥을 빨리 방문하고 싶어.

- 'can't wait to+동사원형'은 '~하기를 몹시 바라다' 또는 '어서 ~하고 싶다'라는 의미로 기대를 나타낼 때 사용하는 표현이다.
- 'can't wait to+동사원형' 대신에 'can't wait for+(동)명사'나 'look forward to+(동)명사', 'expect to+동사원형'을 사용할 수 있다.
- 'I can't wait to' 다음에는 동사원형이 오고, 'I'm looking forward to' 다음에는 명사나 동명사가 오는 것에 유의한다.

I can't wait to take the trip. (나는 어서 여행을 하고 싶다.)
= I can't wait for taking the trip.
= I'm looking forward to taking the trip.
= I'm looking forward to the trip.

기대하는 일을 나타내는 표현

- I can't wait to 동사원형. (나는 어서 ~하고 싶어.)
- I'm looking forward to (동)명사.
- I can't wait for (동)명사.
- I expect to 동사원형. (나는 ~을 기대한다.)

핵심 Check

1. 다음 우리말과 일치하도록 주어진 단어를 배열하여 문장을 만드시오.

A: I am going to have a pizza party this Friday. Can you come?
B: Of course. ________________________ (can't, the, I, wait, party, to, to, go) (나는 어서 파티에 가고 싶어.)

2. 다음 문장과 같은 의미가 되도록 주어진 단어를 이용하여 쓰시오.

I can't wait to try them out on my friends. (나는 어서 내 친구들한테 그것들을 사용해 보고 싶어.)

➡ ____ (look)

2 알고 있는 정보 말하기

A: What are the white things in the picture? 사진의 그 흰 것들은 무엇이니?

B: They are snow rollers. I've heard that they are made by strong wind and sticky snow. 그것들은 두루마리 눈이야. 나는 그것들이 강한 바람과 끈적거리는 눈에 의해 만들어진다는 말을 들었어.

- 'I've heard that ~.'은 '~에 대해 들었다'의 의미로 알고 있거나 들은 것에 대해 말할 때 쓰는 표현이다.
- 일반적으로 현재완료의 형태인 'I've heard that ~.'을 쓰지만 'I heard that ~.'이라고 할 수도 있다. that절이 아닌 전치사 about을 써서 표현할 수도 있다.

알고 있는 정보 말하기

- I've heard that 주어+동사 ~.
- I heard that 주어+동사 ~.
- I know that 주어+동사 ~.
- I've heard about (동)명사 ~.
- I heard about[of] (동)명사 ~. (나는 ~에 대해 들었다.)
- I know about (동)명사 ~. (나는 ~을 알고 있다.)
- I'm aware of (동)명사 ~.

핵심 Check

3. 다음 우리말과 일치하도록 빈칸에 알맞은 말을 쓰시오.

B: I am having trouble with my eyes.
A: I've heard ______________________.
(토마토를 먹는 것이 눈에 좋다고 들었어.)

4. 주어진 문장 이후에 올 대화의 순서를 바르게 배열하시오.

What's wrong?

(A) I've heard that having seaweed is good for your hair.
(B) I'll try to have it more often.
(C) I am having trouble with my hair.

➡ ______________________

Conversation 교과서 대화문 익히기

Listen & Talk 1 A-1

W: David, what's your summer plan?

M: My family is going to China. I ❶can't wait to visit the Rainbow Mountains.

W: The Rainbow Mountains?

M: They are some mountains ❷that ❸look like ❹canvases ❺in rainbow colors.

W: ❻That sounds amazing! ❼Take lots of pictures!

W: David, 여름 계획은 뭐야?
M: 우리 가족은 중국에 갈 거야. 나는 레인보우 산맥을 빨리 방문하고 싶어.
W: 레인보우 산맥?
M: 그것은 무지개 색깔의 화폭처럼 보이는 산들이야.
W: 정말 멋지구나! 사진 많이 찍어!

❶ can't wait to+동사원형: 빨리 ~하고 싶다, ~하기를 몹시 바라다 visit: 방문하다
❷ that은 선행사 some mountains를 수식하고 있는 주격 관계대명사이다.
❸ look like 명사: ~처럼 보이다 / 선행사가 some mountains이므로 복수 동사인 look의 형태를 사용한다.
❹ canvas: 도화지, 캔버스
❺ in rainbow colors: 무지개 색깔로
❻ sound+형용사: ~하게 들리다 amazing: 멋진
❼ take a picture: 사진을 찍다 lots of: 많은

Check(√) True or False

(1) David has no plans for summer. T ☐ F ☐

(2) You can visit the Rainbow Mountains in China. T ☐ F ☐

Listen & Talk 2 A-1

M: Mom, did you watch ❶the weather report today? We ❷will be able to see ❸hundreds of ❹shooting stars tonight!

W: Wow, fantastic! When is the best time ❺to see them?

M: ❻I've heard that the shooting stars will peak between 12 a.m. and 2 a.m.

W: Wow, it will be a special night!

M: 엄마, 오늘 일기예보 보셨어요? 우리는 오늘 밤 수많은 유성을 볼 수 있을 거예요!
W: 와, 환상적이야! 그것들을 보기에 가장 좋은 시간은 언제니?
M: 저는 유성이 오전 12시에서 2시 사이에 절정에 이를 거라고 들었어요.
W: 와, 특별한 밤이 되겠구나!

❶ weather report: 일기 예보
❷ will: ~할 것이다 be able to 동사원형: ~할 수 있다 / 조동사는 2개를 연달아(will can) 사용할 수 없기 때문에 can을 be able to로 바꿔서 사용한다.
❸ hundreds of ~: 수백의 ~, 수많은 ~
❹ shooting star: 유성, 별똥별
❺ to see them에서 them은 shooting stars를 받는 인칭대명사이다. to see them은 the best time을 꾸며주는 형용사적 용법으로 사용되고 있다.
❻ I've heard that ~: ~에 대해 들었다, ~에 대해 알고 있다 peak: 절정[최대한도]에 이르다 between A and B: A와 B 사이에서

Check(√) True or False

(3) There will be many shooting stars tomorrow. T ☐ F ☐

(4) The man knows when the shooting stars will peak. T ☐ F ☐

Listen & Talk 1 A-2

M: Do you ❶want to watch the new 3D movie?
W: Which ❷one?
M: The one about ❸adventures under the sea. ❹It was shot near Australia's Great Barrier Reef.
W: Oh, ❺I've heard of it. It has the most beautiful sea life.
M: Right. I ❻can't wait to watch the movie. ❼Let's go and get the ticket.

M: 너 새로 나온 3D 영화 보고 싶니?
W: 어느 영화?
M: 바다 밑의 모험에 관한 거야. 그것은 오스트레일리아의 Great Barrier Reef 근처에서 촬영되었어.
W: 오, 난 그것에 대해 들어본 적이 있어. 거기에는 가장 아름다운 해양 생물이 있어.
M: 맞아. 난 그 영화를 빨리 보고 싶어. 가서 표를 사자.

❶ want는 'to+동사원형'을 목적어로 취할 수 있다.
❷ one은 a 3D movie를 받는 부정대명사이다.
❸ adventure: 모험 under ~: ~ 아래에
❹ shoot: 촬영하다 (shoot–shot–shot) near: ~ 가까이에서 reef: 암초
주어진 It은 새로 나온 3D 영화 중 하나를 의미한다. 영화가 촬영되었으므로 동사는 수동태인 'be shot'으로 사용되었다.
❺ 'I've heard of it.'은 '그것에 대해 들어 본 적이 있다'의 의미로 알고 있거나 들은 것에 대해 말할 때 쓰는 표현이다. 전치사 of 대신에 about을 사용할 수 있다.
❻ can't wait to+동사원형: 빨리 ~하고 싶다, ~하기를 몹시 바라다(= can't wait for (동)명사 ~ = be looking forward to (동)명사 ~ = expect to 동사원형 ~)
❼ go와 get은 접속사 and로 연결되어 있다. Let's 다음에 동사원형이 나와야 하므로 get도 동사원형으로 사용되었다.

Check(√) True or False

(5) The woman has never heard of the movie about adventures under the sea. T ☐ F ☐

(6) The woman and the man will watch the movie together. T ☐ F ☐

Listen & Talk 2 B

M: Jisu, ❶did you know that the sun never sets in Norway during summer?
W: No, I didn't know ❷that. How interesting!
M: Yeah, and ❸I've heard that people go hiking and even cycling at night ❹because it isn't dark.
W: I'd love to go hiking and cycling ❺in the middle of the night!
M: Me, too. I hope we ❻get the chance ❼to try it someday.

M: 지수야, 여름 동안 노르웨이에서는 해가 지지 않는다는 걸 알고 있니?
W: 아니, 그건 몰랐어. 정말 흥미롭구나!
M: 그래, 그리고 난 사람들이 밤에 어둡지 않아서 하이킹 가고 심지어 자전거를 타러 간다고 들었어.
W: 나는 한밤중에 하이킹 가고 자전거를 타러 가고 싶어!
M: 나도. 언젠가 그것을 해볼 기회가 있으면 좋겠어.

❶ 'Did you know that ~?'은 '~에 대해 알고 있었니?'의 의미로, 알고 있는지 여부를 묻는 표현이다. 같은 의미로 'Are you aware that ~?'나 'Have you heard that ~?'을 사용할 수 있다. set: (해 · 달 등이) 지다 during+명사: ~ 동안에
❷ 대명사 that은 앞 문장의 'the sun never sets in Norway during summer(노르웨이에서는 여름 동안에는 해가 지지 않는다)'의 내용을 받고 있다.
❸ I've heard that ~: ~에 대해 들었다, ~에 대해 알고 있다 go+동사ing: ~하러 가다 at night: 밤에
❹ because(~ 때문에)는 이유를 나타내는 접속사이므로 뒤에 주어와 동사가 와야 한다.
❺ in the middle of the night: 한밤중에
❻ get the chance: 기회를 얻다(= have the chance)
❼ to try it은 앞의 명사 the chance를 수식하는 형용사적 용법으로 사용하였다. try: 시도하다, 해보다

Check(√) True or False

(7) Jisu knew that the sun never sets in Norway during summer. T ☐ F ☐

(8) The man wishes to go hiking and cycling in the middle of the night. T ☐ F ☐

Conversation 교과서 대화문 익히기

Listen & Talk 1 Get Ready

A: The ❶view of the top of the mountain ❷is going to be amazing.
B: Yeah, ❸I can't wait to see the view. ❹Let's run up there!

❶ view: 경치, 풍경, 전망
❷ 주어가 The view로 단수 명사이므로 단수 동사인 is가 어울린다. be going to 동사원형: ~할 것이다
❸ 'can't wait to+동사원형'은 '~하기를 몹시 바라다' 또는 '어서 ~하고 싶다'의 의미로 기대를 나타낼 때 사용하는 표현이다.
❹ 어떤 활동을 함께하자고 제안할 경우에는 'Let's+동사원형'을 사용할 수 있다. run up (to 장소): (~에) 달려가다

Listen & Talk 1 B

W: Dad, my science club ❶is going to go to Dokdo in July.
M: Oh, really? What do you plan to do there?
W: We are going to ❷study the caves on the island and go bird watching.
M: ❸Sounds like it will be an interesting trip.
W: Yeah. I've ❹only read about Dokdo in books. I can't wait to actually visit there.
M: I ❺hope you enjoy your trip!

❶ be going to 동사원형: ~할 예정이다 go to 장소: ~에 가다. 월(month)을 나타내는 명사 앞에는 전치사 in을 사용한다.
❷ study: 연구하다 cave: 동굴 / 접속사 and로 study와 go가 병렬 구조를 이루고 있다.
❸ Sounds like 명사/명사절: ~처럼 들리다, ~일 것 같다
❹ only는 in books를 수식하는 부사이다.
❺ 'I hope (that)+주어+동사 ~.'는 '~를 바란다.'의 의미로 희망이나 바람을 나타내는 표현이다.

Listen & Talk 2 Get Ready

A: ❶The level of yellow dust is really high today.
B: Yeah. ❷I've heard that the yellow dust travels from the deserts of Mongolia to Korea.

❶ level: 정도, 수준 yellow dust: 황사 high: 격심한
❷ I've heard that ~: ~에 대해 들었다, ~에 대해 알고 있다 from A to B: A에서 B로 travel: 이동하다

Listen & Talk 2 A-2

M: Erica, what are the white things in the picture?
W: They are snow rollers. I've heard that ❶ they ❷are made by strong wind and ❸ sticky snow.
M: ❹Interesting! They look like snow rings.
W: Yeah, I'd like to actually see them someday.

❶ they는 snow rollers(두루마리 눈)를 받는 대명사이다.
❷ be made by ~: ~에 의해 만들어지다
❸ sticky: 끈적거리는, 달라붙는
❹ 'Interesting!'은 상대방이 한 말에 대하여 '재미있겠다!'라는 표현으로 'How interesting!'이나 'Sounds interesting!' 등의 표현을 사용할 수 있다.

Communication

M: Let's welcome ❶Ms. Scarlett Lee, the winner of this year's photo competition.
W: Hello, thank you for inviting me. ❷I've honored ❸to receive the award.
M: ❹Let's talk about your photo. I've heard that this photo ❺was taken in the Maldives. Is that true?
W: Yes, ❻this glowing beach is caused by plankton.
M: Wow, it truly is amazing!
W: Yes, it is. I can't wait to take more pictures of amazing beaches.
M: ❼I wish you the best of luck!

❶ Ms. Scarlett Lee와 the winner of this year's photo competition은 동격 관계이다. winner: 우승자 competition: 대회
❷ honor: 영광으로 생각하다
❸ to receive the award는 honored(영광으로 생각하다)의 이유를 설명하고 있으므로, to부정사의 부사적 용법 중 감정의 원인(~해서)으로 사용하고 있다. award: 상
❹ 'Let's talk about ~'는 '~에 대해 이야기해 보자'의 의미로 주제를 소개할 때 사용한다.
❺ that절의 주어인 this photo가 찍히는 것이므로 수동태(be+p.p.)인 'be taken'이 적절하다.
❻ glowing: 빛나는 be caused by ~: ~에 기인하다
❼ wish가 4형식으로 간접목적어(you)와 직접목적어(the best of luck)를 취하고 있다.

● 다음 우리말과 일치하도록 빈칸에 알맞은 말을 쓰시오.

Listen & Talk 1 Get Ready

A: The ________ of the top of the mountain is going to be ________.

B: Yeah, I can't ________ ________ see the view. Let's ________ ________ there!

해석

A: 산꼭대기의 경치는 멋질 거야.

B: 그래, 빨리 경치가 보고 싶어. 저곳으로 뛰어 올라가자!

Listen & Talk 1 A-1

W: David, ________ your summer ________?

M: My family is ________ to China. I can't ________ ________ ________ the Rainbow Mountains.

W: The Rainbow Mountains?

M: They ________ some mountains ________ look ________ canvases in rainbow colors.

W: That ________ amazing! ________ lots of pictures!

W: David, 여름 계획은 뭐야?

M: 우리 가족은 중국에 갈 거야. 나는 레인보우 산맥을 빨리 방문하고 싶어.

W: 레인보우 산맥?

M: 그것은 무지개 색깔의 화폭처럼 보이는 산들이야.

W: 정말 멋지구나! 사진 많이 찍어!

Listen & Talk 1 A-2

M: Do you ________ ________ ________ the new 3D movie?

W: Which one?

M: The one ________ ________ under the sea. It ________ ________ near Australia's Great Barrier Reef.

W: Oh, I've ________ of it. It ________ the most beautiful sea life.

M: Right. I ________ ________ ________ ________ the movie. Let's ________ ________ ________ the ticket.

M: 너 새로 나온 3D 영화 보고 싶니?

W: 어느 영화?

M: 바다 밑의 모험에 관한 거야. 그것은 오스트레일리아의 Great Barrier Reef 근처에서 촬영되었어.

W: 오, 난 그것에 대해 들어본 적이 있어. 거기에는 가장 아름다운 해양 생물이 있어.

M: 맞아. 난 그 영화를 빨리 보고 싶어. 가서 표를 사자.

Listen & Talk 1 B

W: Dad, my science club ________ ________ to go to Dokdo ________ July.

M: Oh, really? ________ do you ________ ________ do there?

W: We are going to ________ the ________ on the island and ________ bird ________.

W: 아빠, 제 과학 동아리는 7월에 독도에 갈 거예요.

M: 오, 정말? 그곳에서 무엇을 할 계획이니?

W: 우리는 섬에 있는 동굴을 연구하고 새를 관찰하러 갈 거예요.

M: Sounds ________ it will be an ________ trip.

W: Yeah. ________ ________ ________ ________ Dokdo in books. I can't ________ ________ ________ ________ there.

M: I ________ you ________ your trip!

해석

M: 흥미로운 여행이 될 것 같구나.
W: 네. 저는 책에서만 독도에 대해서 읽었어요. 빨리 그곳을 실제로 방문하고 싶어요.
M: 즐거운 여행이 되길 바라!

Listen & Talk 2 Get Ready

A: The level of yellow dust ________ really ________ today.

B: Yeah. ________ ________ ________ the yellow dust ________ ________ the deserts of Mongolia ________ Korea.

A: 오늘 황사의 정도가 정말 심해.
B: 그래. 황사는 몽골의 사막에서 한국으로 이동한다고 들었어.

Listen & Talk 2 A-1

M: Mom, did you watch the ________ ________ today? We will be ________ to see hundreds of ________ ________ tonight!

W: Wow, fantastic! ________ is the best time ________ ________ ________?

M: I've ________ ________ the ________ ________ will peak ________ 12 a.m. ________ 2 a.m.

W: Wow, it will be a ________ ________!

M: 엄마, 오늘 일기예보 보셨어요? 우리는 오늘 밤 수많은 유성을 볼 수 있을 거예요!
W: 와, 환상적이야! 그것을 보기에 가장 좋은 시간은 언제니?
M: 저는 유성이 오전 12시에서 2시 사이에 절정에 이를 거라고 들었어요.
W: 와, 특별한 밤이 되겠구나!

Listen & Talk 2 A-2

M: Erica, what ________ the white things in the picture?

W: ________ ________ snow rollers. ________ ________ ________ they are ________ ________ strong wind and ________ snow.

M: Interesting! They look ________ snow rings.

W: Yeah, I'd ________ to ________ see them someday.

M: Erica, 사진 속의 흰 것들은 뭐니?
W: 그것들은 두루마리 눈이야. 나는 그것이 강한 바람과 끈적끈적한 눈으로 만들어진다고 들었어.
M: 흥미롭구나! 그것들은 눈 반지처럼 보여.
W: 그래, 나도 언젠가 그것들을 실제로 보고 싶어.

해석

Listen & Talk 2 B

M: Jisu, did you know ________ the sun never ________ in Norway during summer?

W: No, I didn't know ________. ________ interesting!

M: Yeah, and I've ________ ________ people go hiking and even ________ at night ________ it isn't dark.

W: I'd ________ to go hiking and cycling ________ the middle ________ the night!

M: Me, ________. I hope we get the________ ________ ________ it someday.

M: 지수야, 여름 동안 노르웨이에서는 해가 지지 않는다는 걸 알고 있니?

W: 아니, 그건 몰랐어. 정말 흥미롭구나!

M: 그래, 그리고 난 사람들이 밤에 어둡지 않아서 하이킹 가고 심지어 자전거를 타러 간다고 들었어.

W: 나는 한밤중에 하이킹과 자전거를 타러 가고 싶어!

M: 나도. 언젠가 그것을 해볼 기회가 있으면 좋겠어.

Communication

M: Let's welcome Ms. Scarlett Lee, the ________ of this year's photo competition.

W: Hello, thank you ________ ________ me. I've ________ to receive the award.

M: Let's ________ about your photo. I've ________ ________ this photo ________ ________ in the Maldives. Is that ________?

W: Yes, this glowing beach is ________ ________ plankton.

M: Wow, it truly is ________!

W: Yes, it is. I ________ ________ ________ ________ more pictures of amazing beaches.

M: I ________ you the ________ of luck!

M: 올해 사진 대회 우승자인 Scarlett Lee 양을 환영합시다.

W: 안녕하세요, 초대해 주셔서 감사합니다. 상을 받게 되어 영광으로 생각합니다.

M: 사진에 대해 얘기해 봅시다. 저는 이 사진이 몰디브에서 찍힌 거라고 들었어요. 그게 사실인가요?

W: 네, 이 빛나는 해변은 플랑크톤 때문에 생긴 거예요.

M: 와, 정말 놀랍네요!

W: 네, 그래요. 저는 빨리 멋진 해변의 사진을 더 많이 찍고 싶어요.

M: 행운을 빌어요!

01 다음 대화의 빈칸에 알맞은 것을 모두 고르시오.

W: David, what's your summer plan?
M: My family is going to China. ____________________
W: The Rainbow Mountains?
M: They are some mountains that look like canvases in rainbow colors.
W: That sounds amazing! Take lots of pictures!

① I hope you will enjoy the Rainbow Mountains.
② I can't wait to visit the Rainbow Mountains.
③ I'm sure you will visit the Rainbow Mountains.
④ I can wait to visit the Rainbow Mountains.
⑤ I'm looking forward to visiting the Rainbow Mountains.

02 주어진 문장 다음에 올 대화의 순서를 바르게 배열한 것을 고르시오.

M: Mom, did you watch the weather report today? We will be able to see hundreds of shooting stars tonight!

(A) I've heard that the shooting stars will peak between 12 a.m. and 2 a.m.
(B) Wow, fantastic! When is the best time to see them?
(C) Wow, it will be a special night!

① (A) – (C) – (B) ② (B) – (A) – (C) ③ (B) – (C) – (A)
④ (C) – (A) – (B) ⑤ (C) – (B) – (A)

03 다음 대화의 빈칸에 알맞은 것을 고르시오.

M: Do you want to watch the new 3D movie?
W: Which one?
M: The one about adventures under the sea. It was shot near Australia's Great Barrier Reef.
W: Oh, ______________ It has the most beautiful sea life.
M: Right. I can't wait to watch the movie. Let's go and get the ticket.

① I've heard of it. ② I didn't hear of it.
③ You have no idea of that. ④ I've never heard of it.
⑤ Did you hear about it?

[01~02] 다음 대화를 읽고 물음에 답하시오.

W: Dad, my science club is going to go to Dokdo in July. (①)
M: Oh, really? (②)
W: (③) We are going to study the caves on the island and go bird watching.
M: Sounds like it will be an interesting trip. (④)
W: Yeah. I've only read about Dokdo in books. (⑤) I can't wait to actually visit there.
M: I hope you enjoy your trip!

중요
01 위 대화의 ①~⑤ 중 주어진 문장이 들어갈 알맞은 곳은?

What do you plan to do there?

① ② ③ ④ ⑤

02 위 대화를 읽고 답할 수 없는 질문을 고르시오.

① Has the girl's dad been to Dokdo?
② When will the girl's science club go to Dokdo?
③ What is the girl going to do in Dokdo?
④ Where will the girl's science club go in July?
⑤ Is the girl looking forward to going to Dokdo?

[03~05] 다음 대화를 읽고 물음에 답하시오.

M: Let's welcome Ms. Scarlett Lee, the winner of this year's photo competition. (①)
W: Hello, thank you (A)________ inviting me. I've honored to receive the award. (②)
M: Let's talk about your photo. (③) Is that true?
W: Yes, this glowing beach is caused by plankton. (④)
M: Wow, it truly is amazing! (⑤)
W: Yes, it is. I can't wait to take more pictures of amazing beaches.
M: I wish you the best of luck!

03 위 대화의 ①~⑤ 중 주어진 문장이 들어갈 알맞은 곳은?

I've heard that this photo was taken in the Maldives.

① ② ③ ④ ⑤

서답형
04 빈칸 (A)에 들어갈 전치사를 쓰시오.

➡ ________________

중요
05 위 대화를 읽고 답할 수 없는 질문을 고르시오.

① Why is the beach in the Maldives glowing?
② What are they talking about?
③ Who is the winner of this year's photo competition?
④ What country is Ms. Scarlett Lee going to visit to take more pictures?
⑤ Where did Ms. Scarlett Lee take the award-winning photo?

중요 06 다음 대화의 ⓐ~ⓔ 중 가리키는 것이 다른 하나를 고르시오.

M: Erica, what are ⓐthe white things in the picture?
W: ⓑThey are snow rollers. I've heard that ⓒthey are made by strong wind and sticky snow.
M: Interesting! They look like ⓓsnow rings.
W: Yeah, I'd like to actually see ⓔthem someday.

① ⓐ  ② ⓑ  ③ ⓒ  ④ ⓓ ⑤ ⓔ

07 다음 중 짝지어진 대화가 어색한 것은?

① A: I gained 2 kilograms recently.
B: Don't worry. I've heard that gaining some weight is natural for teens.
② A: Do you have any plans for this weekend?
B: I'm going to climb Halla Mountain. I can't wait to do it.
③ A: I can't wait for next Sunday.
B: What are you going to do then?
④ A: Do you want to go to a rock concert?
B: No, I don't. I can't wait for it.
⑤ A: I can't wait to travel to Hawaii.
B: Have you decided what you will do there?

중요 08 주어진 문장 다음에 올 대화의 순서를 바르게 배열한 것을 고르시오.

Jisu, did you know that the sun never sets in Norway during summer?

(A) Me, too. I hope we get the chance to try it someday.
(B) I'd love to go hiking and cycling in the middle of the night!
(C) No, I didn't know that. How interesting!
(D) Yeah, and I've heard that people go hiking and even cycling at night because it isn't dark.

① (B)–(A)–(C)–(D) ② (B)–(C)–(A)–(D)
③ (C)–(A)–(B)–(D) ④ (C)–(B)–(A)–(D)
⑤ (C)–(D)–(B)–(A)

[09~10] 다음 대화를 읽고 물음에 답하시오.

W: Have you made plans for this vacation?
M: Yeah, I'm going to go to Uyuni Salt Flats in Bolivia. I can't (A)_______ to go bike riding there.

중요 09 빈칸 (A)에 알맞은 말을 고르시오.

① need ② look forward ③ see
④ wait ⑤ keep

서답형 10 위 대화의 내용에 맞게 빈칸을 완성하시오.

The man is _______ to go to _______ _______ _______ in Bolivia this vacation.
He wishes to _______ _______ there.

11 다음 빈칸에 알맞은 말을 고르시오.

A: I've _______ you can walk on the seabed once a year in Jindo, Korea.
B: Sounds interesting! I'd like to go there someday.

① hear that ② heard what
③ heard that ④ know what
⑤ know that

Conversation 서술형 시험대비

[01~02] 다음 대화를 읽고 물음에 답하시오.

M: Mom, ⓐdid you watch the weather report today? ⓑWe will be able to see hundreds of shooting stars tonight!
W: ⓒWow, fantastic! ⓓWhere is the best place to see them?
M: I've heard that the shooting stars will peak between 12 a.m. (A)________ 2 a.m.
W: ⓔWow, it will be a special night!

01 빈칸 (A)에 알맞은 말을 쓰시오.

➡ ______________________

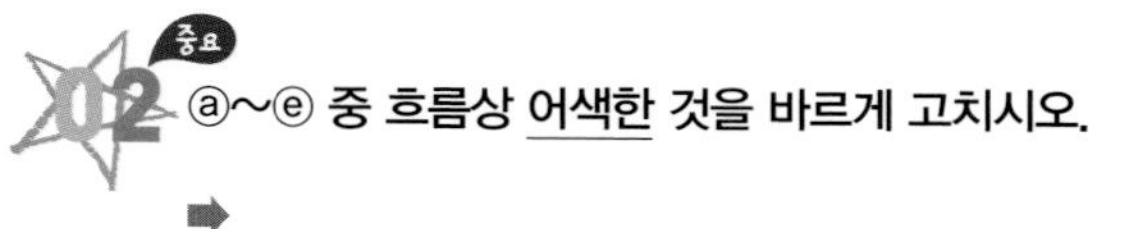

02 ⓐ~ⓔ 중 흐름상 어색한 것을 바르게 고치시오.

➡ ______________________

[03~04] 다음 대화를 읽고 물음에 답하시오.

W: David, what's your summer plan?
M: My family is going to China. (A)나는 빨리 the Rainbow Mountains를 방문하고 싶어.
W: The Rainbow Mountains?
M: They are some mountains that look (B)______ canvases in rainbow colors.
W: That sounds amazing! Take lots of pictures!

03 밑줄 친 (A)의 우리말을 영작하시오.

➡ ______________________

04 빈칸 (B)에 들어갈 말을 쓰시오.

➡ ______________________

[05~06] 다음 대화를 읽고 물음에 답하시오.

M: Do you want to watch the new 3D movie?
W: Which one?
M: The one about adventures under the sea. It (A)________(shoot) near Australia's Great Barrier Reef.
W: Oh, (B)나는 그것에 대해 들었어. It has the most beautiful sea life.
M: Right. I can't wait to watch the movie. Let's go and get the ticket.

05 중요 빈칸 (A)를 괄호 안의 주어진 단어를 이용하여 쓰시오.

➡ ______________________

06 밑줄 친 (B)의 우리말을 주어진 단어를 이용하여 쓰시오.

➡ ______________________ (of, have)

07 빈칸 (A)를 괄호 안에 주어진 단어를 알맞게 배열하여 채우시오.

M: Erica, what are the white things in the picture?
W: They are snow rollers. (A) __________ __________________ (made, and, snow, heard, are, sticky, I've, strong, by, wind, they, that)
M: Interesting! They look like snow rings.
W: Yeah, I'd like to actually see them someday.

➡ ______________________

____

교과서

Grammar

1 to부정사의 의미상의 주어

- Iceland is the best place **for many location scouts** to visit.
  아이슬랜드는 사진 촬영 장소를 찾으러 다니는 사람들이 방문할 가장 좋은 장소이다.
- It's very considerate **of her** to have said so. 그녀가 그렇게 말했다니 참 이해심도 많네요.

■ to부정사의 의미상의 주어
to부정사의 동작을 실제로 하는 주체를 to부정사의 의미상의 주어라고 한다. to부정사의 의미상의 주어는 to부정사 바로 앞에 'for+명사 또는 대명사의 목적격'으로 나타낸다. 이때 문장에 쓰인 형용사가 nice, kind, smart, wise 등과 같이 사람의 성향, 성격을 나타내는 말일 때는 for 대신 of를 쓴다.

- Is three weeks enough time **for you** to finish? 3주면 당신이 충분히 끝낼 수 있는 시간이죠?
- It is impossible **for him** to do that. 그가 그것을 하기는 불가능하다.
- It is quite silly **of you** to try to force him to consent. 네가 강제로 그의 승낙을 받으려는 것은 아주 어리석은 일이다.

■ 비교적 긴 to부정사 부분이 문장의 주어로 쓰일 때 보통 그 to부정사 부분을 문장 제일 뒤에 두고 주어 자리에 가주어 it을 넣어준다.

- **It** is hard **to criticize** the people one loves. 자기가 사랑하는 사람들을 비난하는 것은 어려운 일이다.
  = **To criticize** the people one loves is hard.

■ to부정사의 의미상의 주어가 일반적인 사람일 경우는 보통 생략한다. 또한 to부정사의 부정은 to부정사 앞에 not이나 never를 써서 'not[never]+to부정사'로 나타낸다.

- It is interesting **to compare** their situation and ours. 그들의 상황과 우리의 상황을 비교해 보면 재미있다.
- Try **not to let** him bother you. 그가 당신을 괴롭히게 내버려 두지 말아요.

핵심 Check

1. 빈칸에 알맞은 말을 어법에 맞게 쓰시오.

(1) It is exciting ________ go to the amusement park.
(2) It is interesting ________ me to speak to a foreign friend.
(3) Was it wise ________ you to come to the hotel?

2 현재완료진행형

- **I've been visiting** the forest to study animals for 20 years.
  나는 20년간 동물들을 연구하기 위해 그 숲을 방문하고 있다.
- Scientists **have been suggesting** their possible presence since 1992.
  과학자들은 1992년 이래 그들의 존재 가능성을 제기해 왔다.

■ 현재완료진행형은 'have[has] been+동사원형-ing'의 형태로 보통 for(~ 동안)나 since(~ 이래로)와 함께 쓰여 '~이래로[~ 동안] …해 오고 있다'라고 해석한다.

- The problem **has been bothering** me until now. 그 문제는 지금까지 나를 괴롭혀 왔다.

■ 현재완료진행형은 어떤 상태나 행위가 과거 어느 때부터 시작되어 현재까지 계속 진행되고 있음을 나타내거나 현재까지 계속적으로 반복되고 있는 것을 나타낸다.

- My back **has been bothering** me lately. 요즘은 허리가 영 시원찮다.

■ 현재완료진행형에서 진행형이 가능한 동사는 현재완료진행형으로 동작의 계속을 표현하고, 진행형으로 쓸 수 없는 동사(have(소유), belong, know, like, hate 등)는 현재완료형으로 상태의 계속을 표현한다. 즉, 현재완료진행은 '상태'가 아닌, '동작'만을 나타낸다.

- It **has been snowing** for around 5 days. 약 5일 동안 내내 눈이 내리고 있다. (동작의 계속)
- She **has known** Mary for two years. 그녀는 2년 동안 Mary와 알고 지냈다. (상태의 계속)

■ 현재완료 / 현재완료진행형
현재완료는 동작의 결과에 초점을 맞춘다고 생각할 수 있지만, 현재완료진행형은 계속되고 있는 동작 그 자체에 초점을 맞춘다고 생각할 수 있다.

- What **has** he **done**? (그는 무엇을 했는가?) → 결과에 초점
- What **has** he **been doing**? (그는 무엇을 하고 있는가?) → 동작에 초점

핵심 Check

2. 주어진 어휘를 빈칸에 어법에 맞게 쓰시오.

(1) He has been _______ the guitar for two hours. (play)
(2) Wendy has been _______ the flute since she was six. (play)
(3) Mike has been _______ it in secret. (do)

Grammar 시험대비 기본평가

01 다음 빈칸에 알맞은 것을 고르시오.

A: Is it important ______________________?
B: Yes, it is.

① practice playing the flute
② practices playing the flute
③ to practicing playing the flute
④ for you to practice playing the flute
⑤ of you to practice playing the flute

02 다음 두 문장을 한 문장으로 바꾸어 쓸 때 알맞게 표현한 것을 고르시오.

• The problem started bothering me a long time ago.
• It is still bothering me.

① The problem is bothering me now.
② The problem bothered me a long time ago.
③ The problem has been bothering me for a long time
④ The problem was bothering me for a long time.
⑤ The problem will be bothering me for a long time.

03 다음 괄호 안에서 알맞은 말을 고르시오.

(1) The research has been (suggesting / suggested) that drinking coffee may actually be good for your health.
(2) I (am living / have been living) in New York for 6 years.
(3) It is foolish (for / of) you to think so.
(4) Global warming and water pollution make it harder (for / of) the animals to live.

04 다음 우리말에 맞게 주어진 어휘를 바르게 배열하시오.

학생들이 그들의 숙제를 하는 것은 중요하다.
(students, their homework, important, it, do, is, to, for)

➡ ______________________________

중요
01 다음 중 어법상 올바른 것은?

① It has been rain all day long.
② The argument has been going on since years.
③ Rana has been planted trees in the valleys for the last 31 years.
④ China has been cutting down many trees.
⑤ I've been visiting the forest to study animals since 20 years.

02 다음 중 어법상 올바르지 않은 것은?

① The shopping center is close enough for us to drop by.
② It's necessary for you to talk to her again.
③ This is no time of us to remain idle.
④ It isn't easy for me to teach history to students.
⑤ It was unwise of him not to have booked the travel insurance.

중요
03 다음 빈칸에 알맞은 말이 올바르게 짝지어진 것은?

• Mildred _______ Korean for two years. • Is the book easy enough _______ you to read?

① studies – of
② studied – of
③ is studying – of
④ has been studied – for
⑤ has been studying – for

서답형
04 다음 괄호 안에서 알맞은 말을 고르시오.

(1) How long have you (collect / been collecting) stamps?
(2) She has been living in London (since / for) three years.
(3) They have been shouting at us (since / for) this morning
(4) It is easy (for / of) us to take photos of many kinds of animals.
(5) It's so kind (for / of) you to invite me tonight.

05 다음 대화의 빈칸에 들어갈 말로 알맞은 것은?

M: Is it safe _______ you to play outside at night in Seoul? W: Of course.

① of ② for
③ by ④ at
⑤ to

중요
06 다음 문장의 빈칸에 들어갈 알맞은 것은?

It has been raining cats and dogs _______ this morning.

① since ② for
③ at ④ during
⑤ with

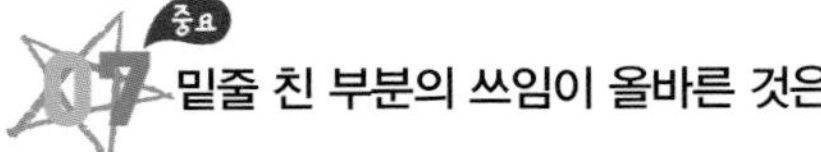

중요
07 밑줄 친 부분의 쓰임이 올바른 것은?

① We have been knowing Emily since she was a child.
② James has been making the film for one year.
③ Fans has been waiting for their favorite stars for two hours.
④ I have been playing computer games 3 hours ago.
⑤ Brian has been studying Korean last night.

서답형
08 우리말과 일치하도록 빈칸에 알맞은 말을 쓰시오.

> 이 컴퓨터는 내가 휴대할 수 있을 정도로 작다.
> = This computer is small enough ________ ________ ________ carry.

서답형
09 주어진 어휘를 이용하여 다음 우리말을 영작하시오.

> 그는 2001년 이래로 NASA의 다양한 분야에서 근무해 오고 있다. (11 단어)
> (fields, NASA, work, various, at, in)

➡ ____________________________

10 다음 문장의 빈칸에 알맞은 말은?

> How stupid ________ to believe such a man!

① for him ② for us
③ for your ④ of him
⑤ of his

11 주어진 우리말을 영어로 바르게 옮긴 것은?

> 우리 가족은 10년이 넘는 동안 그 집에서 살아오고 있다.

① My family lived in the house during over 10 years.
② My family has living in the house since over 10 years.
③ My family has been lived in the house for over 10 years.
④ My family had lived in the house for over 10 years.
⑤ My family has been living in the house for over 10 years.

중요
12 다음 빈칸에 들어갈 말이 나머지와 다른 하나는?

① It is important ________ Rachel to prepare special food.
② The restaurant had delicious foods ________ us to enjoy.
③ It's nice ________ you to come all the way to the airport.
④ It's so difficult ________ him to bring up his children.
⑤ It was hard ________ him to live on his low salary.

서답형
13 괄호 속의 단어들을 자연스럽게 배열하시오.

(1) I (interviewing / have / for / actors / been) one hour.
➡ ____________________________

(2) Julie (knitting / a / been / has / sweater / since) this morning.
➡ ____________________________

서답형

14 다음 문장에서 어법상 어색한 것을 바르게 고쳐 다시 쓰시오.

(1) Mr. Lee has been teach math for more than 30 years.

➡ ______________________

(2) Mariel has been learning Korean at the school 5 years ago.

➡ ______________________

(3) I have been climbing the mountain for Monday.

➡ ______________________

(4) We have been waiting for her since 2 hours.

➡ ______________________

(5) What time would be best of me to talk to you?

➡ ______________________

(6) I think it is very polite for her to ask permission.

➡ ______________________

(7) It will be difficult for the children swimming across this river.

➡ ______________________

서답형

15 다음 문장을 바꾸어 쓸 때 빈칸에 알맞은 말을 쓰시오.

It is natural that she should cry.
= ________ is natural ________ ________ ________ ________.

16 다음 두 문장을 한 문장으로 바르게 연결한 것은?

- Actors and actresses started arriving here at 5 o'clock.
- They are still arriving here.

① Actors and actresses arrived here since 5 o'clock.
② Actors and actresses had arrived here for 5 o'clock.
③ Actors and actresses have arriving here since 5 o'clock.
④ Actors and actresses have been arriving here for 5 o'clock.
⑤ Actors and actresses have been arriving here since 5 o'clock.

중요

17 다음 중 어법상 어색한 것을 고르시오. (3개)

① I have been loving Lily since I met her for the first time.
② The Ice Cube is the best place for David to investigate the climate of the earth.
③ The little girl has been crying an hour ago.
④ It was so rude for you to say so.
⑤ I've been visiting the forest to study animals for 20 years.

서답형

18 다음 주어진 어휘를 이용하여 우리말을 영작하시오.

겨울이 오고 있기 때문에 우리는 겨울을 준비해야 한다. (as, winter, it, come, prepare, necessary, the, 14 단어)

➡ ______________________

고난이도

01 괄호 안의 단어 수대로 주어진 두 문장을 하나의 문장으로 쓰시오.

(1) • Naomi reached the station at two o'clock to take the train.
• She is still waiting for her train. (10 단어)
➡ ____________________
____

(2) • It started raining three hours ago.
• It is still raining. (7 단어)
➡ ____________________

(3) • Women have made important contributions to sports for centuries.
• They are still making contributions. (10 단어)
➡ ____________________
____

02 다음 우리말에 맞게 주어진 어구를 바르게 배열하시오.

(1) 이 책은 네가 읽기엔 너무 어렵다. (you, this book, difficult, read, is, too, for, to)
➡ ____________________

(2) 그는 영리하게도 그 기회를 놓치지 않았다. (it, him, the chance, was, miss, very smart, not, to, of)
➡ ____________________

(3) 나는 부모님의 사랑을 당연한 것으로 받아 들여 왔다. (I, love, my parents', been, granted, taking, have, for)
➡ ____________________

중요

03 그림을 보고, 주어진 어휘를 이용하여 빈칸을 알맞게 채우시오.

(1)

They ____________ her birthday party ____________. (enjoying, two hours)

(2)

It was ____________ the window open. (leave, careless, her)

04 다음 〈보기〉에 주어진 단어를 이용하여 문맥에 맞게 문장을 완성하시오.

보기
since for

(1) My mom has been watching TV ________ two hours.

(2) Nancy has been studying Korean ________ 2010.

05 괄호 안에 주어진 말을 이용하여 어법에 맞게 문장을 완성하시오.

(1) This book is ________________ read. (you, difficult, too)

(2) Is the room ________________ get together? (big, us, enough)

(3) It was ________________ give food to the children. (nice, her, to)

고난이도

06 〈보기〉와 같이 문장을 바꿔 쓸 때 빈칸에 알맞은 말을 쓰시오.

보기

You should choose good friends.
→ It is important for you to choose good friends.

(1) You should listen carefully to the advice.
→ It is important ________________ ________________.

(2) Abigail helped me to stand on my own feet.
→ It was nice ________________ ________________.

07 다음 문장에서 어법상 어색한 것을 바르게 고치시오.

(1) How long have you been thought about joining us?
➡ ________________

(2) I have been waiting for him since 30 minutes.
➡ ________________

(3) He has been collecting insects in a remote desert for 2009.
➡ ________________

(4) The country has been possessing a strong military power.
➡ ________________

(5) I have been living here 5 years ago.
➡ ________________

(6) It is necessary of her to finish the report.
➡ ________________

(7) It was difficult for me finding out what he wanted.
➡ ________________

중요

08 다음 우리말을 괄호 안에 주어진 어휘를 이용하여 영작하시오.

(1) 지난 몇 달 동안 모두가 열심히 공부해 왔다. (everyone, the last few months, hard, studying, 10 단어)
➡ ________________
____

(2) 그는 오랜 시간 동안 그 책을 써 오고 있다. (the book, write, long, 8 단어)
➡ ________________

(3) 그녀는 5월부터 거기서 일해 왔어요. (work, there, May, 7 단어)
➡ ________________

(4) 고맙게도 그녀가 내게 차편을 제공해 주었다. (it, nice, offer me a ride, to, 10 단어)
➡ ________________

(5) 아직 내가 처리해야 할 일이 두 가지 더 있어. (there, still, chores, to do, more, 10 단어)
➡ ________________

교과서

Reading

The World Through My Eyes

"The beauty of nature inspires us all (우리 모두를). Let's find out how people (간접의문문: 의문사+주어+동사) from different fields of work get inspired (동작수동태: get+과거분사) by nature."

Lin Wang, Ecologist
Tsingy, the Stone Forest of Madagascar

I've been visiting (현재완료진행형) the stone forest of Madagascar to study (to부정사의 부사적 용법(목적)) plants and animals for over (~ 이상) 20 years. The spiky stones of this place are true miracles of nature. This amazing shape has been created (현재완료 수동태) by rainfall. Rain has cut down the stones and made them (= the stones) sharp and spiky over (~에 걸쳐) a long period of time. The environment is harsh for animals to live (to부정사의 부사적 용법) in, but they have found (현재완료) ways to survive (to부정사의 형용사적 용법). For example, lemurs, which (that(×)) only live in Madagascar, have frog-like legs that (주격 관계대명사) help them jump (= to jump) from one stone tower to another. For me, the stone forest is like (= is similar to) a jack-in-the-box. It always surprises me and keeps me on my toes (keep ~ on one's toes: ~에게 정신을 바짝 차리게 하다)!

inspire 영감을 주다, 고무[격려]하다
field 분야
forest 숲
spiky 뾰족뾰족한
miracle 기적
shape 모양
rainfall 강우
sharp 날카로운
environment 환경
harsh 가혹한
survive 살아남다, 생존하다
lemur 여우원숭이
from A to B A에서 B로
jack-in-the-box 열면 인형이 튀어나오는 상자

확인문제

● 다음 문장이 본문의 내용과 일치하면 T, 일치하지 않으면 F를 쓰시오.

1 We are all inspired by the beauty of nature. ☐
2 Lin Wang has visited the stone forest of Madagascar more than 20 times. ☐
3 The amazing shape of Tsingy has been created by rainfall. ☐
4 It is comfortable for animals to live in the environment. ☐
5 Lemurs only live in Madagascar. ☐
6 Lemurs have frog-like arms that help them jump from one stone tower to another. ☐

Amber Smith, Fashion Colorist
Caño Cristales, the River of Five Colors of Colombia

The world is filled with (= is full of) millions of (수백만의) different colors. It (가주어) is my job to mix, develop, and create colors for clothing (진주어(to부정사의 명사적 용법)). Over the years, I've been gaining (현재완료진행형) insights from the beautiful colors of Caño Cristales.
You cannot see the wonderful mixed colors of this river anywhere else (다른 어떤 곳에서도) in the world. The combination of colorful plants under the water and sunlight makes (make(×): The combination이 주어임.) the colors more alive (서술 용법(보어로만 쓰임)의 형용사) and bright.
Whenever (= Every time) I visit the Caño Cristales, it makes me think (사역동사+목적어+원형부정사) that maybe there are still countless colors that are (주격 관계대명사+be동사) waiting to be created (to부정사의 수동태).

Danny Mehta, Location Scout
Vatnajökull National Park, Frozen Beauty of Iceland

I'm a location scout and my job is finding (동명사 (보어)) perfect places to shoot (to부정사의 형용사적 용법) movies. Iceland is the best place for many location scouts (to부정사의 의미상의 주어(for+목적격)) to visit (to부정사의 형용사적 용법) due to (~ 때문에) its unusual beauty. My personal favorite is the Vatnajökull National Park. The sharp cliffs, blue glacier caves, and long mountain ranges can stand in for (~을 대신하다(replace)) any place in the world or the universe. In fact (= As a matter of fact. Actually), the recent sci-fi movie we shot ((that) we shot) here was produced without using (전치사의 목적어로 쓰인 동명사) computer graphics! Iceland can help make (= to make) our wildest dreams come true (=realize) on the movie screen.

different 각양각색의, 각기 다른
mix 섞다
clothing 의류, 옷
insight 통찰력
combination 결합
colorful 다채로운
alive (생기 · 감정 · 활기 등이) 넘치는
bright 밝은
countless 무수한, 셀 수 없이 많은
perfect 완벽한
shoot (영화를) 촬영하다
unusual 특이한, 흔치 않은
beauty 아름다움
personal 개인의, 개인적인
cliff 절벽
glacier 빙하

확인문제

● 다음 문장이 본문의 내용과 일치하면 T, 일치하지 않으면 F를 쓰시오.

1 Amber Smith is a fashion colorist. ☐
2 Amber Smith cannot see the wonderful mixed colors of Caño Cristales. ☐
3 The combination of colorful plants under the water and sunlight makes the colors of Caño Cristales more alive and bright. ☐
4 Danny Mehta is a location scout who makes perfect places to shoot movies. ☐
5 Danny Mehta's personal favorite is the Vatnajökull National Park. ☐

Reading 교과서 확인학습 A

• 우리말을 참고하여 빈칸에 알맞은 말을 쓰시오.

1 The World ________ My Eyes

2 "The ________ of nature ________ us all.

3 Let's ________ ________ how people from different ________ ________ ________ ________ ________ by nature."

4 **Lin Wang, ________**

5 **Tsingy, the ________ ________ of Madagascar**

6 ________ ________ ________ the stone forest of Madagascar to study plants and animals ________ ________ 20 years.

7 The ________ stones of this place are ________ ________ of nature.

8 This ________ shape ________ ________ ________ by rainfall.

9 Rain has cut down the stones and made them ________ and ________ ________ a long period of time.

10 The environment is harsh ________ ________ ________ ________ ________, but they have found ways ________ ________.

11 For example, lemurs, ________ only live in Madagascar, have ________ legs ________ help them jump ________ one stone tower ________ another.

12 For me, the stone forest ________ ________ a ____________.

13 It always surprises me and ________ ________ ________ ________ ________!

14 **Amber Smith, ________ ________**

15 **Caño Cristales, the ________ ________ ________ ________ of Colombia**

16 The world ________ ________ ________ millions of different colors.

---

1 내 눈에 비친 세계

2 "자연의 아름다움은 우리 모두에게 영감을 준다.

3 서로 다른 직업 분야의 사람들이 자연에 의해 어떻게 영감을 받는지 알아보자."

4 Lin Wang, **생태학자**

5 Tsingy, **마다가스카르의 석림**

6 나는 20년 이상 동안 식물과 동물을 연구하기 위해서 마다가스카르의 석림을 방문하고 있다.

7 이 지역의 뾰족한 돌들은 진정한 자연의 놀라움이다.

8 이 놀라운 모양은 비에 의해서 만들어졌다.

9 비가 오랜 기간 동안 돌을 침식해서 날카롭고 뾰족하게 만들었다.

10 이런 환경은 동물들이 살기에 험난하지만, 동물들은 생존할 방법들을 찾아냈다.

11 예를 들어, 마다가스카르에서만 사는 여우원숭이는 한 개의 돌탑에서 다른 돌탑으로 뛸 수 있도록 도와주는 개구리와 같은 다리를 가지고 있다.

12 나에게 석림은 '잭인더박스(열면 인형이 튀어나오는 상자)'와 같다.

13 그것은 늘 나를 놀라게 하고 정신을 바짝 차리게 한다!

14 Amber Smith, **패션 색채 전문가**

15 Caño Cristales, **콜롬비아의 다섯 색깔의 강**

16 세계는 수백만의 다양한 색깔로 가득 차 있다.

17 It is my job to mix, develop, and _______ _______ for clothing.

18 Over the years, _______ _______ _______ insights from the beautiful colors of Caño Cristales.

19 You cannot see the wonderful _______ _______ of this river _______ _______ in the world.

20 The _______ of colorful plants under the water and sunlight _______ the colors _______ _______ and _______.

21 _______ I visit the Caño Cristales, it makes me think that maybe there are still _______ colors that are _______ _______ _______ _______.

22 **Danny Mehta, _______ _______**

23 **Vatnajökull National Park, _______ _______ of Iceland**

24 I'm a location scout and my job is finding perfect places _______ _______ _______.

25 Iceland is the best place _______ _______ _______ _______ to visit _______ _______ its _______ _______.

26 _______ _______ _______ is the Vatnajökull National Park.

27 The sharp cliffs, blue glacier caves, and long mountain ranges can _______ _______ _______ _______ _______ in the world or the universe.

28 _______ _______, the recent sci-fi movie _______ _______ _______ was produced _______ _______ computer graphics!

29 Iceland can _______ _______ our wildest dreams _______ _______ on the movie screen.

17 의류를 위해서 색을 섞고, 발전시키고, 만들어 내는 것이 나의 일이다.

18 수년 동안, 나는 카뇨 크리스탈레스의 아름다운 색으로부터 영감을 얻어 오고 있다.

19 이 강의 아름답게 혼합된 색깔은 세상 어느 다른 곳에서도 볼 수 없다.

20 물속의 화려한 식물들과 햇빛의 결합은 그 색깔을 더 생생하고 밝게 만든다.

21 내가 카뇨 크리스탈레스를 방문할 때마다 그 강은 나로 하여금 아마도 여전히 만들어지기를 기다리고 있는 셀 수 없이 많은 색깔이 있음을 생각하게 한다.

22 **Danny Mehta, 장소 섭외가**

23 **Vatnajökull 국립 공원, 아이슬란드의 얼음으로 덮인 아름다움**

24 나는 장소 섭외가이고 나의 일은 영화를 찍기에 완벽한 장소를 찾는 것이다.

25 아이슬란드는 비범한 아름다움 때문에 많은 장소 섭외가들이 방문하기에 최고의 장소이다.

26 내가 개인적으로 가장 선호하는 곳은 바트나이외쿠틀 국립 공원이다.

27 가파른 절벽, 푸른 빙하 동굴, 그리고 긴 산맥들은 세계나 혹은 우주의 어느 장소도 대신할 수 있다.

28 사실상, 우리가 여기서 찍은 최근의 공상 과학 영화는 컴퓨터 그래픽 없이 만들어졌다!

29 아이슬란드는 우리의 가장 무모한 꿈을 영화 스크린에서 실현할 수 있게 해 준다.

Reading 교과서 확인학습 B

• 우리말을 참고하여 본문을 영작하시오.

1 **내 눈에 비친 세계**

➡ ______

2 "자연의 아름다움은 우리 모두에게 영감을 준다.

➡ ______

3 서로 다른 직업 분야의 사람들이 자연에 의해 어떻게 영감을 받는지 알아보자."

➡ ______

4 **Lin Wang, 생태학자**

➡ ______

5 **Tsingy, 마다가스카르의 석림**

➡ ______

6 나는 20년 이상 동안 식물과 동물을 연구하기 위해서 마다가스카르의 석림을 방문하고 있다.

➡ ______

7 이 지역의 뾰족한 돌들은 진정한 자연의 놀라움이다.

➡ ______

8 이 놀라운 모양은 비에 의해서 만들어졌다.

➡ ______

9 비가 오랜 기간 동안 돌을 침식해서 날카롭고 뾰족하게 만들었다.

➡ ______

10 이런 환경은 동물들이 살기에 험난하지만, 동물들은 생존할 방법들을 찾아냈다.

➡ ______

11 예를 들어, 마다가스카르에서만 사는 여우원숭이는 한 개의 돌탑에서 다른 돌탑으로 뛸 수 있도록 도와주는 개구리와 같은 다리를 가지고 있다.

➡ ______

______

12 나에게 석림은 '잭인더박스(열면 인형이 튀어나오는 상자)'와 같다.

➡ ______

13 그것은 늘 나를 놀라게 하고 정신을 바짝 차리게 한다!

➡ ______

14 **Amber Smith, 패션 색채 전문가**

➡ ______

15 **Caño Cristales, 콜롬비아의 다섯 색깔의 강**

➡ ______

16 세계는 수백만의 다양한 색깔로 가득 차 있다.

➡ ______

17 의류를 위해서 색을 섞고, 발전시키고, 만들어 내는 것이 나의 일이다.
➡ ______________________________

18 수년 동안, 나는 카뇨 크리스탈레스의 아름다운 색으로부터 영감을 얻어 오고 있다.
➡ ______________________________

19 이 강의 아름답게 혼합된 색깔은 세상 어느 다른 곳에서도 볼 수 없다.
➡ ______________________________

20 물속의 화려한 식물들과 햇빛의 결합은 그 색깔을 더 생생하고 밝게 만든다.
➡ ______________________________

21 내가 카뇨 크리스탈레스를 방문할 때마다 그 강은 나로 하여금 아마도 여전히 만들어지기를 기다리고 있는 셀 수 없이 많은 색깔이 있음을 생각하게 한다.
➡ ______________________________
____

22 **Danny Mehta, 장소 섭외가**
➡ ______________________________

23 **Vatnajökull 국립 공원, 아이슬란드의 얼음으로 덮인 아름다움**
➡ ______________________________

24 나는 장소 섭외가이고 나의 일은 영화를 찍기에 완벽한 장소를 찾는 것이다.
➡ ______________________________

25 아이슬란드는 비범한 아름다움 때문에 많은 장소 섭외가들이 방문하기에 최고의 장소이다.
➡ ______________________________

26 내가 개인적으로 가장 선호하는 곳은 바트나이외쿠틀 국립 공원이다.
➡ ______________________________

27 가파른 절벽, 푸른 빙하 동굴, 그리고 긴 산맥들은 세계나 혹은 우주의 어느 장소도 대신할 수 있다.
➡ ______________________________
____

28 사실상, 우리가 여기서 찍은 최근의 공상 과학 영화는 컴퓨터 그래픽 없이 만들어졌다!
➡ ______________________________

29 아이슬란드는 우리의 가장 무모한 꿈을 영화 스크린에서 실현할 수 있게 해 준다.
➡ ______________________________

[01~03] 다음 글을 읽고 물음에 답하시오.

Danny Mehta, Location Scout
Vatnajökull National Park, Frozen Beauty of Iceland

I'm a location scout and my job is finding perfect places ⓐto shoot movies. Iceland is the best place for many location scouts to visit due to its unusual beauty. My personal favorite is the Vatnajökull National Park. The sharp cliffs, blue glacier caves, and long mountain ranges can ⓑstand in for any place in the world or the universe. ⓒIn fact, the recent sci-fi movie we shot here was produced by using computer graphics! Iceland can help make our wildest dreams come true on the movie screen.

01 아래 <보기>에서 위 글의 밑줄 친 ⓐto shoot과 to부정사의 용법이 같은 것의 개수를 고르시오.

보기
① She has a few books to read.
② Give me something to eat.
③ I don't like to read books.
④ They came here to see you.
⑤ To speak English is not easy.

① 1개 ② 2개 ③ 3개 ④ 4개 ⑤ 5개

중요
02 위 글의 밑줄 친 ⓑstand in for와 바꿔 쓸 수 있는 말을 모두 고르시오.

① change
② replace
③ remove
④ exchange
⑤ take the place of

서답형
03 위 글의 밑줄 친 ⓒ에서 흐름상 어색한 부분을 찾아 고치시오.

➡ ____________

[04~06] 다음 글을 읽고 물음에 답하시오.

"The beauty of nature inspires us all. Let's find out how people from different fields of work get __ⓐ__ by nature."

Lin Wang, Ecologist
Tsingy, the Stone Forest of Madagascar

I've been __ⓑ__ the stone forest of Madagascar to study plants and animals for over 20 years. (①) The spiky stones of this place are true miracles of nature. (②) This amazing shape has been __ⓒ__ by rainfall. (③) Rain has cut down the stones and made them sharp and spiky over a long period of time. (④) For example, lemurs, which only live in Madagascar, have frog-like legs that help them jump from one stone tower to another. (⑤) For me, the stone forest is like a jack-in-the-box. ⓓIt always surprises me and keeps me on my toes!

서답형
04 위 글의 빈칸 ⓐ, ⓑ, ⓒ에 각각 inspire, visit, create를 알맞은 형태로 쓰시오.

➡ ⓐ________ ⓑ________ ⓒ________

05 위 글의 흐름으로 보아, 주어진 문장이 들어가기에 가장 적절한 곳은?

The environment is harsh for animals to live in, but they have found ways to survive.

① ② ③ ④ ⑤

서답형
06 위 글의 밑줄 친 ⓓIt이 가리키는 것을 본문에서 찾아 쓰시오.

➡ ____________

[07~09] 다음 글을 읽고 물음에 답하시오.

Amber Smith, Fashion Colorist
Caño Cristales, the River of Five Colors of Colombia

ⓐThe world is filled with millions of different colors. It is my job to mix, develop, and create colors for clothing. Over the years, I've been gaining insights from the beautiful colors of Caño Cristales. You cannot see the wonderful (A)[mixing / mixed] colors of this river anywhere else in the world. The combination of colorful plants under the water and sunlight makes the colors more (B)[alive / live] and bright. Whenever I visit the Caño Cristales, it makes me (C)[think / to think] that maybe there are still ⓑcountless colors that are waiting to be created.

07 위 글의 밑줄 친 ⓐ를 다음과 같이 바꿔 쓸 때 빈칸에 들어갈 알맞은 말을 두 단어로 쓰시오.

➡ The world is ________ ________ millions of different colors.

서답형
08 위 글의 괄호 (A)~(C)에서 어법상 알맞은 낱말을 골라 쓰시오.

➡ (A)________ (B)________ (C)________

09 위 글의 밑줄 친 ⓑcountless와 바꿔 쓸 수 없는 말을 고르시오.

① a great many ② numerous
③ a great deal of ④ innumerable
⑤ a good number of

[10~13] 다음 글을 읽고 물음에 답하시오.

"The beauty of nature inspires us all. Let's find out how people from different (A)fields of work get inspired by nature."

Lin Wang, Ecologist
Tsingy, the Stone Forest of Madagascar

I've been visiting the stone forest of Madagascar to study plants and animals ⓐ_____ over 20 years. The spiky stones of this place are true miracles of nature. This amazing shape has been created by rainfall. Rain has cut down the stones and made them sharp and spiky over a long period of time. The environment is harsh for animals to live in, but they have found ways to survive. For example, lemurs, which only live in Madagascar, have frog-like legs that help them jump from one stone tower to another. For me, the stone forest is like a jack-in-the-box. It always surprises me and keeps me ⓑ______ my toes!

10 위 글의 빈칸 ⓐ와 ⓑ에 들어갈 전치사가 바르게 짝지어진 것은?

	ⓐ ⓑ		ⓐ ⓑ
①	for – on	②	during – by
③	in – to	④	during – on
⑤	for – to		

11 위 글의 밑줄 친 (A)fields와 같은 의미로 쓰인 것을 고르시오.

① People were working in the fields.
② Many soldiers died in the fields of battle.
③ His homeland is famous for many beautiful ice fields.
④ How many flying fields are there in this region?
⑤ All of them are experts in their chosen fields.

12 중요 위 글의 제목으로 가장 알맞은 것을 고르시오.

① Visit the Stone Forest to Study Nature!
② How Does Rainfall Create an Amazing Shape?
③ How Did Lin Wang Get Inspired by Nature?
④ The Harsh Environment for Animals to Live in
⑤ Lemurs with Frog-like Legs Can Survive in Tsingy!

13 According to the passage, which is NOT true?

① All of us are inspired by the beauty of nature.
② Lin Wang is an ecologist.
③ Lin has been visiting Tsingy to study plants and animals for over 20 years.
④ The round stones of this place are true miracles of nature.
⑤ For Lin, the stone forest is like a jack-in-the-box.

[14~16] 다음 글을 읽고 물음에 답하시오.

I've been visiting the stone forest of Madagascar to study plants and animals for over 20 years. The spiky stones of this place are true miracles of nature. This amazing shape has been created by rainfall. Rain has cut down the stones and made (A)them sharp and spiky over a long period of time. (B)이런 환경은 동물들이 살기에 험난하다, but (C)they have found ways to survive. ___ⓐ___, lemurs, which only live in Madagascar, have frog-like legs that help them jump from one stone tower to another. For me, the stone forest is like a jack-in-the-box. It always surprises me and keeps me on my toes!

14 위 글의 빈칸 ⓐ에 들어갈 알맞은 말을 고르시오.

① As a result
② For example
③ However
④ In other words
⑤ Therefore

서답형

15 위 글의 밑줄 친 (A)them과 (C)they가 가리키는 것을 본문에서 찾아 쓰시오.

➡ (A) ____________ (C) ____________

서답형

16 위 글의 밑줄 친 (B)의 우리말에 맞게 주어진 어휘를 이용하여 9 단어로 영작하시오.

harsh

➡ ______________________________

[17~20] 다음 글을 읽고 물음에 답하시오.

Amber Smith, Fashion Colorist
Caño Cristales, the River of Five Colors of Colombia

The world is filled with millions of different colors. (A)It is my job to mix, develop, and create colors for clothing. Over the years, I've been ___ⓐ___ insights from the beautiful colors of Caño Cristales. You cannot see the wonderful mixed colors of this river anywhere else in the world. The combination of colorful plants under the water and sunlight makes the colors more alive and bright. Whenever I visit the Caño Cristales, it makes me think that maybe there are (B)still countless colors that are waiting to be created.

서답형

17 위 글의 빈칸 ⓐ에 gain을 알맞은 형태로 쓰시오.

➡ ______________________

18 위 글의 밑줄 친 (A)It과 문법적 쓰임이 같은 것을 모두 고르시오.

① It was raining this morning.
② I find it strange that she doesn't want to go.
③ It is important for you to choose good friends.
④ It is time for you to go to bed.
⑤ It is strange that she says so.

19 위 글의 밑줄 친 (B)still과 같은 의미로 쓰인 것을 모두 고르시오.

① I had a still better idea.
② I'm still hungry!
③ Keep still while I brush your hair.
④ He is still there.
⑤ The weather was cold and wet. Still, we had a great time.

20 Which question CANNOT be answered after reading the passage?

① What is Caño Cristales?
② Where is Caño Cristales?
③ What is Amber Smith's job?
④ What color has Amber Smith created for clothing?
⑤ What makes the colors of Caño Cristales more alive and bright?

[21~24] 다음 글을 읽고 물음에 답하시오.

Danny Mehta, Location Scout

Vatnajökull National Park, Frozen Beauty of Iceland

I'm a location scout and my job is ⓐfinding perfect places to shoot movies. Iceland is the best place for many location scouts to visit due to its unusual beauty. My personal favorite is the Vatnajökull National Park. The sharp cliffs, blue glacier caves, and long mountain ranges can stand in for any place in the world or the universe. ⓑIn fact, ⓒthe recent sci-fi movie we shot here was produced without using computer graphics! Iceland can help make our wildest dreams come true on the movie screen.

21 위 글의 밑줄 친 ⓐfinding과 문법적 쓰임이 같은 것을 모두 고르시오.

① Look at the sleeping baby.
② I forget posting the letter.
③ She was cooking in the kitchen.
④ He is good at speaking English.
⑤ I saw him dancing.

22 위 글의 밑줄 친 ⓑIn fact와 바꿔 쓸 수 있는 말을 모두 고르시오.

① Therefore
② As a matter of fact
③ Actually
④ However
⑤ As a result

서답형

23 위 글의 밑줄 친 문장 ⓒ에 생략된 단어를 넣어 문장을 다시 쓰시오.

➡ ______________________________
____

서답형

24 다음 문장에서 위 글의 내용과 다른 부분을 찾아서 고치시오.

The common beauty of Iceland makes it the best place for many location scouts to visit.

➡ ____________________

[01~04] 다음 글을 읽고 물음에 답하시오.

"The beauty of nature inspires us all. Let's find out ⓐ서로 다른 직업 분야의 사람들이 자연에 의해 어떻게 영감을 받는지."

Lin Wang, Ecologist

Tsingy, the Stone Forest of Madagascar

ⓑI've been visiting the stone forest of Madagascar to study plants and animals for over 20 years. The spiky stones of this place are true miracles of nature. This amazing shape has been created by rainfall. Rain has cut down the stones and made them sharp and spiky over a long period of time. ⓒThe environment is mild for animals to live in, but they have found ways to survive. For example, lemurs, which only live in Madagascar, have frog-like legs that help them jump from one stone tower to another. ⓓFor me, the stone forest is like a jack-in-the-box. It always surprises me and keeps me on my toes!

01 위 글의 밑줄 친 ⓐ의 우리말에 맞게 한 단어를 보충하여, 주어진 어휘를 알맞게 배열하시오.

by / fields / get / people / different / from / inspired / of / nature / work

➡ ____

____

고난이도

02 위 글의 밑줄 친 ⓑ를 다음과 같이 바꿔 쓸 때 빈칸에 들어갈 알맞은 단어를 쓰시오.

➡ I started ________ ________ the stone forest of Madagascar to study plants and animals over 20 years ________, and I am still ________ it.

03 위 글의 밑줄 친 ⓒ에서 흐름상 어색한 부분을 찾아 고치시오.

➡ ____

04 다음 빈칸에 공통으로 들어갈 알맞은 단어를 넣어, Lin Wang이 위 글의 밑줄 친 ⓓ처럼 말한 이유를 완성하시오.

➡ It's because the stone forest always ________ Lin Wang as a jack-in-the-box ________ people when they open the box.

[05~07] 다음 글을 읽고 물음에 답하시오.

Danny Mehta, Location Scout

Vatnajökull National Park, Frozen Beauty of Iceland

I'm a location scout and my job is finding perfect places to shoot movies. Iceland is the best place __ⓐ__ many location scouts to visit due to its unusual beauty. My personal favorite is the Vatnajökull National Park. The sharp cliffs, blue glacier caves, and long mountain ranges can stand in for any place in the world or the universe. __ⓑ__ fact, the recent sci-fi movie we shot here was produced without using computer graphics! Iceland can help (A) 우리의 가장 무모한 꿈을 실현되도록 만들다 on the movie screen.

중요

05 위 글의 빈칸 ⓐ와 ⓑ에 들어갈 전치사가 바르게 짝지어진 것은?

	ⓐ	ⓑ		ⓐ	ⓑ
①	for	To	②	of	In
③	to	In	④	for	In
⑤	of	To			

06 위 글의 밑줄 친 (A)의 우리말에 맞게 6 단어로 영작하시오.

➡ ______________________

고난이도

07 다음 빈칸 (A)와 (B)에 알맞은 단어를 넣어 Vatnajökull National Park에 대한 소개를 완성하시오.

> Vatnajökull National Park is in Iceland and its (A)_______ _______, blue glacier caves, and long mountain ranges can (B)_______ _______ _______ any place in the world or the universe.

[08~10] 다음 글을 읽고 물음에 답하시오.

> **Amber Smith, Fashion Colorist**
> **Caño Cristales, the River of Five Colors of Colombia**
> The world is filled with millions of different colors. It is my job to mix, develop, and create colors for clothing. Over the years, I've been gaining insights from the beautiful colors of Caño Cristales. ⓐYou can see the wonderful mixed colors of this river anywhere else in the world. The combination of colorful plants under the water and sunlight makes the colors more alive and bright. ⓑWhenever I visit the Caño Cristales, it makes me think that maybe ⓒthere are still countless colors that are waiting to be created.

08 위 글의 밑줄 친 ⓐ에서 흐름상 어색한 부분을 찾아 고치시오.

➡ ______________________

중요

09 위 글의 밑줄 친 ⓑ를 다음과 같이 바꿔 쓸 때 빈칸에 들어갈 알맞은 단어를 쓰시오.

➡ When I visit the Caño Cristales, it _______ makes me think

10 위 글의 밑줄 친 ⓒ에서 생략할 수 있는 부분을 찾아 쓰시오.

➡ ______________________

[11~13] 다음 글을 읽고 물음에 답하시오.

> **Lin Wang, Ecologist**
> **Tsingy, the Stone Forest of Madagascar**
> I've been visiting the stone forest of Madagascar to study plants and animals for over 20 years. The spiky stones of this place (A)[is / are] true miracles of nature. ⓐThis amazing shape has been created by rainfall. Rain has cut down the stones and made them sharp and spiky over a long period of time. The environment is harsh for animals to (B)[live / live in], but they have found ways to survive. For example, lemurs, which only live in Madagascar, have frog-like legs that help them (C)[jump / jumping] from one stone tower to another. For me, the stone forest is like a jack-in-the-box. It always surprises me and keeps me on my toes!

중요

11 위 글의 괄호 (A)~(C)에서 어법상 알맞은 낱말을 골라 쓰시오.

➡ (A) _______ (B) _______ (C) _______

12 위 글의 밑줄 친 ⓐ를 능동태로 고치시오.

➡ ______________________

13 다음 빈칸 (A)와 (B)에 알맞은 단어를 넣어 Lin Wang에 대한 소개를 완성하시오.

> Lin Wang is an (A)_______ and has been visiting Tsingy, (B)_______ _______ _______ of Madagascar, to study plants and animals for over 20 years.

교과서

구석구석

Communication Step B

A: Congratulations on receiving the award. I've heard that this photo was taken in India. Is that true?
동명사 (전치사 on의 목적어) / 현재완료 / = this photo was taken in India

B: Yes, this rainbow cloud is caused by thin clouds and water drops.
수동태

A: Wow, it truly is amazing!

B: Yes, it is. I can't wait to take more photos of amazing clouds.
어서 ~하고 싶다

A: I wish you the best of luck!

해석

A: 상 받은 것을 축하해. 이 사진이 인도에서 찍힌 것이라고 들었어. 맞니?
B: 응, 이 무지개 구름은 얇은 구름과 물방울에 의해 생긴 거야.
A: 와, 정말 멋지다!
B: 응, 그래. 어서 더 많은 멋진 구름 사진을 찍고 싶어.
A: 행운을 빌어!

Wrap Up 1

W: Your uncle, John, is coming back from South America this weekend.
come back from ~: ~에서 돌아오다

M: That's great. He has been away for almost 2 years, right?
be away: 떨어져 있다

W: Yeah, he's been in the jungle most of the time to research.
대체로, 대부분의 시간에 / to부정사의 부사적 용법(~하기 위해서)

M: Wow, that's amazing. I can't wait to see him and listen to his stories.
can't wait to+동사원형: 빨리 ~하고 싶다 / see와 병렬 구조

W: Me, too. We're having dinner with him this Saturday, so don't make other plans.

M: Okay, I won't, Mom.
뒤에 make other plans가 생략되어 있다.

구문해설 • almost: 거의 • research: (연구) 조사, 연구

W: 네 삼촌, John이 이번 주말에 남아메리카에서 돌아올 거야.
M: 잘됐네요. 그는 거의 2년 동안 떨어져 있었죠, 그렇죠?
W: 그래, 그는 연구를 위해 대부분의 시간을 정글에 있었어.
M: 와, 정말 놀랍네요. 빨리 그를 보고 그의 이야기를 듣고 싶어요.
W: 나도. 이번 토요일에 그와 저녁 식사를 할 거니까 다른 계획은 세우지 마.
M: 알았어요, 안 그럴게요, 엄마.

Think & Write Step A

Mt. Jiri and Mt. Seorak
Trip for Hiking Fans
- walk along beautiful hiking routes
  ~을 따라 걷다
- learn how to get in shape and keep fit
  의문사+to부정사(명사적 용법) = how you should get

Trip for Soccer Fans
Madrid and Manchester
- meet famous players
- learn how to improve your soccer skills
  의문사 to부정사(명사적 용법) = how you should improve

Paris and London
Trip for Art Fans
- visit famous art museums
- learn how to draw pictures creatively
  의문사+to부정사(명사적 용법) = how you should draw

지리산과 설악산
하이킹 팬들을 위한 여행
- 아름다운 하이킹 길을 따라 걷는다
- 좋은 몸매를 유지하고 건강을 유지하는 법을 배운다

축구 팬들을 위한 여행
마드리드와 맨체스터
- 유명한 선수들을 만난다
- 여러분의 축구 기술을 향상시키는 법을 배운다

파리와 런던
예술 팬들을 위한 여행
- 유명한 미술관을 방문한다
- 창조적으로 그림을 그리는 법을 배운다

구문해설 • route: 길[경로/루트] • get in shape: 좋은 몸 상태(몸매)를 유지하다
• keep fit: 건강을 유지하다 • improve: 개선되다, 향상시키다 • art museum: 미술관

영역별 핵심문제

Words & Expressions

01 접두어 in-의 성격이 다른 하나를 고르시오.

① insight ② indoor
③ income ④ independent
⑤ inside

02 다음 괄호 안의 단어를 문맥에 맞게 고쳐 쓰시오.

(1) We were beginning to worry. It was ________ for David to be so late. (usual)

(2) The new device is a ________ of copier, fax, image scanner, and document printer. (combine)

03 다음 우리말에 맞도록 빈칸에 알맞은 말을 쓰시오. (철자가 주어진 경우 주어진 철자로 시작할 것.)

(1) 황사가 있을 때마다 내 눈과 목이 아파.
➡ My eyes and throat hurt w________ there is ________ ________.

(2) 새로운 상품을 판매하기 위해 시장에 제공하기 전에 시장을 충분히 조사하는 것이 중요하다.
➡ It is important to ________ the market fully before offering a new product for sale.

(3) 호수 가까이에 많은 하이킹 등산로가 있다.
➡ There are c________ hiking trails ________ the lake.

04 다음 빈칸에 들어갈 말을 <보기>에서 찾아 쓰시오.

보기
of at by out to with

(1) To everybody's surprise, temple stays turned ________ to be a popular travel program.

(2) His death was due ________ heart disease.

(3) The songs were made ________ the world's best musicians.

(4) Most ________ the lung cancer is caused by smoking.

Conversation

[05~06] 다음 대화를 읽고 물음에 답하시오.

M: Do you want to watch the new 3D movie? (①)
W: Which one? (②)
M: (③) It was shot near Australia's Great Barrier Reef.
W: Oh, I've heard of it. (④) It has the most beautiful sea life.
M: Right. (⑤) I can't wait to watch the movie. Let's go and get the ticket.

05 위 대화의 빈칸에 들어갈 말로 적절한 것은?

The one about adventures under the sea.

① ② ③ ④ ⑤

06 위 대화의 내용과 일치하지 않는 것을 고르시오.

① The man is going to get the ticket after the conversation.
② The man wants to watch the new 3D movie.
③ Australia's Great Barrier Reef has the most beautiful sea life.
④ The movie is about the sea life at Australia's Great Barrier Reef.
⑤ The woman heard of Great Barrier Reef.

[07~08] 다음 대화를 읽고 물음에 답하시오.

W: Dad, my science club is going to go to Dokdo in July.
M: Oh, really? What do you plan to do there?
W: We are going to study the caves on the island and go bird watching.
M: Sounds (A)________ it will be an interesting trip.
W: Yeah. I've only read about Dokdo in books. (B)____________________________(to, there, can't, actually, I, wait, visit)
M: I hope you enjoy your trip!

07 빈칸 (A)에 알맞은 말을 쓰시오.

➡ ____________________________

08 빈칸 (B)를 괄호 안에 주어진 단어를 알맞게 배열하여 채우시오.

➡ ____

[09~10] 다음 대화를 읽고 물음에 답하시오.

W: Your uncle, John, is coming back from South America this weekend.
M: That's great. He has been away for almost 2 years, right?
W: Yeah, he's been in the jungle most of the time to research.
M: Wow, that's amazing. I can't wait to see him and listen to his stories.
W: Me, too. We're having dinner with him this Saturday, so don't make other plans.
M: Okay, I won't, Mom.

09 위 대화에서 다음 영영풀이에 해당하는 단어를 찾아 쓰시오.

to study a subject in detail, especially in order to discover new facts or test new ideas

➡ ____________________________

10 위 대화를 읽고 답할 수 없는 질문을 고르시오.

① When the man is going to have dinner with his uncle?
② Where is John coming from?
③ How long has John been away?
④ What does John research in the jungle?
⑤ Is the man looking forward to see his uncle, John?

[11~12] 다음 대화를 읽고 물음에 답하시오.

M: Jisu, did you know that the sun never (A)______ in Norway during summer?
W: No, I didn't know that. How interesting!
M: Yeah, and I've heard that people go hiking and even cycling at night (B)_______ it isn't dark.
W: I'd love to go hiking and cycling in the middle of the night!
M: Me, too. (C)________________(we, someday, chance, it, get, hope, the, I, to, try)

11 빈칸 (A)와 (B)에 들어갈 말이 알맞게 짝지어진 것은?

① rises – although ② rises – because
③ sets – unless ④ sets – although
⑤ sets – because

12 빈칸 (C)를 괄호 안에 주어진 단어를 알맞게 배열하여 채우시오.

➡ ______________________

Grammar

13 다음 문장의 빈칸에 알맞은 말이 바르게 짝지어진 것은?

- Grace has been watching TV ______ 30 minutes.
- He has been doing it ______ 10 years ago.

① for – for ② for – since
③ since – for ④ since – since
⑤ during – since

14 다음 중 어색한 문장을 모두 고르시오.

① The children are too noisy for me to concentrate.
② He expects me to visit Korea.
③ How silly for her to tell him such a thing!
④ Emma has been teaching English three years ago.
⑤ Miriam has been growing vegetables since last year.
⑥ It has been snowing heavily for over three hours.

15 그림을 보고, 주어진 어휘를 이용하여 빈칸을 알맞게 채우시오.

It was ______________________ the window.
(break, careless, Mike)

16 다음 빈칸에 들어갈 말이 나머지와 다른 하나는?

① Mr. Jones has been writing a letter ______ 30 minutes.
② My brother has been repairing his computer ______ an hour.
③ He has been using the pen ______ long.
④ He has been learning Spanish ______ five years.
⑤ Eva has been living in this house ______ last year.

17 다음 중 어법상 옳은 것을 모두 고르시오.

① Amanda has been traveling around the world for the past two months.
② Molly has been trying to solve the problem since an hour.
③ It has been raining two days ago.
④ It was not easy for me to choose the best movie.
⑤ This jungle is a wonderful place of animals to live in.

18 다음 두 문장의 의미가 같도록 빈칸에 알맞은 말을 쓰시오.

(1) He was generous to give her that money.
= It was generous ________________.

(2) The book was difficult for her to read.
= It was difficult ________________.

Reading

[19~21] 다음 글을 읽고 물음에 답하시오.

"The beauty of nature inspires us all. Let's find out how people from different fields of work get inspired by nature."

Lin Wang, Ecologist

Tsingy, the Stone Forest of Madagascar

ⓐI've been visiting the stone forest of Madagascar to study plants and animals for over 20 years. The spiky stones of this place are true miracles of nature. This amazing shape has been created by rainfall. Rain has cut down the stones and made them sharp and spiky over a long period of time. The environment is harsh for animals to live in, but they have found ways to survive. For example, lemurs, ___ⓑ___ only live in Madagascar, have frog-like legs that help them jump from one stone tower to another. For me, the stone forest is like a jack-in-the-box. It always surprises me and ⓒ나를 정신을 바짝 차리게 한다!

19 위 글의 밑줄 친 ⓐ와 현재완료의 용법이 같은 것을 모두 고르시오.

① She has gone to Japan.
② She has been sick since last Friday.
③ I've watched the movie twice.
④ She has just come.
⑤ He has lived in Seoul for ten years.

20 위 글의 빈칸 ⓑ에 알맞은 것은?

① that ② who ③ what
④ which ⑤ whose

21 위 글의 밑줄 친 ⓒ의 우리말에 맞게 주어진 어휘를 이용하여 5 단어로 영작하시오.

toes

➡ ________________________

[22~23] 다음 글을 읽고 물음에 답하시오.

Amber Smith, Fashion Colorist

Caño Cristales, the River of Five Colors of Colombia

The world is filled with millions of different colors. It is my job to mix, develop, and create colors for (A)[clothing / clothings]. Over the years, I've been gaining insights from the beautiful colors of Caño Cristales. You cannot see the wonderful mixed colors of this river (B)[anywhere / somewhere] else in the world. The combination of colorful plants under the water and sunlight (C) [make / makes] the colors more alive and bright. Whenever I visit the Caño Cristales, it makes me think that maybe there are still countless colors that are waiting to be created.

22 위 글의 괄호 (A)~(C)에서 어법상 알맞은 낱말을 골라 쓰시오.

➡ (A)________ (B)________ (C)________

23 According to the passage, which is NOT true?

① Amber Smith is a fashion colorist.
② Caño Cristales is the River of Five Colors of Colombia.
③ Amber Smith has been gaining insights from the beautiful colors of Caño Cristales over the years.
④ The colors of Caño Cristales become more alive and bright thanks to the combination of colorful plants under the water and sunlight.
⑤ Amber Smith thinks that maybe there are no more colors that are waiting to be created.

[24~26] 다음 글을 읽고 물음에 답하시오.

THE PLACE THAT INSPIRES ME
01 Tsingy, Madagascar
• Recommended by an ecologist
• The sharp and spiky stones have been created by rainfall(rain). Animals (A)<u>like</u> lemurs have found ways to survive in the harsh environment.
02 Caño Cristales, Colombia
• Recommended by a fashion colorist
• The river has wonderful mixed colors. The colorful plants and the sunlight make the colors more alive and bright.
03 Vatnajökull National Park, Iceland
• Recommended by a location scout
• There are sharp cliffs, blue glacier caves, and long mountain ranges. Sci-fi movies can be ___(B)___ without computer graphics.

24 위 글의 밑줄 친 (A)<u>like</u>와 바꿔 쓸 수 있는 단어를 쓰시오. (두 단어)

➡ ______________________

25 위 글의 빈칸 (B)에 shoot을 알맞은 형태로 쓰시오.

➡ ______________________

26 Which question CANNOT be answered after reading the passage?

① Who recommends Tsingy, Madagascar?
② By what have the sharp and spiky stones of Tsingy been created?
③ What does an ecologist do?
④ Why does a fashion colorist recommend Caño Cristales?
⑤ Where can sci-fi movies be shot without computer graphics?

[27~28] 다음 글을 읽고 물음에 답하시오.

Danny Mehta, Location Scout
Vatnajökull National Park, Frozen Beauty of Iceland
I'm a location scout and my job is finding perfect places to shoot movies. (①) Iceland is the best place for many location scouts to visit ⓐ<u>due to</u> its unusual beauty. (②) My personal favorite is the Vatnajökull National Park. (③) The sharp cliffs, blue glacier caves, and long mountain ranges can stand in for any place in the world or the universe. (④) Iceland can help make our wildest dreams come true on the movie screen. (⑤)

27 위 글의 흐름으로 보아, 주어진 문장이 들어가기에 가장 적절한 곳은?

> In fact, the recent sci-fi movie we shot here was produced without using computer graphics!

① ② ③ ④ ⑤

28 위 글의 밑줄 친 ⓐ<u>due to</u>와 바꿔 쓸 수 있는 말을 고르시오.

① as for
② instead of
③ in place of
④ because of
⑤ in spite of

단원별 예상문제

출제율 100%

01 〈보기〉에 주어진 단어로 빈칸을 채울 수 없는 문장을 고르시오.

보기

countless personal recent unique

① Employees said their job is good for ________ growth.

② Everyone is __________ and people should be encouraged to express their individual identities.

③ The light in here is not __________ enough to read by.

④ They spent _________ hours talking to one another.

⑤ What's been happening in _________ weeks?

출제율 95%

02 다음 빈칸에 공통으로 들어갈 말을 쓰시오.

- Can you stand in ______ me at the meeting next week?
- Thank you so much ______ your call last week.

출제율 90%

03 두 문장이 같은 의미가 되도록 빈칸을 채우시오. (철자가 주어진 경우 주어진 철자로 시작할 것.)

He had to retire because of ill health.
= He had to retire d______ ______ ill health.

출제율 95%

04 〈보기 1〉의 영영풀이에 해당하는 단어를 〈보기 2〉의 문장의 빈칸에 알맞게 연결한 것은?

보기1

(A) a very large mass of ice that moves very slowly
(B) a particular length of time with a beginning and an end
(C) the steep side of an area of high land
(D) something that combines several things

보기2

ⓐ Banana, orange juice, and cream may seem an odd _____, but together they make a delicious drink.
ⓑ Such a rise in temperatures could melt ice sheets and _____s.
ⓒ His playing improved in a very short _____of time.
ⓓ He dives off the edge of the _____ into the sea.

(A) – (B) – (C) – (D)

① ⓐ – ⓑ – ⓒ – ⓓ
② ⓐ – ⓒ – ⓑ – ⓓ
③ ⓑ – ⓒ – ⓐ – ⓓ
④ ⓑ – ⓒ – ⓓ – ⓐ
⑤ ⓑ – ⓓ – ⓐ – ⓒ

[05~07] 다음 대화를 읽고 물음에 답하시오.

M: Mom, did you watch the weather report today? (①)
W: Wow, fantastic! (②) When is the best time to see them? (③)
M: (④) <u>I've heard what the shooting stars will peak between 12 a.m. or 2 a.m.</u> (⑤)
W: Wow, it will be a special night!

출제율 95%

05 ①~⑤ 중 주어진 문장이 들어갈 곳은?

We will be able to see hundreds of shooting stars tonight!

① ② ③ ④ ⑤

출제율 90%

06 위 대화에서 다음 영영풀이에 해당하는 단어를 찾아 쓰시오.

a piece of rock or metal from space, which burns brightly as it falls towards the Earth

➡ ____________________

출제율 95%

07 밑줄 친 문장에서 어색한 부분을 모두 고쳐 완전한 문장으로 쓰시오.

➡ ____________________

____

[08~09] 다음 대화를 읽고 물음에 답하시오.

M: Jisu, did you know (A)[that / what / how] the sun never sets in Norway (B)[from / during / while] summer?

W: No, I didn't know that. (①) (C)[What / How / Which] interesting! (②)

M: Yeah! (③)

W: I'd love to go hiking and cycling in the middle of the night! (④)

M: Me, too. (⑤) I hope we get the chance to try it someday.

출제율 95%

08 ①~⑤ 중 주어진 문장이 들어갈 곳은?

I've heard that people go hiking and even cycling at night because it isn't dark.

① ② ③ ④ ⑤

출제율 90%

09 위 대화의 괄호 (A)~(C)에서 적절한 것을 골라 쓰시오.

➡ (A)________ (B)________ (C)________

[10~12] 다음 대화를 읽고 물음에 답하시오.

W: Look at this picture on Jake's blog. He went indoor rock climbing!

M: Oh, it looks interesting (A)________ seems too hard.

W: Actually, I've heard that there are different levels of courses at the community center.

M: Really? Then, maybe I should visit the center and find (B)______ more about the courses.

W: Let me know how it turns (C)______.

출제율 90%

10 빈칸 (A)에 알맞은 말을 고르시오.

① but ② so ③ because
④ if ⑤ or

출제율 95%

11 빈칸 (B)와 (C)에 공통으로 들어갈 말을 쓰시오.

➡ ____________________

출제율 100%

12 위 대화의 내용과 일치하지 않는 것은?

① There are few indoor rock climbing courses at the community center.
② The man is interested in indoor rock climbing.
③ The man is going to go to the community center to search into the rock climbing courses.
④ There is a picture in which Jake went indoor rock climbing on his blog.
⑤ The woman knows that there are rock climbing courses at the community center.

출제율 100%

13 다음 빈칸에 알맞은 말이 순서대로 짝지어진 것은?

> • It was foolish ____________ to waste his money on such a thing.
> • Kim has been talking on the phone with her friend ________ noon.

① of him – since ② for him – for
③ of him – for ④ for him – since
⑤ for him – ago

출제율 90%

14 다음 빈칸에 알맞지 않은 것은?

> It was __________ for her to solve the problems.

① impossible ② difficult
③ easy ④ wise
⑤ necessary

출제율 100%

15 다음 중 어법상 적절한 문장은?

① My dad has been work in New York for a year.
② Brian has been painting his house since two hours.
③ She has been cleaning her house then.
④ Anne has been listening to the music since an hour ago.
⑤ What's been happened in recent weeks?

출제율 95%

16 다음 빈칸에 들어갈 말이 나머지와 다른 하나는?

① It is necessary _______ Jamie to counsel people because they are far from their family and friends.
② It was very thoughtful ________ you to send her the flowers.
③ It would be dangerous ________ you to stay here.
④ It's an exciting opportunity ______ me to do some traveling.
⑤ It was difficult _______ me to remember things.

출제율 95%

17 다음 괄호 안에 주어진 어휘를 이용하여 빈칸에 알맞게 쓰시오.

> The woman ________ ________ ________ for her husband ________ an hour. (wait)

[18~20] 다음 글을 읽고 물음에 답하시오.

> **Lin Wang, Ecologist**
> **Tsingy, the Stone Forest of Madagascar**
> I've been visiting the stone forest of Madagascar to study plants and animals for over 20 years. The spiky stones of this place are true miracles of nature. This amazing shape has been created by rainfall. Rain has cut down the stones and made them sharp ! and spiky over a long period of time. The environment is harsh for animals ⓐto live in

but they have found ways ⓑto survive. ⓒFor example, lemurs, that only live in Madagascar, have frog-like legs that help them jump from one stone tower to another. For me, the stone forest is like a jack-in-the-box. It always surprises me and keeps me on my toes.

출제율 95%

18 위 글의 밑줄 친 ⓐto live, ⓑto survive와 to부정사의 용법이 같은 것을 각각 모두 고르시오.

보기

① They were happy to survive the crisis.
② I have no house to live in.
③ There are many ways to live in the jungle.
④ Many birds migrate south to survive the cold winter.
⑤ He must be clever to survive on $10 a week.

➡ ⓐ ________, ⓑ ________

출제율 90%

19 위 글의 밑줄 친 ⓒ에서 어법상 틀린 부분을 찾아 고치시오.

➡ ____________________

출제율 100%

20 위 글을 읽고 알 수 없는 것을 고르시오.

① Where is Tsingy?
② How many times has Lin Wang visited Tsingy?
③ By what have the spiky stones of Tsingy been created?
④ Is the environment of Tsingy proper for animals to live in?
⑤ Are there any animals that live in the stone forest of Tsingy?

[21~22] 다음 글을 읽고 물음에 답하시오.

Amber Smith, Fashion Colorist
Caño Cristales, the River of Five Colors of Colombia

The world is filled with millions of different colors. It is my job to mix, develop, and create colors for clothing. Over the years, I've been gaining insights from the beautiful colors of Caño Cristales. You cannot see the wonderful mixed colors of this river anywhere else in the world. ⓐThe combination of colorful plants under the water and sunlight makes the colors more alive and bright. Whenever I visit the Caño Cristales, it makes me think that maybe there are still countless colors ⓑ만들어지기를 기다리고 있는.

출제율 90%

21 다음 빈칸 (A)와 (B)에 알맞은 단어를 넣어 위 글의 밑줄 친 ⓐ가 의미하는 것을 완성하시오.

When the sun shines on the (A)________ ________ under Caño Cristales, the (B)________ of Caño Cristales can be made more alive and bright.

출제율 95%

22 위 글의 밑줄 친 ⓑ의 우리말에 맞게 주어진 어휘를 이용하여 6 단어로 영작하시오.

created

➡ ____________________

서술형 실전문제

01 대화의 흐름상이나 어법상 어색한 것을 골라 바르게 고치시오. (3개)

M: Let's welcome Ms. Scarlett Lee, the winner of this year's photo competition.
W: Hello, thank you for invite me. I've honored to receive the award.
M: Let's talk about your photo. I've heard that this photo took in the Maldives. Is that true?
W: Yes, this glowing beach is caused by plankton.
M: Wow, it truly is amazing!
W: Yes, it is. I can't wait taking more pictures of amazing beaches.
M: I wish you the best of luck!

➡ (1) ____________________
(2) ____________________
____
(3) ____________________
____

[02~03] 다음 대화를 읽고 물음에 답하시오.

W: Your uncle, ⓐJohn is coming back from South America this weekend.
M: That's great. ⓑHe has been away for almost 2 years, right?
W: Yeah, ⓒhe's been in the jungle most of the time to research.
M: Wow, that's amazing. 나는 빨리 그를 보고 그의 이야기 듣고 싶어.
W: Me, too. ⓓWe're having dinner with him this Saturday, so don't make other plans.
M: Okay, ⓔI will, Mom.

02 밑줄 친 우리말을 주어진 단어를 이용하여 영작하시오.

➡ ____________________
(can't, listen, see)

03 ⓐ~ⓔ 중 문맥상이나 어법상 어색한 것을 골라 바르게 고치시오.

➡ ____________________

04 주어진 두 문장을 한 문장으로 바꾸시오.

(1) • I started visiting the Wimbledon tennis tournament when I was in high school.
• I am still visiting it.
➡ ____________________
____

(2) • Phil began repairing mobile phones ten years ago.
• He is still repairing mobile phones.
➡ ____________________

(3) • I am still staying at the hotel.
• I started to stay there a few days ago.
➡ ____________________

05 다음 문장을 it을 사용하여 같은 뜻의 문장으로 바꾸어 쓰시오.

(1) The comic book is fun for me to read.
➡ ____________________

(2) People here need to eat well to stay warm and healthy. (necessary를 이용할 것.)
➡ ____________________
____

(3) This book is too difficult for me to understand.
➡ ____________________

06 다음 문장에서 어법상 어색한 것을 바르게 고쳐 다시 쓰시오.

(1) The airplane has been flying an hour ago.

➡ ______________________

(2) The government has been stealing our public funds since a long time.

➡ ______________________

____

(3) I have been knowing him ever since he was a boy.

➡ ______________________

(4) The room is large enough of all of us to stay in.

➡ ______________________

(5) I think it is nice for you to give books to your brother.

➡ ______________________

(6) The bands played music for many people dance to.

➡ ______________________

[07~09] 다음 글을 읽고 물음에 답하시오.

Lin Wang, Ecologist
Tsingy, the Stone Forest of Madagascar

I've been visiting the stone forest of Madagascar to study plants and animals for over 20 years. The spiky stones of this place are true miracles of nature. This (A)[amazing / amazed] shape has been created by rainfall. Rain has cut down the stones and made them (B)[sharp / sharply] and spiky over a long period of time. The environment is harsh for animals to live in, but they have found ways to survive. ___ⓐ___ example, lemurs, which only live in Madagascar, have frog-like legs that help them jump from one stone tower to another. For me, the stone forest is (C)[like / alike] a jack-in-the-box. It always surprises me and keeps me ___ⓑ___ my toes!

07 위 글의 괄호 (A)~(C)에서 어법상 알맞은 낱말을 골라 쓰시오.

➡ (A)________ (B)________ (C)________

08 위 글의 빈칸 ⓐ와 ⓑ에 각각 들어갈 알맞은 말을 쓰시오.

➡ ⓐ ____________, ⓑ ____________

09 How can lemurs live in the stone forest of Tsingy? Fill in the blanks with suitable words.

> They can live there because they have ________ ________ that help them jump from one stone tower to another.

창의사고력 서술형 문제

01 대화의 흐름에 맞게 빈칸에 주어진 단어를 이용하여 자신의 기대에 관해 쓰시오.

> **A:** I'm going to go to the preview tonight.
> **B:** Wow, that's amazing.
> **A:** ________________________________ (film, wait, see, meet, actors, director)

02 다음 그림을 보고, 주어진 조건에 맞게 영작하시오.

(1) 2:00 p.m. ~ 4:00 p.m.(now) (2) 3:00 p.m.~now

> 조건
> (1) 사진 속 인물의 행동을 묘사할 것.
> (2) since 또는 for를 이용하여 현재완료진행형으로 쓸 것.

(1) ________________________________

(2) ________________________________

03 다음 내용을 바탕으로 여러분이 기획한 테마 여행을 소개하는 글을 쓰시오.

> Q1 For whom is your trip designed?
> A1 My trip is designed for people who are interested in hiking.
>
> Q2 Which places will the tourists visit? Write two places.
> A2 They will visit Mt. Jiri and Mt. Seorak.
>
> Q3 What will the tourists do during the trip?
> A3 They will be able to walk along beautiful hiking routes. They will also learn how to get in shape and keep fit.

> Are you a hiking fan? Then join my trip. It is designed for those who are interested in (A)______________. You'll visit (B)______________. These are the best places for hiking fans to visit. You'll be able to walk along beautiful (C)______________. Also, you'll learn how to (D)______________ and (E)______________. This trip will be the most memorable one!

단원별 모의고사

01 다음 영영풀이가 나타내는 말을 주어진 철자로 시작하여 쓰시오.

> very many, especially more than you think is reasonable

➡ c________________________

02 다음 빈칸을 〈보기〉에 있는 어휘를 이용하여 채우시오.

보기: cut get keep walk

(1) She gets up at six every morning to ________ along the beach.

(2) If you want to ________ in shape, you should do more exercise.

(3) People do not need to ________ down trees and produce paper.

(4) With a test every Friday, she ________ her students on their toes.

03 다음 밑줄 친 부분의 의미로 알맞지 않은 것은?

① The movie has won a number of awards. (상)

② Hundreds of people were killed or wounded. (수백의)

③ I got more insights about him from reading his books than from talking to him. (시야)

④ She bought a few items of clothing. (의류, 옷)

⑤ The glowing blue color is created by X-rays. (빛나는)

04 다음 우리말에 맞도록 빈칸에 알맞은 말을 쓰시오. (철자가 주어진 경우 주어진 철자로 시작할 것.)

(1) 원할 때 언제라도 날 방문해도 좋다.

➡ You can visit me w________ you want.

(2) 당신을 만나서 정말 영광입니다.

➡ I'm really h________ to meet you.

(3) 섬유소가 많고 칼로리가 적은 음식을 골라라.

➡ Choose foods that are h________ in fiber and low in calories.

[05~06] 다음 대화를 읽고 물음에 답하시오.

W: ⓐLook at this picture on Jake's blog. ⓑHe went indoor rock climbing!

M: ⓒOh, it looks interesting but seems too hard.

W: Actually, 지역문화회관에 다른 수준의 코스들이 있다고 들었어. (hear, that, course, at, there, level, center)

M: Really? ⓓThen, maybe I should visit the center and find out more about the courses.

W: ⓔLet me to know how does it turn out.

05 밑줄 친 우리말과 일치하도록 주어진 단어를 이용해 문장을 쓰시오.

➡ ____

____

06 ⓐ~ⓔ 중 어법상 어색한 것을 골라 바르게 고치시오.

➡ ____

____

[07~08] 다음 대화를 읽고 물음에 답하시오.

M: Do you want to watch the new 3D movie?
W: Which one?
M: The one about adventures under the sea. It was shot near Australia's Great Barrier Reef.
W: Oh, I've heard of it. It has the most beautiful sea life.
M: Right. 나는 빨리 그 영화를 보고 싶어. Let's go and get the ticket.

07 위 대화에서 다음 영영풀이에 해당하는 단어를 찾아 쓰시오.

an exciting experience in which dangerous or unusual things happen

➡ ____________________

08 밑줄 친 우리말과 일치하도록 주어진 단어를 이용하여 영작하시오.

➡ ______________________________

(wait, watch, to, 7 단어)

[09~10] 다음 대화를 읽고 물음에 답하시오.

M: Jisu, (A)____________ the sun never sets in Norway during summer?
W: No, I didn't know that. How interesting!
M: Yeah, and (B)______________ people go hiking and even cycling at night because it isn't dark.
W: I'd love to go hiking and cycling in the middle of the night!
M: Me, too. I hope we get the chance to try it someday.

09 다음 빈칸 (A)와 (B)에 들어갈 말이 알맞게 짝지어진 것은?

(A) (B)

① do you know why – I've heard that
② do you know why – I've heard about
③ did you know that – I've heard that
④ did you know that – I didn't know that
⑤ did you know that – I've heard about

10 위 대화의 내용에 맞게 빈칸에 알맞은 말을 쓰시오.

In Norway, people go ______________ ______________ the night during summer because ______________.

[11~13] 다음 대화를 읽고 물음에 답하시오.

W: David, what's your summer plan? (①)
M: My family is going to China. (②)
W: The Rainbow Mountains? (③)
M: They are some mountains (A)that look like canvases in rainbow colors. (④)
W: That sounds amazing! (⑤) Take lots of pictures!

11 ①~⑤ 중 주어진 문장이 들어갈 곳은?

I can't wait to visit the Rainbow Mountains.

① ② ③ ④ ⑤

12 위 대화에서 다음 영영풀이에 해당하는 단어를 찾아 쓰시오.

a large curve of different colors that can appear in the sky when there is both sun and rain

➡ ____________________

13 밑줄 친 (A)that과 쓰임이 같은 것을 고르시오.

① I heard that he was very sick.
② Do you know that ice cream is from China?
③ Do you know the girl that is standing there?
④ I've heard that the school tennis team won the match.
⑤ People didn't know that the earth is round.

14 다음 중 <보기>의 문장과 의미가 같은 것을 고르시오.

보기

He is working now. He began working at 7 p.m.

① He is working at 7 p.m.
② He worked at 7 p.m.
③ He has been working since 7 p.m.
④ He has been worked for 7 p.m.
⑤ He had worked since 7 p.m.

15 다음 중 어법상 옳은 문장을 모두 고르시오.

① Isn't it necessary of us to help them?
② Iceland is the best place for many location scouts to visit.
③ She has been listening to the music since two hours.
④ Alex has been having his father's watch since his father passed away.
⑤ They have been waiting for a doctor for two hours.

16 다음 두 문장의 의미가 같도록 빈칸에 알맞은 말을 쓰시오.

(1) It's important that we should have a sense of belonging.
= It's important ______________________.

(2) It's reasonable that employees should be properly paid.
= It's reasonable ______________________.

17 주어진 표현을 사용하여 질문에 대한 대답을 완성하시오.

(1) Q: How long have both of you been living together?
A: We ______________________.
(5 years)

(2) Q: Since when has Christine been reading the book?
A: She ______________________.
(yesterday)

18 다음 문장에서 어법상 어색한 것을 바르게 고쳐 다시 쓰시오.

(1) The greenhouse in the Ice Cube is warm enough of Mathew to grow fresh vegetables.
➡ ______________________

(2) It was wise for Solomon to make such a careful decision.
➡ ______________________

(3) Jason has been taking horse-riding lessons since three months.
➡ ______________________

(4) Ashley has been learning to play the flute 5 months ago.
➡ ______________________

(5) Lily has been liking Gino since she first met him.
➡ ______________________

[19~21] 다음 글을 읽고 물음에 답하시오.

"①The beauty of nature inspires us all. Let's find out how people from different fields of work get inspired by nature."

Lin Wang, Ecologist

②Tsingy, the Stone Forest of Madagascar

I've been visiting the stone forest of Madagascar to study plants and animals for ③ over 20 years. The spiky stones of this place are true miracles of nature. This amazing shape has been created by rainfall. Rain has cut down the stones and made them sharp and spiky ④over a long period of time. ⓐ The environment is harsh for animals to live in, but they have found ways to survive. For example, lemurs, which only live in Madagascar, have frog-like legs ⓑthat help them jump from one stone tower to another. For me, the stone forest ⑤is like a jack-in-the-box. It always surprises me and keeps me on my toes!

19 다음 중 위 글의 밑줄 친 ①~⑤에 대한 설명을 옳게 하지 못한 사람을 고르시오.

① 수미: 수동태로 고치면 Us all are inspired by the beauty of nature.야.
② 혜경: 콤마는 동격을 나타내서, 'Madagascar에 있는 석림인 Tsingy'라는 뜻이야.
③ 영호: '… 이상'이라는 뜻으로, more than으로 바꿔 쓸 수 있어.
④ 철규: '…에 걸쳐'라는 뜻이야.
⑤ 진성: is similar to로 바꿔 쓸 수 있지.

20 위 글의 밑줄 친 ⓐ처럼 말한 이유를 우리말로 쓰시오.

➡ ______________________________
____

21 위 글의 밑줄 친 ⓑthat과 문법적 쓰임이 같은 것을 모두 고르시오.

① She said that the story was true.
② I can't walk that far.
③ The people that he spoke to were very helpful.
④ It's the best novel that I've ever read.
⑤ It's true that he was a little late.

[22~24] 다음 글을 읽고 물음에 답하시오.

Danny Mehta, Location Scout

Vatnajökull National Park, Frozen Beauty of Iceland

I'm a location scout and my job is finding perfect places to ⓐshoot movies. Iceland is the best place for many location scouts to visit due to its unusual beauty. My personal favorite is the Vatnajökull National Park. The sharp cliffs, blue glacier caves, and long mountain ranges can stand in for any place in the world or the universe. In fact, the recent sci-fi movie we shot here was produced without using computer graphics! ⓑIceland can help make our wildest dreams come true on the movie screen.

22 위 글의 밑줄 친 ⓐshoot와 같은 의미로 쓰인 것을 고르시오.

① Don't shoot beams of light at him.
② The police rarely shoot to kill people.
③ He likes to shoot his film in Hollywood.
④ He tried to shoot the ball to first base.
⑤ This is just a toy gun — it doesn't shoot real bullets.

23 위 글의 밑줄 친 ⓑ를 다음과 같이 바꿔 쓸 때 빈칸에 들어갈 알맞은 말을 두 단어로 쓰시오.

➡ Iceland can help ________ ________ our wildest dreams come true on the movie screen.

24 Which question CANNOT be answered after reading the passage?

① What is Danny Mehta's job?
② Where is the Vatnajökull National Park?
③ Why is Iceland the best place for many location scouts to visit?
④ What place is Danny Mehta's personal favorite?
⑤ How many sci-fi movies were produced in the Vatnajökull National Park?

[25~27] 다음 글을 읽고 물음에 답하시오.

Are you a hiking fan? Then join my trip. It is designed for those who are interested in hiking. You'll visit Mt. Jiri and Mt. Seorak. These are the best places for hiking fans to visit. You'll be able to walk along beautiful hiking routes. Also, you'll learn how to get in shape and keep fit. This trip will be the most memorable ⓐone!

25 위 글의 종류로 알맞은 것을 고르시오.

① article ② essay ③ PR poster
④ review ⑤ book report

26 위 글의 밑줄 친 ⓐone이 가리키는 것을 본문에서 찾아 쓰시오.

➡ ______________________

27 위 글을 읽고 알 수 없는 것을 고르시오.

① For whom is the trip designed?
② How long will it take to go hiking?
③ Which places will the tourists visit?
④ What will the tourists do during the trip?
⑤ Will this trip be unforgettable?

[28~29] 다음 글을 읽고 물음에 답하시오.

Danny Mehta, Location Scout
Vatnajökull National Park, Frozen Beauty of Iceland

I'm a location scout and my job is finding perfect places to shoot movies. Iceland is the best place for many location scouts to visit due to its unusual beauty. My personal favorite is the Vatnajökull National Park. The sharp cliffs, blue glacier caves, and long mountain ranges can stand in for any place in the world or the universe. ___ⓐ___, the recent sci-fi movie we shot here was produced without using computer graphics! Iceland can help make our wildest dreams come true on the movie screen.

28 위 글의 빈칸 ⓐ에 들어갈 알맞은 말을 고르시오.

① Moreover ② In fact
③ Therefore ④ However
⑤ In other words

29 According to the passage, which is NOT true?

① Danny Mehta is a location scout.
② Vatnajökull National Park is located in Iceland.
③ Iceland is the best place for many location scouts to visit due to its unusual beauty.
④ The recent action movie Danny Mehta's team shot here was produced without using computer graphics.
⑤ Iceland can help make our wildest dreams become realized on the movie screen.

[30~31] 다음 글을 읽고 물음에 답하시오.

Amber Smith, Fashion Colorist
Caño Cristales, the River of Five Colors of Colombia

The world is filled with millions of different colors. It is my job to mix, develop, and create colors for clothing. Over the years, I've been gaining insights from the beautiful colors of Caño Cristales. You cannot see the wonderful mixed colors of this river anywhere else in the world. ⓐ물속의 화려한 식물들과 햇빛의 결합은 그 색깔을 더 생생하고 밝게 만든다. Whenever I visit the Caño Cristales, it makes me think that maybe there are still countless colors that are waiting to be created.

30 위 글의 밑줄 친 ⓐ의 우리말에 맞게 한 단어를 보충하여, 주어진 어휘를 알맞게 배열하시오.

sunlight / of colorful plants / and / under the water / the / makes / more alive and bright / the colors

➡ ______________________________
____
____

31 다음 빈칸 (A)와 (B)에 알맞은 단어를 넣어 Amber Smith에 대한 소개를 완성하시오.

Amber Smith is a (A)________ ________ who has been gaining insights from the beautiful colors of (B)________ ________.

[32~34] 다음 글을 읽고 물음에 답하시오.

I'm a location scout and my job is finding perfect places to shoot movies. ⓐ아이슬란드는 비범한 아름다움 때문에 많은 장소 섭외가들이 방문하기에 최고의 장소이다. My personal favorite is the Vatnajökull National Park. The sharp cliffs, blue glacier caves, and long mountain ranges can stand ___ⓑ___ for any place in the world or the universe. In fact, the recent sci-fi movie we shot here was produced without using computer graphics! Iceland can help make our wildest dreams come true on the movie screen.

32 위 글의 밑줄 친 ⓐ의 우리말에 맞게 한 단어를 보충하여, 주어진 어휘를 알맞게 배열하시오.

the best place / is / to visit / Iceland / its unusual beauty / due to / for many location

➡ ______________________________
____

33 위 글의 빈칸 ⓑ에 알맞은 것은?

① in ② to ③ at
④ for ⑤ with

34 What makes the Vatnajökull National Park stand in for any place in the world or the universe? Fill in the blanks (A) and (B) with suitable words.

Its sharp cliffs, blue (A)________ ________, and long (B)________ ________.

For the Love of Our Country

의사소통 기능

- 알고 있는 내용 진술하기
  A: Wasn't Jeong Yakyong a scholar in the Joseon Dynasty?
  B: Yeah, but it is said that he was also a detective.
- 허락 요청하기
  A: Is it okay if I take pictures in the museum?
  B: Sure. Go ahead.

언어 형식

- 접속사 if
  I was not sure **if** he was telling the truth.
- 과거완료
  When I was sixteen years old, my family **had** already **made** an arrangement for me to marry him.

교과서

Words & Expressions

Key Words

- □ **afterwards** [ǽftərdz] 부 나중에, 그 뒤에
- □ **already** [ɔːlrédi] 부 이미, 벌써
- □ **article** [áːrtikl] 명 기사
- □ **biography** [baiágəfi] 명 자서전, 전기
- □ **bring** [briŋ] 동 가져오다
- □ **chest** [tʃest] 명 서랍장, 큰 상자, 장롱
- □ **clinic** [klínik] 명 병원, 진료소
- □ **detective** [ditéktiv] 명 형사, 탐정
- □ **disappointing** [dìsəpɔ́intiŋ] 형 실망시키는
- □ **Dynasty** [dáinəsti] 명 왕조
- □ **embarrassing** [imbǽrəsiŋ] 형 부끄러운, 당황스러운
- □ **female** [fíːmeil] 명 여자 형 여자의, 여성의
- □ **fight** [fait] 동 싸우다
- □ **fortress** [fɔ́ːrtris] 명 요새
- □ **fortune** [fɔ́ːrtʃən] 명 재산, 행운
- □ **gamble** [gǽmbl] 동 도박하다, ~을 도박으로 잃다
- □ **gambling house** 도박장
- □ **general** [dʒénərəl] 명 장군
- □ **horrible** [hɔ́ːrəbl] 형 끔찍한
- □ **husband** [hʌ́zbənd] 명 남편
- □ **include** [inklúːd] 동 ~을 포함하다
- □ **independence** [ìndipéndəns] 명 독립, 광복
- □ **invention** [invénʃən] 명 발명품, 발명
- □ **Japanese** [dʒæ̀pəníːz] 형 일본의 명 일본어
- □ **leave** [liːv] 동 맡기다, 남기다
- □ **locker** [lákər] 명 사물함
- □ **machine** [məʃíːn] 명 기계, 기구
- □ **Manchuria** [mæntʃúərə] 명 만주 형 만주의
- □ **marriage** [mǽridʒ] 명 결혼, 혼인
- □ **marry** [mǽri] 동 결혼하다, 혼인하다
- □ **merchant** [mɔ́ːrtʃənt] 명 상인
- □ **move** [muːv] 동 이동시키다, 이동하다
- □ **movement** [múːvmənt] 명 (정치적 · 사회적) 운동
- □ **museum** [mjuːzíːəm] 명 박물관, 기념관
- □ **musical instrument** 악기
- □ **object** [ábdʒikt] 명 물건
- □ **odd** [ad] 형 이상한
- □ **officer** [ɔ́ːfisər] 명 경찰관, 장교
- □ **pilot** [páilət] 명 조종사, 비행사
- □ **realistic** [rìːəlístik] 형 진짜 같은, 사실적인
- □ **realize** [ríːəlàiz] 동 깨닫다
- □ **ruin** [rúːin] 동 망치다, 파산시키다
- □ **save** [seiv] 동 구하다
- □ **scholar** [skálər] 명 학자
- □ **since** [sins] 접 ~이기 때문에, ~한 이래로
- □ **social studies** 사회
- □ **solve** [salv] 동 해결하다, 풀다
- □ **strange** [streindʒ] 형 낯선, 모르는
- □ **Sudan** [suːdǽn] 명 수단 (민주 공화국)
- □ **truth** [truːθ] 명 진실, 사실
- □ **village** [vílidʒ] 명 마을, 농촌
- □ **whenever** [hwenévər] 접 ~할 때마다, ~하면
- □ **whisper** [hwíspər] 동 속삭이다, (사람 · 일에 대하여) 소곤소곤 이야기하다
- □ **wonder** [wʌ́ndər] 동 궁금하다
- □ **wooden** [wúdn] 형 나무로 된, 목재의
- □ **would** [wəd] 동 (과거에 있어서의 습관 · 습성 · 반복적 동작) ~(하곤) 했다

Key Expressions

- □ **ask for**: 청구하다, 청하다
- □ **at that moment**: 그 순간에
- □ **at this hour**: 이 시간에
- □ **be used to (동)명사**: ~하는 데 익숙하다
- □ **behind one's back**: ~ 몰래, ~의 등 뒤에서
- □ **by 동사ing**: ~함으로써
- □ **devote one's life to 명사**: ~에 일생을 바치다
- □ **hear of[about]** ~: ~에 대해 듣다
- □ **instead of**: ~ 대신에
- □ **Is it okay if I** ~?: 제가 ~해도 될까요?
- □ **It is said that 주어+동사** ~: (사람들이) ~라고 한다
- □ **keep a secret**: 비밀을 지키다
- □ **make an arrangement**: ~을 결정하다
- □ **so+형용사/부사+that 주어+동사**: 너무 ~해서 …하다
- □ **take a look at** ~: ~을 보다
- □ **try on**: 입어 보다, 신어 보다
- □ **yell at**: ~에게 고함치다, ~에게 호통치다

Word Power

※ 명사형 어미 -age(~하는 행위, 상태)

- □ **marry**(결혼하다)+**-age**(~의 상태) → **marriage**(결혼)
- □ **pack**(싸다)+**-age**(~한 것) → **package**(꾸러미, 하나로 묶음)
- □ **use**(사용하다)+**-age**(법) → **usage**(사용법)
- □ **cour**(마음)+**-age**(~의 상태) → **courage**(용기, 용감)
- □ 라틴어 **damnum**(손해)+**-age**(상태, 요금) → **damage**(손해, 손상)
- □ 라틴어 **ab**(~으로)+**ante**(앞)+**-age**(상태) → **advantage**(우위, 우세)

※ 부사형 접미어 -ward(s)(방향, ~쪽으로)

- □ **after**(뒤에, 후에)+**-ward**(~쪽으로) → **afterwards**(후에, 나중에)
- □ **back**(뒤)+**-ward**(~쪽으로) → **backwards**(뒤로)
- □ **up**(위)+**-ward**(~쪽으로) → **upwards**(위로)
- □ **fore**(앞)+**-ward**(~쪽으로) → **forwards**(앞으로)
- □ **in**(안)+**-ward**(~쪽으로) → **inward**(안으로)
- □ **out**(바깥에)+**-ward**(~쪽으로) → **outward**(밖으로)

English Dictionary

□ **article** 기사
→ a piece of writing about a particular subject that is published in a newspaper or magazine
신문이나 잡지에 발행되는 특정한 주제에 대해 쓴 글

□ **biography** 자서전, 전기
→ a book that someone writes about someone else's life
누군가가 다른 누군가의 삶에 대해 쓴 책

□ **chest** 서랍장, 큰 상자, 장롱
→ a large strong heavy box used for storing things
물건을 보관하기 위해 사용되는 크고 무거운 상자

□ **female** 여자의, 여성의
→ relating to women or girls
여자나 여자아이와 관련된

□ **fortress** 요새
→ a large strong building used for defending an important place
중요한 장소를 방어하기 위해 사용되는 크고 튼튼한 건물

□ **fortune** 재산
→ a very large amount of money
매우 많은 돈

□ **general** 장군
→ an officer of very high rank in the army or air force
육군이나 공군에서 높은 계급을 가진 장교

□ **include** ~을 포함하다
→ to contain someone or something as a part
사람이나 사물을 어떤 것의 일부로 내포하다

□ **independence** 독립
→ freedom from control by another country or organization
다른 나라나 조직에 의한 통제로부터 벗어난 자유

□ **merchant** 상인
→ someone who buys and sells goods in large quantities
많은 양의 물건을 사고파는 사람

□ **movement** (정치적 · 사회적) 운동
→ a gradual development or change of an attitude, opinion, or policy
태도, 의견 또는 정책의 점진적인 발전 또는 변화

□ **ruin** 망치다, 파산시키다
→ to make someone lose all their money or power
누군가로 하여금 그들의 돈이나 권력을 모두 잃게 만들다

□ **scholar** 학자
→ someone who studies a particular subject and knows a lot about it, especially a subject that is not scientific
특히 과학적인 주제가 아닌 특정 주제에 대해 공부하고 많이 아는 사람

□ **save** 구하다
→ to make someone or something safe from danger, harm, or destruction
위험, 해로움, 또는 파괴로부터 사람이나 사물을 안전하게 만들다

Words & Expressions 시험대비 실력평가 Step2

[01~02] 다음 밑줄 친 부분과 바꿔 쓸 수 있는 말을 고르시오.

01

> We were rescued from the sinking ship by a passing fishing boat.

① trapped ② protected ③ saved
④ rushed ⑤ searched

02

> Buffett made a lot of money through intelligent investments.

① a move ② a result ③ a chance
④ a fortune ⑤ a poverty

03 중요 다음 밑줄 친 부분의 의미로 알맞지 않은 것은?

① He is a writer rather than a scholar. (학자)
② She was clearly speaking the truth. (진실)
③ The soldiers were ready to defend the fortress. (요새)
④ Have you ever been to the War Memorial Museum of Korea? (기념관)
⑤ He was recently promoted to general. (일반적인 것)

04 다음 빈칸에 들어갈 말을 고르시오.

> It was really ________ to find all our money stolen.

① terrific ② confident ③ boring
④ horrible ⑤ exciting

05 다음 제시된 단어를 사용하여 자연스러운 문장을 만들 수 없는 것은? (형태 변화 가능)

> hear make take try

① Let's ________ an arrangement of our destination.
② She said she would ________ her life to public service.
③ Do you have any jackets I could ________ on?
④ It's an interesting place. Do you want to ________ a look around?
⑤ Have you ________ about the garage sale?

서답형
06 두 문장이 같은 의미가 되도록 빈칸을 채우시오. (주어진 철자로 시작할 것)

> You should talk to Karen because she's the one responsible for it.
> = You should talk to Karen s________ she's the one responsible for it.

07 중요 다음 영영풀이가 나타내는 말을 고르시오.

> a gradual development or change of an attitude, opinion, or policy

① movement ② culture
③ model ④ volunteer
⑤ activity

중요
01 우리말 해석에 맞게 주어진 단어를 알맞게 배열하시오.

(1) 그는 새로운 안경에 익숙해지려고 노력하면서 늙은이처럼 걸었다.
➡ He walked like an old man __________ ________________. (glasses, be, to, trying, to, new, used)

(2) 사람들은 그녀가 전 세계를 다녀왔다고 말한다.
➡ ________________________________
(that, all, said, world, she, is, the, been, over, it, has)

(3) 나는 그의 등 뒤에서 이렇게 얘기하는 것을 싫어한다.
➡ ________________________________
(talking, behind, like, back, his, hate, this, I)

(4) 내가 사진을 찍어도 괜찮을까요?
➡ ________________________________
(a, okay, picture, I, if, it, take, is)

02 빈칸에 적절한 말을 주어진 단어를 변형하여 채우시오.

She took part in the March 1st Movement for Korea's __________. (depend)

03 두 문장이 같은 의미가 되도록 주어진 단어를 이용하여 빈칸을 채우시오.

He was strong enough to lift it. = He was ________ strong ________ ________ ________ lift it. (can)

고난이도
04 다음 제시된 의미에 맞는 단어를 주어진 철자로 시작하여 빈칸에 쓰고, 알맞은 것을 골라 문장을 완성하시오.

• i________: to contain someone or something as a part • r________: to make someone lose all their money or power • s________: to make someone or something safe from danger, harm, or destruction

(1) Some say spoilers ________ the story.
(2) Wearing a seat belt can help ________ your life.
(3) The price for the hotel ________s breakfast.

05 다음 빈칸에 공통으로 들어갈 말을 쓰시오.

• The building was destroyed ________ fire in 2004. • She earns extra money ________ babysitting.

06 다음 우리말에 맞도록 빈칸에 알맞은 말을 쓰시오.

(1) LA Times에 직장 내 괴롭힘에 대한 흥미로운 기사가 있었다.
➡ There was an interesting ________ in the LA Times about bullying at work.

(2) 우리는 자주 저녁 산책을 하곤 했다.
➡ We ________ often have a walk of an evening.

교과서

Conversation

1 알고 있는 내용 진술하기

A: Wasn't Jeong Yakyong a scholar in the Joseon Dynasty?

정약용이 조선왕조 때의 학자가 아니었나요?

B: Yeah, but it is said that he was also a detective.

네, 하지만 그는 또한 탐정이었다는 말이 있어요.

- 'It is said that 주어+동사 ~.'는 '(사람들이) ~라고 한다.'라는 뜻으로 that절의 내용에 대해 진술할 때 사용한다. 'is said'가 수동태 형태임에 주의한다.
- 'It is said that 주어+동사 ~.'는 말하는 사람이 구체적으로 정해져 있지 않고 '(사람들이) ~라고 말했다'라는 의미로 사용하므로, 일반인인 'they[people]'를 주어로 'They[People] say that 주어+동사'.로 바꿔 쓸 수 있다.

알고 있는 내용 진술하기

- It is said that 주어+동사 ~. (~라고 한다.)
- It is believed that 주어+동사 ~. (~라고 믿어진다.)
- It is thought that 주어+동사 ~. (~라고 생각된다.)
- They[People] say (that) 주어+동사 ~. (사람들이 ~라고 말한다.)

핵심 Check

1. 우리말과 일치하도록 주어진 단어를 알맞게 배열하여 문장을 만드시오.

A: ______________________________ in front of the City Hall this weekend.
(that, is, will, a, said, it, there, be, festival, big)
B: I'm interested in that. How about going there?

2. 다음 문장과 같은 의미가 되도록 주어진 단어를 이용하여 쓰시오.

They say that he is a liar.

➡ ______________________________ (said)

3. 다음 우리말과 일치하도록 빈칸에 알맞은 말을 쓰시오.

보라색은 클레오파트라가 가장 좋아하는 색이었다고 한다.

➡ ______________________________ a favorite color of Cleopatra.

2 허락 요청하기

A: Is it okay if I take pictures in the museum? 박물관에서 사진을 찍어도 괜찮나요?
B: Sure. Go ahead. 물론이죠. 그렇게 하세요.

- 'Is it okay if I ~?'는 '제가 ~해도 될까요?'라는 뜻으로 어떤 행동을 하기 전에 허가를 요청할 때 사용하는 표현이다. if 다음에는 허락을 구하는 내용을 쓴다.
- 허가를 묻는 다른 표현으로 'Can I ~?', 'Are we allowed to 동사원형 ~?', I'm wondering if I ~. 등이 있다.

허락 요청하기

- Is it okay if I ~?
- Can[May] I ~?
- Would it be all right if I ~?
- Is it possible that I ~?
- I'm wondering if I ~.
- Are we allowed to 동사원형 ~?

허락을 요청하는 질문에 답하기

〈허락하기〉
- Sure.
- Of course.
- Certainly.
- Why not?
- No problem.

〈거절하기〉
- I'm sorry, but you can't[may not].
- I'm afraid not.
- You're not allowed to 동사원형.
- You can't do that.
- I'm afraid you can't.
- No way!
- You're not permitted to do that.
- Not right now.

핵심 Check

4. 다음 우리말과 일치하도록 주어진 말을 이용해 빈칸을 완성하시오.

A: ______________________ (okay, if, the guitar) (제가 기타를 연습해도 될까요?)
B: OK, but you're not allowed to practice after 10 p.m.

5. 우리말과 일치하도록 주어진 단어를 배열하여 영작하시오.

A: ____________________________ (okay, to, it, you, if, is, next, sit, I)
(내가 당신 옆에 앉아도 될까요?)
B: No problem.

Listen & Talk 1 A-1

M: Lisa, ❶what are you reading?
W: I'm reading a ❷biography of Gwon Giok.
M: ❸I haven't heard about her. Who is she?
W: She was the first ❹female pilot in Korea. ❺It is said that she had over 7,000 hours of flying time.
M: Wow, I didn't know that.

M: Lisa, 너 뭐 읽고 있니?
W: 권기옥의 전기를 읽고 있어.
M: 그녀에 대해 들어본 적이 없어. 그녀는 누구니?
W: 그녀는 한국의 첫 번째 여성 조종사야. 그녀는 비행시간이 7,000 시간이 넘는다고 해.
M: 와, 난 몰랐어.

❶ 무엇을 읽고 있는지 현재진행형(be동사+동사ing)을 이용해 질문하고 있다.
❷ biography: 자서전, 전기
❸ hear about ~: ~에 대해 듣다
❹ female: 여자; 여자의, 여성의 pilot: 조종사, 비행사
❺ 'It is said that 주어+동사 ~.'는 '(사람들이) ~라고 한다.'라는 뜻으로 that절의 내용에 대해 진술할 때 사용한다. over: ~을 넘어, ~보다 많은

Check(√) True or False

(1) Lisa is reading a novel about Gwon Giok. T ☐ F ☐
(2) The man didn't know who Gwon Giok was. T ☐ F ☐
(3) Gwon Giok was the first female pilot in Korea. T ☐ F ☐

Listen & Talk 2 A-1

W: Excuse me, you ❶can't take your backpack ❷inside the museum.
M: Oh, I didn't know that. Is it okay if I ❸bring in my water bottle?
W: ❹Yes, that's fine. You can ❺leave your bag in the locker.
M: Okay, thank you.

W: 죄송합니다만, 박물관에 가방을 가지고 들어갈 수 없어요.
M: 아, 몰랐어요. 물병은 가지고 들어가도 괜찮나요?
W: 네, 그건 괜찮아요. 가방은 라커에 두시면 돼요.
M: 알았어요. 감사합니다.

❶ 어떤 일이 가능한지 묻고 답할 때 조동사 can을 사용할 수 있다.
❷ inside: ~ 안에
❸ bring in: 들여가다
❹ 'that's fine.'은 '그것은 괜찮다.'라는 의미로 상대방이 허락을 구하는 말을 했을 때 허락하는 표현이다. 이외의 허락의 표현에는 'Of course.', 'Certainly.', 'No problem.' 등이 있다.
❺ leave: 남기다, 맡기다

Check(√) True or False

(4) The museum allows people to take their backpack inside it. T ☐ F ☐
(5) The woman can't bring in her water bottle. T ☐ F ☐

Listen & Talk 1 B

W: Hey, Mark, ❶do you know about Father Lee Taeseok?

M: Yeah, ❷I've heard of him. Why?

W: ❸Take a look at this article. He is going to ❹be included in the social studies textbook in South Sudan.

M: Wow, that's great.

W: Yeah, he helped the children ❺by building a clinic and a school. ❻It is said that such stories will be included in the textbook.

M: It is good to hear ❼that students will learn about such a great person.

W: 어이, Mark, 너 이태석 신부에 대해 아니?
M: 응, 그에 대해 들어본 적이 있어. 왜?
W: 이 기사를 봐. 그는 남수단의 사회 교과서에 실릴 거야.
M: 와, 그거 대단하구나.
W: 그래, 그는 병원과 학교를 지어 아이들을 도와주었어. 그런 이야기들이 교과서에 실릴 거라고 해.
M: 학생들이 그토록 훌륭한 사람에 대해 배울 거라는 말을 들으니 좋군.

❶ 'Do you know about ~?'은 '~에 대해서 알고 있어?'라는 의미로 상대방에게 알고 있는지 묻는 표현이다. 'Have you heard about ~?'이나 'Are you aware of ~?'로 바꿔 쓸 수 있다.

❷ 'I've heard of[about] ~'은 '~에 대해 들었다'라는 뜻으로 알고 있거나 들은 것에 대해 말할 때 쓰는 표현이다. 일반적으로 현재완료의 형태로 쓰지만 'I heard of[about] ~'라고 할 수도 있다

❸ take a look at ~: ~을 보다 article: 기사 ❹ include: ~을 포함하다 ❺ by 동사ing: ~함으로써

❻ 'It is said that 주어+동사 ~.'는 말하는 사람이 구체적으로 정해져 있지 않고 '(사람들이) ~라고 말한다'라는 의미로 사용하므로, 일반인인 'they[people]'를 주어로 'They[People] say that 주어+동사 ~.'로 바꿔 쓸 수 있다. (= They[People] say that such stories will be included in the textbook.)

❼ 동사 hear 뒤에 명사절을 이끄는 접속사 that이 사용되고 있다.

Check(√) True or False

(6) The woman read the article about how to be a great person. T ☐ F ☐

(7) Mark wasn't aware of Father Lee Taeseok. T ☐ F ☐

Communication Step B

A: This ❶is called the *Geojunggi*.

B: Wow, this ❷looks interesting.

A: This is a machine ❸that moves heavy objects. It is said that ❹it helped to build the Hwaseong Fortress only in 28 months.

B: How amazing! Is it okay if I take a closer look at it?

A: Sure.

A: 이것은 거중기라고 불려.
B: 와, 이거 흥미 있어 보이는데.
A: 이것은 무거운 물체들을 옮기는 기계야. 그것은 화성 요새를 겨우 28개월 만에 짓는 데 도움이 되었다고 해.
B: 정말 놀랍다! 그걸 더 자세히 봐도 괜찮겠니?
A: 물론이지.

❶ call이 5형식으로 사용하여 '[사람 · 물건을] (어떤 이름으로) 부르다, 이름을 붙이다'로 쓰일 수 있다. 원래는 'People call this the *Geojunggi*.'인 문장을 수동태로 바꾼 것이다.

❷ look+형용사: ~하게 보이다 / interesting은 현재분사형의 형용사로 '~하게 하는'의 뜻으로 감정을 유발하는 대상에 쓰인다.

❸ that은 주격 관계대명사로 which와 바꿔 쓸 수 있다. 주격 관계대명사는 생략할 수 없다.

❹ help (to+) 동사원형: ~ 하는 데 도움이 되다

Check(√) True or False

(8) They are looking at the *Geojunggi*. T ☐ F ☐

(9) *B* is interested in *Geojunggi*. T ☐ F ☐

Listen & Talk 1 Get Ready

A: Kim Deuksin was a painter.

B: ❶No! I read a book and ❷it is said that he was a scholar.

C: Don't fight. You are ❸both right.

❶ 다음에 'He was not a painter.'가 생략되어 있다.
❷ scholar: 학자 ❸ both: 둘 다

Listen & Talk 1 A-2

M: I watched an interesting movie yesterday. Jeong Yakyong was a ❶detective in it.

W: Jeong Yakyong? Wasn't he a scholar in the Joseon ❷Dynasty?

M: Yeah, but it is said that he was also a detective. He ❸solved ❹about 90 cases.

W: Oh, I didn't know that he was also a detective.

❶ detective: 형사, 탐정 in it에서 it은 남자가 어제 본 영화를 의미한다.
❷ Dynasty: 왕조 ❸ solve: 해결하다, 풀다
❹ 숫자 앞의 about은 '대략, 약'의 의미를 가진다.

Listen & Talk 2 A-2

W: Hi, ❶welcome to the National Museum. How can I help you?

M: Hi, is it okay if I ❷take pictures in the museum?

W: Yes, but please ❸don't use a flash.

M: Oh, I see. Thank you.

❶ welcome to 장소: (장소에) 오신 것을 환영합니다
❷ take pictures: 사진 찍다
❸ 명령문은 동사로 시작한다. 하지 말라고 할 때는 그 앞에 'Don't'를 붙인다. flash: (카메라) 플래시

Listen & Talk 2 B

M: Hello, Ms. Jackson. How was your tour of the *Hanok Village*?

W: It was wonderful. The houses were really beautiful.

M: That's great.

W: Actually, I didn't ❶get the chance to have dinner. Is it okay if I cook in the kitchen at this hour?

M: Yes, but please remember ❷that the kitchen ❸closes at 10 p.m.

W: Okay. The kitchen is on the 5th floor, right?

M: Yes, it is. ❹Let me know if you need anything.

❶ get a chance: 기회를 가지다(= have a chance) 'to have dinner'는 앞의 the chance를 수식하는 형용사적 용법이다. ❷ that은 remember의 목적어인 명사절을 이끄는 접속사이다. ❸ 반복되는 사실에 대해서 현재시제를 사용할 수 있다. ❹ 상대방에게 어떤 일을 나에게 알려 달라고 부탁할 때 'let me know'를 이용해 말할 수 있다. let은 사역동사이므로 목적격보어 자리에 동사원형인 know를 사용한다.

Wrap Up 1

W: James, ❶what are you watching?

M: Oh, I'm watching a video about Yi Sunsin.

W: Isn't he the one ❷that saved Joseon from Japan?

M: Right. It is said that he won the war only with twelve wooden ships.

W: Wow, ❸how can that be possible?

M: He was a wise general who made creative plans.

❶ 무엇을 읽는 중인지 현재진행형(be동사+ing)을 사용하여 질문하고 있다.
❷ 주격 관계대명사(= who) ❸ '그것이 어떻게 가능하겠어요?'의 의미로 놀람을 나타내는 표현이며, 여기서는 가능하게 된 이유를 물어보고 있다.

교과서 확인학습

● 다음 우리말과 일치하도록 빈칸에 알맞은 말을 쓰시오.

Listen & Talk 1 Get Ready

A: Kim Deuksin ________ a painter.

B: No! I ________ a book and ________ ________ ________ that he was a scholar.

C: Don't fight. You are ________ right.

해석

A: 김득신은 화가였어.
B: 아니야! 내가 책을 읽었는데 그는 학자였다고 해.
C: 싸우지 마. 너희 둘 다 옳아.

Listen & Talk 1 A-1

M: Lisa, ________ are you ________?

W: I'm reading a ________ of Gwon Giok.

M: I ________ ________ about her. Who is she?

W: She was ________ ________ ________ pilot in Korea. ________ ________ ________ ________ she had ________ 7,000 hours of flying time.

M: Wow, I didn't know that.

M: Lisa, 너 뭐 읽고 있니?
W: 권기옥의 전기를 읽고 있어.
M: 그녀에 대해 들어본 적이 없어. 그녀는 누구니?
W: 그녀는 한국의 첫 번째 여성 조종사야. 그녀는 비행시간이 7,000 시간이 넘는다고 해.
M: 와, 난 몰랐어.

Listen & Talk 1 A-2

M: I watched an ________ movie yesterday. Jeong Yakyong was a ________ in it.

W: Jeong Yakyong? Wasn't he a ________ in the Joseon Dynasty?

M: Yeah, ________ ________ ________ ________ ________ ________ ________ ________ a detective. He ________ about 90 cases.

W: Oh, I ________ ________ ________ he was also a detective.

M: 난 어제 흥미 있는 영화를 보았어. 그 영화에서 정약용이 탐정이었어.
W: 정약용? 그는 조선 왕조의 학자 아니었니?
M: 응, 하지만 그는 탐정이기도 했다고 해. 그는 약 90개의 사건을 해결했어.
W: 아, 그가 또한 탐정이었다는 건 몰랐어.

Listen & Talk 1 B

W: Hey, Mark, do you ________ ________ Father Lee Taeseok?

M: Yeah, I've ________ of him. Why?

W: ________ ________ ________ ________ this article. He is going ________ ________ ________ in the social studies textbook in South Sudan.

M: Wow, that's great.

W: Yeah, he ________ the children ________ ________ ________ ________ and a school. It is said ________ ________ will ________ ________ ________ the textbook.

M: It is good ________ hear that students will learn about ________ a great person.

W: 어이, Mark, 너 이태석 신부에 대해 아니?
M: 응, 그에 대해 들어본 적이 있어. 왜?
W: 이 기사를 봐. 그는 남수단의 사회 교과서에 실릴 거야.
M: 와, 그거 대단하구나.
W: 그래, 그는 병원과 학교를 지어 아이들을 도와주었어. 그런 이야기들이 교과서에 실릴 거라고 해.
M: 학생들이 그토록 훌륭한 사람에 대해 배울 거라는 말을 들으니 좋군.

Listen & Talk 2 A-1

W: Excuse me, you ________ ________ your backpack inside the ________.

M: Oh, I didn't know that. ________ ________ ________ if I bring in my water bottle?

W: Yes, that's fine. You can ________ your bag ________ the locker.

M: Okay, thank you.

해석

W: 죄송합니다만, 박물관에 가방을 가지고 들어갈 수 없어요.
M: 아, 몰랐어요. 물병은 가지고 들어가도 괜찮나요?
W: 네, 그건 괜찮아요. 가방은 라커에 두시면 돼요.
M: 알았어요. 감사합니다.

Listen & Talk 2 A-2

W: Hi, welcome ________ the National Museum. ________ can I help you?

M: Hi, ________ ________ ________ ________ ________ ________ ________ ________ the museum?

W: Yes, but please ________ use a flash.

M: Oh, I see. Thank you.

W: 안녕하세요, 국립박물관에 오신 걸 환영합니다. 무엇을 도와드릴까요?
M: 안녕하세요, 박물관에서 사진을 찍어도 괜찮나요?
W: 네, 하지만 플래시는 사용하지 마세요.
M: 아, 알겠습니다. 감사합니다.

Listen & Talk 2 B

M: Hello, Ms. Jackson. ________ ________ your tour of the *Hanok Village*?

W: It was wonderful. The houses ________ really beautiful.

M: That's great.

W: Actually, I didn't ________ ________ ________ ________ have dinner. Is it ________ ________ ________ cook in the kitchen at this hour?

M: Yes, but please ________ ________ the kitchen closes ________ 10 p.m.

W: Okay. The kitchen is ________ the 5th floor, right?

M: Yes, it is. ________ ________ ________ ________ you need anything.

M: 안녕하세요, Jackson 씨. 한옥 마을 관광은 어땠어요?
W: 굉장했어요. 집들이 정말 아름다웠습니다.
M: 대단하네요.
W: 사실 전 저녁식사를 할 기회가 없었어요. 이 시간에 부엌에서 요리해도 괜찮나요?
M: 네, 하지만 부엌이 오후 10시에 문을 닫는 걸 기억하세요.
W: 알겠습니다. 부엌은 5층에 있죠, 맞나요?
M: 네, 그래요. 무언가 필요하시면 제게 말씀해 주세요.

Communication Step A

M: All right, everyone! This way, please. Now, we ________ ________ ________ the Joseon Dynasty. ________ ________ ________ ________, there were ________ interesting ________. This one ________ ________ the *Jagyeongnu*.

W: Is it a ________ ________?

M: Actually, this is a water clock. ________ ________ ________ ________ ________ ________ the oldest and the ________ water clock in Korea.

W: ________ amazing! ________ ________ ________ ________ I take a picture of it?

M: Sure.

해석

M: 좋아요, 여러분! 이쪽으로 오세요. 이제, 우리는 조선 왕조로 옮겨갑니다. 보시다시피, 많은 흥미 있는 발명품들이 있습니다. 이것은 자격루라고 불립니다.

W: 그것은 악기인가요?

M: 사실은 이것은 물시계입니다. 그것은 한국에서 가장 오래되고, 가장 큰 물시계라고 합니다.

W: 정말 놀랍군요. 그것을 사진 찍어도 괜찮나요?

M: 물론입니다.

Wrap Up 1

W: James, ________ are you watching?

M: Oh, I'm ________ a video about Yi Sunsin.

W: ________ ________ the one that saved Joseon from Japan?

M: Right. ________ ________ ________ ________ ________ ________ the war only with twelve wooden ships.

W: Wow, ________ can that be ________?

M: He was a wise ________ ________ ________ ________ plans.

W: James, 뭘 보고 있니?

M: 아, 이순신에 관한 비디오를 보고 있어.

W: 그는 일본으로부터 조선을 구한 사람 아니니?

M: 맞아. 그는 겨우 12척의 목선으로 전쟁에 이겼다고 해.

W: 와, 그게 어떻게 가능할 수 있지?

M: 그는 창의적인 계획을 세운 현명한 장군이었어.

Wrap Up 2

W: Excuse me, sir. ________ ________ ________ ________ have curry or *bibimbap*?

M: ________ ________ ________ have *bibimbap*, please.

W: ________ you are.

M: Thank you. Oh, ________ ________ ________ ________ I use the bathroom now?

W: Sure, but ________ the seat light is ________, you should ________ in your seat.

M: Okay, thank you.

W: 실례합니다, 선생님. 카레를 드시겠어요 아니면 비빔밥을 드시겠어요?

M: 비빔밥을 먹고 싶습니다.

W: 여기 있습니다.

M: 고마워요. 아, 지금 화장실을 이용해도 괜찮나요?

W: 그럼요, 하지만 좌석 불이 켜져 있으면 선생님 좌석에 있으셔야 합니다.

M: 알았어요, 감사합니다.

01 주어진 문장 이후에 올 대화의 순서를 바르게 배열한 것을 고르시오.

Lisa, what are you reading?

(A) Wow, I didn't know that.
(B) She was the first female pilot in Korea. It is said that she had over 7,000 hours of flying time.
(C) I'm reading a biography of Gwon Giok.
(D) I haven't heard about her. Who is she?

① (B) – (A) – (C) – (D)　② (B) – (C) – (A) – (D)
③ (C) – (A) – (B) – (D)　④ (C) – (B) – (A) – (D)
⑤ (C) – (D) – (B) – (A)

[02~03] 다음 대화를 읽고 물음에 답하시오.

W: Hi, welcome to the National Museum. How can I help you?
M: Hi, is it okay (A)________ I take pictures in the museum?
W: (B)________, but please don't use a flash.
M: Oh, I see. Thank you.

02 빈칸 (A)에 알맞은 말을 고르시오

① that　② if　③ while
④ what　⑤ though

03 빈칸 (B)에 알맞은 말을 모두 고르시오.

① No, you can't　② Okay　③ Of course not
④ Sure, go ahead　⑤ Yes

04 밑줄 친 우리말을 주어진 단어를 이용해 영작하시오.

A: 내가 창문을 열어도 되나요?
B: Sorry, you can't.

➡ ________________________________ (if, okay)

[01~02] 다음 대화를 읽고 물음에 답하시오.

M: I watched an interesting movie yesterday. (①) Jeong Yakyong was a (A)________ in it. (②)
W: Jeong Yakyong? (③)
M: Yeah, but it is said that he was also a (B)__________. (④) He solved about 90 cases. (⑤)
W: Oh, I didn't know that he was also a (C)__________.

01 중요 위 대화의 ①~⑤ 중 주어진 문장이 들어갈 알맞은 곳은?

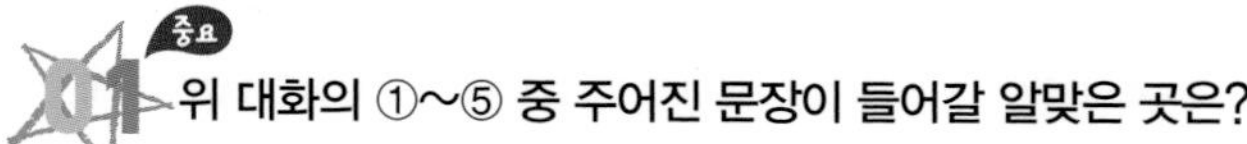
Wasn't he a scholar in the Joseon Dynasty?

① ② ③ ④ ⑤

02 밑줄 친 부분을 근거로 (A)~(C)에 알맞은 말을 고르시오.

① diplomat ② detective
③ reporter ④ victim
⑤ painter

[03~04] 다음 대화를 읽고 물음에 답하시오.

M: Lisa, what are you reading? (①)
W: I'm reading a biography of Gwon Giok. (②)
M: I haven't heard about her. (③)
W: She was the first female pilot in Korea. (④) It is said that she had over 7,000 hours of flying time.
M: Wow, I didn't know that. (⑤)

03 위 대화의 ①~⑤ 중 주어진 문장이 들어갈 알맞은 곳은?

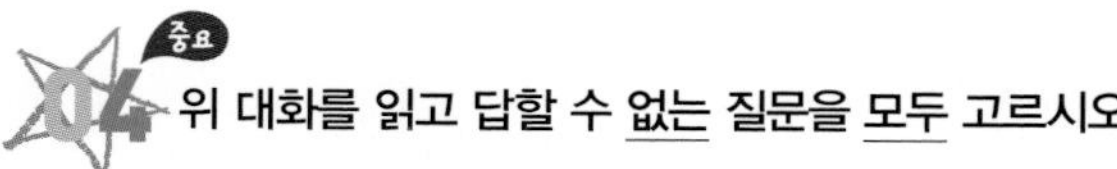
Who is she?

① ② ③ ④ ⑤

04 중요 위 대화를 읽고 답할 수 없는 질문을 모두 고르시오.

① What kind of book is Lisa reading?
② How many hours of flying time did Gwon Giok have?
③ Who was the first male pilot in Korea?
④ Why is Lisa reading the book about Gwon Giok?
⑤ Has the man heard about Gwon Giok?

05 다음 중 짝지어진 대화가 어색한 것은?

① A: Is it okay if I turn on the air conditioning?
B: I'm afraid not. I feel so cold now.
② A: You didn't hand in the homework?
B: I'm sorry. Is it okay if I submit it tomorrow?
③ A: May I turn on the heater?
B: Sure. Go ahead.
④ A: Is it possible that I use your cellphone?
B: Certainly. I didn't bring it today.
⑤ A: Is it okay if I go out and play?
B: I'm sorry, but it's too late.

06 대화가 자연스럽게 연결되도록 (A)~(D)를 순서대로 가장 적절하게 배열한 것은?

M: Hello, Ms. Jackson. How was your tour of the *Hanok Village*?
W: ______________________
M: ______________________
W: ______________________
M: ______________________
W: Okay. The kitchen is on the 5th floor, right?
M: Yes, it is. Let me know if you need anything.

(A) That's great.
(B) Actually, I didn't get the chance to have dinner. Is it okay if I cook in the kitchen at this hour?
(C) It was wonderful. The houses were really beautiful.
(D) Yes, but please remember that the kitchen closes at 10 p.m.

① (B) – (A) – (C) – (D)
② (B) – (C) – (A) – (D)
③ (C) – (A) – (B) – (D)
④ (C) – (B) – (A) – (D)
⑤ (C) – (D) – (B) – (A)

[07~09] 다음 대화를 읽고 물음에 답하시오.

W: Hey, Mark, (A)______________
M: Yeah, I've heard of him. (①) Why?
W: (B)__________ a look at this article. (②) He is going to be included in the social studies textbook in South Sudan. (③)
M: Wow. that's great. (④)
W: Yeah, he helped the children by building a clinic and a school. (⑤)
M: It is good to hear that students will learn about such a great person.

07 위 대화의 ①~⑤ 중 주어진 문장이 들어갈 알맞은 곳은?

It is said that such stories will be included in the textbook.

① ② ③ ④ ⑤

08 빈칸 (A)에 알맞지 않은 말을 모두 고르시오.

① what do you think about Father Lee Taeseok?
② do you know about Father Lee Taeseok?
③ are you reading about Father Lee Taeseok?
④ have you heard of Father Lee Taeseok?
⑤ do you know who Father Lee Taeseok is?

09 빈칸 (B)에 알맞은 말을 고르시오.

① Take ② See ③ Make
④ Stay ⑤ Find

10 빈칸 (A)에 알맞지 않은 말을 모두 고르시오.

A: Do you know who Kim Deuksin is?
B: Yes. Isn't he a scholar from the Joseon Dynasty?
A: Right. I saw a TV show and it is (A)________ that he read one book over 10,000 times.

① said ② allowed
③ thought ④ possible
⑤ believed

[01~02] 다음 대화를 읽고 물음에 답하시오.

A: Do you know (A)_______________?
B: Yes. Isn't she an artist from the Joseon Dynasty?
A: Right. I saw a TV show and (B)________ ____________________. (that, painted, so, paintings, gathered, were, birds, is, the, that, realistic, her, tree, said, around, it)

01 Who is Shin Saimdang?을 빈칸 (A)에 어법에 맞게 써 넣으시오.

➡ ________________________________

중요
02 빈칸 (B)를 괄호 안에 주어진 단어를 알맞게 배열하여 채우시오.

➡ ________________________________
____

[03~04] 다음 대화를 읽고 물음에 답하시오.

W: Hi, welcome to the National Museum. How can I help you?
M: Hi, is it okay (A)_______ I take pictures in the museum?
W: (B)_______, but please don't use a flash.
M: Oh, I see. Thank you.

03 빈칸 (A)에 알맞은 말을 쓰시오.

➡ ______________________

중요
04 빈칸 (B)에 알맞은 말을 3개 이상 쓰시오.

➡ ________________________________

[05~07] 다음 대화를 읽고 물음에 답하시오.

W: Hey, Mark, do you know about Father Lee Taeseok?
M: Yeah, I've heard of him. Why?
W: Take a look at this article. He is going to be included in the social studies textbook in South Sudan.
M: Wow. that's great.
W: Yeah, he helped the children (A)______ building a clinic and a school. It is said that (B)_______ stories will be included in the textbook.
M: It is good to hear that students will learn about (C)______ a great person.

중요
05 빈칸 (A)에 알맞은 전치사를 쓰시오.

➡ ______________________

06 빈칸 (B)와 (C)에 공통으로 들어갈 말을 쓰시오.

➡ ______________________

07 위 대화의 내용에 맞게 빈칸에 알맞은 말을 쓰시오.

Father Lee Taeseok's story that he ________ a clinic and a school to help the children ________ ________ ________ in the social studies textbook in ________ ________.

08 밑줄 친 우리말과 일치하도록 주어진 단어를 이용하여 영작하시오.

A: 내가 너의 모자를 써 보아도 될까?
B: Yes, go ahead.

➡ ______________________ (okay, try, on)

교과서

Grammar

1 접속사 if

- I was not sure **if** he was telling the truth. 나는 그가 진실을 말하고 있는지 확신할 수 없었다.
- I don't know **if** Sarah will like the idea. 사라가 그 아이디어를 좋아할지 모르겠어요.

■ '~인지 (아닌지)'라는 의미의 접속사로 어떠한 사실의 여부를 확인하거나 불확실함을 나타낼 때 쓰이며, 주로 ask, find out, know, see, tell, wonder, be not sure 등의 동사의 목적어 역할을 하는 명사절을 이끈다. if 뒤에 오는 절은 의문사가 없는 간접의문문으로 'if[whether]+주어+동사'의 어순으로 쓴다.

- I asked him **if** I could borrow his car. 나는 그에게 차를 빌려 달라고 부탁했다.
- I wonder **if** he is at home. 그가 집에 있을지 모르겠다.
- I can't tell **if** it will rain or not. 비가 올지 안 올지 모르겠다.
- I'm not sure. + Can I ask this kind of question?
  → I'm not sure **if** I can ask this kind of question. 이런 질문해도 될까 모르겠네요.

■ if가 명사절을 이끄는 접속사로 그 명사절이 문장 내에서 동사의 목적어로 쓰일 때는 whether로 바꿔 쓸 수 있다. whether가 이끄는 절이 주어 역할을 할 경우에는 if로 바꿔 쓸 수 없으며, whether 다음에는 or not을 바로 붙여 쓸 수 있지만, if는 바로 붙여 쓸 수 없다.

- When they asked me **if** I wanted the job, I said yes. 그들이 나에게 그 직장을 원하느냐고 물었을 때 난 그렇다고 대답했다. [목적어]
  = When they asked me **whether** I wanted the job, I said yes.
- **Whether** it's true or not doesn't matter. 그것이 진실이든 아니든 중요하지 않다. [주어]
  = If it's true or not doesn't matter. (×)
- It's questionable **whether** or not that will be true. 그게 사실일지 어쩔지는 의심스럽다.
  = It's questionable if or not that will be true. (×)

cf. if가 조건의 부사절을 이끌 때는 '만약 ~라면'이라는 의미로 쓰이며, whether가 부사절을 이끌 경우에는 '~이든 (아니든)'이라는 '양보'의 의미로 쓰인다.

- **If** anyone calls, tell them I'm not at home. 누구든 전화하면 나 집에 없다고 해. [조건]
- I'm going **whether** you like it or not. 네가 좋아하든 안 하든 난 갈 거야. [양보]

핵심 Check

1. 다음 〈보기〉에서 알맞은 말을 골라 빈칸을 채우시오.

보기

whether, if

(1) I wonder __________ he is at home.

(2) Tell me __________ or not you are willing to believe it.

(3) I don't know __________ you can help me.

2 과거완료

- When I was sixteen years old, my family **had** already **made** an arrangement for me to marry him. 내가 열여섯 살 때 나의 가족은 이미 내가 그와 결혼하기로 합의했다.
- I was in a hotel, and I **had** just **finished** shaving. 전 그때 호텔에 있었는데 막 면도를 끝냈어요.

■ 과거완료는 과거 이전에 일어난 일이 과거의 어느 시점까지 영향을 미칠 때 쓰며, 'had+과거분사'의 형태로 쓴다. 과거완료도 현재완료처럼 완료, 경험, 계속, 결과의 용법이 있다. 또한 과거의 어느 시점보다 먼저 일어난 일이나 상태를 나타낼 때도 쓰이며 이것을 보통 '대과거'라고 한다.

- A young businessman **had** just **started** his own firm. (한 젊은 사업가가 막 자신의 회사를 열었다.) 〈완료〉
- He **had** never **learned** to read and write. (그는 읽고 쓰기를 전혀 배우지 못했다.) 〈경험〉
- She **had written** the letter for two hours. (그녀는 2시간 동안 그 편지를 쓰고 있었다.) 〈계속〉
- He **had gone** to America leaving his family in Korea. (그는 가족을 한국에 남겨 두고 미국으로 가버렸다.) 〈결과〉
- She wasn't recognizable after she **had had** plastic surgery. (성형 수술 후 그녀를 알아볼 수 없었다.) 〈대과거〉

■ 한 문장에 두 가지 과거의 일이 나올 때, 두 동작이 거의 동시에 일어났거나 시간차가 거의 없이 연속적으로 일어났을 경우에는 단순과거로 표현한다. 또, 접속사 after나 before가 쓰여 두 동작의 전후 관계가 명백할 때도 단순과거로 표현할 수 있다.

- He **closed** the door and **went** away. (그는 문을 닫고 가버렸다.) 〈시간차가 거의 없는 연속 동작〉
- His father **died** before he **was** born. (그의 아버지는 그가 태어나기 전에 돌아가셨다.) 〈전후 관계가 명백함〉

핵심 Check

2. 괄호 안에서 알맞은 말을 고르시오.

(1) She couldn't believe what she (has just heard / had just heard).
(2) Their friends knew that they (had lost / lost) their son a week before.
(3) His face grew dark after he (has heard / heard) the news.

01 다음 빈칸에 들어갈 말로 알맞은 것은?

He remembered that he ________ them onto the table.

① toss ② tosses ③ tossed
④ has tossed ⑤ had tossed

02 다음 괄호 안에서 알맞은 말을 고르시오.

(1) When I arrived at the station, the train (already left / had already left).
(2) He confessed to me that he (broke / had broken) the vase.
(3) I don't know (if / that) he will be able to come.
(4) Decide (if / whether) or not the answer is correct.

03 다음 빈칸에 알맞은 것은?

I asked her ________ she was ready to go, and she nodded.

① that ② what ③ which
④ if ⑤ unless

04 다음 우리말에 맞게 주어진 어휘를 바르게 배열하시오.

(1) 제 딸은 그때까지 아팠던 적이 한 번도 없어요.
(my daughter, been, then, sick, had, until, never)
➡ ________________________________
(2) 잠이 막 들었을 때 누군가가 문을 노크했다. (I로 시작할 것)
(I, someone, the door, asleep, fallen, knocked, had, when, just, at)
➡ ________________________________
(3) 그녀는 자신이 미래에 돌아올지 여부에 대해 확신하지 못한다.
(she, she, the future, will, is, return, sure, not, if, in)
➡ ________________________________

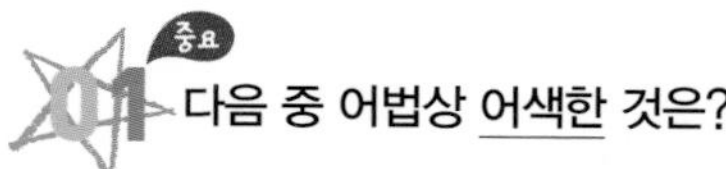

Grammar 시험대비 실력평가

Step3

중요

01 다음 중 어법상 어색한 것은?

① I was so excited because I had never played yut before.
② When she arrived at the station, the first train already left.
③ They described a bear that had threatened them.
④ Tom has lived in LA for 12 years.
⑤ This was the first gold medal that Korea had ever won.

02 다음 중 어법상 바르지 않은 것은?

① I am not sure if he had lunch already.
② I asked her if she wanted to join our meeting.
③ If my guess is right, he must be about forty.
④ He asked her nicely that he could see her license.
⑤ Let your friends know that Thursday's the deadline.

중요

03 다음 빈칸에 알맞은 말이 바르게 짝지어진 것은?

• I wonder ________ my child expresses himself well in English.
• I came across a pen that I ________ last week.

① if – had lost
② because – had lost
③ if – lost
④ because – lost
⑤ whether – have lost

서답형

04 다음 괄호 안에서 알맞은 말을 고르시오.

(1) She was the most remarkable woman he had ever (encounters / encountered).
(2) I walked the dog which Dad (had bought / bought) for me.
(3) Sartre (had practiced / practiced) playing the piano since childhood.
(4) Please tell me (whether / that) he is at home.
(5) Carol wants to know (if / that) the seat is vacant.
(6) We're debating (whether / if) or not to go skiing this winter.

05 주어진 문장의 틀린 부분을 찾아, 올바르게 고친 것을 고르시오.

When Dave got there, Juliet already entered the theater by herself.

① When Dave got there, Juliet already enters the theater by herself.
② When Dave got there, Juliet has already entered the theater by herself.
③ When Dave got there, Juliet had already entered the theater by herself.
④ When Dave had got there, Juliet already entered the theater by herself.
⑤ When Dave had got there, Juliet already had entered the theater by herself.

06 중요 다음 문장의 밑줄 친 부분 중 어법상 어색한 것은?

> I ⓐhave been, I ⓑthought, a ⓒbalanced reporter ⓓfor ⓔ26 years.

① ⓐ ② ⓑ ③ ⓒ
④ ⓓ ⑤ ⓔ

07 빈칸 (A)와 (B)에 알맞은 것으로 바르게 짝지어진 것은?

> Sara wanted to know ___(B)___ the bag ___(A)___ away or not.

	(A)	(B)
①	whether	was thrown
②	that	was thrown
③	if	has been thrown
④	that	had been thrown
⑤	if	had been thrown

서답형
08 〈보기〉에서 알맞은 접속사를 골라 다음 빈칸을 채우시오. (한 번씩만 쓸 것.)

> 보기
> whether, though, if, when, unless

(1) We will go on a picnic __________ it rains.
(2) She will forgive you __________ you apologize to her.
(3) Cross the road carefully __________ there is no car coming.
(4) Alicia put on a mask __________ working as a spy.
(5) They have never decided __________ or not he was killed.

[09~10] 다음 문장의 빈칸에 알맞은 말을 고르시오.

09

> When I got back home, my parents __________ out for a walk.

① goes ② went ③ going
④ has gone ⑤ had gone

10 중요

> I wonder ________ this soup will keep till tomorrow.

① since ② unless ③ if
④ after ⑤ though

11 다음 우리말을 바르게 영작한 것을 고르시오.

> 그 일을 끝냈는지 물어봐도 될까요?

① May I ask though you finished the work?
② May I ask if you finished the work?
③ May I ask unless you finished the work?
④ May I ask as you finished the work?
⑤ May I ask since you finished the work?

서답형
12 다음 두 문장을 한 문장으로 바꿔 쓰고자 한다. 빈칸에 들어갈 알맞은 말을 쓰시오.

> • Cathy started to play the violin when she was 6.
> • Cathy played the violin successfully at the contest yesterday.
> = Cathy played the violin successfully at the contest yesterday as she __________ it since she was 6.

13 다음 밑줄 친 과거완료의 용법이 <보기>와 같은 것은?

보기

Kim <u>had been</u> ill for a couple of years.

① He <u>had</u> just <u>arrived</u> from the countryside.
② It was the best chicken soup I <u>had</u> ever <u>had</u>.
③ When you hired him, how long <u>had</u> he <u>practiced</u> law?
④ The people <u>had lost</u> faith in their politicians and faith in their government.
⑤ He realized that it <u>had been</u> a bad decision on his part.

서답형

14 다음 문장에서 어법상 어색한 것을 바르게 고쳐 다시 쓰시오.

(1) Please tell me what your sister is in her room.
➡ ____________________

(2) If he wants or not isn't that important.
➡ ____________________

(3) I suddenly remembered that I left the windows open.
➡ ____________________
____

(4) I had never been to the big city ago.
➡ ____________________

(5) I found out that someone broke the lamp.
➡ ____________________

[15~16] 다음 우리말에 맞게 영작한 것을 고르시오.

15

그는 내게 고전 음악을 좋아하느냐고 물었다.

① He asked me that I liked classic music.
② He asked me what I liked classic music.
③ He asked me which I liked classic music.
④ He asked me if I liked classic music.
⑤ He asked me if or not I liked classic music.

16

나는 네게 얘기했던 카메라를 샀다.

① I bought the camera that I told you about.
② I bought the camera that I told you.
③ I bought the camera that I have told you about.
④ I bought the camera that I had told you.
⑤ I bought the camera that I had told you about.

중요

17 다음 중 어법상 어색한 것을 고르시오. (2개)

① He asked me if or not the book was boring.
② I remembered that I turned the stove on.
③ He had never been to any foreign countries.
④ When I arrived at the theater, the movie had already begun.
⑤ John wants to ask if you are going to go on a world tour this year.

Grammar 서술형 시험대비

01 시간 흐름에 따른 사건 전개에 맞게 빈칸을 채워 문장을 완성하시오.

> (1) My boy friend bought a ring for me the day before. → Yesterday I lost the ring.
> (2) Clare received flowers last Saturday. → Today her little brother threw them away.

(1) Yesterday I lost the ring that my boy friend ________________ the day before.

(2) Today Clare's little brother threw away the flowers that ________________ last Saturday.

02 (중요) 다음을 when을 이용하여 한 문장으로 연결할 때 빈칸을 알맞게 채우시오. (시제에 유의할 것.)

(1) I went to the restaurant to have lunch with my friends. I arrived there. I remembered that I did not lock the door.
→ When I arrived at the restaurant to have lunch with my friends, I remembered that I ________________ the door.

(2) I was supposed to meet Harry at the library. I went there very late. He already went back to his home. So, I couldn't meet him.
→ When I got to the library to meet Harry, ________________ back to his home.

03 (고난이도) 다음 우리말에 맞게 주어진 단어를 바르게 배열하시오.

(1) 이 음식들이 입맛에 맞으실지 모르겠군요. (I, your taste, these dishes, suit, wonder, will, if)
➡ ________________

(2) 그가 집에 있는지 사무실에 있는지 모른다. (I, he, at the office, at home, is, don't, know, whether, or)
➡ ________________

(3) 우리는 우리가 같은 학교에 다녔다는 걸 알게 되었다. (we, we, school, found, been, had, the, that, same, out, at)
➡ ________________
____

(4) 내가 파리에 한 번도 못 가 보았다는 것에 그녀가 몹시 놀라는 눈치였다. (I, she, Paris, had, astonished, seemed, been, that, never, to)
➡ ________________
____

04 다음 문장에서 잘못된 것을 알맞게 고치시오.

(1) If you said so or not doesn't matter now.
➡ ________________

(2) This approach may be useful in assessing if or not the programme was of value.
➡ ________________

(3) I couldn't decide if to have pizza or a hamburger.
➡ ________________

중요

05 그림을 보고, 주어진 어휘를 이용하여 빈칸을 알맞게 채우시오.

(1) The elderly man was afraid of skiing because he ________________ skiing before. (never, learn)

(2) He wonders ________________ about the appointment. (she, forgot)

06 알맞은 접속사를 이용하여 주어진 두 문장을 하나의 문장으로 쓰시오.

(1) • The man isn't sure.
• He can help her.
➡ ________________________________

(2) • They don't know.
• Will he be promoted?
➡ ________________________________

(3) • Would you tell me?
• He needs surgery or not.
➡ ________________________________
____

07 다음 두 문장을 because를 사용하여 한 문장으로 연결하시오. (두 사건의 시간차가 드러나도록 할 것.)

(1) • He won the contest.
• He practiced a lot for the contest.
➡ ________________________________
____

(2) • I couldn't take the class.
• The class was canceled.
➡ ________________________________
____

고난이도

08 다음 문장에서 어법상 어색한 것을 바르게 고쳐 다시 쓰시오.

(1) He told me that he stole the money the other day.
➡ ________________________________
____

(2) No computer won even one game against a human player until then.
➡ ________________________________
____

(3) I found my bag that I lost on the bus.
➡ ________________________________

(4) I asked the lady that I could use the bathroom.
➡ ________________________________

(5) I'm not sure if Santa gives me a nice gift or not.
➡ ________________________________

(6) I couldn't decide if to buy it.
➡ ________________________________

교과서

Reading

The Secret of My Father

In 1946, a strange man visited me and asked, "Are you Mr. Kim Yonghwan's daughter?"

For me, this (= Are you Mr. Kim Yonghwan's daughter?) was an odd question because I was more used to being (be used to ~ing: ~하는 데 익숙하다) called the daughter of a *parakho*.

"I'm your father's friend. You may wonder if (= whether) it is true, but your father...," the man said.

At that moment, I was expecting disappointing (disappointed(×)) news since (이유를 나타내는 접속사) I did not have good memories of my father.

Back in the 1920's (과거 1920년대에), whenever people saw me in the village, they would (과거의 불규칙적 습관을 나타내는 조동사(~하곤 했다)) say, "There goes the *parakho*'s daughter."

My father was a son from a very rich family. Instead of (~하는 대신에) living (동명사) the life of a *seonbi*, he was always at the gambling house. That is why (because(×)) he was called a *parakho*, which (계속적 용법의 관계대명사(= and it)) means someone who (= that) ruins his family's fortune.

"Your father has gambled away (gamble away: 도박으로 ~을 다 날리다[잃다]) all of the money, and now he's asking for (요청하다) more. Go and tell him that we have no more money left (더 이상 돈이 남아 있지 않다)," my mother would (과거의 불규칙적 습관을 나타내는 조동사(~하곤 했다)) tell me whenever she sent me to the gambling house.

Then, my father would yell at me angrily, "Why did you come empty-handed (주격 보어로 쓰인 유사분사(명사+ed))? Bring me more money!"

strange 이상한, 낯선
odd 이상한
moment 순간
disappointing 실망스러운
back 돌아가서, 과거로 거슬러
whenever ~할 때마다
instead of ~하는 대신에
gambling 도박
ruin 망치다, 파산시키다
fortune 재산
yell 소리치다
angrily 화가 나서
empty-handed 빈손으로

확인문제

- 다음 문장이 본문의 내용과 일치하면 T, 일치하지 않으면 F를 쓰시오.

1 The writer was more used to being called the daughter of a *parakho* than Mr. Kim Yonghwan's daughter. ☐

2 The writer was expecting terrific news though she did not have good memories of her father. ☐

3 The writer's father lived the life of a *seonbi*. ☐

When I was sixteen years old, my family had already made an arrangement for me to marry Mr. Seo. As part of the wedding tradition, Mr. Seo's family sent my family some money to buy a new chest for clothes.

과거완료의 완료 용법 / marry with(×) / 형용사적 용법(money를 수식)

Right before the wedding day, my mother came into my room and said, "Your father has taken the money for the chest."

~ 직전에

I asked angrily, "How could he do such a horrible thing? What should we do now?"

앞 문장의 "Your father has taken the money for the chest."를 가리킨다.

"We have no choice. You'll have to take your aunt's old chest," my mother said.

"How embarrassing for the family," people would whisper behind my back.

embarrassed(×)

Since the first day of marriage, life at my husband's house had been difficult for me.

~ 이후에 / 계속을 나타내는 과거 완료

"Your father, my dear friend...," my father's friend continued his story. "He was not a gambler. Your father sent the family money to the independence fighters in Manchuria. He made himself look like a gambler to keep this a secret from the Japanese officers."

사역동사(made)+목적어+원형부정사, look like+명사: ~처럼 보이다 / 목적을 나타내는 부사적 용법

At first, I was not sure if he was telling the truth. But afterwards, I found out the truth about my father and I realized that I had been wrong about him. Ever since that moment, I have been proud to be the daughter of a *parakho* who had devoted his life to the independence movement.

= whether / realized보다 먼저 일어난 일을 가리키므로 과거완료로 씀. / 언제나 / devote A to B: A를 B에 바치다

arrangement 협의, 합의
wedding 결혼, 결혼식
tradition 전통
chest 상자, 장롱
horrible 지긋지긋한, 끔찍한
choice 선택
embarrassing 난처한, 당혹스러운
behind one's back ~ 몰래, ~의 등 뒤에서
whisper 속삭이다
continue 계속하다
officer 경찰관
at first 처음에
truth 사실
afterwards 나중에, 그 후에
realize 깨닫다, 알아차리다

● 다음 문장이 본문의 내용과 일치하면 T, 일치하지 않으면 F를 쓰시오.

1 Mr. Seo's family sent the writer's family some money to buy a new chest for clothes. ☐

2 The writer's father sent the family money to the independence fighters in Manchuria. ☐

3 The writer's father devoted his life to gambling. ☐

Reading 교과서 확인학습 A

• 우리말을 참고하여 빈칸에 알맞은 말을 쓰시오.

1 The ________ of My Father

2 In 1946, ________ ________ ________ visited me and asked, "Are you Mr. Kim Yonghwan's daughter?"

3 For me, this was ________ ________ ________ because I ________ ________ ________ ________ ________ ________ the daughter of a *parakho*.

4 "I'm ________ ________ ________.

5 You may ________ ________ it is true, but your father...," the man said.

6 At that moment, I was expecting ________ news since I did not have ________ ________ of my father.

7 ________ in the 1920's, ________ people saw me in the village, they would say, "________ ________ the *parakho*'s daughter."

8 My father was a son ________ a very rich family.

9 ________ ________ the life of a *seonbi*, he was always at the gambling house.

10 ________ ________ ________ he was called a *parakho*, ________ means someone who ________ his family's fortune.

11 "Your father ________ ________ ________ all of the money, and now he's asking for more.

12 Go and tell him that we ________ ________ ________ ________ ________," my mother ________ tell me ________ she sent me to the gambling house.

13 Then, my father ________ ________ ________ me angrily, "Why did you come ________?

14 ________ me more money!"

1 아버지의 비밀

2 1946년에, 낯선 남자가 나를 찾아와 물었다. "당신이 김용환 씨의 딸입니까?"

3 나는 파락호의 딸이라고 불리는 것이 더 익숙했으므로 나에게 이것은 이상한 질문이었다.

4 "나는 당신 아버지의 친구입니다.

5 당신은 이것이 사실인지 의아하겠지만, 당신의 아버지는…,"이라고 그 남자는 말했다.

6 나는 내 아버지에 대해 좋은 기억을 가지고 있지 않았으므로 그 순간에 실망스러운 소식을 예상하고 있었다.

7 1920년대에 마을에서 사람들이 나를 볼 때마다 그들은 "저기에 파락호의 딸이 가네."라고 말하곤 했다.

8 나의 아버지는 매우 부유한 집안의 아들이었다.

9 선비의 삶을 사는 대신, 아버지는 항상 도박장에 계셨다.

10 그것이 그가 집안의 재산을 탕진하는 사람이라는 뜻의 파락호로 불린 이유이다.

11 "네 아버지는 도박으로 모든 돈을 써 버리고 지금 더 요구하고 계신다.

12 가서 더 이상 남아 있는 돈이 없다고 말씀드려라."라고 나의 어머니는 나를 도박장으로 보낼 때마다 말씀하시곤 했다.

13 그러면, 아버지는 나에게 화를 내시며 소리치셨다. "왜 빈손으로 왔니?

14 돈을 더 가져와!"

15 When I was sixteen years old, my family _______ _______ _______ _______ _______for me to marry Mr. Seo.

16 _______ _______ _______ the wedding tradition, Mr. Seo's family sent my family some money to buy _______ _______ _______ _______ _______.

17 _______ _______ the wedding day, my mother came into my room and said, "Your father _______ _______ _______ _______ for the chest."

18 I asked angrily, "How could he do _______ _______ _______ _______?

19 _______ should we do now?"

20 "We have _______ _______.

21 _______ _______ _______ _______ your aunt's old chest," my mother said.

22 "_______ _______ for the family," people would whisper _______ _______ _______.

23 Since the first day of marriage, life at my husband's house _______ _______ _______ _______ _______.

24 "Your father, my dear friend...," my father's friend _______ _______ _______.

25 "He was not _______ _______.

26 Your father sent the family money to the _______ _______ in Manchuria.

27 He _______ _______ look like a gambler to _______ _______ _______ _______ _______ the Japanese officers."

28 At first, I was not sure _______ he was telling the truth.

29 But _______, I found out the truth about my father and I realized that I _______ _______ _______ about him.

30 Ever since that moment, I have been proud to be the daughter of a *parakho* who _______ _______ _______ _______ _______ the independence movement.

15 내가 16살이 되었을 때, 나의 가족은 나를 서 씨와 결혼시키기로 이미 결정을 했었다.

16 결혼 풍습의 일부로, 서 씨네 가족은 새 장롱을 사라고 우리 가족에게 돈을 보냈다.

17 결혼식 바로 전날, 나의 어머니는 내 방에 들어오셔서 말씀하셨다. "네 아버지가 장롱을 살 돈을 가져가 버렸다."

18 나는 화가 나서 물었다 "어떻게 그리 끔찍한 일을 하실 수 있나요?

19 우린 이제 어떡해요?"

20 "우리에게 선택권은 없구나.

21 큰어머니의 옛 장롱을 가져가야겠구나."라고 어머니가 말씀하셨다.

22 "가문에 부끄러운 일이야."라고 사람들이 내 뒤에서 속삭이곤 했다.

23 결혼 첫날부터, 남편의 집에서의 생활은 나에게 힘겨웠다.

24 "당신의 아버지, 나의 친애하는 친구…," 나의 아버지의 친구분은 그의 이야기를 이어가셨다.

25 "그는 도박꾼이 아니었어요.

26 당신의 아버지는 가족의 돈을 만주에 있는 독립운동가들에게 보냈답니다.

27 그는 이것을 일본 순사들에게 비밀로 하기 위해 그 자신을 도박꾼처럼 보이게 했어요."

28 처음엔, 나는 그분이 사실을 얘기하시는 건지 확신할 수 없었다.

29 그러나 나중에, 나는 나의 아버지에 대한 진실을 알게 되었고 내가 아버지에 관해 오해하고 있었다는 것을 깨달았다.

30 그 순간부터, 나는 독립운동에 그의 인생을 헌신하신 파락호의 딸인 것이 자랑스러웠다.

Reading 교과서 확인학습 B

• 우리말을 참고하여 본문을 영작하시오.

1 아버지의 비밀

➡ ______________________________

2 1946년에, 낯선 남자가 나를 찾아와 물었다. "당신이 김용환 씨의 딸입니까?"

➡ ______________________________

3 나는 파락호의 딸이라고 불리는 것이 더 익숙했으므로 나에게 이것은 이상한 질문이었다. .

➡ ______________________________

4 "나는 당신 아버지의 친구입니다.

➡ ______________________________

5 당신은 이것이 사실인지 의아하겠지만, 당신의 아버지는…,"이라고 그 남자는 말했다.

➡ ______________________________

6 나는 내 아버지에 대해 좋은 기억을 가지고 있지 않았으므로 그 순간에 실망스러운 소식을 예상하고 있었다.

➡ ______________________________

7 1920년대에 마을에서 사람들이 나를 볼 때마다 그들은 "저기에 파락호의 딸이 가네."라고 말하곤 했다.

➡ ______________________________

____

8 나의 아버지는 매우 부유한 집안의 아들이었다.

➡ ______________________________

9 선비의 삶을 사는 대신, 아버지는 항상 도박장에 계셨다.

➡ ______________________________

10 그것이 그가 집안의 재산을 탕진하는 사람이라는 뜻의 파락호로 불린 이유이다.

➡ ______________________________

11 "네 아버지는 도박으로 모든 돈을 써 버리고 지금 더 요구하고 계신다.

➡ ______________________________

12 가서 더 이상 남아 있는 돈이 없다고 말씀드려라."라고 나의 어머니는 나를 도박장으로 보낼 때마다 말씀하시곤 했다.

➡ ______________________________

____

13 그러면, 아버지는 나에게 화를 내시며 소리치셨다. "왜 빈손으로 왔니?

➡ ______________________________

14 돈을 더 가져와!"

➡ ______________________________

15 내가 16살이 되었을 때, 나의 가족은 나를 서 씨와 결혼시키기로 이미 결정을 했었다.

➡ ____________________

16 결혼 풍습의 일부로, 서 씨네 가족은 새 장롱을 사라고 우리 가족에게 돈을 보냈다.

➡ ____________________

____

17 결혼식 바로 전날, 나의 어머니는 내 방에 들어오셔서 말씀하셨다. "네 아버지가 장롱을 살 돈을 가져가 버렸다."

➡ ____________________

____

18 나는 화가 나서 물었다 "어떻게 그리 끔찍한 일을 하실 수 있나요?

➡ ____________________

19 우린 이제 어떡해요?"

➡ ____________________

20 "우리에게 선택권은 없구나.

➡ ____________________

21 큰어머니의 옛 장롱을 가져가야겠구나."라고 어머니가 말씀하셨다.

➡ ____________________

22 "가문에 부끄러운 일이야."라고 사람들이 내 뒤에서 속삭이곤 했다.

➡ ____________________

23 결혼 첫날부터, 남편의 집에서의 생활은 나에게 힘겨웠다.

➡ ____________________

24 "당신의 아버지, 나의 친애하는 친구…," 나의 아버지의 친구분은 그의 이야기를 이어가셨다.

➡ ____________________

25 "그는 도박꾼이 아니었어요.

➡ ____________________

26 당신의 아버지는 가족의 돈을 만주에 있는 독립운동가들에게 보냈답니다.

➡ ____________________

27 그는 이것을 일본 순사들에게 비밀로 하기 위해 그 자신을 도박꾼처럼 보이게 했어요."

➡ ____________________

28 처음엔, 나는 그분이 사실을 얘기하시는 건지 확신할 수 없었다.

➡ ____________________

29 그러나 나중에, 나는 나의 아버지에 대한 진실을 알게 되었고 내가 아버지에 관해 오해하고 있었다는 것을 깨달았다.

➡ ____________________

____

30 그 순간부터, 나는 독립운동에 그의 인생을 헌신하신 파락호의 딸인 것이 자랑스러웠다.

➡ ____________________

____

[01~03] 다음 글을 읽고 물음에 답하시오.

In 1946, a strange man visited me and asked, "Are you Mr. Kim Yonghwan's daughter?"

For me, ⓐthis was a(n) (A)[familiar / odd] question because I was more used to (B)[be / being] called the daughter of a *parakho*.

"I'm your father's friend. You may wonder (C)[if / that] it is true, but your father...," the man said.

At that moment, I was expecting disappointing news ⓑsince I did not have good memories of my father.

서답형

01 위 글의 밑줄 친 ⓐthis가 가리키는 것을 본문에서 찾아 쓰시오.

➡ ________________________________

서답형

02 위 글의 괄호 (A)~(C)에서 문맥이나 어법상 알맞은 낱말을 골라 쓰시오.

➡ (A)________ (B)________ (C)________

03 위 글의 밑줄 친 ⓑsince와 같은 의미로 쓰인 것을 모두 고르시오.

① She's been off work since Tuesday.
② Since you're already here, you might as well stay.
③ We've lived here since 1994.
④ Since then, I had wondered where he lived.
⑤ Since we're not very busy just now, I can get away from the office.

[04~05] 다음 글을 읽고 물음에 답하시오.

"Your father, my dear friend...," my father's friend continued his story. "He was not a gambler. Your father sent the family money to the independence fighters in Manchuria. He made himself look like a gambler to keep this a secret from the Japanese officers."

At first, I was not sure ⓐif he was telling the truth. But afterwards, I found out the truth about my father and I realized that I had been wrong about him. Ever since that moment, I have been proud to be the daughter of a *parakho* who had devoted his life to the independence movement.

04 위 글의 밑줄 친 ⓐif와 문법적 쓰임이 같은 것을 모두 고르시오.

① If necessary, I can come at once.
② If you run all the way, you'll get there in time.
③ I don't care if you agree with me.
④ He asked me if I knew Spanish.
⑤ I will tell him if he comes.

중요

05 위 글을 읽고 알 수 없는 것을 고르시오.

① Was the writer's father a gambler?
② To whom did the writer's father send the family money?
③ Why did the writer's father make himself look like a gambler?
④ How much money did the writer's father send to the independence fighters?
⑤ How did the writer find out the truth about her father?

[06~08] 다음 글을 읽고 물음에 답하시오.

Back in the 1920's, whenever people saw me in the village, they would say, "There goes the *parakho*'s daughter." (①)

My father was a son from a very rich family. (②) That is why he was called a *parakho*, which means someone who ruins his family's fortune. (③)

"Your father has gambled away all of the money, and now he's asking ___ⓐ___ more. (④) Go and tell him that we have no more money left," my mother would tell me whenever she sent me to the gambling house. (⑤)

Then, my father would yell ___ⓑ___ me angrily, "Why did you come empty-handed? Bring me more money!"

06 위 글의 빈칸 ⓐ와 ⓑ에 들어갈 전치사가 바르게 짝지어진 것은?

	ⓐ ⓑ		ⓐ ⓑ
①	for – at	②	in – to
③	in – for	④	on – at
⑤	for – for		

07 위 글의 흐름으로 보아, 주어진 문장이 들어가기에 가장 적절한 곳은?

> Instead of living the life of a *seonbi*, he was always at the gambling house.

① ② ③ ④ ⑤

중요 **08** According to the passage, which is NOT true?

① The writer's father was a son from a very rich family.
② The writer's father lived the life of a *seonbi*.
③ A *parakho* means someone who ruins his family's fortune.
④ The writer's father gambled away all of the money.
⑤ The writer's family had no more money left.

09 주어진 글 다음에 이어질 글의 순서로 가장 적절한 것은?

> "Your father, my dear friend...," my father's friend continued his story.

(A) "He was not a gambler. Your father sent the family money to the independence fighters in Manchuria. He made himself look like a gambler to keep this a secret from the Japanese officers."

(B) Ever since that moment, I have been proud to be the daughter of a *parakho* who had devoted his life to the independence movement.

(C) At first, I was not sure if he was telling the truth. But afterwards, I found out the truth about my father and I realized that I had been wrong about him.

① (A)–(C)–(B) ② (B)–(A)–(C)
③ (B)–(C)–(A) ④ (C)–(A)–(B)
⑤ (C)–(B)–(A)

[10~12] 다음 글을 읽고 물음에 답하시오.

When I was sixteen years old, my family had (A)[already / yet] made an arrangement for me to marry Mr. Seo. ⓐ<u>As</u> part of the wedding tradition, Mr. Seo's family sent my family some money to buy a new chest for clothes.

Right before the wedding day, my mother came into my room and said, "Your father has taken the money for the chest."

I asked angrily, "How could he do such a horrible thing? (B)[How / What] should we do now?"

"We have no choice. You'll have to take your aunt's old chest," my mother said.

(C)[For / Since] the first day of marriage, life at my husband's house had been difficult for me.

10 위 글의 괄호 (A)~(C)에서 어법상 알맞은 낱말을 골라 쓰시오.

➡ (A)________ (B)________ (C)________

11 위 글의 밑줄 친 ⓐAs와 같은 의미로 쓰인 것을 고르시오.

① She came up as I was speaking.
② Her anger grew as she talked.
③ This is twice as large as that.
④ Leave it as it is.
⑤ This box will be used as a table.

12 중요 Which question CANNOT be answered after reading the passage?

① Whom did the writer's family make an arrangement for the writer to marry?
② Why did Mr. Seo's family send the writer's family some money?
③ Could the writer buy a new chest for clothes?
④ Where did the writer's father spend the money for the chest?
⑤ Was the writer's life at Mr. Seo's house easy for her?

[13~15] 다음 글을 읽고 물음에 답하시오.

Back in the 1920's, whenever people saw me in the village, they would say, "There goes ①the *parakho*'s daughter."

My father was a son from a very rich family. __ⓐ__ living the life of a *seonbi*, ②he was always at the gambling house. That is why he was called a *parakho*, which means someone who ruins ③his family's fortune.

"Your father has gambled away all of the money, and now he's asking for more. Go and tell ④him that we have no more money left," my mother ⓑwould tell me whenever she sent me to the gambling house.

Then, my father would yell at me angrily, "Why did you come empty-handed? Bring ⑤me more money!"

13 위 글의 빈칸 ⓐ에 들어갈 알맞은 말을 고르시오.

① In spite of
② Because of
③ As well as
④ Instead of
⑤ In addition to

14 중요 밑줄 친 ①~⑤ 중에서 가리키는 대상이 나머지 넷과 다른 것은?

① ② ③ ④ ⑤

15 위 글의 밑줄 친 ⓑwould와 문법적 쓰임이 같은 것을 고르시오.

① He said he would be here at eight o'clock.
② Would you open the door for me, please?
③ I would rather come with you.
④ When my parents were away, my grandmother would take care of me.
⑤ Would you like a sandwich?

[16~17] 다음 글을 읽고 물음에 답하시오.

"Your father, my dear friend...," my father's friend continued his story. "He was not a gambler. Your father sent the family money to the independence fighters in Manchuria. He made himself look like a gambler to keep this a secret from the Japanese officers."

At first, ⓐ그분이 사실을 얘기하시는 건지 확신할 수 없었다. But afterwards, I found out the truth about my father and I realized that I had been wrong about him. Ever since that moment, I have been proud to be the daughter of a *parakho* who had devoted his life to the independence movement.

서답형

16 위 글의 밑줄 친 ⓐ의 우리말에 맞게 한 단어를 보충하여, 주어진 어휘를 알맞게 배열하시오.

the truth / not / telling / was / sure / I / was / he

➡ ________________

중요

17 위 글의 제목으로 알맞은 것을 고르시오.

① The Miserable Life of a *Parakho*
② Not a *Parakho* But a Secret Independence Fighter
③ The Secret Independence Fighters in Manchuria
④ History of Independence Movement
⑤ The Life as a Daughter of a *Parakho*

[18~21] 다음 글을 읽고 물음에 답하시오.

Back in the 1920's, whenever people saw me in the village, they (A)[should / would] say, "There goes the *parakho*'s daughter."

My father was a son from a very rich family. Instead of living the life of a *seonbi*, he was always at the gambling house. That is ___ⓐ___ he was called a *parakho*, ⓑwhich means someone who (B)[increases / ruins] his family's fortune.

"Your father has gambled away all of the money, and now he's asking for more. Go and tell him that ⓒ우리는 더 이상 남아 있는 돈이 없다," my mother would tell me whenever she sent me to the gambling house.

Then, my father would yell at me angrily, "Why did you come (C)[empty-hand / empty-handed]? Bring me more money!"

18 위 글의 빈칸 ⓐ에 들어갈 알맞은 말을 모두 고르시오.

① how ② the reason
③ why ④ when
⑤ where

서답형

19 위 글의 괄호 (A)~(C)에서 문맥이나 어법상 알맞은 낱말을 골라 쓰시오.

➡ (A) ________ (B) ________ (C) ________

서답형

20 위 글의 밑줄 친 ⓑ를 접속사를 사용하여 두 단어로 바꿔 쓰시오.

➡ ________________

서답형

21 위 글의 밑줄 친 ⓒ의 우리말에 맞게 주어진 어휘를 이용하여 6 단어로 영작하시오.

more, left

➡ ________________

[01~03] 다음 글을 읽고 물음에 답하시오.

Back in the 1920's, (A)whenever people saw me in the village, they would say, "There goes the *parakho*'s daughter."

My father was a son from a very rich family. Instead of living the life of a *seonbi*, he was always at the gambling house. (B)That is why he was called a *parakho*, which means someone who ruins his family's fortune.

"Your father has gambled away all of the money, and now he's asking for more. Go and tell him that we have no more money ⓐ_____," my mother would tell me whenever she sent me to the gambling house.

Then, my father would yell at me angrily, "Why did you come empty-handed? Bring me more money!"

01 위 글의 빈칸 ⓐ에 leave를 알맞은 형태로 쓰시오.

➡ ____________________

고난이도

02 위 글의 밑줄 친 (A)whenever와 바꿔 쓸 수 있는 말을 쓰시오.

➡ ____________________

03 위 글의 밑줄 친 (B)That이 가리키는 것을 본문에서 찾아 쓰시오.

➡ ____________________
____

[04~07] 다음 글을 읽고 물음에 답하시오.

"Your father, my dear friend...," my father's friend continued his story. "He was not a gambler. (A)Your father sent the family money to the independence fighters in Manchuria. He made himself look like a gambler to keep this a secret from the Japanese officers."

(B)At first, I was not sure if he was telling the truth. But afterwards, I found out the truth about my father and I realized that I had been wrong about him. Ever since that moment, I have been proud to be the daughter of a *parakho* who ⓐ his life to the independence movement.

04 위 글의 빈칸 ⓐ에 devote를 알맞은 형태로 쓰시오.

➡ ____________________

중요

05 위 글의 밑줄 친 (A)를 4형식 문장으로 고치시오.

➡ ____________________
____

중요

06 위 글의 밑줄 친 (B)를 다음과 같이 바꿔 쓸 때 빈칸에 들어갈 알맞은 단어를 쓰시오.

➡ At first, I was not sure _______ he was telling the truth.

07 다음 빈칸 (A)와 (B)에 알맞은 단어를 넣어 필자가 아버지에 대해 오해한 내용을 완성하시오.

The writer mistook her father for a *parakho* but in fact he sent the family money to the (A)_______ _______ in Manchuria and made himself look like a gambler to keep this (B)_______ _______ from the Japanese officers.

[08~10] 다음 글을 읽고 물음에 답하시오.

When I was sixteen years old, my family had already made an arrangement for me to marry Mr. Seo. As ⓐpart of the wedding tradition, Mr. Seo's family sent my family some money to buy a new chest for (A)[cloths / clothes].

Right before the wedding day, my mother came into my room and said, "Your father has taken the money for the chest."

I asked angrily, "How could he do such a (B)[horrible / terrific] thing? What should we do now?"

"We have no choice. You'll have to take your aunt's old chest," my mother said.

"How (C)[embarrassing / embarrassed] for the family," people would whisper behind my back.

Since the first day of marriage, life at my husband's house had been difficult for me.

고난이도

08 다음 빈칸에 알맞은 말을 넣어 위 글의 밑줄 친 ⓐ에 대한 설명을 완성하시오.

The family of the bridegroom sent (A)_______ _______ to buy a (B)_______ _______ for clothes to the family of the bride.

09 위 글의 괄호 (A)~(C)에서 문맥이나 어법상 알맞은 낱말을 골라 쓰시오.

➡ (A) _______ (B) _______ (C) _______

10 주어진 영영풀이에 해당하는 단어를 본문에서 찾아 쓰시오.

a large, heavy box used for storing things

➡ ____________________

[11~13] 다음 글을 읽고 물음에 답하시오.

Back in the 1920's, whenever people saw me in the village, they would say, "ⓐ저기에 파락호의 딸이 간다."

My father was a son from a very rich family. Instead of living the life of a *seonbi*, he was always at the gambling house. ⓑThat is why he was called a *parakho*, that means someone who ruins his family's fortune.

"Your father has gambled away all of the money, and now he's asking for more. Go and tell him that we have no more money left," my mother would tell me whenever she sent me to the gambling house.

Then, my father would yell at me angrily, "Why did you come empty-handed? Bring me more money!"

11 위 글의 밑줄 친 ⓐ의 우리말에 맞게 주어진 어휘를 알맞게 배열하시오.

there / the *parakho*'s daughter / goes

➡ ____________________

중요

12 위 글의 밑줄 친 ⓑ에서 어법상 틀린 부분을 찾아 고치시오.

➡ ____________________

13 다음 빈칸 (A)와 (B)에 알맞은 단어를 넣어 글쓴이의 아버지에 대한 소개를 완성하시오.

The writer's father was called a (A)_______ because he (B)_______ away his family's fortune.

교과서

구석구석

Grammar in Real Life A

Mary Jane, your fans have many questions about your plans.

1. Are you going to release a new song this month?
2. Are you interested in various music genres?
   = a variety of
3. Do you have any plans to work with other artists?
   부정사의 형용사적 용법
4. Are you going to go on a world tour this year?

구문해설 • release: 발표[발매]하다 • genre: 유형(類型), 양식, 장르

해석

Mary Jane, 너의 팬들은 너의 계획에 대해 많은 질문들을 가지고 있어.

1. 넌 이 달에 새 노래를 발표할 거니?
2. 넌 다양한 음악 장르에 관심이 있니?
3. 넌 다른 아티스트들과 일할 계획을 가지고 있니?
4. 넌 금년에 월드 투어를 떠날 거니?

Grammar in Real Life B

When I got back home, my parents had gone out for a walk. The house was dark and quiet, but it seemed a little bit strange. I remembered that I had left the door in my room open. I saw that someone had broken the lamp. I found out that someone had eaten my cookies on the table. At last I knew who did it! I found small footprints of my dog, Lucy, and the cat next door.

(When: 때를 나타내는 접속사 / had gone: 대과거 / strange: strangely(×) / had left: 대과거 / had broken: 대과거 / had eaten: 대과거 / who did it: 간접의문문 / the cat: (footprints of) the cat)

구문해설 • a little bit: 조금 (a bit에 little이 붙은 말; 뜻은 a bit과 같음) • at last: 마침내
• next door: 옆집에

내가 집에 돌아왔을 때 나의 부모님은 산보를 나가셨다. 집은 어둡고 조용했지만, 조금 이상해 보였다. 나는 내 방 문을 열어둔 것이 기억났다. 나는 누군가가 램프를 깨뜨린 것을 알았다. 나는 누군가가 식탁 위에 있던 내 쿠키를 먹은 것을 알아냈다. 마침내 나는 누가 그런 일을 했는지 알았다! 나는 내 개 Lucy와 옆집 고양이의 작은 발자국들을 발견했다.

After You Read: Read and Write A

The Secret of My Father

I thought my father was ...

My father was known as a *parakho*. He was born into a rich family but he gambled away all of the money. He even took the money for a new chest for clothes.

(was known as: be known as: ~로 알려지다 / gambled away all of the money: 노름으로 모든 돈을 탕진했다 / clothes: cloth의 복수: 의복)

Actually my father was ...

My father was not a gambler. He sent the family money to the independence fighters in Manchuria. He made himself look like a gambler to keep this a secret from the Japanese officers.

(to: send는 to를 사용하여 3형식으로 고친다. / himself: him(×) / to keep: to부정사의 부사적 용법(목적))

구문해설 • secret: 비밀 • gamble away: 도박으로 ~을 다 날리다 • chest: 궤 • gambler: 노름꾼
• independence fighter: 독립 운동가 • keep+O+O.C.+from A: A로부터 ~을 …로 지키다

나의 아버지의 비밀

나는 아버지가 …라고 생각했다.

나의 아버지는 '파락호'라고 알려져 있었다. 그는 부잣집에 태어났지만, 모든 돈을 노름으로 날렸다. 그는 심지어 새 장롱을 살 돈도 가져갔다.

사실 나의 아버지는 …이었다.

나의 아버지는 노름꾼이 아니었다. 그는 가족의 돈을 만주에 있는 독립 운동가들에게 보냈다. 그는 일본 경찰들로부터 이것을 비밀로 지키려고 스스로를 노름꾼처럼 보이게 했다.

영역별 핵심문제

Words & Expressions

01 다음 밑줄 친 부분의 의미로 알맞지 않은 것을 모두 고르시오.

① The odd thing was that he didn't recognize me. (이상한)
② The country has made great advances since independence. (독립)
③ He followed the impressionist movement. (이동)
④ Did you leave the kids with Grandma on Saturday? (떠나다)
⑤ Don't whisper with your neighbors. (속삭이다)

02 다음 짝지어진 두 단어의 관계가 같도록 빈칸에 알맞은 말을 쓰시오.

solve: solution = marry : ________

[03~04] 다음 빈칸에 공통으로 들어갈 말을 쓰시오.

03

- Have you ever heard ________ a band called Big Star?
- Could I have tuna instead ________ ham?

04

- Most humans are not very good at ________ secrets.
- Paul was ________ awake by drinking lots of strong black coffee.

Conversation

[05~07] 다음 대화를 읽고 물음에 답하시오.

A: This (A)[called / is called] the *Geojunggi*.
B: Wow, this looks interesting.
A: This is a machine that moves heavy objects. It is said that it helped to build the Hwaseong Fortress only in 28 months.
B: How amazing! Is it okay (B)[that / if / what] I take a closer look at it?
A: Sure.

05 위 대화의 괄호 (A)와 (B)에서 적절한 것을 골라 쓰시오.

➡ (A) ____________, (B) ____________

06 위 대화에서 다음 영영풀이에 해당하는 단어를 찾아 쓰시오.

a large strong building used for defending an important place

➡ ____________________

07 위 대화의 내용과 일치하는 것은 모두 몇 개인지 고르시오.

ⓐ *Geojunggi* was used for building the Hwaseong Fortress.
ⓑ *B* wants to watch Hwaseong Fortress closely.
ⓒ Hwaseong Fortress was built in 28 months.
ⓓ *Geojunggi* is a kind of machine.
ⓔ *A* knows about what *Geojunggi* is.

①1개 ② 2개 ③ 3개 ④ 4개 ⑤ 5개

[08~09] 다음 대화를 읽고 물음에 답하시오.

M: Hello, Ms. Jackson. (①)
W: It was wonderful. (②) The houses were really beautiful.
M: That's great.
W: Actually, I didn't get the chance ⓐ_____ have dinner. (③) Is it okay ⓑ_____ I cook in the kitchen at this hour?
M: Yes, but please remember ⓒ_____ the kitchen closes ⓓ_____ 10 p.m. (④)
W: Okay. The kitchen is on the 5th floor, right? (⑤)
M: Yes, it is. Let me know ⓔ_____ you need anything.

08 ①~⑤ 중 주어진 문장이 들어갈 곳은?

> How was your tour of the *Hanok Village*?

① ② ③ ④ ⑤

09 빈칸 ⓐ~ⓔ에 들어가지 않는 말을 고르시오.

① for ② at ③ if ④ that ⑤ to

[10~12] 다음 대화를 읽고 물음에 답하시오.

W: James, what are you watching?
M: Oh, I'm watching a video about Yi Sunsin.
W: Isn't he the one that saved Joseon from Japan?
M: (A)[No, he isn't. / Right.] It is said that he won the war only with twelve (a)_____(wood) ships.
W: Wow, how can that be possible?
M: He was a wise general (B)[who / which] (C)[made / is made] creative plans.

10 괄호 안의 단어를 문맥에 맞게 고쳐 빈칸 (a)에 쓰시오.

➡ ____________________

11 위 대화의 괄호 (A)~(C)에서 적절한 것을 골라 쓰시오.

➡ (A)_______ (B)_______ (C)_______

12 위 대화에서 다음 영영풀이에 해당하는 단어를 찾아 쓰시오.

> an officer of very high rank in the army or air force

➡ ____________________

Grammar

13 다음 밑줄 친 부분과 바꿔 쓸 수 있는 것은?

> You were the one who asked me if I had anything to say.

① unless ② that ③ what
④ which ⑤ whether

14 다음 문장 중에서 어법상 어색한 문장을 고르시오.

① When I got home, Mom had already prepared our dinner.
② I found out that someone had eaten my cookies on the table.
③ Cathy lost the necklace that I had bought for her.
④ When Megan had arrived at the station, the train already left for London.
⑤ He had gone out for a walk when I arrived at his home.

15 다음 그림을 보고 주어진 어휘를 이용하여 빈칸을 알맞게 채우시오.

➡ A man visited his teacher, and asked him ______________________.
(his fault, forgive, will)

16 다음 ⓐ~ⓖ 중 어법상 옳은 것을 모두 고르시오.

ⓐ The movie has been over when I arrived at the theater.
ⓑ I realized that I had been wrong about him.
ⓒ I had eaten the sandwich which Mom made the night before.
ⓓ David would like to know if you have any plans to work with other artists.
ⓔ Can you tell me if she's a new student in our class?
ⓕ Let me ask you which you want to buy something nice.
ⓖ I wonder that the dress looks good on me.

➡ ______________________

17 다음 문장의 빈칸에 들어갈 수 없는 말은?

When Scott arrived at the station, __________ ______________________.

① the train had already left for London
② the train had just arrived at the platform
③ he had already his lunch
④ he remembered that he had left his smart phone at the restaurant
⑤ Lily had already gone

18 다음 두 문장을 한 문장으로 쓰시오.

(1) • I was not sure.
• He was telling the truth.
➡ ______________________

(2) • Rob wants to know.
• More men than women like gardening.
➡ ______________________
____

(3) • I asked her.
• I could have a drink.
➡ ______________________

19 다음 빈칸에 들어갈 말이 다른 하나는?

① Try this food and see ______ you like it.
② I wonder ______ the movie is still showing on the theater.
③ Lucy wants to know ______ you are going to release a new song this month.
④ I am not sure ______ Rachel can play the cello.
⑤ I can't believe ______ it will be New Year's Day soon.

Reading

[20~21] 다음 글을 읽고 물음에 답하시오.

Back in the 1920's, whenever people saw me in the village, they would say, "There goes the *parakho*'s daughter."

ⓐMy father was a son from a very rich family. Instead of living the life of a *seonbi*, he was always at the gambling house. ⓑThat is because he was called a *parakho*, which means someone who ruins his family's fortune.

"Your father has gambled away all of the money, and now he's asking for more. Go and tell him that we have no more money left," my mother would tell me whenever she sent me to the gambling house.

Then, my father would yell at me angrily, "Why did you come empty-handed? Bring me more money!"

20 위 글의 ⓐMy father에 관한 내용으로 옳지 않은 것은?

① He was born into a rich family.
② He didn't live the life of a *seonbi*.
③ He was always at the gambling house.
④ He was called a *parakho*.
⑤ He won a lot of money by gambling.

21 위 글의 밑줄 친 ⓑ에서 흐름상 어색한 부분을 찾아 고치시오.

➡ ______________________

[22~24] 다음 글을 읽고 물음에 답하시오.

When I was sixteen years old, my family had already made an arrangement for me to marry Mr. Seo. (①)

ⓐRight before the wedding day, my mother came into my room and said, "Your father has taken the money for the chest." (②) I asked angrily, "How could he do such a horrible thing? (③) What should we do now?" (④)

"We have no choice. (⑤) You'll have to take your aunt's old chest," my mother said.

"How embarrassing for the family," people would whisper behind my back.

Since the first day of marriage, life at my husband's house had been difficult for me.

22 위 글의 흐름으로 보아, 주어진 문장이 들어가기에 가장 적절한 곳은?

> As part of the wedding tradition, Mr. Seo's family sent my family some money to buy a new chest for clothes.

① ② ③ ④ ⑤

23 위 글의 밑줄 친 ⓐRight과 같은 의미로 쓰인 것을 고르시오.

① What gives you the right to do that?
② The bus came right on time.
③ You were quite right to criticize him.
④ Next time we'll get it right.
⑤ I don't feel quite right today.

24 본문의 내용과 일치하도록 다음 빈칸 (A)와 (B)에 알맞은 단어를 쓰시오.

> The writer got married to Mr. Seo, but because of (A)________ ________, she couldn't buy a (B)________ ________ for clothes.

[25~27] 다음 글을 읽고 물음에 답하시오.

"Your father, my dear friend...," my father's friend continued his story. "He was not a gambler. Your father sent the family money to the independence fighters in Manchuria. He made (A)[him / himself] look like a gambler to (B)[keep / stop] this a secret from the Japanese officers."

(C)[At first / For the first time], I was not sure if he was telling the truth. But afterwards, I found out the truth about my father and I realized that I had been wrong about him. Ever since that moment, I ⓐhave been proud to be the daughter of a *parakho* who had devoted his life to the independence movement.

25 위 글의 괄호 (A)~(C)에서 문맥이나 어법상 알맞은 낱말을 골라 쓰시오.

➡ (A)________ (B)________ (C)________

26 위 글의 밑줄 친 ⓐhave been과 현재완료 용법이 다른 것을 모두 고르시오.

① I have worn these jeans for 3 years.
② I have never met a student like him.
③ How long has Jim been here?
④ She has gone to Paris.
⑤ He hasn't eaten his hamburger yet.

27 위 글에서 알 수 있는 아버지에 대한 'I'의 심경 변화로 가장 알맞은 것을 고르시오.

① ashamed → surprised
② respectful → satisfied
③ bored → disappointed
④ ashamed → respectful
⑤ surprised → proud

[28~30] 다음 글을 읽고 물음에 답하시오.

Have you heard of Nam Jahyun? She was a female independence fighter. When her husband died during the war, she decided to fight for independence. In 1919, Nam Jahyun moved to Manchuria. Then, she built schools and educated women there. When she was arrested by the Japanese in 1933, she had tried to kill Japanese officers. After she ⓐ______ in prison for six months, she was released and died shortly after. In 1962, to honor her work fighting for independence, the government gave her an award.

28 위 글의 빈칸 ⓐ에 be동사를 알맞은 형태로 쓰시오.

➡ ____________________

29 위 글의 종류로 알맞은 것을 고르시오.

① e-mail
② biography
③ diary
④ article
⑤ autobiography

30 위 글의 남자현에 관한 내용으로 옳지 않은 것은?

① 여성 독립 운동가였다.
② 그녀의 남편이 죽은 뒤에 만주로 갔다.
③ 만주에서 학교를 세우고 여성들을 가르쳤다.
④ 일본 경찰에 체포된 뒤에 감옥에서 죽었다.
⑤ 1962년 정부가 그녀에게 상을 주었다.

단원별 예상문제

출제율 90%

01 접미사 -ward(s)를 붙여 부사로 만들 수 없는 것을 고르시오.

① in ② over ③ after
④ back ⑤ fore

출제율 100%

02 다음 빈칸에 알맞은 단어를 〈보기〉에서 골라 쓰시오.

보기
any most so some such

(1) Everything has changed ________ much that I can hardly recognize the place.
(2) He came to ________ a sudden stop that we almost hit him.

출제율 95%

03 빈칸 (A)와 (B)에 들어갈 말로 알맞은 것끼리 짝지어진 것을 고르시오.

• He's always unwilling to ask (A)_______ anyone's help.
• She announced that she would devote her life (B)_______ art.

(A) (B)
① out – for
② out – to
③ for – for
④ for – to
⑤ around – for

출제율 90%

04 다음 주어진 우리말에 맞게 빈칸을 채우시오. (철자가 주어진 경우 주어진 철자로 시작할 것.)

(1) 그녀는 포기하지 않고 유명한 중국 장군을 만나러 갔다.
➡ She did not give up and went to see a famous Chinese g________.
(2) 너무 많은 결혼들이 이혼으로 끝난다.
➡ Too many ________ end in divorce.
(3) 하늘에 이상한 물체가 있다.
➡ There's a strange o________ in the sky.
(4) 내가 휴가 갈 것이기 때문에, 그 회의에 참석할 수 없을 것 같다.
➡ I won't be able to attend the meeting s________ I'll be on vacation.

[05~07] 다음 대화를 읽고 물음에 답하시오.

W: Excuse me, sir. (①)
M: I'd like to have *bibimbap*, please. (②)
W: Here you are. (③)
M: Thank you. (④) Oh, 지금 화장실을 이용해도 될까요?
W: Sure, but if the seat light is on, you should stay in your seat. (⑤)
M: Okay, thank you.

출제율 90%

05 ①~⑤ 중 주어진 문장이 들어갈 곳은?

Would you like to have curry or *bibimbap*?

① ② ③ ④ ⑤

출제율 90%

06 Where is this conversation taking place?

① bus ② train ③ hotel
④ airplane ⑤ factory

출제율 95%

07 밑줄 친 우리말과 일치하도록 주어진 단어를 이용해 문장을 만드시오.

➡ ________________________________

(okay, bathroom, use)

[08~10] 다음 대화를 읽고 물음에 답하시오.

M: Lisa. (A)______________________________
W: I'm reading a biography of Gwon Giok.
M: I haven't heard about her. (B)__________
W: She was the first ⓐ[male / female] pilot in Korea. It ⓑ[says / said / is said] ⓒ[which / what / that] she had over 7,000 hours of flying time.
M: Wow, I didn't know that.

출제율 95%

08 위 대화의 빈칸 (A)와 (B)에 알맞은 것을 〈보기〉에서 골라 쓰시오.

보기
- Is it okay if I take a picture of it?
- Who is she?
- Why did she become a pilot?
- What are you reading?
- How was your reading?
- How can it be possible?

➡ (A) ______________________________
(B) ______________________________

출제율 90%

09 위 대화의 괄호 ⓐ~ⓒ에서 적절한 것을 골라 쓰시오.

➡ ⓐ________ ⓑ________ ⓒ________

출제율 90%

10 위 대화에서 다음 영영풀이에 해당하는 단어를 찾아 쓰시오.

a book that someone writes about someone else's life

➡ ______________________________

[11~12] 다음 대화를 읽고 물음에 답하시오.

M: All right, everyone! This way, please. Now, we are moving onto the Joseon Dynasty. (A)______, there were many interesting (B)_______(invent). This one is called the *Jagyeongnu*.
W: Is it a musical instrument?
M: Actually, this is a water clock. It is said that it is the oldest and the largest water clock in Korea.
W: How amazing! Is it okay if I take a picture of it?
M: Sure.

출제율 95%

11 빈칸 (A)에 알맞은 말을 고르시오.

① Besides
② However
③ Instead
④ As it is
⑤ As you can see

출제율 95%

12 괄호 안의 단어를 문맥에 맞게 고쳐 빈칸 (B)에 쓰시오.

➡ ______________________________

출제율 95%

13 다음 그림을 보고 주어진 어휘를 사용하여 빈칸을 알맞게 채우시오.

Jonathan asked Bells __________________
_________ with him. (go, she, can, out)

출제율 95%

14 다음 중 밑줄 친 if의 쓰임이 다른 하나는?

① It does not matter if you answer yes or no.
② I'm not sure if I'm well prepared.
③ I asked him if he was sorry for what he had done.
④ Please let me know if he comes.
⑤ You may wonder if it is true or not.

출제율 100%

15 다음 중 어법상 적절한 문장은?

① I had told the story that I have read in the book.
② I couldn't find the pen which Dad had gave to me.
③ After she was in prison for 6 months, she had been released and died short after.
④ I couldn't meet him because he had left the town when I got back.
⑤ It was proved that the officials took bribes from him months before.

[16~17] 다음 글을 읽고 물음에 답하시오.

Back in the 1920's, whenever people saw me in the village, they would say, "There goes the *parakho*'s daughter."

My father was a son from a very rich family. Instead of ⓐliving the life of a *seonbi*, he was always at the gambling house. That is why he was called a *parakho*, which means someone who ruins his family's fortune.

"Your father has gambled away all of the money, and now he's asking for more. Go and tell him that we have no more money left," my mother would tell me whenever she sent me to the gambling house.

Then, my father would yell at me angrily, "Why did you come empty-handed? Bring me more money!"

출제율 100%

16 위 글의 밑줄 친 ⓐliving과 문법적 쓰임이 다른 것을 모두 고르시오.

① He is good at playing tennis.
② We enjoy swimming after school.
③ She is cooking in the kitchen.
④ They stopped eating the food.
⑤ They sat studying in the room.

출제율 90%

17 Why was the writer's father called a *parakho*? Fill in the blanks below with suitable words. (2 words)

Because he was always at the ________ ________ instead of living the life of a *seonbi*.

[18~20] 다음 글을 읽고 물음에 답하시오.

ⓐWhen I was sixteen years old, my family has already made an arrangement for me to marry Mr. Seo. As part of the wedding tradition, Mr. Seo's family sent my family some money to buy a new chest for clothes.

Right before the wedding day, my mother came into my room and said, "Your father has taken the money for the chest."

I asked angrily, "How could he do ⓑ그런 끔찍한 일? What should we do now?"

"We have no choice. You'll have to take your aunt's old chest," my mother said.

"How embarrassing for the family," people would whisper ⓒ나 몰래.

Since the first day of marriage, life at my husband's house had been difficult for me.

출제율 95%

18 위 글의 밑줄 친 ⓑ와 ⓒ의 우리말에 맞게 주어진 어휘를 이용하여, 각각 4 단어와 3 단어로 영작하시오.

ⓑ horrible ⓒ back

➡ ⓑ ________________ ⓒ ________________

출제율 90%

19 위 글의 밑줄 친 ⓐ에서 어법상 틀린 부분을 찾아 고치시오.

➡ ______________________

출제율 100%

20 According to the passage, which is NOT true?

① The writer's husband's family name was Seo.
② As part of the wedding tradition, the writer received some money from Mr. Seo's family.
③ The money that Mr. Seo's family sent was for buying a new chest for clothes.
④ The writer's father took the money for the chest on the wedding day.
⑤ The writer had to take her aunt's old chest.

[21~23] 다음 글을 읽고 물음에 답하시오.

"Your father, my dear friend...," my father's friend continued his story. "He was not a gambler. Your father sent the family money to the independence fighters in Manchuria. He made himself look like a gambler (A)to keep this a secret ⓐ the Japanese officers."

At first, I was not sure if he was telling the truth. But afterwards, I found out (B)the truth about my father and I realized that I had been wrong about him. Ever since that moment, I have been proud to be the daughter of a parakho who had devoted his life ⓑ the independence movement.

출제율 90%

21 위 글의 빈칸 ⓐ와 ⓑ에 들어갈 전치사가 바르게 짝지어진 것은?

	ⓐ ⓑ		ⓐ ⓑ
①	from – on	②	to – at
③	to – on	④	for – to
⑤	from – to		

출제율 95%

22 위 글의 밑줄 친 (A)to keep과 to부정사의 용법이 다른 것을 모두 고르시오.

① I don't have any friends to talk with.
② He went to Africa in 1990, never to return.
③ He can't be rich to ask me for some money.
④ She encouraged me to try once again.
⑤ She came here to ask a question.

출제율 95%

23 다음 빈칸 (A)와 (B)에 알맞은 단어를 넣어 (B)the truth에 대한 설명을 완성하시오.

> The writer's father was not a *parakho* but he made himself (A)________ ________ a gambler to keep the fact that he sent the family money to the independence fighters in Manchuria a secret from the (B)________ ________.

[24~25] 다음 글을 읽고 물음에 답하시오.

I thought my father was ...

My father was known as a *parakho*. He was born into a rich family but he gambled away all of the money. He even took the money for a new chest for clothes.

Actually my father was ...

My father was not a gambler. He sent the family money to the independence fighters in Manchuria. ⓐHe made himself to look a gambler to keep ⓑthis a secret from the Japanese officers.

출제율 100%

24 위 글의 밑줄 친 ⓐ에서 어법상 틀린 부분을 찾아 고치시오.

➡ ______________________

출제율 95%

25 위 글의 밑줄 친 ⓑthis가 가리키는 것을 본문에서 찾아 쓰시오.

➡ ______________________

____

서술형 실전문제

[01~02] 다음 대화를 읽고 물음에 답하시오.

W: Hey, Mark, do you know about Father Lee Taeseok?
M: Yeah, I've heard of him. ⓐWho?
W: ⓑTake a look at this article. ⓒHe is going to include in the social studies textbook in South Sudan.
M: Wow. that's great.
W: Yeah, ⓓhe helped the children by building a clinic and a school. 사람들이 그러한 이야기들이 교과서에 포함된다고 말했어.
M: ⓔIt is bad to hear that students will learn about such a great person.

01 밑줄 친 ⓐ~ⓔ 중 문맥상 또는 어법상 어색한 것을 모두 골라 바르게 고치시오.

➡ ______________________________
____
____
____

02 밑줄 친 우리말을 주어진 단어를 이용하여 영작하시오.

➡ ______________________________
______________________________ (say, it)
➡ ______________________________
______________________________ (people)

03 주어진 단어를 이용하여 빈칸에 알맞은 말을 쓰시오.

(1) I remembered that I ______________ the door of my room open. (leave)
(2) The library ______________ when I got there. (closed)

04 밑줄 친 우리말을 주어진 단어를 이용하여 영작하시오.

W: Excuse me, you can't take your backpack inside the museum.
M: Oh, I didn't know that. 물병을 가지고 들어가도 될까요?
W: Yes, that's fine. You can leave your bag in the locker.
M: Okay, thank you.

➡ ______________________________ (okay)
➡ ______________________________ (can)

05 다음 문장에서 틀린 것을 고쳐 다시 쓰시오.

(1) It was the most interesting game that I ever played.
➡ ______________________________
____

(2) His wife was surprised to learn that he was already fired without any warning.
➡ ______________________________
____

(3) He could not decide that this was a fairy tale or a nightmare.
➡ ______________________________
____

(4) I'm considering if to accept his offer.
➡ ______________________________

06 다음 우리말을 주어진 어휘를 이용하여 영작하시오.

(1) 나는 그가 그녀에게 추천서를 줄 수 있는지 알고 싶다. (give her a recommendation, 11 단어)

➡ ______________________

(2) 그녀는 열쇠를 학교에 두고 왔기 때문에 문을 열 수가 없었다. (at school, leave, the door, the key, because, open, 14 단어)

➡ ______________________

[07~08] 다음 글을 읽고 물음에 답하시오.

Back in the 1920's, whenever people saw me in the village, they would say, "There goes the *parakho*'s daughter."

My father was a son from a very rich family. ⓐInstead of living the life of a *seonbi*, he was always at the gambling house. That is why he was called a *parakho*, which means someone who ruins his family's fortune.

"Your father has gambled away all of the money, and now he's asking for more. Go and tell him that we have no more money left," my mother would tell me whenever she sent me to the gambling house.

Then, my father would yell at me angrily, "Why did you come empty-handed? ⓑBring me more money!"

07 위 글의 밑줄 친 ⓐ를 다음과 같이 바꿔 쓸 때 빈칸에 들어갈 알맞은 단어를 쓰시오.

➡ He did ________ live the life of a *seonbi*, ________ he was always at the gambling house.

08 위 글의 밑줄 친 ⓑ를 3형식 문장으로 고치시오.

➡ ______________________

[09~11] 다음 글을 읽고 물음에 답하시오.

ⓐWhen I was sixteen years old, my family had already made an arrangement for me to marry with Mr. Seo. As part of the wedding tradition, Mr. Seo's family sent my family some money to buy a new chest for clothes.

Right before the wedding day, my mother came into my room and said, "Your father has taken the money for the chest."

I asked angrily, "How could he do ⓑsuch a horrible thing? What should we do now?"

"We have no choice. You'll have to take your aunt's old chest," my mother said.

"How embarrassing for the family," people would whisper behind my back.

Since the first day of marriage, life at my husband's house had been difficult for me.

09 위 글의 밑줄 친 ⓐ에서 어법상 틀린 부분을 찾아 고치시오.

➡ ______________________

10 위 글의 밑줄 친 ⓑsuch a horrible thing이 가리키는 내용을 우리말로 쓰시오.

➡ ______________________

11 Why did people whisper behind the writer's back that it was very embarrassing for the family? Fill in the blanks below with suitable words.

Because ________ ________ took the ________ for the chest.

창의사고력 서술형 문제

01 그림을 보고 허락을 요청하는 말을 이용해 문장을 완성하시오. 괄호 안에 주어진 말을 이용하시오.

A: ______________________________

____

(borrow, 2개 이상)

B: ______________________________

(sorry, broken)

02 그림을 참고하고, 주어진 어휘를 이용하여 대화를 완성하시오.

(1)  (2) 

(1) A: Do you know ______________________ a comic book? (she, read)

B: I'm not sure, but she likes to read comic books.

(2) A: How was your play yesterday?

B: It was terrible. I forgot the lines that I __________________ during our practice. (memorize)

03 다음 내용을 바탕으로 독립운동가 남자현의 전기문을 쓰시오.

Biography of Nam Jahyun, a female independence fighter
1873: born in Yeongyang
1919: Her husband died during the war.
• moved to Manchuria • built schools and educated women there
1919: decided to fight for independence
1924~1933: tried to kill Japanese officers
1933: • arrested by the Japanese • had been in prison for six months
• died on Aug 22nd
1962: The government gave her an award.

Have you heard of Nam Jahyun? She was a (A)________________________. When her husband died during the war, she decided (B)________________________. In 1919, Nam Jahyun moved to Manchuria. Then, she (C)________________________ there. When she was arrested by the Japanese in 1933, she had tried to kill Japanese officers. After she had been in prison for (D)______________, she was released and died shortly after. In 1962, to honor her work fighting for independence, the government gave her (E)____________.

단원별 모의고사

01 다음 문장 중 자연스럽지 않은 것을 찾아 고치시오.

ⓐ The road surface became so hot that it melted.
ⓑ Children are used to spend much of their free time watching TV.
ⓒ I wanted to buy a new car by selling my house.

➡ ____________________

02 다음 빈칸에 공통으로 들어갈 말을 고르시오.

• Right _______ that moment, you came up to me and issued a ticket without giving me a chance to explain.
• Don't yell _______ me like that!

03 다음 빈칸을 〈보기〉에 있는 어휘를 이용하여 채우시오.

보기
biography detective female locker

(1) I have read a __________ of Abraham Lincoln.
(2) Oh Eun-sun is a Korean __________ mountaineer.
(3) Where can I get a key for my __________?
(4) The __________ found some evidence.

04 다음 우리말에 맞도록 빈칸에 알맞은 말을 쓰시오. (철자가 주어진 경우 주어진 철자로 시작할 것.)

(1) 미국의 많은 가정, 호텔, 학교에서 이 운동에 참여했습니다.
➡ Many American families, hotels, and schools participated in this __________.
(2) 그의 많은 발명품 덕분에 그는 많은 돈을 벌었습니다.
➡ He made a lot of money thanks to his many __________.
(3) 그는 일찍 일어나는 데 익숙하다.
➡ He is used to __________ up early.

[05~06] 다음 대화를 읽고 물음에 답하시오.

W: Excuse me, you can't ⓐ__________ your backpack inside the museum.
M: Oh, I didn't ⓑ________ that. Is it okay if I ⓒ________ in my water bottle?
W: Yes, that's fine. You can ⓓ________ your bag in the locker.
M: Okay, thank you.

05 빈칸 ⓐ~ⓔ에 들어가지 않는 말을 고르시오.

① know ② help ③ leave
④ bring ⑤ take

06 위 대화를 읽고 답할 수 없는 질문을 고르시오.

① Can the man carry the water bottle inside the museum?
② Where is the man now?
③ Is there a locker in the museum?
④ Can the man take pictures inside the museum?
⑤ Can the man take his backpack inside the museum?

[07~09] 다음 대화를 읽고 물음에 답하시오.

M: All right, everyone! This way, please. Now, we are moving onto the Joseon Dynasty. As you can see, there were many interesting inventions. This one (A)[called / is called] the *Jagyeongnu*.
W: Is it a musical instrument?
M: (a)Actually, this is a water clock. (b)그것은 한국에서 가장 오래되고 가장 큰 물시계라고 합니다.
W: How amazing! Is it okay if I take a picture of (B)[it / them]?
M: Sure.

07 위 대화의 괄호 (A)와 (B)에서 적절한 것을 고르시오.

➡ (A)______________ (B)______________

08 밑줄 친 (a)Actually와 바꿔 쓸 수 있는 말을 고르시오.

① However ② Rather
③ In fact ④ In the end
⑤ On the other hand

09 밑줄 친 (b)의 우리말과 일치하도록 주어진 단어를 이용하여 영작하시오.

➡ ________________________________

____

(large, say, in, old)

[10~13] 다음 대화를 읽고 물음에 답하시오.

M: I watched an interesting movie yesterday. (①)
W: Jeong Yakyong? (②) Wasn't he a scholar in the Joseon Dynasty? (③)
M: Yeah, but (A)그는 또한 탐정이었다고 한다. (④) He solved about 90 cases. (⑤)
W: Oh, I didn't know (B)______ he was also a detective.

10 ①~⑤ 중 주어진 문장이 들어갈 곳은?

Jeong Yakyong was a detective in it.

① ② ③ ④ ⑤

11 위 대화에서 다음 영영풀이에 해당하는 단어를 찾아 쓰시오.

someone who studies a particular subject and knows a lot about it, especially a subject that is not scientific

➡ ______________________

12 밑줄 친 (A)의 우리말과 일치하도록 영작하시오. (9 단어)

➡ ________________________________

13 빈칸 (B)에 알맞은 말을 고르시오.

① how ② what ③ which
④ that ⑤ if

14 Which is grammatically WRONG?

① The woman wants to know if there is a bank near here.
② I want to ask Wendy if she likes ice cream or not.
③ Try this food and see if or not you like it.
④ Can you tell me whether you will go shopping tonight?
⑤ I'm not sure whether Mina can join the picnic or not.

15 다음 두 문장을 한 문장으로 바꿔 쓸 때 빈칸에 알맞은 말을 쓰시오.

(1) • I want to know.
• Is the school lunch delicious?
➡ I want to know ________________
______________________________.

(2) • I'll ask Sarah.
• It's all right to sit next to her.
➡ I'll ask Sarah ________________
______________________________.

(3) • Jim didn't feel hungry.
• Jim ate lunch already.
➡ Jim didn't feel hungry because he ________________ lunch.

16 다음 문장에서 어법상 어색한 것을 바르게 고쳐 다시 쓰시오.

(1) Would you please check that I filled out this card right?
➡ ______________________________
____

(2) I don't know that my mom likes potato pizza.
➡ ______________________________
____

(3) I am not sure that Mike will meet Judy at 3 o'clock.
➡ ______________________________
____

(4) He insisted that he never heard a girl crying that night.
➡ ______________________________
____

(5) I decided to come home earlier than I planned.
➡ ______________________________

17 다음 중 어법상 어색한 문장을 고르시오.

① I knew that Mike had won first prize at the singing contest.
② Lisa doesn't know whether I can ride a bike.
③ Whether Juliet likes Romeo is not certain.
④ Lily wonders if you are interested in various music genres.
⑤ I'm not sure if or not she made a mistake.

18 다음 두 문장의 뜻이 같도록 빈칸에 알맞은 말을 쓰시오.

(1) I went to the store, but all the flowers were sold out.
= All the flowers ________________ when I went to the store.

(2) I didn't know who she was. I never met her.
= I didn't know who she was since I ________________ her.

[19~20] 다음 글을 읽고 물음에 답하시오.

In 1946, a strange man visited me and asked, "Are you Mr. Kim Yonghwan's daughter?"

For me, this was an odd question because I was more used to ⓐbeing called the daughter of a *parakho*.

"I'm your father's friend. You may wonder if it is true, but your father...," the man said.

At that moment, I was expecting disappointing news since I did not have good memories of my father.

19 위 글의 밑줄 친 ⓐbeing과 문법적 쓰임이 같은 것을 모두 고르시오.

① His hobby is collecting stamps.
② Playing the piano is fun.
③ I finished doing my homework.
④ Kirl was playing chess.
⑤ Look at the smiling girl.

20 When the writer heard the man's words, why was she expecting disappointing news? Fill in the blanks below with suitable words. (2 words)

Because she did not have ________ ________ of her father.

21 위 글의 밑줄 친 ⓐ를 능동태로 고치시오.

➡ ______________________________

22 아래 〈보기〉에서 위 글의 밑줄 친 ⓑwho와 문법적 쓰임이 다른 것의 개수를 고르시오.

보기
① Anyone who wants to come is welcome.
② There's a student who wants to see you.
③ This is the person who made me a kite yesterday.
④ Nobody knew who he was.
⑤ He was the only one who trusted me.

① 1개 ② 2개 ③ 3개 ④ 4개 ⑤ 5개

[21~22] 다음 글을 읽고 물음에 답하시오.

Back in the 1920's, whenever people saw me in the village, they would say, "There goes the *parakho*'s daughter."

My father was a son from a very rich family. Instead of living the life of a *seonbi*, he was always at the gambling house. That is why ⓐhe was called a *parakho*, which means someone ⓑwho ruins his family's fortune.

"Your father has gambled away all of the money, and now he's asking for more. Go and tell him that we have no more money left," my mother would tell me whenever she sent me to the gambling house.

Then, my father would yell at me angrily, "Why did you come empty-handed? Bring me more money!"

[23~24] 다음 글을 읽고 물음에 답하시오.

When I was sixteen years old, my family (A)had already made an arrangement for me to marry Mr. Seo. As part of the wedding tradition, Mr. Seo's family sent my family some money to buy a new chest for clothes.

Right before the wedding day, my mother came into my room and said, "Your father has taken the money for the chest."

I asked angrily, "How could he do such a horrible thing? What should we do now?"

"We have no choice. You'll have to take your aunt's old chest," my mother said.

"How __ⓐ__ for the family," people would whisper behind my back.

Since the first day of marriage, life at my husband's house had been difficult for me.

23 위 글의 빈칸 ⓐ에 들어갈 알맞은 말을 고르시오.

① exciting ② satisfying
③ boring ④ embarrassing
⑤ amazing

24 위 글의 밑줄 친 (A)had made와 과거완료의 용법이 같은 것을 모두 고르시오.

① I found that I had lost my watch.
② When she came, I had not finished my homework yet.
③ When I called on her, she had been ill for two weeks.
④ The train had just left when he got to the station.
⑤ I did not tell him at first, for I had never seen him before.

[25~28] 다음 글을 읽고 물음에 답하시오.

"Your father, my dear friend...," my father's friend continued his story. "He was not a gambler. Your father sent the family money to the independence fighters in Manchuria. He made ⓐhim look like a gambler to keep this a secret from the Japanese officers."

__ⓑ__ first, I was not sure if he was telling the truth. But afterwards, I found out the truth about my father and I realized that I had been wrong about him. Ever since that moment, I have been proud to be the daughter of a *parakho* ⓒ독립운동에 그의 인생을 헌신하신.

25 밑줄 친 ⓐhim을 알맞은 형으로 고치시오.

➡ ____________________

26 빈칸 ⓑ에 알맞은 것은?

① In ② At
③ For ④ With
⑤ From

27 위 글의 밑줄 친 ⓐ의 우리말에 맞게 주어진 어휘를 이용하여 9 단어로 영작하시오.

had devoted, life, movement

➡ ____________________
____

28 According to the passage, which is NOT true?

① The writer's father was not a gambler.
② The writer's father sent the family money to the independence fighters in Manchuria.
③ The writer's father wanted to look like a gambler to keep his secret identity from the independence fighters.
④ The writer realized that she had been wrong about her father.
⑤ The writer's father was a *parakho* who had devoted his life to the independence movement.

MEMO

Music to My Ears!

의사소통 기능

- 상대방의 의견 묻기
  A: **Do you find it** helpful to listen to music before you swim?
  B: Yes, it helps me focus.
- 앞으로의 계획 묻기
  A: **Are you planning to** perform at the talent show?
  B: Yeah, I am.

언어 형식

- 분사
  They played instruments **made** out of garbage.
- it(가목적어) ~ to부정사(진목적어)
  I found **it** possible **to inspire** people by music.

교과서
Words & Expressions

Key Words

- ☐ **anchor** [ǽŋkər] 명 (뉴스 등의) 진행자
- ☐ **attention** [əténʃən] 명 관심, 주목
- ☐ **background** [bǽkgraund] 명 배경
- ☐ **balloon** [bəlú:n] 명 풍선
- ☐ **beat** [bi:t] 명 울림, 맥박 동 때리다, 두드리다
- ☐ **broadcast** [brɔ́:dkæst] 동 방송하다
- ☐ **choir** [kwaiər] 명 합창단
- ☐ **compete** [kəmpí:t] 동 (경기 등에) 출전하다
- ☐ **concentrate** [kánsəntrèit] 동 집중하다
- ☐ **conductor** [kəndʌ́ktər] 명 지휘자
- ☐ **congratulation** [kəngrætʃuléiʃən] 명 축하
- ☐ **consider** [kənsídər] 동 ~이라고 여기다, 생각하다
- ☐ **deliver** [dilívər] 동 전하다
- ☐ **endless** [éndlis] 형 끝없는, 무한한
- ☐ **entirely** [intáiərli] 부 완전히, 전부
- ☐ **environmental** [invàiərənméntl] 형 환경의, 환경과 관련된
- ☐ **famous** [féiməs] 형 유명한
- ☐ **garbage** [gá:rbidʒ] 명 쓰레기
- ☐ **imagine** [imǽdʒin] 동 상상하다
- ☐ **index finger** 집게손가락
- ☐ **instrument** [ínstrəmənt] 명 악기
- ☐ **local** [lóukəl] 형 현지의, 지역의
- ☐ **mostly** [móustli] 부 주로, 대부분
- ☐ **musical** [mjú:zikəl] 형 음악의
- ☐ **musician** [mju:zíʃən] 명 음악가
- ☐ **nail** [neil] 명 손톱
- ☐ **notice** [nóutis] 동 ~을 알아차리다
- ☐ **orchestra** [ɔ́:rkəstrə] 명 오케스트라, 관현악단
- ☐ **pain** [pein] 명 고통, 아픔
- ☐ **perform** [pərfɔ́:rm] 동 공연하다, 수행하다
- ☐ **picker** [píkər] 명 줍는 사람, 채집자
- ☐ **positive** [pázətiv] 형 긍정적인
- ☐ **pure** [pjuər] 형 깨끗한, 순수한
- ☐ **quickly** [kwíkli] 부 빠르게
- ☐ **recommend** [rèkəménd] 동 추천하다
- ☐ **recycle** [ri:sáikl] 명 재활용하다
- ☐ **return** [ritə́:rn] 동 돌아오다
- ☐ **review** [rivjú:] 동 재검토하다, 복습하다
- ☐ **serious** [síəriəs] 형 심각한
- ☐ **share** [ʃεər] 동 나누다
- ☐ **shiny** [ʃáini] 형 빛나는, 반짝거리는
- ☐ **shocked** [ʃakt] 형 충격을 받은
- ☐ **solo** [sóulou] 명 독주, 독창
- ☐ **talented** [tǽləntid] 형 재능이 있는
- ☐ **tank** [tæŋk] 명 (물, 기름 등의) 저장 통
- ☐ **thumb** [θʌm] 명 엄지손가락
- ☐ **title** [táitl] 명 제목
- ☐ **touch** [tʌtʃ] 동 감동시키다
- ☐ **treasure** [tréʒər] 명 보물, 보물 같은 것
- ☐ **water pipe** 수도관
- ☐ **worthless** [wə́:rθlis] 형 쓸모없는, 가치 없는

Key Expressions

- ☐ **add ~ to ...** ~을 …에 추가하다
- ☐ **as long as** ~하는 한
- ☐ **be eager to** ~하고 싶어 하다
- ☐ **be filled with** ~로 가득 차다
- ☐ **be similar to** ~와 비슷하다
- ☐ **bring ~ to one's attention** ~에 …가 주목하게 하다
- ☐ **calm down** 진정하다
- ☐ **draw on** ~을 활용하다
- ☐ **in harmony with** ~와 조화를 이루어
- ☐ **in the beginning** 처음에, 초반에
- ☐ **keep a journal** 일기를 쓰다
- ☐ **keep ~ awake** ~을 깨어 있게 하다
- ☐ **put one's heart into** ~에 정열을 쏟다, ~에 열중하다
- ☐ **send back** ~을 돌려주다
- ☐ **sign up for** ~을 신청하다, ~에 가입하다
- ☐ **stand on one's head** 물구나무서다
- ☐ **Where are you off to?** 어디 가니?
- ☐ **work out** 운동하다

Word Power

※ 서로 비슷한 뜻을 가진 어휘

- □ **concentrate** 집중하다 - **focus** 집중하다
- □ **entirely** 완전히, 전부 - **totally** 전적으로
- □ **mostly** 주로, 대부분 - **largely** 주로
- □ **touch** 감동시키다 - **move** 감동을 주다
- □ **consider** ~이라고 여기다 - **regard** ~이라고 여기다
- □ **garbage** 쓰레기 - **waste** 쓰레기
- □ **positive** 긍정적인 - **affirmative** 긍정적인
- □ **worthless** 쓸모없는 - **useless** 쓸모없는

※ 서로 반대의 뜻을 가진 어휘

- □ **positive** 긍정적인 ↔ **negative** 부정적인
- □ **worthless** 가치 없는 ↔ **worthwhile** 가치 있는
- □ **pure** 깨끗한, 순수한 ↔ **impure** 순수하지 못한
- □ **entirely** 전부 ↔ **partly** 부분적으로

※ re+동사

- □ **re-+cycle** = **recycle** (재활용하다)
- □ **re-+view** = **review** (재검토하다)
- □ **re-+play** = **replay** (재생하다, 다시 보다)
- □ **re-+turn** = **return** (되돌아오다, 돌아오다)
- □ **re-+form** = **reform** (다시 만들다, 개선하다)

※ 명사 - 형용사

- □ **environment** 환경 - **environmental** 환경의
- □ **music** 음악 - **musical** 음악의
- □ **nature** 자연 - **natural** 자연스러운
- □ **nation** 국가 - **national** 국가의, 국가 소유의
- □ **culture** 문화 - **cultural** 문화적인, 문화의
- □ **magic** 마술 - **magical** 마술의

※ 동사 - 명사

- □ **arrive** 도착하다 - **arrival** 도착
- □ **rehears** 연습하다 - **rehearsal** 리허설, 예행 연습
- □ **approve** 승인하다 - **approval** 승인
- □ **propose** 제안하다 - **proposal** 제안
- □ **remove** 제거하다 - **removal** 제거
- □ **survive** 살아남다 - **survival** 생존

English Dictionary

□ **conductor** 지휘자
→ a person who directs the performance of an orchestra or choir
오케스트라나 합창단의 공연을 지휘하는 사람

□ **endless** 끝없는, 무한한
→ having no end
끝이 없는

□ **garbage** 쓰레기
→ things that are no longer useful and that have been thrown out
더 이상 쓸모가 없어 버려지는 것들

□ **instrument** 악기
→ a device that is used to make music
음악을 하기 위하여 사용되는 도구

□ **picker** 줍는 사람, 채집자
→ a person or machine that gathers something
무언가를 모으는 사람이나 기계

□ **positive** 긍정적인
→ giving cause for hope and confidence
희망이나 자신감의 원인을 제공하는

□ **recycle** 재활용하다
→ to use something again for a different purpose
다른 목적으로 무언가를 다시 사용하다

□ **shiny** 빛나는, 반짝거리는
→ having a smooth, shining, bright appearance
매끄럽고, 반짝거리고, 밝은 겉모습을 가진

□ **talented** 재능이 있는
→ having a special ability to do something well
어떤 것을 잘하는 특별한 능력을 가진

□ **tank** (물, 기름 등의) 저장 통
→ a container for holding a liquid or gas
액체나 기체를 담는 용기

□ **treasure** 보물, 보물 같은 것
→ a very valuable object
매우 소중한 물건

□ **worthless** 쓸모없는, 가치 없는
→ having no real value or use
실제적인 가치나 쓸모가 없는

Words & Expressions

시험대비 실력평가

Step2

서답형

01 다음 짝지어진 단어의 관계가 같도록 빈칸에 알맞은 말을 쓰시오.

pure : impure = ________ : negative

02 다음 영영풀이가 가리키는 것을 고르시오.

a person who directs the performance of an orchestra or choir

① conductor ② anchor
③ picker ④ treasure
⑤ solo

중요

03 다음 주어진 문장의 밑줄 친 beat과 같은 의미로 쓰인 것은?

I like this rap song because of the strong <u>beats</u>.

① I heard several loud <u>beats</u> on the drum.
② Have you heard somebody <u>beating</u> at the door?
③ My brother used to <u>beat</u> the window when he didn't have a key.
④ I saw the thief <u>beat</u> the car with a baseball bat.
⑤ My child <u>beat</u> on the table with his chopsticks.

중요

04 다음 밑줄 친 부분의 의미로 알맞지 않은 것은?

① Is he learning an <u>instrument</u>? (악기)
② The decision is <u>entirely</u> yours. (부분적으로)
③ He asked us to <u>imagine</u> a world without poverty or war. (상상하다)
④ You didn't <u>notice</u> that I got my hair cut. (알아차리다)
⑤ She put on the silky dress, white stockings, and <u>shiny</u> black boots. (빛나는, 반짝거리는)

서답형

05 다음 문장의 빈칸에 들어갈 말을 〈보기〉에서 골라 쓰시오.

보기
thumb / shocked / pure / treasure / recommend

(1) On Christmas, I used to play ________ hunt with my brother.
(2) I was ________ when I listened to the news.
(3) Henry hit his ________ by mistake.
(4) I brought a bottle of ________ water.
(5) Would you ________ an interesting novel?

서답형

06 다음 우리말에 맞게 주어진 단어를 활용하여 영작하시오.

(1) 우리는 현지 식당에서 저녁을 먹었다. (had, dinner, at)
➡ ____________________
(2) 그는 체리 채집자로서 근무했다. (as, cherry, pick)
➡ ____________________
(3) 내 삶은 음악이 없다면 가치 없을 것이다. (would, without, worth)
➡ ____________________

01 다음 짝지어진 단어의 관계가 같도록 빈칸에 알맞은 말을 쓰시오.

clean : dirty = __________ : narrow

중요
02 다음 우리말에 맞게 빈칸에 알맞은 말을 주어진 철자로 시작하여 쓰시오.

(1) 나의 형에게 대학을 가지 않은 것은 심각한 실수였다.
➡ For my brother, not going to college was a s________ mistake.

(2) 그는 정오에 연설을 할 것이다.
➡ He will d________ the speech at noon.

(3) 그 책은 국가적 관심을 이끌었다.
➡ The book has attracted national a________.

(4) 시험을 보기 전에 노트를 복습하도록 노력해라.
➡ Try to r________ your notes before you take a test.

(5) 중세시대의 보물은 박물관에 보관된다.
➡ The t________ from the Middle Ages is kept in the museum.

03 다음 우리말을 주어진 단어를 활용하여 영작하시오.

(1) 은행에 끝없는 줄이 있었다. (end)
➡ ______________________________

(2) 모든 구성원들은 독특하고 재능이 있다. (talent)
➡ ______________________________

(3) 미세 먼지는 환경 재난이다. (fine dust, environment)
➡ ______________________________

고난이도
04 다음 문장의 빈칸에 들어갈 말을 <보기>에서 골라 쓰시오.

보기
as long as / eager to / in harmony with / calm down / draw on

(1) You can __________ your imagination.

(2) I think this color is __________ the background.

(3) I told him to __________ and not to be so excited.

(4) Mike is __________ become the ace of the team.

(5) We'll go on a picnic __________ the weather is good.

05 우리말과 일치하도록 주어진 단어를 모두 배열하여 영작하시오.

(1) 지문 감식기 위에 집게손가락을 올려놓으세요.
(finger / your / the / on / scanner / place / index / finger)
➡ Please ______________________________
______________________________.

(2) 그 노인은 멋진 구두를 만드는 것에 그의 열정을 쏟는다.
(nice / the / shoes / old / into / man / puts / heart / his / making)
➡ ______________________________
____

(3) 우리는 그들이 그 문제에 주목하게 해야 한다.
(the / to / their / attention / we / bring / should / matter)
➡ ______________________________

교과서

Conversation

1 상대방의 의견 묻기

A: Do you find it helpful to listen to music before you swim?

너는 수영하기 전에 음악을 듣는 것이 도움이 된다고 생각하니?

B: Yes, it helps me focus. 물론이지. 그것은 집중하도록 도와줘.

■ 경험한 일을 바탕으로 하여 상대방의 의견이나 감정을 물을 때는 'Do you find it ~?(너는 ~가 …하다고 생각하니?)'를 사용한다. 주로 'find it+형용사+to부정사'의 형태로, 여기에 사용되는 it은 가목적어이고, 그 다음에는 다양한 형용사가 나올 수 있다. 예를 들어, 친구가 기타를 연주할 줄 아는데 기타를 연주하는 것이 쉬운지 어려운지 친구의 의견을 묻고 싶으면, 'Do you find it easy/hard to play the guitar?(너는 기타 연주하는 것이 쉽다고/어렵다고 생각하니?)'와 같이 말한다.

■ 상대방의 의견을 물어보는 표현으로 'Would you find it easy/hard to play the guitar if you had the chance to play it?(만약 네가 기타를 연주할 기회가 있다면 너는 그것을 연주하는 것이 쉽다고/어렵다고 생각하니?)'를 사용할 수 있고, think를 사용하여 'Do you think it is easy/hard to play the guitar?(너는 기타 치는 것이 쉽다고/어렵다고 생각하니?)'와 같이 물어볼 수 있다.

■ 막연하게 상대방의 의견을 물어보는 표현일 때는 'How do you feel about ~?(~에 대하여 어떻게 생각하니?)', 'What do you think about ~?(~에 대하여 어떻게 생각하니?)', 'What's your opinion about ~?(~에 대한 의견이 무엇이니?)'와 같이 물어볼 수 있다.

상대방의 의견 묻기

- Would you find it easy/hard to ~ if you had the chance to ~? (만약 네가 ~할 기회가 있다면 너는 ~을 쉽다고/어렵다고 생각하니?)
- Do you think it is easy/hard to ~? (너는 ~하는 것을 쉽다고/어렵다고 생각하니?)
- How do you feel about ~? (~에 대하여 어떻게 생각하니?)
- What do you think about ~? (~에 대하여 어떻게 생각하니?)
- What's your opinion about ~? (~에 대한 의견이 무엇이니?)

핵심 Check

1. 주어진 단어를 포함하여, 다음 우리말과 일치하도록 빈칸에 알맞은 말을 쓰시오.

M: Hi, Sally. Where are you off to?

W: I'm going to the music room. I have choir practice.

M: Oh, yeah. I forgot that you've joined the choir. ______________________ ______________________ (it, find, interesting) (너는 합창단에서 노래하는 것이 재미있다고 생각하니?)

W: Yeah, it's great to sing in harmony with others.

2 앞으로의 계획 묻기

A: Are you planning to perform at the talent show? 너는 장기 자랑에서 공연할 계획이니?
B: Yeah, I am. 응, 그래.

- 상대방에게 앞으로의 계획을 물을 때 'Are you planning to ~?(너는 ~할 계획이니?)'를 사용할 수 있다. 예를 들어, 방학 동안 해외여행을 갈 계획을 하고 있는지 알고 싶을 때, 'Are you planning to travel abroad during the vacation?(너는 여름 방학 동안 해외여행을 갈 계획이니?)'와 같이 물을 수 있다.
- 앞으로의 계획을 물어볼 때는 'be going to ~(~할 것이다, ~할 예정이다)'를 사용하여 'Are you going to ~?(너는 ~할 거니?)'라고 할 수 있고, 'Do you have plans to ~?(너는 ~할 계획을 가지고 있니?)' 또는 'Do you intend to ~?(너는 ~할 의도이니?)'와 같이 물어볼 수 있다.
- 상대방이 계획하는 일에 대하여서 아는 바가 없이 막연하게 앞으로의 계획이 무엇인지를 물어볼 때는 'What are you going to do?(너는 무엇을 할 거니?)', 'What are you planning to do?(너는 무엇을 할 계획이니?)', 'What's your plan?(네 계획이 무엇이니?)' 등으로 물어볼 수 있다.
- 계획이 무엇인지를 묻는 말에 대한 대답은 'will', 'be going to', 'plan to부정사' 등을 사용하여 'I will ~.(나는 ~할 것이다.)', 'I am going to ~.(나는 ~할 예정이다)', 'I am planning to ~.(나는 ~할 계획이다)', 'I have a plan to ~.(나는 ~할 계획을 가지고 있다.)' 등으로 대답할 수 있다.

앞으로의 계획 묻기

- Are you planning to ~? (너는 ~할 계획이니?)
- Are you going to ~? (너는 ~할 거니?)
- Do you have plans to ~? (너는 ~할 계획을 가지고 있니?)
- Do you intend to ~? (너는 ~할 의도이니?)
- What are you going/planning to do? (너는 무엇을 할 거니?)
- What's your plan? (네 계획이 무엇이니?)

핵심 Check

2. 다음 대화를 자연스러운 순서로 배열하시오.

W: Hey, Tommy. When is the last day to sign up for the talent show?
(A) How cool! What are you going to do?
(B) Yeah, I'm going to perform with a couple of people.
(C) This Friday. Are you planning to sign up for it, Megan?
W: We will play K-pop music with the violin and cello.

Listen and Talk 1-B

Sujin: Hi, Jason. Great to see you again. I've heard the new rap song, *Young and Wild*, ❶that you recorded. It's really cool.
Jason: Oh, thanks.
Sujin: I really like your songs. ❷Do you find it easy to write them?
Jason: Well, it was hard ❸in the beginning, but now it's getting easier. I ❹draw on my experiences and ❺keep a journal.
Sujin: Wow! As they say, "No pain, no gain." Best of luck with your new song!
Jason: Thank you.

Sujin: 안녕하세요, Jason. 다시 만나서 반갑습니다. 녹음하신 새로운 랩 노래, '젊고 무모한(Young and Wild)'을 들었어요. 정말 멋지던데요.
Jason: 오, 고마워요.
Sujin: 당신 노래들은 정말 좋아요. 곡을 쓰는 일이 쉬우세요?
Jason: 글쎄요, 처음에는 어려웠어요, 하지만 지금은 쉬워지고 있어요. 저는 제 경험을 활용해서 일기를 쓰고 있거든요.
Sujin: 와! '고통 없이는 얻는 것도 없다.'라는 말이 있잖아요. 새 노래가 잘 되길 바랍니다!
Jason: 고마워요.

❶ 목적격 관계대명사로 which로 바꾸어 쓸 수 있다.
❷ 상대방의 의견을 묻는 표현으로 'find it+형용사+to부정사"의 형태로, 여기에 사용되는 it은 가목적어이다.
❸ in the beginning: 처음에, 초반에 ❹ draw on: ~을 활용하다 ❺ keep a journal: 일기를 쓰다

Check(√) True or False

(1) It was difficult for Jason to write the song in the beginning. T ☐ F ☐
(2) Jason recommended keeping a journal to write a song to Sujin. T ☐ F ☐

Communication

Emma: Hey, Anthony. ❶Can you help me with something?
Anthony: Sure, what's up?
Emma: I'm going to a concert at the Arts Center, but I don't know ❷ which seat I should choose.
Anthony: ❸Are you planning to go to the orchestra concert?
Emma: Yes. I'm going to watch the orchestra concert.
Anthony: Then, you should get the seats on the second floor. You can hear the beautiful sounds of various ❹musical instruments better.
Emma: Oh, do you find it better to hear the performance from the second floor?
Anthony: Yes. I find it better than from other seats.

Emma: 저기, Anthony, 나 뭐 좀 도와줄래?
Anthony: 물론, 무슨 일이야?
Emma: 예술 회관에서 하는 공연에 가려고 하는데, 어떤 좌석을 골라야 할지 모르겠어.
Anthony: 오케스트라 공연에 갈 계획이니?
Emma: 응. 나는 오케스트라 공연을 보려고 해.
Anthony: 그럼, 너는 2층 좌석을 얻는 게 좋아. 다양한 악기들의 아름다운 소리를 더 잘 들을 수 있거든.
Emma: 오, 2층에서 공연을 듣는 것이 더 낫다는 거니?
Anthony: 응. 다른 좌석들보다 더 낫다고 생각해.

❶ 도움을 요청하는 표현으로 'Can you give me a hand?' 등으로 바꾸어 표현할 수 있다.
❷ 간접의문문 어순으로 '의문사+주어+동사'의 순서로 이어진다.
❸ 상대방에게 앞으로의 계획을 묻는 표현으로 'Are you going to go to the orchestra concert?'로 바꾸어 표현할 수 있다.
❹ musical instrument: 악기

Check(√) True or False

(3) Emma had a difficulty choosing the seat for the orchestra concert. T ☐ F ☐
(4) Anthony had a plan to watch the concert at the second floor. T ☐ F ☐

Listen and Talk 1-A-1

W: Hey, Jake. I saw ❶you won the swimming ❷competition yesterday. Congratulations!
M: Thanks, Anna.
W: You always seem to listen to music before you compete. ❸Do you find it helpful to listen to music before you swim?
M: Yes, it ❹keeps me awake and it helps me focus.

❶ 목적어 역할을 하는 명사절을 이끄는 접속사 that이 생략되어 있다.
❷ competition: 대회
❸ 상대방의 의견을 묻는 표현으로 'Do you think it is helpful to listen to music before you swim?' 등으로 바꾸어 표현할 수 있다.
❹ keep ~ awake: ~을 깨어 있게 하다

Listen and Talk 1-A-2

M: Hi, Sally. ❶Where are you off to?
W: I'm going to the music room. I have ❷choir practice.
M: Oh, yeah. I forgot that you've joined the choir. Do you find it interesting to sing in the choir?
W: Yeah, it's great to sing ❸in harmony with others.

❶ Where are you off to?: 어디 가니?
❷ choir: 합창단 ❸ in harmony with: ~와 조화를 이루어

Listen and Talk 2-A-1

W: Hey, Tommy. When is the last day to ❶ sign up for the talent show?
M: This Friday. Are you planning to sign up for ❷it, Megan?
W: Yeah, ❸I'm going to perform with a couple of people.
M: How cool! What are you going to do?
W: We will play K-pop music with the violin and cello.

❶ sign up for: ~을 신청하다, ~에 가입하다
❷ it은 the talent show를 가리킨다.
❸ 앞으로의 계획을 설명하는 표현으로 'I have a plan to perform with a couple of people.'로 바꾸어 쓸 수 있다.

Listen and Talk 2-A-2

W: Hello, ❶I'd like to sign up for a drum class.
M: Okay. ❷Are you planning to take the class during the week or during the weekend?
W: I'm planning to take a weekday class. When do you offer them?
M: There is a class on Tuesday and ❸another one on Thursday. Both classes start at 6 o'clock.
W: Great. I'd like to sign up for the Tuesday class.

❶ I'd like to ~. = I would like to ~.: ~하고 싶다. ❷ Are you planning to ~? = Are you going to ~?: 너는 ~할 거니? ❸ another one = another class

Listen and Talk 2-B

W: Are you planning to learn a musical instrument? I'd like to recommend the *kalimba*, a small African musical instrument. The sound ❶it makes ❷is similar to ❸that of a music box. Playing the *kalimba* is very easy. You can learn to use your ❹thumb nails to play beautiful music in just one lesson!

❶ it는 *kalimba*를 가리킨다. ❷ be similar to ~: ~와 비슷하다
❸ that은 the sound를 가리킨다. ❹ thumb: 엄지손가락

Wrap Up

M: Hey, Alice.
W: Hi, Sam. ❶How have you been?
M: Great. Actually, ❷I've read a lot of pop news from your blog.
W: Oh, have you? Thanks for visiting my blog!
M: Do you find it interesting to post ❸the latest pop news?
W: Yes, I love to spread news to people.

❶ '어떻게 지냈니?'라고 안부를 묻는 표현이다.
❷ 'have + p.p.' 형태의 현재완료 시제이다. ❸ the latest ~: 가장 최근의 ~

Conversation 교과서 확인학습

● 다음 우리말과 일치하도록 빈칸에 알맞은 말을 쓰시오.

Listen & Talk 1 A-1

W: Hey, Jake. I saw you ________ the swimming ________ yesterday. ________!

M: Thanks, Anna.

W: You always seem to listen to music before you ________. Do you ________ ________ ________ to listen to music before you swim?

M: Yes, it ________ me ________ and it helps me focus.

해석

W: 안녕, Jake. 어제 수영 대회에서 네가 이긴 것을 봤어. 축하해!
M: 고마워, Anna.
W: 너는 경기하기 전에 항상 음악을 듣는 것 같더라. 수영하기 전에 음악을 듣는 게 도움이 되니?
M: 응, 그것은 나를 깨어 있게 하고 집중하는 데 도움을 줘.

Listen & Talk 1 A-2

M: Hi, Sally. Where are you ________ to?

W: I'm going to the music room. I have ________ ________.

M: Oh, yeah. I ________ that you've joined the ________. Do you ________ it ________ to sing in the choir?

W: Yeah, it's great to sing ________ ________ ________ others.

M: 안녕, Sally. 어디 가는 길이야?
W: 음악실에 가는 중이야. 합창단 연습이 있거든.
M: 오, 그래. 네가 합창단에 들어간 걸 잊고 있었어. 합창단에서 노래하는 것은 재미있니?
W: 응, 다른 사람들과 조화를 이루어 노래하는 게 좋아.

Listen & Talk 1-B

W: Hi, Jason. Great to see you again. I've heard the new rap song, *Young and Wild*, that ________ ________. It's really cool.

M: Oh, thanks.

W: I really like your songs. Do you ________ ________ ________ ________ ________ ________?

M: Well, it was hard in the ________, but now it's getting easier. I ________ ________ my experiences and ________ ________ ________.

W: Wow! As they say, "________ ________, ________ ________." Best of luck with your new song!

M: Thank you.

W: 안녕하세요, Jason. 다시 만나서 반갑습니다. 녹음하신 새로운 랩 노래, '젊고 무모한(Young and Wild)'을 들었어요. 정말 멋지던데요.
M: 오, 고마워요.
W: 당신 노래들은 정말 좋아요. 곡을 쓰는 일이 쉬우세요?
M: 글쎄요, 처음에는 어려웠어요, 하지만 지금은 쉬워지고 있어요. 저는 제 경험을 활용해서 일기를 쓰고 있거든요.
W: 와! '고통 없이는 얻는 것도 없다.'라는 말이 있잖아요. 새 노래가 잘 되길 바랍니다!
M: 고마워요.

Listen & Talk 2 A-1

W: Hey, Tommy. When is the last day to ________ ________ ________ the talent show?

M: This Friday. ________ ________ ________ ________ sign up for it, Megan?

W: Yeah, I'm going to ________ with a couple of people.

M: How cool! What are you going to do?

W: We will play K-pop music with the ________ and ________.

W: 안녕, Tommy. 장기 자랑 등록 마감이 언제야?
M: 이번 주 금요일이야. 너 그거 등록할 계획이니, Megan?
W: 응, 나는 몇 사람과 함께 공연할 거야.
M: 정말 멋지다! 무엇을 할 거야?
W: 우리는 케이팝 음악을 바이올린과 첼로로 연주할 거야.

Listen & Talk 2 A-2

W: Hello, I'd like to ________ ________ ________ a drum class.

M: Okay. Are you planning to ________ ________ ________ during the week or during the weekend?

W: I'm ________ to take a weekday class. When do you ________ them?

M: There is a class on Tuesday and ________ ________ on Thursday. ________ classes start at 6 o'clock.

W: Great. I'd like to ________ ________ for the Tuesday class.

해석

W: 안녕하세요, 드럼 수업에 등록하고 싶은데요.
M: 알겠습니다. 수업을 주중에 들으실 건가요, 주말에 들으실 건가요?
W: 주중 수업을 들을 계획이에요. 수업이 언제 있나요?
M: 화요일 수업이 하나 있고 또 하나는 목요일에 있어요. 두 수업 모두 6시 정각에 시작합니다.
W: 좋아요. 화요일 수업에 등록할게요.

Listen & Talk 2-B

W: Are you planning to learn a ________ ________? I'd like to ________ the *kalimba*, a small African musical instrument. The sound it makes ________ ________ ________ that of a music box. ________ the *kalimba* is very easy. You can learn to use your ________ ________ to play beautiful music in just one lesson!

W: 악기를 배울 계획인가요? 아프리카의 작은 악기인 '칼림바'를 추천하고 싶습니다. 그 악기가 내는 소리는 음악 상자의 소리와 비슷합니다. '칼림바'를 연주하는 것은 아주 쉬워요. 단 한 번의 수업으로 엄지손톱을 사용해 아름다운 음악을 연주하는 걸 배울 수 있어요!

Communication

W: Hey, Anthony. Can you help me with ________?

M: Sure, what's ________?

W: I'm going to a concert at the Arts Center, but I don't know ________ ________ ________ ________ ________.

M: Are you planning to go to the ________ concert?

W: Yes. I'm going to watch the ________ concert.

M: Then, you should ________ ________ ________ on the second floor. You can hear the beautiful sounds of ________ ________ ________ better.

W: Oh, do you find it better to hear the performance ________ ________ ________ ________?

M: Yes. I ________ ________ ________ than from other seats.

W: 저기, Anthony. 나 뭐 좀 도와줄래?
M: 물론, 무슨 일이야?
W: 예술 회관에서 하는 공연에 가려고 하는데, 어떤 좌석을 골라야 할지 모르겠어.
M: 오케스트라 공연에 갈 계획이니?
W: 응. 나는 오케스트라 공연을 보려고 해.
M: 그럼, 너는 2층 좌석을 얻는 게 좋아. 다양한 악기들의 아름다운 소리를 더 잘 들을 수 있거든.
W: 오, 2층에서 공연을 듣는 것이 더 낫다는 거니?
M: 응. 다른 좌석들보다 더 낫다고 생각해.

Wrap Up

M: Hey, Alice.

W: Hi, Sam. How have you ________?

M: Great. Actually, ________ ________ a lot of pop news from your blog.

W: Oh, ________ ________? Thanks ________ ________ my blog!

M: Do you ________ it interesting to ________ the ________ pop news?

W: Yes, I love to ________ news to people.

M: 안녕, Alice.
W: 안녕, Sam. 어떻게 지내?
M: 좋아. 사실, 네 블로그에서 팝 소식을 많이 읽었어.
W: 오, 그랬어? 내 블로그를 방문해 줘서 고마워!
M: 최신 팝 소식을 올리는 게 재미있니?
W: 응, 사람들에게 소식을 전하는 게 좋아.

01 다음 대화의 빈칸에 들어갈 말을 <보기>에 주어진 단어들을 모두 배열하여 영작하시오.

Minho: Hi, Sally. Where are you off to?
Sally: I'm going to the music room. I have choir practice.
Minho: Oh, yeah. I forgot that you've joined the choir. __________
Sally: Yeah, it's great to sing in harmony with others.

보기
in / you / it / do / to / sing / the / find / choir / interesting / ?

➡ ______________________________

02 다음 대화의 내용과 일치하지 않는 것은?

Chris: Hi, Julie. Where are you going?
Julie: Hi, Chris. I'm going to my guitar lesson. Our band has a concert at the hospital this Sunday.
Chris: This Sunday? Are you planning to perform at the Happy Children's Hospital?
Julie: Yes. How do you know about the concert?
Chris: Oh, my sister is going to play the piano there, so I'm going to the concert, too.
Julie: Great. Come and watch our performance!

① Julie는 기타 수업에 가는 길이다.
② Julie의 밴드는 이번 주 일요일에 병원에서 공연을 할 것이다.
③ Julie는 Happy 아동 병원에서 공연을 할 계획이다.
④ Chris의 여동생은 공연에서 피아노를 연주할 것이다.
⑤ Julie는 Chris의 여동생을 공연에 초대했다.

03 다음 대화가 자연스럽게 이어지도록 순서대로 배열하시오.

(A) How cool! What are you going to do?
(B) We will play K-pop music with the violin and cello.
(C) Yeah, I'm going to perform with a couple of people.
(D) This Friday. Are you planning to sign up for it, Megan?
(E) Hey, Tommy. When is the last day to sign up for the talent show?

➡ ______________________________

[01~02] 다음 대화를 읽고 물음에 답하시오.

Sujin: Hi, Jason. Great to see you again. I've heard the new rap song, *Young and Wild*, that you recorded. It's really cool.
Jason: Oh, thanks.
Sujin: I really like your songs. (A)__________
Jason: Well, it was hard in the beginning, but now it's getting easier. I draw on my experiences and keep a journal.
Sujin: Wow! As they say, "No pain, no gain." Best of luck with your new song!
Jason: Thank you.

서답형

01 위 대화의 빈칸 (A)에 들어갈 말을 〈보기〉에 주어진 단어들을 배열하여 영작하시오.

보기

you / it / do / to / write / them / find / easy / ?

➡ ______________________

02 위 대화의 내용과 일치하지 않는 것은?

① 수진은 Jason을 처음 만났다.
② 수진은 Jason의 새로운 노래를 정말 좋아한다.
③ Jason은 경험을 활용해 일기를 쓰고 있다.
④ '젊고 무모한(*Young and Wild*)'은 Jason의 새로운 랩 노래이다.
⑤ Jason은 곡을 쓰는 일이 처음에는 어려웠지만 지금은 점점 쉬워지고 있다.

[03~04] 다음 대화를 읽고 물음에 답하시오.

Anna: Hey, Jake. I saw you ⓐwon the swimming competition yesterday. ⓑCongratulations!
Jake: Thanks, Anna.
Anna: You always seem to listen to music before you ⓒcompeting. Do you find it ⓓhelpful to listen to music before you swim?
Jake: Yes, it keeps me ⓔawake and it helps me focus.

03 위 대화의 밑줄 친 ⓐ~ⓔ 중 어법상 틀린 것을 찾아 바르게 고치시오.

➡ ______________________

중요

04 위 대화의 내용과 일치하지 않는 것은?

① Jake took part in the swimming competition yesterday.
② Jake won the swimming competition yesterday.
③ Jake always listens to music before he competes.
④ It is helpful for Jake to listen to music to keep awake.
⑤ It is necessary for Jake to swim to focus on his work.

[05~06] 다음 대화를 읽고 물음에 답하시오.

Megan: Hey, Tommy. When is the last day to sign up for the talent show?
Tommy: This Friday. Are you planning to sign up for it, Megan?
Megan: Yeah, I'm going to perform with a couple of people.
Tommy: How cool! What are you going to do?
Megan: We will play K-pop music with the violin and cello.

서답형
05 Until when should Megan sign up for the talent show?

➡ ______________________

서답형
06 What is Megan's plan for the talent show? Use the words 'people', 'play', and 'violin and cello'.

➡ ______________________
____

[07~09] 다음 글을 읽고 물음에 답하시오.

W: Are you planning to learn a musical instrument? I'd like to recommend the *kalimba*, a small African musical instrument. The sound it makes is similar to that of a music box. Playing the *kalimba* is very easy. You can learn to use your thumb nails to play beautiful music in just one lesson!

서답형
07 What is the *kalimba*?

➡ ______________________

서답형
08 What is the sound the *kalimba* makes similar to?

➡ ______________________

서답형
09 What should you use to play the *kalimba*?

➡ ______________________

중요
10 다음 짝지어진 대화가 어색한 것은?

① A: Do you find it helpful to listen to music before you swim?
B: Yes, it helps me focus.

② A: Are you planning to perform at the talent show?
B: Yeah, I am.

③ A: Do you find it interesting to learn how to cook?
B: Yes, I am. It's so interesting.

④ A: Do you think it is fun to play baseball?
B: No, I don't. How about you?

⑤ A: Are you planning to visit Jejudo this summer?
B: Well, I'm not sure yet.

[11~12] 다음 대화를 읽고 물음에 답하시오.

Sue: (A) Hello, I'd like to sign up for a drum class.
Mike: (B) Okay. Are you planning to take the class during the week or during the weekend?
Sue: (C) When do you offer them?
Mike: (D) There is a class on Tuesday and another one on Thursday. Both classes start at 6 o'clock.
Sue: (E) Great. I'd like to sign up for the Tuesday class.

11 위 대화의 (A)~(E) 중 주어진 문장이 들어가기에 적절한 곳은?

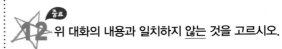

I'm planning to take a weekday class.

① (A) ② (B) ③ (C) ④ (D) ⑤ (E)

중요
12 위 대화의 내용과 일치하지 않는 것을 고르시오.

① Sue는 드럼 수업에 등록하고 싶다.
② Sue는 주중 수업을 들을 계획이다.
③ 주중 드럼 수업은 화요일과 목요일에 있다.
④ 주중 드럼 수업 시간은 서로 다르다.
⑤ Sue는 화요일 수업에 등록하고 싶다.

[01~02] 다음 대화를 읽고 물음에 답하시오.

Megan: Hey, Tommy. When is the last day to sign up for the talent show?
Tommy: This Friday. (A)너 그거 등록할 계획이니?(it, planning, sign), Megan?
Megan: Yeah, I'm going to perform with a couple of people.
Tommy: How cool! What are you going to do?
Megan: We will play K-pop music with the violin and cello.

01 위 대화의 밑줄 친 (A)의 우리말을 주어진 어휘를 이용하여 8 단어로 영작하시오.

➡ ______________________

중요
02 What kind of musical instruments is Megan's team going to play?

➡ ______________________

[03~04] 다음 글을 읽고 물음에 답하시오.

W: (A)악기를 배울 계획인가요?(musical, planning) I'd like to recommend the *kalimba*, a small African musical instrument. The sound it makes (B)_______(be) similar to that of a music box. (C)______(play) the *kalimba* is very easy. You can learn to use your thumb nails to play beautiful music in just one lesson!

중요
03 위 글의 밑줄 친 (A)의 우리말을 주어진 어휘를 이용하여 영작하시오.

➡ ______________________

04 위 글의 빈칸 (B)와 (C)에 괄호 안에 주어진 단어를 알맞은 형태로 쓰시오.

➡ (B) ____________ (C) ____________

고난이도
05 다음 대화의 내용과 일치하도록 빈칸을 완성하시오.

Anna: Hey, Jake. I saw you won the swimming competition yesterday. Congratulations!
Jake: Thanks, Anna.
Anna: You always seem to listen to music before you compete. Do you find it helpful to listen to music before you swim?
Jake: Yes, it keeps me awake and it helps me focus.

⬇

Anna congratulated Jake on (A)__________ __________ competition yesterday. She wanted to know why Jake always listens to music before (B)__________. Jake told her that (C)__________ ______________________.

06 다음 대화의 밑줄 친 (A)의 우리말을 주어진 어구를 배열하여 영작하시오.

Sam: Hey, Alice.
Alice: Hi, Sam. How have you been?
Sam: Great. Actually, I've read a lot of pop news from your blog.
Alice: Oh, have you? Thanks for visiting my blog!
Sam: (A)최근 팝 소식을 올리는 게 재미있니?
Alice: Yes, I love to spread news to people.

보기
the / it / you / to / pop news / post / interesting / do / find / latest

➡ ______________________

교과서

Grammar

1 분사(현재분사 • 과거분사)

- They played instruments **made** out of garbage. 그들은 쓰레기로 만들어진 악기를 연주했다.
- She soothed the **crying** baby by patting it on the back.
  그녀는 우는 아기를 토닥거리며 달랬다.

■ 분사는 동사의 활용형으로, 동사의 성격을 지니면서 형용사의 역할을 할 수 있게 변형한 것을 말한다. 분사는 명사의 앞이나 뒤에서 명사를 꾸며주며, 현재분사는 '능동'이나 '진행'의 의미가 있고, 과거분사는 '수동'이나 '완료'의 의미가 있다.

- Do you know the baby **sleeping** in the cradle? (너는 요람에서 자고 있는 아기를 아니?: 뒤에서 수식하는 현재분사 '진행')
- I put the **sleeping** baby down gently. (나는 자고 있는 아기를 살며시 내려놓았다.: 앞에서 수식하는 현재분사 '진행')
- Do you have a client **named** Peters? (당신에게 Peters라는 이름을 가진 고객이 있습니까?: 뒤에서 수식하는 과거분사 '수동')
- She felt sure the letter had some **hidden** meaning. (그녀는 그 편지에 무슨 숨은 의미가 있다고 확신했다.: 앞에서 수식하는 과거분사 '수동')

■ 분사가 단독으로 명사를 수식할 때는 명사 앞에 붙지만 분사에 다른 어구(목적어, 수식어구 등)가 함께 있을 때는 뒤에서 명사를 수식한다.

- John is a student of **proven** ability. (John은 증명된 능력을 지닌 학생이다.)
- Look at the man **taking** pictures. (사진을 찍고 있는 남자를 보세요.)

■ 명사를 뒤에서 수식하는 경우에는 그 앞에 '주격 관계대명사+be동사'가 생략된 것으로 생각할 수 있다.

- I like the books (which were) **written** in plain English. (나는 평이한 영어로 쓰여진 책들을 좋아한다.)
- Look at the man (who is) **taking** pictures. (사진을 찍고 있는 남자를 보세요.)

■ 동명사와 현재분사는 둘 다 '동사원형+-ing'의 형태이지만, 동명사는 문장 내에서 명사의 역할을 하고, 현재분사는 문장 내에서 형용사의 역할을 한다.

- a **sleeping** baby (잠자는 아기: 현재분사)
- a **sleeping** bag (침낭: 동명사: 목적이나 용도를 나타냄.)

핵심 Check

1. 괄호 안에 주어진 어휘를 이용하여 빈칸을 알맞게 채우시오.

(1) She showed me the letter __________ in English. (write)

(2) There are eight men __________ on the stage. (sing)

(3) A __________ stone gathers no moss. (roll)

2 it(가목적어) ~ to부정사(진목적어)

• I found **it** possible **to inspire** people by music.
나는 음악으로 사람들에게 영감을 주는 것이 가능하다는 것을 알았다.

■ '주어+동사+목적어+목적격보어'로 이루어진 문장은 5형식 문장이라고 한다.

• They made me repeat the whole story. (그들은 내게 그 이야기 전체를 반복하게 만들었다.)

■ 길이가 긴 to부정사구가 목적어로 쓰일 때, 목적어 자리에 가목적어 it을 쓰고 to부정사는 문장의 맨 뒤에 쓴다. 이때 진목적어는 to 이하이다.

• I think **it** important **to read** books. (나는 독서가 중요하다고 생각한다.)
이 문장에서 it이 의미하는 것은 to read books이다. it 자리에 to부정사를 넣어 해석한다.

■ 가목적어는 대개 목적격보어가 있는 5형식 문장에서 쓰인다.

• Social media has made **it** possible for older people **to reconnect** with old friends. (소셜 미디어는 나이가 든 사람들이 옛 친구들과 다시 연결되는 것을 가능하게 해준다.)
이 문장에서 possible은 목적어를 보충해 주는 목적격보어이다. 목적어 자리에 it이 쓰였지만, 가목적어 it은 아무 의미가 없는 단어이며, 목적격보어는 to부정사의 의미를 보충해 준다.(for older people to reconnect with old friends → possible) 특히 find, make, think 등은 to부정사(구)가 목적어로 나올 경우 가목적어 it을 쓴다.

■ 의미상의 주어
전체 문장과 to부정사구의 행위의 주체가 다른 경우 to부정사구의 주체를 의미상의 주어라고 하며, 주로 'for+목적격'의 형태로 to부정사 앞에 쓴다.

• I thought **it** necessary for her **to do** so. (나는 그녀가 그렇게 하는 게 필요하다고 생각했다.)

■ 가목적어 it은 to부정사를 문장의 맨 뒤로 보내고 그 목적어 자리에 it을 쓴 것이고, 가주어 it은 주어 역할을 하는 to부정사를 뒤로 보내고 가짜 주어인 it을 그 자리에 쓴 것이다.

• They considered **it** impossible for us **to climb** the mountain. (그들은 우리가 그 산에 오르지 못할 것으로 생각했다.) 〈가목적어 it〉

• **It** is quite reasonable for you **to act** that way. (네가 그렇게 행동해도 도리에 어긋나지 않는다.) 〈가주어 it〉

핵심 Check

2. 다음 빈칸에 알맞은 말을 쓰시오.

(1) Do you find __________ easy to write poems?
(2) My dad considers it important __________ stay healthy.

01 다음 빈칸에 들어갈 말로 알맞은 것은?

I think ________ important to read books.

① this ② that ③ what
④ which ⑤ it

02 다음 괄호 안에서 알맞은 말을 고르시오.

(1) The girl (smiling / smiled) over there is beautiful.
(2) There are no (hiding / hidden) costs.
(3) She is talking with a girl (wearing / wears) glasses.
(4) He watered the trees (planting / planted) in the garden.

03 다음 우리말을 바르게 영작한 것을 고르시오.

나는 해외로 여행하는 것이 신난다는 것을 알았다.

① I found that exciting to take a trip abroad.
② I found what exciting to take a trip abroad.
③ I found it exciting to take a trip abroad.
④ I found it exciting taking a trip abroad.
⑤ I found to take a trip abroad exciting.

04 다음 우리말에 맞게 주어진 어휘를 바르게 배열하시오.

(1) 음악회는 한 소녀가 자신의 반짝이는 첼로로 바흐의 <첼로 모음곡 1번>을 연주하는 것으로 시작되었다. (her, Bach's *Cello Suite No. 1*, the concert, a girl, cello, began, playing, shiny, on, with)

➡ ________________________________

(2) 그는 한국에서 만들어진 차를 샀다. (he, Korea, car, bought, made, a, in)

➡ ________________________________

(3) Anna는 피아노를 치는 것이 재미있다고 생각한다. (it, the piano, Anna, play, finds, fun, to)

➡ ________________________________

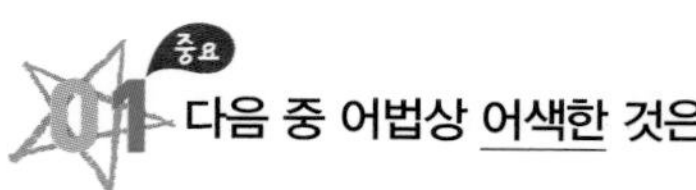

01 중요 다음 중 어법상 어색한 것은?

① Do you find it interesting to learn how to cook?
② The new law made for teenagers to drive possible.
③ I believe it helpful to listen to music while I study alone.
④ Some people think it impolite to ask someone's age.
⑤ It is advisable for you to go right now.

02 다음 중 어법상 어색한 것은?

① The woman attacked by a dog suffered severe injuries.
② Look at the crying baby.
③ Sam was surprised by the results posting on the Internet.
④ Graham saw a man lying on the bed.
⑤ The package containing the samples of accessories was received today.

03 중요 다음 빈칸에 알맞은 말이 바르게 짝지어진 것은?

- Look at the children ________ on the stage.
- Minsu found ______ exciting to dance in front of many people.

① singing – it
② singing – that
③ sung – what
④ sung – it
⑤ sing – that

04 서답형 다음 괄호 안에서 알맞은 말을 고르시오.

(1) He thought it logical (for / of) her to delay the plan.
(2) Do you find (it / that) fun to watch that kind of musical?
(3) The combined effort of everyone has made it possible (achieve / to achieve) this goal.
(4) I know the girl (talking / talked) to her teacher.
(5) The child (frightening / frightened) by the burning candle started to cry.
(6) He sent a personal letter to the (complaining / complained) customer.

05 중요 주어진 문장의 밑줄 친 부분의 쓰임이 나머지 넷과 다른 것은?

① *Yesterday* is a famous song sung by The Beatles.
② The army attacked by the enemy finally defeated them.
③ They made their desires known to the mayor.
④ His house is crowded with people invited to the party.
⑤ The boy has already taken a lot of pictures of the sea.

중요
06 다음 문장의 밑줄 친 부분 중 어법상 어색한 것은?

She ⓐmade ⓑit ⓒpossible ⓓfor us ⓔ singing in the talent show.

① ⓐ ② ⓑ ③ ⓒ
④ ⓓ ⑤ ⓔ

07 Which is suitable for the blank?

The desert fox is famous for appearing in *The Little Prince* ________ by Antoine de Saint Exupery.

① write ② wrote ③ written
④ writing ⑤ to write

중요
08 다음 중 밑줄 친 it[It]의 용법이 나머지와 다른 하나는?

① It was 10 o'clock in the morning.
② Last Saturday, it rained on and off all day long.
③ It isn't that far from here to the museum.
④ Do you think it easy to play the guitar?
⑤ In the summer when it was really hot, she would send me over to the small house to get her a bottle of water.

09 다음 우리말을 바르게 영작한 것을 고르시오.

편지를 쓰고 있는 소년을 보아라.

① Look at the writing a letter boy.
② Look at the boy writing a letter.
③ Look at the boy written a letter.
④ Look at the writing boy a letter.
⑤ Look at the boy write a letter.

중요
10 다음 두 문장을 한 문장으로 바꿔 쓸 때 가장 적절한 것은?

• To play dodge ball is fun.
• Some students think so.

① Some students think to play dodge ball fun.
② Some students think fun to play dodge ball.
③ Some students think fun to play dodge ball it.
④ Some students think it fun to play dodge ball.
⑤ Some students think fun it to play dodge ball.

11 다음 문장의 빈칸에 들어갈 수 없는 것은?

Fake Love is a famous song ________ by many teenagers.

① singing ② sung
③ which is sung ④ loved
⑤ which is loved

중요
12 다음 중 밑줄 친 it[It]이 가목적어로 쓰인 것을 고르시오.

① It gave me goose bumps just to think about it.
② It weighed between nine and ten kilos.
③ I consider it necessary to sleep at least six hours.
④ When it was really cold, we would sit on the floor and cover with a blanket.
⑤ He picked up a stone and then threw it at a crow.

13 다음 문장의 빈칸에 들어갈 수 없는 말은?

The girl ____________ is my daughter.

① taking a walk in the park
② invited to the party
③ playing in the garden
④ reads a book
⑤ wearing a pink dress

중요
14 다음 빈칸에 it[It]이 들어갈 수 없는 것은?

① I know ______ many employees drive alone to work.
② ______ was she that became the first of three queens to rule the Silla Dynasty.
③ I make ______ a rule to go to bed at 11 o'clock.
④ ______ is not easy for Tom to climb the mountain.
⑤ Do you find ______ better to watch the performance on the left side?

15 다음 빈칸에 알맞은 말이 순서대로 바르게 짝지어진 것을 고르시오.

• The results of the meeting ________ at the centre will be announced tomorrow. • They turned their attention to food ________ at the restaurant.

① held – serving
② held – served
③ hold – serves
④ holding – served
⑤ holding – serving

16 다음 우리말에 맞게 영작한 것을 모두 고르시오.

나는 대부분이 쓰레기로 가득 차 있는 마을에 살고 있는 어린이들을 보았습니다.

① I saw children lived in a town that was mostly filling with garbage.
② I saw children lived in a town that was mostly filled with garbage.
③ I saw children living in a town that was mostly filling with garbage.
④ I saw children living in a town that was mostly filled with garbage.
⑤ I saw children living in a town mostly filled with garbage.

서답형
17 다음 문장에서 생략되어 있는 것을 찾아 어법에 맞게 다시 쓰시오.

(1) An autograph is something written by a person, not a machine.
➡ ________________________________
____

(2) The image of a girl playing chess with the statue was taken on Jan. 7.
➡ ________________________________
____

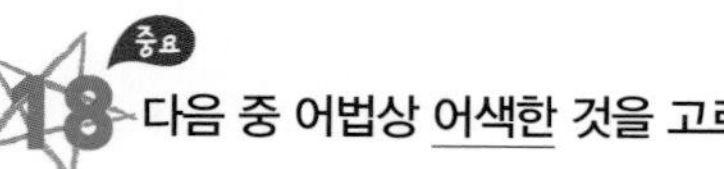

중요
18 다음 중 어법상 어색한 것을 고르시오. (2개)

① I found it easy to play the game.
② Nick thought that hard to sing a solo well.
③ The police officer helped a man lain on the street.
④ He wrote about his experience in a book titled 'Journey Man.'
⑤ Sarah opened the big box filled with a lot of books.

01 다음 빈칸에 알맞은 말을 쓰시오.

(1) I consider ________ important to keep a diary.

(2) He helped make it possible ________ children to play music with instruments made out of garbage.

(3) The situation made it hard for them ________ decide which direction they should go.

고난이도

02 다음 우리말에 맞게 주어진 어구를 바르게 배열하시오.

(1) 나는 가치 없는 것도 영감을 주는 음악을 만들어 낼 수 있다는 것을 사람들이 알게 되기를 원합니다. (I, people, something, music, know, can, want, make, inspiring, that, even, worthless, to)

➡ ________________________________

____

(2) 선생님은 학생들이 숙제를 할 것을 분명히 했다. (the teacher, their homework, the students, it, do, made, clear, for, to)

➡ ________________________________

____

(3) Stravinsky는 매일 아침 15분 동안 물구나무 서는 것이 도움이 된다고 생각했다. (Stravinsky, his head, morning, it, 15 minutes, helpful, considered, stand, every, to, on, for)

➡ ________________________________

____

03 다음 문장에서 생략된 것을 넣어 다시 쓰시오.

(1) There is an old family photo hanging on the wall.

➡ ________________________________

____

(2) Only the people invited to the meeting can attend the meeting.

➡ ________________________________

____

04 다음 문장의 it[It]이 대신하고 있는 것을 찾아 쓰시오.

(1) The gifted boy thinks it easy to draw pictures using his imagination.

➡ ________________________________

(2) Some students find it more interesting to do experiments at a science lab.

➡ ________________________________

(3) It is hard to memorize all the poems in the book.

➡ ________________________________

중요

05 괄호 안에 있는 단어를 어법에 맞게 고쳐 쓰시오.

(1) So here we have an artist (paint) her image.

➡ ____________________

(2) It has a chocolate flower (paint) in real gold dust.

➡ ____________________

(3) Who is that man (wear) a cowboy hat?

➡ ____________________

(4) My teacher got thank-you letters (write) by students.

➡ ____________________

06 그림을 보고, 주어진 어휘를 이용하여 빈칸을 알맞게 채우시오.

(1) The teacher is looking at the students ________ soccer. (play)

(2) Look at the teacher ________ with the letter ________ by the student. (satisfy)

(3) There is a girl ________ the guitar. (play)

07 중요 두 문장의 의미가 같도록 빈칸에 알맞은 말을 쓰시오.

(1) Mary thought that it is fun to play the guitar.
= Mary thought ________ fun ________ ________ the guitar.

(2) Do you find that it is helpful to listen to music before you swim?
= Do you find ________ helpful ________ ________ to music before you swim?

08 중요 다음 문장에서 어법상 어색한 것을 바르게 고치시오.

(1) We met a little girl walked with her sister in the park.
➡ ________________

(2) He found a strange man lain motionless on the street.
➡ ________________

(3) We're going to find out how a musical group calling "The Junk Orchestra" was formed.
➡ ________________

(4) Do you find that interesting to watch old movies?
➡ ________________

(5) The severe pain made it hard of her to work.
➡ ________________

(6) Is it possible for us visiting Mars someday?
➡ ________________

(7) I think to carry out our design at once necessary.
➡ ________________
____

09 다음 문장을 같은 뜻의 문장으로 바꿔 쓸 때 빈칸에 알맞은 말을 쓰시오.

(1) I believe that it is difficult to support them.
= I believe it difficult ________ them.

(2) I think that you should do it at once.
= I think it necessary ________ at once.

교과서

Reading

The Junk Orchestra

– written by a music blogger, Lucy White

"The world sends us garbage, we send back music." This was written on the back of a concert ticket I was given. The musical group was called "The Junk Orchestra." They played instruments made entirely out of garbage. I could not imagine what kind of sound these instruments would make, so I was eager to find out.

(on the back of: ~의 뒤에 / I was given은 앞에 목적격 관계대명사 which[that]가 생략 / made entirely out of garbage: 앞의 instruments를 후치 수식하는 과거 분사구 / what kind ~ would make: 동사 imagine의 목적어 역할을 하는 간접의문문)

Before the concert, I thought that the instruments might sound strange. After a few minutes, a group of young people began to walk on the stage. The first thing I noticed was their instruments: a cello made out of a shiny oil tank, a violin made with forks, and a flute made with a water pipe and buttons. The concert began with a girl playing Bach's *Cello Suite No. 1* on her shiny cello. I was shocked by the deep sound. I was so into the music that I forgot that they were playing with instruments made from recycled materials.

(might: may의 과거형 / I noticed 앞에 목적격 관계대명사 which[that]가 생략 / made out of a shiny oil tank: a cello를 후치 수식하는 과거분사구 / begin with+명사: ~로 시작하다 / playing ~ cello: a girl을 후치 수식하는 현재분사구 / be into+명사: ~에 푹 빠지다, ~을 매우 좋아하다 / so+형용사[부사]+that+주어+동사: 너무 ~해서 그 결과 …하다 / made from recycled materials: instruments를 후치 수식하는 과거분사구, recycled는 뒤의 materials를 앞에서 수식하는 과거분사로 뒤에 다른 어구가 없으므로 명사를 앞에서 수식하고 있다.)

After the concert, I was eager to write a story about the orchestra. I met Favio Chávez, the conductor, and asked him about the orchestra.

(Favios Chávez의 바로 뒤에 나오는 콤마(,)는 동격의 콤마. Favio Chávez의 직업이 the conductor임을 의미)

Lucy White: Why did you start The Junk Orchestra?

Favio Chávez: When I went to a small town called Cateura in Paraguay to work on a recycling program in 2005, I saw children living in a town that was mostly filled with garbage.

(called 이하: 과거분사구로 town을 후치 수식 / to work: to부정사의 부사적 용법(목적) / living in a town: 앞의 children을 수식하는 현재분사구. that: 주격 관계대명사)

garbage 쓰레기
instrument 악기
entirely 완전히, 전부
imagine 상상하다
send back ~을 돌려주다
be eager to ~하고 싶어 하다
notice ~을 알아차리다
shiny 빛나는, 반짝거리는
tank (물, 기름 등의) 저장 통
shocked 충격을 받은
recycle 재활용하다
conductor 지휘자
mostly 주로, 대부분

확인문제

● 다음 문장이 본문의 내용과 일치하면 T, 일치하지 않으면 F를 쓰시오.

1 The Junk Orchestra played instruments made entirely out of garbage. ☐

2 Lucy didn't long to find out what kind of sound these instruments would make. ☐

3 Before the concert, Lucy thought that the instruments might sound strange. ☐

4 The concert began with a girl playing Bach's *Cello Suite No. 1* on her shiny violin. ☐

I wanted to add something positive to their lives, so I decided to share my love of music with them.

positive가 앞에 있는 something을 꾸며 준다.

Lucy White: Why did you use garbage to make instruments?

Favio Chávez: One person's garbage is another person's treasure. Nicolás Gómez, a local garbage picker, helped me a lot. He made it possible for children to play music by making instruments out of garbage. The wonderful thing about these instruments was that the children didn't have to worry about spending a lot of money on them.

주격보어로, 주어 One person's garbage의 의미를 보충해 주는 내용. 즉 garbage = treasure임을 의미 / Nicolás Gómez를 설명해 주는 동격어구, 동격의 콤마(,)를 사용 / 가목적어 / 의미상의 주어 / 진목적어 / ~을 이용해서, ~을 재료로 하여 / ~할 필요가 없었다 / = much

Lucy White: What do you want people to learn through your music?

Favio Chávez: I want people to know that even something worthless can make inspiring music.

music을 앞에서 수식

After interviewing Chávez, I realized that it really doesn't matter what instrument you play with as long as you put your heart into playing it. The children of Cateura showed me that an orchestra is formed by people, not by instruments.

after+동명사 / 가주어 / 중요하다 / 진주어, 간접의문문(의문사+주어+동사의 어순 / ~하는 한 / be동사(is)+과거분사(formed)+by+목적격: 수동태

Comments

Annie: (23 seconds ago) So moving to see how music can change lives. The power of music is endless!

원인을 나타내는 부사적 용법

Thomas: (1 minute ago) After the concert, I found it possible to inspire people by music played with recycled instruments.

가목적어 / music을 후치 수식하는 과거분사 / instruments를 독립적으로 앞에서 꾸며 주는 과거분사

Kate: (5 days ago) Not only do these talented young people deliver great music, but they also bring serious environmental problems to our attention.

Not only라는 부사가 문장 맨 앞에 쓰였기 때문에, 조동사 do가 주어보다 앞에 쓰여 도치를 이룸. / not only A but also B: A뿐만 아니라 B도

positive 긍정적인
share 나누다
add ~ to ~을 …에 추가하다
treasure 보물, 보물 같은 것
local 현지의, 지역의
picker 줍는 사람, 채집자
worthless 쓸모없는, 가치 없는
as long as ~하는 한
put one's heart into ~에 정열을 쏟다, ~에 열중하다
endless 끝없는, 무한한
talented 재능이 있는
deliver 전하다, 배달하다
serious 심각한
environmental 환경의, 환경과 관련된
attention 관심, 주목
bring ~ to one's attention ~에 …가 주목하게 하다

확인문제

- 다음 문장이 본문의 내용과 일치하면 T, 일치하지 않으면 F를 쓰시오.

1 Nicolás Gómez, a local garbage picker, helped Favio Chávez a lot. ☐

2 Favio Chávez wants people to know that even something priceless can make inspiring music. ☐

3 The children of Cateura showed the writer that an orchestra is formed by people, not by instruments. ☐

4 Thomas found it possible to inspire people by music played with musical instruments. ☐

• 우리말을 참고하여 빈칸에 알맞은 말을 쓰시오.

1 **The ________ Orchestra**

2 ________ ________ a music blogger, Lucy White

3 "The world sends us ________, we send back ________."

4 This was written ________ ________ ________ ________ a concert ticket I was given.

5 The musical group ________ ________ "The Junk Orchestra."

6 They played instruments ________ ________ ________ ________ garbage.

7 I could not imagine what kind of sound these instruments would make, so I ________ ________ ________ ________ ________.

8 Before the concert, I thought that the instruments might ________ ________.

9 ________ ________ ________ ________, a group of young people began to walk on the stage.

10 ________ ________ ________ ________ ________ was their instruments: a cello made out of a shiny oil tank, a violin made with forks, and a flute made with a water pipe and buttons.

11 The concert began ________ ________ ________ ________ Bach's *Cello Suite No. 1* ________ her shiny cello.

12 I ________ ________ ________ the deep sound.

13 I ________ so ________ the music that I forgot that they were playing with instruments ________ ________ ________ ________.

14 After the concert, I ________ ________ ________ ________ a story about the orchestra.

15 I met Favio Chávez, ________ ________, and asked him about the orchestra.

16 **Lucy White**: ________ ________ ________ ________ **The Junk Orchestra?**

17 **Favio Chávez**: When I went to a small town called Cateura in Paraguay ________ ________ ________ a recycling program in 2005, I saw children living in a town that ________ ________ ________ ________ garbage.

1 정크 오케스트라
2 음악 블로거 Lucy White 씀
3 "세상이 우리에게 쓰레기를 보내면, 우리는 음악을 돌려준다."
4 이것은 내가 받은 음악회 입장권의 뒷면에 쓰여 있었다.
5 그 음악 그룹은 '정크 오케스트라'라고 불렸다.
6 그들은 완전히 쓰레기로만 만들어진 악기를 연주했다.
7 나는 그런 악기들이 어떤 종류의 소리를 낼지 상상할 수 없었고, 그래서 나는 알아보고 싶어졌다.
8 음악회가 시작되기 전에 나는 그 악기들이 이상한 소리를 낼지도 모른다고 생각했다.
9 몇 분 후에 한 무리의 젊은이들이 무대 위로 걸어 올라오기 시작했다.
10 내가 처음으로 알아차린 것은 그들의 악기였는데, 그것들은 반짝이는 기름통으로 만들어진 첼로, 포크로 만들어진 바이올린, 수도관과 단추로 만들어진 플루트였다.
11 음악회는 한 소녀가 자신의 반짝이는 첼로로 바흐의 〈첼로 모음곡 1번〉을 연주하는 것으로 시작되었다.
12 나는 그 깊은 소리에 충격을 받았다.
13 나는 음악에 너무 심취해서 그들이 재활용된 재료들로 만들어진 악기를 연주하고 있다는 것을 잊었다.
14 음악회가 끝나고, 나는 그 오케스트라에 대한 이야기를 몹시 쓰고 싶었다.
15 나는 지휘자인 Favio Chávez를 만나서 그에게 오케스트라에 대해 물었다.
16 Lucy White: 왜 당신은 정크 오케스트라를 시작하셨나요?
17 Favio Chávez: 2005년에 재활용 프로그램에서 일을 하기 위해서 내가 파라과이의 카테우라라고 불리는 작은 마을에 갔을 때, 나는 대부분이 쓰레기로 가득 차 있는 마을에 살고 있는 어린이들을 보았습니다.

18 I wanted to add _______ _______ to their lives, so I decided to _______ my love of music _______ them.

19 Lucy White: Why did you use garbage _______ _______ _______?

20 **Favio Chávez**: One person's _______ is another person's _______.

21 Nicolás Gómez, _______ _______ _______ _______, helped me a lot.

22 He made it possible for children to play music by making instruments _______ _______ _______.

23 _______ _______ _______ about these instruments was that the children _______ _______ _______ _______ _______ spending a lot of money on them.

24 Lucy White: What do you want people to learn _______ your music?

25 **Favio Chávez**: I want people to know that even something _______ can make _______ _______.

26 After interviewing Chávez, I realized that it really doesn't matter what instrument you play with _______ _______ _______ you put your heart _______ playing it.

27 The children of Cateura showed me that an orchestra is formed by people, _______ _______ _______.

28 **Comments**

29 **Annie**: (23 seconds ago) So moving to see _______ music can change lives.

30 The power of music is _______!

31 **Thomas**: (1 minute ago) After the concert, I found it possible to inspire people by music _______ _______ recycled instruments.

32 **Kate**: (5 days ago) _______ _______ _______ these talented young people deliver great music, but they also _______ serious environmental problems _______ _______ _______.

18 나는 그들의 삶에 긍정적인 무엇인가를 더해 주고 싶어서, 음악에 대한 나의 사랑을 그들과 나누기로 결정했습니다.

19 Lucy White: 왜 당신은 악기를 만들기 위해 쓰레기를 이용했나요?

20 Favio Chávez: 한 사람의 쓰레기는 다른 사람의 보물입니다.

21 그 지역의 쓰레기 줍는 사람인 Nicolás Gámez가 나를 많이 도와주었습니다.

22 그는 쓰레기로 악기를 만들어 줌으로써 어린이들이 음악을 연주하는 것이 가능하도록 만들었습니다.

23 이 악기들의 멋진 점은 어린이들이 악기에 많은 돈을 쓸 것을 걱정하지 않아도 된다는 점이었죠.

24 Lucy White: 당신의 음악을 통해서 사람들이 무엇을 배우기를 원하십니까?

25 Favio Chávez: 나는 가치 없는 것도 영감을 주는 음악을 만들어 낼 수 있다는 것을 사람들이 알게 되기를 원합니다.

26 Chávez를 인터뷰한 후에 나는 사람들이 악기를 연주하는 데 마음을 쏟아붓는 한, 그 사람이 연주하는 악기가 무엇인지는 별로 중요하지 않다는 것을 깨달았다.

27 카테우라의 어린이들은 나에게 오케스트라는 악기에 의해서가 아니라 사람에 의해 이루어지는 것이라는 것을 보여 주었다.

28 감상평

29 Annie: (23초 전) 음악이 삶을 바꿀 수 있다는 것을 보아서 너무 가슴이 뭉클하다.

30 음악의 힘은 끝이 없다!

31 Thomas: (1분 전) 음악회가 끝난 후, 나는 재활용 악기로 연주되는 음악으로 사람들에게 영감을 주는 것이 가능하다는 것을 알았다.

32 Kate: (5일 전) 이 재능 있는 젊은이들은 훌륭한 음악을 전할 뿐만 아니라, 또한 심각한 환경 문제에 우리가 주목하게 한다.

Reading 교과서 확인학습 B

• 우리말을 참고하여 본문을 영작하시오.

1 정크 오케스트라
➡ ______________________________

2 음악 블로거 Lucy White 씀
➡ ______________________________

3 "세상이 우리에게 쓰레기를 보내면, 우리는 음악을 돌려준다."
➡ ______________________________

4 이것은 내가 받은 음악회 입장권의 뒷면에 쓰여 있었다.
➡ ______________________________

5 그 음악 그룹은 '정크 오케스트라'라고 불렸다.
➡ ______________________________

6 그들은 완전히 쓰레기로만 만들어진 악기를 연주했다.
➡ ______________________________

7 나는 그런 악기들이 어떤 종류의 소리를 낼지 상상할 수 없었고, 그래서 나는 알아보고 싶어졌다.
➡ ______________________________

8 음악회가 시작되기 전에 나는 그 악기들이 이상한 소리를 낼지도 모른다고 생각했다.
➡ ______________________________

9 몇 분 후에 한 무리의 젊은이들이 무대 위로 걸어 올라오기 시작했다.
➡ ______________________________

10 내가 처음으로 알아차린 것은 그들의 악기였는데, 그것들은 반짝이는 기름통으로 만들어진 첼로, 포크로 만들어진 바이올린, 수도관과 단추로 만들어진 플루트였다.
➡ ______________________________
____

11 음악회는 한 소녀가 자신의 반짝이는 첼로로 바흐의 〈첼로 모음곡 1번〉을 연주하는 것으로 시작되었다.
➡ ______________________________

12 나는 그 깊은 소리에 충격을 받았다.
➡ ______________________________

13 나는 음악에 너무 심취해서 그들이 재활용된 재료들로 만들어진 악기를 연주하고 있다는 것을 잊었다.
➡ ______________________________

14 음악회가 끝나고, 나는 그 오케스트라에 대한 이야기를 몹시 쓰고 싶었다.
➡ ______________________________

15 나는 지휘자인 Favio Chávez를 만나서 그에게 오케스트라에 대해 물었다.
➡ ______________________________

16 Lucy White: 왜 당신은 정크 오케스트라를 시작하셨나요?
➡ ______________________________

17 Favio Chávez: 2005년에 재활용 프로그램에서 일을 하기 위해서 내가 파라과이의 카테우라라고 불리는 작은 마을에 갔을 때, 나는 대부분이 쓰레기로 가득 차 있는 마을에 살고 있는 어린이들을 보았습니다.
➡ ______________________________
____

18 나는 그들의 삶에 긍정적인 무엇인가를 더해 주고 싶어서, 음악에 대한 나의 사랑을 그들과 나누기로 결정했습니다.

➡ ______

19 Lucy White: 왜 당신은 악기를 만들기 위해 쓰레기를 이용했나요?

➡ ______

20 Favio Chávez: 한 사람의 쓰레기는 다른 사람의 보물입니다.

➡ ______

21 그 지역의 쓰레기 줍는 사람인 Nicolás Gámez가 나를 많이 도와주었습니다.

➡ ______

22 그는 쓰레기로 악기를 만들어 줌으로써 어린이들이 음악을 연주하는 것이 가능하도록 만들었습니다.

➡ ______

23 이 악기들의 멋진 점은 어린이들이 악기에 많은 돈을 쓸 것을 걱정하지 않아도 된다는 점이었죠.

➡ ______

______

24 Lucy White: 당신의 음악을 통해서 사람들이 무엇을 배우기를 원하십니까?

➡ ______

25 Favio Chávez: 나는 가치 없는 것도 영감을 주는 음악을 만들어 낼 수 있다는 것을 사람들이 알게 되기를 원합니다.

➡ ______

26 Chávez를 인터뷰한 후에 나는 사람들이 악기를 연주하는 데 마음을 쏟아붓는 한, 그 사람이 연주하는 악기가 무엇인지는 별로 중요하지 않다는 것을 깨달았다.

➡ ______

______

27 카테우라의 어린이들은 나에게 오케스트라는 악기에 의해서가 아니라 사람에 의해 이루어지는 것이라는 것을 보여 주었다.

➡ ______

28 감상평

➡ ______

29 Annie: (23초 전) 음악이 삶을 바꿀 수 있다는 것을 보아서 너무 가슴이 뭉클하다.

➡ ______

30 음악의 힘은 끝이 없다!

➡ ______

31 Thomas: (1분 전) 음악회가 끝난 후, 나는 재활용 악기로 연주되는 음악으로 사람들에게 영감을 주는 것이 가능하다는 것을 알았다.

➡ ______

______

32 Kate: (5일 전) 이 재능 있는 젊은이들은 훌륭한 음악을 전할 뿐만 아니라, 또한 심각한 환경 문제에 우리가 주목하게 한다.

➡ ______

______

[01~03] 다음 글을 읽고 물음에 답하시오.

"The world sends us garbage, we send back music." This was written on the back of a concert ticket I was given. The musical group was called "The Junk Orchestra." ⓐ They played instruments made entirely into garbage. I could not imagine what kind of sound these instruments would make, so I ⓑ was eager to find out.

서답형

01 위 글의 밑줄 친 ⓐ에서 흐름상 어색한 부분을 찾아 고치시오.

➡ ______________________

02 위 글의 밑줄 친 ⓑwas eager to와 바꿔 쓸 수 있는 말을 모두 고르시오.

① was worried to
② was anxious to
③ was likely to
④ paid attention to
⑤ longed to

중요

03 위 글의 뒤에 올 내용으로 가장 알맞은 것을 고르시오.

① the reason the world sends us garbage
② the way to send back music
③ to find out the sound of these instruments
④ the kinds of musical instruments
⑤ how to make a harmonious sound

[04~06] 다음 글을 읽고 물음에 답하시오.

Before the concert, I thought that the instruments might sound strange. After a few minutes, a group of young people began to walk on the stage. The first thing I noticed was their instruments: a cello made out of a shiny oil tank, a violin made with forks, and a flute made with a water pipe and buttons. The concert began ___ⓐ___ a girl playing Bach's *Cello Suite No. 1* ___ⓑ___ her shiny cello. I was shocked by the deep sound. I was so into the music that I forgot that they were playing with instruments made from recycled materials.

04 위 글의 빈칸 ⓐ와 ⓑ에 들어갈 전치사가 바르게 짝지어진 것은?

	ⓐ ⓑ		ⓐ ⓑ
①	for – on	②	with – in
③	on – by	④	for – by
⑤	with – on		

중요

05 위 글의 제목으로 알맞은 것을 고르시오.

① A Strange Sound from Instruments Made out of Garbage
② How about Enjoying Bach's *Cello Suite No. 1*?
③ Unbelievable! Such a Deep Sound from Instruments Made out of Garbage?
④ The Difficulty of Making Instruments from Recycled Materials
⑤ Unbelievable! Such a Young Girl Plays Bach's *Cello Suite No. 1*!

중요

06 위 글에서 알 수 있는 글쓴이의 심경 변화로 가장 알맞은 것을 고르시오.

① nervous → disappointed
② anxious → satisfied
③ excited → nervous
④ bored → pleased
⑤ surprised → bored

[07~09] 다음 글을 읽고 물음에 답하시오.

After the concert, I was eager to write a story about the orchestra. I met Favio Chávez, the conductor, and asked him about the orchestra.

Lucy White: ⓐ ______________________

Favio Chávez: When I went to a small town called Cateura in Paraguay ⓑto work on a recycling program in 2005, I saw children living in a town that was mostly filled with garbage. I wanted to add something positive to their lives, ⓒso I decided to share my love of music with them.

07 위 글의 빈칸 ⓐ에 들어갈 알맞은 질문을 고르시오.

① Why did you use garbage to make instruments?
② How did you start The Junk Orchestra?
③ Why did you start The Junk Orchestra?
④ How many children joined The Junk Orchestra?
⑤ What do you want people to learn through your music?

중요

08 위 글의 밑줄 친 ⓑto work와 to부정사의 용법이 같은 것을 모두 고르시오.

① I was happy to work on a recycling program.
② Why did you want to work on a recycling program?
③ Who is the right man to work on a recycling program?
④ He was eager to work on a recycling program.
⑤ I think it worthwhile to work on a recycling program.

서답형

09 위 글의 밑줄 친 ⓒ를 다음과 같이 바꿔 쓸 때 빈칸에 들어갈 알맞은 단어를 쓰시오.

➡ so I decided to ________ my love of music in common with them

[10~12] 다음 글을 읽고 물음에 답하시오.

Before the concert, I thought that the instruments might sound strange. After a few minutes, a group of young people began to walk on the stage. The first thing I noticed was their instruments: a cello made out of a shiny oil tank, a violin made with forks, and a flute made with a water pipe and buttons. The concert began ⓐ한 소녀가 바흐의 <첼로 모음곡 1번>을 연주하는 것으로 on her shiny cello. I was shocked by the deep sound. I was so into the music that I forgot that they were playing with instruments made from recycled materials.

10 위 글에 나오는 악기의 재료에 속하지 않는 것을 고르시오.

① an oil tank
② spoons
③ a water pipe
④ forks
⑤ buttons

서답형

11 위 글의 밑줄 친 ⓐ의 우리말에 맞게 주어진 어휘를 이용하여 9 단어로 영작하시오.

with, Bach's *Cello Suite No. 1*

➡ ______________________

중요

12 According to the passage, which is NOT true?

① The writer thought that the instruments might sound strange before listening to their music.
② The first thing the writer noticed was their instruments.
③ The musicians of the concert were a group of young people.
④ The first music of the concert was a violin piece.
⑤ The musicians were playing with instruments made from recycled materials.

[13~15] 다음 글을 읽고 물음에 답하시오.

After the concert, I was eager to write a story about the orchestra. I met Favio Chávez, the conductor, and asked him about the orchestra.
Lucy White: Why did you start The Junk Orchestra?
Favio Chávez: When I went to a small town called Cateura in Paraguay to work on a recycling program in 2005, I saw children living in a town that was mostly filled with garbage. I wanted to add something __ⓐ__ to their lives, so I decided to share my love of music with ⓑthem.

13 위 글의 빈칸 ⓐ에 들어갈 알맞은 말을 고르시오.

① passive ② positive
③ temporary ④ general
⑤ permanent

서답형

14 위 글의 밑줄 친 ⓑthem이 가리키는 것을 본문에서 찾아 쓰시오.

➡ ______________________

서답형

15 Why did the writer meet Favio Chávez, the conductor, after the concert? Fill in the blanks with suitable words.

Because the writer wanted to write a story about ________ ________ very much.

[16~18] 다음 글을 읽고 물음에 답하시오.

Lucy White: Why did you use garbage to make instruments?
Favio Chávez: One person's garbage is another person's treasure. Nicolás Gómez, a local garbage picker helped me a lot. He made ⓐit possible ①of children to play music ②by making instruments out of garbage. The wonderful thing ③about these instruments was that the children didn't have to worry about spending a lot of money ④on them.
Lucy White: What do you want people to learn ⑤through your music?
Favio Chávez: I want people to know that even something worthless can make inspiring music.

서답형

16 위 글의 밑줄 친 ①~⑤에서 전치사의 쓰임이 적절하지 않은 것을 찾아 알맞게 고치시오.

➡ ______________________

17 위 글의 밑줄 친 ⓐit과 문법적 쓰임이 같은 것을 고르시오.

① It was raining this morning.
② He took a stone and threw it.
③ It is important for you to choose good friends.
④ It was she who told me the story.
⑤ I make it a rule to get up early.

중요
18 위 글을 읽고 알 수 없는 것을 고르시오.

① Why did Favio Chávez use garbage to make instruments?
② Who was Nicolás Gómez?
③ Why did Nicolás Gómez help Favio Chávez a lot?
④ What was the wonderful thing about the instruments?
⑤ What does Favio Chávez want people to learn through his music?

[19~20] 다음 글을 읽고 물음에 답하시오.

After interviewing Chávez, I realized that ⓐit really doesn't matter what instrument you play with ⓑas long as you put your heart into playing it. The children of Cateura showed me that an orchestra is formed by people, not by instruments.

서답형
19 위 글의 밑줄 친 ⓐ를 다음과 같이 바꿔 쓸 때 빈칸에 들어갈 알맞은 단어를 쓰시오.

➡ it isn't really ________

20 위 글의 밑줄 친 ⓑas long as와 바꿔 쓸 수 있는 말을 모두 고르시오.

① as far as
② as well as
③ as much as
④ as soon as
⑤ so long as

[21~23] 다음 글을 읽고 물음에 답하시오.

The Junk Orchestra
The world sends us garbage, we send back, music.
Comments
Annie: (23 seconds ago) So ⓐmoving to see how music can change lives. The power of music is endless!
Thomas: (1 minute ago) ⓑAfter the concert, I found it possible to inspire people by music played with recycling instruments.
Kate: (5 days ago) ⓒ이 재능 있는 젊은이들은 훌륭한 음악을 전할 뿐만 아니라, but they also bring serious environmental problems to our attention.

서답형
21 위 글의 밑줄 친 ⓐmoving과 바꿔 쓸 수 있는 말을 쓰시오.

➡ ________________

서답형
22 위 글의 밑줄 친 ⓑ에서 어법상 틀린 부분을 찾아 고치시오.

➡ ________________

서답형
23 위 글의 밑줄 친 ⓒ의 우리말에 맞게 한 단어를 보충하여, 주어진 어휘를 알맞게 배열하시오.

not only / great music / deliver / these talented young people

➡ ________________________
____

[01~03] 다음 글을 읽고 물음에 답하시오.

"(A)The world sends us garbage, we send back music." This was written on the back of a concert ticket I ___ⓐ___ . The musical group was called "The Junk Orchestra." They played instruments made entirely out of garbage. (B)나는 그런 악기들이 어떤 종류의 소리를 낼지 상상할 수 없었고, so I was eager to find out.

01 위 글의 빈칸 ⓐ에 give를 알맞은 형태로 쓰시오.

➡ ____________________

중요
02 다음 빈칸 (a)와 (b)에 알맞은 단어를 넣어 위 글의 밑줄 친 (A)의 의미를 완성하시오.

We make musical instruments by recycling (a)________, and perform (b)________ playing the instruments.

03 위 글의 밑줄 친 (B)의 우리말에 맞게 주어진 어휘를 알맞게 배열하시오.

instruments / would / what kind of sound / imagine / I / these / make / could not

➡ ____________________
____

[04~06] 다음 글을 읽고 물음에 답하시오.

Before the concert, I thought that the instruments might sound (A)[strange / strangely]. After a few minutes, a group of young people began to walk on the stage. The first thing I noticed was their instruments: a cello made out of a shiny oil tank, a violin made with forks, and a flute made with a water pipe and buttons. The concert began with a girl playing Bach's *Cello Suite No. 1* on her shiny cello. I was (B)[shocking / shocked] by the deep sound. I was so into the music that I forgot that they were playing with instruments made from (C)[recycling / recycled] materials.

중요
04 위 글의 괄호 (A)~(C)에서 어법상 알맞은 낱말을 골라 쓰시오.

➡ (A) ________ (B) ________ (C) ________

05 What did the writer notice first when a group of young people began to walk on the stage? Fill in the blank with a suitable word.

➡ The writer first noticed their __________.

고난이도
06 본문의 내용과 일치하도록 다음 빈칸에 알맞은 단어를 쓰시오.

The concert began with a girl playing Bach's *Cello Suite No. 1* on her cello which was made out of ________ ________ ________ ________.

[07~08] 다음 글을 읽고 물음에 답하시오.

After interviewing Chávez, I realized that it really doesn't matter what instrument you play with as long as you put your heart into playing ⓐit. ⓑThe children of Cateura showed me that an orchestra is formed by people, not by instruments.

07 위 글의 밑줄 친 ⓐit이 가리키는 것을 두 단어로 쓰시오.

➡ ______________________

중요 **08** 위 글의 밑줄 친 ⓑ를 다음과 같이 바꿔 쓸 때 빈칸에 들어갈 알맞은 말을 한 단어씩 쓰시오.

➡ The children of Cateura showed me that an orchestra is formed ________ by instruments ________ by people.

[09~11] 다음 글을 읽고 물음에 답하시오.

After the concert, I was eager to write a story about the orchestra. I met Favio Chávez, the conductor, and asked him about the orchestra.

Lucy White: Why did you start The Junk Orchestra?

Favio Chávez: When I went to a small town ⓐ____ Cateura in Paraguay to work on a recycling program in 2005, ⓑI saw children living in a town that was mostly filled with garbage. I wanted to add something positive to their lives, so I decided to share my love of music with them.

중요 **09** 위 글의 빈칸 ⓐ에 call을 알맞은 형태로 쓰시오.

➡ ______________________

10 위 글의 밑줄 친 ⓑ에서 생략할 수 있는 부분을 생략하고 문장을 다시 쓰시오.

➡ ______________________________

____

고난이도 **11** 본문의 내용과 일치하도록 다음 빈칸 (A)와 (B)에 알맞은 단어를 쓰시오.

When Favio Chávez went to Cateura in Paraguay to work on a recycling program in 2005, he decided to share (A)________ ________ ________ ________ with the children living in a town that was mostly filled with garbage in order to add (B)________ ________ to their lives.

[12~13] 다음 글을 읽고 물음에 답하시오.

Lucy White: Why did you use garbage to make instruments?

Favio Chávez: One person's garbage is another person's treasure. Nicolás Gómez, a local garbage picker helped me a lot. He made it possible for children to play music by making instruments out of garbage. ⓐThe wonderful thing about these instruments was that the children didn't have to worry about spending a lot of money on them.

Lucy White: What do you want people to learn through your music?

Favio Chávez: ⓑI want people to know that even something priceless can make inspiring music.

12 위 글의 밑줄 친 ⓐ를 다음과 같이 바꿔 쓸 때 빈칸에 들어갈 알맞은 말을 한 단어로 쓰시오.

➡ The wonderful thing about these instruments was that the children didn't ________ to worry about spending a lot of money on them.

중요 **13** 위 글의 밑줄 친 ⓑ에서 흐름상 어색한 부분을 찾아 고치시오.

➡ ______________________

교과서

구석구석

After You Read A

The Junk Orchestra
The world sends us garbage, we send back music.
garbage to us(3형식)

About the concert
– The young people played instruments made out of garbage.
(which were) made
– It started with a girl playing the cello made out of a shiny oil tank.
(which were) made
– I was shocked by the deep sound.

The Interview with Mr. Chávez
– He went to Cateura in Paraguay to work on a recycling program.
to부정사의 부사적 용법(목적)
– He decided to share his love of music with the children.
share A with B: A를 B와 공유하다
– A local garbage picker helped him.

⇒ An orchestra is formed by people, not by instruments.
= not by instruments but by people

구문해설 • garbage: 쓰레기 • send back: ~을 돌려주다 • instrument: 악기 • shiny: 빛나는, 반짝거리는 • tank: (물, 기름 등의) 저장 통 • shocked: 충격을 받은 • recycle: 재활용하다 • share: 나누다

해석

정크 오케스트라
세상이 우리에게 쓰레기를 보내면 우리는 음악을 돌려준다.
음악회에 관해
• 젊은이들은 쓰레기로 만들어진 악기를 연주했다.
• 음악회는 한 소녀의 반짝이는 기름통으로 만들어진 첼로 연주로 시작되었다.
• 나는 그 깊은 소리에 충격을 받았다.
Chávez 씨와의 인터뷰
• 그는 재활용 프로그램에서 일을 하기 위해 파라과이의 카테우라에 갔다.
• 그는 그의 음악에 대한 사랑을 아이들과 나누기로 결정했다.
• 그 지역의 쓰레기 줍는 사람이 그를 도와주었다.
⇒ 오케스트라는 악기에 의해서가 아니라 사람에 의해 이루어지는 것이다.

Grammar in Real Life

I visited a broadcasting company. In the news room, I sat at the desk where (관계부사) anchors give the news. There were two screens hanging (two screens를 수식하는 현재분사) on the wall. I could read aloud sentences moving (sentences를 수식하는 현재분사) across the screen. After I came out of the room, I could see myself (주어와 목적어가 같으므로 재귀대명사) recorded (myself를 수식하는 과거분사) on the TV screen. I really liked the background created (background를 수식하는 과거분사) with computer graphics.

구문해설 • broadcasting company: 방송국 • background: 배경

나는 방송국을 방문했다. 뉴스 룸에서 나는 앵커들이 뉴스를 전하는 책상에 앉았다. 벽에는 두 개의 스크린이 걸려 있었다. 나는 화면을 가로질러 움직이는 문장들을 소리 내어 읽을 수 있었다. 방에서 나온 후 TV 화면에 녹화된 내 모습을 볼 수 있었다. 나는 컴퓨터 그래픽으로 만들어진 배경이 정말 마음에 들었다.

Wrap Up 2

M: Hi, Julie. Where are you going?
= Where are you off to?
W: Hi, Chris. I'm going to my guitar lesson. Our band has a concert at the hospital this Sunday.
M: This Sunday? Are you planning to perform at the Happy Children's Hospital? = Are you going to = Do you have a plan to
W: Yes. How do you know about the concert?
M: Oh, my sister is going to play the piano there, so I'm going to the concert, too.
W: Great. Come and watch our performance!

구문해설 • performance: 공연

M: 안녕, Julie. 어디 가는 길이니?
W: 안녕, Chris. 나는 기타 수업에 가는 길이야. 우리 밴드가 이번 주 일요일에 병원에서 공연을 하거든.
M: 이번 주 일요일? Happy 아동 병원에서 공연할 계획이니?
W: 응. 그 공연에 대해 어떻게 알고 있어?
M: 아, 내 여동생이 거기서 피아노를 연주할 거라서 나도 그 공연에 갈 거야.
W: 잘됐다. 와서 우리 공연을 봐!

영역별 핵심문제

Words & Expressions

01 다음 짝지어진 단어의 관계가 같도록 빈칸에 알맞은 말을 쓰시오.

arrive : arrival = survive : ________

02 다음 영영풀이가 가리키는 것을 고르시오.

to use something again for a different purpose

① recommend ② share
③ recycle ④ deliver
⑤ perform

03 다음 우리말에 맞게 빈칸에 알맞은 말을 쓰시오.

(1) 너는 물구나무를 설 수 있니?
➡ Can you ________ ________ ________ ________?

(2) 나는 깨어 있기 위해 많은 커피를 마신다.
➡ I drink much coffee to ________ me ________.

(3) 재즈 댄스 수업에 어떻게 신청합니까?
➡ How do I ________ ________ ________ the jazz dance class?

(4) 나는 거의 매일 체육관에서 운동한다.
➡ I ________ ________ at the gym almost every day.

04 다음 중 밑줄 친 부분의 뜻풀이가 바르지 않은 것은?

① I filled the gas tank before I left. (저장 통)
② She was shocked by his sudden death. (충격을 받은)
③ Why not recycle Christmas cards as gift tags? (재활용하다)
④ He has served as the conductor of the orchestra. (지휘자)
⑤ The people at the concert were mostly old people. (최대한)

05 다음 문장에 공통으로 들어갈 말을 고르시오.

• Minsu showed up without any ________. • The first thing I ________(e)d in the room was the smell. • Did you ________ how upset I was?

① compete ② deliver
③ concentrate ④ imagine
⑤ notice

06 다음 주어진 문장의 밑줄 친 touched와 같은 의미로 쓰인 것은?

Her story touched us all deeply.

① I touched him lightly on the arm.
② You have never touched your food.
③ My mom touched my forehead.
④ He hardly touched the ball during the game.
⑤ I was so touched that I almost cried.

Conversation

07 다음 대화의 빈칸 (A)에 들어갈 말로 적절한 것은?

> **Anna:** Hey, Jake. I saw you won the swimming competition yesterday. Congratulations!
> **Jake:** Thanks, Anna.
> **Anna:** You always seem to listen to music before you compete. (A)__________
> **Jake:** Yes, it keeps me awake and it helps me focus.

① What do you think about listening to music before you swim?
② How do you feel when you listen to music before you swim?
③ Do you find it helpful to listen to music before you swim?
④ What's your opinion about listening to music before you swim?
⑤ What kind of music do you listen to music before you swim?

08 다음 대화의 (A)~(C)에 들어갈 말이 바르게 짝지어진 것은?

> **Minho:** Hi, Sally. Where are you (A)[on / off] to?
> **Sally:** I'm going to the music room. I have choir practice.
> **Minho:** Oh, yeah. I forgot (B)[that / which] you've joined the choir. Do you find it (C)[interested / interesting] to sing in the choir?
> **Sally:** Yeah, it's great to sing in harmony with others.

	(A)	(B)	(C)
①	on	that	interested
②	on	which	interesting
③	off	that	interesting
④	off	which	interested
⑤	off	that	interested

[09~11] 다음 대화를 읽고 물음에 답하시오.

> **Sujin:** Hi, Jason. Great to see you again. I've heard the new rap song, *Young and Wild*, that you recorded. It's really cool.
> **Jason:** (A) Oh, thanks.
> **Sujin:** (B) I really like your songs. Do you find it easy to write them?
> **Jason:** (C) I draw on my experiences and keep a journal.
> **Sujin:** (D) Wow! As they say, "No pain, no gain." Best of luck with your new song!
> **Jason:** (E) Thank you.

09 위 대화의 (A)~(E) 중 주어진 문장이 들어가기에 적절한 곳은?

> Well, it was hard in the beginning, but now it's getting easier.

① (A) ② (B) ③ (C) ④ (D) ⑤ (E)

10 위 대화에서 나타난 수진과 Jason의 관계로 적절한 것은?

① interviewer – rapper
② musician – dancer
③ guide – tourist
④ doctor – patient
⑤ teacher – student

11 위 대화를 읽고 대답할 수 없는 것은?

① What is the title of Jason's new song?
② What does Sujin think about Jason's new song?
③ What does Jason do to write the songs?
④ What proverb does Sujin use to describe Jason's effort?
⑤ How many times has Sujin heard Jason's new rap song?

[12~13] 다음 대화를 읽고 물음에 답하시오.

Emma: Hey, Anthony. Can you help me with something?
Anthony: Sure, what's up?
Emma: I'm going to a concert at the Arts Center, but I don't know which seat ⓐshould I choose.
Anthony: Are you planning ⓑto go to the orchestra concert?
Emma: Yes. I'm going to watch the orchestra concert.
Anthony: Then, you should get the seats ⓒon the second floor. You can hear the beautiful sounds of various musical instruments ⓓbetter.
Emma: Oh, do you find it better ⓔto hear the performance from the second floor?
Anthony: Yes. I find it better than from other seats.

12 위 대화의 밑줄 친 ⓐ~ⓔ 중 어법상 틀린 것을 찾아 바르게 고치시오.

➡ ______________________

13 위 대화의 내용과 일치하지 않는 것은?

① Emma는 예술 회관에서 하는 오케스트라 공연에 가려고 한다.
② Emma는 좌석을 고르는 데 있어 Anthony에게 도움을 요청했다.
③ Anthony는 2층 좌석을 얻는 것을 추천한다.
④ Anthony는 2층 좌석은 다양한 악기들의 아름다운 소리를 더 잘 들을 수 있기 때문에 추천한다.
⑤ Anthony는 2층에서 공연을 더 잘 볼 수 있었다.

Grammar

14 다음 문장 중에서 어법상 어색한 문장을 모두 고르시오.

① Falling leaves are under the trees.
② They may feel discouraged to see the celebrities enjoying special treatments.
③ This is the newest smartphone make in Korea.
④ Mina sent me the photos taken last Saturday.
⑤ There were some girls swimming in the pool.

15 다음 빈칸에 들어갈 말로 알맞은 것은?

Does Amy think ______________ to the top of the mountain?

① impossible to get
② to get impossible
③ it to get impossible
④ impossible it to get
⑤ it impossible to get

16 다음 그림을 참고하여, 괄호 안에 주어진 어휘를 이용하여 빈칸에 알맞게 쓰시오.

Becky thought __________ easy __________ __________ the clothes. (sew)

17 다음 두 문장의 의미가 같도록 빈칸에 알맞은 말을 쓰시오.

(1) I knew the students satisfied with the game result.
= I knew the students ___________ satisfied with the game result.

(2) It started with a girl playing the cello made out of a shiny oil tank.
= It started with a girl ___________ playing the cello ___________ made out of a shiny oil tank.

18 밑줄 친 it의 쓰임이 나머지 넷과 다른 것은?

① Brian considered it exciting to play the main character.
② I found it was not easy to drive through the narrow streets.
③ The audience thought it fun to see their friends singing and dancing.
④ I found it helpful to listen to music when I was in the hospital.
⑤ Some students think it more relaxing to watch movies.

19 다음 ⓐ~ⓕ 중 어법상 옳은 것을 모두 고르시오.

ⓐ I consider it wonderful to have so many talented students in my school.
ⓑ The picture stealing from the museum was found.
ⓒ Be quiet not to awake the sleeping baby.
ⓓ There were many dogs run here and there in the field.
ⓔ Does John find it interesting to read books?
ⓕ My mom made to exercise every Sunday a rule.

➡ ___________

Reading

[20~21] 다음 글을 읽고 물음에 답하시오.

Before the concert, I thought that the instruments might sound strange. After a few minutes, a group of young people began to walk on the stage. The first thing I noticed was their instruments: a cello made out of a shiny oil tank, a violin made with forks, and a flute made with a water pipe and buttons. The concert began with a girl playing Bach's *Cello Suite No. 1* on her shiny cello. ⓐI was shocked by the deep sound. I was so into the music that I forgot that ⓑthey were playing with instruments made from recycled materials.

20 위 글의 밑줄 친 ⓐ를 능동태로 고치시오.

➡ ___________

21 위 글의 밑줄 친 ⓑthey가 가리키는 것을 본문에서 찾아 쓰시오.

➡ ___________

[22~23] 다음 글을 읽고 물음에 답하시오.

After the concert, I was eager to write a story about the orchestra. I met Favio Chávez, the conductor, and asked him about the orchestra.

Lucy White: Why did you start The Junk Orchestra?

Favio Chávez: When I went to a small town called Cateura in Paraguay to work on a recycling program in ⓐ2005, I saw children living in a town that was mostly filled with garbage. I wanted to add something positive to their lives, so I decided to share my love of music with them.

22 위 글의 밑줄 친 ⓐ2005를 영어로 읽는 법을 쓰시오.

➡ ______________________

23 According to the passage, which is NOT true?

① After the concert, the writer was eager to write a story about the orchestra.
② After the concert, the writer met Favio Chávez, the conductor.
③ Favio Chávez was living in a town that was mostly filled with garbage.
④ Favio Chávez wanted to add something positive to the children's lives.
⑤ Favio Chávez made a decision to share his love of music with the children.

[24~26] 다음 글을 읽고 물음에 답하시오.

Lucy White: Why did you use garbage to make instruments?
Favio Chávez: One person's garbage is another person's treasure. Nicolás Gómez, a local garbage picker helped me a lot. He made it possible for children to play music by making instruments out of garbage. The wonderful thing about these instruments was that the children didn't have to worry about spending a lot of money on them.
Lucy White: What do you want people to learn through your music?
Favio Chávez: I want people to know that ⓐ가치 없는 것도 영감을 주는 음악을 만들어 낼 수 있다.

24 What was the wonderful thing about the instruments made out of garbage? Answer in English beginning with "It".

➡ ______________________
____

25 위 글의 주제로 알맞은 것을 고르시오.

① the reason a local garbage picker helped Favio Chávez a lot.
② how to play music by making instruments out of garbage
③ the wonderful thing about the instruments made out of garbage
④ the worry about spending much money on the instruments
⑤ the reason and the goal to make instruments using garbage

26 위 글의 밑줄 친 ⓐ의 우리말에 맞게 주어진 어휘를 알맞게 배열하시오.

worthless / music / even / inspiring / make / something / can

➡ ______________________
____

[27~28] 다음 글을 읽고 물음에 답하시오.

I want to recommend a song to those who need to ___ⓐ___. The title of the song is "*Happy*," and the singer is Allan Hamilton. This song is about looking on the bright side of life and staying happy. I want to recommend this song because I found it helpful to listen to it when I was in the hospital. ⓑIt cheered up me and gave me hope. <the writer: a girl>

27 위 글의 빈칸 ⓐ에 cheer up을 알맞은 형태로 쓰시오.

➡ ______________________

28 위 글의 밑줄 친 ⓑ에서 어법상 틀린 부분을 찾아 고치시오.

➡ ______________________

단원별 예상문제

[01~03] 다음 대화를 읽고 물음에 답하시오.

Emma: Hey, Anthony. Can you help me with something?
Anthony: Sure, what's up?
Emma: I'm going to a concert at the Arts Center, but I don't know which seat I should choose.
Anthony: Are you planning to go to the orchestra concert?
Emma: Yes. I'm going to watch the orchestra concert.
Anthony: Then, you should get the seats on the second floor. You can hear the beautiful sounds of various musical instruments better.
Emma: Oh, (A)<u>2층에서 공연을 듣는 것이 더 낫다는 거니?</u>
Anthony: Yes. I find it better than from other seats.

출제율 90%

01 위 대화의 밑줄 친 (A)의 우리말을 〈보기〉에 주어진 어구를 배열하여 영작하시오.

보기

from / it / to / you / do / find / the second / the performance / hear / floor / better

➡ ______________________________

____

출제율 100%

02 위 대화를 읽고 대답할 수 <u>없는</u> 것은?

① Where is Emma planning to go?
② Where is the orchestra concert held?
③ Which seat does Anthony recommend?
④ Where does Anthony think Emma can hear the beautiful sounds better?
⑤ With whom is Emma going to watch the orchestra concert?

출제율 90%

03 위 대화의 내용과 일치하도록 Emma의 일기를 완성하시오.

I had a plan to watch the orchestra concert. But I was confused which (A)__________ I should choose. I asked Anthony to help me to select the seat. Anthony recommended (B)________________, because he found it better to (C)______________________________. He said I could hear (D)______________________________ better. It was very helpful information for me. I'm looking forward to watching the concert soon.

[04~06] 다음 대화를 읽고 물음에 답하시오.

Anna: Hey, Jake. I saw you won the swimming competition yesterday. Congratulations!
Jake: Thanks, Anna.
Anna: You always seem to listen to music before you compete. Do you find it helpful to listen to music before you swim?
Jake: Yes, it keeps me awake and it helps me focus.

출제율 90%

04 What competition did Jake win yesterday?

➡ ______________________________

출제율 95%

05 What does Jake always do before he competes?

➡ ______________________________

출제율 95%

06 How is it helpful for Jake to listen to music before he competes?

➡ ______________________

[07~09] 다음 글을 읽고 물음에 답하시오.

W: (A)Are you planning to learn a musical instrument? (plan, do) I'd like to recommend the *kalimba*, a small African musical instrument. The sound it makes is similar to that of a music box. Playing the *kalimba* is very easy. You can learn to use your (B)__________ to play beautiful music in just one lesson!

출제율 95%

07 위 글의 밑줄 친 (A)와 의도가 같도록 괄호 안에 주어진 단어를 사용하여 다시 쓰시오.

➡ ______________________

출제율 90%

08 위 글의 빈칸 (B)에 '엄지손톱'을 나타내는 말을 두 단어로 쓰시오.

➡ ______________________

출제율 100%

09 위 글의 내용과 일치하지 않는 것은?

① 여자는 칼림바를 배워 볼 것을 추천하고 있다.
② 칼림바는 아프리카의 작은 악기이다.
③ 악기가 내는 소리는 음악 상자의 소리와 비슷하다.
④ 엄지손톱을 사용해 아름다운 음악을 연주할 수 있다.
⑤ 칼림바를 배우는 데 약 한 달 정도 걸린다.

출제율 95%

10 다음 대화가 자연스럽게 이어지도록 순서대로 배열하시오.

(A) You always seem to listen to music before you compete. Do you find it helpful to listen to music before you swim?
(B) Yes, it keeps me awake and it helps me focus.
(C) Hey, Jake. I saw you won the swimming competition yesterday. Congratulations!
(D) Thanks, Anna.

➡ ______________________

출제율 95%

11 다음 중 어법상 적절한 문장은?

① The book borrowing from the library is heavy.
② These talenting young people deliver great music and bring serious environmental problems to our attention.
③ Do you like the cheese made from the milk from the farm?
④ She made it possible of us to sing in the talent show.
⑤ She thinks to sleep more relaxing.

출제율 95%

12 괄호 안에 주어진 말을 이용해 밑줄 친 명사를 수식하는 문장으로 다시 쓰시오.

(1) Can you tell me a name? (begin with M)
➡ ______________________

(2) There was a small boy. (call "Mr. Big" in my school)
➡ ______________________
____

(3) The dog is Mike's. (lie under the table)
➡ ______________________

출제율 90%

13 다음 문장에서 밑줄 친 it이 가리키는 것을 찾아 쓰시오.

(1) Mr. Thompson considers it important to have breakfast every day.

➡ ________________

(2) Molly found it difficult to write lyrics.

➡ ________________

(3) Do you think it is important to exercise every day?

➡ ________________

출제율 95%

14 다음 우리말을 괄호 안에 주어진 어휘를 이용하여 영작하시오.

(1) 드럼을 치고 있는 그 남자는 유명한 음악가이다. (beat, drums, famous musician)

➡ ________________

(2) 나는 Cateura라고 불리는 작은 마을에 갔다. (call)

➡ ________________

(3) 우리 엄마는 내가 바이올린을 연주할 수 있도록 했다. (my mom, made, possible, to)

➡ ________________

(4) 그 소녀는 외국어를 배우는 것이 어렵다고 생각한다. (think, hard, foreign languages, to)

➡ ________________

[15~16] 다음 글을 읽고 물음에 답하시오.

"The world sends us garbage, we send back music." ⓐThis was written on the back of a concert ticket I was given. The musical group was called "The Junk Orchestra." They played instruments made entirely out of garbage. ⓑ I could not imagine what kind of sound these instruments would make, as I was eager to find out.

출제율 90%

15 위 글의 밑줄 친 ⓐThis가 가리키는 것을 본문에서 찾아 쓰시오.

➡ ________________

출제율 100%

16 위 글의 밑줄 친 ⓑ에서 흐름상 어색한 부분을 찾아 고치시오.

➡ ________________

[17~18] 다음 글을 읽고 물음에 답하시오.

After the concert, I was eager to write a story about the orchestra. I met Favio Chávez, the conductor, and asked him about the orchestra.

Lucy White: Why did you start The Junk Orchestra?

Favio Chávez: When I went to a small town called Cateura in Paraguay to work on a recycling program in 2005, I saw children living in a town that was mostly filled ⓐ______ garbage. I wanted to add something positive to their lives, so I decided to share my love of music ⓑ______ them.

출제율 95%

17 위 글의 빈칸 ⓐ와 ⓑ에 공통으로 들어갈 알맞은 전치사를 쓰시오.

➡ ________________

출제율 95%

18 Why did Favio Chávez go to a small town called Cateura in Paraguay in 2005? Fill in the blanks with suitable words.

He went there in order that he might work on ________ ________ ________.

[19~21] 다음 글을 읽고 물음에 답하시오.

Lucy White: ⓐ ______________________

Favio Chávez: One person's garbage is another person's treasure. Nicolás Gómez, a local garbage picker helped me a lot. He made it possible for children to play music by making instruments out of garbage. The wonderful thing about these instruments was that the children didn't have to worry about spending a lot of money on them.

Lucy White: What do you want people to learn through your music?

Favio Chávez: I want people to know that even something ⓑworthless can make inspiring music.

출제율 100%

19 위 글의 빈칸 ⓐ에 들어갈 알맞은 질문을 고르시오.

① How do you make people play music?
② Why did Nicolás Gómez help you?
③ How did Nicolás Gómez make instruments out of garbage?
④ Why did you use garbage to make instruments?
⑤ Why did you start The Junk Orchestra?

출제율 90%

20 위 글의 밑줄 친 ⓑworthless와 바꿔 쓸 수 있는 말을 고르시오.

① invaluable ② valueless
③ worthwhile ④ valuable
⑤ priceless

출제율 95%

21 According to the passage, which is NOT true?

① Favio Chávez thinks that one person's garbage is another person's treasure.
② Nicolás Gómez was a local garbage picker.
③ Favio Chávez helped Nicolás Gómez a lot.
④ Nicolás Gómez made instruments out of garbage.
⑤ The children didn't have to worry about spending much money on the instruments made out of garbage.

[22~23] 다음 글을 읽고 물음에 답하시오.

After interviewing Chávez, I realized that it really doesn't matter what instrument you play with ⓐ사람들이 악기를 연주하는 데 마음을 쏟아 붓는 한. The children of Cateura showed me that an orchestra is formed by people, not by instruments.

출제율 90%

22 위 글의 밑줄 친 ⓐ의 우리말에 맞게 주어진 어휘를 이용하여 10 단어로 영작하시오.

as long as, put, into, you

➡ ______________________

출제율 95%

23 다음 문장에서 위 글의 내용과 다른 부분을 찾아서 고치시오.

What instrument you play with is really of importance.

➡ ______________________

서술형 실전문제

[01~03] 다음 대화를 읽고 물음에 답하시오.

Sujin: Hi, Jason. Great to see you again. I've heard the new rap song, *Young and Wild*, that you recorded. It's really cool.
Jason: Oh, thanks.
Sujin: I really like your songs. Do you find it easy to write them?
Sujin: Well, it was hard in the beginning, but now it's getting easier. I draw on my experiences and keep a journal.
Sujin: Wow! As they say, "No pain, no gain." Best of luck with your new song!
Jason: Thank you.

01 What does Sujin think about the new rap song that Jason recorded?

➡ ____________________

02 What does Jason do to write songs?

➡ ____________________

____

03 What proverb does Sujin use to describe Jason's effort?

➡ ____________________

04 다음 문장에서 어법상 어색한 것을 바르게 고쳐 다시 쓰시오.

(1) Einstein considered to solve math problems fun.

➡ ____________________

(2) We found enjoyable to sing the song writing by children.

➡ ____________________

____

(3) The woman made a cake is my mother.

➡ ____________________

(4) We studied at desks making out of trees from the nearby mountain.

➡ ____________________

____

05 다음 문장에서 틀린 것을 고쳐 다시 쓰시오.

(1) The played the piano girl on the stage is my sister.

➡ ____________________

____

(2) The box carrying into the building is very big.

➡ ____________________

(3) I found that possible to inspire people by music played with recycled instruments.

➡ ____________________

____

(4) Rebecca thought to sing in front of others difficult even though she is a great singer.

➡ ____________________

____

[06~08] 다음 글을 읽고 물음에 답하시오.

Before the concert, I thought that the instruments might sound strange. After a few minutes, a group of young people began to walk on the stage. The first thing I noticed was their instruments: a cello made out of a shiny oil tank, a violin made with forks, and a flute made with a water pipe and buttons. The concert began with a girl playing Bach's *Cello Suite No. 1* on her shiny cello. I was shocked by the deep sound. ⓐI was so into the music that I forgot that they were playing with instruments made from recycled materials.

06 위 글의 밑줄 친 ⓐ를 다음과 같이 바꿔 쓸 때 빈칸에 들어갈 알맞은 단어를 쓰시오.

➡ I was so ________ in the music

07 What was the violin made with? Answer in English in a full sentence. (5 words)

➡ ________________________________

08 본문의 내용과 일치하도록 다음 빈칸 (A)와 (B)에 알맞은 단어를 쓰시오.

Before the concert, the writer thought that the sound of the instruments might be (A)________, but when the concert began with a girl playing Bach's *Cello Suite No. 1* on her shiny cello, the writer was shocked by the (B)________ ________.

[09~11] 다음 글을 읽고 물음에 답하시오.

Lucy White: Why did you use garbage to make instruments?

Favio Chávez: ⓐ한 사람의 쓰레기는 다른 사람의 보물입니다. Nicolás Gómez, a local garbage picker helped me a lot. He made it possible for children to play music by making instruments out of garbage. The wonderful thing about these instruments was that the children didn't have to worry about spending a lot of money on ⓑthem.

Lucy White: What do you want people to learn through your music?

Favio Chávez: I want people to know that even something worthless can make inspiring music.

09 위 글의 밑줄 친 ⓐ의 우리말에 맞게 주어진 어휘를 이용하여 7 단어로 영작하시오.

one person's, another, treasure

➡ ________________________________

____

10 위 글의 밑줄 친 ⓑthem이 가리키는 것을 본문에서 찾아 쓰시오.

➡ ________________________

11 본문의 내용과 일치하도록 다음 빈칸 (A)와 (B)에 알맞은 단어를 쓰시오.

Through his music, Favio Chávez wants people to know that even something (A)________ can make (B)________ music.

창의사고력 서술형 문제

01 다음 대화의 내용과 일치하도록 빈칸을 완성하시오.

Sujin: Hi, Jason. Great to see you again. I've heard the new rap song, *Young and Wild*, that you recorded. It's really cool.
Jason: Oh, thanks.
Sujin: I really like your songs. Do you find it easy to write them?
Jason: Well, it was hard in the beginning, but now it's getting easier. I draw on my experiences and keep a journal.
Sujin: Wow! As they say, "No pain, no gain." Best of luck with your new song!
Jason: Thank you.

A rapper, Jason, released a new song, *Young and Wild*. His songs were cool. He said that writing songs was (A)__________ in the beginning, but it was getting (B)__________. To write songs, he draws on his (C)__________ and (D)_______________. I wished him my best luck.

02 다음 내용을 바탕으로 상황에 어울리는 노래를 찾아 추천하는 글을 쓰시오.

Q1 To whom do you want to recommend a song?
A1 I want to recommend a song to those who need to be cheered up.
Q2 What is the title of the song, and who is the singer?
A2 The title of the song is "*Happy*," and the singer is Allan Hamilton.
Q3 What is the song about?
A3 It is about looking on the bright side of life and staying happy.
Q4 Why do you want to recommend the song?
A4 I found it helpful to listen to it when I was in the hospital. It cheered me up and gave me hope.

I want to recommend a song to those who need to (A)_______________. The title of the song is "*Happy*," and the singer is (B)_______________. This song is about looking on the (C)_______________ of life and staying happy. I want to recommend this song because I found it helpful to listen to it when I was (D)_______________. It cheered me up and (E)_______________.

단원별 모의고사

01 다음 영영풀이가 가리키는 고르시오.

things that are no longer useful and that have been thrown out

① tank ② thumb
③ treasure ④ nail
⑤ garbage

02 다음 문장에 공통으로 들어갈 말을 고르시오.

- Stop biting your ________s.
- I need to drive a ________ into a board.
- The cat scratched me with its ________s.

① nail ② pain
③ title ④ treasure
⑤ finger

03 다음 우리말에 맞게 빈칸에 알맞은 말을 쓰시오.

(1) 우리는 환경과 조화를 이루며 살아야 할 필요가 있다.
➡ We need to live ________ ________ ________ our environment.

(2) 엄마는 처음에는 요리를 잘 못하셨다.
➡ My mom wasn't good at cooking ________ ________ ________.

(3) 나는 왜 그녀가 나에게 나의 선물을 돌려보냈는지 모르겠다.
➡ I don't know why she ________ ________ my present to me.

(4) 나는 영어로 일기를 쓰려고 노력한다.
➡ I try to ________ ________ in English.

04 다음 우리말을 주어진 단어를 이용하여 영작하시오.

(1) 그의 방은 책들과 서류들로 가득하다. (filled) (8 words)
➡ ________________________

(2) 내 가방이 네 것과 비슷하지만 내 것이 더 크다. (similar) (10 words)
➡ ________________________

[05~06] 다음 대화를 읽고 물음에 답하시오.

> **Minho:** Hi, Sally. Where are you off to?
> **Sally:** I'm going to the music room. I have choir practice.
> **Minho:** Oh, yeah. I forgot that you've joined the choir. Do you find it interesting to sing in the choir?
> **Sally:** Yeah, it's great to sing in harmony with others.

05 Why is Sally going to the music room?

➡ ________________________

06 What does Sally think about singing in the choir?

➡ ________________________
____

[07~08] 다음 대화를 읽고 물음에 답하시오.

> **Megan:** Hey, Tommy. When is the last day to sign up for the talent show?
> **Tommy:** This Friday. (A)____________, Megan?
> **Megan:** Yeah, I'm going to perform with a couple of people.
> **Tommy:** How cool! What are you going to do?
> **Megan:** We will play K-pop music with the violin and cello.

07 위 대화의 빈칸 (A)에 들어갈 말로 나머지와 의도가 다른 것은?

① Are you going to sign up for it
② Do you have a plan to sign up for it
③ Do you intend to sign up for it
④ Are you planning to sign up for it
⑤ Are you aware of signing up for it

08 위 대화의 내용과 일치하지 않는 것은?

① 장기 자랑 등록 마감은 이번 주 금요일이다.
② Megan은 장기 자랑에 등록할 계획이다.
③ Megan은 몇 사람과 함께 공연을 할 것이다.
④ Megan은 케이팝 음악을 연주할 계획이다.
⑤ Megan은 바이올린과 첼로로 연주되는 케이팝 공연을 관람할 것이다.

09 다음 주어진 문장이 자연스럽게 이어지도록 순서대로 배열하시오.

Sujin: Hi, Jason. Great to see you again. I've heard the new rap song, *Young and Wild*, that you recorded. It's really cool.
(A) Well, it was hard in the beginning, but now it's getting easier. I draw on my experiences and keep a journal.
(B) I really like your songs. Do you find it easy to write them?
(C) Wow! As they say, "No pain, no gain." Best of luck with your new song!
(D) Oh, thanks.

➡ ____________________

[10~11] 다음 대화를 읽고 물음에 답하시오.

Sue: Hello, I'd like to sign up for a drum class.
Mike: Okay. Are you planning to take the class during the week or during the weekend?
Sue: I'm planning to take a weekday class. When do you offer them?
Mike: There is a class on Tuesday and another one on Thursday. Both classes start at 6 o'clock.
Sue: Great. I'd like to sign up for the Tuesday class.

10 What kind of music class is Sue planning to sign up for?

➡ ____________________

11 What day and time is Sue going to take the class?

➡ ____________________

12 다음 짝지어진 대화가 어색한 것은?

① A: Are you planning to go to the K-pop concert Saturday afternoon?
B: No, I'm not. I'm thinking of watching the hip-hop dance competition.
② A: Are you going to enter the singing contest on Saturday morning?
B: Yes, I am.
③ A: Do you have a plan to hear an African dance Sunday afternoon?
B: I think you will enter the singing contest.
④ A: Are you planning to take the one-day cooking class?
B: Yes, I am. I'm looking forward to it.
⑤ A: What are you planning to do this Sunday?
B: I'm planning to have dinner with my grandmother.

13 다음 문장에서 밑줄 친 it이 가리키는 것을 찾아 쓰시오.

(1) Would you find it easy to play the guitar if you had the chance to play it?

➡ ____________________

(2) The weather made it impossible for everybody to come.

➡ ____________________

(3) It is helpful to clarify the objectives of the listening task.

➡ ____________________

14 다음 두 문장을 한 문장으로 바꿔 썼을 때 가장 적절한 것은?

• I received a letter. • The letter was written by the student.

① I wrote a letter received by the student.
② I wrote a letter receiving by the student.
③ I received a letter writing by the student.
④ I received a letter write by the student.
⑤ I received a letter written by the student.

15 다음 주어진 단어의 형태를 알맞게 바꿔 문장을 완성하시오.

(1) My parents are drinking wine ________ from grapes we picked last year. (make)

(2) The farmer ________ cheese is my uncle. (make)

16 다음 문장에서 어법상 어색한 것을 바르게 고쳐 다시 쓰시오.

(1) Sally finds that bored to sing in the choir.

➡ ____________________

(2) She thinks to make good friends a key factor to success.

➡ ____________________

____

(3) He made possible for children playing music by making instruments out of garbage.

➡ ____________________

____

(4) The singer wore a T-shirt which designed by an artist.

➡ ____________________

____

____

(5) The man is taking pictures of people posed in front of the monuments.

➡ ____________________

____

17 다음 빈칸에 들어갈 말이 적절하게 짝지어진 것을 고르시오.

Look at the woman ________ on the stage that was _______ with flowers.

① stand – cover
② stood – covering
③ stood – covered
④ standing – covering
⑤ standing – covered

[18~19] 다음 글을 읽고 물음에 답하시오.

Before the concert, I thought that the instruments might sound strange. After a few minutes, a group of young people began to walk on the stage. The first thing I noticed was their instruments: a cello made out of a shiny oil tank, a violin made with forks, and a flute made with a water pipe and buttons. The concert began with a girl playing Bach's *Cello Suite No. 1* on her shiny cello. I was shocked by the deep sound. ⓐI was so into the music that I forgot that they were playing with instruments making from recycled materials.

18 What was the flute made with? Answer in English in a full sentence. (9 words)

➡ ______________________________

19 위 글의 밑줄 친 ⓐ에서 어법상 틀린 부분을 찾아 고치시오.

➡ ______________________________

[20~21] 다음 글을 읽고 물음에 답하시오.

The Junk Orchestra
The world sends us garbage, we send back music.

Comments

Annie: (23 seconds ago) So ⓐmoving to see how music can change lives. The power of music is endless!

Thomas: (1 minute ago) After the concert, I found it possible to inspire people by music played with recycled instruments.

Kate: (5 days ago) ⓑNot only do these talented young people deliver great music, but they also bring serious environmental problems to our attention.

20 위 글의 밑줄 친 ⓐmoving과 같은 의미로 쓰인 것을 고르시오.

① Ann is moving her chair to the corner.
② Look at the fast-moving water.
③ Shoot at the moving target.
④ He paid the moving expenses.
⑤ She cried to hear a moving story.

21 위 글의 밑줄 친 ⓑ를 as well as를 사용하여 고칠 때, 빈칸에 들어갈 알맞은 말을 쓰시오.

➡ These talented young people ____________ ______________________________, as well as ____________________.

[22~23] 다음 글을 읽고 물음에 답하시오.

After the concert, ⓐI was eager to write a story about the orchestra. I met Favio Chávez, the conductor, and asked him about the orchestra.

Lucy White: Why did you start The Junk Orchestra?

Favio Chávez: When I went to a small town called Cateura in Paraguay to work on a recycling program in 2005, ⓑ나는 대부분이 쓰레기로 가득 차 있는 마을에 살고 있는 어린이들을 보았습니다. I wanted to add something positive to their lives, so I decided to share my love of music with them.

22 위 글의 밑줄 친 ⓐ를 다음과 같이 바꿔 쓸 때 빈칸에 들어갈 알맞은 말을 쓰시오.

➡ I was eager for ________ a story about the orchestra.

23 위 글의 밑줄 친 ⓑ의 우리말에 맞게 주어진 어휘를 이용하여 13 단어로 영작하시오.

a town, that, mostly, with, garbage

➡ ________________________________
____

[24~25] 다음 글을 읽고 물음에 답하시오.

Lucy White: Why did you use garbage ⓐto make instruments?
Favio Chávez: One person's garbage is another person's treasure. Nicolás Gómez, a local garbage picker helped me a lot. ⓑHe made it possible for children to play music by making instruments out of garbage. The wonderful thing about these instruments was that the children didn't have to worry about spending a lot of money on them.

24 아래 〈보기〉에서 위 글의 밑줄 친 ⓐto make와 to부정사의 용법이 다른 것의 개수를 고르시오.

보기
① It is difficult to make instruments.
② What did you use to make instruments?
③ He had no money to make instruments with.
④ He promised me to make instruments.
⑤ She had the talent to make instruments.

① 1개 ② 2개 ③ 3개 ④ 4개 ⑤ 5개

25 위 글의 밑줄 친 ⓑ를 다음과 같이 바꿔 쓸 때 빈칸에 알맞은 말을 쓰시오.

➡ Thanks ________ his help, children ________ play music by making instruments out of garbage.

[26~27] 다음 글을 읽고 물음에 답하시오.

The Junk Orchestra
The world sends us garbage, we send back music.
About the concert
– The young people played instruments ①made out of garbage.
– It started with a girl ②played the cello ③made out of a shiny oil tank.
– I was ④shocked by the deep sound.
The Interview with Mr. Chávez
– He went to Cateura in Paraguay to work on a recycling program.
– He decided to share his love of music with the children.
– A local garbage picker helped him.
⇒ An orchestra is ⑤formed by people, not by instruments.

26 위 글의 밑줄 친 ①~⑤ 중 어법상 틀린 것을 찾아 고치시오.

➡ ________________________________

27 Which question CANNOT be answered after reading the passage?

① What was the cello at the concert made of?
② How did the instrument sound?
③ Why did Mr. Chávez go to Cateura in Paraguay?
④ What did Mr. Chávez decide to do?
⑤ What was the name of the local garbage picker?

MEMO

Middle School 3-1

학교시험 완벽 대비

1학기 전과정

적중100 plus

영어 기출문제집

영어 중3

비상 | 김진완

Best Collection

내용문의 중등영어발전소 적중100 편집부 TEL 070-7707-0457

INSIGHT
on the textbook

교과서 파헤치기

영어 기출 문제집

적중100 plus
1학기 전과정

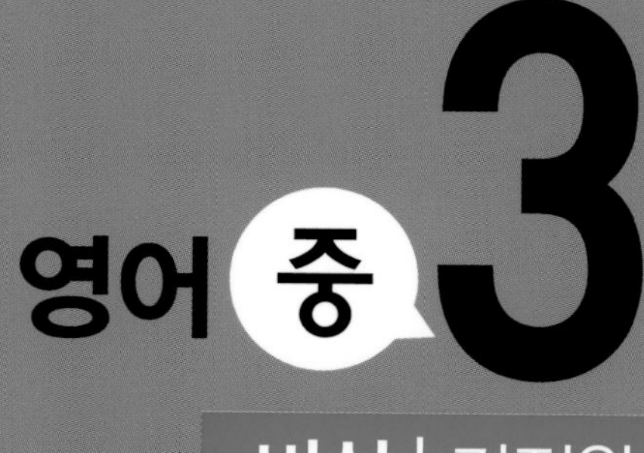

비상 | 김진완

INSIGHT on the textbook

교과서 파헤치기

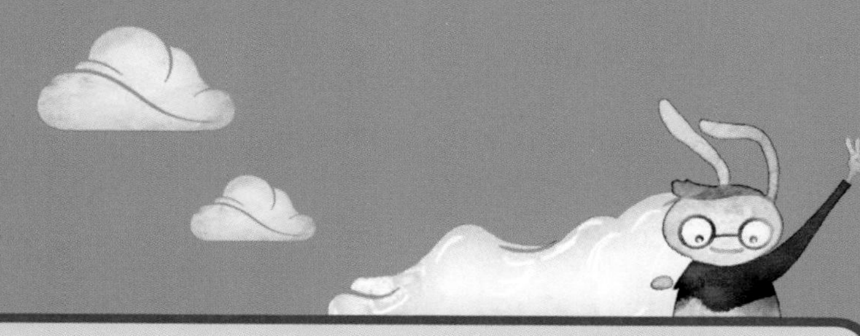

단어 Test

Step1

※ 다음 영어를 우리말로 쓰시오.

01 prevent ______________
02 demand ______________
03 detail ______________
04 argument ______________
05 careless ______________
06 concentrate ______________
07 actually ______________
08 direct ______________
09 uncomfortable ______________
10 effectively ______________
11 argue ______________
12 express ______________
13 prepare ______________
14 hide ______________
15 solve ______________
16 mad ______________
17 mean ______________
18 consider ______________
19 probably ______________
20 request ______________
21 disappointed ______________
22 reason ______________
23 relationship ______________
24 simply ______________
25 trouble ______________
26 instead ______________
27 long face ______________
28 upset ______________
29 somewhere ______________
30 helpful ______________
31 pick ______________
32 seem ______________
33 focus ______________
34 loudly ______________
35 work out ______________
36 cut ~ off ______________
37 keep ~ in mind ______________
38 be ready to 동사원형 ______________
39 get cold feet ______________
40 free from ______________
41 be upset about ~ ______________
42 let the cat out of the bag ______________
43 point the finger at ______________

단어 Test

Step2

※ 다음 우리말을 영어로 쓰시오.

01 주장, 논쟁 ______________

02 부주의한, 조심성 없는 ______________

03 딱 부러지는, 단도직입적인 ______________

04 어딘가에 ______________

05 아마도 ______________

06 집중하다 ______________

07 도움이 되는, 유용한 ______________

08 화난, 기분 나쁜 ______________

09 숨기다, 감추다 ______________

10 그 대신에 ______________

11 말다툼하다, 언쟁하다 ______________

12 불편한 ______________

13 시험 ______________

14 못된, 심술궂은 ______________

15 배려하다, 고려하다 ______________

16 실망한, 낙담한 ______________

17 해결하다 ______________

18 효과적으로 ______________

19 우울한 얼굴 ______________

20 선택하다, 고르다 ______________

21 준비하다 ______________

22 단순히 ______________

23 사실은 ______________

24 막다, 예방하다 ______________

25 요구 ______________

26 요청 ______________

27 구체적 내용, 자세한 내용 ______________

28 이유 ______________

29 관계 ______________

30 두려워하는, 겁먹은 ______________

31 표현하다, 나타내다 ______________

32 감정, 느낌 ______________

33 (~처럼) 보이다, ~인 듯하다 ______________

34 고민, 문제 ______________

35 ~에게 자꾸 이래라저래라 하다 ______________

36 요구하다 ______________

37 먼저, 무엇보다도 ______________

38 ~할 준비가 되다 ______________

39 ~을 명심하다 ______________

40 정시에, 제때에 ______________

41 ~의 도중에, ~의 중간에 ______________

42 결국 ~하게 되다 ______________

43 ~을 중단시키다, ~을 잘라내다 ______________

단어 Test

Step3

※ 다음 영영풀이에 알맞은 단어를 <보기>에서 골라 쓴 후, 우리말 뜻을 쓰시오.

1 __________: cruel or not kind: __________

2 __________: frightened, or worried: ____________

3 __________: feeling sad or upset: ____________

4 __________: useful, or providing help: ____________

5 __________: an angry disagreement between people: __________

6 __________: very sad, worried, or angry about something: ____________

7 __________: to give all your attention to the thing you are doing: __________

8 __________: a sad, disappointed, or serious expression on someone's face: __________

9 __________: to think about someone's feelings or reactions: ____________

10 __________: to put something in a place so that no one can find or see it: __________

11 __________: to find a solution to something that is causing difficulties: __________

12 __________: to stop something from happening or existing: __________

13 __________: to tell someone about a feeling, opinion, or goal by speaking or writing about it: ____________

14 __________: one of many small facts or pieces of information relating to a situation: ______________

15 __________: unhappy because something that you hoped for or expected did not happen or because someone or something was not as good as you expected: __________

16 __________: a fact, situation, or intention that explains why something happened, why someone did something, or why something is true: __________

보기

disappointed	concentrate	hide	helpful
detail	long face	express	scared
reason	upset	consider	unhappy
prevent	argument	solve	mean

대화문 Test

Step1

※ 다음 우리말과 일치하도록 빈칸에 알맞은 말을 쓰시오.

Listen & Talk 1 Get Ready

A: ________ do you ________ so ________?

B: I'm upset ________ Roy. He always ________ me.

A: Don't ________ ________ so ________.

A: 너는 왜 침울해 보이니?
B: 나는 Roy한테 화가 나. 그는 항상 나를 따라 해.
A: 너무 속상해 하지 마.

Listen & Talk 1 A-1

M: Sally, ________ ________ you don't talk much ________ Anna ________ ________?

W: Well, I'm ________ ________ ________ ________ we had.

M: ________ are you ________?

W: She kept ________ ________ ________ ________ the middle of my sentences, so I got ________. We argued and I ________ ________ ________ her.

M: Oh, I'm ________ ________ ________ that.

M: Sally야, 요즘에 왜 Anna와 별로 대화를 하지 않니?
W: 음, 나는 우리가 한 논쟁 때문에 화가 나.
M: 왜 화가 난 거야?
W: 그녀가 계속해서 내가 말을 하고 있는 도중에 끊어서 화가 났어. 우리는 논쟁을 했고, 나는 그녀와 이야기를 하지 않았어.
M: 오, 그거 유감이구나.

Listen & Talk 1 A-2

W: ________ is your science homework ________?

M: Not good. ________ ________ ________ my science group.

W: What's ________?

M: The group members only speak and never listen. ________ ________ ________ ________ we can finish the homework ________ ________.

W: That's ________ ________.

W: 너의 과학 숙제는 어떻게 되어 가고 있니?
M: 좋지 않아. 나는 나의 과학 그룹에 화가 나.
W: 뭐가 문제인데?
M: 그룹 구성원들이 말만 하고 전혀 듣지 않아. 나는 우리가 숙제를 제시간에 끝낼 수 있을 거라고 생각하지 않아.
W: 그것 참 안 되었구나.

Listen & Talk 1 B

M: ________the ________ ________, Julie?

W: I got ________ ________ my sister yesterday and ________ ________ ________ things to her.

M: Oh, ________ were you ________?

W: I was really tired and I wanted ________ ________. ________ she was ________ ________ ________ ________ ________. I was really ________ about that.

M: 왜 그렇게 우울한 얼굴이니, Julie?
W: 어제 여동생한테 화가 나서 그녀에게 심술궂은 말을 했어.
M: 오, 왜 화가 났니?
W: 정말 피곤해서 자고 싶었어. 하지만 여동생은 전화로 큰 소리로 이야기하고 있었어. 나는 그것에 대해 정말 화가 났어.

M: I see. And you two ________ ________ ________ ________ yet?

W: No, not yet. I want to say I'm sorry ________ I was ________ to her, ________ ________ ________ ________ ________.

M: ________ ________ you write her a note or ________ her a text message?

W: Hmm, that's a good idea. Thanks.

M: 그렇구나. 그리고 너희 둘은 아직 화해하지 않았니?
W: 아니, 아직이야. 내가 여동생에게 심술궂게 굴어서 미안하다고 말하고 싶지만, 방법을 모르겠어.
M: 그녀에게 편지를 쓰거나 문자 메시지를 보내는 게 어때?
W: 음, 좋은 생각이야. 고마워.

Listen & Talk 1 Get Ready

A: Don't ________ ________ ________ ________ ________ ________ ________ about Clara's ________ ________.

B: A cat? I don't have a cat.

A: ________ ________ ________ I meant. ________ her party ________ ________.

A: Clara의 깜짝 파티에 대해 비밀을 누설하지 마.
B: 고양이? 나는 고양이가 없어.
A: 그건 그런 뜻이 아니야. 그녀의 파티를 비밀로 해.

Listen & Talk 2 A-1

W: Mr. Brown, I want to ________ a good ________ ________ English. ________ ________ I do?

M: Well, Sujin, you should ________ in class, ________ ________ ________. I see you often ________ ________ ________ ________ ________ ________.

W: Clouds? I can't ________ ________ ________ from inside the classroom.

M: ________ ________ ________ ________ ________. I ________ you don't ________ in class.

W: Brown 선생님, 저는 영어에서 좋은 점수를 받고 싶어요. 어떻게 해야 하죠?
M: 음, 수진아, 너는 우선 수업에 집중해야 해. 난 네가 종종 공상에 잠겨 있는 것을 본단다.
W: 구름이요? 교실 안에서는 하늘을 볼 수 없어요.
M: 그건 그런 뜻이 아니야. 내 말은 네가 수업에 집중하지 않는다는 거야.

Listen & Talk 2 A-2

W: Did you finally ________ ________ yesterday, Nick?

M: ________, I ________ ________ ________, Mina.

W: That's too bad. How did you ________ ________ ________?

M: No, Mina. That's not ________ I meant. ________ ________ ________ I got ________, so I didn't dive.

W: Nick, 어제 드디어 다이빙하러 갔니?
M: 미나야, 사실 난 겁이 났어.
W: 그거 안 됐구나. 어떻게 감기에 걸렸니?
M: 아니, 미나야. 그건 그런 뜻이 아니야. 내가 겁을 먹어서 다이빙을 안 했다는 뜻이야.

Listen & Talk 2 B

W: I'm so ________ ________ ________ my exams, Jinsu.

M: Yeah, me, too. We have ________ ________ ________ ________.

W: After ________ my exams, I want to ________ ________ ________ trip and just let my ________ ________.

M: You want to change your ________ ________?

W: No, that's not ________ ________ ________. I want to go somewhere and ________ ________ all my ________.

W: 진수야, 나는 시험에 대해 너무 스트레스를 받아.
M: 그래, 나도. 우리는 볼 시험이 두 개 더 있어.
W: 시험을 마친 후, 나는 여행을 가서 느긋하게 쉬고 싶어.
M: 머리 스타일을 바꾸고 싶다고?
W: 아니, 그런 뜻이 아니야. 난 어디 가서 내 모든 고민에서 벗어나고 싶어.

Communication

W: Hey, Jason. You ________ upset. Anything ________?

M: People ________ ________ ________ ________ I'm too ________. I'm ________ about that.

W: Hmm.... I kind of know ________ ________ ________ ________.

M: ________ do you ________?

W: Well, sometimes you ________ ________ ________ ________ ________ your mind too ________.

M: ________ I just ________ ________, then?

W: ________ ________ ________ ________ ________. You can ________ ________ ________ others' ________.

M: I see. I'll ________ that.

W: 안녕, Jason. 화나 보여. 무슨 문제라도 있니?
M: 사람들은 내가 너무 단도직입적이라고 계속 말해. 나는 그것에 대해 화가 나.
W: 흠…. 난 그들이 무슨 이야기를 하는지 어느 정도 알아.
M: 무슨 의미야?
W: 음, 가끔 넌 네 마음에 있는 것을 너무 강하게 말하는 경향이 있어.
M: 그럼, 그냥 조용히 있어야 하니?
W: 내 말은 그게 아니야. 너는 다른 사람의 감정을 고려하도록 노력하면 돼.
M: 알겠어. 그렇게 해 보도록 할게.

대화문 Test

※ 다음 우리말에 맞도록 대화를 영어로 쓰시오.

Listen & Talk 1 Get Ready

A: ________________

B: ________________

A: ________________

A: 너는 왜 침울해 보이니?
B: 나는 Roy한테 화가 나. 그는 항상 나를 따라 해.
A: 너무 속상해 하지 마.

Listen & Talk 1 A-1

M: ________________

W: ________________

M: ________________

W: ________________

____

M: ________________

M: Sally야, 요즘에 왜 Anna와 별로 대화를 하지 않니?
W: 음, 나는 우리가 한 논쟁 때문에 화가 나.
M: 왜 화가 난 거야?
W: 그녀가 계속해서 내가 말을 하고 있는 도중에 끊어서 화가 났어. 우리는 논쟁을 했고, 나는 그녀와 이야기를 하지 않았어.
M: 오, 그거 유감이구나.

Listen & Talk 1 A-2

W: ________________

M: ________________

W: ________________

M: ________________

____

W: ________________

W: 너의 과학 숙제는 어떻게 되어 가고 있니?
M: 좋지 않아. 나는 나의 과학 그룹에 화가 나.
W: 뭐가 문제인데?
M: 그룹 구성원들이 말만 하고 전혀 듣지 않아. 나는 우리가 숙제를 제시간에 끝낼 수 있을 거라고 생각하지 않아.
W: 그것 참 안 되었구나.

Listen & Talk 1 B

M: ________________

W: ________________

M: ________________

W: ________________

____

M: 왜 그렇게 우울한 얼굴이니, Julie?
W: 어제 여동생한테 화가 나서 그녀에게 심술궂은 말을 했어.
M: 오, 왜 화가 났니?
W: 정말 피곤해서 자고 싶었어. 하지만 여동생은 전화로 큰 소리로 이야기하고 있었어. 나는 그것에 대해 정말 화가 났어.

M: ______

W: ______

______

M: ______

W: ______

M: 그렇구나. 그리고 너희 둘은 아직 화해하지 않았니?
W: 아니, 아직이야. 내가 여동생에게 심술궂게 굴어서 미안하다고 말하고 싶지만, 방법을 모르겠어.
M: 그녀에게 편지를 쓰거나 문자 메시지를 보내는 게 어때?
W: 음, 좋은 생각이야. 고마워.

Listen & Talk 1 Get Ready

A: ______

B: ______

A: ______

A: Clara의 깜짝 파티에 대해 비밀을 누설하지 마.
B: 고양이? 나는 고양이가 없어.
A: 그건 그런 뜻이 아니야. 그녀의 파티를 비밀로 해.

Listen & Talk 2 A-1

W: ______

M: ______

______

W: ______

M: ______

W: Brown 선생님, 저는 영어에서 좋은 점수를 받고 싶어요. 어떻게 해야 하죠?
M: 음, 수진아, 너는 우선 수업에 집중해야 해. 난 네가 종종 공상에 잠겨 있는 것을 본단다.
W: 구름이요? 교실 안에서는 하늘을 볼 수 없어요.
M: 그건 그런 뜻이 아니야. 내 말은 네가 수업에 집중하지 않는다는 거야.

Listen & Talk 2 A-2

W: ______________________________

M: ______________________________

W: ______________________________

M: ______________________________

W: Nick, 어제 드디어 다이빙하러 갔니?
M: 미나야, 사실 난 겁이 났어.
W: 그거 안 됐구나. 어떻게 감기에 걸렸니?
M: 아니, 미나야. 그건 그런 뜻이 아니야. 내가 겁을 먹어서 다이빙을 안 했다는 뜻이야.

Listen & Talk 2 B

W: ______________________________

M: ______________________________

W: ______________________________

M: ______________________________

W: ______________________________

____

W: 진수야, 나는 시험에 대해 너무 스트레스를 받아.
M: 그래, 나도. 우리는 볼 시험이 두 개 더 있어.
W: 시험을 마친 후, 나는 여행을 가서 느긋하게 쉬고 싶어.
M: 머리 스타일을 바꾸고 싶다고?
W: 아니, 그런 뜻이 아니야. 난 어디 가서 내 모든 고민에서 벗어나고 싶어.

Communication

W: ______________________________

M: ______________________________

W: ______________________________

M: ______________________________

W: ______________________________

M: ______________________________

W: ______________________________

M: ______________________________

W: 안녕, Jason. 화나 보여. 무슨 문제라도 있니?
M: 사람들은 내가 너무 단도직입적이라고 계속 말해. 나는 그것에 대해 화가 나.
W: 흠…. 난 그들이 무슨 이야기를 하는지 어느 정도 알아.
M: 무슨 의미야?
W: 음, 가끔 넌 네 마음에 있는 것을 너무 강하게 말하는 경향이 있어.
M: 그럼, 그냥 조용히 있어야 하니?
W: 내 말은 그게 아니야. 너는 다른 사람의 감정을 고려하도록 노력하면 돼.
M: 알겠어. 그렇게 해 보도록 할게.

※ 다음 우리말과 일치하도록 빈칸에 알맞은 것을 골라 쓰시오.

1 ________ Your ________ ________
A. Mind B. Speak C. Effectively

2 ________ ________ "All about ________."
A. Teens B. to C. welcome

3 I'm ________ ________.
A. Carter B. Dr.

4 Today, we're going to talk about ________ good communication ________ to ________ ourselves more ________.
A. skills B. using C. effectively D. express

5 ________ start ________ our first ________ about Brian.
A. with B. let's C. clip

6 When he ________ to talk to his brother, he always ________ ________ ________ with his brother.
A. up B. tries C. arguing D. ends

7 Let's ________ ________ the ________ ________ he has this problem.
A. out B. reason C. find D. why

8 **Brian: *You* ________ *my earphones again.* ________ *are you* ________ ________?**
A. careless B. lost C. why D. so

9 Brian is starting a ________ ________ "you" to ________ his ________.
A. feelings B. sentence C. express D. with

10 ________, he should ________ the "________."
A. use B. instead C. I-message

11 Starting with "I" can help him ________ ________ what he feels or thinks ________ ________ point the finger at his brother.
A. on B. than C. rather D. focus

12 **Brian: I'm *really* ________ ________ *my* ________ *earphones are* ________.**
A. lost B. upset C. favorite D. because

13 ________ is ________.
A. Calli B. next

14 She is ________ to talk to her mother, but she is ________ ________ to go to ________.
A. work B. trying C. preparing D. busy

15 Let's ________ ________ ________.
A. look B. a C. have

1 당신의 마음을 효과적으로 말하라
2 '십 대들의 모든 것'에 오신 걸 환영합니다.
3 저는 Carter 박사입니다.
4 오늘 우리는 자신을 더 효과적으로 표현하기 위해 적절한 의사소통 기술을 사용하는 것에 대해 이야기해 보겠습니다.
5 Brian에 대한 첫 번째 동영상으로 시작해 보죠.
6 Brian이 남동생과 이야기하려고 할 때, 그는 결국 동생과 항상 말다툼을 하게 돼요.
7 그에게 이런 문제가 있는 이유를 알아봅시다.
8 Brian: "너 또 내 이어폰 잃어버렸지. 너는 왜 그렇게 조심성이 없니?"
9 Brian은 그의 감정을 표현하기 위해 '너'로 문장을 시작하고 있군요.
10 대신에 그는 '나 메시지'를 써야 해요.
11 '나'로 시작하는 것은 그가 남동생을 비난하기보다는 자신이 느끼거나 생각하는 것에 집중하도록 도울 수 있답니다.
12 Brian: "내가 가장 좋아하는 이어폰이 없어져서 난 정말 속상해."
13 다음은 Calli입니다.
14 그녀는 어머니와 이야기하려고 하지만, 어머니는 출근 준비로 바쁘시군요.
15 한번 보시죠.

16 **Calli:** ***Hey, Mom.*** ________ ***I*** ________ ***to you about*** ________***?***
A. something B. talk C. could

17 Calli ________ to ________ the ________ ________ to talk to her mom.
A. right B. needs C. find D. time

18 Maybe Calli's mom ________ to listen ________ ________ Calli was ________ to say.
A. what B. going C. wanted D. to

19 But she didn't have ________ ________ ________ talk ________ her daughter.
A. time B. with C. enough D. to

20 Calli should ________ a time when her mom is ________ ________ ________.
A. ready B. pick C. listen D. to

21 **Calli:** ***Hey, Mom.*** ________ ***I talk to you*** ________ ________***?***
A. about B. could C. something

22 ________**:** ________**.**
A. sure B. Mom

23 Now, let's ________ a ________ ________ our last clip.
A. at B. take C. look

24 Anna and Julie are best friends, but Anna ________ ________ Julie's ________.
A. feelings B. hurts C. often

25 **Anna:** ________ ________ ***your bag*** ________ ***my desk!***
A. put B. don't C. on

26 Julie probably ________ ________ because Anna made a ________ ________ the word "don't."
A. using B. uncomfortable C. demand D. felt

27 People ________ don't like ________ ________.
A. orders B. simply C. taking

28 Anna should ________ ________ use words ________ ________ "can," "could," or "please."
A. as B. to C. such D. try

29 Then, ________ she says will sound ________ a ________ rather than a ________.
A. like B. demand C. what D. request

30 **Anna:** ________ ***you*** ________ ***your bag*** ________ ***your desk?***
A. put B. on C. could

31 As we saw in the video clips, a small ________ in the way we ________ ourselves can ________ or even ________ communication problems.
A. express B. prevent C. change D. solve

32 Let's ________ these tips ________ ________!
A. mind B. keep C. in

16 Calli: "저기, 엄마. 엄마랑 뭔가에 대해 이야기 좀 할 수 있을까요?"
16 Calli는 어머니와 이야기를 나눌 적절한 때를 찾아야 해요.
16 Calli의 어머니도 아마 Calli가 말하려고 했던 것을 듣고 싶어 하셨을 거예요.
16 그러나 어머니에게는 딸과 이야기할 시간이 충분하지 않았어요.
20 Calli는 어머니가 들으실 준비가 된 때를 골라야 해요.
21 Calli: "저기, 엄마. 엄마랑 뭔가에 대해 이야기 좀 할 수 있을까요?"
22 Mom: "물론이지."
23 이제 마지막 동영상을 봅시다.
24 Anna와 Julie는 가장 친한 친구 사이이지만, Anna가 종종 Julie의 마음을 상하게 합니다.
25 Anna: "네 가방을 내 책상에 놓지 마!"
26 Anna가 don't라는 단어를 써서 요구했기 때문에 Julie는 아마 불편하게 느꼈을 거예요.
27 사람들은 명령 받는 것을 전혀 좋아하지 않아요.
28 Anna는 can, could 또는 please와 같은 말을 사용하도록 노력해야 해요.
29 그러면 그녀가 하는 말이 요구보다는 요청처럼 들릴 거예요.
30 Anna: "네 가방은 네 책상에 놔 두겠니?"
31 우리가 동영상에서 본 것처럼, 우리 자신을 표현하는 방식을 조금만 바꾸어도 의사소통의 문제를 해결하거나 심지어 막을 수도 있답니다.
32 이 조언들을 명심합시다!

※ 다음 우리말과 일치하도록 빈칸에 알맞은 말을 쓰시오.

1 Speak Your _______ _______

2 _______ _______ "All about _______."

3 _______ Dr. Carter.

4 Today, we're going to talk about _______ _______ _______ _______ to express _______ more _______.

5 _______ start with _______ _______ _______ about Brian.

6 When he _______ _______ talk to his brother, he always _______ _______ _______ with his brother.

7 Let's _______ _______ _______ _______ _______ he has this problem.

8 **Brian:** ***You*** _______ ***my earphones again. Why are you so*** _______**?**

9 Brian is starting a _______ _______ "you" _______ _______ _______ _______.

10 _______, he should use the "_______."

11 Starting with "I" can help him _______ _______ what he feels or thinks _______ _______ _______ _______ _______ _______ his brother.

12 **Brian:** _______ ***really*** _______ ***because my favorite earphones*** _______ _______.

13 _______ is Calli.

14 She is trying to talk to her mother, but she _______ _______ _______ to go to work.

15 Let's _______ _______ _______.

1 당신의 마음을 효과적으로 말하라

2 '십 대들의 모든 것'에 오신 걸 환영합니다.

3 저는 Carter 박사입니다.

4 오늘 우리는 자신을 더 효과적으로 표현하기 위해 적절한 의사소통 기술을 사용하는 것에 대해 이야기해 보겠습니다.

5 Brian에 대한 첫 번째 동영상으로 시작해 보죠.

6 Brian이 남동생과 이야기하려고 할 때, 그는 결국 동생과 항상 말다툼을 하게 돼요.

7 그에게 이런 문제가 있는 이유를 알아봅시다.

8 Brian: "너 또 내 이어폰 잃어버렸지. 너는 왜 그렇게 조심성이 없니?"

9 Brian은 그의 감정을 표현하기 위해 '너'로 문장을 시작하고 있군요.

10 대신에 그는 '나 메시지'를 써야 해요.

11 '나'로 시작하는 것은 그가 남동생을 비난하기보다는 자신이 느끼거나 생각하는 것에 집중하도록 도울 수 있답니다.

12 Brian: "내가 가장 좋아하는 이어폰이 없어져서 난 정말 속상해."

13 다음은 Calli입니다.

14 그녀는 어머니와 이야기하려고 하지만, 어머니는 출근 준비로 바쁘시군요.

15 한번 보시죠.

16 **Calli: *Hey, Mom.* _______ _______ *talk to you about something?***

17 Calli _______ _______ find _______ _______ _______ to talk to her mom.

18 Maybe Calli's mom wanted to listen to _______ Calli was _______ _______ _______.

19 But she didn't have _______ _______ _______ _______ with her daughter.

20 Calli should _______ _______ _______ when her mom _______ _______ _______ _______.

21 **Calli: *Hey, Mom.* _______ _______ *talk to you about something?***

22 **Mom: _______.**

23 Now, let's _______ _______ _______ _______ our last clip.

24 Anna and Julie are best friends, but Anna often _______ Julie's _______.

25 **Anna: _______ _______ *your bag on my desk!***

26 Julie probably _______ _______ because Anna _______ _______ _______ using the word "don't."

27 People _______ don't like _______ _______.

28 Anna _______ _______ to use words _______ _______ "can," "could," or "please."

29 Then, _______ she says will _______ _______ a _______ rather than a _______.

30 **Anna: _______ _______ *put your bag on your desk?***

31 As we saw in the video clips, _______ _______ _______ in the way we _______ _______ can solve or even _______ _______ _______.

32 Let's _______ these tips _______ _______!

16 Calli: "저기, 엄마. 엄마랑 뭔가에 대해 이야기 좀 할 수 있을까요?"

16 Calli는 어머니와 이야기를 나눌 적절한 때를 찾아야 해요.

16 Calli의 어머니도 아마 Calli가 말하려고 했던 것을 듣고 싶어 하셨을 거예요.

16 그러나 어머니에게는 딸과 이야기할 시간이 충분하지 않았어요.

20 Calli는 어머니가 들으실 준비가 된 때를 골라야 해요.

21 Calli: "저기, 엄마. 엄마랑 뭔가에 대해 이야기 좀 할 수 있을까요?"

22 Mom: "물론이지."

23 이제 마지막 동영상을 봅시다.

24 Anna와 Julie는 가장 친한 친구 사이이지만, Anna가 종종 Julie의 마음을 상하게 합니다.

25 Anna: "네 가방을 내 책상에 놓지 마!"

26 Anna가 don't라는 단어를 써서 요구했기 때문에 Julie는 아마 불편하게 느꼈을 거예요.

27 사람들은 명령 받는 것을 전혀 좋아하지 않아요.

28 Anna는 can, could 또는 please와 같은 말을 사용하도록 노력해야 해요.

29 그러면 그녀가 하는 말이 요구보다는 요청처럼 들릴 거예요.

30 Anna: "네 가방은 네 책상에 놔 두겠니?"

31 우리가 동영상에서 본 것처럼, 우리 자신을 표현하는 방식을 조금만 바꾸어도 의사소통의 문제를 해결하거나 심지어 막을 수도 있답니다.

32 이 조언들을 명심합시다!

본문 Test

Step3

※ 다음 문장을 우리말로 쓰시오.

1 Speak Your Mind Effectively

➡ ______________________

2 Welcome to "All about Teens."

➡ ______________________

3 I'm Dr. Carter.

➡ ______________________

4 Today, we're going to talk about using good communication skills to express ourselves more effectively.

➡ ______________________

5 Let's start with our first clip about Brian.

➡ ______________________

6 When he tries to talk to his brother, he always ends up arguing with his brother.

➡ ______________________

7 Let's find out the reason why he has this problem.

➡ ______________________

8 Brian: You lost my earphones again. Why are you so careless?

➡ ______________________

9 Brian is starting a sentence with "you" to express his feelings.

➡ ______________________

10 Instead, he should use the "I-message."

➡ ______________________

11 Starting with "I" can help him focus on what he feels or thinks rather than point the finger at his brother.

➡ ______________________

12 Brian: I'm really upset because my favorite earphones are lost.

➡ ______________________

13 Next is Calli.

➡ ______________________

14 She is trying to talk to her mother, but she is busy preparing to go to work.

➡ ______________________

15 Let's have a look.

➡ ______________________

16 Calli: Hey, Mom. Could I talk to you about something?

➡ ______________________________

17 Calli needs to find the right time to talk to her mom.

➡ ______________________________

18 Maybe Calli's mom wanted to listen to what Calli was going to say.

➡ ______________________________

19 But she didn't have enough time to talk with her daughter.

➡ ______________________________

20 Calli should pick a time when her mom is ready to listen.

➡ ______________________________

21 Calli: Hey, Mom. Could I talk to you about something?

➡ ______________________________

22 Mom: Sure.

➡ ______________________________

23 Now, let's take a look at our last clip.

➡ ______________________________

24 Anna and Julie are best friends, but Anna often hurts Julie's feelings.

➡ ______________________________

25 Anna: Don't put your bag on my desk!

➡ ______________________________

26 Julie probably felt uncomfortable because Anna made a demand using the word "don't."

➡ ______________________________

27 People simply don't like taking orders.

➡ ______________________________

28 Anna should try to use words such as "can," "could," or "please."

➡ ______________________________

29 Then, what she says will sound like a request rather than a demand.

➡ ______________________________

30 Anna: Could you put your bag on your desk?

➡ ______________________________

31 As we saw in the video clips, a small change in the way we express ourselves can solve or even prevent communication problems.

➡ ______________________________

____

32 Let's keep these tips in mind!

➡ ______________________________

Step4

※ 다음 괄호 안의 단어들을 우리말에 맞도록 바르게 배열하시오.

1 (Your / Speak / Effectively / Mind)
➡ ______

2 (to / Welcome / about / "All / Teens.")
➡ ______

3 (Carter. / Dr. / I'm)
➡ ______

4 (we're / today, / to / going / about / talk / using / communication / good / to / skills / express / more / ourselves / effectively.)
➡ ______

5 (start / let's / our / with / clip / first / Brian. / about)
➡ ______

6 (he / when / to / tries / talk / his / to / brother, / always / he / up / ends / with / arguing / brother. / his)
➡ ______

7 (find / let's / out / reason / the / he / why / this / problem. / has)
➡ ______

8 (Brian: / lost / you / earphones / my / again. // are / why / so / you / careless?)
➡ ______

9 (is / Brian / a / starting / with / sentence / to / "you" / his / express / feelings.)
➡ ______

10 (he / instead, / use / should / "I-message." / the)
➡ ______

11 (with / starting / can / "I" / help / him / help / focus / what / on / feels / he / thinks / or / than / rather / the / point / at / finger / his / brother.)
➡ ______

12 (Brian: / really / I'm / because / upset / favorite / my / earphones / lost. / are)
➡ ______

13 (Calli. / is / next)
➡ ______

14 (is / she / to / trying / talk / her / to / mother, / she / but / is / preparing / busy / go / to / work. / to)
➡ ______

15 (have / let's / look. / a)
➡ ______

1 당신의 마음을 효과적으로 말하라

2 '십 대들의 모든 것'에 오신 걸 환영합니다.

3 저는 Carter 박사입니다.

4 오늘 우리는 자신을 더 효과적으로 표현하기 위해 적절한 의사소통 기술을 사용하는 것에 대해 이야기해 보겠습니다.

5 Brian에 대한 첫 번째 동영상으로 시작해 보죠.

6 Brian이 남동생과 이야기하려고 할 때, 그는 결국 동생과 항상 말다툼을 하게 돼요.

7 그에게 이런 문제가 있는 이유를 알아봅시다.

8 Brian: "너 또 내 이어폰 잃어버렸지. 너는 왜 그렇게 조심성이 없니?"

9 Brian은 그의 감정을 표현하기 위해 '너'로 문장을 시작하고 있군요.

10 대신에 그는 '나 메시지'를 써야 해요.

11 '나'로 시작하는 것은 그가 남동생을 비난하기보다는 자신이 느끼거나 생각하는 것에 집중하도록 도울 수 있답니다.

12 Brian: "내가 가장 좋아하는 이어폰이 없어져서 난 정말 속상해."

13 다음은 Calli입니다.

14 그녀는 어머니와 이야기하려고 하지만, 어머니는 출근 준비로 바쁘시군요.

15 한번 보시죠.

16 (Calli: / Mom. / hey, // I / could / to / talk / about / you / something?)
➡ ______________________________

17 (needs / Calli / find / to / right / the / to / time / to / talk / mom. / her)
➡ ______________________________

18 (Calli's / maybe / wanted / mom / listen / to / what / to / was / Calli / going / say. / to)
➡ ______________________________

19 (she / but / have / didn't / time / enough / talk / to / her / with / daughter.)
➡ ______________________________

20 (should / Calli / pick / time / a / her / when / is / mom / to / ready / listen.)
➡ ______________________________

21 (Calli: / Mom. / hey, // I / could / talk / you / to / something? / about)
➡ ______________________________

22 (sure. / Mom:)
➡ ______________________________

23 (let's / now, / a / take / at / look / clip. / last)
➡ ______________________________

24 (Julie / and / Anna / best / are / friends, / Anna / but / hurts / often / feelings. / Julie's)
➡ ______________________________

25 (Anna: / put / don't / bag / your / on / desk! / my)
➡ ______________________________

26 (Julie / felt / probably / because / uncomfortable / made / Anna / demand / a / using / word / "don't." / the)
➡ ______________________________
____

27 (simply / people / like / don't / orders. / taking)
➡ ______________________________

28 (should / Anna / to / try / words / use / as / such /. "could," / or / "can," / "please.")
➡ ______________________________

29 (what / then, / says / she / sound / will / a / like / rather / request / than / demand. / a)
➡ ______________________________

30 (Anna: / you / could / your / put / bag / your / on / desk?)
➡ ______________________________

31 (we / as / in / saw / video / the / clips, / small / a / change / the / in / way / express / we / can / ourselves / solve / or / prevent / even / problems. / communication)
➡ ______________________________
____

32 (keep / let's / tips / these / mind! / in)
➡ ______________________________

16 Calli: "저기, 엄마. 엄마랑 뭔가에 대해 이야기 좀 할 수 있을까요?"

16 Calli는 어머니와 이야기를 나눌 적절한 때를 찾아야 해요.

16 Calli의 어머니도 아마 Calli가 말하려고 했던 것을 듣고 싶어 하셨을 거예요.

16 그러나 어머니에게는 딸과 이야기할 시간이 충분하지 않았어요.

20 Calli는 어머니가 들으실 준비가 된 때를 골라야 해요.

21 Calli: "저기, 엄마. 엄마랑 뭔가에 대해 이야기 좀 할 수 있을까요?"

22 Mom: "물론이지."

23 이제 마지막 동영상을 봅시다.

24 Anna와 Julie는 가장 친한 친구 사이이지만, Anna가 종종 Julie의 마음을 상하게 합니다.

25 Anna: "네 가방을 내 책상에 놓지 마!"

26 Anna가 don't라는 단어를 써서 요구했기 때문에 Julie는 아마 불편하게 느꼈을 거예요.

27 사람들은 명령 받는 것을 전혀 좋아하지 않아요.

28 Anna는 can, could 또는 please와 같은 말을 사용하도록 노력해야 해요.

29 그러면 그녀가 하는 말이 요구보다는 요청처럼 들릴 거예요.

30 Anna: "네 가방은 네 책상에 놔두겠니?"

31 우리가 동영상에서 본 것처럼, 우리 자신을 표현하는 방식을 조금만 바꾸어도 의사소통의 문제를 해결하거나 심지어 막을 수도 있답니다.

32 이 조언들을 명심합시다!

본문 Test

Step5

※ 다음 우리말을 영어로 쓰시오.

1 당신의 마음을 효과적으로 말하라

➡ ______________________________

2 '십 대들의 모든 것'에 오신 걸 환영합니다.

➡ ______________________________

3 저는 Carter 박사입니다.

➡ ______________________________

4 오늘 우리는 자신을 더 효과적으로 표현하기 위해 적절한 의사소통 기술을 사용하는 것에 대해 이야기해 보겠습니다.

➡ ______________________________

5 Brian에 대한 첫 번째 동영상으로 시작해 보죠.

➡ ______________________________

6 Brian이 남동생과 이야기하려고 할 때, 그는 결국 동생과 항상 말다툼을 하게 돼요.

➡ ______________________________

7 그에게 이런 문제가 있는 이유를 알아봅시다.

➡ ______________________________

8 Brian: "너 또 내 이어폰 잃어버렸지. 너는 왜 그렇게 조심성이 없니?"

➡ ______________________________

9 Brian은 그의 감정을 표현하기 위해 '너'로 문장을 시작하고 있군요.

➡ ______________________________

10 대신에 그는 '나 메시지'를 써야 해요.

➡ ______________________________

11 '나'로 시작하는 것은 그가 남동생을 비난하기보다는 자신이 느끼거나 생각하는 것에 집중하도록 도울 수 있답니다.

➡ ______________________________

12 Brian: "내가 가장 좋아하는 이어폰이 없어져서 난 정말 속상해."

➡ ______________________________

13 다음은 Calli입니다.

➡ ______________________________

14 그녀는 어머니와 이야기하려고 하지만, 어머니는 출근 준비로 바쁘시군요.

➡ ______________________________

15 한번 보시죠.

➡ ______________________________

16 Calli: “저기, 엄마. 엄마랑 뭔가에 대해 이야기 좀 할 수 있을까요?”

➡ ______________________________

17 Calli는 어머니와 이야기를 나눌 적절한 때를 찾아야 해요.

➡ ______________________________

18 Calli의 어머니도 아마 Calli가 말하려고 했던 것을 듣고 싶어 하셨을 거예요.

➡ ______________________________

19 그러나 어머니에게는 딸과 이야기할 시간이 충분하지 않았어요.

➡ ______________________________

20 Calli는 어머니가 들으실 준비가 된 때를 골라야 해요.

➡ ______________________________

21 Calli: “저기, 엄마. 엄마랑 뭔가에 대해 이야기 좀 할 수 있을까요?”

➡ ______________________________

22 Mom: “물론이지.”

➡ ______________________________

23 이제 마지막 동영상을 봅시다.

➡ ______________________________

24 Anna와 Julie는 가장 친한 친구 사이이지만, Anna가 종종 Julie의 마음을 상하게 합니다.

➡ ______________________________

25 Anna: “네 가방을 내 책상에 놓지 마!”

➡ ______________________________

26 Anna가 don't라는 단어를 써서 요구했기 때문에 Julie는 아마 불편하게 느꼈을 거예요.

➡ ______________________________

27 사람들은 명령 받는 것을 전혀 좋아하지 않아요.

➡ ______________________________

28 Anna는 can, could 또는 please와 같은 말을 사용하도록 노력해야 해요.

➡ ______________________________

29 그러면 그녀가 하는 말이 요구보다는 요청처럼 들릴 거예요.

➡ ______________________________

30 Anna: “네 가방은 네 책상에 놔두겠니?”

➡ ______________________________

31 우리가 동영상에서 본 것처럼, 우리 자신을 표현하는 방식을 조금만 바꾸어도 의사소통의 문제를 해결하거나 심지어 막을 수도 있답니다.

➡ ______________________________

____

32 이 조언들을 명심합시다!

➡ ______________________________

구석구석 지문 Test

Step1

※ 다음 우리말과 일치하도록 빈칸에 알맞은 말을 쓰시오.

Wrap Up 1

1. M: You ________ ________, Anna. What's ________?
2. W: Well, I'm ________ ________ my sister, Elsa.
3. M: ________ are you ________ ________ her?
4. W: She ________ ________ me ________.
5. M: Oh, maybe you should ________ ________ ________ ________ ________.

1. M: 너 화나 보여, Anna. 무슨 일 있니?
2. W: 음, 난 내 여동생 Elsa에 대해 화가 나.
3. M: 왜 Elsa 때문에 화가 났니?
4. W: 그녀는 계속 나한테 이래라저래라 해.
5. M: 오, 어쩌면 네가 어떻게 느끼는지 그녀에게 말해야 할지도 몰라.

Wrap Up 2

1. W: Hey, Mike! ________ ________ you ________ ________ to my birthday party yesterday?
2. M: Sorry. I really ________ ________ ________ ________ ________ yesterday.
3. W: ________ did you hit your books? ________ you ________ ________ something?
4. M: Oh no, that's ________ ________ I ________. I ________ ________ ________ yesterday ________ I had an exam this morning.

1. W: 안녕, Mike! 너는 왜 어제 내 생일 파티에 안 왔니?
2. M: 미안해. 나는 어제 정말 'hit the books(공부하다)' 해야 했어.
3. W: 왜 책을 쳤니? 너 뭔가에 화가 났니?
4. M: 아 아니, 그런 뜻이 아니야. 나는 오늘 아침에 시험이 있어서 어제 공부를 해야 했어.

Read and Think B

1. ________ ________ was ________ ________ ________ to you, and why?
2. ________ the "I-message" was ________ ________ ________.
3. I often ________ ________ ________ ________ my sister, and now I understand ________ ________.

1. 어떤 조언이 너에게 가장 도움이 되었니, 그리고 이유는?
2. "나 메세지"를 사용하는 것이 가장 도움이 되었어.
3. 나는 자주 내 여동생과 논쟁을 벌이곤 했는데, 이제 그 이유를 이해해.

After You Read A. Read and Write

1. ________ ________ good communication skills, we can ________ ________ more ________.
2. ⓐ ________ the "I-message."
3. You can ________ ________ ________ you feel or think ________ ________ point the finger at others.
4. ⓑ ________ the ________ ________.
5. Others will listen to you when they have ________ ________ ________ ________ ________ you.
6. ⓒ ________ a ________.
7. Use words ________ ________ "can," "could," or "please."

1. 좋은 대화 기술을 사용함으로써, 우리는 스스로를 더 효과적으로 표현할 수 있다.
2. ⓐ "나 메세지"를 사용하라.
3. 남을 비난하기보다 당신이 느끼거나 생각하는 것에 초점을 맞출 수 있다.
4. ⓑ 올바른 시간을 선택하라.
5. 다른 사람들은 그들이 당신과 이야기할 충분한 시간이 있을 때 당신의 말을 들을 것이다.
6. ⓒ 요청을 하라.
7. "can," "could, " 또는 "please"와 같은 말을 사용하라.

구석구석 지문 Test

Step2

※ 다음 우리말을 영어로 쓰시오.

Wrap Up 1

1. M: 너 화나 보여, Anna. 무슨 일 있니?
➡ ______
2. W: 음, 난 내 여동생 Elsa에 대해 화가
➡ ______
3. M: 왜 Elsa 때문에 화가 났니?
➡ ______
4. W: 그녀는 계속 나한테 이래라저래라 해.
➡ ______
5. M: 오, 어쩌면 네가 어떻게 느끼는지 그녀에게 말해야 할지도 몰라.
➡ ______

Wrap Up 2

1. W: 안녕, Mike! 너는 왜 어제 내 생일 파티에 안 왔니?
➡ ______
2. M: 미안해. 나는 어제 정말 'hit the books(공부하다)' 해야 했어.
➡ ______
3. W: 왜 책을 쳤니? 너 뭔가에 화가 났니?
➡ ______
4. M: 아 아니, 그런 뜻이 아니야. 나는 오늘 아침에 시험이 있어서 어제 공부를 해야 했어.
➡ ______

Read and Think B

1. 어떤 조언이 너에게 가장 도움이 되었니, 그리고 이유는?
➡ ______
2. "나 메세지"를 사용하는 것이 가장 도움이 되었어.
➡ ______
3. 나는 자주 내 여동생과 논쟁을 벌이곤 했는데, 이제 그 이유를 이해해.
➡ ______

After You Read A. Read and Write

1. 좋은 대화 기술을 사용함으로써, 우리는 스스로를 더 효과적으로 표현할 수 있다.
➡ ______
2. ⓐ "나 메세지"를 사용하라.
➡ ______
3. 남을 비난하기보다 당신이 느끼거나 생각하는 것에 초점을 맞출 수 있다.
➡ ______
4. ⓑ 올바른 시간을 선택하라.
➡ ______
5. 다른 사람들은 그들이 당신과 이야기할 충분한 시간이 있을 때 당신의 말을 들을 것이다.
➡ ______
6. ⓒ 요청을 하라.
➡ ______
7. "can," "could," 또는 "please"와 같은 말을 사용하라.
➡ ______

단어 Test

Step1

※ 다음 영어를 우리말로 쓰시오.

01 shape ____________

02 unique ____________

03 spiky ____________

04 unusual ____________

05 yellow dust ____________

06 investigate ____________

07 view ____________

08 sticky ____________

09 combination ____________

10 peak ____________

11 shoot ____________

12 shooting star ____________

13 location ____________

14 period ____________

15 survive ____________

16 rainfall ____________

17 glacier ____________

18 competition ____________

19 countless ____________

20 develop ____________

21 alive ____________

22 ecologist ____________

23 cliff ____________

24 improve ____________

25 insight ____________

26 personal ____________

27 miracle ____________

28 research ____________

29 glow ____________

30 harsh ____________

31 honor ____________

32 inspire ____________

33 clothing ____________

34 colorist ____________

35 stand in for ____________

36 be[get] inspired by ____________

37 come true ____________

38 be filled with ____________

39 get in shape ____________

40 keep ~ on one's toes ____________

41 due to 명사 ____________

42 be made by ~ ____________

43 walk along ____________

단어 Test

Step2

※ 다음 우리말을 영어로 쓰시오.

01 통찰력 ______________

02 절벽 ______________

03 많은, 셀 수 없는 ______________

04 절정[최대한도]에 이르다 ______________

05 의류, 옷 ______________

06 개선하다, 향상시키다 ______________

07 색채화가 ______________

08 위치, 장소 ______________

09 조합 ______________

10 놀라운 일, 기적 ______________

11 모양, 형태 ______________

12 만들다, 발전하다 ______________

13 생태학자 ______________

14 빛나다 ______________

15 암초 ______________

16 (날씨, 생활환경이) 혹독한 ______________

17 촬영하다 ______________

18 영감을 주다, 고무하다 ______________

19 빙하 ______________

20 조사하다 ______________

21 끝이 뾰족한 ______________

22 살아남다, 생존하다 ______________

23 조사하다, 연구하다 ______________

24 영광으로 생각하다 ______________

25 강우 ______________

26 끈적거리는, 달라붙는 ______________

27 생기 넘치는, 살아 있는 ______________

28 특이한, 흔치 않은 ______________

29 풍경, 전망 ______________

30 모험 ______________

31 개인적인 ______________

32 황사 ______________

33 실제로 ______________

34 최근의 ______________

35 수백만의 ______________

36 발견하다, 알아보다 ______________

37 ~에 기인하다 ______________

38 ~을 대신하다 ______________

39 ~에 의해 영감을 받다 ______________

40 ~로 가득차다 ______________

41 좋은 몸 상태를 유지하다 ______________

42 ~ 때문에 ______________

43 자르다 ______________

단어 Test

Step3

※ 다음 영영풀이에 알맞은 단어를 <보기>에서 골라 쓴 후, 우리말 뜻을 쓰시오.

1 __________: to shine with a soft light: __________

2 __________: the steep side of an area of high land: __________

3 __________: very special, unusual, or good: __________

4 __________: to reach the highest point or level: _______________

5 __________: a large hole in the side of a hill or under the ground: __________

6 __________: difficult to live in and very uncomfortabl: _______________

7 __________: something that combines several things: __________

8 __________: a particular length of time with a beginning and an end: __________

9 __________: a very large mass of ice that moves very slowly: __________

10 __________: consisting of several different types of things or people: __________

11 __________: an exciting experience in which dangerous or unusual things happen: __________

12 __________: very many, especially more than you think is reasonable: __________

13 __________: a scientist who studies the environment and the way that plants, animals, and humans live together and affect each other: __________

14 __________: to encourage someone by making them feel confident and eager to do something: ____________________

15 __________: to study a subject in detail, especially in order to discover new facts or test new ideas: ____________

16 __________: a piece of rock or metal from space that burns brightly as it falls towards the Earth: __________

보기

harsh	shooting star	cave	adventure
period	ecologist	combination	research
cliff	glacier	glow	inspire
peak	countless	unique	mixed

대화문 Test

※ 다음 우리말과 일치하도록 빈칸에 알맞은 말을 쓰시오.

Listen & Talk 1 Get Ready

A: The ________ of the ________ of the mountain is going to be ________.

B: Yeah, I ________ ________ ________ see the view. Let's ________ ________ there!

A: 산꼭대기의 경치는 멋질 거야.
B: 그래, 빨리 경치가 보고 싶어. 저곳으로 뛰어 올라가자!

Listen & Talk 1 A-1

W: David, ________ your summer ________?

M: My family is ________ ________ China. I can't ________ ________ ________ the Rainbow Mountains.

W: The Rainbow Mountains?

M: They ________ some mountains ________ ________ ________ in rainbow colors.

W: That ________ amazing! ________ ________ ________ pictures!

W: David, 여름 계획은 뭐야?
M: 우리 가족은 중국에 갈 거야. 나는 레인보우 산맥을 빨리 방문하고 싶어.
W: 레인보우 산맥?
M: 그것은 무지개 색깔의 화폭처럼 보이는 산들이야.
W: 정말 멋지구나! 사진 많이 찍어!

Listen & Talk 1 A-2

M: Do you ________ ________ ________ the new 3D movie?

W: ________ one?

M: The one ________ ________ ________ the sea. It ________ ________ near Australia's Great Barrier Reef.

W: Oh, I've ________ ________ it. It ________ the most beautiful ________ ________.

M: Right. I ________ ________ ________ ________ the movie. Let's ________ ________ ________ the ticket.

M: 너 새로 나온 3D 영화 보고 싶니?
W: 어느 영화?
M: 바다 밑의 모험에 관한 거야. 그것은 오스트레일리아의 Great Barrier Reef 근처에서 촬영되었어.
W: 오, 난 그것에 대해 들어본 적이 있어. 거기에는 가장 아름다운 해양 생물이 있어.
M: 맞아. 난 그 영화를 빨리 보고 싶어. 가서 표를 사자.

Listen & Talk 1 B

W: Dad, my science club ________ ________ ________ ________ to Dokdo ________ July.

M: Oh, really? ________ do you ________ ________ do there?

W: We are ________ ________ ________ the ________ on the island and ________ bird ________.

W: 아빠, 제 과학 동아리는 7월에 독도에 갈 거예요.
M: 오, 정말? 그곳에서 무엇을 할 계획이니?
W: 우리는 섬에 있는 동굴을 연구하고 새를 관찰하러 갈 거예요.

M: Sounds ________ it will be an ________ ________.

W: Yeah. ________ ________ ________ ________ Dokdo in books. I can't ________ ________ ________ ________ there.

M: I ________ you ________ your ________!

M: 흥미로운 여행이 될 것 같구나.
W: 네. 저는 책에서만 독도에 대해서 읽었어요. 빨리 그곳을 실제로 방문하고 싶어요.
M: 즐거운 여행이 되길 바라!

Listen & Talk 2 Get Ready

A: The level of yellow dust ________ really ________ today.

B: Yeah. ________ ________ ________ the yellow dust ________ ________ the deserts of Mongolia ________ Korea.

A: 오늘 황사의 정도가 정말 심해.
B: 그래. 황사는 몽골의 사막에서 한국으로 이동한다고 들었어.

Listen & Talk 2 A-1

M: Mom, did you watch the ________ ________ today? We will be ________ to see ________ ________ ________ ________ tonight!

W: Wow, fantastic! ________ is the best time ________ ________ ________?

M: I've ________ ________ the ________ ________ will peak ________ 12 a.m. ________ 2 a.m.

W: Wow, it will be a ________ ________!

M: 엄마, 오늘 일기예보 보셨어요? 우리는 오늘 밤 수많은 유성을 볼 수 있을 거예요!
W: 와, 환상적이야! 그것을 보기에 가장 좋은 시간은 언제니?
M: 저는 유성이 오전 12시에서 2시 사이에 절정에 이를 거라고 들었어요.
W: 와, 특별한 밤이 되겠구나!

Listen & Talk 2 A-2

M: Erica, what ________ the white things in the picture?

W: ________ ________ snow rollers. ________ ________ ________ they are ________ ________ strong wind and ________ snow.

M: Interesting! They ________ ________ snow rings.

W: Yeah, I'd ________ to ________ see them ________.

M: Erica, 사진 속의 흰 것들은 뭐니?
W: 그것들은 두루마리 눈이야. 나는 그것이 강한 바람과 끈적끈적한 눈으로 만들어진다고 들었어.
M: 흥미롭구나! 그것들은 눈 반지처럼 보여.
W: 그래, 나도 언젠가 그것들을 실제로 보고 싶어.

Listen & Talk 2 B

M: Jisu, did you know ________ the sun never ________ in Norway ________ ________?

W: No, I didn't know ________. ________ ________!

M: Yeah, and I've ________ ________ people go hiking and ________ ________ at night ________ it isn't dark.

W: I'd ________ to go hiking and cycling ________ ________ ________ ________ the night!

M: Me, ________. I hope we ________ the________ ________ ________ it ________.

M: 지수야, 여름 동안 노르웨이에서는 해가 지지 않는다는 걸 알고 있니?

W: 아니, 그건 몰랐어. 정말 흥미롭구나!

M: 그래, 그리고 난 사람들이 밤에 어둡지 않아서 하이킹 가고 심지어 자전거를 타러 간다고 들었어.

W: 나는 한밤중에 하이킹과 자전거를 타러 가고 싶어!

M: 나도. 언젠가 그것을 해볼 기회가 있으면 좋겠어.

Communication

M: Let's welcome Ms. Scarlett Lee, the ________ of this year's photo ________.

W: Hello, thank you ________ ________ me. I've ________ ________ ________ the award.

M: Let's ________ about your photo. I've ________ ________ this photo ________ ________ in the Maldives. Is that ________?

W: Yes, this ________ ________ is ________ ________ plankton.

M: Wow, it truly is ________!

W: Yes, it is. I ________ ________ ________ ________ more pictures of ________ ________.

M: I ________ you the ________ of luck!

M: 올해 사진 대회 우승자인 Scarlett Lee 양을 환영합시다.

W: 안녕하세요, 초대해 주셔서 감사합니다. 상을 받게 되어 영광으로 생각합니다.

M: 사진에 대해 얘기해 봅시다. 저는 이 사진이 몰디브에서 찍힌 거라고 들었어요. 그게 사실인가요?

W: 네, 이 빛나는 해변은 플랑크톤 때문에 생긴 거예요.

M: 와, 정말 놀랍네요!

W: 네, 그래요. 저는 빨리 멋진 해변의 사진을 더 많이 찍고 싶어요.

M: 행운을 빌어요!

대화문 Test

Step2

※ 다음 우리말에 맞도록 대화를 영어로 쓰시오.

해석

Listen & Talk 1 Get Ready

A: ______________________________

B: ______________________________

A: 산꼭대기의 경치는 멋질 거야.
B: 그래, 빨리 경치가 보고 싶어. 저곳으로 뛰어 올라가자!

Listen & Talk 1 A-1

W: ______________________________

M: ______________________________

W: ______________________________

M: ______________________________

W: ______________________________

W: David, 여름 계획은 뭐야?
M: 우리 가족은 중국에 갈 거야. 나는 레인보우 산맥을 빨리 방문하고 싶어.
W: 레인보우 산맥?
M: 그것은 무지개 색깔의 화폭처럼 보이는 산들이야.
W: 정말 멋지구나! 사진 많이 찍어!

Listen & Talk 1 A-2

M: ______________________________

W: ______________________________

M: ______________________________

____

W: ______________________________

M: ______________________________

M: 너 새로 나온 3D 영화 보고 싶니?
W: 어느 영화?
M: 바다 밑의 모험에 관한 거야. 그것은 오스트레일리아의 Great Barrier Reef 근처에서 촬영되었어.
W: 오, 난 그것에 대해 들어본 적이 있어. 거기에는 가장 아름다운 해양 생물이 있어.
M: 맞아. 난 그 영화를 빨리 보고 싶어. 가서 표를 사자.

Listen & Talk 1 B

W: ______________________________

M: ______________________________

W: ______________________________

W: 아빠, 제 과학 동아리는 7월에 독도에 갈 거예요.
M: 오, 정말? 그곳에서 무엇을 할 계획이니?
W: 우리는 섬에 있는 동굴을 연구하고 새를 관찰하러 갈 거예요.

M: ______________________________

W: ______________________________

M: ______________________________

M: 흥미로운 여행이 될 것 같구나.
W: 네. 저는 책에서만 독도에 대해서 읽었어요. 빨리 그곳을 실제로 방문하고 싶어요.
M: 즐거운 여행이 되길 바라!

Listen & Talk 2 Get Ready

A: ______________________________

B: ______________________________

____

A: 오늘 황사의 정도가 정말 심해.
B: 그래. 황사는 몽골의 사막에서 한국으로 이동한다고 들었어.

Listen & Talk 2 A-1

M: ______________________________

____

W: ______________________________

M: ______________________________

W: ______________________________

M: 엄마, 오늘 일기예보 보셨어요? 우리는 오늘 밤 수많은 유성을 볼 수 있을 거예요!
W: 와, 환상적이야! 그것을 보기에 가장 좋은 시간은 언제니?
M: 저는 유성이 오전 12시에서 2시 사이에 절정에 이를 거라고 들었어요.
W: 와, 특별한 밤이 되겠구나!

Listen & Talk 2 A-2

M: ______________________________

W: ______________________________

____

M: ______________________________

W: ______________________________

M: Erica, 사진 속의 흰 것들은 뭐니?
W: 그것들은 두루마리 눈이야. 나는 그것이 강한 바람과 끈적끈적한 눈으로 만들어진다고 들었어.
M: 흥미롭구나! 그것들은 눈 반지처럼 보여.
W: 그래, 나도 언젠가 그것들을 실제로 보고 싶어.

Listen & Talk 2 B

M: ____________________

W: ____________________

M: ____________________

____

W: ____________________

M: ____________________

M: 지수야, 여름 동안 노르웨이에서는 해가 지지 않는다는 걸 알고 있니?
W: 아니, 그건 몰랐어. 정말 흥미롭구나!
M: 그래, 그리고 난 사람들이 밤에 어둡지 않아서 하이킹 가고 심지어 자전거를 타러 간다고 들었어.
W: 나는 한밤중에 하이킹과 자전거를 타러 가고 싶어!
M: 나도. 언젠가 그것을 해볼 기회가 있으면 좋겠어.

Communication

M: ____________________

W: ____________________

M: ____________________

____

W: ____________________

M: ____________________

W: ____________________

M: ____________________

M: 올해 사진 대회 우승자인 Scarlett Lee 양을 환영합시다.
W: 안녕하세요, 초대해 주셔서 감사합니다. 상을 받게 되어 영광으로 생각합니다.
M: 사진에 대해 얘기해 봅시다. 저는 이 사진이 몰디브에서 찍힌 거라고 들었어요. 그게 사실인가요?
W: 네, 이 빛나는 해변은 플랑크톤 때문에 생긴 거예요.
M: 와, 정말 놀랍네요!
W: 네, 그래요. 저는 빨리 멋진 해변의 사진을 더 많이 찍고 싶어요.
M: 행운을 빌어요!

본문 Test

※ 다음 우리말과 일치하도록 빈칸에 알맞은 것을 골라 쓰시오.

1 The ________ ________ My ________
A. Eyes B. Through C. World

2 "The ________ of ________ ________ us all.
A. nature B. beauty C. inspires

3 Let's ________ ________ how people from different ________ of work get ________ by nature."
A. out B. inspired C. fields D. find

4 ________ **Wang,** ________
A. Ecologist B. Lin

5 **Tsingy, the ________ ________ of Madagascar**
A. Forest B. Stone

6 I've ________ ________ the stone forest of Madagascar to study plants and animals ________ ________ 20 years.
A. for B. been C. over D. visiting

7 The ________ stones of this place are ________ ________ of nature.
A. true B. spiky C. miracles

8 This ________ shape ________ ________ ________ by rainfall.
A. created B. has C. amazing D. been

9 Rain has cut ________ the stones and made them ________ and ________ ________ a long period of time.
A. over B. down C. spiky D. sharp

10 The ________ is ________ for ________ to live in, but they have found ways to ________.
A. harsh B. survive C. animals D. environment

11 For example, lemurs, ________ only live in Madagascar, have ________ legs ________ help them jump from one stone tower to ________.
A. frog-like B. which C. another D. that

12 ________ me, the stone forest ________ ________ a jack-in-the-box.
A. like B. is C. for

13 It always ________ me and ________ me ________ my ________!
A. keeps B. surprises C. toes D. on

14 **Amber Smith,** ________ ________
A. Colorist B. Fashion

15 **Caño Cristales, the ________ ________ ________ ________ of Colombia**
A. Colors B. River C. Five D. of

16 The world is ________ ________ millions of ________ colors.
A. with B. different C. filled

1 내 눈에 비친 세계

2 "자연의 아름다움은 우리 모두에게 영감을 준다.

3 서로 다른 직업 분야의 사람들이 자연에 의해 어떻게 영감을 받는지 알아보자."

4 **Lin Wang, 생태학자**

5 **Tsingy, 마다가스카르의 석림**

6 나는 20년 이상 동안 식물과 동물을 연구하기 위해서 마다가스카르의 석림을 방문하고 있다.

7 이 지역의 뾰족한 돌들은 진정한 자연의 놀라움이다.

8 이 놀라운 모양은 비에 의해서 만들어졌다.

9 비가 오랜 기간 동안 돌을 침식해서 날카롭고 뾰족하게 만들었다.

10 이런 환경은 동물들이 살기에 험난하지만, 동물들은 생존할 방법들을 찾아냈다.

11 예를 들어, 마다가스카르에서만 사는 여우원숭이는 한 개의 돌탑에서 다른 돌탑으로 뛸 수 있도록 도와주는 개구리와 같은 다리를 가지고 있다.

12 나에게 석림은 '잭인더박스(열면 인형이 튀어나오는 상자)'와 같다.

13 그것은 늘 나를 놀라게 하고 정신을 바짝 차리게 한다!

14 **Amber Smith, 패션 색채 전문가**

15 **Caño Cristales, 콜롬비아의 다섯 색깔의 강**

16 세계는 수백만의 다양한 색깔로 가득 차 있다.

17 It is my job to ________, ________, and ________ colors for ________.

A. clothing B. mix C. create D. develop

18 ________ the years, I've ________ ________ ________ from the beautiful colors of Caño Cristales.

A. insights B. over C. gaining D. been

19 You cannot see the wonderful ________ colors of this river ________ ________ in the ________.

A. else B. mixed C. anywhere D. world

20 The ________ of ________ plants under the water and sunlight makes the colors more ________ and ________.

A. alive B. combination C. bright D. colorful

21 ________ I visit the Caño Cristales, it makes me think that maybe there are still ________ colors that are ________ to be ________.

A. countless B. waiting C. whenever D. created

22 **Danny Mehta,** ________ ________

A. Scout B. Location

23 **Vatnajökull** ________ **Park,** ________ ________ **of Iceland**

A. Beauty B. National C. Frozen

24 I'm a ________ scout and my job is finding ________ places to ________ movies.

A. shoot B. location C. perfect

25 Iceland is the best place ________ many location scouts to visit ________ ________ its unusual ________.

A. due B. beauty C. to D. for

26 ________ ________ ________ is the Vatnajökull National Park.

A. favorite B. personal C. my

27 The sharp cliffs, blue ________ caves, and long mountain ________ can ________ in for any ________ in the world or the universe.

A. glacier B. stand C. ranges D. place

28 In fact, the ________ sci-fi movie we ________ here was produced ________ ________ computer graphics!

A. using B. shot C. without D. recent

29 Iceland can ________ ________ our wildest dreams ________ ________ on the movie screen.

A. come B. make C. true D. help

17 의류를 위해서 색을 섞고, 발전시키고, 만들어 내는 것이 나의 일이다.

18 수년 동안, 나는 카뇨 크리스탈레스의 아름다운 색으로부터 영감을 얻어 오고 있다.

19 이 강의 아름답게 혼합된 색깔은 세상 어느 다른 곳에서도 볼 수 없다.

20 물속의 화려한 식물들과 햇빛의 결합은 그 색깔을 더 생생하고 밝게 만든다.

21 내가 카뇨 크리스탈레스를 방문할 때마다 그 강은 나로 하여금 아마도 여전히 만들어지기를 기다리고 있는 셀 수 없이 많은 색깔이 있음을 생각하게 한다.

22 **Danny Mehta, 장소 섭외가**

23 **Vatnajökull 국립 공원, 아이슬란드의 얼음으로 덮인 아름다움**

24 나는 장소 섭외가이고 나의 일은 영화를 찍기에 완벽한 장소를 찾는 것이다.

25 아이슬란드는 비범한 아름다움 때문에 많은 장소 섭외가들이 방문하기에 최고의 장소이다.

26 내가 개인적으로 가장 선호하는 곳은 바트나이외쿠틀 국립 공원이다.

27 가파른 절벽, 푸른 빙하 동굴, 그리고 긴 산맥들은 세계나 혹은 우주의 어느 장소도 대신할 수 있다.

28 사실상, 우리가 여기서 찍은 최근의 공상 과학 영화는 컴퓨터 그래픽 없이 만들어졌다!

29 아이슬란드는 우리의 가장 무모한 꿈을 영화 스크린에서 실현할 수 있게 해 준다.

본문 Test

※ 다음 우리말과 일치하도록 빈칸에 알맞은 말을 쓰시오.

1 The ________ ________ My Eyes

2 "The ________ of nature ________ ________ ________.

3 ________ ________ ________ how people from different ________ ________ ________ ________ ________ by nature."

4 **Lin Wang, ________**

5 **Tsingy, the ________ ________ of Madagascar**

6 ________ ________ ________ the ________ ________ of Madagascar to study plants and animals ________ ________ 20 years.

7 The ________ ________ of this place are ________ ________ of nature.

8 This ________ shape ________ ________ ________ ________ ________.

9 Rain has ________ ________ the stones and made them ________ and ________ ________ a long period of time.

10 The environment is ________ ________ ________ ________ ________ ________, but they have found ways ________ ________.

11 For example, lemurs, ________ only live in Madagascar, have ________ legs ________ ________ them ________ ________ one stone tower ________ ________.

12 For me, the stone forest ________ ________ a ____________.

13 It always ________ me and ________ ________ ________ ________ ________!

14 **Amber Smith, ________ ________**

15 **Caño Cristales, the ________ ________ ________ ________ of Colombia**

16 The world ________ ________ ________ ________ ________ different colors.

---

1 내 눈에 비친 세계

2 "자연의 아름다움은 우리 모두에게 영감을 준다.

3 서로 다른 직업 분야의 사람들이 자연에 의해 어떻게 영감을 받는지 알아보자."

4 **Lin Wang, 생태학자**

5 **Tsingy, 마다가스카르의 석림**

6 나는 20년 이상 동안 식물과 동물을 연구하기 위해서 마다가스카르의 석림을 방문하고 있다.

7 이 지역의 뾰족한 돌들은 진정한 자연의 놀라움이다.

8 이 놀라운 모양은 비에 의해서 만들어졌다.

9 비가 오랜 기간 동안 돌을 침식해서 날카롭고 뾰족하게 만들었다.

10 이런 환경은 동물들이 살기에 험난하지만, 동물들은 생존할 방법들을 찾아냈다.

11 예를 들어, 마다가스카르에서만 사는 여우원숭이는 한 개의 돌탑에서 다른 돌탑으로 뛸 수 있도록 도와주는 개구리와 같은 다리를 가지고 있다.

12 나에게 석림은 '잭인더박스(열면 인형이 튀어나오는 상자)'와 같다.

13 그것은 늘 나를 놀라게 하고 정신을 바짝 차리게 한다!

14 **Amber Smith, 패션 색채 전문가**

15 **Caño Cristales, 콜롬비아의 다섯 색깔의 강**

16 세계는 수백만의 다양한 색깔로 가득 차 있다.

17 It is my job to _______, _______, and _______ _______ for clothing.

18 Over the years, _______ _______ _______ insights from the _______ _______ of Caño Cristales.

19 You cannot see the _______ _______ _______ of this river _______ _______ in the world.

20 The _______ of _______ _______ under the water and sunlight _______ the colors _______ _______ and _______.

21 _______ I visit the Caño Cristales, it _______ me _______ that maybe there are still _______ colors that are _______ _______ _______ _______.

22 **Danny Mehta,** _______ _______

23 **Vatnajökull National Park,** _______ _______ **of Iceland**

24 I'm a location scout and my job is finding _______ _______ _______ _______ _______.

25 Iceland is the best place _______ _______ _______ _______ to visit _______ _______ its _______ _______.

26 _______ _______ _______ is the Vatnajökull National Park.

27 The sharp _______, blue _______ _______, and long mountain ranges can _______ _______ _______ _______ _______ in the world or the universe.

28 _______ _______, the recent sci-fi movie _______ _______ _______ was _______ _______ _______ computer graphics!

29 Iceland can _______ _______ our wildest dreams _______ _______ on the movie screen.

17 의류를 위해서 색을 섞고, 발전시키고, 만들어 내는 것이 나의 일이다.

18 수년 동안, 나는 카뇨 크리스탈레스의 아름다운 색으로부터 영감을 얻어 오고 있다.

19 이 강의 아름답게 혼합된 색깔은 세상 어느 다른 곳에서도 볼 수 없다.

20 물속의 화려한 식물들과 햇빛의 결합은 그 색깔을 더 생생하고 밝게 만든다.

21 내가 카뇨 크리스탈레스를 방문할 때마다 그 강은 나로 하여금 아마도 여전히 만들어지기를 기다리고 있는 셀 수 없이 많은 색깔이 있음을 생각하게 한다.

22 **Danny Mehta, 장소 섭외가**

23 **Vatnajökull 국립 공원, 아이슬란드의 얼음으로 덮인 아름다움**

24 나는 장소 섭외가이고 나의 일은 영화를 찍기에 완벽한 장소를 찾는 것이다.

25 아이슬란드는 비범한 아름다움 때문에 많은 장소 섭외가들이 방문하기에 최고의 장소이다.

26 내가 개인적으로 가장 선호하는 곳은 바트나이외쿠틀 국립 공원이다.

27 가파른 절벽, 푸른 빙하 동굴, 그리고 긴 산맥들은 세계나 혹은 우주의 어느 장소도 대신할 수 있다.

28 사실상, 우리가 여기서 찍은 최근의 공상 과학 영화는 컴퓨터 그래픽 없이 만들어졌다!

29 아이슬란드는 우리의 가장 무모한 꿈을 영화 스크린에서 실현할 수 있게 해 준다.

본문 Test

※ 다음 문장을 우리말로 쓰시오.

1 The World Through My Eyes

➡ ______________________________

2 "The beauty of nature inspires us all.

➡ ______________________________

3 Let's find out how people from different fields of work get inspired by nature."

➡ ______________________________

4 Lin Wang, Ecologist

➡ ______________________________

5 Tsingy, the Stone Forest of Madagascar

➡ ______________________________

6 I've been visiting the stone forest of Madagascar to study plants and animals for over 20 years.

➡ ______________________________

7 The spiky stones of this place are true miracles of nature.

➡ ______________________________

8 This amazing shape has been created by rainfall.

➡ ______________________________

9 Rain has cut down the stones and made them sharp and spiky over a long period of time.

➡ ______________________________

10 The environment is harsh for animals to live in, but they have found ways to survive.

➡ ______________________________

11 For example, lemurs, which only live in Madagascar, have frog-like legs that help them jump from one stone tower to another.

➡ ______________________________

____

12 For me, the stone forest is like a jack-in-the-box.

➡ ______________________________

13 It always surprises me and keeps me on my toes!

➡ ______________________________

14 Amber Smith, Fashion Colorist

➡ ______________________________

15 Caño Cristales, the River of Five Colors of Colombia

➡ ______________________________

16 The world is filled with millions of different colors.

➡ ______________________________

17 It is my job to mix, develop, and create colors for clothing.

➡ ______________________________

18 Over the years, I've been gaining insights from the beautiful colors of Caño Cristales.

➡ ______________________________

19 You cannot see the wonderful mixed colors of this river anywhere else in the world.

➡ ______________________________

20 The combination of colorful plants under the water and sunlight makes the colors more alive and bright.

➡ ______________________________

21 Whenever I visit the Caño Cristales, it makes me think that maybe there are still countless colors that are waiting to be created.

➡ ______________________________

____

22 Danny Mehta, Location Scout

➡ ______________________________

23 Vatnajökull National Park, Frozen Beauty of Iceland

➡ ______________________________

24 I'm a location scout and my job is finding perfect places to shoot movies.

➡ ______________________________

25 Iceland is the best place for many location scouts to visit due to its unusual beauty.

➡ ______________________________

26 My personal favorite is the Vatnajökull National Park.

➡ ______________________________

27 The sharp cliffs, blue glacier caves, and long mountain ranges can stand in for any place in the world or the universe.

➡ ______________________________

28 In fact, the recent sci-fi movie we shot here was produced without using computer graphics!

➡ ______________________________

29 Iceland can help make our wildest dreams come true on the movie screen.

➡ ______________________________

본문 Test

※ 다음 괄호 안의 단어들을 우리말에 맞도록 바르게 배열하시오.

1 (World / The / My / Eyes / Through)
➡ ______________________________

2 (beauty / "the / nature / of / us / all. / inspires)
➡ ______________________________

3 (find / let's / out / people / how / different / from / of / fields / work / by / get / inspired / nature.")
➡ ______________________________
____

4 (Wang, / Lin / Ecologist)
➡ ______________________________

5 (the / Tsingy, / Stone / of / Forest / Madagascar)
➡ ______________________________

6 (been / I've / the / visiting / stone / of / forest / Madagascar / study / to / and / plants / for / animals / 20 / over / years.)
➡ ______________________________
____

7 (spiky / the / of / stones / this / are / place / true / of / miracles / nature.)
➡ ______________________________

8 (amazing / this / has / shape / been / by / rainfall. / created)
➡ ______________________________

9 (has / rain / down / cut / stones / the / and / them / made / sharp / over / and / spiky / long / a / of / period / time.)
➡ ______________________________
____

10 (environment / the / is / for / harsh / to / animals / in, / live / but / have / they / found / ways / survive. / to)
➡ ______________________________
____

11 (example, / for / which / lemurs, / only / in / live / Madagascar, / frog-like / have / that / legs / them / help / from / jump / stone / one / to / another. / tower)
➡ ______________________________
____

12 (me, / for / stone / the / is / forest / a / like / jack-in-the-box.)
➡ ______________________________

13 (always / it / me / surprises / and / me / keeps / my / on / toes!)
➡ ______________________________

14 (Smith, / Amber / Colorist / Fashion)
➡ ______________________________

15 (Cristales, / Caño / River / the / Five / of / Colors / Colombia / of)
➡ ______________________________

16 (world / the / filled / is / with / of / millions / colors. / different)
➡ ______________________________

1 내 눈에 비친 세계

2 "자연의 아름다움은 우리 모두에게 영감을 준다.

3 서로 다른 직업 분야의 사람들이 자연에 의해 어떻게 영감을 받는지 알아보자."

4 **Lin Wang, 생태학자**

5 **Tsingy, 마다가스카르의 석림**

6 나는 20년 이상 동안 식물과 동물을 연구하기 위해서 마다가스카르의 석림을 방문하고 있다.

7 이 지역의 뾰족한 돌들은 진정한 자연의 놀라움이다.

8 이 놀라운 모양은 비에 의해서 만들어졌다.

9 비가 오랜 기간 동안 돌을 침식해서 날카롭고 뾰족하게 만들었다.

10 이런 환경은 동물들이 살기에 험난하지만, 동물들은 생존할 방법들을 찾아냈다.

11 예를 들어, 마다가스카르에서만 사는 여우원숭이는 한 개의 돌탑에서 다른 돌탑으로 뛸 수 있도록 도와주는 개구리와 같은 다리를 가지고 있다.

12 나에게 석림은 '잭인더박스(열면 인형이 튀어나오는 상자)'와 같다.

13 그것은 늘 나를 놀라게 하고 정신을 바짝 차리게 한다!

14 **Amber Smith, 패션 색채 전문가**

15 **Caño Cristales, 콜롬비아의 다섯 색깔의 강**

16 세계는 수백만의 다양한 색깔로 가득 차 있다.

Step4

17 (is / it / job / my / mix, / to / and / develop, / colors / create / clothing. / for)
➡ ______________________________

18 (over / years, / the / been / I've / insights / gaining / the / from / colors / beautiful / of / Cristales. / Caño)
➡ ______________________________
____

19 (cannot / you / see / wonderful / the / mixed / of / colors / this / river / else / anywhere / the / in / world.)
➡ ______________________________
____

20 (combination / the / colorful / of / under / plants / water / the / and / makes / sunlight / colors / the / alive / more / bright. / and)
➡ ______________________________
____

21 (I / whenever / vist / Caño / the / Cristales, / makes / it / think / me / maybe / that / are / there / countless / still / that / colors / are / to / waiting / created. / be)
➡ ______________________________
____

22 (Mehta, / Danny / Scout / Location)
➡ ______________________________

23 (Vatnajökull / Park, / National / Beauty / Frozen / Iceland / of)
➡ ______________________________

24 (a / I'm / scout / location / and / job / my / finding / is / places / perfect / shoot / to / movies.)
➡ ______________________________

25 (is / Iceland / the / place / best / many / for / scouts / location / to / due / visit / to / unusual / its / beauty.)
➡ ______________________________
____

26 (personal / my / is / favorite / the / National / Vatnajökull / Park.)
➡ ______________________________

27 (sharp / the / cliffs, / glacier / blue / caves, / long / and / ranges / mountain / can / in / stand / for / place / any / the / in / world / the / or / universe.)
➡ ______________________________
____

28 (fact, / in / recent / the / sci-fi / we / movie / shot / was / here / without / produced / computer / using / graphics!)
➡ ______________________________
____

29 (can / Iceland / make / help / wildest / our / dreams / true / come / the / on / screen. / movie)
➡ ______________________________
____

17 의류를 위해서 색을 섞고, 발전시키고, 만들어 내는 것이 나의 일이다.

18 수년 동안, 나는 카뇨 크리스탈레스의 아름다운 색으로부터 영감을 얻어 오고 있다.

19 이 강의 아름답게 혼합된 색깔은 세상 어느 다른 곳에서도 볼 수 없다.

20 물속의 화려한 식물들과 햇빛의 결합은 그 색깔을 더 생생하고 밝게 만든다.

21 내가 카뇨 크리스탈레스를 방문할 때마다 그 강은 나로 하여금 아마도 여전히 만들어지기를 기다리고 있는 셀 수 없이 많은 색깔이 있음을 생각하게 한다.

22 **Danny Mehta, 장소 섭외가**

23 **Vatnajökull 국립 공원, 아이슬란드의 얼음으로 덮인 아름다움**

24 나는 장소 섭외가이고 나의 일은 영화를 찍기에 완벽한 장소를 찾는 것이다.

25 아이슬란드는 비범한 아름다움 때문에 많은 장소 섭외가들이 방문하기에 최고의 장소이다.

26 내가 개인적으로 가장 선호하는 곳은 바트나이외쿠틀 국립 공원이다.

27 가파른 절벽, 푸른 빙하 동굴, 그리고 긴 산맥들은 세계나 혹은 우주의 어느 장소도 대신할 수 있다.

28 사실상, 우리가 여기서 찍은 최근의 공상 과학 영화는 컴퓨터 그래픽 없이 만들어졌다!

29 아이슬란드는 우리의 가장 무모한 꿈을 영화 스크린에서 실현할 수 있게 해 준다.

본문 Test

※ 다음 우리말을 영어로 쓰시오.

1 **내 눈에 비친 세계**

➡ ______________________________

2 "자연의 아름다움은 우리 모두에게 영감을 준다.

➡ ______________________________

3 서로 다른 직업 분야의 사람들이 자연에 의해 어떻게 영감을 받는지 알아보자."

➡ ______________________________

4 **Lin Wang, 생태학자**

➡ ______________________________

5 **Tsingy, 마다가스카르의 석림**

➡ ______________________________

6 나는 20년 이상 동안 식물과 동물을 연구하기 위해서 마다가스카르의 석림을 방문하고 있다.

➡ ______________________________

7 이 지역의 뾰족한 돌들은 진정한 자연의 놀라움이다.

➡ ______________________________

8 이 놀라운 모양은 비에 의해서 만들어졌다.

➡ ______________________________

9 비가 오랜 기간 동안 돌을 침식해서 날카롭고 뾰족하게 만들었다.

➡ ______________________________

10 이런 환경은 동물들이 살기에 험난하지만, 동물들은 생존할 방법들을 찾아냈다.

➡ ______________________________

11 예를 들어, 마다가스카르에서만 사는 여우원숭이는 한 개의 돌탑에서 다른 돌탑으로 뛸 수 있도록 도와주는 개구리와 같은 다리를 가지고 있다.

➡ ______________________________

____

12 나에게 석림은 '잭인더박스(열면 인형이 튀어나오는 상자)'와 같다.

➡ ______________________________

13 그것은 늘 나를 놀라게 하고 정신을 바짝 차리게 한다!

➡ ______________________________

14 **Amber Smith, 패션 색채 전문가**

➡ ______________________________

15 **Caño Cristales, 콜롬비아의 다섯 색깔의 강**

➡ ______________________________

16 세계는 수백만의 다양한 색깔로 가득 차 있다.

➡ ______________________________

17 의류를 위해서 색을 섞고, 발전시키고, 만들어 내는 것이 나의 일이다.

➡ ________________________________

18 수년 동안, 나는 카뇨 크리스탈레스의 아름다운 색으로부터 영감을 얻어 오고 있다.

➡ ________________________________

19 이 강의 아름답게 혼합된 색깔은 세상 어느 다른 곳에서도 볼 수 없다.

➡ ________________________________

20 물속의 화려한 식물들과 햇빛의 결합은 그 색깔을 더 생생하고 밝게 만든다.

➡ ________________________________

21 내가 카뇨 크리스탈레스를 방문할 때마다 그 강은 나로 하여금 아마도 여전히 만들어지기를 기다리고 있는 셀 수 없이 많은 색깔이 있음을 생각하게 한다.

➡ ________________________________

____

22 **Danny Mehta, 장소 섭외가**

➡ ________________________________

23 **Vatnajökull 국립 공원, 아이슬란드의 얼음으로 덮인 아름다움**

➡ ________________________________

24 나는 장소 섭외가이고 나의 일은 영화를 찍기에 완벽한 장소를 찾는 것이다.

➡ ________________________________

25 아이슬란드는 비범한 아름다움 때문에 많은 장소 섭외가들이 방문하기에 최고의 장소이다.

➡ ________________________________

26 내가 개인적으로 가장 선호하는 곳은 바트나이외쿠틀 국립 공원이다.

➡ ________________________________

27 가파른 절벽, 푸른 빙하 동굴, 그리고 긴 산맥들은 세계나 혹은 우주의 어느 장소도 대신할 수 있다.

➡ ________________________________

____

28 사실상, 우리가 여기서 찍은 최근의 공상 과학 영화는 컴퓨터 그래픽 없이 만들어졌다!

➡ ________________________________

29 아이슬란드는 우리의 가장 무모한 꿈을 영화 스크린에서 실현할 수 있게 해 준다.

➡ ________________________________

※ 다음 우리말과 일치하도록 빈칸에 알맞은 말을 쓰시오.

Communication Step B

1. A: Congratulations ________ ________ the award. ________ ________ that this photo ________ ________ in India. Is that ________?
2. B: Yes, this rainbow cloud ________ ________ ________ thin clouds and water ________.
3. A: Wow, it ________ ________ ________!
4. B: Yes, it is. I ________ ________ ________ ________ more photos of ________ ________.
5. A: I ________ you ________ ________ ________ ________!

1. A: 상 받은 것을 축하해. 이 사진이 인도에서 찍힌 것이라고 들었어. 맞니?
2. B: 응, 이 무지개 구름은 얇은 구름과 물방울에 의해 생긴 거야.
3. A: 와, 정말 멋지다!
4. B: 응, 그래. 어서 더 많은 멋진 구름 사진을 찍고 싶어.
5. A: 행운을 빌어!

Wrap Up 1

1. W: Your uncle, John, is ________ ________ ________ South America this weekend.
2. M: That's great. He ________ ________ ________ for almost 2 years, ________?
3. W: Yeah, he's been in the jungle ________ ________ ________ ________ ________ ________.
4. M: Wow, that's amazing. I ________ ________ ________ ________ him and ________ ________ his stories.
5. W: Me, too. We're ________ ________ with him this Saturday, so ________ ________ ________ ________.
6. M: Okay, I ________, Mom.

1. W: 네 삼촌, John이 이번 주말에 남아메리카에서 돌아올 거야.
2. M: 잘됐네요. 그는 거의 2년 동안 떨어져 있었죠, 그렇죠?
3. W: 그래, 그는 연구를 위해 대부분의 시간을 정글에 있었어.
4. M: 와, 정말 놀랍네요. 빨리 그를 보고 그의 이야기를 듣고 싶어요.
5. W: 나도. 이번 토요일에 그와 저녁 식사를 할 거니까 다른 계획은 세우지 마.
6. M: 알았어요, 안 그럴게요. 엄마.

Think & Write Step A

1. ________ Jiri and Mt. Seorak
2. ________ for ________ Fans
3. • ________ ________ beautiful hiking ________
4. • learn how to get ________ ________ and ________ ________
5. ________ for ________ Fans
6. Madrid and ________
7. • meet ________ ________
8. • learn ________ ________ ________ your soccer skills
9. ________ and London
10. ________ ________ ________ Fans
11. • visit ________ ________ ________
12. • learn ________ ________ ________ pictures ________

1. 지리산과 설악산
2. 하이킹 팬들을 위한 여행
3. • 아름다운 하이킹 길을 따라 걷는다
4. • 좋은 몸매를 유지하고 건강을 유지하는 법을 배운다
5. 축구 팬들을 위한 여행
6. 마드리드와 맨체스터
7. • 유명한 선수들을 만난다
8. • 여러분의 축구 기술을 향상시키는 법을 배운다
9. 파리와 런던
10. 예술 팬들을 위한 여행
11. • 유명한 미술관을 방문한다
12. • 창조적으로 그림을 그리는 법을 배운다

구석구석 지문 Test

Step2

※ 다음 우리말을 영어로 쓰시오.

Communication Step B

1. A: 상 받은 것을 축하해. 이 사진이 인도에서 찍힌 것이라고 들었어. 맞니?
➡ ______
2. B: 응, 이 무지개 구름은 얇은 구름과 물방울에 의해 생긴 거야.
➡ ______
3. A: 와, 정말 멋지다!
➡ ______
4. B: 응, 그래. 어서 더 많은 멋진 구름 사진을 찍고 싶어.
➡ ______
5. A: 행운을 빌어!
➡ ______

Wrap Up 1

1. W: 네 삼촌, John이 이번 주말에 남아메리카에서 돌아올 거야.
➡ ______
2. M: 잘됐네요. 그는 거의 2년 동안 떨어져 있었죠, 그렇죠?
➡ ______
3. W: 그래, 그는 연구를 위해 대부분의 시간을 정글에 있었어.
➡ ______
4. M: 와, 정말 놀랍네요. 빨리 그를 보고 그의 이야기를 듣고 싶어요.
➡ ______
5. W: 나도. 이번 토요일에 그와 저녁 식사를 할 거니까 다른 계획은 세우지 마.
➡ ______
6. M: 알았어요, 안 그럴게요. 엄마.
➡ ______

Think & Write Step A

1. 지리산과 설악산
➡ ______
2. 하이킹 팬들을 위한 여행
➡ ______
3. • 아름다운 하이킹 길을 따라 걷는다
➡ ______
4. • 좋은 몸매를 유지하고 건강을 유지하는 법을 배운다
➡ ______
5. 축구 팬들을 위한 여행
➡ ______
6. 마드리드와 맨체스터
➡ ______
7. • 유명한 선수들을 만난다
➡ ______
8. • 여러분의 축구 기술을 향상시키는 법을 배운다
➡ ______
9. 파리와 런던
➡ ______
10. 예술 팬들을 위한 여행
➡ ______
11. • 유명한 미술관을 방문한다
➡ ______
12. • 창조적으로 그림을 그리는 법을 배운다
➡ ______

단어 Test

Step1

※ 다음 영어를 우리말로 쓰시오.

01 horrible ____________
02 article ____________
03 biography ____________
04 ruin ____________
05 husband ____________
06 detective ____________
07 fortress ____________
08 gamble ____________
09 disappointing ____________
10 afterwards ____________
11 fortune ____________
12 general ____________
13 include ____________
14 locker ____________
15 whenever ____________
16 independence ____________
17 movement ____________
18 wooden ____________
19 odd ____________
20 officer ____________
21 realistic ____________
22 invention ____________
23 embarrassing ____________
24 strange ____________
25 female ____________
26 whisper ____________
27 marriage ____________
28 chest ____________
29 since ____________
30 merchant ____________
31 clinic ____________
32 solve ____________
33 truth ____________
34 scholar ____________
35 instead of ____________
36 yell at ____________
37 be used to (동)명사 ____________
38 devote one's life to 명사 ____________
39 at that moment ____________
40 make an arrangement ____________
41 keep a secret ____________
42 behind one's back ____________
43 It is said that 주어+동사 ~ ____________

단어 Test

Step2

※ 다음 우리말을 영어로 쓰시오.

01 나중에, 그 뒤에 ____________
02 상인 ____________
03 자서전, 전기 ____________
04 서랍장, 큰 상자, 장롱 ____________
05 (정치적 · 사회적) 운동 ____________
06 망치다, 파산시키다 ____________
07 실망시키는 ____________
08 부끄러운, 당황스러운 ____________
09 독립, 광복 ____________
10 이상한 ____________
11 재산, 행운 ____________
12 도박하다, ~을 도박으로 잃다 ____________
13 사회 ____________
14 장군 ____________
15 소곤소곤 이야기하다 ____________
16 ~을 포함하다 ____________
17 기계, 기구 ____________
18 학자 ____________
19 발명품, 발명 ____________
20 끔찍한 ____________
21 기사 ____________
22 결혼, 혼인 ____________
23 여자; 여자의, 여성의 ____________
24 궁금하다 ____________
25 물건 ____________
26 요새 ____________
27 병원, 진료소 ____________
28 진짜 같은, 사실적인 ____________
29 형사, 탐정 ____________
30 구하다 ____________
31 남편 ____________
32 나무로 된, 목재의 ____________
33 사물함 ____________
34 낯선, 모르는 ____________
35 비밀을 지키다 ____________
36 ~에게 고함치다 ____________
37 ~을 보다 ____________
38 청구하다, 청하다 ____________
39 그 순간에 ____________
40 ~ 대신에 ____________
41 입어 보다, 신어 보다 ____________
42 ~을 결정하다 ____________
43 ~하는 데 익숙하다 ____________

단어 Test

Step3

※ 다음 영영풀이에 알맞은 단어를 <보기>에서 골라 쓴 후, 우리말 뜻을 쓰시오.

1 __________: relating to women or girls: ____________

2 __________: a very large amount of money: __________

3 __________: the man that somebody is married to: __________

4 __________: a large strong heavy box used for storing things: ____________

5 __________: to make someone lose all their money or power: ____________

6 __________: an officer of very high rank in the army or air force: __________

7 __________: to contain someone or something as a part: __________

8 __________: a book that someone writes about someone else's life: __________

9 __________: someone who buys and sells goods in large quantities: __________

10 __________: to make someone or something safe from danger, harm, or destruction: __________

11 __________: a large strong building used for defending an important place: __________

12 __________: freedom from control by another country or organization: __________

13 __________: a piece of writing about a particular subject that is published in a newspaper or magazine: __________

14 __________: a gradual development or change of an attitude, opinion, or policy: ____________

15 __________: a small cabinet that can be locked, where you can leave your clothes, bags, etc. while you play a sport or go somewhered: __________

16 __________: someone who studies a particular subject and knows a lot about it, especially a subject that is not scientific: __________

보기

article	husband	save	fortress
locker	ruin	include	chest
movement	female	merchant	fortune
scholar	independence	biography	general

대화문 Test

Step1

※ 다음 우리말과 일치하도록 빈칸에 알맞은 말을 쓰시오.

Listen & Talk 1 Get Ready

A: Kim Deuksin ________ ________ ________.

B: No! I ________ a book and ________ ________ ________ that he was a ________.

C: Don't ________. You are ________ ________.

해석

A: 김득신은 화가였어.
B: 아니야! 내가 책을 읽었는데 그는 학자였다고 해.
C: 싸우지 마. 너희 둘 다 옳아.

Listen & Talk 1 A-1

M: Lisa, ________ are you ________?

W: I'm ________ a ________ of Gwon Giok.

M: I ________ ________ about her. Who is she?

W: She was ________ ________ ________ pilot in Korea. ________ ________ ________ ________ she had ________ 7,000 hours of ________ ________.

M: Wow, I didn't know that.

M: Lisa, 너 뭐 읽고 있니?
W: 권기옥의 전기를 읽고 있어.
M: 그녀에 대해 들어본 적이 없어. 그녀는 누구니?
W: 그녀는 한국의 첫 번째 여성 조종사야. 그녀는 비행시간이 7,000 시간이 넘는다고 해.
M: 와, 난 몰랐어.

Listen & Talk 1 A-2

M: I watched an ________ movie yesterday. Jeong Yakyong was a ________ in it.

W: Jeong Yakyong? Wasn't he a ________ in the Joseon Dynasty?

M: Yeah, ________ ________ ________ ________ ________ ________ ________ ________ a detective. He ________ about 90 ________.

W: Oh, I ________ ________ ________ he was also a ________.

M: 난 어제 흥미 있는 영화를 보았어. 그 영화에서 정약용이 탐정이었어.
W: 정약용? 그는 조선 왕조의 학자 아니었니?
M: 응, 하지만 그는 탐정이기도 했다고 해. 그는 약 90개의 사건을 해결했어.
W: 아, 그가 또한 탐정이었다는 건 몰랐어.

Listen & Talk 1 B

W: Hey, Mark, do you ________ ________ Father Lee Taeseok?

M: Yeah, I've ________ of him. Why?

W: ________ ________ ________ ________ this article. He is going ________ ________ ________ in the ________ ________ textbook in South Sudan.

M: Wow, that's great.

W: Yeah, he ________ the children ________ ________ ________ ________ and a school. It is said ________ ________________ will ________ ________ ________ the textbook.

M: ________ is good ________ hear ________ students will learn about ________ a great person.

W: 어이, Mark, 너 이태석 신부에 대해 아니?
M: 응, 그에 대해 들어본 적이 있어. 왜?
W: 이 기사를 봐. 그는 남수단의 사회 교과서에 실릴 거야.
M: 와, 그거 대단하구나.
W: 그래, 그는 병원과 학교를 지어 아이들을 도와주었어. 그런 이야기들이 교과서에 실릴 거라고 해.
M: 학생들이 그토록 훌륭한 사람에 대해 배울 거라는 말을 들으니 좋군.

Listen & Talk 2 A-1

W: Excuse me, you ________ ________ your backpack inside the ________.

M: Oh, I didn't know that. ________ ________ ________ if I bring in my ________ ________?

W: Yes, that's fine. You can ________ your bag ________ the locker.

M: Okay, thank you.

W: 죄송합니다만, 박물관에 가방을 가지고 들어갈 수 없어요.
M: 아, 몰랐어요. 물병은 가지고 들어가도 괜찮나요?
W: 네, 그건 괜찮아요. 가방은 라커에 두시면 돼요.
M: 알았어요. 감사합니다.

Listen & Talk 2 A-2

W: Hi, ________ ________ the National Museum. ________ can I help you?

M: Hi, ________ ________ ________ ________ ________ ________ ________ ________ the museum?

W: Yes, but please ________ ________ a flash.

M: Oh, I see. Thank you.

W: 안녕하세요, 국립박물관에 오신 걸 환영합니다. 무엇을 도와드릴까요?
M: 안녕하세요, 박물관에서 사진을 찍어도 괜찮나요?
W: 네, 하지만 플래시는 사용하지 마세요.
M: 아, 알겠습니다. 감사합니다.

Listen & Talk 2 B

M: Hello, Ms. Jackson. ________ ________ your tour of the *Hanok Village*?

W: It was wonderful. The houses ________ really beautiful.

M: That's great.

W: Actually, I didn't ________ ________ ________ ________ have dinner. Is it ________ ________ ________ cook in the kitchen at this hour?

M: Yes, but please ________ ________ the kitchen ________ ________ 10 p.m.

W: Okay. The kitchen is ________ the ________ ________, right?

M: Yes, it is. ________ ________ ________ ________ you need anything.

M: 안녕하세요. Jackson 씨. 한옥 마을 관광은 어땠어요?
W: 굉장했어요. 집들이 정말 아름다웠습니다.
M: 대단하네요.
W: 사실 전 저녁식사를 할 기회가 없었어요. 이 시간에 부엌에서 요리해도 괜찮나요?
M: 네, 하지만 부엌이 오후 10시에 문을 닫는 걸 기억하세요.
W: 알겠습니다. 부엌은 5층에 있죠, 맞나요?
M: 네, 그래요. 무언가 필요하시면 제게 말씀해 주세요.

Communication Step A

M: All right, everyone! This way, please. Now, we ________ ________ ________ the Joseon Dynasty. ________ ________ ________ ________, there were ________ interesting ________. This one ________ ________ the *Jagyeongnu*.

W: Is it a ________ ________?

M: Actually, this is a ________ ________. ________ ________ ________ ________ ________ ________ the ________ and ________ ________ water clock in Korea.

W: ________ amazing! ________ ________ ________ ________ I take a ________ ________ it?

M: Sure.

M: 좋아요, 여러분! 이쪽으로 오세요. 이제, 우리는 조선 왕조로 옮겨갑니다. 보시다시피, 많은 흥미 있는 발명품들이 있습니다. 이것은 자격루라고 불립니다.
W: 그것은 악기인가요?
M: 사실은 이것은 물시계입니다. 그것은 한국에서 가장 오래되고, 가장 큰 물시계라고 합니다.
W: 정말 놀랍군요. 그것을 사진 찍어도 괜찮나요?
M: 물론입니다.

Wrap Up 1

W: James, ________ are you ________?

M: Oh, I'm ________ a video about Yi Sunsin.

W: ________ ________ the one that ________ Joseon from Japan?

M: Right. ________ ________ ________ ________ ________ ________ the war only with twelve ________ ________.

W: Wow, ________ can that be ________?

M: He was a ________ ________ ________ ________ ________ plans.

W: James, 뭘 보고 있니?
M: 아, 이순신에 관한 비디오를 보고 있어.
W: 그는 일본으로부터 조선을 구한 사람 아니니?
M: 맞아. 그는 겨우 12척의 목선으로 전쟁에 이겼다고 해.
W: 와, 그게 어떻게 가능할 수 있지?
M: 그는 창의적인 계획을 세운 현명한 장군이었어.

Wrap Up 2

W: Excuse me, sir. ________ ________ ________ ________ have curry or *bibimbap*?

M: ________ ________ ________ have *bibimbap*, please.

W: ________ you are.

M: Thank you. Oh, ________ ________ ________ ________ I use the ________ now?

W: Sure, but ________ the seat light is ________, you should ________ in ________ ________.

M: Okay, thank you.

W: 실례합니다, 선생님. 카레를 드시겠어요 아니면 비빔밥을 드시겠어요?
M: 비빔밥을 먹고 싶습니다.
W: 여기 있습니다.
M: 고마워요. 아, 지금 화장실을 이용해도 괜찮나요?
W: 그럼요, 하지만 좌석 불이 켜져 있으면 선생님 좌석에 있으셔야 합니다.
M: 알았어요, 감사합니다.

대화문 Test

※ 다음 우리말에 맞도록 대화를 영어로 쓰시오.

Listen & Talk 1 Get Ready

A: ______________________

B: ______________________

C: ______________________

A: 김득신은 화가였어.
B: 아니야! 내가 책을 읽었는데 그는 학자였다고 해.
C: 싸우지 마. 너희 둘 다 옳아.

Listen & Talk 1 A-1

M: ______________________

W: ______________________

M: ______________________

W: ______________________

____

M: ______________________

M: Lisa, 너 뭐 읽고 있니?
W: 권기옥의 전기를 읽고 있어.
M: 그녀에 대해 들어본 적이 없어. 그녀는 누구니?
W: 그녀는 한국의 첫 번째 여성 조종사야. 그녀는 비행시간이 7,000 시간이 넘는다고 해.
M: 와, 난 몰랐어.

Listen & Talk 1 A-2

M: ______________________

W: ______________________

M: ______________________

W: ______________________

M: 난 어제 흥미 있는 영화를 보았어. 그 영화에서 정약용이 탐정이었어.
W: 정약용? 그는 조선 왕조의 학자 아니었니?
M: 응, 하지만 그는 탐정이기도 했다고 해. 그는 약 90개의 사건을 해결했어.
W: 아, 그가 또한 탐정이었다는 건 몰랐어.

Listen & Talk 1 B

W: ______________________

M: ______________________

W: ______________________

____

M: ______________________

W: ______________________

____

M: ______________________

W: 어이, Mark, 너 이태석 신부에 대해 아니?
M: 응, 그에 대해 들어본 적이 있어. 왜?
W: 이 기사를 봐. 그는 남수단의 사회 교과서에 실릴 거야.
M: 와, 그거 대단하구나.
W: 그래, 그는 병원과 학교를 지어 아이들을 도와주었어. 그런 이야기들이 교과서에 실릴 거라고 해.
M: 학생들이 그토록 훌륭한 사람에 대해 배울 거라는 말을 들으니 좋군.

Listen & Talk 2 A-1

W: ______________________________

M: ______________________________

W: ______________________________

M: ______________________________

W: 죄송합니다만, 박물관에 가방을 가지고 들어갈 수 없어요.
M: 아, 몰랐어요. 물병은 가지고 들어가도 괜찮나요?
W: 네, 그건 괜찮아요. 가방은 라커에 두시면 돼요.
M: 알았어요. 감사합니다.

Listen & Talk 2 A-2

W: ______________________________

M: ______________________________

W: ______________________________

M: ______________________________

W: 안녕하세요, 국립박물관에 오신 걸 환영합니다. 무엇을 도와드릴까요?
M: 안녕하세요, 박물관에서 사진을 찍어도 괜찮나요?
W: 네, 하지만 플래시는 사용하지 마세요.
M: 아, 알겠습니다. 감사합니다.

Listen & Talk 2 B

M: ______________________________

W: ______________________________

M: ______________________________

W: ______________________________

____

M: ______________________________

W: ______________________________

M: ______________________________

M: 안녕하세요, Jackson 씨. 한옥 마을 관광은 어땠어요?
W: 굉장했어요. 집들이 정말 아름다웠습니다.
M: 대단하네요.
W: 사실 전 저녁식사를 할 기회가 없었어요. 이 시간에 부엌에서 요리해도 괜찮나요?
M: 네, 하지만 부엌이 오후 10시에 문을 닫는 걸 기억하세요.
W: 알겠습니다. 부엌은 5층에 있죠, 맞나요?
M: 네, 그래요. 무언가 필요하시면 제게 말씀해 주세요.

Communication Step A

M: ____________________

____

____

W: ____________________

M: ____________________

____

W: ____________________

M: ____________________

M: 좋아요, 여러분! 이쪽으로 오세요. 이제, 우리는 조선 왕조로 옮겨갑니다. 보시다시피, 많은 흥미 있는 발명품들이 있습니다. 이것은 자격루라고 불립니다.
W: 그것은 악기인가요?
M: 사실은 이것은 물시계입니다. 그것은 한국에서 가장 오래되고, 가장 큰 물시계라고 합니다.
W: 정말 놀랍군요. 그것을 사진 찍어도 괜찮나요?
M: 물론입니다.

Wrap Up 1

W: ____________________

M: ____________________

W: ____________________

M: ____________________

W: ____________________

M: ____________________

W: James, 뭘 보고 있니?
M: 아, 이순신에 관한 비디오를 보고 있어.
W: 그는 일본으로부터 조선을 구한 사람 아니니?
M: 맞아. 그는 겨우 12척의 목선으로 전쟁에 이겼다고 해.
W: 와, 그게 어떻게 가능할 수 있지?
M: 그는 창의적인 계획을 세운 현명한 장군이었어.

Wrap Up 2

W: ____________________

M: ____________________

W: ____________________

M: ____________________

W: ____________________

M: ____________________

W: 실례합니다, 선생님. 카레를 드시겠어요 아니면 비빔밥을 드시겠어요?
M: 비빔밥을 먹고 싶습니다.
W: 여기 있습니다.
M: 고마워요. 아, 지금 화장실을 이용해도 괜찮나요?
W: 그럼요, 하지만 좌석 불이 켜져 있으면 선생님 좌석에 있으셔야 합니다.
M: 알았어요, 감사합니다.

본문 Test

Step1

※ 다음 우리말과 일치하도록 빈칸에 알맞은 것을 골라 쓰시오.

1 The ________ of ________ ________
A. Father B. Secret C. My

2 In 1946, a ________ man ________ me and ________, "Are you Mr. Kim Yonghwan's ________?"
A. visited B. daughter C. asked D. strange

3 For me, this was am ________ question because I was more ________ ________ ________ called the daughter of a *parakho*.
A. used B. odd C. to D. being

4 "I'm ________ ________ ________.
A. father's B. your C. friend

5 You may ________ ________ it is ________, but your father...," the man said.
A. if B. wonder C. true

6 At that ________, I was ________ ________ news since I did not have good ________ of my father.
A. disappointing B. memories C. moment D. expecting

7 ________ in the 1920's, ________ people saw me in the village, they would say, "________ ________ the parakho's daughter."
A. goes B. back C. there D. whenever

8 My father was a son ________ a very ________ ________.
A. rich B. from C. family

9 ________ of ________ the life of a *seonbi*, he was ________ at the ________ house.
A. gambling B. living C. instead D. always

10 That is ________ he was called a *parakho*, ________ means someone who ________ his family's ________.
A. which B. why C. fortune D. ruins

11 "Your father has ________ ________ all of the money, and now he's ________ ________ more.
A. away B. asking C. gambled D. for

12 Go and tell him that we ________ no more money ________," my mother________ tell me ________ she sent me to the gambling house.
A. left B. whenever C. would D. have

13 Then, my father would ________ ________ me ________, "Why did you come ________?
A. angrily B. empty-handed C. at D. yell

14 ________ me ________ money!"
A. more B. bring

1 아버지의 비밀

2 1946년에, 낯선 남자가 나를 찾아와 물었다. "당신이 김용환 씨의 딸입니까?"

3 나는 파락호의 딸이라고 불리는 것이 더 익숙했으므로 나에게 이것은 이상한 질문이었다.

4 "나는 당신 아버지의 친구입니다.

5 당신은 이것이 사실인지 의아하겠지만, 당신의 아버지는…."이라고 그 남자는 말했다.

6 나는 내 아버지에 대해 좋은 기억을 가지고 있지 않았으므로 그 순간에 실망스러운 소식을 예상하고 있었다.

7 1920년대에 마을에서 사람들이 나를 볼 때마다 그들은 "저기에 파락호의 딸이 가네."라고 말하곤 했다.

8 나의 아버지는 매우 부유한 집안의 아들이었다.

9 선비의 삶을 사는 대신, 아버지는 항상 도박장에 계셨다.

10 그것이 그가 집안의 재산을 탕진하는 사람이라는 뜻의 파락호로 불린 이유이다.

11 "네 아버지는 도박으로 모든 돈을 써 버리고 지금 더 요구하고 계신다.

12 가서 더 이상 남아 있는 돈이 없다고 말씀드려라."라고 나의 어머니는 나를 도박장으로 보낼 때마다 말씀하시곤 했다.

13 그러면, 아버지는 나에게 화를 내시며 소리치셨다. "왜 빈손으로 왔니?

14 돈을 더 가져와!"

15 When I was sixteen years old, my family ________ ________ ________ an ________for me to marry Mr. Seo.
A. arrangement B. already C. made D. had

16 As ________ of the wedding ________, Mr. Seo's family sent my family some money to buy a new ________ for ________.
A. part B. chest C. tradition D. clothes

17 ________ ________ the wedding day, my mother came into my room and said, "Your father has ________ the ________ for the chest."
A. before B. taken C. right D. money

18 I asked ________, "How could he do ________ a ________ ________?
A. thing B. such C. horrible D. angrily

19 ________ ________ we ________ now?"
A. do B. should C. what

20 "We ________ ________ ________.
A. choice B. no C. have

21 You'll ________ ________ ________ your aunt's old ________," my mother said.
A. chest B. to C. have D. take

22 "________ ________ for the family," people would whisper ________ my ________.
A. embarrassing B. back C. how D. behind

23 ________ the first day of ________, life at my husband's house had ________ ________ for me.
A. marriage B. difficult C. since D. been

24 "Your father, my ________ friend...," my father's friend ________ his ________.
A. continued B. dear C. story

25 "He ________ ________ a ________.
A. not B. was C. gambler

26 Your father sent the ________ ________ to the ________ ________ in Manchuria.
A. money B. fighters C. family D. independence

27 He ________ ________ look like a gambler to ________ this a ________ from the Japanese officers."
A. secret B. himself C. keep D. made

28 At first, I was not ________ ________ he was ________ the ________.
A. telling B. if C. truth D. sure

29 But ________, I found ________ the truth about my father and I ________ that I had been ________ about him.
A. wrong B. afterwards C. out D. realized

30 Ever ________ that moment, I have been ________ to be the daughter of a *parakho* who had ________ his life to the independence ________.
A. proud B. devoted C. since D. movement

15 내가 16살이 되었을 때, 나의 가족은 나를 서 씨와 결혼시키기로 이미 결정을 했었다.

16 결혼 풍습의 일부로, 서 씨네 가족은 새 장롱을 사라고 우리 가족에게 돈을 보냈다.

17 결혼식 바로 전날, 나의 어머니는 내 방에 들어오셔서 말씀하셨다. "네 아버지가 장롱을 살 돈을 가져가 버렸다."

18 나는 화가 나서 물었다 "어떻게 그리 끔찍한 일을 하실 수 있나요?

19 우린 이제 어떡해요?"

20 "우리에게 선택권은 없구나.

21 큰어머니의 옛 장롱을 가져가야겠구나."라고 어머니가 말씀하셨다.

22 "가문에 부끄러운 일이야."라고 사람들이 내 뒤에서 속삭이곤 했다.

23 결혼 첫날부터, 남편의 집에서의 생활은 나에게 힘겨웠다.

24 "당신의 아버지, 나의 친애하는 친구…," 나의 아버지의 친구분은 그의 이야기를 이어가셨다.

25 "그는 도박꾼이 아니었어요.

26 당신의 아버지는 가족의 돈을 만주에 있는 독립운동가들에게 보냈답니다.

27 그는 이것을 일본 순사들에게 비밀로 하기 위해 그 자신을 도박꾼처럼 보이게 했어요."

28 처음엔, 나는 그분이 사실을 얘기하시는 건지 확신할 수 없었다.

29 그러나 나중에, 나는 나의 아버지에 대한 진실을 알게 되었고 내가 아버지에 관해 오해하고 있었다는 것을 깨달았다.

30 그 순간부터, 나는 독립운동에 그의 인생을 헌신하신 파락호의 딸인 것이 자랑스러웠다.

본문 Test

Step2

※ 다음 우리말과 일치하도록 빈칸에 알맞은 말을 쓰시오.

1 The ________ of My ________

2 In 1946, ________ ________ ________ ________ me and ________, "Are you Mr. Kim Yonghwan's daughter?"

3 For me, this was ________ ________ ________ because I ________ ________ ________ ________ ________ ________ the daughter of a *parakho*.

4 "I'm ________ ________ ________.

5 You may ________ ________ it is ________, but your father...," the man said.

6 At that moment, I was ________ ________ news ________ I did not have ________ ________ of my father.

7 ________ in the 1920's, ________ people saw me in the village, they would say, "________ ________ the parakho's daughter."

8 My father was a son ________ a very ________ ________.

9 ________ ________ ________ the life of a *seonbi*, he was always at the ________ ________.

10 ________ ________ ________ he ________ ________ a *parakho*, ________ means someone who ________ his family's fortune.

11 "Your father ________ ________ ________ all of the money, and now he's ________ ________ more.

12 Go and tell him that we ________ ________ ________ ________ ________," my mother ________ tell me ________ she ________ me to the gambling house.

13 Then, my father ________ ________ ________ me ________, "Why did you come ________?

14 ________ ________ more ________!"

1 아버지의 비밀

2 1946년에, 낯선 남자가 나를 찾아와 물었다. "당신이 김용환 씨의 딸입니까?"

3 나는 파락호의 딸이라고 불리는 것이 더 익숙했으므로 나에게 이것은 이상한 질문이었다.

4 "나는 당신 아버지의 친구입니다.

5 당신은 이것이 사실인지 의아하겠지만, 당신의 아버지는…,"이라고 그 남자는 말했다.

6 나는 내 아버지에 대해 좋은 기억을 가지고 있지 않았으므로 그 순간에 실망스러운 소식을 예상하고 있었다.

7 1920년대에 마을에서 사람들이 나를 볼 때마다 그들은 "저기에 파락호의 딸이 가네."라고 말하곤 했다.

8 나의 아버지는 매우 부유한 집안의 아들이었다.

9 선비의 삶을 사는 대신, 아버지는 항상 도박장에 계셨다.

10 그것이 그가 집안의 재산을 탕진하는 사람이라는 뜻의 파락호로 불린 이유이다.

11 "네 아버지는 도박으로 모든 돈을 써 버리고 지금 더 요구하고 계신다.

12 가서 더 이상 남아 있는 돈이 없다고 말씀드려라."라고 나의 어머니는 나를 도박장으로 보낼 때마다 말씀하시곤 했다.

13 그러면, 아버지는 나에게 화를 내시며 소리치셨다. "왜 빈손으로 왔니?

14 돈을 더 가져와!"

15 When I was sixteen years old, my family _______ _______ _______ _______ _______ for me to _______ Mr. Seo.

16 _______ _______ _______ the wedding tradition, Mr. Seo's family sent my family some money to buy _______ _______ _______ _______ _______.

17 _______ _______ the wedding day, my mother _______ _______ my room and said, "Your father _______ _______ _______ _______ for the chest."

18 I asked _______, "How could he do _______ _______ _______ _______?

19 _______ should we do now?"

20 "We have _______ _______.

21 _______ _______ _______ _______ your aunt's old chest," my mother said.

22 "_______ _______ for the family," people would _______ _______ _______ _______.

23 Since the first day of _______, life at my husband's house _______ _______ _______ _______ _______.

24 "Your father, my dear friend...," my father's friend _______ _______ _______.

25 "He was not _______ _______.

26 Your father sent the family money to the _______ _______ in Manchuria.

27 He _______ _______ look like a gambler to _______ _______ _______ _______ _______ the _______ _______."

28 At first, I was not sure _______ he was _______ the _______.

29 But _______, I found out the truth about my father and I realized that I _______ _______ _______ about him.

30 Ever since that moment, I have been proud to be the daughter of a *parakho* who _______ _______ _______ _______ _______ the _______ _______.

15 내가 16살이 되었을 때, 나의 가족은 나를 서 씨와 결혼시키기로 이미 결정을 했었다.

16 결혼 풍습의 일부로, 서 씨네 가족은 새 장롱을 사라고 우리 가족에게 돈을 보냈다.

17 결혼식 바로 전날, 나의 어머니는 내 방에 들어오셔서 말씀하셨다. "네 아버지가 장롱을 살 돈을 가져가 버렸다."

18 나는 화가 나서 물었다 "어떻게 그리 끔찍한 일을 하실 수 있나요?

19 우린 이제 어떡해요?"

20 "우리에게 선택권은 없구나.

21 큰어머니의 옛 장롱을 가져가야겠구나."라고 어머니가 말씀하셨다.

22 "가문에 부끄러운 일이야."라고 사람들이 내 뒤에서 속삭이곤 했다.

23 결혼 첫날부터, 남편의 집에서의 생활은 나에게 힘겨웠다.

24 "당신의 아버지, 나의 친애하는 친구…." 나의 아버지의 친구분은 그의 이야기를 이어가셨다.

25 "그는 도박꾼이 아니었어요.

26 당신의 아버지는 가족의 돈을 만주에 있는 독립운동가들에게 보냈답니다.

27 그는 이것을 일본 순사들에게 비밀로 하기 위해 그 자신을 도박꾼처럼 보이게 했어요."

28 처음엔, 나는 그분이 사실을 얘기하시는 건지 확신할 수 없었다.

29 그러나 나중에, 나는 나의 아버지에 대한 진실을 알게 되었고 내가 아버지에 관해 오해하고 있었다는 것을 깨달았다.

30 그 순간부터, 나는 독립운동에 그의 인생을 헌신하신 파락호의 딸인 것이 자랑스러웠다.

※ 다음 문장을 우리말로 쓰시오.

1 The Secret of My Father

➡ ______________________________

2 In 1946, a strange man visited me and asked, “Are you Mr. Kim Yonghwan’s daughter?

➡ ______________________________

3 For me, this was an odd question because I was more used to being called the daughter of a *parakho*.

➡ ______________________________

4 “I’m your father’s friend.

➡ ______________________________

5 You may wonder if it is true, but your father...,” the man said.

➡ ______________________________

6 At that moment, I was expecting disappointing news since I did not have good memories of my father.

➡ ______________________________

7 Back in the 1920’s, whenever people saw me in the village, they would say, “There goes the *parakho’s* daughter.”

➡ ______________________________

8 My father was a son from a very rich family.

➡ ______________________________

9 Instead of living the life of a seonbi, he was always at the gambling house.

➡ ______________________________

10 That is why he was called a parakho, which means someone who ruins his family’s fortune.

➡ ______________________________

11 “Your father has gambled away all of the money, and now he’s asking for more.

➡ ______________________________

12 Go and tell him that we have no more money left,” my mother would tell me whenever she sent me to the gambling house.

➡ ______________________________

13 Then, my father would yell at me angrily, “Why did you come empty-handed?

➡ ______________________________

14 Bring me more money!”

➡ ______________________________

15 When I was sixteen years old, my family had already made an arrangement for me to marry Mr. Seo.

➡ ______________________________

16 As part of the wedding tradition, Mr. Seo's family sent my family some money to buy a new chest for clothes.

➡ ______________________________

17 Right before the wedding day, my mother came into my room and said, "Your father has taken the money for the chest."

➡ ______________________________

18 I asked angrily, "How could he do such a horrible thing?

➡ ______________________________

19 What should we do now?"

➡ ______________________________

20 "We have no choice.

➡ ______________________________

21 You'll have to take your aunt's old chest," my mother said.

➡ ______________________________

22 "How embarrassing for the family," people would whisper behind my back.

➡ ______________________________

23 Since the first day of marriage, life at my husband's house had been difficult for me.

➡ ______________________________

24 "Your father, my dear friend...," my father's friend continued his story.

➡ ______________________________

25 "He was not a gambler.

➡ ______________________________

26 Your father sent the family money to the independence fighters in Manchuria.

➡ ______________________________

27 He made himself look like a gambler to keep this a secret from the Japanese officers."

➡ ______________________________

28 At first, I was not sure if he was telling the truth.

➡ ______________________________

29 But afterwards, I found out the truth about my father and I realized that I had been wrong about him.

➡ ______________________________

30 Ever since that moment, I have been proud to be the daughter of a parakho who had devoted his life to the independence movemen

➡ ______________________________

본문 Test

Step4

※ 다음 괄호 안의 단어들을 우리말에 맞도록 바르게 배열하시오.

1 (Secret / The / My / of / Father)
➡ ______________________

2 (1946, / in / strange / a / visited / man / me / asked, / and / "are / Mr. / you / Kim / daughter?" / Yonghwan's)
➡ ______________________

3 (me, / for / was / this / odd / an / question / I / because / was / used / more / to / called / being / daughter / the / a / of / *parakho*.)
➡ ______________________

4 (your / "I'm / friend. / father's)
➡ ______________________

5 (may / you / wonder / it / if / true, / is / but / father...," / your / man / the / said.)
➡ ______________________

6 (that / at / moment, / was / I / expecting / news / disappointing / since / did / I / have / not / good / of / memories / father. / my)
➡ ______________________

7 (in / back / 1920's, / the / whenever / saw / people / me / the / in / village, / would / they / say, / goes / "there / *parakho*'s / the / daughter.")
➡ ______________________

8 (father / my / a / was / son / a / from / rich / very / family.)
➡ ______________________

9 (of / instead / living / life / the / a / of / *seonbi*, / was / he / at / always / the / house. / gambling)
➡ ______________________

10 (is / that / why / was / he / called / *parakho*, / a / means / which / who / someone / ruins / family's / his / fortune.)
➡ ______________________

11 (father / your / has / away / gambled / all / the / of / money, / now / and / he's / for / asking / more.)
➡ ______________________

12 (tell / and / go / him / we / that / no / have / money / more / left," / mother / my / tell / would / whenever / me / she / me / sent / to / gambling / the / house.)
➡ ______________________

13 (my / then, / father / yell / would / me / at / angrily, / did / "why / come / you / empty-handed?)
➡ ______________________

14 (me / bring / money!" / more)
➡ ______________________

1 아버지의 비밀

2 1946년에, 낯선 남자가 나를 찾아와 물었다. "당신이 김용환 씨의 딸입니까?"

3 나는 파락호의 딸이라고 불리는 것이 더 익숙했으므로 나에게 이것은 이상한 질문이었다.

4 "나는 당신 아버지의 친구입니다.

5 당신은 이것이 사실인지 의아하겠지만, 당신의 아버지는…,"이라고 그 남자는 말했다.

6 나는 내 아버지에 대해 좋은 기억을 가지고 있지 않았으므로 그 순간에 실망스러운 소식을 예상하고 있었다.

7 1920년대에 마을에서 사람들이 나를 볼 때마다 그들은 "저기에 파락호의 딸이 가네."라고 말하곤 했다.

8 나의 아버지는 매우 부유한 집안의 아들이었다.

9 선비의 삶을 사는 대신, 아버지는 항상 도박장에 계셨다.

10 그것이 그가 집안의 재산을 탕진하는 사람이라는 뜻의 파락호로 불린 이유이다.

11 "네 아버지는 도박으로 모든 돈을 써 버리고 지금 더 요구하고 계신다.

12 가서 더 이상 남아 있는 돈이 없다고 말씀드려라."라고 나의 어머니는 나를 도박장으로 보낼 때마다 말씀하시곤 했다.

13 그러면, 아버지는 나에게 화를 내시며 소리치셨다. "왜 빈손으로 왔니?

14 돈을 더 가져와!"

15 (I / when / was / years / sixteen / old, / family / my / already / had / an / made / arrangement / me / for / marry / to / Seo. / Mr.)
➡ ______________________________
____

16 (part / as / the / of / tradition, / wedding / Seo's / Mr. / sent / family / my / some / family / money / buy / to / a / chest / new / clothes. / for)
➡ ______________________________
____

17 (before / right / the / day, / wedding / mother / my / into / came / room / my / and / said, / father / "your / taken / has / the / for / money / chest." / the)
➡ ______________________________
____

18 (asked / I / angrily, / could / "how / do / he / a / such / thing? / horrible)
➡ ______________________________

19 (should / what / do / we / now?")
➡ ______________________________

20 (have / "we / choice. / no)
➡ ______________________________

21 (have / you'll / take / to / aunt's / your / chest," / old / mother / my / said.)
➡ ______________________________

22 (embarrassing / "how / the / for / family," / would / people / whisper / my / behind / back.)
➡ ______________________________

23 (the / since / day / first / marriage, / of / life / my / at / husband's / had / house / been / for / difficult / me.)
➡ ______________________________
____

24 (father / "your / dear / my / friend...," / father's / my / continued / friend / story. / his)
➡ ______________________________

25 (was / "he / a / not / gambler.)
➡ ______________________________

26 (father / your / sent / family / the / to / money / the / fighters / independence / Manchuria. / in)
➡ ______________________________

27 (made / he / look / himself / like / gambler / a / keep / to / this / secret / a / from / Japanese / the / officers.")
➡ ______________________________
____

28 (first, / at / was / I / sure / not / he / if / telling / was / truth. / the)
➡ ______________________________

29 (afterwards, / but / found / I / the / out / truth / about / father / my / and / realized / I / that / been / had / about / him. / wrong)
➡ ______________________________
____

30 (since / ever / moment, / that / have / I / been / to / proud / be / daughter / the / a / of / *parakho* / who / devoted / had / life / his / the / to / movement. / independence)
➡ ______________________________
____

15 내가 16살이 되었을 때, 나의 가족은 나를 서 씨와 결혼시키기로 이미 결정을 했었다.

16 결혼 풍습의 일부로, 서 씨네 가족은 새 장롱을 사라고 우리 가족에게 돈을 보냈다.

17 결혼식 바로 전날, 나의 어머니는 내 방에 들어오셔서 말씀하셨다. "네 아버지가 장롱을 살 돈을 가져가 버렸다."

18 나는 화가 나서 물었다 "어떻게 그리 끔찍한 일을 하실 수 있나요?

19 우린 이제 어떡해요?"

20 "우리에게 선택권은 없구나.

21 큰어머니의 옛 장롱을 가져가야겠구나."라고 어머니가 말씀하셨다.

22 "가문에 부끄러운 일이야."라고 사람들이 내 뒤에서 속삭이곤 했다.

23 결혼 첫날부터, 남편의 집에서의 생활은 나에게 힘겨웠다.

24 "당신의 아버지, 나의 친애하는 친구…," 나의 아버지의 친구분은 그의 이야기를 이어가셨다.

25 "그는 도박꾼이 아니었어요.

26 당신의 아버지는 가족의 돈을 만주에 있는 독립운동가들에게 보냈답니다.

27 그는 이것을 일본 순사들에게 비밀로 하기 위해 그 자신을 도박꾼처럼 보이게 했어요."

28 처음엔, 나는 그분이 사실을 얘기하시는 건지 확신할 수 없었다.

29 그러나 나중에, 나는 나의 아버지에 대한 진실을 알게 되었고 내가 아버지에 관해 오해하고 있었다는 것을 깨달았다.

30 그 순간부터, 나는 독립운동에 그의 인생을 헌신하신 파락호의 딸인 것이 자랑스러웠다.

본문 Test

Step5

※ 다음 우리말을 영어로 쓰시오.

1 아버지의 비밀

➡ ______________________________

2 1946년에, 낯선 남자가 나를 찾아와 물었다. "당신이 김용환 씨의 딸입니까?"

➡ ______________________________

3 나는 파락호의 딸이라고 불리는 것이 더 익숙했으므로 나에게 이것은 이상한 질문이었다.

➡ ______________________________

4 "나는 당신 아버지의 친구입니다.

➡ ______________________________

5 당신은 이것이 사실인지 의아하겠지만, 당신의 아버지는…,"이라고 그 남자는 말했다.

➡ ______________________________

6 나는 내 아버지에 대해 좋은 기억을 가지고 있지 않았으므로 그 순간에 실망스러운 소식을 예상하고 있었다.

➡ ______________________________

7 1920년대에 마을에서 사람들이 나를 볼 때마다 그들은 "저기에 파락호의 딸이 가네."라고 말하곤 했다.

➡ ______________________________

____

8 나의 아버지는 매우 부유한 집안의 아들이었다.

➡ ______________________________

9 선비의 삶을 사는 대신, 아버지는 항상 도박장에 계셨다.

➡ ______________________________

10 그것이 그가 집안의 재산을 탕진하는 사람이라는 뜻의 파락호로 불린 이유이다.

➡ ______________________________

11 "네 아버지는 도박으로 모든 돈을 써 버리고 지금 더 요구하고 계신다.

➡ ______________________________

12 가서 더 이상 남아 있는 돈이 없다고 말씀드려라."라고 나의 어머니는 나를 도박장으로 보낼 때마다 말씀하시곤 했다.

➡ ______________________________

____

13 그러면, 아버지는 나에게 화를 내시며 소리치셨다. "왜 빈손으로 왔니?

➡ ______________________________

14 돈을 더 가져와!"

➡ ______________________________

15 내가 16살이 되었을 때, 나의 가족은 나를 서 씨와 결혼시키기로 이미 결정을 했었다.

➡

16 결혼 풍습의 일부로, 서 씨네 가족은 새 장롱을 사라고 우리 가족에게 돈을 보냈다.

➡

17 결혼식 바로 전날, 나의 어머니는 내 방에 들어오셔서 말씀하셨다. "네 아버지가 장롱을 살 돈을 가져가 버렸다."

➡

18 나는 화가 나서 물었다 "어떻게 그리 끔찍한 일을 하실 수 있나요?

➡

19 우린 이제 어떡해요?"

➡

20 "우리에게 선택권은 없구나.

➡

21 큰어머니의 옛 장롱을 가져가야겠구나."라고 어머니가 말씀하셨다.

➡

22 "가문에 부끄러운 일이야."라고 사람들이 내 뒤에서 속삭이곤 했다.

➡

23 결혼 첫날부터, 남편의 집에서의 생활은 나에게 힘겨웠다.

➡

24 "당신의 아버지, 나의 친애하는 친구…," 나의 아버지의 친구분은 그의 이야기를 이어가셨다.

➡

25 "그는 도박꾼이 아니었어요.

➡

26 당신의 아버지는 가족의 돈을 만주에 있는 독립운동가들에게 보냈답니다.

➡

27 그는 이것을 일본 순사들에게 비밀로 하기 위해 그 자신을 도박꾼처럼 보이게 했어요."

➡

28 처음엔, 나는 그분이 사실을 얘기하시는 건지 확신할 수 없었다.

➡

29 그러나 나중에, 나는 나의 아버지에 대한 진실을 알게 되었고 내가 아버지에 관해 오해하고 있었다는 것을 깨달았다.

➡

30 그 순간부터, 나는 독립운동에 그의 인생을 헌신하신 파락호의 딸인 것이 자랑스러웠다.

➡

구석구석 지문 Test

Step1

※ 다음 우리말과 일치하도록 빈칸에 알맞은 말을 쓰시오.

Grammar in Real Life A

1. Mary Jane, your fans ________ ________ ________ about ________ ________.
2. 1. ________ you ________ ________ ________ a new song this month?
3. 2. Are you ________ ________ ________ music ________?
4. 3. Do you have any ________ ________ ________ ________ ________ ________?
5. 4. Are you ________ ________ ________ ________ a ________ ________ this year?

1. Mary Jane, 너의 팬들은 너의 계획에 대해 많은 질문들을 가지고 있어.
2. 1. 넌 이 달에 새 노래를 발표할 거니?
3. 2. 넌 다양한 음악 장르에 관심이 있니?
4. 3. 넌 다른 아티스트들과 일할 계획을 가지고 있니?
5. 4. 넌 금년에 월드 투어를 떠날 거니?

Grammar in Real Life B

1. When I ________ ________ ________, my parents ________ ________ out for a walk.
2. The house was dark and quiet, but it ________ ________ ________ ________ ________.
3. I ________ that I ________ ________ the door in my room open.
4. I ________ that someone ________ ________ the lamp.
5. I ________ ________ that someone ________ ________ my cookies on the table.
6. ________ ________ I knew ________ ________ ________!
7. I ________ ________ ________ of my dog, Lucy, and the cat next door

1. 내가 집에 돌아왔을 때 나의 부모님은 산보를 나가셨다.
2 집은 어둡고 조용했지만, 조금 이상해 보였다.
3. 나는 내 방문을 열어둔 것이 기억났다.
4. 나는 누군가가 램프를 깨뜨린 것을 알았다.
5. 나는 누군가가 식탁 위에 있던 내 쿠키를 먹은 것을 알아냈다.
6. 마침내 나는 누가 그런 일을 했는지 알았다!
7. 나는 내 개 Lucy와 옆집 고양이의 작은 발자국들을 발견했다.

After You Read: Read and Write A

1. The ________ of My Father
2. I ________ my father was ...
3. My father ________ ________ ________ a *parakho*.
4. He ________ ________ ________ a rich family but he ________ ________ all of the money.
5. He ________ ________ the money for ________ ________ ________ ________ ________.
6. ________ my father was ...
7. My father was not a gambler.
8. He ________ the family money to the ________ ________ in Manchuria.
9. He ________ ________ ________ ________ a gambler to ________ ________ ________ ________ from the Japanese officers.

1. 나의 아버지의 비밀
2. 나는 아버지가 …라고 생각했다.
3. 나의 아버지는 '파락호'라고 알려져 있었다.
4. 그는 부잣집에 태어났지만, 모든 돈을 노름으로 날렸다.
5. 그는 심지어 새 장롱을 살 돈도 가져갔다.
6. 사실 나의 아버지는 …이었다.
7. 나의 아버지는 노름꾼이 아니었다.
8. 그는 가족의 돈을 만주에 있는 독립 운동가들에게 보냈다.
9. 그는 일본 경찰들로부터 이것을 비밀로 지키려고 스스로를 노름꾼처럼 보이게 했다.

구석구석 지문 Test

※ 다음 우리말을 영어로 쓰시오.

Grammar in Real Life A

1. Mary Jane, 너의 팬들은 너의 계획에 대해 많은 질문들을 가지고 있어.
➡ ______
2. 1. 넌 이 달에 새 노래를 발표할 거니?
➡ ______
3. 2. 넌 다양한 음악 장르에 관심이 있니?
➡ ______
4. 3. 넌 다른 아티스트들과 일할 계획을 가지고 있니?
➡ ______
5. 4. 넌 금년에 월드 투어를 떠날 거니?
➡ ______

Grammar in Real Life B

1. 내가 집에 돌아왔을 때 나의 부모님은 산보를 나가셨다.
➡ ______
2. 집은 어둡고 조용했지만, 조금 이상해 보였다.
➡ ______
3. 나는 내 방문을 열어둔 것이 기억났다.
➡ ______
4. 나는 누군가가 램프를 깨뜨린 것을 알았다.
➡ ______
5. 나는 누군가가 식탁 위에 있던 내 쿠키를 먹은 것을 알아냈다.
➡ ______
6. 마침내 나는 누가 그런 일을 했는지 알았다!
➡ ______
7. 나는 내 개 Lucy와 옆집 고양이의 작은 발자국들을 발견했다.
➡ ______

After You Read: Read and Write A

1. 나의 아버지의 비밀
➡ ______
2. 나는 아버지가 …라고 생각했다.
➡ ______
3. 나의 아버지는 '파락호'라고 알려져 있었다.
➡ ______
4. 그는 부잣집에 태어났지만, 모든 돈을 노름으로 날렸다.
➡ ______
5. 그는 심지어 새 장롱을 살 돈도 가져갔다.
➡ ______
6. 사실 나의 아버지는 …이었다.
➡ ______
7. 나의 아버지는 노름꾼이 아니었다.
➡ ______
8. 그는 가족의 돈을 만주에 있는 독립 운동가들에게 보냈다.
➡ ______
9. 그는 일본 경찰들로부터 이것을 비밀로 지키려고 스스로를 노름꾼처럼 보이게 했다.
➡ ______

단어 Test

Step1

※ 다음 영어를 우리말로 쓰시오.

01 background ______
02 anchor ______
03 conductor ______
04 deliver ______
05 thumb ______
06 imagine ______
07 beat ______
08 recommend ______
09 talented ______
10 instrument ______
11 broadcast ______
12 choir ______
13 local ______
14 pain ______
15 mostly ______
16 endless ______
17 touch ______
18 attention ______
19 concentrate ______
20 treasure ______
21 consider ______

22 compete ______
23 positive ______
24 entirely ______
25 worthless ______
26 garbage ______
27 review ______
28 environmental ______
29 recycle ______
30 orchestra ______
31 notice ______
32 shiny ______
33 perform ______
34 pure ______
35 in the beginning ______
36 calm down ______
37 in harmony with ______
38 be similar to ______
39 send back ______
40 sign up for ______
41 be filled with ______
42 as long as ______
43 be eager to ______

단어 Test

Step2

※ 다음 우리말을 영어로 쓰시오.

01 방송하다 ____________

02 합창단 ____________

03 완전히, 전부 ____________

04 (뉴스 등의) 진행자 ____________

05 감동시키다 ____________

06 관심, 주목 ____________

07 주로, 대부분 ____________

08 긍정적인 ____________

09 배경 ____________

10 상상하다 ____________

11 집게손가락 ____________

12 악기 ____________

13 현지의, 지역의 ____________

14 (경기 등에) 출전하다 ____________

15 재능이 있는 ____________

16 쓰레기 ____________

17 집중하다 ____________

18 울림, 맥박; 때리다, 두드리다 ____________

19 ~이라고 여기다, 생각하다 ____________

20 쓸모없는, 가치 없는 ____________

21 재검토하다, 복습하다 ____________

22 끝없는, 무한한 ____________

23 공연하다, 수행하다 ____________

24 재활용하다 ____________

25 고통, 아픔 ____________

26 엄지손가락 ____________

27 지휘자 ____________

28 전하다 ____________

29 추천하다 ____________

30 보물, 보물 같은 것 ____________

31 ~을 알아차리다 ____________

32 깨끗한, 순수한 ____________

33 심각한 ____________

34 환경의, 환경과 관련된 ____________

35 ~하는 한 ____________

36 진정하다 ____________

37 ~을 돌려주다 ____________

38 ~로 가득 차다 ____________

39 ~을 신청하다, ~에 가입하다 ____________

40 ~을 하고 싶어 하다 ____________

41 처음에, 초반에 ____________

42 ~와 비슷하다 ____________

43 ~와 조화를 이루어 ____________

단어 Test

Step3

※ 다음 영영풀이에 알맞은 단어를 <보기>에서 골라 쓴 후, 우리말 뜻을 쓰시오.

1 ________: having no end: ________

2 ________: a device that is used to make music: ________

3 ________: giving cause for hope and confidence: ________

4 ________: a very valuable object: ________

5 ________: a person who writes, sings, or plays music: ________

6 ________: having no real value or use: ________

7 ________: having a special ability to do something well: ________

8 ________: a person or machine that gathers something: ________

9 ________: to use something again for a different purpose: ________

10 ________: having a smooth, shining, bright appearance: ________

11 ________: a container for holding a liquid or gas: ________

12 ________: to entertain an audience by singing, acting, etc.: ________

13 ________: to give your attention to the thing you are doing, reading, etc.: ________

14 ________: a person who directs the performance of an orchestra or choir: ________

15 ________: things that are no longer useful and that have been thrown out: ________

16 ________: to tell someone that something is good or useful, or that someone would be suitable for a particular job, etc.: ________

보기

tank	worthless	recycle	picker
recommend	talented	conductor	endless
shiny	instrument	perform	musician
garbage	treasure	concentrate	positive

대화문 Test

※ 다음 우리말과 일치하도록 빈칸에 알맞은 말을 쓰시오.

Listen & Talk 1 A-1

W: Hey, Jake. I saw you ________ the ________ ________ yesterday. ________!

M: Thanks, Anna.

W: You always seem to listen to music before you ________. Do you ________ ________ ________ to listen to music before you swim?

M: Yes, it ________ me ________ and it ________ me ________.

W: 안녕, Jake. 어제 수영 대회에서 네가 이긴 것을 봤어. 축하해!
M: 고마워, Anna.
W: 너는 경기하기 전에 항상 음악을 듣는 것 같더라. 수영하기 전에 음악을 듣는 게 도움이 되니?
M: 응, 그것은 나를 깨어 있게 하고 집중하는 데 도움을 줘.

Listen & Talk 1 A-2

M: Hi, Sally. Where are you ________ ________?

W: I'm ________ to the music room. I have ________ ________.

M: Oh, yeah. I ________ that you've joined the ________. Do you ________ it ________ ________ ________ in the choir?

W: Yeah, it's great to sing ________ ________ ________ ________.

M: 안녕, Sally. 어디 가는 길이야?
W: 음악실에 가는 중이야. 합창단 연습이 있거든.
M: 오, 그래. 네가 합창단에 들어간 걸 잊고 있었어. 합창단에서 노래하는 것은 재미있니?
W: 응, 다른 사람들과 조화를 이루어 노래하는 게 좋아.

Listen & Talk 1-B

W: Hi, Jason. Great to see you again. I've ________ the new rap song, *Young and Wild*, that ________ ________. It's really cool.

M: Oh, thanks.

W: I really like your songs. Do you ________ ________ ________ ________ ________ ________?

M: Well, it was hard in the ________, but now it's getting easier. I ________ ________ my experiences and ________ ________ ________.

W: Wow! As they say, "________ ________, ________ ________." Best of luck ________ your new song!

M: Thank you.

W: 안녕하세요, Jason. 다시 만나서 반갑습니다. 녹음하신 새로운 랩 노래, '젊고 무모한(Young and Wild)'을 들었어요. 정말 멋지던데요.
M: 오, 고마워요.
W: 당신 노래들은 정말 좋아요. 곡을 쓰는 일이 쉬우세요?
M: 글쎄요, 처음에는 어려웠어요, 하지만 지금은 쉬워지고 있어요. 저는 제 경험을 활용해서 일기를 쓰고 있거든요.
W: 와! '고통 없이는 얻는 것도 없다.'라는 말이 있잖아요. 새 노래가 잘 되길 바랍니다!
M: 고마워요.

Listen & Talk 2 A-1

W: Hey, Tommy. When is the last day to ________ ________ ________ the talent show?

M: This Friday. ________ ________ ________ ________ ________ ________ ________ it, Megan?

W: Yeah, I'm going ________ ________ ________ a couple of people.

M: How cool! What ________ you ________ ________ do?

W: We will play K-pop music ________ the ________ and ________.

W: 안녕, Tommy. 장기 자랑 등록 마감이 언제야?
M: 이번 주 금요일이야. 너 그거 등록할 계획이니, Megan?
W: 응, 나는 몇 사람과 함께 공연할 거야.
M: 정말 멋지다! 무엇을 할 거야?
W: 우리는 케이팝 음악을 바이올린과 첼로로 연주할 거야.

Listen & Talk 2 A-2

W: Hello, I'd like to ________ ________ ________ a drum class.

M: Okay. Are you ________ ________ ________ ________ ________ during the week or ________ the weekend?

W: I'm ________ to take a ________ ________. When do you ________ them?

M: There is a class on Tuesday and ________ ________ on Thursday. ________ classes start at 6 o'clock.

W: Great. I'd like to ________ ________ for the Tuesday class.

W: 안녕하세요, 드럼 수업에 등록하고 싶은데요.
M: 알겠습니다. 수업을 주중에 들으실 건가요, 주말에 들으실 건가요?
W: 주중 수업을 들을 계획이에요. 수업이 언제 있나요?
M: 화요일 수업이 하나 있고 또 하나는 목요일에 있어요. 두 수업 모두 6시 정각에 시작합니다.
W: 좋아요. 화요일 수업에 등록할게요.

Listen & Talk 2-B

W: Are you planning to learn a ________ ________? I'd like to ________ the *kalimba*, a small African musical instrument. The sound it makes ________ ________ ________ that of a music box. ________ the *kalimba* is very easy. You can learn ________ ________ your ________ ________ ________ ________ beautiful music in just one lesson!

W: 악기를 배울 계획인가요? 아프리카의 작은 악기인 '칼림바'를 추천하고 싶습니다. 그 악기가 내는 소리는 음악 상자의 소리와 비슷합니다. '칼림바'를 연주하는 것은 아주 쉬워요. 단 한 번의 수업으로 엄지손톱을 사용해 아름다운 음악을 연주하는 걸 배울 수 있어요!

Communication

W: Hey, Anthony. Can you ________ me ________ ________?

M: Sure, what's ________?

W: I'm going to a concert at the Arts Center, but I don't know ________ ________ ________ ________ ________.

M: Are you ________ ________ go to the ________ concert?

W: Yes. I'm going to watch the ________ concert.

M: Then, you should ________ ________ ________ on the ________ ________. You can hear the beautiful sounds of ________ ________ ________ better.

W: Oh, do you find it ________ ________ ________ the performance ________ ________ ________ ________?

M: Yes. I ________ ________ ________ than from ________ ________.

W: 저기, Anthony. 나 뭐 좀 도와줄래?
M: 물론, 무슨 일이야?
W: 예술 회관에서 하는 공연에 가려고 하는데, 어떤 좌석을 골라야 할지 모르겠어.
M: 오케스트라 공연에 갈 계획이니?
W: 응. 나는 오케스트라 공연을 보려고 해.
M: 그럼, 너는 2층 좌석을 얻는 게 좋아. 다양한 악기들의 아름다운 소리를 더 잘 들을 수 있거든.
W: 오, 2층에서 공연을 듣는 것이 더 낫다는 거니?
M: 응. 다른 좌석들보다 더 낫다고 생각해.

Wrap Up

M: Hey, Alice.

W: Hi, Sam. How ________ you ________?

M: Great. Actually, ________ ________ a lot of pop news from your blog.

W: Oh, ________ ________? Thanks ________ ________ my blog!

M: Do you ________ it interesting to ________ the ________ pop news?

W: Yes, I love to ________ ________ to people.

M: 안녕, Alice.
W: 안녕, Sam. 어떻게 지내?
M: 좋아. 사실, 네 블로그에서 팝 소식을 많이 읽었어.
W: 오, 그랬어? 내 블로그를 방문해 줘서 고마워!
M: 최신 팝 소식을 올리는 게 재미있니?
W: 응, 사람들에게 소식을 전하는 게 좋아.

대화문 Test

※ 다음 우리말에 맞도록 대화를 영어로 쓰시오.

Listen & Talk 1 A-1

W: ______________________________

M: ______________________________

W: ______________________________

____

M: ______________________________

W: 안녕, Jake. 어제 수영 대회에서 네가 이긴 것을 봤어. 축하해!
M: 고마워, Anna.
W: 너는 경기하기 전에 항상 음악을 듣는 것 같더라. 수영하기 전에 음악을 듣는 게 도움이 되니?
M: 응, 그것은 나를 깨어 있게 하고 집중하는 데 도움을 줘.

Listen & Talk 1 A-2

M: ______________________________

W: ______________________________

M: ______________________________

____

W: ______________________________

M: 안녕, Sally. 어디 가는 길이야?
W: 음악실에 가는 중이야. 합창단 연습이 있거든.
M: 오, 그래. 네가 합창단에 들어간 걸 잊고 있었어. 합창단에서 노래하는 것은 재미있니?
W: 응, 다른 사람들과 조화를 이루어 노래하는 게 좋아.

Listen & Talk 1-B

W: ______________________________

____

M: ______________________________

W: ______________________________

M: ______________________________

____

W: ______________________________

M: ______________________________

W: 안녕하세요, Jason. 다시 만나서 반갑습니다. 녹음하신 새로운 랩 노래, '젊고 무모한(Young and Wild)'을 들었어요. 정말 멋지던데요.
M: 오, 고마워요.
W: 당신 노래들은 정말 좋아요. 곡을 쓰는 일이 쉬우세요?
M: 글쎄요, 처음에는 어려웠어요, 하지만 지금은 쉬워지고 있어요. 저는 제 경험을 활용해서 일기를 쓰고 있거든요.
W: 와! '고통 없이는 얻는 것도 없다.'라는 말이 있잖아요. 새 노래가 잘 되길 바랍니다!
M: 고마워요.

Listen & Talk 2 A-1

W: ______________________________

M: ______________________________

W: ______________________________

M: ______________________________

W: ______________________________

W: 안녕, Tommy. 장기 자랑 등록 마감이 언제야?
M: 이번 주 금요일이야. 너 그거 등록할 계획이니, Megan?
W: 응, 나는 몇 사람과 함께 공연할 거야.
M: 정말 멋지다! 무엇을 할 거야?
W: 우리는 케이팝 음악을 바이올린과 첼로로 연주할 거야.

Listen & Talk 2 A-2

W:
M:
W:
M:

W:

W: 안녕하세요, 드럼 수업에 등록하고 싶은데요.
M: 알겠습니다. 수업을 주중에 들으실 건가요, 주말에 들으실 건가요?
W: 주중 수업을 들을 계획이에요. 수업이 언제 있나요?
M: 화요일 수업이 하나 있고 또 하나는 목요일에 있어요. 두 수업 모두 6시 정각에 시작합니다.
W: 좋아요. 화요일 수업에 등록할게요.

Listen & Talk 2-B

W:

W: 악기를 배울 계획인가요? 아프리카의 작은 악기인 '칼림바'를 추천하고 싶습니다. 그 악기가 내는 소리는 음악 상자의 소리와 비슷합니다. '칼림바'를 연주하는 것은 아주 쉬워요. 단 한 번의 수업으로 엄지손톱을 사용해 아름다운 음악을 연주하는 걸 배울 수 있어요!

Communication

W:
M:
W:

M:
W:
M:

W:
M:

W: 저기, Anthony, 나 뭐 좀 도와줄래?
M: 물론, 무슨 일이야?
W: 예술 회관에서 하는 공연에 가려고 하는데, 어떤 좌석을 골라야 할지 모르겠어.
M: 오케스트라 공연에 갈 계획이니?
W: 응, 나는 오케스트라 공연을 보려고 해.
M: 그럼, 너는 2층 좌석을 얻는 게 좋아. 다양한 악기들의 아름다운 소리를 더 잘 들을 수 있거든.
W: 오, 2층에서 공연을 듣는 것이 더 낫다는 거니?
M: 응, 다른 좌석들보다 더 낫다고 생각해.

Wrap Up

M:
W:
M:
W:
M:
W:

M: 안녕, Alice.
W: 안녕, Sam. 어떻게 지내?
M: 좋아. 사실, 네 블로그에서 팝 소식을 많이 읽었어.
W: 오, 그랬어? 내 블로그를 방문해 줘서 고마워!
M: 최신 팝 소식을 올리는 게 재미있니?
W: 응, 사람들에게 소식을 전하는 게 좋아.

본문 Test

※ 다음 우리말과 일치하도록 빈칸에 알맞은 것을 골라 쓰시오.

1 The ________ ________
A. Orchestra B. Junk

2 ________ ________ a music ________, Lucy White
A. by B. blogger C. written

3 "The world ________ us ________, we send ________ ________."
A. back B. garbage C. sends D. music

4 This was ________ ________ the ________ of a concert ticket I was ________.
A. back B. given C. written D. on

5 The ________ group ________ ________ "The Junk Orchestra."
A. called B. musical C. was

6 They played instruments ________ ________ ________ ________ garbage.
A. out B. made C. of D. entirely

7 I could not ________ what ________ of sound these instruments would make, so I was ________ to find ________.
A. eager B. out C. kind D. imagine

8 Before the concert, I ________ that the instruments ________ ________ ________.
A. strange B. might C. sound D. thought

9 After a ________ ________, a group of young people began to ________ on the ________.
A. minutes B. stage C. few D. walk

10 The first ________ I ________ was their instruments: a cello made out of a shiny oil tank, a violin ________ with forks, and a flute made ________ a water pipe and buttons.
A. made B. noticed C. with D. thing

11 The concert began ________ a girl ________ Bach's *Cello Suite No. 1* ________ her ________ cello.
A. on B. with C. playing D. shiny

12 I ________ ________ ________ the ________ sound.
A. deep B. shocked C. was D. by

13 I was so ________ the music that I forgot that they were playing ________ instruments ________ from ________ materials.
A. recycled B. into C. with D. made

14 ________ the concert, I was ________ to ________ a story ________ the orchestra.
A. eager B. after C. write D. about

15 I ________ Favio Chávez, the ________, and ________ him about the ________.
A. asked B. conductor C. met D. orchestra

16 **Lucy White:** ________ ________ ________ ________ **The Junk Orchestra?**
A. did B. why C. start D. you

17 **Favio Chávez**: When I went to a small town called Cateura in Paraguay to ________ ________ a recycling program in 2005, I saw children living in a town that was mostly ________ ________ garbage.
A. on B. filled C. work D. with

---

1 정크 오케스트라
2 음악 블로거 Lucy White 씀
3 "세상이 우리에게 쓰레기를 보내면, 우리는 음악을 돌려준다."
4 이것은 내가 받은 음악회 입장권의 뒷면에 쓰여 있었다.
5 그 음악 그룹은 '정크 오케스트라'라고 불렸다.
6 그들은 완전히 쓰레기로만 만들어진 악기를 연주했다.
7 나는 그런 악기들이 어떤 종류의 소리를 낼지 상상할 수 없었고, 그래서 나는 알아보고 싶어졌다.
8 음악회가 시작되기 전에 나는 그 악기들이 이상한 소리를 낼지도 모른다고 생각했다.
9 몇 분 후에 한 무리의 젊은이들이 무대 위로 걸어 올라오기 시작했다.
10 내가 처음으로 알아차린 것은 그들의 악기였는데, 그것들은 반짝이는 기름통으로 만들어진 첼로, 포크로 만들어진 바이올린, 수도관과 단추로 만들어진 플루트였다.
11 음악회는 한 소녀가 자신의 반짝이는 첼로로 바흐의 〈첼로 모음곡 1번〉을 연주하는 것으로 시작되었다.
12 나는 그 깊은 소리에 충격을 받았다.
13 나는 음악에 너무 심취해서 그들이 재활용된 재료들로 만들어진 악기를 연주하고 있다는 것을 잊었다.
14 음악회가 끝나고, 나는 그 오케스트라에 대한 이야기를 몹시 쓰고 싶었다.
15 나는 지휘자인 Favio Chávez를 만나서 그에게 오케스트라에 대해 물었다.
16 Lucy White: 왜 당신은 정크 오케스트라를 시작하셨나요?
17 Favio Chávez: 2005년에 재활용 프로그램에서 일을 하기 위해서 내가 파라과이의 카테우라라고 불리는 작은 마을에 갔을 때, 나는 대부분이 쓰레기로 가득 차 있는 마을에 살고 있는 어린이들을 보았습니다.

18 I wanted to add ________ ________ to their lives, so I decided to ________ my love of music ________ them.
A. share B. positive C. with D. something

19 **Lucy White: Why did you ________ garbage ________ ________ ________?**
A. make B. to C. instruments D. use

20 **Favio Chávez**: One person's ________ is ________ person's ________.
A. another B. garbage C. treasure

21 Nicolás Gómez, a ________ ________ ________, helped me a ________.
A. lot B. local C. picker D. garbage

22 He made it ________ for children to play music by ________ instruments ________ of ________.
A. out B. possible C. making D. garbage

23 The wonderful ________ about these ________ was that the children didn't have to ________ about ________ a lot of money on them.
A. thing B. spending C. instruments D. worry

24 **Lucy White: What do you ________ people ________ ________ ________ your music?**
A. to B. through C. want D. learn

25 **Favio Chávez**: I want people to know that ________ something ________ can make ________ ________.
A. worthless B. music C. even D. inspiring

26 After interviewing Chávez, I realized that it really doesn't ________ what instrument you play with ________ ________ as you put your heart ________ playing it.
A. into B. matter C. long D. as

27 The children of Cateura showed me that an orchestra is ________ by people, ________ ________ ________.
A. formed B. by C. not D. instruments

28 **Comments**

29 **Annie**: (23 ________ ago) So ________ to see ________ music can change ________.
A. moving B. lives C. how D. seconds

30 The ________ of ________ is ________!
A. endless B. power C. music

31 **Thomas**: (1 minute ago) After the concert, I ________ it ________ to inspire people by music ________ with ________ instruments.
A. possible B. recycled C. found D. played

32 **Kate**: (5 days ago) Not only do these ________ young people ________ great music, but they also bring ________ environmental problems to our ________.
A. attention B. deliver C. serious D. talented

18 나는 그들의 삶에 긍정적인 무엇인가를 더해 주고 싶어서, 음악에 대한 나의 사랑을 그들과 나누기로 결정했습니다.

19 Lucy White: 왜 당신은 악기를 만들기 위해 쓰레기를 이용했나요?

20 Favio Chávez: 한 사람의 쓰레기는 다른 사람의 보물입니다.

21 그 지역의 쓰레기 줍는 사람인 Nicolás Gámez가 나를 많이 도와주었습니다.

22 그는 쓰레기로 악기를 만들어 줌으로써 어린이들이 음악을 연주하는 것이 가능하도록 만들었습니다.

23 이 악기들의 멋진 점은 어린이들이 악기에 많은 돈을 쓸 것을 걱정하지 않아도 된다는 점이었죠.

24 Lucy White: 당신의 음악을 통해서 사람들이 무엇을 배우기를 원하십니까?

25 Favio Chávez: 나는 가치 없는 것도 영감을 주는 음악을 만들어 낼 수 있다는 것을 사람들이 알게 되기를 원합니다.

26 Chávez를 인터뷰한 후에 나는 사람들이 악기를 연주하는 데 마음을 쏟아붓는 한, 그 사람이 연주하는 악기가 무엇인지는 별로 중요하지 않다는 것을 깨달았다.

27 카테우라의 어린이들은 나에게 오케스트라는 악기에 의해서가 아니라 사람에 의해 이루어지는 것이라는 것을 보여 주었다.

28 감상평

29 Annie: (23초 전) 음악이 삶을 바꿀 수 있다는 것을 보아서 너무 가슴이 뭉클하다.

30 음악의 힘은 끝이 없다!

31 Thomas: (1분 전) 음악회가 끝난 후, 나는 재활용 악기로 연주되는 음악으로 사람들에게 영감을 주는 것이 가능하다는 것을 알았다.

32 Kate: (5일 전) 이 재능 있는 젊은이들은 훌륭한 음악을 전할 뿐만 아니라, 또한 심각한 환경 문제에 우리가 주목하게 한다.

본문 Test

※ 다음 우리말과 일치하도록 빈칸에 알맞은 말을 쓰시오.

1 **The ________ Orchestra**

2 ________ ________ a ________ ________, Lucy White

3 "The world sends us ________, we ________ ________ ________."

4 This was ________ ________ ________ ________ ________ a concert ticket I ________ ________.

5 The musical group ________ ________ "The Junk Orchestra."

6 They played instruments ________ ________ ________ ________ ________.

7 I could not imagine what kind of sound these instruments would make, so I ________ ________ ________ ________ ________.

8 Before the concert, I ________ that the instruments ________ ________ ________.

9 ________ ________ ________ ________, a group of young people ________ ________ ________ on the stage.

10 ________ ________ ________ ________ ________ was their instruments: a cello ________ ________ ________ a shiny oil tank, a violin made with forks, and a flute made with a water pipe and buttons.

11 The concert began ________ ________ ________ ________ Bach's *Cello Suite No. 1* ________ her ________ ________.

12 I ________ ________ ________ the ________ ________.

13 I ________ so ________ the music that I forgot that they were playing with instruments ________ ________ ________ ________.

14 After the concert, I ________ ________ ________ ________ a story about the orchestra.

15 I met Favio Chávez, ________ ________, and ________ him about the orchestra.

16 **Lucy White**: ________ ________ ________ ________ **The Junk Orchestra?**

17 **Favio Chávez**: When I went to a small town called Cateura in Paraguay ________ ________ ________ a recycling program in 2005, I ________ children ________ in a town that ________ ________ ________ ________ ________.

1 정크 오케스트라
2 음악 블로거 Lucy White 씀
3 "세상이 우리에게 쓰레기를 보내면, 우리는 음악을 돌려준다."
4 이것은 내가 받은 음악회 입장권의 뒷면에 쓰여 있었다.
5 그 음악 그룹은 '정크 오케스트라'라고 불렸다.
6 그들은 완전히 쓰레기로만 만들어진 악기를 연주했다.
7 나는 그런 악기들이 어떤 종류의 소리를 낼지 상상할 수 없었고, 그래서 나는 알아보고 싶어졌다.
8 음악회가 시작되기 전에 나는 그 악기들이 이상한 소리를 낼지도 모른다고 생각했다.
9 몇 분 후에 한 무리의 젊은이들이 무대 위로 걸어 올라오기 시작했다.
10 내가 처음으로 알아차린 것은 그들의 악기였는데, 그것들은 반짝이는 기름통으로 만들어진 첼로, 포크로 만들어진 바이올린, 수도관과 단추로 만들어진 플루트였다.
11 음악회는 한 소녀가 자신의 반짝이는 첼로로 바흐의 〈첼로 모음곡 1번〉을 연주하는 것으로 시작되었다.
12 나는 그 깊은 소리에 충격을 받았다.
13 나는 음악에 너무 심취해서 그들이 재활용된 재료들로 만들어진 악기를 연주하고 있다는 것을 잊었다.
14 음악회가 끝나고, 나는 그 오케스트라에 대한 이야기를 몹시 쓰고 싶었다.
15 나는 지휘자인 Favio Chávez를 만나서 그에게 오케스트라에 대해 물었다.
16 Lucy White: 왜 당신은 정크 오케스트라를 시작하셨나요?
17 Favio Chávez: 2005년에 재활용 프로그램에서 일을 하기 위해서 내가 파라과이의 카테우라라고 불리는 작은 마을에 갔을 때, 나는 대부분이 쓰레기로 가득 차 있는 마을에 살고 있는 어린이들을 보았습니다.

18 I wanted to add _______ _______ to their lives, _______ I decided to _______ my love of music _______ them.

19 **Lucy White: Why did you use garbage _______ _______ _______?**

20 **Favio Chávez**: One person's _______ is _______ _______ _______.

21 Nicolás Gómez, _______ _______ _______ _______, helped me _______ _______.

22 He made _______ possible _______ _______ to play music by making instruments _______ _______ _______.

23 _______ _______ _______ about these instruments was that the children _______ _______ _______ _______ _______ _______ a lot of money on them.

24 **Lucy White: What do you want people _______ _______ _______ your music?**

25 **Favio Chávez**: I want people to know that _______ _______ can make _______ _______.

26 After _______ Chávez, I realized that it really _______ _______ what instrument you play with _______ _______ _______ you put your heart _______ playing it.

27 The children of Cateura showed me that an orchestra is _______ _______ people, _______ _______ _______.

28 _______

29 **Annie**: (23 _______ ago) So moving to see _______ music can change _______.

30 The power of music is _______!

31 **Thomas**: (1 minute ago) After the concert, I found it possible to inspire people by music _______ _______ recycled instruments.

32 **Kate**: (5 days ago) _______ _______ _______ these _______ _______ people _______ great music, but they also _______ serious environmental problems _______ _______ _______.

18 나는 그들의 삶에 긍정적인 무엇인가를 더해 주고 싶어서, 음악에 대한 나의 사랑을 그들과 나누기로 결정했습니다.

19 Lucy White: 왜 당신은 악기를 만들기 위해 쓰레기를 이용했나요?

20 Favio Chávez: 한 사람의 쓰레기는 다른 사람의 보물입니다.

21 그 지역의 쓰레기 줍는 사람인 Nicolás Gámez가 나를 많이 도와주었습니다.

22 그는 쓰레기로 악기를 만들어 줌으로써 어린이들이 음악을 연주하는 것이 가능하도록 만들었습니다.

23 이 악기들의 멋진 점은 어린이들이 악기에 많은 돈을 쓸 것을 걱정하지 않아도 된다는 점이었죠.

24 Lucy White: 당신의 음악을 통해서 사람들이 무엇을 배우기를 원하십니까?

25 Favio Chávez: 나는 가치 없는 것도 영감을 주는 음악을 만들어 낼 수 있다는 것을 사람들이 알게 되기를 원합니다.

26 Chávez를 인터뷰한 후에 나는 사람들이 악기를 연주하는 데 마음을 쏟아붓는 한, 그 사람이 연주하는 악기가 무엇인지는 별로 중요하지 않다는 것을 깨달았다.

27 카테우라의 어린이들은 나에게 오케스트라는 악기에 의해서가 아니라 사람에 의해 이루어지는 것이라는 것을 보여 주었다.

28 감상평

29 Annie: (23초 전) 음악이 삶을 바꿀 수 있다는 것을 보아서 너무 가슴이 뭉클하다.

30 음악의 힘은 끝이 없다!

31 Thomas: (1분 전) 음악회가 끝난 후, 나는 재활용 악기로 연주되는 음악으로 사람들에게 영감을 주는 것이 가능하다는 것을 알았다.

32 Kate: (5일 전) 이 재능 있는 젊은이들은 훌륭한 음악을 전할 뿐만 아니라, 또한 심각한 환경 문제에 우리가 주목하게 한다.

본문 Test

※ 다음 문장을 우리말로 쓰시오.

1 The Junk Orchestra

➡ ______________________________

2 written by a music blogger, Lucy White

➡ ______________________________

3 "The world sends us garbage, we send back music."

➡ ______________________________

4 This was written on the back of a concert ticket I was given.

➡ ______________________________

5 The musical group was called "The Junk Orchestra."

➡ ______________________________

6 They played instruments made entirely out of garbage.

➡ ______________________________

7 I could not imagine what kind of sound these instruments would make, so I was eager to find out.

➡ ______________________________

8 Before the concert, I thought that the instruments might sound strange.

➡ ______________________________

9 After a few minutes, a group of young people began to walk on the stage.

➡ ______________________________

10 The first thing I noticed was their instruments: a cello made out of a shiny oil tank, a violin made with forks, and a flute made with a water pipe and buttons.

➡ ______________________________

____

11 The concert began with a girl playing Bach's *Cello Suite No. 1* on her shiny cello

➡ ______________________________

12 I was shocked by the deep sound.

➡ ______________________________

13 I was so into the music that I forgot that they were playing with instruments made from recycled materials.

➡ ______________________________

14 After the concert, I was eager to write a story about the orchestra.

➡ ______________________________

15 I met Favio Chávez, the conductor, and asked him about the orchestra.

➡ ______________________________

16 Lucy White: Why did you start The Junk Orchestra?

➡ ______________________________

17 Favio Chávez: When I went to a small town called Cateura in Paraguay to work on a recycling program in 2005, I saw children living in a town that was mostly filled with garbage.

➡ ______________________________

____

18 I wanted to add something positive to their lives, so I decided to share my love of music with them.

➡ ______________________________

19 Lucy White: Why did you use garbage to make instruments?

➡ ______________________________

20 Favio Chávez: One person's garbage is another person's treasure.

➡ ______________________________

21 Nicolás Gómez, a local garbage picker, helped me a lot.

➡ ______________________________

22 He made it possible for children to play music by making instruments out of garbage.

➡ ______________________________

23 The wonderful thing about these instruments was that the children didn't have to worry about spending a lot of money on them.

➡ ______________________________

24 Lucy White: What do you want people to learn through your music?

➡ ______________________________

25 Favio Chávez: I want people to know that even something worthless can make inspiring music.

➡ ______________________________

26 After interviewing Chávez, I realized that it really doesn't matter what instrument you play with as long as you put your heart into playing it.

➡ ______________________________

____

27 The children of Cateura showed me that an orchestra is formed by people, not by instruments.

➡ ______________________________

28 Comments

➡ ______________________________

29 Annie: (23 seconds ago) So moving to see how music can change lives.

➡ ______________________________

30 The power of music is endless!

➡ ______________________________

31 Thomas: (1 minute ago) After the concert, I found it possible to inspire people by music played with recycled instruments.

➡ ______________________________

____

32 Kate: (5 days ago) Not only do these talented young people deliver great music, but they also bring serious environmental problems to our attention.

➡ ______________________________

본문 Test

※ 다음 괄호 안의 단어들을 우리말에 맞도록 바르게 배열하시오.

1 (Junk / The / Orchestra)
➡ ______________________________

2 (by / written / music / a / blogger, / White / Lucy)
➡ ______________________________

3 (world / "the / us / sends / garbage, / send / we / music." / back)
➡ ______________________________

4 (was / this / on / written / back / the / a / of / ticket / concert / was / I / given.)
➡ ______________________________

5 (musical / the / was / group / called / Junk / "The / Orchestra.")
➡ ______________________________

6 (played / they / instruments / entirely / made / out / garbage. / of)
➡ ______________________________

7 (could / I / imagine / not / kind / what / sound / of / these / would / instruments / make / I / so / eager / was / to / out. / find)
➡ ______________________________
____

8 (the / before / concert, / thought / I / the / that / might / instruments / strange. / sound)
➡ ______________________________

9 (a / after / minutes, / few / group / a / young / of / began / people / walk / to / on / stage. / the)
➡ ______________________________
____

10 (first / the / I / thing / was / noticed / instruments: / their / cello / a / out / made / of / shiny / a / tank, / oil / violin / a / with / made / forks, / a / and / flute / with / made / a / pipe / water / buttons. / and)
➡ ______________________________
____
____

11 (concert / the / with / began / girl / a / Bach's / playing / *Cello* / *No.* / *Suite* / *1* / her / on / cello. / shiny)
➡ ______________________________
____

12 (was / I / by / shocked / deep / the / sound.)
➡ ______________________________

13 (was / I / so / the / into / music / I / that / forgot / they / that / playing / were / instruments / with / made / recycled / from / materials.)
➡ ______________________________
____

14 (the / after / concert, / was / I / to / eager / a / write / about / story / orchestra. / the)
➡ ______________________________

15 (met / I / Cháves, / Favio / conductor, / the / and / him / asked / the / about / orchestra.)
➡ ______________________________

16 (Lucy White: / did / why / start / you / Junk / The / Orchestra?)
➡ ______________________________

17 (Favio Chávez: / I / when / to / went / small / a / town / Cateura / called / Paraguay / in / work / to / a / on / program / recycling / 2005, / in / saw / I / children / living / a / in / that / town / mostly / was / with / filled / garbage.)
➡ ______________________________
____
____

1 정크 오케스트라
2 음악 블로거 Lucy White 씀
3 "세상이 우리에게 쓰레기를 보내면, 우리는 음악을 돌려준다."
4 이것은 내가 받은 음악회 입장권의 뒷면에 쓰여 있었다.
5 그 음악 그룹은 '정크 오케스트라'라고 불렸다.
6 그들은 완전히 쓰레기로만 만들어진 악기를 연주했다.
7 나는 그런 악기들이 어떤 종류의 소리를 낼지 상상할 수 없었고, 그래서 나는 알아보고 싶어졌다.
8 음악회가 시작되기 전에 나는 그 악기들이 이상한 소리를 낼지도 모른다고 생각했다.
9 몇 분 후에 한 무리의 젊은이들이 무대 위로 걸어 올라오기 시작했다.
10 내가 처음으로 알아차린 것은 그들의 악기였는데, 그것들은 반짝이는 기름통으로 만들어진 첼로, 포크로 만들어진 바이올린, 수도관과 단추로 만들어진 플루트였다.
11 음악회는 한 소녀가 자신의 반짝이는 첼로로 바흐의 〈첼로 모음곡 1번〉을 연주하는 것으로 시작되었다.
12 나는 그 깊은 소리에 충격을 받았다.
13 나는 음악에 너무 심취해서 그들이 재활용된 재료들로 만들어진 악기를 연주하고 있다는 것을 잊었다.
14 음악회가 끝나고, 나는 그 오케스트라에 대한 이야기를 몹시 쓰고 싶었다.
15 나는 지휘자인 Favio Chávez를 만나서 그에게 오케스트라에 대해 물었다.
16 Lucy White: 왜 당신은 정크 오케스트라를 시작하셨나요?
17 Favio Chávez: 2005년에 재활용 프로그램에서 일을 하기 위해서 내가 파라과이의 카테우라라고 불리는 작은 마을에 갔을 때, 나는 대부분이 쓰레기로 가득 차 있는 마을에 살고 있는 어린이들을 보았습니다.

18 (wanted / I / add / to / positive / something / their / to / lives, / I / so / to / decided / my / share / love / music / of / them. / with)
➡ ______________________________
____

19 (Lucy White: / did / why / use / you / to / garbage / instruments? / make)
➡ ______________________________

20 (Favio Chávez: / person's / one / is / garbage / another / treasure. / person's)
➡ ______________________________

21 (Gómez, / Nicolás / local / a / picker / garbage / me / helped / lot. / a)
➡ ______________________________

22 (made / he / possible / it / children / for / play / to / by / music / instruments / making / of / out / garbage.)
➡ ______________________________
____

23 (wonderful / the / about / thing / instrements / these / that / was / children / the / have / didn't / to / about / worry / spending / lot / a / of / money / them. / on)
➡ ______________________________
____

24 (Lucy White: / do / what / want / you / to / people / learn / your / through / music?)
➡ ______________________________

25 (Favio Chávez: / want / I / to / people / that / know / something / even / can / worthless / make / music. / inspiring)
➡ ______________________________
____

26 (interviewing / after / Chávez, / realized / I / it / that / doesn't / really / what / matter / instrument / play / you / with / long / as / you / as / put / heart / your / into / it. / playing)
➡ ______________________________
____

27 (children / the / Cateura / of / me / showed / that / orchestra / an / formed / is / people, / by / by / not / instruments.)
➡ ______________________________
____

28 Coments

29 (Annie: (seconds / (23 / ago) // moving / so / see / to / music / how / change / can / lives.)
➡ ______________________________

30 (power / the / music / of / endless! / is)
➡ ______________________________

31 (Thomas: / minute / (1 / ago) // the / after / concert, / found / I / it / to / possible / inspire / by / people / played / music / recycled / with / instruments.)
➡ ______________________________
____

32 (Kate: / days / (5 / ago) // only / not / these / do / young / talented / people / deliver / people / music, / great / they / but / bring / also / serious / problems / environmental / out / to / attention.)
➡ ______________________________
____
____

18 나는 그들의 삶에 긍정적인 무엇인가를 더해 주고 싶어서, 음악에 대한 나의 사랑을 그들과 나누기로 결정했습니다.
19 Lucy White: 왜 당신은 악기를 만들기 위해 쓰레기를 이용했나요?
20 Favio Chávez: 한 사람의 쓰레기는 다른 사람의 보물입니다.
21 그 지역의 쓰레기 줍는 사람인 Nicolás Gámez가 나를 많이 도와주었습니다.
22 그는 쓰레기로 악기를 만들어 줌으로써 어린이들이 음악을 연주하는 것이 가능하도록 만들었습니다.
23 이 악기들의 멋진 점은 어린이들이 악기에 많은 돈을 쓸 것을 걱정하지 않아도 된다는 점이었죠.
24 Lucy White: 당신의 음악을 통해서 사람들이 무엇을 배우기를 원하십니까?
25 Favio Chávez: 나는 가치 없는 것도 영감을 주는 음악을 만들어 낼 수 있다는 것을 사람들이 알게 되기를 원합니다.
26 Chávez를 인터뷰한 후에 나는 사람들이 악기를 연주하는 데 마음을 쏟아붓는 한, 그 사람이 연주하는 악기가 무엇인지는 별로 중요하지 않다는 것을 깨달았다.
27 카테우라의 어린이들은 나에게 오케스트라는 악기에 의해서가 아니라 사람에 의해 이루어지는 것이라는 것을 보여 주었다.
28 감상평
29 Annie: (23초 전) 음악이 삶을 바꿀 수 있다는 것을 보아서 너무 가슴이 뭉클하다.
30 음악의 힘은 끝이 없다!
31 Thomas: (1분 전) 음악회가 끝난 후, 나는 재활용 악기로 연주되는 음악으로 사람들에게 영감을 주는 것이 가능하다는 것을 알았다.
32 Kate: (5일 전) 이 재능 있는 젊은이들은 훌륭한 음악을 전할 뿐만 아니라, 또한 심각한 환경 문제에 우리가 주목하게 한다.

본문 Test

※ 다음 우리말을 영어로 쓰시오.

1 정크 오케스트라

➡ ______________________

2 음악 블로거 Lucy White 씀

➡ ______________________

3 "세상이 우리에게 쓰레기를 보내면, 우리는 음악을 돌려준다."

➡ ______________________

4 이것은 내가 받은 음악회 입장권의 뒷면에 쓰여 있었다.

➡ ______________________

5 그 음악 그룹은 '정크 오케스트라'라고 불렸다.

➡ ______________________

6 그들은 완전히 쓰레기로만 만들어진 악기를 연주했다.

➡ ______________________

7 나는 그런 악기들이 어떤 종류의 소리를 낼지 상상할 수 없었고, 그래서 나는 알아보고 싶어졌다.

➡ ______________________

8 음악회가 시작되기 전에 나는 그 악기들이 이상한 소리를 낼지도 모른다고 생각했다.

➡ ______________________

9 몇 분 후에 한 무리의 젊은이들이 무대 위로 걸어 올라오기 시작했다.

➡ ______________________

10 내가 처음으로 알아차린 것은 그들의 악기였는데, 그것들은 반짝이는 기름통으로 만들어진 첼로, 포크로 만들어진 바이올린, 수도관과 단추로 만들어진 플루트였다.

➡ ______________________

____

11 음악회는 한 소녀가 자신의 반짝이는 첼로로 바흐의 〈첼로 모음곡 1번〉을 연주하는 것으로 시작되었다.

➡ ______________________

12 나는 그 깊은 소리에 충격을 받았다.

➡ ______________________

13 나는 음악에 너무 심취해서 그들이 재활용된 재료들로 만들어진 악기를 연주하고 있다는 것을 잊었다.

➡ ______________________

14 음악회가 끝나고, 나는 그 오케스트라에 대한 이야기를 몹시 쓰고 싶었다.

➡ ______________________

15 나는 지휘자인 Favio Chávez를 만나서 그에게 오케스트라에 대해 물었다.

➡ ______________________

16 Lucy White: 왜 당신은 정크 오케스트라를 시작하셨나요?

➡ ______________________

17 Favio Chávez: 2005년에 재활용 프로그램에서 일을 하기 위해서 내가 파라과이의 카테우라라고 불리는 작은 마을에 갔을 때, 나는 대부분이 쓰레기로 가득 차 있는 마을에 살고 있는 어린이들을 보았습니다.

➡ ______________________

____

18 나는 그들의 삶에 긍정적인 무엇인가를 더해 주고 싶어서, 음악에 대한 나의 사랑을 그들과 나누기로 결정했습니다.

➡ ________________

19 Lucy White: 왜 당신은 악기를 만들기 위해 쓰레기를 이용했나요?

➡ ________________

20 Favio Chávez: 한 사람의 쓰레기는 다른 사람의 보물입니다.

➡ ________________

21 그 지역의 쓰레기 줍는 사람인 Nicolás Gámez가 나를 많이 도와주었습니다.

➡ ________________

22 그는 쓰레기로 악기를 만들어 줌으로써 어린이들이 음악을 연주하는 것이 가능하도록 만들었습니다.

➡ ________________

23 이 악기들의 멋진 점은 어린이들이 악기에 많은 돈을 쓸 것을 걱정하지 않아도 된다는 점이었죠.

➡ ________________

____

24 Lucy White: 당신의 음악을 통해서 사람들이 무엇을 배우기를 원하십니까?

➡ ________________

25 Favio Chávez: 나는 가치 없는 것도 영감을 주는 음악을 만들어 낼 수 있다는 것을 사람들이 알게 되기를 원합니다.

➡ ________________

26 Chávez를 인터뷰한 후에 나는 사람들이 악기를 연주하는 데 마음을 쏟아붓는 한, 그 사람이 연주하는 악기가 무엇인지는 별로 중요하지 않다는 것을 깨달았다.

➡ ________________

____

27 카테우라의 어린이들은 나에게 오케스트라는 악기에 의해서가 아니라 사람에 의해 이루어지는 것이라는 것을 보여 주었다.

➡ ________________

28 감상평

➡ ________________

29 Annie: (23초 전) 음악이 삶을 바꿀 수 있다는 것을 보아서 너무 가슴이 뭉클하다.

➡ ________________

30 음악의 힘은 끝이 없다!

➡ ________________

31 Thomas: (1분 전) 음악회가 끝난 후, 나는 재활용 악기로 연주되는 음악으로 사람들에게 영감을 주는 것이 가능하다는 것을 알았다.

➡ ________________

____

32 Kate: (5일 전) 이 재능 있는 젊은이들은 훌륭한 음악을 전할 뿐만 아니라, 또한 심각한 환경 문제에 우리가 주목하게 한다.

➡ ________________

____

구석구석 지문 Test

Step1

※ 다음 우리말과 일치하도록 빈칸에 알맞은 말을 쓰시오.

After You Read A

1. The ________ ________
2. The world ________ ________ ________, we ________ ________ music.
3. ________ the ________
4. The young people ________ ________ ________ ________ ________ ________.
5. It started ________ ________ ________ ________ ________ ________ made out of ________ ________ ________ ________.
6. I ________ ________ ________ the deep sound.
7. ________ ________ ________ Mr. Chávez
8. He went to Cateura in Paraguay ________ ________ ________ ________ ________ ________.
9. He ________ ________ ________ his love of music ________ the children.
10. A ________ ________ ________ helped him.
11. An orchestra is formed ________ ________, ________ ________ ________.

1. 정크 오케스트라
2. 세상이 우리에게 쓰레기를 보내면 우리는 음악을 돌려준다.
3. 음악회에 관해
4. 젊은이들은 쓰레기로 만들어진 악기를 연주했다.
5. 음악회는 한 소녀의 반짝이는 기름통으로 만들어진 첼로 연주로 시작되었다.
6. 나는 그 깊은 소리에 충격을 받았다.
7. Chávez 씨와의 인터뷰
8. 그는 재활용 프로그램에서 일을 하기 위해 파라과이의 카테우라에 갔다.
9. 그는 그의 음악에 대한 사랑을 아이들과 나누기로 결정했다.
10. 그 지역의 쓰레기 줍는 사람이 그를 도와주었다.
11. 오케스트라는 악기에 의해서가 아니라 사람에 의해 이루어지는 것이다.

Grammar in Real Life

1. I ________ a ________ ________.
2. In the news room, I ________ ________ the desk ________ anchors give the news.
3. ________ ________ two screens ________ ________ ________ ________.
4. I could ________ ________ ________ ________ ________ the screen.
5. After I ________ ________ ________ the room, I could see ________ ________ on the TV screen.
6. I really ________ ________ ________ ________ ________ computer graphics.

1. 나는 방송국을 방문했다.
2. 뉴스 룸에서 나는 앵커들이 뉴스를 전하는 책상에 앉았다.
3. 벽에는 두 개의 스크린이 걸려 있었다.
4. 나는 화면을 가로질러 움직이는 문장들을 소리 내어 읽을 수 있었다.
5. 방에서 나온 후 TV 화면에 녹화된 내 모습을 볼 수 있었다.
6. 나는 컴퓨터 그래픽으로 만들어진 배경이 정말 마음에 들었다.

Wrap Up 2

1. M: Hi, Julie. ________ ________ you ________?
2. W: Hi, Chris. I'm ________ to my guitar lesson. Our band has a concert at the hospital ________ ________.
3. M: This Sunday? ________ you ________ ________ ________ at the Happy Children's Hospital?
4. W: Yes. ________ do you ________ ________ the concert?
5. M: Oh, my sister ________ ________ ________ ________ ________ ________ there, so I'm ________ ________ the concert, ________.
6. W: Great. ________ and ________ our ________!

1. M: 안녕, Julie. 어디 가는 길이니?
2. W: 안녕, Chris. 나는 기타 수업에 가는 길이야. 우리 밴드가 이번 주 일요일에 병원에서 공연을 하거든.
3. M: 이번 주 일요일? Happy 아동 병원에서 공연할 계획이니?
4. W: 응. 그 공연에 대해 어떻게 알고 있어?
5. M: 아, 내 여동생이 거기서 피아노를 연주할 거라서 나도 그 공연에 갈 거야.
6. W: 잘됐다. 와서 우리 공연을 봐!

구석구석 지문 Test

Step2

※ 다음 우리말을 영어로 쓰시오.

After You Read A

1. 정크 오케스트라
➡ ______
2. 세상이 우리에게 쓰레기를 보내면 우리는 음악을 돌려준다.
➡ ______
3. 음악회에 관해
➡ ______
4. 젊은이들은 쓰레기로 만들어진 악기를 연주했다.
➡ ______
5. 음악회는 한 소녀의 반짝이는 기름통으로 만들어진 첼로 연주로 시작되었다.
➡ ______
6. 나는 그 깊은 소리에 충격을 받았다.
➡ ______
7. Chávez 씨와의 인터뷰
➡ ______
8. 그는 재활용 프로그램에서 일을 하기 위해 파라과이의 카테우라에 갔다.
➡ ______
9. 그는 그의 음악에 대한 사랑을 아이들과 나누기로 결정했다.
➡ ______
10. 그 지역의 쓰레기 줍는 사람이 그를 도와주었다.
➡ ______
11. 오케스트라는 악기에 의해서가 아니라 사람에 의해 이루어지는 것이다.
➡ ______

Grammar in Real Life

1. 나는 방송국을 방문했다.
➡ ______
2. 뉴스 룸에서 나는 앵커들이 뉴스를 전하는 책상에 앉았다.
➡ ______
3. 벽에는 두 개의 스크린이 걸려 있었다.
➡ ______
4. 나는 화면을 가로질러 움직이는 문장들을 소리 내어 읽을 수 있었다.
➡ ______
5. 방에서 나온 후 TV 화면에 녹화된 내 모습을 볼 수 있었다.
➡ ______
6. 나는 컴퓨터 그래픽으로 만들어진 배경이 정말 마음에 들었다.
➡ ______

Wrap Up 2

1. M: 안녕, Julie. 어디 가는 길이니?
➡ ______
2. W: 안녕, Chris. 나는 기타 수업에 가는 길이야. 우리 밴드가 이번 주 일요일에 병원에서 공연을 하거든.
➡ ______
3. M: 이번 주 일요일? Happy 아동 병원에서 공연할 계획이니?
➡ ______
4. W: 응. 그 공연에 대해 어떻게 알고 있어?
➡ ______
5. M: 아, 내 여동생이 거기서 피아노를 연주할 거라서 나도 그 공연에 갈 거야.
➡ ______
6. W: 잘됐다. 와서 우리 공연을 봐!
➡ ______

MEMO

1학기 전과정
적중100 plus
영어 기출 문제집

영어 기출 문제집

적중100 plus
1학기 전과정

1학기

정답 및 해설

비상 | 김진완

중3

적중100

영어 기출 문제집

적중100

중3

적중100

Lesson 1

The Art of Communication

시험대비 실력평가 p.08

01 ③	02 ④	03 ②	04 ③
05 ②	06 ③	07 ①, ⑤	

01 upset: 화난, 기분 나쁜
02 focus on: ~에 집중하다 concentrate on: ~에 집중하다
03 ①, ④번은 (2)의 뜻으로, ③, ⑤번은 (1)의 뜻으로 사용되었다. ②번의 mean은 '잔인한 또는 친절하지 않은'의 의미로 사용되어 '그것은 친구에게 하는 못된 장난이다.'로 해석된다.
04 stressed out: 스트레스로 지친, 스트레스가 쌓인 / 학기 말에 나는 스트레스로 완전히 지쳐 있었다. work out: 해결하다 / 모든 일이 잘 해결돼서 다행이다.
05 get cold feet: 긴장하다, 겁을 먹다 have one's head in the clouds: 공상에 잠겨 있다(to be out of touch with reality and have impractical ideas about achieving success) hit the books: 공부하다 let one's hair down: 느긋하게 쉬다 let the cat out of the bag: 비밀을 누설하다
06 (A) free from: ~이 없는 (B) find out: 발견하다, 알아내다 (C) first of all: 먼저, 무엇보다도
07 take[have] a look at: ~을 보다

서술형 시험대비 p.09

01 ⓑ ready leaving → ready to leave
ⓒ end up to spend → end up spending
02 (c)old (f)eet
03 (K)eep, in mind
04 (1) effectively (2) (d)isappointed (3) hid
(4) (r)eason
05 long
06 (1) Many trees can help to prevent landslides from flood.
(2) She can help you solve your problem.
(3) This coat is uncomfortable to wear.
(4) Instead, your effort is important.

01 ⓐ be busy 동사ing: ~하느라 바쁘다 / 나는 중간고사 준비하느라고 바쁘다. ⓑ be ready to 동사원형: ~할 준비가 되다 / 우린 아직 떠날 준비가 안 되었어! ⓒ end up 동사ing: 결국 ~하게 되다 / 고객들은 결국 써야 할 돈보다 더 많은 돈을 써 버리고 맙니다.
02 get cold feet: 긴장하다, 겁을 먹다
03 keep ~ in mind: ~을 명심하다
04 (1) effectively: 효과적으로 (2) disappointed: 실망한, 낙담한 (3) hide: 숨다, 감추다 bush: 덤불 (4) reason: 이유
05 long: 긴 / 올해는 춥고 긴 겨울이 계속되네요. long face: 우울한 얼굴 / 그는 시험에 떨어진 후 침울한 얼굴을 하고 있다.
06 (1) prevent: 막다, 예방하다 (2) solve: 해결하다 (3) uncomfortable: 불편한 (4) instead: 그 대신에

교과서

Conversation

핵심 Check p.10~11

1 I am upset with my friend. 2 (C) → (B) → (A)
3 I'm very angry at[with] my sisters.
4 That's not what I meant. I meant
5 (B) → (C) → (A)

교과서 대화문 익히기

Check(√) True or False p.12~13

1 T 2 F 3 F 4 T 5 F 6 T 7 T 8 F

교과서 확인학습 p.15~17

Listen & Talk 1 Get Ready
Why, unhappy / about / take it

Listen & Talk 1 A-1
come, with, these days / upset about an argument / Why / cutting me off in / mad, talking to

Listen & Talk 1 A-2
How, going / I'm upset about / I don't think that, on

Listen & Talk 1 B
Why, long / angry at, said some mean / to sleep, But, talking loudly on the phone / upset / haven't worked it / that, but I don't know how / Why, send

Listen & Talk 2 Get Ready
let the cat out of the bag / That's not what, a secret

Listen & Talk 2 A-1

get, in, should / concentrate, first of all, have your head in the clouds / see the sky / That's not what I meant, meant, focus

Listen & Talk 2 A-2

go diving / got cold feet / get a cold / I meant that, scared

Listen & Talk 2 B

stressed out about / two more to go / finishing, go on a, hair down / hair style / what I meant, feel free from

Communication

seem / keep telling me that, direct, upset / what they're talking about / tend to say what's on, strongly / Should / That's not what I meant, try to consider / try

시험대비 기본평가 p.18

01 ③ 02 ③ 03 ④
04 That's not what I meant.

01 That's not what I meant.는 '그런 뜻이 아니야.'라는 의미이며, 상대방이 자신의 말의 의도를 오해할 때 정정하기 위해 쓰는 표현이다. 'That's not what I meant to say.', 'I'm afraid you don't understand what I'm saying.', 'I didn't mean to say that.', 'I hope there is no misunderstanding.' 등도 비슷한 표현이다.

02 (B) 동생에게 화가 났다는 말에 (C) 무슨 일인지 질문하자 (A) 여동생이 물어보지 않고, 옷을 입는다고 화난 이유에 관해 설명한다. upset: 화난, 기분 나쁜 without: ~ 없이

03 'I got cold feet.'에 대해 여자가 감기 걸린 것으로 이해해서 남자가 'I meant that I got scared.(내가 무서웠다는 말이야.)'로 말하며 자신이 의도하고 싶었던 내용을 말한다.

04 That's not what I meant.: 내가 의미한 것은 그게 아니야.

시험대비 실력평가 p.19~20

01 ③ 02 ⑤ 03 ① 04 ③
05 unhappy 06 ⑤ 07 ① 08 ②
09 ④ 10 ③

01 (C) 좋은 영어 성적을 얻기 위한 조언을 부탁하자 (A) Brown 선생님은 무엇보다도 수업 시간에 집중하라고 말하며 수진이가 종종 공상에 잠겨 있다고(have your head in the clouds) 말하자 (B) 교실에서 하늘을 볼 수 없다고 말하고 (D) 선생님은 그 뜻이 아니라 수업 시간에 집중을 안 한다는 의미로 말했다고 설명한다.

02 'That's not what I meant.(내가 의미한 것은 그게 아니야.)'는 상대방이 자신의 말의 의도를 오해할 때 정정하기 위해 쓰는 표현이다. 자신의 말의 의도를 정정해 주는 'You can try to consider others' feelings.(다른 사람들의 감정을 이해하려고 노력해 봐.)'란 말 앞에 오는 것이 적절하다.

03 여자가 사람들이 Jason에 대해 말한 것을 어느 정도 이해한다고 말하고, 남자의 질문에 이에 대한 자세한 설명을 하고 있으므로 'What do you mean?(무슨 의미야?)'이 어울린다.

04 사람들은 Jason이 단도직입적이라고 말했고 이에 대해 Jason이 화가 났다.

05 'I'm upset about Roy.(Roy에게 화가 났어.)'라고 말하고 있으므로 happy(행복한)는 어울리지 않는다. unhappy: 불만스러운, 불행한

06 'I am upset about ~.(나는 ~에 화가 나.)', 'I can't stand ~.(나는 ~을 참을 수 없어.)' 둘 다 화가 난 감정을 나타낼 때 사용하는 표현이다.

07 왜 우울한 얼굴을 하고 있는지(무슨 일이 있는지) 질문하자 (B) 여동생에게 화가 나서 그녀에게 심술궂은 말을 했다고 대답한다. (A) 왜 화가 났는지 이유를 물어보자 (C) 피곤해서 자려고 했는데 동생이 전화로 시끄럽게 통화해서 화가 났다고 대답한다. (D) 아직 화해를 했는지 남자가 여자에게 물어보고 여자는 아직 못 했다고 대답하며 어떻게 화해할지 모르겠다고 말한다.

08 'let the cat out of the bag(비밀을 누설하다)'을 고양이를 가방에서 꺼내는 것으로 받아들이고 있는 상대방에게 자신이 말한 의도는 그것이 아니었다고 말하며, 말하고 싶어하는 내용을 다시 말하고 있다.

09 A는 B가 Clara의 생일 파티를 비밀로 유지하기를 원하고 있다.

10 남동생에게 화가 났다는 말에, 그가 시험을 잘못 봤다는 말은 어울리지 않는다.

서술형 시험대비 p.21

01 I am upset about an argument we had.
02 off
03 Why are you upset about her?
04 ordering
05 out
06 go
07 I didn't mean to say that.
08 ⓔ that → what

01 upset: 화난, 기분 나쁜 'be upset about ~'은 '~에 대해서 화가 나다'라는 의미로 화가 난 감정을 나타낼 때 사용하는 표현이다. an argument와 we had 사이에 목적격 관계대명사가 생략되어 있다.

02 cut ~ off: ~을 중단시키다, 잘라내다

03 be upset about ~: ~에게 화가 나다

04 keep 동사ing: ~을 계속하다 order 사람 around: ~에게 자꾸 이래라저래라 하다

05 stressed out: 스트레스로 지친, 스트레스가 쌓인

06 go: (일의 진행이 어떻게) 되어가다, 진전되다 go on a trip: 여행가다

07 mean: 의미하다 say: 말하다

08 That's not what I meant.는 '그런 뜻이 아니야.'라는 의미이며, 상대방이 자신의 말의 의도를 오해할 때 정정하기 위해 쓰는 표현이다. meant의 목적어가 없고 not 뒤에 보어가 없기 때문에 선행사를 포함한 관계대명사 what을 사용해야 한다.

교과서

Grammar

핵심 Check p.22~23

1 (1) what (2) what (3) What
2 (1) when (2) where (3) why

시험대비 기본평가 p.24

01 ② 02 ④ 03 ⑤
04 (1) Spring is a beautiful time when the flowers bloom.
(2) Is there any reason why you are here?
(3) Don't live in a town where there are no doctors.

01 선행사가 the house이므로 where가 적절하다.

02 know의 목적어와 think의 목적어 역할을 할 수 있는 것으로 선행사를 포함하는 관계대명사 what이 나와야 한다.

03 선행사 the way와 관계부사 how는 함께 쓸 수 없으며 the way나 how만 써야 하며, 선행사가 the way일 때 how 대신에 that을 쓸 수 있다.

04 (1) 선행사가 time이므로 when이 적절하다. (2) 선행사가 reason이므로 why가 적절하다. (3) 선행사가 a town이므로 where가 적절하다.

시험대비 실력평가 p.25~27

01 ② 02 ③ 03 ④
04 (1) why (2) that (3) when (4) what (5) that
05 ⑤ 06 ① 07 ③ 08 ②, ④
09 Christmas is a time when we share with families.
10 that → what 11 ⑤ 12 ①
13 ② 14 ⑤
15 I found the reality quite different from what I had imagined. 16 ①, ④
17 (1) He didn't let us know the way(또는 how, the way that) he solved the problem.
(2) Judy went to the restaurant in[at] which(또는 where) she had dinner with her friends.
(3) Yuna remembers the day when she won the Olympic gold medal.
(4) I can't believe what you're saying.
(5) I like the bag that[which] I bought yesterday.
(6) I would like to do what I want when I want.
18 1950 is the year when the Korean War broke out.

01 ① This is the house where Anne was born. ③ This is the park where I met Sophie. ④ Tell me how[the way] you solved the problem. ⑤ I remember the day when I met her first.

02 두 개의 동사 believe의 목적어 역할을 할 수 있도록 that을 what으로 고쳐야 한다.

03 첫 번째 문장에서 was doing의 목적어와 would be의 주어 역할을 할 수 있는 것은 What이다. 두 번째 문장에서 the hotel이 선행사이므로 관계부사 where가 적절하다.

04 (1) the reason이 선행사이므로 관계부사 why가 적절하다. (2) the way가 있으므로 how를 쓸 수 없으며 that을 쓸 수 있다. (3) times가 선행사이므로 관계부사 when이 적절하다. (4) for의 목적어가 없으므로 what이 이끄는 절이 sell의 목적어가 되도록 해야 한다. (5) 선행사로 all이 있으므로 관계대명사 that이 적절하다. all을 없애고 what만 써도 어법상 바른 문장이다.

05 had의 목적어와 was의 주어 역할을 할 수 있는 what이 적절하다.

06 the place가 선행사이므로 관계부사 where가 적절하다.

07 관계부사 how는 선행사 the way와 함께 쓸 수 없고 반드시 둘 중 하나는 생략해야 한다.

08 what이 관계대명사인지 의문대명사인지 구분하는 문제로 보통 의문사 what은 '무엇이 ~인(한)지'로, 관계대명사 what은 '~하는 것'으로 해석한다. ① 의문대명사 ② 관계대명사 ③ 의문대명사 ④ 관계대명사 ⑤ 의문대명사

09 a time이 선행사이므로 관계부사 when을 쓴다.

10 what is called: 소위, 이른바

11 the thing which[that]의 역할을 하는 what을 이용하여 나타내도록 한다.

12 ①번은 선행사가 the house로 where가 들어가야 하고, 나머지는 선행사가 시간이므로 when이 적절하다.

13 ②번은 the bank라는 선행사가 있으므로 which나 that이 들어가야 하고 나머지는 선행사가 없으므로 what[What]이 적절하다.

14 관계부사 where는 '전치사 in+which'로 바꿔 쓸 수 있다.

15 선행사를 포함하는 관계대명사 what을 추가하여 쓴다.

16 ① for와 did의 목적어 역할을 해야 하므로 that을 what으로 고쳐야 한다. ④ 선행사가 the day이므로 how를 when으로 고쳐야 한다.

17 (1) 관계부사 how는 선행사 the way와 함께 쓸 수 없고 반드시 둘 중 하나는 생략해야 한다. 또는 the way that을 쓴다. (2) the restaurant이 선행사이지만 뒤에 이어지는 절이 완전하므로 in which나 관계부사 where를 써야 한다. (3) 선행사가 the day이므로 관계부사 when을 써야 한다. (4) that을 believe와 saying의 목적어 역할을 할 수 있는 what으로 고쳐야 한다. (5) the bag이 선행사로 나왔으므로 what이 아니라 which나 that을 써야 한다. (6) that을 do와 want의 목적어 역할을 할 수 있는 what으로 고쳐야 한다.

18 the year가 선행사이므로 when을 이용한다.

서술형 시험대비 p.28~29

01 (1) Do you know the reason why he came here?
Do you know the reason for which he came here?
Do you know the reason which he came here for?
(2) Natural disasters damage the place where people live.
Natural disasters damage the place in which people live.
Natural disasters damage the place which people live in.

02 (1) She has the right to do what she wants to do in her life.
(2) What I want to do is to adopt a dog.
(3) May I ask you the reason why you made that decision?

03 (1) where we stayed
(2) what I want

04 (1) where[at which]
(2) how[the way]
(3) why[for which]

05 (1) He politely denied what I suggested.
(2) He did not listen to what I said.
(3) What was proposed by him was not allowed.
(4) Love is what helps mend a broken heart.

06 (1) I don't know the reason why he hides it.
(2) Bill didn't know the time when she would arrive.
(3) Avoid the area where the accident took place.
(4) We studied how computers store information.
(5) Cambridge Park is a nice park where you can sit on the grass.

07 (1) that은 앞에 있는 선행사를 수식하는 주격 관계대명사이며 형용사절을 이끈다.
(2) what은 선행사를 포함하는 관계대명사로 명사절을 이끌어 does의 목적어 역할을 한다.

08 (1) where → which[that]
(2) the way how → the way(또는 how 또는 the way that 또는 the way in which)
(3) which → when(또는 at which), 또는 which he is least busy → which he is least busy at
(4) what → that, 또는 the things 삭제
(5) That → What (6) that → what

01 (1) why는 'for+which'로 바꿔 쓸 수 있으며, 이때 for는 which의 바로 앞이나 관계사절의 마지막에 쓸 수 있다. (2) where는 'in+which'로 바꿔 쓸 수 있으며, 이때 in은 which의 바로 앞이나 관계사절의 마지막에 쓸 수 있다.

02 (1)~(2) 선행사를 포함하는 관계대명사 what을 이용한다. what이 선행사를 포함하므로 문장에서 두 가지의 역할을 함에 유의한다. (3) the reason이 선행사로 나올 때는 관계부사 why를 쓴다.

03 (1) 선행사가 the hotel이므로 관계부사 where를 이용한다. (2) 선행사를 포함하는 관계대명사 what을 이용한다.

04 (1) where는 'at which'로, (3) why는 'for which'로 바꿔 쓸 수 있다. (2) 완전한 절이 이어지므로 내용상 관계부사how가 적절하다. how 대신 the way를 써도 좋다.

05 the things which[that]의 역할을 하는 what을 이용하여 하나의 문장으로 쓴다.

06 관계부사는 두 문장을 연결하는 접속사의 역할과 부사의 역할을 동시에 하며 선행사에 따라 관계부사 when(시간), where(장소), why(이유), how(방법)를 쓴다.

07 what = the thing[something] that

08 (1) 이어지는 절에서 built의 목적어가 없으므로 where를 관계대명사 that이나 which로 고쳐야 한다. (2) 관계부사 how는 선행사 the way와 함께 쓰지 않고 반드시 둘 중의 하나만 써야

하며 the way that이나 the way in which를 쓸 수 있다. (3) 이어지는 절이 완전하고 선행사로 the time이 나왔으므로 관계대명사 which를 when이나 at which로 고쳐야 한다. at을 관계사절의 끝에 써도 된다. (4) the things라는 선행사가 있으므로 what을 that으로 고쳐 쓴다. 또는 the things를 삭제한다. (5) That을 do의 목적어와 is의 주어 역할을 할 수 있는 What으로 고쳐야 한다. (6) understand와 said의 목적어 역할을 할 수 있도록 that을 what으로 고쳐야 한다.

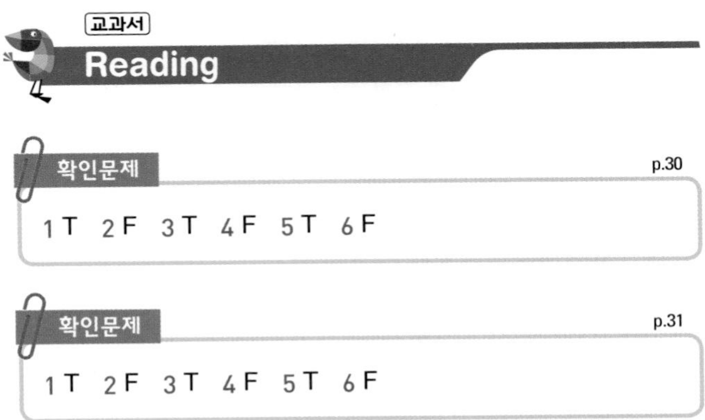

교과서

Reading

확인문제 p.30

1 T 2 F 3 T 4 F 5 T 6 F

확인문제 p.31

1 T 2 F 3 T 4 F 5 T 6 F

교과서 확인학습 A p.32~33

01 Effectively 02 Welcome to 03 I'm
04 using good communication skills
05 our first clip 06 ends up arguing
07 the reason why 08 *careless*
09 to express his feelings
10 Instead, I-message
11 focus on, rather than
12 *I'm, upset, are lost* 13 Next
14 is busy preparing
15 have a look
16 *Could I*
17 the right time
18 what 19 enough time
20 pick a time, is ready to listen
21 *Could I* 22 *Sure*
23 take a look at 24 hurts 25 *Don't put*
26 felt uncomfortable
27 taking orders 28 such as
29 what, request, demand
30 *Could you*
31 a small change, prevent communication problems
32 keep, in mind

교과서 확인학습 B p.34~35

1 Speak Your Mind Effectively
2 Welcome to "All about Teens."
3 I'm Dr. Carter.
4 Today, we're going to talk about using good communication skills to express ourselves more effectively.
5 Let's start with our first clip about Brian.
6 When he tries to talk to his brother, he always ends up arguing with his brother.
7 Let's find out the reason why he has this problem.
8 Brian: You lost my earphones again. Why are you so careless?
9 Brian is starting a sentence with "you" to express his feelings..
10 Instead, he should use the "I-message."
11 Starting with "I" can help him focus on what he feels or thinks rather than point the finger at his brother.
12 Brian: I'm really upset because my favorite earphones are lost.
13 Next is Calli.
14 She is trying to talk to her mother, but she is busy preparing to go to work.
15 Let's have a look.
16 Calli: Hey, Mom. Could I talk to you about something?
17 Calli needs to find the right time to talk to her mom.
18 Maybe Calli's mom wanted to listen to what Calli was going to say.
19 But she didn't have enough time to talk with her daughter.
20 Calli should pick a time when her mom is ready to listen.
21 Calli: Hey, Mom. Could I talk to you about something?
22 Mom: Sure.
23 Now, let's take a look at our last clip.
24 Anna and Julie are best friends, but Anna often hurts Julie's feelings.
25 Anna: Don't put your bag on my desk!
26 Julie probably felt uncomfortable because Anna made a demand using the word "don't."
27 People simply don't like taking orders.
28 Anna should try to use words such as "can," "could," or "please."
29 Then, what she says will sound like a request

rather than a demand.
30 Anna: Could you put your bag on your desk?
31 As we saw in the video clips, a small change in the way we express ourselves can solve or even prevent communication problems.
32 Let's keep these tips in mind!

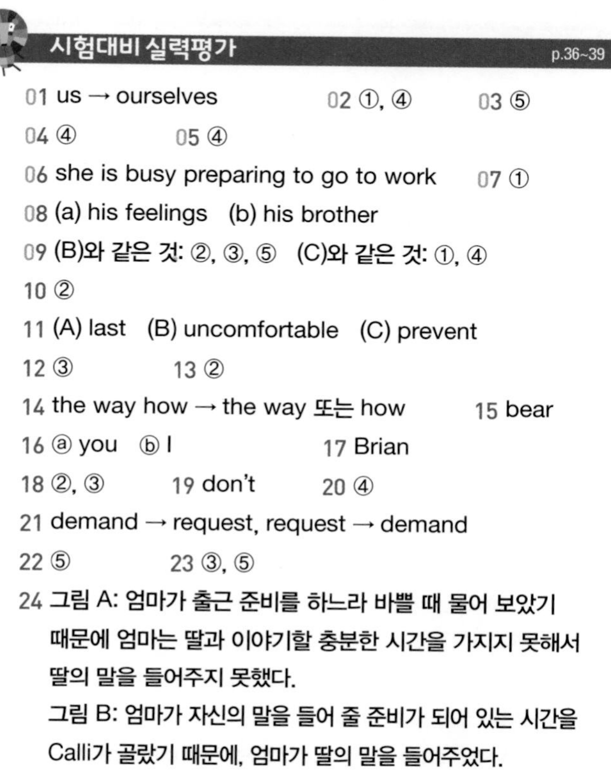

시험대비 실력평가 p.36~39

01 us → ourselves 02 ①, ④ 03 ⑤
04 ④ 05 ④
06 she is busy preparing to go to work 07 ①
08 (a) his feelings (b) his brother
09 (B)와 같은 것: ②, ③, ⑤ (C)와 같은 것: ①, ④
10 ②
11 (A) last (B) uncomfortable (C) prevent
12 ③ 13 ②
14 the way how → the way 또는 how 15 bear
16 ⓐ you ⓑ I 17 Brian
18 ②, ③ 19 don't 20 ④
21 demand → request, request → demand
22 ⑤ 23 ③, ⑤
24 그림 A: 엄마가 출근 준비를 하느라 바쁠 때 물어 보았기 때문에 엄마는 딸과 이야기할 충분한 시간을 가지지 못해서 딸의 말을 들어주지 못했다.
그림 B: 엄마가 자신의 말을 들어 줄 준비가 되어 있는 시간을 Calli가 골랐기 때문에, 엄마가 딸의 말을 들어주었다.

01 주어와 목적어가 같으므로 재귀대명사로 고치는 것이 적절하다.

02 ⓐ와 ①, ④: 명사적 용법, ②, ⑤: 부사적 용법, talk over a cup of coffee: 커피를 마시면서 이야기하다, ③: 형용사적 용법

03 ⑤ '브라이언과 남동생 사이의 말다툼을 하게 된 이유에 대해 알아보자'고 했으므로, 위 글에서는 그 이유를 알 수 없다. ① All about Teens. ② Dr. Carter. ③ Using good communication skills to express ourselves more effectively(자신을 더 효과적으로 표현하기 위해 좋은 의사소통 기술을 사용하는 것). ④ The reason of the argument between Brian and his brother. subject: (논의 등의) 주제, 대상, 화제

04 ④ '아마' Calli의 엄마는 Calli가 말하려고 하는 것을 듣고 싶었을 것이라고 하는 것이 적절하다. Maybe: 아마, ① 그 결과, 따라서, ② 정확히, ③, ⑤: 특히

05 ④는 Calli가 아니라 'Calli의 엄마'를 지칭한다.

06 be busy ~ing: ~하느라 바쁘다

07 ⓐ focus on: (관심, 노력 등을) 집중하다, 초점을 맞추다, ⓑ point the finger at: …을 비난[책망]하다

08 Brian은 '그의 감정'을 표현하기 위해 "너"로 문장을 시작하면서 그의 남동생을 비난하기 때문에, 그는 결국 언제나 '남동생'과 말다툼을 하게 된다.

09 (B)와 ②, ③, ⑤: 현재분사, (C)와 ①, ④: 동명사

10 앞 문장에서 Julie는 Anna가 "don't"라는 단어를 사용하며 요구했기 때문에 아마 불편하게 느꼈을 것이라고 했기 때문에, 사람들은 단순히 '명령을 받는 것'을 좋아하지 않는다고 하는 것이 적절하다. take orders: 명령을 받다, ① ask advice: 충고를 구하다, ③ give advice: 충고를 하다, ④ take turns: 교대로 하다, ⑤ give orders: 지시하다

11 (A) 몇 개의 동영상 중에서 '마지막' 동영상을 말하는 것이므로 last가 적절하다. last: 마지막의, latest: 최근의, (B) 'feel+형용사 보어'를 써야 하므로 uncomfortable이 적절하다. (C) 의사소통의 문제를 '막을 수 있다'고 해야 하므로 prevent가 적절하다. prevent: 막다[예방/방지하다], protect: 보호하다

12 이 글은 '사람들은 단순히 명령을 받는 것을 좋아하지 않으므로 "can," "could," 또는 "please"와 같은 단어들을 사용하려고 노력해야 한다.'는 내용의 글이므로, 어울리는 속담으로는 ③번 '가는 말이 고우면 오는 말도 곱다.'가 적절하다. ① 늦더라도 않는 것보다 낫다. ② 어려울 때 친구가 진정한 친구이다. ④ 깃털이 같은 새들이 함께 모인다.(유유상종) ⑤ 손 안에 든 새 한 마리가 숲 속에 있는 두 마리보다 낫다.

13 ⓐ와 ②: …처럼, …하는 대로, ① [비례] …함에 따라, …할수록, ③ …일 때, ④ (자격·기능 등이) …로(서)(전치사), ⑤ [이유·원인] …이므로, …이기 때문에

14 the way와 how는 같이 쓸 수 없다.

15 keep ~ in mind = bear ~ in mind: 명심하다

16 ⓐ Brian은 그의 감정을 표현하기 위해 "너"로 문장을 시작하고 있다. ⓑ "나"로 시작하는 것은 그의 남동생을 비난하기보다 자신이 느끼거나 생각하는 것에 집중하도록 도울 수 있다.

17 Brian을 가리킨다.

18 ② 비판[비난]하다, ③ …을 탓하다, ① (…해야 한다고) 고집하다[주장하다/우기다], ④ (~이 어떠한지를) 말하다[서술하다], ⑤ (아이디어·계획을) 제안[제의]하다

19 Julie는 Anna가 "don't"라는 단어를 사용하며 요구했기 때문에 아마 불편하게 느꼈을 것이라고 하는 것이 적절하다.

20 ⓑ와 ④: 명령, take orders: 명령을 받다, ① 순서, ② 정돈, ③ (사회적) 질서, ⑤ (상품의) 주문 restore: 복구하다

21 Anna가 "can," "could" 또는 "please"와 같은 말을 사용하려고 노력하면, 그녀가 하는 말이 '요구'라기보다는 '요청'처럼 들릴 것이라고 하는 것이 적절하다.

22 ⓐ와 ⑤: 알맞은, ① 오른쪽의, ② 옳은, ③ 정확히, 바로(부사), ④ 권리[권한](명사)

23 ⓑ와 ③, ⑤: 형용사적 용법, ①, ②: 부사적 용법, ④: 명사적

용법

24 Calli가 엄마에게 말을 걸 적절한 때를 찾아내어 물어보았는지 아닌지를 구별해서 대답하면 정답이다.

서술형 시험대비 p.40~41

01 why

02 (1) in order (2) so as (3) in order that
(4) so that, can[may]

03 he always ends up arguing with his brother

04 preparing

05 the thing which[that]

06 (A) find the right time (B) is ready to listen

07 starting a sentence

08 **자신이 느끼거나 생각하는 것에 집중하도록 "나"로 문장을 시작하는 것이다.**

09 point the finger at his brother → focus on what he feels or thinks, focus on what he feels or thinks → point the finger at his brother

10 have, look at

11 Could[Can] you put your bag on your desk? **또는** Please put your bag on your desk.

12 request, demand / demand, request / demand, request

13 to use words such as "can," "could," or "please"

14 "don't" / "can", "could", "please"

01 선행사가 the reason이므로, 관계부사 why가 적절하다.

02 부사적 용법(목적)을 나타내는 to부정사는 in order to = so as to = in order that ~ can[may] = so that ~ can[may]으로 바꿔 쓸 수 있다.

03 end up ~ing: 결국 ~하게 되다

04 be busy ~ing: ~하느라 바쁘다

05 관계대명사 what은 선행사를 포함한 관계대명사이다. 지금은 동사가 was이므로 선행사를 단수 형태인 the thing으로 쓰는 것이 적절하다.

06 문제점: Calli는 엄마에게 말을 걸 적절한 때를 찾아내지 못했다. 효과적인 의사소통 방법: Calli는 엄마가 들어 줄 준비가 되어 있는 시간을 골라야 한다.

07 그의 감정을 표현하기 위해 "너"로 '문장을 시작하는' 대신에 뒤에 이어지는 내용을 쓰면 된다.

08 뒤에 이어지는 내용을 쓰면 된다.

09 rather than 앞과 뒤의 말들을 서로 바꿔 쓰는 것이 적절하다. B rather than A: A라기보다는 B

10 take a look at = have a look at = look at

11 "can," "could," 또는 "please"와 같은 말을 사용하면 요구라기보다는 요청처럼 들릴 것이라고 했다.

12 A라기보다는 B: B rather than A = rather[more] B than A = not so much A as B = less A than B

13 "can," "could" 또는 "please"와 같은 말을 사용하는 것이다.

14 사용하지 말아야 할 단어: '요구'하는 것처럼 들리는 단어, 사용하려고 노력해야 하는 단어들: '요청'하는 것처럼 들리는 단어들

영역별 핵심문제 p.43~47

01 ④ 02 Keep(keep)

03 (1) off (2) on (3) in 04 ② 05 ④

06 argument 07 ②, ③ 08 ① 09 ⑤

10 ④ 11 ①, ⑤ 12 ④

13 I'm so stressed out about my exams

14 ① 15 ② 16 ③ 17 ⑤

18 (1) What she said (2) what I've missed (3) what I ate

19 (1) My parents got married on the day.
(2) I make gimchi in the way.

20 (1) The house where Anne lives has a small garden.
(2) The house in which Anne lives has a small garden.
(3) The house which Anne lives in has a small garden.

21 ⓐ, ⓒ, ⓔ, ⓕ 22 ③, ④

23 Whenever 24 for which 25 ③ 26 ④

27 maybe **또는** perhaps

28 what she says will sound like a request rather than a demand

29 (A) made a demand (B) can, could, please

30 ② 31 Calli's mother 32 ⑤

01 pre-는 '미리, 먼저(before, beforehand)'의 의미가 있는 접두어이다. precaution: 조심, 예방책 preview: 미리 보기 prepare: 준비하다 prevent: 막다, 예방하다 premium: 고급의

02 keep ~ in mind: ~을 명심하다 / 이 교훈을 명심해라. keep 동사ing: ~을 계속하다, 반복하다 / 그녀가 그에게 설거지하라고 말해서 그는 계속해서 TV를 볼 수 없었다.

03 (1) cut ~ off: ~을 중단시키다, 잘라내다 / 내가 말할 때 내 말을 자르지 마. (2) focus on: ~에 집중하다 / 그는 사진 찍는 데 집중했다. (3) in the middle of: ~ 도중에, ~ 중간에 / 나는 지금 꽤 중요한 일을 하는 중이다.

04 mean: 못된, 심술궂은 / 잔인한 또는 친절하지 않은

05 how come: 어찌하여, 왜

07 ① Anna가 Sally의 말을 중간에 끊었다. ④ 남자가 Sally에게 왜 그녀가 Anna와 말을 안 하는지 물은 것을 보아 왜 사이가 안

좋았는지에 대해 모르고 있었다. ⑤ Sally는 Anna의 행동에 화가 났다.

08 'What should I do?'는 '어떻게 해야 하지?'의 의미로 충고를 구할 때 쓰는 표현으로 Brown씨가 수업에 집중하라고 충고해 주고 있는 대답의 질문으로 적절하다.

09 first of all: 먼저, 무엇보다도 / 좋은 영어 성적을 얻기 위해 무엇을 해야 하는지 충고를 구하는 말에 무엇보다도 수업 시간에 집중하라는 충고를 해 주고 있다.

10 ④번은 상대방이 내가 한 말을 정확히 이해했다는 의미이며, 이외의 나머지 보기들은 상대방이 자신의 말을 이해하지 못했을 때 쓸 수 있는 표현들이다.

11 자신이 화났음을 표현할 때 upset을 사용해서 'I am upset about[with, because of] ~. (나는 ~에 대해[~에게, ~ 때문에] 화가 나)'라고 말할 수 있다.

12 언니가 Anna에게 이래라저래라 하는 것에 화가 난다고 말하고 있으므로 남자아이는 Anna가 느끼는 감정을 언니인 Elsa에게 말해야 한다고 충고하고 있다.

13 stressed out: 스트레스로 지친, 스트레스가 쌓인

14 let one's hair down: 느긋하게 쉬다

15 관계부사 where는 의미에 맞게 '전치사(in, at, on 등)+관계대명사 which'로 바꿔 쓸 수 있다. 여기서 where는 in which나 at which로 바꿔 쓸 수 있다.

16 I like what she bought for me. 선행사가 없으므로 선행사를 포함하는 관계대명사 what을 이용하여 '~하는 것'을 나타낸다.

17 <보기>와 ⑤번은 관계부사이다. ① 의문사, ② 의문사, ③ 접속사, ④ 명사

18 선행사를 포함한 관계대명사 what(= the thing(s) which[that])을 이용한다.

19 관계부사는 '전치사+관계대명사(which)'로 바꿔 쓸 수 있다. when = in/on/at which, how = in which

20 관계부사는 '전치사+관계대명사(which)'로 바꿔 쓸 수 있는데, which를 쓸 때는 전치사를 which 바로 앞에 쓰거나 관계부사절의 끝에 쓴다. where = in which

21 ⓑ that → what ⓓ which → where ⓖ the way how → the way 또는 how 또는 the way that 또는 the way in which

22 ⓐ와 ③, ④: 동명사, ①, ②, ⑤: 현재분사, ② 빈 수레가 요란하다(실속은 없는데 허세를 부릴 때 자주 쓰는 속담).

23 When ~, always = Whenever: ~할 때마다

24 관계부사 why는 for which로 고칠 수 있다.

25 ③번 다음 문장의 But에 주목한다. 주어진 문장의 내용과 상반되는 내용을 이끌고 있으므로 ③번이 적절하다.

26 'Calli's mom' didn't have enough time to talk with 'her daughter.'

27 probably = maybe= perhaps: 아마

28 'what'을 보충하면 된다.

29 문제점: Anna는 "don't"라는 단어를 사용하며 '요구했다.' 효과적인 의사소통 방법: Anna는 "can," "could," 또는 "please"와 같은 말을 사용함으로써 그녀가 말하는 것이 요구라기보다는 요청처럼 들리게 만들어야 한다.

30 선행사가 시간이므로 관계부사 when이 적절하다.

31 'Calli의 엄마'를 가리킨다.

32 Calli가 얼마나 자주 그녀의 엄마와 이야기할 수 있는지는 대답할 수 없다. ① No. ② When her mom is busy preparing to go to work. ③ She needs to find the right time to talk to her mom. ④ Yes.

단원별 예상문제 p.48~51

01 uncomfortable 02 ② 03 got
04 ⑤ 05 ① 06 ③
07 I'm upset about my science group. 08 ③
09 ③ 10 ② 11 What 12 ③
13 ④ 14 ②
15 (1) The report showed what I wanted to know.
(2) He was proud of what he did.
(3) This telescope can do what others cannot.
(4) July is the month when the summer heat actually begins.
(5) We stayed in a village where time has stood still.
(6) The Internet is changing the way people shop.
16 ⓐ relationship ⓑ I will keep my promises. Also I will try to be honest with her.
17 (1) 엄마와의 약속을 지키지 않은 것
(2) 엄마에게 거짓말을 한 것 18 better
19 They will listen to you when they have enough time to talk with you.
20 (1) 1) Use the "I-message."
(2) Pick the right time.
(3) Make a request. 21 ①
22 focus on what he feels or thinks rather than point the finger at his brother 23 ⑤

01 comfortable: 편안한 uncomfortable: 불편한 'What's the problem?(무엇이 문제입니까?)'의 문장으로 보아 음식에 대해 편안한 것이 아니라 불편한 것을 나타내는 말이 나와야 어울린다.

02 express: 표현하다, 나타내다 ④ 그것에 관해 말하거나 써서 감정, 의견 또는 목표를 말하다 / 사람들은 울음으로써 슬픔을 표현한다. solve: 해결하다 ① 어려움을 유발하는 어떤 것에 대

한 해결책을 찾다 / 너는 문제를 해결하기에 충분히 똑똑하다. disappointed: 실망한, 낙담한 ⑤ 바라거나 예상했던 것이 일어나지 않았거나, 예상했던 누군가나 어떤 것이 예상만큼 좋지 않아 행복하지 않은 / 경기에서 져서 실망스럽니? helpful: 도움이 되는, 유용한 ③ 유용한, 도움을 제공하는 / 그 책은 그 시험을 준비하는 데 정말 도움이 되었다. ② reason: 이유 / 왜 어떤 일이 발생했는지, 왜 누군가가 그것을 행했는지, 또는 왜 그것이 진짜인지 등에 대해 설명하는 사실이나 상황 또는 의도

03 get cold feet: 긴장하다, 겁을 먹다 / Sally는 마지막 순간에 겁을 먹고 결혼을 취소했다. get a good grade: 좋은 성적을 얻다 / 나는 지난 토요일에 피아노 축제에서 좋은 점수를 얻었다.

04 make a demand: 요구하다 / 너는 지금 요구할 위치에 있지 않다.

05 빈칸에 이어 'Not good.(좋지 않아.)'이란 대답이 온 것과 다음의 질문에 그룹 구성원들이 말만 하고 듣지 않아서 제시간에 과제를 끝낼 수 없다는 말로 보아 과학 숙제가 어떻게 되어 가고 있는지 묻는 것이 어울린다.

06 남자는 그룹 구성원들이 말만 하고 전혀 듣지 않아 주어진 시간에 끝낼 수 있을 것이라고 생각하고 있지 않다.

07 be upset about ~: ~에 대해서 화나다

08 주어진 문장은 '너희 둘 아직 화해 못 했니?'라는 의미의 질문으로 여자가 'No, not yet.'이라고 대답하고 있으므로 ③에 들어가는 것이 적절하다.

09 대화에서 mean은 '못된, 심술궂은'의 의미로 사용했다. ① 수단 ②, ④, ⑤ 의미하다 ③ 못된, 심술궂은 / 너의 여동생에게 못되게 굴지 마라.

10 ② Julie가 화가 나서 동생한테 큰 소리로 얘기한 것이 아니라, Julie의 동생이 크게 전화 통화를 해서 화가 났다. ① Julie는 피곤해서 자기를 원했다. ③ Julie는 그녀의 동생에게 한 일 때문에 우울하다. ④ Julie는 그녀의 여동생에게 문자 메시지를 보낼 것 같다. ⑤ Julie는 그녀의 여동생에게 미안하다고 얘기하고 싶어 한다.

11 관계대명사 what은 선행사를 포함한 관계대명사로 the thing(s) which[that]를 나타낸다.

12 첫 번째 문장에서는 선행사가 없으므로 선행사를 포함하는 관계대명사 What이 적절하다. 두 번째 문장에서는 the reason이 선행사로 나와 있으므로 관계부사 why가 적절하다.

13 ① Calli's mom wanted to listen to what Calli was going to say. ② What I want for breakfast is just a glass of juice. ③ The painting is what you saw in the house. ⑤ I'd rather talk about the things that are happening. 또는 I'd rather talk about what are happening.

14 뒤에 나오는 절이 완전하며 선행사가 the TV station이므로 which를 where로 바꾸는 것이 적절하다.

15 (1)~(3) 선행사를 포함한 관계대명사 what을 이용한다. (4)~(6) 이어지는 절이 완전한 경우 관계부사를 이용한다. 선행사가 시간을 나타내는 경우 when을 쓰고, 장소를 나타내는 경우 where를 쓰고, 방법을 나타내는 경우 how나 the way를 쓴다.

16 ⓐ '관계', ⓑ '엄마와의 약속을 지킬 것이다. 또한, 엄마에게 정직하려고 노력할 것이다.'를 가리킨다.

17 글쓴이는 '엄마와의 약속을 지키지 않아서' 엄마를 화나게 했고, '엄마에게 거짓말을 해서' 엄마를 실망시켰다.

18 글쓴이는 엄마와의 관계를 '더 좋게' 만들기를 원한다.

19 그들이 당신과 이야기할 충분한 시간을 가질 때 그들은 당신의 말을 들을 것이다.

20 (1) "나 메세지"를 사용하라. (2) 적절한 때를 골라라. (3) 요청을 하라.

21 ⓐ와 ①, ③, ④, ⑤: 부사적 용법, ②: 명사적 용법

22 B rather than A: A라기보다는 B.

23 "나"로 시작하는 것은 '그의 남동생을 비난하기보다' 자신이 느끼고 생각하는 것에 집중하도록 도울 수 있다고 했다.

서술형 실전문제 p.52~53

01 That's not what I meant.
I didn't mean to say that.
You misunderstood me.

02 She kept cutting me off in the middle of my sentences, so I got mad.

03 ⓓ stopped to talk → stopped talking

04 (1) What he remembers
(2) what you want to wear
(3) what she wanted to explain

05 (1) I don't know the reason why Jane is crying. / I don't know the reason for which Jane is crying.
(2) Smart phones have changed the way people live. / Smart phones have changed how people live. / Smart phones have changed the way that people live.

06 (1) Do you remember the library where we studied together?
(2) Do you know the date when Jake will get married?

07 (1) the place (2) the reason

08 what

09 pointing

10 (A) you (B) what he feels or thinks

11 arguing

12 (a) the reason (b) his brother

13 Brian이 남동생과 이야기를 하려고 할 때, 결국 언제나 동생과 말다툼을 하게 되는 것.

01 빈칸 다음에 의미를 다시 이야기하고 있는 것으로 보아 빈칸에는 오해를 지적하는 말이 들어가야 한다. 오해를 지적하는 말에 'That's not what I meant.(내가 의미한 것은 그게 아니야.)', 'I didn't mean to say that.(그 말을 하려던 것이 아니었어.)', 'You misunderstood me.(너는 나를 오해했어.)' 등이 올 수 있다.

02 keep 동사ing: ~을 계속하다, 반복하다 cut ~ off: ~을 중단시키다, 잘라내다 in the middle of: ~ 도중에, ~ 중간에 get+감정형용사: ~하게 되다

03 싸워서 말하는 것을 멈췄다는 말이 어울리므로 stopped to talk를 stopped talking으로 바꾸는 것이 적절하다. stop to 동사원형: ~하기 위해서 멈추다 stop 동사ing: ~을 그만두다, ~하지 않게 되다

04 what은 선행사를 포함한 관계대명사로 '~하는 것'으로 해석하며, the thing(s) which[that]를 나타낸다.

05 (1) 선행사가 '이유'를 나타낼 때 관계부사는 why를 쓰며 이때의 why는 'for which'로 바꿔 쓸 수 있다. (2) 선행사가 '방법'을 나타낼 때 관계부사는 how를 쓰며 이때 how와 함께 the way를 쓰지 않는다는 것을 주의한다. the way나 how 또는 the way that이나 the way in which를 쓴다.

06 (1) 선행사가 the library이므로 관계부사 where를 쓴다. (2) 선행사가 the date이므로 관계부사 when을 쓴다.

07 관계부사의 선행사가 the place, the reason, the time 등일 경우에는 생략할 수 있다.

08 how는 think의 목적어가 될 수 없으므로 what이 적절하다.

09 instead of 뒤에 동명사를 쓰는 것이 적절하다.

10 문제점: Brian은 그의 감정을 표현하기 위해 "너"로 문장을 시작하고 있다. 효과적인 의사소통 방법: 그는 "나 메세지"를 사용해야 한다. 그러면, 그는 그의 남동생을 비난하기보다 '자신이 느끼고 생각하는 것'에 집중할 수 있다.

11 end up ~ing: 결국 ~하게 되다

12 이 동영상은 동생과 이야기를 하려는 Brian의 시도가 결국 항상 동생과 그 사이의 말다툼으로 끝나게 되는 이유를 보여준다. end up ~ing (with+명사): 결국 ~하게 되다

13 앞 문장의 내용을 쓰면 된다.

창의사고력 서술형 문제 p.54

|모범답안|

01 That's not what I meant. I mean our project is postponed.

02 (1) This is my grandparents' house where my first birthday party was held.
(2) Can you show me the way this copy machine works?
(3) Saturday is the day when I don't go to school.
(4) Do you know the reason why she left early?

03 (A) |모범답안| worst (B) |모범답안| got angry
(C)|모범답안| disappointed
(D)|모범답안| keep my promises
(E)|모범답안| to be honest with her

01 That's not what I meant.는 '그런 뜻이 아니야.'라는 의미이며, 상대방이 자신의 말의 의도를 오해할 때 정정하기 위해 쓰는 표현이다. postpone: 미루다, 연기하다 mean: 의미하다

단원별 모의고사 p.55~58

01 (p)oint the finger
02 ⓑ keep to work → keep working 03 ⑤
04 uncertain 05 got 06 ③, ⑤ 07 ②
08 ⑤ 09 ④ 10 ⑤
11 It means to study. 12 ①
13 (A) to talk (B) many (C) quiet (D) to talk
14 detail 15 ② 16 why
17 (1) that → what
(2) what → that[which], 또는 the thing what → what
(3) the way how → the way 또는 how 또는 the way that
(4) which → when 또는 in which 18 ⑤
19 (1) I know a restaurant where we can have delicious *samgyupsal*.
(2) Winter is the season when leaves fall.
20 ①, ④ 21 clip 22 ③ 23 ②
24 Calli should pick a time when her mom is ready to listen.
25 Calli → Calli's mom, mom → daughter, school→work

01 point the finger at: ~을 비난하다

02 ⓐ stop 동사ing: ~을 그만두다, ~하지 않게 되다 / 의사가 그에게 담배 피는 것을 그만 둘 것을 충고했다. ⓑ keep 동사ing: ~을 계속하다, 반복하다 / 계속 노력하면 너는 그 시험에 통과할 것이다. ⓒ tend to 동사원형: ~하는 경향이 있다 / 그 체육관은 6시 정도에 매우 바빠지는 경향이 있다. ⓓ try to 동사원형: ~을 노력하다 / 나는 불필요한 말싸움을 피하려고 한다.

03 (A) order+사람+around: ~에게 자꾸 이래라저래라 하다 / 그녀가 이래라저래라 명령하도록 내버려 두지 마. (B) concentrate on: ~에 집중하다 / 그들은 공부에 집중하지 못했다. (C) work out: 해결하다 / 우리는 어려움을 해결했다.

04 주어진 단어의 관계는 반의어이다. honest 정직한 dishonest 부정직한 certain: 확실한 uncertain: 불확실한

05 get cold feet: 긴장하다, 겁을 먹다 get+감정형용사: ~하게 되

다 scared: 두려워하는, 겁먹은

06 ① Nick은 어제 다이빙을 했는가?(아니오) ② "get cold feet"은 무슨 의미인가?(겁을 먹다) ③ 왜 Nick은 다이빙을 하는 것이 겁이 났는가? ④ 왜 Nick은 다이빙을 안 했는가?(무서워져서) ⑤ 어디로 Nick은 다이빙을 하러 갔는가?

07 ② go: (일의 진행이 어떻게) 되어가다, 진전되다 / 프로그램이 진행될 때, 연출자는 조정실에 앉아 있는다. 나머지 보기들은 '가다'의 의미로 사용되었다.

08 individual: 개인의 / 과학 숙제는 개인 과제가 아니라 그룹 과제였다.

09 어제 왜 생일 파티에 안 왔느냐는 질문에, 남자는 "hit the books"를 해야 했기 때문에 못 갔다고 말했는데, 이것을 이해하지 못한 여자가 왜 책을 쳤는지 물어보며, 무언가에 대해 화났는지 물어보는 것이 어울리므로 ④가 적절하다.

10 '오늘 아침에 시험이 있었다.'와 '나는 어제 공부를 해야 했다.'의 두 문장은 원인과 결과로 이어질 수 있다.

11 hit the books: 공부하다

12 주어진 문장에서 that은 사람들이 자신이 너무 많이 말한다고 계속 말하는 것을 의미한다. 그러므로 사람들이 말한 내용에 이어서 그것에 대해 화가 난다고 말하는 것이 어울린다.

13 (A) tend to 동사원형: ~하는 경향이 있다 (B) details는 셀 수 있는 명사로 s가 붙어 있으므로 셀 수 있는 명사를 수식할 수 있는 many(많은)가 어울린다. (C) A는 자신이 계속 말하고, 세부 사항에 대해 말하는 자신의 경향에 대해 듣고 그러면 자신이 계속 조용히 있어야 하는지를 질문하고 있다. (D) try to 동사원형: ~을 노력하다

14 detail: 구체적 내용, 자세한 내용 / 어떤 상황에 관계된 많은 사소한 사실들이나 정보 중의 하나

15 선행사가 '이유'를 나타낼 때 관계부사는 why를 쓴다. 관계부사 why는 'for+which'로 바꿔 쓸 수 있는데, 전치사를 which 바로 앞에 쓰거나 관계부사절의 끝에 쓴다.

16 선행사로 the reason이 있으므로 why가 적절하며 the reason은 생략 가능하다.

17 (1) that을 wear와 want의 목적어 역할을 할 수 있는 what으로 고치는 것이 적절하다. (2) what = the thing that[which] (3) 선행사 the way와 관계부사 how는 함께 쓸 수 없으며 the way나 how만 써야 하며, 선행사가 the way일 때 how 대신에 that을 쓸 수 있다. (4) 선행사가 시간을 나타내는 the year이므로 which를 when으로 고치는 것이 적절하다. when은 'in which'와 바꿔 쓸 수 있으므로 in which로 고쳐도 좋다.

18 ⑤번은 이어지는 절이 완전하므로 접속사 that이 들어가야 하지만 나머지는 이어지는 절이 불완전하므로 선행사를 포함하는 관계대명사 what이 들어가는 것이 적절하다.

19 (1) a restaurant을 선행사로 하는 관계부사 where를 이용한다. (2) the season을 선행사로 하는 관계부사 when을 이용한다.

20 ⓐ와 ①, ④: 부사적 용법, ②, ⑤: 명사적 용법, ③: 형용사적 용법

21 동영상 / 인터넷 웹사이트에서 볼 수 있는 짧은 비디오 녹화

22 ⓐ와 ②, ④: 현재분사, ①, ③, ⑤: 동명사

23 ② 'Anna'가 자주 'Julie'의 감정을 상하게 한다.

24 be ready to: ~할 준비가 되어 있다

25 'Calli의 엄마'가 '출근' 준비를 하느라고 바빠서 '그녀의 딸'과 이야기할 시간이 없었다.

Lesson 2

Wonderful Nature

시험대비 실력평가 p.62

01 ① 02 ① 03 ③ 04 ④
05 ⑤ 06 ②

01 harsh: (날씨·생활 환경이) 혹독한 / 혹독한 날씨 때문에, 마라톤이 2주 동안 연기되었다.

02 peak: 절정[최대한도]에 이르다 / 석유 생산은 1980년대 초에 최고조에 달했다.

03 ① in fact: 사실상, 실제로 / 나는 그 시장을 매우 잘 안다. 사실 나는 지난주에 그녀와 저녁을 먹었다. ② in the middle of the night: 한밤중에 / 한밤중에 전화가 울렸다. ③ be[get] inspired by: ~에 의해 영감을 받다 / 그 영화는 실제 사건에 의해 영감을 받았다. ④ stand in for: ~을 대신하다 / 위험한 장면에서는 한 여성 스턴트가 Goldie Hawn을 대신했다. ⑤ get in shape: 좋은 몸 상태를 유지하다 / 나는 정말 여름 전에 좋은 몸 상태를 유지하고 싶다.

04 ① 나는 그것을 아직 볼 기회가 없었다. ② Keith는 공학 학위를 가지고 있지만 그의 분야에서 직장을 찾지 못했다. ③ 우리의 문제는 형편없는 경영과 경험의 부족이 결합된 것 때문이었다. ④ try: 맛보다 / 만약 내가 외식하러 나간다면, 나는 다른 것을 맛보는 것을 선호한다. ⑤ 그들은 피카소가 훌륭한 색채 화가였다는 것을 잊었다.

05 inspire: 영감을 주다, 고무하다, 격려하다 / 우리는 그 팀을 고무시킬 수 있는 누군가가 필요하다. 그들은 그의 음악이 사람들에게 영감을 주고 사람들을 감동시킨다고 생각한다.

06 (A) find out: 발견하다, 알아보다 / 하지만 학부모들과 교사들은 그 경기에 문제점이 있다는 것을 발견했다. (B) make plans (for): (~의) 계획을 세우다 / 너는 여름 방학 계획을 세웠니?

서술형 시험대비 p.63

01 Whenever
02 insight
03 ⓐ lone → alone
04 come
05 to
06 (1) aurora's (2) is caused by (3) ecologists
(4) stand in for
07 (1) keep (2) turned (3) cut (4) filled

01 whenever+주어+동사: ~할 때마다 / 내가 세차를 할 때마다 그 다음 날 비가 온다.

02 insight: 통찰력 / 그 연구는 우리가 언어를 처리하는 방식에 대한 새로운 통찰력을 제공한다.

03 ⓐ lone은 보통 한정적 용법으로 사용되고, alone은 서술적 용법으로만 사용된다.

04 come back from ~: ~에서 돌아오다 / 언제 미국에서 돌아왔어요? come true: 실현되다, 사실이 되다 / 이곳은 꿈이 실현되는 장소이다.

05 from A to B: A에서 B로 / 나는 단지 집에서 역으로 나를 데려다 줄 차가 필요하다. due to 명사: ~ 때문에 / 이 기획은 자금의 부족 때문에 내년에 계속되지 않을 것이다.

06 (1) aurora: 오로라 (2) be caused by ~: ~에 의해 야기되다 (3) ecologist: 생태학자 (4) stand in for: ~을 대신하다

07 (1) keep ~ on one's toes: ~을 계속 긴장하게 하다 / 그들은 일하는 사람들이 긴장을 늦추지 않게 하기 위해 무작위로 검사한다. (2) turn out: (일·진행·결과가 특정 방식으로) 되다 / 힘든 시기였지만 결국 상황이 모두 좋게 되었다. (3) cut down: 자르다 / 사람들은 너무 많은 나무를 잘라내고 야생 동물의 서식지를 파괴한다. (4) be filled with: ~로 가득 차다 / 공기가 장미의 향기로 가득 찼다.

교과서

Conversation

핵심 Check p.64~65

1 I can't wait to go to the party.
2 I'm looking forward to trying them out on my friends.
3 that having[eating] a tomato is good for eyes
2 (C) → (A) → (B)

교과서 대화문 익히기

Check(√) True or False p.66~67

1 F 2 T 3 F 4 T 5 F 6 T 7 F 8 T

교과서 확인학습 p.69~71

Listen & Talk 1 Get Ready

view, amazing / wait to, run up

Listen & Talk 1 A-1

what's, plan / going, wait to visit / are, that, like / sounds, Take

Listen & Talk 1 A-2

want to watch / about adventures, was shot / heard, has / can't wait to watch, go and get

Listen & Talk 1 B

is going, in / What, plan to / study, caves, go, watching / like, interesting / I've only read about, wait to actually visit / hope, enjoy

Listen & Talk 2 Get Ready

is, high / I've heard that, travels from, to

Listen & Talk 2 A-1

weather report, able, shooting stars / When, to see them / heard that, shooting starts / between, and / special night

Listen & Talk 2 A-2

are / They are, I've heard that, made by, sticky / like / like, actually

Listen & Talk 2 B

that, sets / that, How / heard that, cycling, because / love, in, of / too, chance to try

Communication

winner / for inviting, honored / talk, heard that, was taken, true / caused by / amazing / can't wait to take / wish, best

시험대비 기본평가 p.72

01 ②, ⑤　02 ②　03 ①

01 'can't wait to+동사원형'은 '~하기를 몹시 바라다.' 또는 '어서 ~하고 싶다.'라는 의미로 기대를 나타낼 때 사용하는 표현이다. 'can't wait to+동사원형' 대신에 'can't wait for+(동)명사'나 'look forward to+(동)명사', 'expect to 동사원형'을 사용할 수 있다.

02 일기예보를 봤느냐고 질문하며 오늘 밤에 많은 유성을 볼 수 있을 거라고 언급하고 (B) 놀랍다고 얘기하며 언제 보는 것이 좋은지 질문하자 (A) 오전 12시에서 2시 사이에 가장 절정이라고 대답한다. (C) 다시 감탄하며, 특별한 밤이 될 것이라고 말한다.

03 남자가 새로 나온 3D 영화 중 하나가 바다 밑의 모험에 관한 것이며 호주의 Great Barrier Reef에서 찍은 거라고 말하자 여자는 그곳에 아름다운 해양 생물이 있다고 대답하고 있으므로, 남자가 말하는 사실에 대해 알고 있는 것을 표현하는 'I've heard of ~.(나는 ~에 대해 들었다)'를 쓰는 것이 적절하다.

시험대비 실력평가 p.73~74

01 ②　02 ①　03 ③　04 for
05 ④　06 ④　07 ④　08 ⑤
09 ④　10 going, Uyuni Salt Flats, bike riding
11 ③

01 주어진 문장은 거기서 무엇을 할 건지 계획을 묻는 것이므로 'We are going to study the caves on the island and go bird watching.(섬에 있는 동굴을 연구하고 새 관찰을 하러 갈 거예요.)'의 질문으로 적절하므로 ②번이 어울린다.

02 ① 소녀의 아빠는 독도를 가본 적이 있는가? ② 언제 소녀의 과학 클럽은 독도에 가는가?(7월) ③ 소녀는 독도에서 무엇을 할 예정인가? (동굴을 연구하고 새 관찰을 하러 갈 것이다.) ④ 소녀의 과학 클럽은 7월에 어디를 가는가?(독도) ⑤ 소녀는 독도를 가는 것을 기대하고 있는가?(네)

03 주어진 문장은 사진이 몰디브에서 찍혔다는 것을 들었다는 것으로 ③ 다음에 나온 문장에서 몰디브에서 찍은 것이 사실인지 물어보는 것과 어울리므로 ③에 들어가는 것이 알맞다.

04 thank you는 감사를 표현하는 말로 뒤에 for를 붙여 감사하는 이유를 적는다.

05 ① 몰디브의 해변은 왜 반짝이는가?(플랑크톤 때문에) ② 그들은 무엇에 관해 이야기하고 있는가?(Ms. Scarlett Lee가 찍은 사진) ③ 누가 금년의 사진 대회의 우승자인가?(Ms. Scarlett Lee) ④ Ms. Scarlett Lee는 어느 나라로 사진을 찍으러 갈 것인가?(멋진 해변의 사진을 찍을 것을 기대한다고 말했지 특정한 나라에 대한 언급은 없었다.) ⑤ Ms. Scarlett Lee가 수상한 사진을 어디에서 찍었는가?(몰디브)

06 ⓓ를 제외한 것은 'snow rollers(두루마기 눈)'를 가리킨다. ⓓ는 snow rollers가 snow rings(눈 반지)처럼 생겼다고 말하는 것이지 snow rollers를 의미하는 것은 아니다.

07 ④ 록 콘서트를 가기를 원하는지 묻는 말에 아니라고 대답하고 기대된다고 말하는 것은 어색하다.

08 노르웨이에서는 여름 동안 해가 지지 않는 것을 알고 있느냐고 질문하니, (C) 알지 못했다고 대답하며, 흥미롭다고 감탄한다. (D) 밤에 어둡지 않기 때문에 밤에 하이킹을 가고 자전거를 타러 간다고 들은 것에 대해 말을 하자 (B) 지수도 한밤중에 하이킹과 자전거를 타러 가고 싶다고 말하며 자신의 바람을 얘기한다. (A) 남자도 역시 그렇게 하고 싶다고 말하면서 언젠가 우리가 그런 기회를 가지기를 희망한다고 말한다.

09 can't wait to+동사원형: 빨리 ~하고 싶다, ~하기를 몹시 바라다

10 be going to 동사원형: ~할 예정이다 go to 장소: ~에 가다 this vacation: 이번 방학에

11 'I've heard ~.' 이후에는 완전한 문장이 나오므로 접속사 that

을 사용한다. 'I've heard that ~.'은 '~에 대해 들었다.'나 '~에 대해 알고 있다.'는 뜻으로 알고 있거나 들은 것에 대해 말할 때 쓰는 표현이다.

서술형 시험대비 p.75

01 and
02 ⓓ Where is the best place → When is the best time
03 I can't wait to visit the Rainbow Mountains.
04 like
05 was shot
06 I have heard of it.
07 I've heard that they are made by strong wind and sticky snow.

01 between A and B: A와 B 사이에서

02 유성이 자정에서 새벽 2시 사이에 가장 최고조가 된다는 말이 이어지고 있으므로 유성을 보기 좋은 장소를 묻는 질문이 아니라 언제 보기 좋은지 시간에 관해서 묻는 질문이 어울린다.

03 can't wait to+동사원형: 빨리 ~하고 싶다, ~하기를 몹시 바라다 visit: 방문하다

04 look like 명사: ~처럼 보이다

05 shoot: 촬영하다 / 주어진 It은 새로 나온 3D 영화 중 하나를 의미하므로, 동사는 수동태인 'be shot'으로 사용되며 과거에 촬영된 것이므로 'was shot'이 적절하다.

06 I have heard about[of] (동)명사 ~: 나는 ~에 대해 들었다 / have heard 다음에 완전한 문장이 나오면 that절을 이어 쓰고, 명사가 오면 전치사 of나 about을 사용한다.

07 I've heard that ~: ~에 대해 들었다, ~에 대해 알고 있다 be made by ~: ~에 의해 만들어지다 sticky: 끈적거리는, 달라붙는

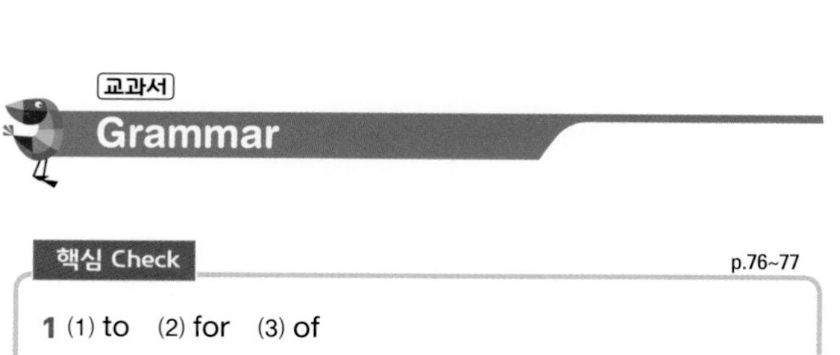

교과서

Grammar

핵심 Check p.76~77

1 (1) to (2) for (3) of
2 (1) playing (2) playing (3) doing

시험대비 기본평가 p.78

01 ④ 02 ③
03 (1) suggesting (2) have been living (3) of (4) for
04 It is important for students to do their homework.

01 it을 가주어로 하고 to부정사를 진주어로 하며 의미상의 주어로 'for you'를 쓰고 있는 ④번이 적절하다.

02 오래 전에 괴롭히기 시작하여 현재까지 계속 진행되고 있으므로 현재완료진행형이 적절하다.

03 (1) 연구 결과가 밝히고 있는 것이므로 현재완료진행형이 적절하다. (2) 6년 동안 살아오고 있는 것이므로 현재완료진행형이 적절하다. (3) 문장에 쓰인 형용사가 nice, kind, smart, wise 등과 같이 사람의 성향, 성격을 나타내는 말일 때는 'of+명사 또는 대명사의 목적격'으로 쓴다. (4) to부정사의 의미상의 주어는 to부정사 바로 앞에 'for+목적격'으로 나타낸다.

04 it을 가주어로 하고 to부정사를 진주어로 하는 구문을 이용한다. 의미상의 주어로 'for+목적격'을 쓴다.

시험대비 실력평가 p.79~81

01 ④ 02 ③ 03 ⑤
04 (1) been collecting (2) for (3) since (4) for (5) of
05 ② 06 ① 07 ②
08 for me to
09 He has been working in various fields at NASA since 2001. 10 ④ 11 ⑤
12 ③
13 (1) have been interviewing actors for
(2) has been knitting a sweater since
14 (1) Mr. Lee has been teaching math for more than 30 years.
(2) Mariel learned Korean at the school 5 years ago. 또는 Mariel has been learning Korean at the school since 5 years ago.
(3) I have been climbing the mountain since Monday.
(4) We have been waiting for her for 2 hours.
(5) What time would be best for me to talk to you?
(6) I think it is very polite of her to ask permission.
(7) It will be difficult for the children to swim across this river. 15 It, for her to cry
16 ⑤ 17 ①, ③, ④
18 As winter is coming, it is necessary for us to prepare for the winter.

01 ① It has been raining all day long. ② The argument has been going on for years. ③ Rana has been planting trees in the valleys for the last 31 years. ⑤ I've been visiting the forest to study animals for 20 years.

02 문장에 쓰인 형용사가 사람의 성향, 성격을 나타내는 말이 아니므로 to부정사의 의미상의 주어로 'for+목적격'을 써야 한다. insurance 보험

03 첫 번째 문장에서는 2년 동안 계속 한국어를 공부해 오고 있는 것이므로 현재완료진행형이 적절하다. 두 번째 문장에서는 to부정사의 의미상의 주어로 'for+목적격'이 적절하다.

04 (1) 현재완료진행형은 'have[has] been+동사원형-ing'의 형태이다. (2), (3) 현재완료진행형에서 since는 '시간'을 나타내는 명사(구)와 함께 쓰이고 for는 '기간'을 나타내는 명사(구)와 함께 쓰인다. (4), (5) to부정사의 의미상의 주어는 'for+목적격'으로 나타낸다. 이때 문장에 쓰인 형용사가 사람의 성향, 성격을 나타내는 말일 때는 'of+목적격'으로 쓴다.

05 to부정사의 의미상의 주어로 'for+목적격'이 적절하다.

06 현재완료진행형에서 since는 '시간'을 나타내는 명사(구)와 함께 쓰이고 for는 '기간'을 나타내는 명사(구)와 함께 쓰인다.

07 현재완료진행형은 'have[has] been+동사원형-ing'의 형태이며 과거를 나타내는 어구와 함께 쓰이지 않는다. ①번은 know가 진행형으로 쓰이지 않는 동사임에 유의한다.

08 to부정사의 의미상의 주어로 'for+목적격'이 적절하다.

09 현재완료진행형을 이용하여 쓴다.

10 문장에 사람의 성격을 나타내는 형용사가 있는 경우 의미상의 주어로 'of+목적격'을 쓴다.

11 과거 어느 때부터 시작되어 현재까지 계속 진행되고 있음을 나타내는 현재완료진행형이 적절하다.

12 ③번은 사람의 성향, 성격을 나타내는 형용사 nice가 있으므로 of를 써야 한다. 나머지는 모두 for를 써야 한다.

13 현재완료진행형은 'have[has] been+동사원형-ing'의 형태이다. since는 '시간'을 나타내는 명사(구)와 함께 쓰이고 for는 '기간'을 나타내는 명사(구)와 함께 쓰인다.

14 (1) 현재완료진행형은 'have[has] been+동사원형-ing'의 형태이다. (2) 현재완료진행형은 과거를 나타내는 어구와 함께 쓰이지 않는다. (3), (4) 현재완료진행형에서 since는 '시간'을 나타내는 명사(구)와 함께 쓰이고 for는 '기간'을 나타내는 명사(구)와 함께 쓰인다. (5), (6) to부정사의 의미상의 주어는 'for+목적격'으로 나타낸다. 이때 문장에 쓰인 형용사가 사람의 성향, 성격을 나타내는 말일 때는 'of+목적격'으로 쓴다. (7) 의미상의 주어로 'for+목적격'이 나왔으므로 진주어로 to부정사를 쓴다.

15 to부정사와 의미상의 주어로 'for her'가 나왔으므로 가주어로 It을 쓰고 진주어로 to부정사를 쓴다.

16 5시부터 도착하기 시작하여 아직도 도착하고 있는 것이므로 현재완료진행형을 이용하여 나타낸다.

17 ① 현재완료진행은 '상태'가 아닌, '동작'만을 나타낸다. ③ 현재완료진행형은 과거를 나타내는 어구와 함께 쓰이지 않는다. ④ 사람의 성향, 성격을 나타내는 형용사(rude)가 나왔으므로 'of you'가 적절하다.

18 이유를 이끄는 as와, 'It(가주어) ~ for ...(의미상의 주어) to부정사(진주어)' 구문을 이용하여 쓴다.

서술형 시험대비 p.82~83

01 (1) Naomi has been waiting for her train since two o'clock.
(2) It has been raining for three hours.
(3) Women have been making important contributions to sports for centuries.

02 (1) This book is too difficult for you to read.
(2) It was very smart of him not to miss the chance.
(3) I have been taking my parents' love for granted.

03 (1) have been enjoying, for two hours
(2) careless of her to leave

04 (1) for (2) since

05 (1) too difficult for you to (2) big enough for us to
(3) nice of her to

06 (1) for you to listen carefully to the advice
(2) of Abigail to help me to stand on my own feet

07 (1) thought → thinking (2) since → for
(3) for → since
(4) has been possessing → has possessed
(5) 5 years ago → for 5 years, 또는 have been living→ lived
(6) of → for (7) finding → to find

08 (1) Everyone has been studying hard for the last few months.
(2) He has been writing the book for long.
(3) She has been working there since May.
(4) It was nice of her to offer me a ride.
(5) There are still two more chores for me to do.

01 과거에 시작하여 지금까지 계속되고 있는 것이므로 현재완료진행형을 이용한다.

02 (1)~(2) to부정사의 의미상의 주어는 'for+목적격'으로 나타내지만 문장에 쓰인 형용사가 사람의 성향, 성격을 나타내는 말일 때는 'of+목적격'으로 쓴다. (3) 과거 어느 때부터 시작되어 현재까지 계속 진행되고 있음을 나타내는 현재완료진행형 구문을 이용한다. take A for granted: A를 당연한 것으로 여기다

03 (1) enjoying이 있으므로 현재완료진행형을 이용한다. two hours라는 기간을 나타내는 명사구가 있으므로 for를 사용한다. (2) 진주어로 to부정사를 쓰고 careless가 사람의 성격을

나타내는 말이므로 'of+목적격'으로 쓴다.

04 현재완료진행형에서 since는 '시간'을 나타내는 명사(구)와 함께 쓰이고 for는 '기간'을 나타내는 명사(구)와 함께 쓰인다.

05 to부정사의 의미상의 주어는 'for+목적격'으로 나타내지만, 문장에 쓰인 형용사가 사람의 성향, 성격을 나타내는 말일 때는 'of+목적격'으로 쓴다.

06 to부정사의 의미상의 주어는 'for+목적격'으로 나타내지만, 문장에 쓰인 형용사가 사람의 성향, 성격을 나타내는 말일 때는 'of+목적격'으로 쓴다.

07 (1) 계속 생각해 오고 있는 것이므로 현재완료진행형으로 나타낸다. (2), (3) 현재완료진행형에서 since는 '시간'을 나타내는 명사(구)와 함께 쓰이고 for는 '기간'을 나타내는 명사(구)와 함께 쓰인다. (4) possess는 소유를 나타내는 동사로 진행형을 쓸 수 없으므로 has been possessing을 has possessed로 고친다. (5) 현재완료진행형은 과거를 나타내는 어구와 함께 쓰이지 않는다. (6) necessary는 사람의 성질을 나타내는 형용사가 아니므로 of를 for로 고친다. (7) 의미상의 주어로 'for me'가 나와 있으므로 finding을 to find로 고친다.

08 (1)~(3) 과거 어느 때부터 시작되어 현재까지 계속 진행되고 있음을 나타내는 현재완료진행형을 이용한다. (4) it을 가주어로 하고 nice가 있으므로 'of her'를 의미상의 주어로 쓴다. (5) 'to do'가 있으므로 'for me'를 의미상의 주어로 쓰고 'There are ~'로 '~이 있다'를 나타낸다.

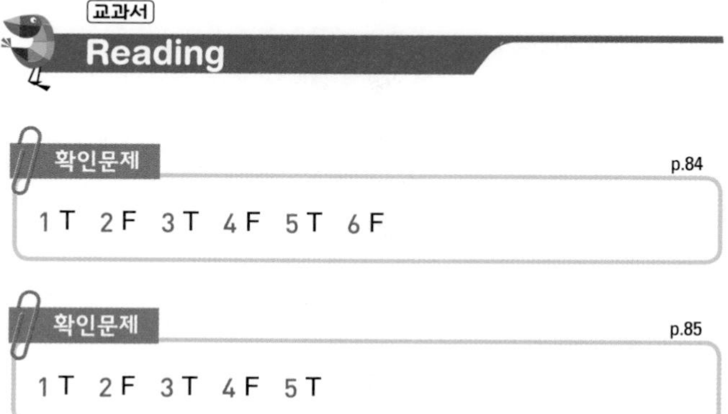

교과서

Reading

확인문제 p.84

1 T 2 F 3 T 4 F 5 T 6 F

확인문제 p.85

1 T 2 F 3 T 4 F 5 T

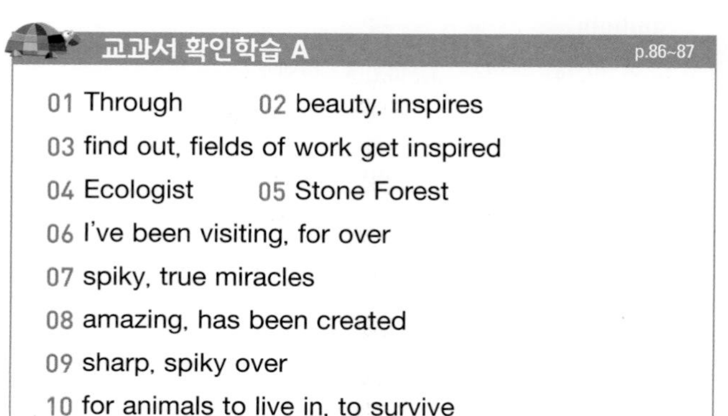

교과서 확인학습 A p.86~87

01 Through 02 beauty, inspires
03 find out, fields of work get inspired
04 Ecologist 05 Stone Forest
06 I've been visiting, for over
07 spiky, true miracles
08 amazing, has been created
09 sharp, spiky over
10 for animals to live in, to survive
11 which, frog-like, that, from, to
12 is like, jack-in-the-box
13 keeps me on my toes
14 Fashion Colorist
15 River of Five Colors 16 is filled with
17 create colors
18 I've been gaining
19 mixed colors, anywhere else
20 combination, makes, more alive, bright
21 Whenever, countless, waiting to be created
22 Location Scout 23 Frozen Beauty
24 to shoot movies
25 for many location scouts, due to, unusual beauty
26 My personal favorite
27 stand in for any place
28 In fact, we shot here, without using
29 help make, come true

교과서 확인학습 B p.88~89

1 The World Through My Eyes
2 "The beauty of nature inspires us all.
3 Let's find out how people from different fields of work get inspired by nature."
4 Lin Wang, Ecologist
5 Tsingy, the Stone Forest of Madagascar
6 I've been visiting the stone forest of Madagascar to study plants and animals for over 20 years.
7 The spiky stones of this place are true miracles of nature.
8 This amazing shape has been created by rainfall.
9 Rain has cut down the stones and made them sharp and spiky over a long period of time.
10 The environment is harsh for animals to live in, but they have found ways to survive.
11 For example, lemurs, which only live in Madagascar, have frog-like legs that help them jump from one stone tower to another.
12 For me, the stone forest is like a jack-in-the-box.
13 It always surprises me and keeps me on my toes!
14 Amber Smith, Fashion Colorist
15 Caño Cristales, the River of Five Colors of Colombia
16 The world is filled with millions of different colors.
17 It is my job to mix, develop, and create colors for clothing.
18 Over the years, I've been gaining insights from the

beautiful colors of Caño Cristales.

19 You cannot see the wonderful mixed colors of this river anywhere else in the world.

20 The combination of colorful plants under the water and sunlight makes the colors more alive and bright.

21 Whenever I visit the Caño Cristales, it makes me think that maybe there are still countless colors that are waiting to be created.

22 Danny Mehta, Location Scout

23 Vatnajökull National Park, Frozen Beauty of Iceland

24 I'm a location scout and my job is finding perfect places to shoot movies.

25 Iceland is the best place for many location scouts to visit due to its unusual beauty.

26 My personal favorite is the Vatnajökull National Park.

27 The sharp cliffs, blue glacier caves, and long mountain ranges can stand in for any place in the world or the universe.

28 In fact, the recent sci-fi movie we shot here was produced without using computer graphics!

29 Iceland can help make our wildest dreams come true on the movie screen.

시험대비 실력평가 p.90~93

01 ② 02 ②, ⑤ 03 by → without
04 ⓐ inspired ⓑ visiting ⓒ created
05 ④ 06 the stone forest 07 full of
08 (A) mixed (B) alive (C) think
09 ③ 10 ① 11 ⑤
12 ③ 13 ④ 14 ②
15 (A) the stones (C) animals
16 The environment is harsh for animals to live in
17 gaining 18 ③, ⑤ 19 ②, ④ 20 ④
21 ②, ④ 22 ②, ③
23 the recent sci-fi movie that[which] we shot here was produced 24 common → unusual

01 ⓐ와 ①, ②는 형용사적 용법, ③, ⑤는 명사적 용법, ④는 부사적 용법

02 ⓑ와 ②, ⑤: 대신하다, ③ 제거하다, ④ 교환하다

03 컴퓨터 그래픽을 사용하지 '않고'라고 하는 것이 적절하다.

04 ⓐ 동작 수동태가 되도록 과거분사를, ⓑ 현재완료진행형이 되도록 현재분사를 ⓒ 현재완료수동태가 되도록 과거분사를 쓰는 것이 적절하다.

05 ④번 다음 문장의 For example에 주목한다. 주어진 문장의 예를 들고 있으므로 ④번이 적절하다.

06 '석림'을 가리킨다.

07 be filled with = be full of: ~로 가득 차다

08 (A) '혼합된'이라고 해야 하므로 mixed가 적절하다. (B) 목적격보어 자리이므로 alive가 적절하다. alive: 보어로만 쓰인다. live: 살아 있는, 생방송의(형용사: 주로 명사 앞에 씀), (C) 사역동사 makes의 목적격보어에 해당하므로 think가 적절하다.

09 ③ a great deal of: 다량의, ⓑ와 나머지는 모두 '수'가 많을 때 사용, countless: 무수한, 셀 수 없이 많은

10 ⓐ 'for+숫자', 'during+기간을 나타내는 명사', ⓑ keep ~ on one's toes: ~을 긴장을 늦추지 않게 하다

11 (A)와 ⑤: 분야, ① 들판, ② 싸움터, 전장(battlefield), ③ [보통 합성어에서 특정한 것으로 덮여 있거나 무엇이 많이 나는] 지역, ice fields: 빙원, ④ (어떤 용도에 쓰는) 지면(地面)

12 이 글은 생태학자인 Lin Wang이 어떻게 자연에 의해 영감을 받았는지에 대한 글이므로, 제목으로는 'Lin Wang은 어떻게 자연에 의해 영감을 받았는가?'가 적절하다.

13 Tsingy는 '뾰족한' 돌로 이루어진 숲이다.

14 앞의 내용의 예가 나오고 있으므로 For example이 가장 적절하다. ① 그 결과, ④ 즉, 다시 말해, ⑤ 그러므로

15 (A)는 '돌', (C)는 '동물들'을 가리킨다.

16 to부정사의 의미상의 주어를 'for+목적격'으로 쓰는 것이 적절하다.

17 현재완료진행형으로 써야 하므로 gaining이 적절하다.

18 (A)와 ③, ⑤: 가주어, ①, ④: 비인칭주어, ② 가목적어

19 (B)와 ②, ④: 아직(도), 여전히, ① (비교급을 강조하여) 더욱, 훨씬, ③ 가만히 있는, 고요한(형용사), ⑤ 그럼에도 불구하고(부사)

20 Amber Smith가 의류를 위해 무슨 색을 만들었는지는 대답할 수 없다. ① It is the river of five colors of Colombia. ② In Colombia. ③ She is a fashion colorist and her job is to mix, develop, and create colors for clothing. ⑤ The combination of colorful plants under the water and sunlight.

21 ⓐ와 ②, ④: 동명사, ①, ③, ⑤: 현재분사

22 ⓑ와 ②, ③: 사실, ① 그러므로, ⑤ 그 결과

23 목적격 관계대명사 'that[which]'이 생략되어 있다.

24 Iceland의 '비범한' 아름다움이 그곳을 많은 장소 섭외가들이 방문하기에 최고의 장소가 되도록 만든다고 하는 것이 적절하다. common: 흔한, 보통의, 평범한거운

서술형 시험대비

p.94~95

01 how people from different fields of work get inspired by nature
02 to visit, ago, visiting
03 mild → harsh 04 surprises
05 ④
06 make our wildest dreams come true
07 (A) sharp cliffs (B) stand in for
08 can → cannot 09 always
10 that are
11 (A) are (B) live in (C) jump
12 Rainfall has created this amazing shape.
13 (A) ecologist (B) the stone forest

01 'how'를 보충하면 된다.
02 for over 20 years를 over 20 years ago로 바꿔 쓰는 것이 적절하다.
03 동물들이 살기에는 환경이 '가혹하지만', 그들은 생존할 방법들을 찾아내 왔다고 해야 하므로 harsh와 같은 '가혹한'이란 의미의 단어로 고치는 것이 적절하다.
04 석림은 항상 Lin Wang을 '놀라게' 하기 때문이다. jack-in-the-box: 열면 인형이 튀어나오는 상자
05 ⓐ to부정사의 의미상의 주어로 'for+목적격'이 적절하다. ⓑ in fact: 사실
06 come true: 실현되다
07 Vatnajökull 국립 공원은 아이슬란드에 있고, 그곳의 '가파른 절벽', 푸른 빙하 동굴, 그리고 긴 산맥들은 세계나 우주의 어느 장소도 대신할 수 있다.
08 세상 다른 어느 곳에서도 이 강의 아름답게 혼합된 색깔을 '볼 수 없다'고 하는 것이 적절하다.
09 Whenever = When+always
10 '주격 관계대명사+ be동사'를 생략할 수 있다.
11 (A) 주어가 'The spiky stones'이므로 are가 적절하다. (B) It is harsh for animals to live in the environment에서 the environment를 주어로 바꾼 것이므로 live in이 적절하다. (C) 'help+목적어+원형부정사 또는 to부정사'이므로 jump가 적절하다.
12 rainfall을 주어로 해서 고치는 것이 적절하다.
13 Lin Wang은 '생태학자'이고, 식물과 동물을 연구하기 위해 마다가스카르의 '석림'인 Tsingy를 20년 이상 동안 방문해 오고 있다.

영역별 핵심문제

p.97~101

01 ④ 02 (1) unusual (2) combination
03 (1) (w)henever, yellow dust (2) research
(3) (c)ountless, near
04 (1) out (2) to (3) by (4) of 05 ③
06 ④ 07 like
08 I can't wait to actually visit there.
09 research 10 ④ 11 ⑤
12 I hope we get the chance to try it someday.
13 ② 14 ③, ④
15 careless of Mike to break 16 ⑤
17 ①, ④
18 (1) of him to give her that money
(2) for her to read the book 19 ②, ⑤
20 ④ 21 keeps me on my toes
22 (A) clothing (B) anywhere (C) makes
23 ⑤ 24 such as 25 shot 26 ③
27 ④ 28 ④

01 ④ 이외의 단어들에서 접두어 in-은 '안에'의 의미로 사용되었다. ④는 반대, 부정의 의미이다. dependent: 의존하는 independent: 독립적인
02 (1) usual: 흔히 있는 unusual: 특이한, 흔치 않은 (2) combine: 결합하다 combination: 조합, 복합
03 (1) whenever+주어+동사: ~할 때마다 yellow dust: 황사 (2) research: 조사하다, 연구하다 (3) countless: 많은, 셀 수 없는 near: ~ 가까이에
04 (1) turn out: (일·진행·결과가 특정 방식으로) 되다 / 모든 사람들이 놀랍게도 템플 스테이는 인기 있는 여행 프로그램이 되었다. (2) due to: ~ 때문에 / 그의 죽음은 심장병 때문이었다. (3) be made by ~: ~에 의해 만들어지다 / 그 노래들은 세계 최고의 음악가들이 만들었다. (4) most of: 대부분의 ~ / 대부분의 폐암은 흡연에 기인한다.
05 새로 나온 3D 영화 중에서 'Which one?(어느 것)'인지 묻고 있는 질문에 바다 밑의 모험에 관한 것이 대답으로 어울리므로 ③이 적절하다.
06 ④ 영화의 내용은 'Australia's Great Barrier Reef'의 바다 생물에 관한 내용이 아니라 바다 속의 모험에 관한 내용이다.
07 sound like 명사/명사절: ~처럼 들리다, ~일 것 같다
08 can't wait to+동사원형: 빨리 ~하고 싶다, ~하기를 몹시 바라다 actually: 실제로 visit: 방문하다
09 research: 조사하다, 연구하다 / 특히 새로운 사실을 발견하거나 새로운 생각을 검사하기 위해 자세히 어떤 대상을 연구하다
10 ① 언제 남자는 그의 삼촌과 저녁을 먹을 것인가? (이번 주 토요일) ② John은 어디에서 오는가? (남아메리카) ③ 얼마나 John은 떠나 있었는가? (2년) ④ John은 정글에서 무엇을 연구하는가? ⑤ 남자는 John을 만나는 것을 기대하는가? (네)
11 (A) set: (해·달 등이) 지다. 한밤중에 하이킹을 가고 자전거를 타러 나갈 수 있으려면 해가 지지 않아야 하므로 set이 어울린다. (B) 어둡지 않기 때문에 한밤중에 하이킹 하러 간다는 내용이 어울리므로 이유의 접속사 because가 적절하다.
12 hope 희망하다 get the chance: 기회를 가지다 chance+to부

정사: ~할 기회

13 현재완료진행형에서 since는 '시간'을 나타내는 명사(구)와 함께 쓰이고 for는 '기간'을 나타내는 명사(구)와 함께 쓰인다.

14 ③ How silly of her to tell him such a thing! ④ Emma has been teaching English for three years.

15 진주어로 to부정사를 쓰고 careless가 사람의 성격을 나타내는 말이므로 'of+목적격'으로 쓴다.

16 현재완료진행형에서 since는 '시간'을 나타내는 명사(구)와 함께 쓰이고 for는 '기간'을 나타내는 명사(구)와 함께 쓰인다. ⑤번은 since가 들어가야 하고 나머지는 모두 for가 적절하다.

17 ② since → for ③ two days ago → for two days 또는 has been raining → rained ⑤ of → for

18 to부정사의 의미상의 주어는 'for+목적격'으로 나타내지만, 문장에 쓰인 형용사가 사람의 성향, 성격을 나타내는 말일 때는 'of+목적격'으로 쓴다.

19 ⓐ와 ②, ⑤: 계속 용법, ① 결과 용법, ③ 경험 용법, ④ 완료 용법

20 선행사가 동물이고 계속적 용법이므로 which가 알맞다.

21 keep ~ on one's toes: ~에게 정신을 바짝 차리게 하다

22 (A) clothing은 '의류'라는 뜻의 집합명사이고 복수형으로 쓸 수 없으므로 clothing, (B) 부정문이므로 anywhere, (C) 'The combination'이 주어이므로 makes가 적절하다.

23 Amber Smith는 아마도 여전히 만들어지기를 기다리고 있는 '셀 수 없이 많은 색깔이 있을 것' 이라고 생각한다.

24 like = such as: ~와 같은

25 수동태이므로 과거분사로 쓰는 것이 적절하다.

26 생태학자가 무엇을 하는지는 대답할 수 없다. ① An ecologist. ② By rainfall[rain]. ④ Because the river has wonderful mixed colors. ⑤ In Vatnajökull National Park, Iceland.

27 앞의 내용을 추가해서 설명할 때 사용하는 In fact가 주어진 문장에 쓰인 것을 주목한다. ④번 앞 문장의 내용을 추가해서 설명하는 말이므로 ④번이 적절하다.

28 ⓐ와 ④: ~ 때문에, ① ~에 대해서 말하자면, ② ~ 대신에, ③ ~을 대신하여, ⑤ ~에도 불구하고

단원별 예상문제

p.102~105

01 ③ 02 for 03 (d)ue to
04 ④ 05 ① 06 shooting star
07 I've heard that the shooting stars will peak between 12 a.m. and 2 a.m.
08 ③ 09 (A) that (B) during (C) How
10 ① 11 out 12 ① 13 ①
14 ④ 15 ④ 16 ②
17 has been waiting, for 18 ⓐ ①, ④, ⑤, ⓑ ②, ③
19 that → which 20 ②
21 (A) colorful plants (B) colors
22 that[which] are waiting to be created

01 ① personal: 개인적인 / 직원들은 그들의 직업이 개인적인 성장에 도움이 된다고 말했다. ② unique: 독특한, 특별한 / 모든 사람은 특별하고 사람들은 자신의 정체성을 표현하는 것을 격려받아야 한다. ③ bright: 밝은, 빛나는 / 여기의 불은 읽기에 충분히 밝지 않다. ④ countless: 많은, 셀 수 없는 / 그들은 서로 말하는 데 많은 시간을 썼다. ⑤ recent: 최근의 / 최근 몇 주간 무슨 일이 일어난 것일까요?

02 stand in for: ~을 대신하다 thank you for ~: ~해서 감사합니다

03 due to 명사: ~ 때문에 / 그는 좋지 못한 건강 때문에 은퇴를 해야 했다.

04 (A) ⓑ glacier: 빙하 / 매우 느리게 움직이는 아주 큰 얼음 덩어리 / 이러한 기온의 증가는 얼음층과 빙하를 녹일 수 있다. (B) ⓒ period: 기간 / 처음과 끝을 가진 특정한 시간의 길이 / 그의 경기는 아주 짧은 시간에 향상되었다. (C) ⓓ cliff: 절벽 / 높은 땅이 있는 지역의 가파른 면 / 그는 절벽 가장자리에서 바다로 다이빙한다. (D) ⓐ combination: 조합 / 몇몇 개의 것들을 결합시킨 것 / 바나나, 오렌지 주스와 크림은 이상한 조합처럼 들리지만, 함께 섞으면 맛있는 음료가 된다.

05 'When is the best time to see them?'에서 them이 shooting stars를 의미하기 때문에 ①이 적절하다.

06 shooting star: 유성, 별똥별 / 지구로 떨어질 때 밝은 빛을 내며 타는 우주로부터 온 돌이나 금속 조각

07 I've heard that ~: ~에 대해 들었다, ~에 대해 알고 있다 between A and B: A와 B 사이에서

08 남자가 노르웨이에서는 여름 동안 해가 지지 않는다고 말했을 때 여자는 몰랐다고 대답했으므로 ①과 ②는 어울리지 않고, 이어서 남자가 노르웨이 사람들이 밤에 어둡지 않아서 하이킹이나 자전거 타러 간다는 것을 들었다고 얘기하는 것이 적절하다.

09 (A) 'Did you know that 주어 동사 ~?'로 상대방에게 무언가에 대해 알고 있는지 물어볼 수 있다. that은 접속사이므로 뒤에 주어와 동사로 이루어진 완전한 문장이 온다. (B) 내용상 '여름 동안'의 의미이므로 during이 어울린다. while은 접속사이기 때문에 주어와 동사가 뒤에 나와야 한다. (C) 감탄문은 느낌이나 감탄을 나타내는 것으로 how 또는 what으로 시작하며 '정말 ~하구나!'로 해석한다. how로 시작할 때는 'How+형용사/부사(+주어+동사)!'로, what으로 시작하는 감탄문은 'What+(a/an)+형용사+명사(+주어+동사)!'이다. 그러므로 여기서는 How가 어울린다.

10 흥미로워 보인다와 너무 어려워 보인다는 두 문장은 '그러나, 하지만'의 의미를 지닌 접속사 but으로 연결될 수 있다.

11 (B) find out: 발견하다, 알아보다 (C) turn out: (일·진행·결과가 특정 방식으로) 되다

12 ① few: 거의 없는, 지역문화회관에는 다른 레벨의 코스들이 있다고 언급되고 있다. / 지역문화회관에는 실내 암벽등반 수업이

거의 없다. ② 남자는 실내 암벽등반에 관심이 있다. ③ 남자는 실내 암벽등반에 관한 것을 조사하기 위해 지역문화회관을 방문할 것이다. ④ Jake의 블로그에 그가 실내 암벽등반을 하러 간 사진이 있다. ⑤ 여자는 지역문화회관에 실내 암벽등반 수업이 있다는 것을 알고 있다.

13 첫 번째 문장에서는 foolish가 사람의 성향, 성격을 나타내는 말이므로 'of+목적격'이 적절하다. 두 번째 문장에서는 noon이라는 시간을 나타내는 명사가 있으므로 since가 적절하다.

14 의미상의 주어 앞에 전치사 for가 있으므로 빈칸에는 사람의 성격을 나타내는 형용사인 wise는 알맞지 않다.

15 ① My dad has been working in New York for a year. ② Brian has been painting his house for two hours. ③ She cleaned her house then. ⑤ What's been happening in recent weeks?

16 ②에는 사람의 성격이나 성질을 나타내는 형용사(thoughtful)가 왔으므로 의미상의 주어로 'of+목적격'이 적절하다. 나머지는 모두 'for+목적격'이 적절하다.

17 과거 어느 때부터 시작되어 현재까지 계속 진행되고 있음을 나타내는 현재완료진행형을 이용한다. '기간'을 나타내는 an hour가 있으므로 for를 쓴다.

18 ⓐ와 ①, ④, ⑤: 부사적 용법, ⓑ와 ②, ③: 형용사적 용법

19 관계대명사 that은 계속적 용법으로 쓸 수 없기 때문에, which로 고치는 것이 적절하다.

20 Lin Wang이 Tsingy를 몇 번 방문했는지는 알 수 없다. ① In Madagascar. ③ By rainfall. ④ No. ⑤ Yes.

21 햇빛이 Caño Cristales 아래의 '화려한 식물'에 비칠 때, Caño Cristales의 '색깔'은 더 생생하고 밝게 될 수 있다.

22 주격 관계대명사 that[which]을 사용하는 것이 적절하다.

서술형 실전문제

p.106~107

01 (1) thank you for invite me → thank you for inviting me
(2) I've heard that this photo took in the Maldives. → I've heard that this photo was taken in the Maldives.
(3) I can't wait taking more pictures of amazing beaches. → I can't wait to take more pictures of amazing beaches.

02 I can't wait to see him and listen to his stories.

03 ⓔ I will → I won't

04 (1) I have been visiting the Wimbledon tennis tournament since I was in high school.
(2) Phil has been repairing mobile phones for ten years.
(3) I have been staying at the hotel for a few days.

05 (1) It is fun for me to read the comic book.
(2) It is necessary for people here to eat well to stay warm and healthy.
(3) It is too difficult for me to understand this book.

06 (1) The airplane has been flying since an hour ago.
(2) The government has been stealing our public funds for a long time.
(3) I have known him ever since he was a boy.
(4) The room is large enough for all of us to stay in.
(5) I think it is nice of you to give books to your brother.
(6) The bands played music for many people to dance to.

07 (A) amazing (B) sharp (C) like

08 ⓐ For ⓑ on

09 frog-like legs

01 (1) thank you for ~: ~해서 감사합니다 / 전치사 for 다음에는 명사나 동명사가 올 수 있다. (2) take a picture: 사진을 찍다 / 사진은 찍혀지는 대상이므로 수동태로 써야 한다. (3) can't wait to+동사원형: 빨리 ~하고 싶다, ~하기를 몹시 바라다

02 can't wait to+동사원형: 빨리 ~하고 싶다, ~하기를 몹시 바라다

03 이번 주 토요일에 그의 삼촌과 저녁을 할 예정이라고 다른 계획을 잡지 말라는 말에 남자는 'Okay'라고 대답했으므로 '계획을 안 잡을 게요.'란 말이 내용상 적절하므로 will이 아닌 won't가 어울린다. won't 다음에 make other plans가 생략되었다.

04 과거에 시작해서 현재도 진행 중이므로 현재완료진행형으로 쓴다. since는 '시간'을 나타내는 명사(구)와 함께 쓰이고 for는 '기간'을 나타내는 명사(구)와 함께 쓰인다.

05 가주어 it을 사용하고 to부정사를 진주어로 쓴다. 의미상의 주어를 빠뜨리지 말아야 한다.

06 (1) 현재완료진행형은 과거를 나타내는 어구와 함께 쓰이지 않는다. (2) 현재완료진행형에서 since는 '시간'을 나타내는 명사(구)와 함께 쓰이고 for는 '기간'을 나타내는 명사(구)와 함께 쓰인다. (3) know는 진행형으로 쓸 수 없는 동사이므로 현재완료시제로 나타낸다. (4), (5) to부정사의 의미상의 주어는 'for+목적격'으로 나타낸다. 이때 문장에 쓰인 형용사가 사람의 성향, 성격을 나타내는 말일 때는 'of+목적격'으로 쓴다. (6) 의미상의 주어 'for+목적격'이 있으므로 to부정사를 쓴다.

07 (A) 감정을 나타내는 동사는 감정을 유발할 때 현재분사를 쓰는 것이 적절하다. (B) 'make+목적어+목적격보어' 구문이므로, 목

적격보어로 형용사 sharp를 쓰는 것이 적절하다. (C) A is like B: ~와 같다, alike 뒤에는 목적어를 쓸 수 없다.

08 ⓐ for example: 예를 들면 ⓑ keep ~ on one's toes: ~을 계속 긴장하게 하다

09 그들이 한 개의 돌탑에서 다른 돌탑으로 뛸 수 있도록 도와주는 '개구리 같은 다리'를 가지고 있기 때문에 그곳에서 살 수 있다.

창의사고력 서술형 문제 p.108

|모범답안|

01 I can't wait to see a new film and meet a director and actors.

02 (1) |모범답안| They have been playing basketball for two hours.

(2) |모범답안| He has been playing the cello since 3 o'clock.

03 (A) hiking (B) Mt. Jiri and Mt. Seorak (C) hiking routes (D) get in shape (E) keep fit

01 preview: 시사회 can't wait to+동사원형: 빨리 ~하고 싶다, ~하기를 몹시 바라다 director: 감독 actor: 배우

단원별 모의고사 p.109~112

01 (c)ountless

02 (1) walk (2) get (3) cut (4) keeps 03 ③

04 (1) (w)henever (2) (h)onored (3) (h)igh

05 I've heard that there are different levels of courses at the community center.

06 ⓔ Let me to know how does it turn out. → Let me know how it turns out.

07 adventure

08 I can't wait to watch the movie. 09 ③

10 hiking and cycling in the middle of, it isn't dark

11 ② 12 rainbow 13 ③ 14 ③

15 ②, ⑤

16 (1) for us to have a sense of belonging

(2) for employees to be properly paid

17 (1) have been living together for 5 years

(2) has been reading the book since yesterday

18 (1) The greenhouse in the Ice Cube is warm enough for Mathew to grow fresh vegetables.

(2) It was wise of Solomon to make such a careful decision.

(3) Jason has been taking horse-riding lessons for three months.

(4) Ashley has been learning to play the flute for 5 months. 또는 Ashley learned to play the flute 5 months ago.

(5) Lily has liked Gino since she first met him.

19 ①

20 비가 오랜 기간 동안 돌을 침식해서 날카롭고 뾰족하게 만들었기 때문이다.

21 ③, ④ 22 ③ 23 to make

24 ⑤ 25 ③ 26 trip 27 ②

28 ② 29 ④

30 The combination of colorful plants under the water and sunlight makes the colors more alive and bright.

31 (A) fashion colorist (B) Caño Cristales

32 Iceland is the best place for many location scouts to visit due to its unusual beauty. 33 ①

34 (A) glacier caves (B) mountain ranges

01 countless: 많은, 셀 수 없이 많은 / 매우 많은, 특히 당신이 생각하기에 합당한 것보다 더 많은

02 (1) walk along: ~을 따라 산책하다 / 그녀는 해변을 산책하기 위해 매일 아침 6시에 일어난다. (2) get in shape: 좋은 몸 상태를 유지하다 / 네가 좋은 몸 상태를 유지하기를 원한다면, 더 많은 운동을 해야 한다. (3) cut down: 자르다 / 나무를 베어서 종이를 만들 필요가 없습니다. (4) keep ~ on one's toes: ~에게 긴장을 늦추지 않게 하다 / 매주 금요일마다 보는 시험으로 그녀는 학생들이 긴장을 늦추지 않게 한다.

03 insight: 통찰력

04 (1) whenever+주어+동사: ~할 때마다 (2) honor: 영광으로 생각하다 (3) high: 많은

05 I've heard that ~: ~에 대해 들었다, ~에 대해 알고 있다 community center: 지역문화회관

06 let는 '~에게 …하게 하다'라는 의미를 가지는 사역동사로, 목적어와 목적격보어가 능동의 관계이면 목적격보어 자리에 동사원형을 쓴다. know의 목적어로 의문사 how가 들어간 의문문을 사용할 때는 '의문사+주어+동사'의 순서로 쓴다.

07 adventure: 모험 / 위험하고 흔치 않은 일이 발생하는 신나는 경험

08 can't wait to+동사원형: 빨리 ~하고 싶다, ~하기를 몹시 바라다

09 (A) 여름 동안 해가 안 진다는 것을 알고 있는지 물어보고 있다. (B) 사람들이 밤에 하이킹과 자전거를 타러 간다는 사실을 들어서 알고 있음을 표현하고 있다. (B) 다음에 주어와 동사가 들어간 문장이 나오므로 전치사가 아닌 접속사 that이 적절하다.

10 in the middle of the night: 한밤중에

11 여자가 남자에게 여름방학 계획에 대해 묻고, 남자가 중국에 간다는 대답을 한다. 이후에 여자가 'The Rainbow

Mountains?'라고 묻고 있으므로 'The Rainbow Mountains'에 대한 언급을 남자가 먼저 했어야 하므로 ②가 적절하다.

12 rainbow: 무지개 / 태양과 비 둘 다 있을 때 하늘에 나타날 수 있는 여러 가지의 색깔을 가진 큰 곡선

13 대화에서 that은 주격 관계대명사로 사용하였다. ③ 이외의 보기는 타동사의 목적어 자리에 들어가는 명사절을 이끄는 접속사로 사용했다.

14 과거 어느 때부터 시작되어 현재까지 계속 진행되고 있음을 나타내는 현재완료진행형을 이용한다.

15 ① Isn't it necessary for us to help them? ③ She has been listening to the music for two hours. ④ Alex has had his father's watch since his father passed away.

17 현재완료진행형에서 since는 '시간'을 나타내는 명사(구)와 함께 쓰이고 for는 '기간'을 나타내는 명사(구)와 함께 쓰인다.

18 (1), (2) to부정사의 의미상의 주어는 to부정사 바로 앞에 'for+명사의 목적격'으로 나타내지만 문장에 쓰인 형용사가 nice, kind, smart, wise 등과 같이 사람의 성향, 성격을 나타내는 말일 때는 'of+목적격'으로 쓴다. (3) 현재완료진행형에서 since는 '시간'을 나타내는 명사(구)와 함께 쓰이고 for는 '기간'을 나타내는 명사(구)와 함께 쓰인다. (4) 현재완료진행형은 과거를 나타내는 어구인 5 months ago와 함께 쓰이지 않는다. (5) 진행형으로 쓸 수 없는 동사인 like는 현재완료형으로 상태의 계속을 표현한다.

19 수동태로 고치면 We all are inspired by the beauty of nature.가 된다.

20 앞 문장의 내용을 쓰는 것이 적절하다.

21 ⓑ와 ③, ④: 관계대명사, ①, ⑤: 접속사, ② 그렇게(지시부사)

22 ⓐ와 ③: 촬영하다, ① [빛 등을] 갑자기 발하다, ②, ⑤: [총·대포를] 발사[발포]하다, ④ 던지다

23 help 뒤에 원형부정사나 to부정사를 쓸 수 있다.

24 Vatnajökull 국립 공원에서 몇 편의 sci-fi 영화가 만들어졌는지는 대답할 수 없다. ① He is a location scout and his job is finding perfect places to shoot movies. ② In Iceland. ③ Due to its unusual beauty. ④ The Vatnajökull National Park.

25 ③ 위 글은 '홍보 포스터'이다. ① (신문·잡지의) 글, 기사, ② 수필, ④ (책·연극·영화 등에 대한) 논평[비평], 감상문, ⑤ 독후감

26 '여행'을 가리킨다.

27 하이킹하는 데 시간이 얼마 걸릴지는 알 수 없다. ① For people who are interested in hiking. ③ Mt. Jiri and Mt. Seorak. ④ They will be able to walk along beautiful hiking routes and will also learn how to get in shape and keep fit. ⑤ Yes. unforgettable: 잊지 못할[잊을 수 없는], memorable: 기억할 만한

28 앞의 내용을 추가해서 설명하고 있으므로 In fact가 가장 적절하다. ① 게다가, 더욱이, ③ 그러므로, ⑤ 즉, 다시 말해

29 Danny Mehta의 팀이 컴퓨터 그래픽을 사용하지 않고 최근에 촬영한 영화는 'action' 영화가 아니라 'sci-fi' 영화였다.

30 'combination'을 보충하면 된다.

31 Amber Smith는 'Caño Cristales'의 아름다운 색으로부터 영감을 얻어온 '패션 색채 전문가'이다.

32 scouts를 보충하면 된다.

33 stand in for: ~을 대신하다

34 그곳의 가파른 절벽, 푸른 '빙하 동굴', 그리고 긴 '산맥들'은 세계나 우주의 어느 장소도 대신할 수 있다.

Lesson 3

For the Love of Our Country

시험대비 실력평가

p.118

01 ③	02 ④	03 ⑤	04 ④
05 ②	06 (s)ince	07 ①	

01 rescue: 구하다, 구조[구출/구제]하다 save: 구하다 / 우리는 지나가는 낚싯배에 의해서 가라앉는 배에서부터 구조되었다.

02 fortune: 재산 / 버핏은 영리한 투자를 통해서 큰 돈을 벌었다.

03 ① 그는 학자라기보다는 오히려 작가이다. ② 그녀는 분명히 진실을 말하고 있었다. ③ 병사들은 요새를 방어할 준비가 되어 있었다. ④ 너는 한국 전쟁 기념관에 가 본 적이 있니? ⑤ general: 장군 / 그는 최근에 장군으로 진급했다.

04 horrible: 끔찍한 / 우리의 모든 돈이 도난당했다는 것을 알았을 때 정말로 끔찍했다.

05 ① make, make an arrangement: ~을 결정하다 / 우리의 목적지를 결정하자. ② devote, devote one's life to 명사: ~에 일생을 바치다 / 그녀는 공직에 일생을 바칠 것이라고 말했습니다. ③ try. try on: 입어 보다, 신어 보다 / 입어 볼 만한 재킷 좀 있나요? ④ take, take a look around ~: ~ 주위를 둘러보다 / 이곳은 재미있는 곳이에요. 한번 둘러보시겠어요? ⑤ heard, hear of[about] ~: ~에 대해 듣다 / 너는 차고 세일에 대해 들어 본 적 있니?

06 since: ~이기 때문에

07 movement: (정치적·사회적) 운동 / 태도, 의견 또는 정책의 점진적인 발전 또는 변화

서술형 시험대비

p.119

01 (1) trying to be used to new glasses
(2) It is said that she has been all over the world.
(3) I hate talking like this behind his back.
(4) Is it okay if I take a picture?

02 independence

03 so, that he could

04 (i)nclude (r)uin (s)ave
(1) ruin (2) save (3) include

05 by

06 (1) article (2) would

01 (1) be used to (동)명사: ~하는 데 익숙하다 (2) It is said that 주어+동사 ~: (사람들이) ~라고 한다 (3) behind one's back: 등 뒤에서 (4) Is it okay if I ~?: 제가 ~해도 될까요? take a picture: 사진을 찍다

02 depend: 의존하다 independence: 독립 / 그녀는 대한민국 독립을 위한 3.1 운동에 참여했다.

03 so+형용사/부사+that 주어+동사: 너무 ~해서 …하다

04 include: ~을 포함하다 / 사람이나 사물을 어떤 것의 일부로 내포하다 ruin: 망치다, 파산시키다 / 누군가로 하여금 그들의 돈이나 권력을 모두 잃게 만들다 save: 구하다 / 위험, 해로움, 또는 파괴로부터 사람이나 사물을 안전하게 만들다 (1) 어떤 사람들은 스포일러가 이야기를 망친다고 말한다. (2) 안전띠를 매는 것은 너의 생명을 구할 수 있다. (3) 호텔비는 아침식사를 포함한다.

05 be+p.p+by 행위자(수동태) / 그 빌딩은 2004년 화재에 의해 파괴되었다. by 동사ing: ~함으로써 / 그녀는 아이들을 돌봄으로써 여분의 돈을 번다.

06 (1) article: 기사 (2) would: (과거에 있어서의 습관·습성·반복적 동작) ~하곤 했다

교과서

Conversation

핵심 Check

p.120~121

1 It is said that there will be a big festival
2 It is said that he is a liar.
3 It is said that purple was
4 Is it okay if I practice the guitar?
5 Is it okay if I sit next to you?

교과서 대화문 익히기

Check(√) True or False

p.122~123

1 F 2 T 3 T 4 F 5 F 6 F 7 F 8 T 9 T

교과서 확인학습 p.125~127

Listen & Talk 1 Get Ready

was / read, it is said / both

Listen & Talk 1 A-1

what, reading / biography / haven't heard / the first female, It is said that, over

Listen & Talk 1 A-2

interesting, detective / scholar / but it is said that he was also, solved / didn't know that

Listen & Talk 1 B

know about / heard / Take a look at, to be included / helped, by building a clinic, that such stories, be included in / to, such

Listen & Talk 2 A-1

can't take, museum / Is it okay / leave, in

Listen & Talk 2 A-2

to, How / is it okay if I take pictures in / don't

Listen & Talk 2 B

How was / were / get the chance to, okay if I / remember that, at / on / Let me know if

Communication Step A

are moving onto, As you can see, many, inventions, is called / musical instrument / It is said that it is, largest / How, Is it okay if

Wrap Up 1

what / watching / Isn't he / It is said that he won / how, possible / general who made creative

Wrap Up 2

Would you like to / I'd like to / Here / is it okay if / if, on, stay

시험대비 기본평가 p.128

01 ⑤ 02 ② 03 ②, ④, ⑤

04 Is it okay if I open the window?

01 무엇을 읽고 있는지 물어보는 질문에, (C) 권기옥의 자서전을 읽고 있다고 대답한다. (D) 그녀(권기옥)에 대해 들어본 적이 없다고 말하며, 그녀가 누구인지 질문한다. (B) 그녀는 한국 최초의 여자 비행 조종사라고 얘기하며 비행시간이 7,000시간 이상이었다는 사실을 추가해서 말한다. (A) 놀라움을 표현하며, 그러한 사실을 몰랐다고 반응한다.

02 'Is it okay if I ~?'는 '제가 ~해도 될까요?'라는 뜻으로 어떤 행동을 하기 전에 허가를 요청할 때 사용하는 표현이다.

03 빈칸 다음에 접속사 but(하지만)이 나오고 플래시를 사용하지 말라는 내용이 나오는 것으로 보아 미술관 안에서 사진을 찍는 것을 허락하고 당부하는 말을 덧붙인 것으로 볼 수 있다.

04 Is it okay if I ~?: 제가 ~해도 될까요? open: 열다

시험대비 실력평가 p.129~130

01 ③	02 ②	03 ③	04 ③, ④
05 ④	06 ③	07 ⑤	08 ①, ③
09 ①	10 ②, ④		

01 주어진 문장은 조선 시대에 그가 학자가 아니었는지 묻는 것으로 여기서 그는 정약용을 말한다. 남자가 정약용이 학자이지만, 또한 형사였다고 말하는 것이 주어진 문장에 대한 대답이 될 수 있으므로 ③에 들어가는 것이 적절하다.

02 밑줄 친 부분은 대략 90개의 사건을 해결했다는 의미이므로, 사건을 해결할 수 있는 detective(형사, 탐정)가 가장 어울린다. ① diplomat: 외교관 ③ reporter: 기자 ④ victim: 피해자 ⑤ painter: 화가

03 주어진 문장에서 she는 여자가 읽고 있는 자서전의 주인공인 권기옥을 의미한다. 남자는 그녀(권기옥)에 대해 들어 본 적이 없다고 말하며 이어서 그녀가 누구인지 여자에게 묻는 것이 어울리므로 ③이 적절하다.

04 ① Lisa는 어떤 종류의 책을 읽고 있는가? (자서전) ② 얼마나 많은 비행 시간을 권기옥은 가지고 있었는가? (7,000시간 이상) ③ 누가 한국에서 최초의 남성 비행사였는가? (최초의 여성 비행사에 대한 정보만 있으므로 알 수 없다.) ④ Lisa는 왜 권기옥에 관한 책을 읽고 있는가? (책을 읽는 이유에 대해서는 언급되어 있지 않다.) ⑤ 남자는 권기옥에 대해서 들어본 적이 있는가? (아니요)

05 ④ 상대방의 핸드폰을 사용할 수 있는지 허락을 묻는 질문에 긍정으로 대답하고 핸드폰을 안 가져왔다고 말하는 것은 어울리지 않는다.

06 한옥 마을이 어땠는지 감상을 묻는 질문에 (C) 좋았다고 대답하며 집들이 예뻤다고 대답한다. (A) 잘 되었다고 말한다. (B) 여자가 저녁을 먹을 기회가 없었다고 하면서, 부엌을 이 시간에 쓰는 것에 대해 허락을 요청하자 (D) 괜찮다고 대답하며, 하지만 부엌이 10시에 닫는다는 사실을 상기시켜 준다.

07 주어진 문장에서 such stories는 여자가 말한 이태석 신부가 병원과 학교를 지음으로써 아이들을 도왔다는 이야기를 의미하므로 그 문장 다음에 나와야 적절하다.

08 남자가 이태석 신부에 대해서 들어 본 적이 있다고 대답하고 있으므로, 이태석 신부에 대해서 들어 본 적이 있는지 아니면 이태석 신부에 대해서 알고 있는지 물어보는 것이 적절하다.

09 take a look at ~: ~을 보다

10 알고 있는 내용을 진술할 때 'It is said that 주어+동사 ~.(~라고 한다)', 'It is believed that 주어+동사 ~. (~라고 믿어진다.)', 'It is thought that 주어+동사 ~. (~라고 생각된다.)'라고 말할 수 있다.

서술형 시험대비 p.131

01 who Shin Saimdang is
02 it is said that her paintings were so realistic that birds gathered around the painted tree
03 if
04 Sure / Of course / Certainly / No problem
05 by
06 such
07 built, will be included, South Sudan
08 Is it okay if I try on your hat?

01 간접의문문의 어순은 '의문사+주어+동사'이다.
02 It is said that 주어+동사 ~: (사람들이) ~라고 한다 so+형용사/부사+that 주어+동사: 너무 ~해서 …하다 realistic: 진짜 같은, 사실적인 gather: 모이다
03 Is it okay if I ~?: 제가 ~해도 될까요?
04 사진을 찍어도 되는지 허가를 묻는 말에 허락의 말이 나오고 접속사 but 다음에 카메라의 플래시를 터뜨리지 말라는 말이 나오는 것이 어울린다.
05 by 동사ing: ~함으로써
06 such: (형) 이러한, 그러한 such (a(n))+형용사+명사: 너무 ~한 명사
07 build: 짓다(built-built) include: ~을 포함하다 social studies: 사회 Sudan: 수단 (민주 공화국) / 이태석 신부가 아이들을 돕기 위해서 병원과 학교를 지은 이야기는 남수단의 사회 교과서에 포함될 것이다.
08 Is it okay if I ~?: 제가 ~해도 될까요? try on: 입어[써] 보다, 신어 보다

교과서

Grammar

핵심 Check p.132~133

1 (1) if[whether] (2) whether (3) if[whether]
2 (1) had just heard (2) had lost (3) heard

시험대비 기본평가 p.134

01 ⑤
02 (1) had already left (2) had broken (3) if (4) whether
03 ④
04 (1) My daughter had never been sick until then.
(2) I had just fallen asleep when someone knocked at the door.
(3) She is not sure if she will return in the future.

01 주절의 동사가 remembered로 과거이고 그것들을 탁자 위에 던져 놓은 것은 그 이전의 사실이므로 과거완료(대과거)를 써야 한다.
02 (1) 도착한 것보다 기차가 떠난 것이 앞서는 것이므로 과거완료가 적절하다. (2) 꽃병을 깼음(앞선 사실)을 고백하는 것이므로 과거완료가 적절하다. (3) 내용상 '올 수 있다는 것을 모른다'는 어색하다. 사실의 여부를 확인하거나 불확실함을 나타내는 if가 적절하다. (4) 바로 뒤에 or not이 이어지고 있으므로 whether가 적절하다.
03 asked의 직접목적어가 나와야 하는데 '~인지 (아닌지)'라는 의미로 명사절을 이끄는 접속사 if가 적절하다.
04 (1) 경험을 나타내는 과거완료를 이용한다. (2) 노크하기 전에 잠이 막 들은 것이므로 과거완료로 나타낸다. (3) '~인지 (아닌지)'라는 의미의 접속사로 어떠한 사실의 여부를 확인하거나 불확실함을 나타낼 때 쓰이는 if를 이용한다.

시험대비 실력평가 p.135~137

01 ② 02 ④ 03 ①
04 (1) encountered (2) had bought (3) had practiced (4) whether (5) if (6) whether
05 ③ 06 ① 07 ⑤
08 (1) unless (2) if (3) though (4) when (5) whether
09 ⑤ 10 ③ 11 ②
12 had played 13 ③
14 (1) Please tell me if[whether] your sister is in her room.
(2) Whether he wants or not isn't that important.
(3) I suddenly remembered that I had left the windows open.
(4) I had never been to the big city before.
(5) I found out that someone had broken the lamp.
15 ④ 16 ⑤ 17 ①, ②

01 When she arrived at the station, the first train had already left.
02 He asked her nicely if he could see her license.
03 첫 번째 빈칸에는 '~인지 (아닌지)'라는 의미의 접속사 if가 적절하다. 두 번째 빈칸에는 잃어버린 것이 우연히 찾은 것보다 앞서므로 과거완료가 적절하다.

04 (1) 과거완료는 'had+과거분사'의 형태이므로 encountered가 적절하다. (2) 산책시킨 시점보다 아빠가 사주신 시점이 앞서므로 had bought가 적절하다. (3) since(~ 이래로)가 있으므로 had practiced가 적절하다. (4) 내용상 '~인지 (아닌지)'라는 의미의 접속사 whether가 적절하다. (5) 내용상 '~인지 (아닌지)'라는 의미의 접속사 if가 적절하다. (6) 뒤에 or not이 바로 이어서 나오고 있으므로 whether가 적절하다.

05 도착했을 때(과거) 이미 극장에 들어간 것이므로 과거완료로 써야 한다.

06 I thought보다 앞선 시제이므로 ⓐ의 have been은 had been으로 고쳐야 한다.

07 뒤에 or not이 있고 내용상 '~인지 (아닌지)'라는 의미가 자연스러우므로 if나 whether가 적절하고, 알고 싶어 하는 것보다 가방이 버려진 시점이 앞선 시제이므로 과거완료가 적절하다.

08 (1) 조건의 unless가 적절하다. (2) 조건의 부사절을 이끄는 if가 적절하다. (3) 서로 상반되는 내용이 나오므로 though가 적절하다. (4) 뒤에 '주어+be동사'가 생략된 형태로 when이 적절하다. (5) or not이 바로 뒤에 이어지므로 whether가 적절하다.

09 집에 도착한 것보다 산책을 나간 것이 앞서므로 과거완료가 적절하다.

10 '~인지 (아닌지)'라는 의미의 명사절을 이끄는 if가 적절하다.

11 ask의 목적어로 '~인지 (아닌지)'라는 의미의 명사절을 이끄는 if가 적절하다.

12 6살에 연주하기 시작했으므로 6살 이래로 연주해 왔다고 과거완료로 나타낼 수 있다.

13 <보기>는 계속적 용법이다. ① 완료, ② 경험, ③ 계속, ④ 결과, ⑤ 대과거

14 (1) what이 문장 내에서 하는 역할이 없으므로 '~인지 (아닌지)'라는 의미의 접속사로 쓰이는 if나 whether로 고치는 것이 적절하다. (2) if가 이끄는 명사절은 주어 역할을 할 수 없으므로 whether로 고치는 것이 적절하다. (3) 창문을 열어 놓은 것이 기억하는 시점보다 앞서므로 과거완료로 고치는 것이 적절하다. (4) 완료시제와 어울리는 것은 ago가 아니라 before이다. (5) 누군가 램프를 깨뜨린 것이 발견한 것보다 앞서므로 과거완료가 적절하다.

15 '~인지 (아닌지)'라는 의미의 접속사 if가 적절하며 if 다음에는 or not을 바로 붙여 쓰지 않는다.

16 사기 전에 말했던 것이므로 과거완료로 나타내는 것이 적절하다. 전치사 about을 빠뜨리지 않도록 주의한다.

17 ① He asked me whether or not the book was boring. ② I remembered that I had turned the stove on.

서술형 시험대비

p.138~139

01 (1) had bought for me (2) she had received

02 (1) had not locked (2) he had already gone

03 (1) I wonder if these dishes will suit your taste.
(2) I don't know whether he is at home or at the office.
(3) We found out that we had been at the same school.
(4) She seemed astonished that I had never been to Paris.

04 (1) If → Whether (2) if → whether (3) if → whether

05 (1) had never learned (2) if[whether] she forgot

06 (1) The man isn't sure if[whether] he can help her.
(2) They don't know if[whether] he will be promoted.
(3) Would you tell me if[whether] he needs surgery or not?

07 (1) He won the contest because he had practiced a lot for the contest.
(2) I couldn't take the class because it had been canceled.

08 (1) He told me that he had stolen the money the other day.
(2) No computer had won even one game against a human player until then.
(3) I found my bag that I had lost on the bus.
(4) I asked the lady if[whether] I could use the bathroom.
(5) I'm not sure if Santa will give me a nice gift or not.
(6) I couldn't decide whether to buy it.

01 각각 과거보다 앞선 시제에 행한 것을 나타내는 과거완료를 이용한다.

02 (1) 과거완료의 대과거 용법을 이용한다. (2) 과거완료의 결과 용법을 이용한다.

03 (1) if가 명사절을 이끌도록 한다. (2) whether가 명사절을 이끌도록 한다. (3), (4) 하나 앞서는 시제에 과거완료를 이용한다.

04 (1) 문두에서 주어를 이끄는 역할을 하고 있으므로 If를 Whether로 고치는 것이 적절하다. (2) 뒤에 or not이 바로 이어서 나오고 있으므로 if를 whether로 고치는 것이 적절하다. (3) whether 다음에 to부정사를 쓸 수 있지만 if는 to부정사와 함께 쓰이지 않는다.

05 (1) 과거보다 앞서는 일이나 상태를 나타내는 과거완료(대과거)를 이용한다. (2) 명사절을 이끄는 if[whether]를 이용한다.

06 명사절을 이끄는 if나 whether를 이용하여 두 문장을 연결한다.

07 시간차가 드러나도록 하라고 했으므로 앞서는 사건을 과거완료 시제로 나타낸다.

08 (1) 말했을 때보다 그가 훔친 시점이 앞서므로 과거완료가 적절하다. (2) until then으로 보아 그때까지의 경험을 나타내는 과거완료가 적절하다. (3) 잃어버린 후에 발견한 것이므로 잃어버린 것을 과거완료로 쓰는 것이 적절하다. (4) 명사절을 이끄는 if나 whether를 쓰는 것이 적절하다. (5) if가 이끄는 절이 명사절이므로 미래는 미래시제로 나타내야 한다. (6) whether 다음에 to부정사를 쓸 수 있지만 if는 to부정사와 함께 쓰이지 않는다.

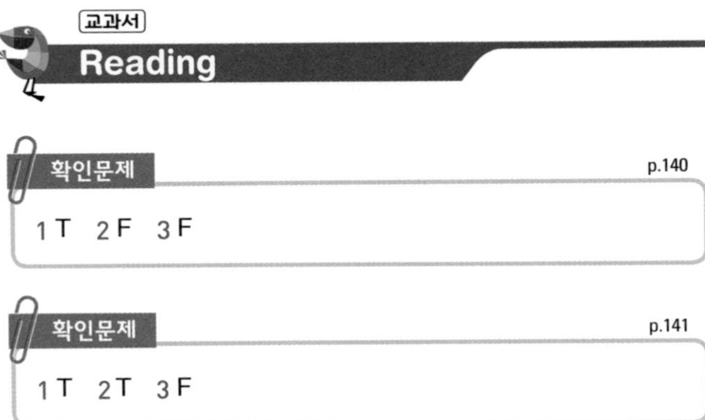

교과서

Reading

확인문제 p.140

1 T 2 F 3 F

확인문제 p.141

1 T 2 T 3 F

교과서 확인학습 A p.142~143

01 Secret
02 a strange man
03 an odd question, was more used to being called
04 your father's friend
05 wonder if
06 disappointing, good memories
07 Back, whenever, There goes
08 from 09 Instead of living
10 That is why, which, ruins
11 has gambled away
12 have no more money left, would, whenever
13 would yell at, empty-handed
14 Bring
15 had already made an arrangement
16 As part of, a new chest for clothes
17 Right before, has taken the money
18 such a horrible thing
19 What 20 no choice
21 You'll have to take
22 How embarrassing, behind my back
23 had been difficult for me
24 continued his story
25 a gambler 26 independence fighters
27 made himself, keep this a secret from
28 if
29 afterwards, had been wrong
30 had devoted his life to

교과서 확인학습 B p.144~145

1 The Secret of My Father
2 In 1946, a strange man visited me and asked, "Are you Mr. Kim Yonghwan's daughter?"
3 For me, this was an odd question because I was more used to being called the daughter of a *parakho*.
4 "I'm your father's friend.
5 You may wonder if it is true, but your father...," the man said.
6 At that moment, I was expecting disappointing news since I did not have good memories of my father.
7 Back in the 1920's, whenever people saw me in the village, they would say, "There goes the *parakho*'s daughter."
8 My father was a son from a very rich family.
9 Instead of living the life of a seonbi, he was always at the gambling house.
10 That is why he was called a *parakho*, which means someone who ruins his family's fortune.
11 "Your father has gambled away all of the money, and now he's asking for more.
12 Go and tell him that we have no more money left," my mother would tell me whenever she sent me to the gambling house.
13 Then, my father would yell at me angrily, "Why did you come empty-handed?
14 Bring me more money!"
15 When I was sixteen years old, my family had already made an arrangement for me to marry Mr. Seo.
16 As part of the wedding tradition, Mr. Seo's family sent my family some money to buy a new chest for clothes.
17 Right before the wedding day, my mother came into my room and said, "Your father has taken the money for the chest."
18 I asked angrily, "How could he do such a horrible thing?
19 What should we do now?"
20 "We have no choice.

21 You'll have to take your aunt's old chest," my mother said.
22 "How embarrassing for the family," people would whisper behind my back.
23 Since the first day of marriage, life at my husband's house had been difficult for me.
24 "Your father, my dear friend...," my father's friend continued his story.
25 "He was not a gambler.
26 Your father sent the family money to the independence fighters in Manchuria.
27 He made himself look like a gambler to keep this a secret from the Japanese officers."
28 At first, I was not sure if he was telling the truth.
29 But afterwards, I found out the truth about my father and I realized that I had been wrong about him.
30 Ever since that moment, I have been proud to be the daughter of a *parakho* who had devoted his life to the independence movement.

시험대비 실력평가

p.146~149

01 Are you Mr. Kim Yonghwan's daughter?
02 (A) odd (B) being (C) if
03 ②, ⑤ 04 ③, ④ 05 ④ 06 ①
07 ② 08 ② 09 ①
10 (A) already (B) What (C) Since 11 ⑤
12 ④ 13 ④ 14 ③ 15 ④
16 I was not sure if[whether] he was telling the truth
17 ② 18 ②, ③
19 (A) would (B) ruins (C) empty-handed
20 and it
21 we have no more money left

01 낯선 남자가 물어본 내용을 가리킨다.

02 (A) 나는 파락호의 딸이라고 불리는 것이 더 익숙했기 때문에 이것은 나에게 '이상한' 질문이었다고 해야 하므로 odd가 적절하다. familiar: 익숙한, 친숙한, odd: 이상한, 특이한, (B) 나는 파락호의 딸이라고 불리는 것에 더 '익숙했다'고 해야 하므로 being이 적절하다. be used to ~ing: ~하는 데 익숙하다, be used to 동사원형: ~하기 위해 사용되다, (C) wonder if: ~ 여부를 궁금해 하다, that은 목적어의 내용이 확실할 때 사용한다.

03 ⓑ와 ②, ⑤: [이유를 나타내어] …이므로, …이니까, ①, ③, ④: …부터[이후]

04 ⓐ와 ③, ④: ~인지 아닌지, ①, ②, ⑤: 만약

05 필자의 아버지가 독립운동가들에게 얼마나 많은 돈을 보냈는지는 알 수 없다. ① No. ② To the independence fighters in Manchuria. ③ To keep the fact that he sent the family money to the independence fighters in Manchuria a secret from the Japanese officers. ⑤ Her father's friend told her the truth.

06 ⓐ ask for: 요청하다, ⓑ yell at: ~에게 소리를 지르다

07 ②번 다음 문장의 That에 주목한다. 주어진 문장의 내용을 받고 있으므로 ②번이 적절하다.

08 글쓴이의 아버지는 '선비'의 삶을 사는 대신 항상 도박장에 계셨다.

09 ① (C)의 첫 부분은 (A)의 내용을 가리키므로 (A) 다음에 (C)가 이어지고 (B)의 that moment가 (C)에서 아버지에 대한 사실을 알게 된 다음을 가리키므로 (C) 다음에 (B)가 와야 한다. 그러므로 (A)-(C)-(B)의 순서가 적절하다.

10 (A) 긍정문이므로 already를 쓰는 것이 적절하다. yet: 부정문(아직), 의문문(벌써), (B) do의 목적어를 써야 하므로 What이 적절하다. (C) 결혼 첫날 '이래'라고 해야 하므로 Since가 적절하다. for+기간(~ 동안), since+기점(~부터[이후])

11 ⓐ와 ⑤: [역할·자격·기능·성질 따위를 나타내어] …으로서(전치사), ① …할 때(접속사), ② [비례] …함에 따라(접속사) ③ [보통 as ~ as ...로 형용사·부사 앞에서] …와 같은 정도로(앞의 as는 지시부사, 뒤의 as는 접속사), ④ [상태] …한 대로(접속사)

12 글쓴이의 아버지가 장롱을 살 돈을 어디에 썼는지는 대답할 수 없다. ① Mr. Seo. ② To buy a new chest for clothes. ③ No. ⑤ No.

13 선비의 삶을 사는 '대신에'라고 해야 하므로 instead of가 적절하다. instead of: ~ 대신에, ① ~에도 (불구하고), ② ~ 때문에, ③ ~에 더하여, 게다가, ⑤ ~에 더하여

14 ③의 his는 글쓴이의 아버지가 아니라 일반적인 '파락호'를 지칭한다.

15 ⓑ와 ④: ~하곤 했다(과거의 불규칙적 습관), ① 시제 일치에 의해 will(…일[할] 것이다)을 과거형 would로 쓴 것임. ② 정중히 요청을 할 때 씀, ③ would rather 동사원형(~했으면 좋겠다), ⑤ 정중한 제의·초대를 할 때 씀

16 if[whether]를 보충하면 된다.

17 이 글은 필자의 아버지가 파락호로 신분을 숨기고 독립 운동 자금을 대었다는 내용의 글이므로, 제목으로는 ②번 '파락호가 아니라 비밀 독립운동가'가 적절하다.

18 the reason why는 선행사와 관계부사 중에서 the reason이나 why 어느 한 쪽만 써도 된다.

19 (A) '말하곤 했다'라고 해야 하므로 과거의 불규칙적 습관을 나타내는 would가 적절하다. (B) 집안의 '재산을 탕진하는' 사람

이라고 해야 하므로 ruins가 적절하다. ruin one's fortune: 재산을 탕진하다, (C) 명사에 ed를 붙인 유사분사가 주격보어로 쓰인 것이므로 empty-handed가 적절하다. empty-handed: 빈손인

20 계속적 용법의 관계대명사는 '접속사+인칭대명사'로 바꿔 쓸 수 있다.

21 have no more money left: 남은 돈이 없다

서술형 시험대비

p.150~151

01 left
02 every time 또는 each time
03 Instead of living the life of a *seonbi*, he was always at the gambling house.
04 had devoted
05 Your father sent the independence fighters in Manchuria the family money.
06 whether
07 (A) independence fighters (B) a secret
08 (A) some money (B) new chest
09 (A) clothes (B) horrible (C) embarrassing
10 chest
11 There goes the *parakho's* daughter
12 that → which
13 (A) *parakho* (B) gambled

01 have no more money left: 더 이상 남은 돈이 없다

02 whenever = every time = each time: …할 때는 언제든지

03 앞 문장의 내용('선비의 삶을 사는 대신 그는 항상 도박장에 계셨다.')을 가리킨다.

04 독립 운동에 생애를 바친 것이 먼저 일어난 일이므로 과거완료로 쓰는 것이 적절하다.

05 to를 생략하고 '간접목적어+직접목적어' 순서로 쓰는 것이 적절하다.

06 if = whether: ~인지 아닌지

07 필자는 아버지를 파락호라고 오해했지만, 사실 그의 아버지는 가족의 돈을 만주에 있는 독립운동가들에게 보냈고 그 사실을 일본 순사들에게 비밀로 하기 위해 도박꾼처럼 보이게 했다.

08 신랑측 가족이 신부측 가족에게 옷을 넣을 새 장롱을 살 약간의 돈을 보내 주었다.

09 (A) '옷'을 넣을 장롱이라고 해야 하므로 clothes가 적절하다. cloths: cloth(옷감, 천)의 복수 clothes: 옷, 의복, (B) 그런 '끔찍한' 일이라고 해야 하므로 horrible이 적절하다. horrible: 끔찍한, terrific: 아주 좋은, 멋진, (C) 감정을 나타내는 동사는 감정을 유발할 때 현재분사를 쓰는 것이 적절하므로 embarrassing이 적절하다.

10 chest: (보통 나무로 만든) 상자, 장롱, 물건을 보관하기 위해 사용되는 크고 무거운 상자

11 There+동사+명사 주어

12 관계대명사 that은 계속적 용법으로 쓸 수 없기 때문에, which로 고치는 것이 적절하다.

13 gamble away one's fortune: 노름으로 가산을 탕진하다

영역별 핵심문제

p.153~157

01 ③, ④ 02 marriage 03 of
04 keeping 05 (A) is called (B) if 06 fortress
07 ④ 08 ① 09 ①
10 wooden 11 (A) Right. (B) who (C) made
12 general 13 ⑤ 14 ④
15 if[whether] he would forgive his fault
16 ⓑ, ⓓ, ⓔ 17 ③
18 (1) I was not sure if[whether] he was telling the truth.
(2) Rob wants to know if[whether] more men than women like gardening.
(3) I asked her if[whether] I could have a drink.
19 ⑤ 20 ⑤
21 because → why 22 ① 23 ②
24 (A) her father (B) new chest
25 (A) himself (B) keep (C) At first
26 ②, ④, ⑤ 27 ④ 28 had been 또는 was
29 ② 30 ④

01 ① 이상한 것은 그가 나를 못 알아본다는 점이었다. ② 이 나라는 독립 이후로 많은 발전을 이룩했다. ③ movement: (정치적·사회적) 운동 / 그는 인상주의 운동을 추종했다. ④ leave: 맡기다, 남기다 / 너는 아이들을 토요일에 할머니한테 맡겼니? ⑤ 옆 사람과 속삭이지 마세요.

02 주어진 단어는 동사와 명사의 관계이다. marry는 뒤에 –age를 붙여 명사형을 만든다. solve: 해결하다, 풀다 solution: 해결 marry: 결혼하다 marriage: 결혼

03 hear of ~: ~에 대해 듣다 / Big Star라고 불리는 밴드에 대해 들어 본 적 있니? instead of: ~ 대신에 / 내가 햄 대신에 참치를 먹어도 되나요?

04 keep a secret: 비밀을 지키다 / 대부분의 사람들은 비밀을 지키는 것을 잘하지 못한다. keep: (~한 상태를) 유지하다 awake: 깨어 있는 / Paul은 강한 블랙 커피를 많이 마심으로써 깨어 있었다.

05 (A) call이 5형식으로 사용하여 '[사람·물건을] (어떤 이름으로) 부르다, 이름을 붙이다'로 쓰일 수 있다. 원래는 'People call this the Geojunggi.'인 문장을 수동태로 바꿨으므로 is

called가 적절하다. (B) 어떤 일을 하기 전에 해도 되는지 허가 여부를 물을 때 'Is it okay if I ~?(제가 ~해도 될까요?)'라고 질문한다.

06 fortress: 요새 / 중요한 장소를 방어하기 위해 사용되는 크고 튼튼한 건물

07 ⓐ 거중기는 화성 요새를 지을 때 사용되었다.(○) ⓑ B는 화성 요새를 더 가까이 보기를 원했다. (화성 요새가 아닌 거중기를 더 가까이 보고 싶어 했다.) ⓒ 화성 요새는 28개월 동안에 지어졌다.(○) ⓓ 거중기는 기계의 일종이다. (○) ⓔ A는 거중기가 무엇인지 알고 있다.(○)

08 'How was ~?'는 상대방의 경험에 대해 묻는 표현으로, 대답 'It was wonderful.(좋았어요.)'과 어울리므로 ①이 적절하다.

09 ⓐ to, the chance to 동사원형: ~할 기회, to부정사가 the chance를 꾸며주고 있다. ⓑ if, Is it okay if I ~?: 제가 ~해도 될까요? ⓒ that, that은 remember의 목적어 자리에 들어가는 명사절을 이끄는 접속사로 사용됐다. ⓓ at, 시간 앞에는 전치사 at을 사용한다. ⓔ if, if: (접) ~한다면

10 ships를 수식하는 형용사가 들어갈 자리이다. wood: 나무, 목재 wooden: 나무로 된, 목재의

11 (A) (사람들이) 그가 12척의 나무 배로(목선으로) 전쟁을 이겼다고 말했으므로, 긍정의 대답이 나와야 한다. (B) 여기서 general은 '장군'이므로 사람을 선행사로 하는 주격 관계대명사 who[that]가 적절하다. (C) 목적어 creative plans가 있으므로 능동이 어울린다.

12 general: 장군 / 육군이나 공군에서 높은 계급을 가진 장교

13 명사절을 이끄는 접속사 if는 whether로 바꿔 쓸 수 있다.

14 When Megan arrived at the station, the train had already left for London. 도착하기 전에 이미 출발한 것이므로 도착한 것은 과거로, 출발한 것은 과거완료로 써야 한다.

15 명사절을 이끄는 접속사 if나 whether를 이용하고 주절이 과거시제이므로 will을 would로 써야 하는 것에 유의한다.

16 ⓐ has → had ⓒ had eaten → ate, made → had made ⓕ which → if[whether] ⓖ that → if[whether]

17 already로 보아 had already eaten과 같은 과거완료가 나와야 한다.

18 명사절을 이끄는 접속사 if[whether]를 이용한다.

19 ⑤번은 believe의 목적어를 이끄는 접속사 that이 적절하고 나머지는 모두 '~인지 (아닌지)'라는 의미의 명사절을 이끄는 접속사 if[whether]가 적절하다.

20 win a lot of money by gambling: 노름으로 돈을 많이 따다

21 '그것이 그가 파락호라고 불린 이유이다'라고 해야 하므로, because를 why로 고치는 것이 적절하다.

22 ①번 다음 문장의 the money에 주목한다. 주어진 문장의 some money를 받고 있으므로 ①번이 적절하다.

23 ⓐ와 ② 꼭, 바로(부사), ① 권리(명사), ③ 옳은(형용사) ④ 제대로 된(형용사), ⑤ (상태가) 좋은(형용사)

24 글쓴이는 Mr. Seo와 결혼하게 되었지만, '그녀의 아버지' 때문에 옷을 넣을 '새 장롱'을 살 수 없었다.

25 (A) 주어와 목적어가 같으므로 재귀대명사 himself가 적절하다. (B) '일본 경찰들로부터 이것을 비밀로 지키려고'라고 해야 하므로 keep이 적절하다. keep+O+O.C.+from A: A로부터 ~을 …로 지키다, stop A from B: A가 B하는 것을 막다, (C) '처음에는'이라고 해야 하므로 At first가 적절하다. for the first time: 처음으로

26 ⓐ와 ①, ③: 계속 용법, ② 경험 용법, ④ 결과 용법, ⑤ 완료 용법

27 'I realized that I had been wrong about him'을 통해 'ashamed'를, 'I have been proud'를 통해 'respectful'을 찾을 수 있다. ① ashamed: 부끄러운, ② respectful: 존경심을 보이는, ③ disappointed: 실망한

28 after가 있을 때는 시간의 전후관계가 분명하므로, 과거완료를 과거로 쓸 수 있다.

29 ② 위 글은 '전기'이다. ④ (신문•잡지의) 글, 기사, ⑤ 자서전

30 석방된 직후에 죽었다.

단원별 예상문제 p.158~161

01 ② 02 (1) so (2) such 03 ④
04 (1) (g)eneral (2) marriages (3) (o)bject (4) (s)ince
05 ① 06 ④
07 is it okay if I use the bathroom now?
08 (A) What are you reading? (B) Who is she?
09 ⓐ female ⓑ is said ⓒ that
10 biography 11 ⑤ 12 inventions
13 if[whether] she could go out 14 ④
15 ④ 16 ③, ⑤ 17 gambling house
18 ⓑ such a horrible thing ⓒ behind my back
19 has → had 20 ④ 21 ⑤
22 ①, ④ 23 (A) look like (B) Japanese officers
24 to look → look like
25 He sent the family money to the independence fighters in Manchuria.

01 ②번을 제외한 보기들은 뒤에 –ward(s)를 붙여 부사를 만들 수 있다. ① inward: 안으로 ③ afterwards: 후에, 나중에 ④ backwards: 뒤로 ⑤ forwards: 앞으로

02 (1) so+형용사/부사+that 주어 동사: 너무 ~해서 …하다 / 모든 것이 너무 변해서 나는 그 장소를 알아차리지 못했다. (2) such (a(n))+형용사+명사: 너무 ~한 명사 / 그는 너무 갑작스럽게 멈춰서 우리가 거의 그를 칠 뻔 했다.

03 (A) unwilling: 꺼려하는, 싫어하는 ask for: 청구하다, 청

하다 / 그는 항상 다른 사람에게 부탁하기를 꺼려한다. (B) devote one's life to 명사: ~에 일생을 바치다 / 그녀는 예술에 자신의 일생을 바치겠다고 발표했다.

04 (1) general: 장군 (2) marriage: 결혼, 혼인 (3) object: 물체, 물건 (4) since: ~이기 때문에

05 주어진 문장은 카레랑 비빔밥 중 무엇을 먹을지 묻는 질문이다. 이에 대한 대답으로 'I'd like to have *bibimbap*, please.'가 어울리므로 ①이 적절하다.

06 마지막 부분에서 여자가 좌석 불이 켜지면 좌석에 앉아야 한다고 말하는 것을 볼 때 대화는 항공기 안에서 이뤄지고 있다.

07 Is it okay if I ~?: 제가 ~해도 될까요? if 다음에는 주어와 동사 순으로 나온다. use: 사용하다 bathroom: 화장실

08 (A) Lisa가 권기옥에 대한 책을 읽고 있는 중이라고 대답하였으므로 무엇을 하고 있는지 묻는 질문이 어울린다. (B) Lisa가 권기옥에 대한 설명을 하고 있으므로, 그녀(권기옥)가 누구인지 물어보는 질문이 적절하다

09 ⓐ She가 주어이므로 female이 어울린다. male: 남성; 남성의 female: 여자; 여자의, 여성의 ⓑ, ⓒ It is said that 주어+동사 ~: (사람들이) ~라고 한다.

10 biography: 전기 / 누군가가 다른 누군가의 삶에 대해 쓴 책

11 남자는 조선 시대로 넘어가자고 얘기하면서 조선 시대의 유물들을 보여주며 그 중 하나인 자격루를 소개하고 있는 상황이다. As you can see: 보시다시피

12 invent: 발명하다 invention: 발명품, 발명

13 명사절을 이끄는 접속사 if나 whether를 이용하고 주절이 과거 시제이므로 will을 would로 써야 하는 것에 유의한다.

14 ④번은 '만약 ~한다면'의 의미로 부사절을 이끄는 접속사로 쓰였지만 나머지는 모두 '~인지 아닌지'라는 의미로 명사절을 이끄는 접속사로 쓰였다.

15 ① I told the story that I had read in the book. ② I couldn't find the pen which Dad had given to me. ③ After she had been[was] in prison for 6 months, she was released and died short after. ⑤ It was proved that the officials had taken bribes from him months before. bribe: 뇌물

16 ⓐ와 ①, ②, ④: 동명사, ③, ⑤: 현재분사

17 선비의 삶을 사는 대신 항상 '도박장'에 계셨기 때문이다.

18 ⓑ 'such a 형용사+명사'의 순서로 쓰는 것이 적절하다. ⓒ behind one's back: ~ 몰래

19 기준 시점보다 더 이전에 일어난 일이므로, 과거완료로 쓰는 것이 적절하다.

20 '결혼식 직전'에 돈을 가져갔다.

21 ⓐ keep+O+O.C.+from A: A로부터 ~을 …로 지키다, ⓑ devote A to B: A를 B에 바치다

22 (A)와 ②, ③, ⑤: 부사적 용법, ① 형용사적 용법, ④ 명사적 용법

23 필자의 아버지는 파락호가 아니라 가족의 돈을 만주에 있는 독립운동가들에게 보내는 사실을 '일본 순사들'에게 비밀로 하기 위해 그 자신을 도박꾼처럼 보이게 했다.

24 사역동사(made)+목적어+원형부정사, look like+명사: ~처럼 보이다

25 '그가 가족의 돈을 만주에 있는 독립 운동가들에게 보냈다.'는 것을 가리킨다.

서술형 실전문제 p.162~163

01 ⓐ Why? ⓒ He is going to be included in the social studies textbook in South Sudan.
ⓔ It is good to hear that students will learn about such a great person.

02 It is said that such stories will be included in the textbook. / People say that such stories will be included in the textbook.

03 (1) had left (2) had been closed

04 Is it okay if I bring in my water bottle? / Can I bring in my water bottle?

05 (1) It was the most interesting game that I had ever played.
(2) His wife was surprised to learn that he had already been fired without any warning.
(3) He could not decide if[whether] this was a fairy tale or a nightmare.
(4) I'm considering whether to accept his offer.

06 (1) I want to know if[whether] he can give her a recommendation.
(2) She could not open the door because she had left the key at school.

07 not, but

08 Bring more money to me!

09 marry with → marry

10 글쓴이의 아버지가 장롱을 살 돈을 가지고 간 것

11 her father, money

01 ⓐ 남자가 그 사람에 대해서 들어본 적이 있다고 했는데, 그 사람이 누구인지 묻는 것은 앞뒤가 맞지 않는다. 여자가 이태석 신부의 이야기가 교과서에 실린다는 말을 하고 있으므로 남자는 이태석 신부를 아는지 물어본 이유에 대해서 질문하는 것이 적절하다. ⓒ 그의 이야기가 교과서에 포함되어지는 것이므로 수동태로 써야 한다. ⓔ 학생들이 훌륭한 사람에 대해서 배우는 일은 듣기 좋은 것이므로 bad를 good으로 바꿔야 한다.

02 알고 있는 내용을 진술할 때 'It is said that 주어+동사 ~.'나

'They[People] say (that) 주어+동사 ~.'을 쓸 수 있다.

03 (1) 기억하는 시점보다 앞선 시점에 문을 열어 놓은 것이므로 과거완료를 이용한다. (2) 도착한 시점보다 앞선 시점에 문이 닫힌 것이므로 과거완료를 이용한다. 수동태로 써야 하는 것에 주의한다.

04 'Is it okay if I ~?'는 '제가 ~해도 될까요?'라는 뜻으로 어떤 행동을 하기 전에 허가를 요청할 때 사용하는 표현이다. 이외의 허가를 구하는 다른 표현으로 'Can I ~?' 가 있다.

05 (1) 과거의 어느 시점까지 게임을 해 본 것이므로 과거완료로 나타내는 것이 적절하다. (2) 해고된 것이 앞선 일이고 already가 있으므로 과거완료로 나타내는 것이 적절하다. (3) 뒤에 or a nightmare가 나오므로 that을 if나 whether로 고치는 것이 적절하다. (4) if는 to부정사와 함께 쓰이지 않으므로 if를 whether로 고치는 것이 적절하다. nightmare: 악몽

06 (1) '~인지 (아닌지)'라는 의미의 명사절을 이끄는 접속사 if[whether]를 이용한다. (2) 열쇠를 두고 온 것이 문을 열지 못하는 시점보다 앞서므로 과거완료로 써야 한다.

07 not A but B = instead of A, B = B instead of A

08 bring은 to를 사용하여 3형식으로 고친다.

09 marry는 타동사이므로 전치사 with 없이 목적어를 쓰는 것이 적절하다.

10 글쓴이의 어머니가 말한 "Your father has taken the money for the chest."를 가리킨다.

11 '그녀의 아버지'가 장롱을 살 '돈'을 가져갔기 때문이다.

창의사고력 서술형 문제 p.164

|모범답안|

01 A: Is it okay if I borrow your bicycle? / Can[May] I borrow your bicycle? / I'm wondering if I can borrow your bicycle.
B: I'm sorry. It's broken.

02 (1) if[whether] she is reading
(2) had memorized

03 (A) female independence fighter
(B) to fight for independence
(C) built schools and educated women
(D) six months (E) an award

01 'Is it okay if I ~?'는 '제가 ~해도 될까요?'라는 뜻으로 어떤 행동을 하기 전에 허가를 요청할 때 사용하는 표현이다. if 다음에는 허락을 구하는 내용을 쓴다. 허가를 묻는 다른 표현으로는 'Can I ~?' 등이 있다. borrow: 빌리다 broken: 고장 난

단원별 모의고사 p.165~169

01 ⓑ to spend → to spending 02 at
03 (1) biography (2) female (3) locker (4) detective
04 (1) movement (2) inventions (3) getting
05 ② 06 ④
07 (A) is called (B) it 08 ③
09 It is said that it is the oldest and the largest water clock in Korea.
10 ① 11 scholar
12 It is said that he was also a detective.
13 ④ 14 ③
15 (1) if[whether] the school lunch is delicious
(2) if[whether] it's all right to sit next to her
(3) had already eaten
16 (1) Would you please check if[whether] I filled out this card right?
(2) I don't know if[whether] my mom likes potato pizza.
(3) I am not sure if[whether] Mike will meet Judy at 3 o'clock.
(4) He insisted that he had never heard a girl crying that night.
(5) I decided to come home earlier than I had planned. 17 ⑤
18 (1) had been sold out (2) had never met
19 ①, ②, ③ 20 good memories
21 they called him a *parakho* 22 ①
23 ④ 24 ②, ④ 25 himself 26 ②
27 who[that] had devoted his life to the independence movement 28 ③

01 ⓐ so+형용사/부사+that 주어+동사: 너무 ~해서 …하다 / 땅의 표면이 너무 뜨거워서 녹았다. ⓑ be used to 동명사: ~하는 데 익숙하다 / 아이들은 그들의 많은 자유 시간을 TV 보는 데 쓰는 것에 익숙하다. ⓒ by 동사ing: ~함으로써 / 나는 내 집을 팔아서 새 차를 사기를 바랐다.

02 at that moment: 그 순간에 / 바로 그 순간, 당신은 나에게 다가와서 내게 설명할 기회도 주지 않고 딱지를 끊었어요. yell at: ~에게 고함치다 / 나에게 그렇게 소리치지 마.

03 (1) biography: 전기 / 나는 아브라함 링컨의 전기를 읽었다. (2) female: 여자; 여자의, 여성의 / 오은선은 한국의 여성 등반가이다. (3) locker: 사물함 / 제 사물함 열쇠를 어디서 받을 수 있나요? (4) detective: 형사, 탐정 / 그 탐정은 약간의 증거를 찾았다.

04 (1) movement: (정치적·사회적) 운동 (2) invention: 발명품, 발명 (3) be used to 동명사 ~하는 데 익숙하다

05 ⓐ take ⓑ know ⓒ bring ⓓ leave

06 ① 남자가 물병을 박물관 안에 가지고 들어갈 수 있나요? (네) ② 남자는 지금 어디에 있는가? (박물관) ③ 박물관에 사물함이 있나요? (네) ④ 박물관 안에서 사진을 찍을 수 있나요?(답할 수 없음) ⑤ 남자가 가방을 박물관 안에 가지고 들어갈 수 있나요? (아니요)

07 (A) 이것이 '자격루'라고 불리는 것이므로 수동태를 사용해야 한다. (B) *Jagyeongnu*를 가리키고 있으므로 'it'으로 받아야 한다.

08 actually: 사실은, 실제로 in fact: 사실은

10 주어진 문장의 it은 남자가 본 영화를 의미이므로 ①번이 적절하다.

11 scholar: 학자 / 특히 과학적인 주제가 아닌 특정한 주제에 대해 공부하고 많이 아는 사람

12 It is said that 주어+동사 ~: (사람들이) ~라고 한다 also: 또한 detective: 형사, 탐정

13 동사 know 뒤에 목적어 자리로 명사절을 이끄는 접속사 that이 어울린다.

14 if는 'if or not'의 형태로 쓰이지 않으므로 if만 쓰거나 or not을 '~ it or not.'의 형태로 문장의 뒷부분에 써야 한다.

15 (1) 의문사가 없는 간접의문문에 쓰인 if[whether]이다. (2) 명사절을 이끄는 접속사 if[whether]를 이용한다. (3) 점심을 먹은 것이 앞선 시점이고 already가 있으므로 과거완료로 쓰는 것이 적절하다.

16 (1) 명사절을 이끄는 접속사 if[whether]를 이용한다. (2) 의문사가 없는 간접의문문에 쓰인 if[whether]이다. (3) I am not sure의 목적어로는 접속사 if[whether]를 이용하는 것이 적절하다. (4) 주장하는 시점보다 듣지 못한 시점이 앞서므로 과거완료로 쓰는 것이 적절하다. (5) 결정하는 시점보다 계획한 시점이 앞서므로 과거완료로 쓰는 것이 적절하다.

17 ⑤ I'm not sure if she made a mistake or not.

18 과거의 어느 시점보다 먼저 일어난 일이나 상태를 나타낼 때 과거완료를 사용한다.

19 ⓐ와 ①, ②, ③: 동명사, ④, ⑤: 현재분사

20 아버지에 대한 '좋은 기억'을 가지고 있지 않았기 때문이다.

21 they를 주어로 하여 능동태로 고치는 것이 적절하다.

22 ⓐ와 ①, ②, ③, ⑤: 관계대명사, ④: 의문대명사

23 신랑 집에서 장롱을 사라고 준 돈을 신부의 아버지가 결혼식 전에 가져가 버렸기 때문에, '난처한'이 적절하다. ② 만족스러운, ⑤ (감탄스럽도록) 놀라운

24 ⓐ와 ②, ④: 완료 용법, ① 결과 용법, ③ 계속 용법, ⑤ 경험 용법

25 주어와 목적어가 같은 사람이므로 재귀대명사를 써야 한다.

26 at first: 처음에

27 devote A to B: A를 B에 바치다

28 필자의 아버지는 '일본 순사들'로부터 자신의 신분을 비밀로 지키려고 도박꾼처럼 보이기를 원했다.

Music to My Ears!

시험대비 실력평가 p.174

01 positive 02 ① 03 ① 04 ②
05 (1) treasure (2) shocked (3) thumb (4) pure (5) recommend
06 (1) We had dinner at a local restaurant.
(2) He worked as a cherry picker.
(3) My life would be worthless without music.

01 주어진 단어는 반의어 관계이다. positive: 긍정적인, negative: 부정적인
02 '오케스트라나 합창단의 공연을 지휘하는 사람'을 가리키는 말은 'conductor(지휘자)'이다.
03 주어진 문장에서 beat은 박자를 나타내며 이와 같은 의미로 쓰인 것은 ①번이다. 나머지는 모두 '때리다, 두드리다'를 나타낸다.
04 entirely: 전적으로, 완전히
05 thumb: 엄지손가락, shocked: 충격을 받은, pure: 깨끗한, 순수한, treasure: 보물, recommend: 추천하다
06 local: 현지의, picker: 채집자, worthless: 가치 없는

서술형 시험대비 p.175

01 wide
02 (1) (s)erious (2) (d)eliver (3) (a)ttention (4) (r)eview (5) (t)reasure
03 (1) There was an endless line at the bank.
(2) All the members are unique and talented.
(3) Fine dust is an environmental disaster.
04 (1) draw on (2) in harmony with (3) calm down (4) eager to (5) as long as
05 (1) place your index finger on the finger scanner
(2) The old man puts his heart into making nice shoes.
(3) We should bring the matter to their attention.

01 주어진 단어는 반의어 관계이다. wide: 넓은, narrow: 좁은
02 serious: 심각한, deliver a speech: 연설하다 attention: 관심, review: 복습하다, treasure: 보물
03 endless: 끝없는, talented: 재능 있는, environmental: 환경의, fine dust: 미세 먼지
04 as long as: ~하는 한, be eager to: ~하고 싶어 하다, in harmony with: ~와 조화를 이루어, calm down: 진정하다, draw on: ~을 활용하다
05 index finger: 집게손가락, put one's heart into: ~에 정열을 쏟다, ~에 열중하다, bring ~ to one's attention: ~에 …가 주목하게 하다

교과서
Conversation

핵심 Check p.176~177

1 Do you find it interesting to sing in the choir?
2 (C) → (B) → (A)

교과서 대화문 익히기

Check(√) True or False p.178

1 T 2 F 3 T 4 F

교과서 확인학습 p.180~181

Listen & Talk 1 A-1
won, competition, Congratulations / compete, find it helpful / keeps, awake

Listen & Talk 1 A-2
off / choir practice / forgot, choir, find, interesting / in harmony with

Listen & Talk 1-B
you recorded / find it easy to write them / beginning, draw on, keep a journal / No pain, no gain

Listen & Talk 2 A-1
sign up for / Are you planning to / perform / violin, cello

Listen & Talk 2 A-2
sign up for / take the class / planning, offer / another one, Both / sign up

Listen & Talk 2-B
musical instrument, recommend, is similar to, Playing, thumb nails

Communication

something / up / which seat I should choose / orchestra / orchestra / get the seats, various musical instruments / from the second floor / find it better

Wrap Up

been / I've read / have you / for visiting / find / post, latest / spread

시험대비 기본평가 p.182

01 Do you find it interesting to sing in the choir?

02 ⑤ 03 (E) → (D) → (C) → (A) → (B)

02 Chris는 동생의 연주를 보러 콘서트에 갈 것이다.

03 (E) 장기 자랑 등록 기한 질문 → (D) 대답 및 계획 질문 → (C) 장기 자랑 계획 대답 → (A) 반응 및 구체적 계획 질문 → (B) 구체적 계획 대답

시험대비 실력평가 p.183~184

01 Do you find it easy to write them? 02 ①

03 ⓒ → compete 04 ⑤

05 She should sign up for the talent show by Friday.

06 Her plan is to play K-pop music with the violin and cello with a couple of people.

07 It is a small African musical instrument.

08 It is similar to the sound of a music box.

09 I should use my thumb nails to play the *kalimba*.

10 ③ 11 ③ 12 ④

02 수진이 '다시 만나 반갑습니다.'라고 인사한 것으로 보아 Jason을 처음 만난 것이 아님을 알 수 있다.

03 접속사 뒤에 절이 이어지므로 동사 compete가 적절하다.

04 Jake가 일에 집중하기 위해 수영할 필요가 있다는 설명은 대화의 내용과 일치하지 않는다.

05 Megan은 금요일까지 장기 자랑 등록을 마쳐야 한다.

06 Megan은 몇 사람과 함께 공연을 할 것이다.

07 칼림바는 아프리카의 작은 악기이다.

08 칼림바는 음악 상자의 소리와 비슷하다.

09 칼림바를 연주하기 위해 엄지손톱을 사용해야 한다.

10 'Yes, I do.'라는 대답이 적절하다.

11 주어진 문장은 수업을 주중에 들을 건지 주말에 들을 건지에 대한 대답으로 적절하므로 (C)에 와야 한다.

12 주중 드럼 수업은 정각 6시로 서로 같다.

서술형 시험대비 p.185

01 Are you planning to sign up for it

02 Her team is going to play the violin and cello.

03 Are you planning to learn a musical instrument?

04 (B) is (C) Playing

05 (A) winning the swimming (B) he competes
(C) it keeps him awake and it helps him focus

06 Do you find it interesting to post the latest pop news?

02 Megan의 팀은 바이올린과 첼로를 연주할 것이다.

04 (B) 주어가 3인칭 단수이므로 'is', (C)는 주어로 동명사 'Playing'이 적절하다.

05 Anna는 Jake에게 어제 수영대회에서 우승한 것을 축하했다. 그녀는 왜 Jake가 항상 경기 전에 음악을 듣는지 알고 싶었다. Jake는 이것이 그를 깨어 있게 하고 집중하는 데 도움을 준다고 말했다.

교과서

Grammar

핵심 Check p.186~187

1 (1) written (2) singing (3) rolling

2 (1) it (2) to

시험대비 기본평가 p.188

01 ⑤

02 (1) smiling (2) hidden (3) wearing (4) planted

03 ③

04 (1) The concert began with a girl playing Bach's *Cello Suite No. 1* on her shiny cello.
(2) He bought a car made in Korea.
(3) Anna finds it fun to play the piano.

01 to부정사구가 목적어로 쓰일 때, to부정사를 문장의 맨 뒤에 쓰고 목적어 자리에 가목적어 it을 쓴 것이다.

02 (1) 소녀가 웃고 있는 것이므로 능동의 의미를 갖는 현재분사가 적절하다. (2) 비용이 감춰진 것이므로 수동의 의미를 갖는 과거분사가 적절하다. (3) 소녀가 안경을 끼는 것이므로 능동의 의미를 갖는 현재분사가 적절하다. (4) 나무들이 심겨진 것이므로 수동의 의미를 갖는 과거분사가 적절하다.

03 목적격보어가 있는 5형식 문장에서 길이가 긴 to부정사구가 목적어로 쓰일 때, 보통 목적어 자리에 가목적어 it을 쓰고 to부정사는 문장의 맨 뒤에 쓴다. 이때 진목적어는 to 이하이다.

04 (1) 'playing Bach's *Cello Suite No. 1* on her shiny cello'가 a girl을 뒤에서 수식하도록 영작한다. (2) 차가 만들어지는 것이므로 수동의 의미를 갖는 과거분사를 이용한다. (3) it을 가목적어로 하고 to부정사를 진목적어로 하여 영작한다.

시험대비 실력평가

p.189~191

01 ② 02 ③ 03 ①
04 (1) for (2) it (3) to achieve (4) talking (5) frightened (6) complaining
05 ⑤ 06 ⑤ 07 ③ 08 ④
09 ② 10 ④ 11 ① 12 ③
13 ④ 14 ① 15 ② 16 ④, ⑤
17 (1) An autograph is something that[which] is written by a person, not a machine.
(2) The image of a girl who[that] is playing chess with the statue was taken on Jan. 7.
18 ②, ③

01 make 동사는 to부정사가 목적어로 나올 때 반드시 가목적어 it을 써야 한다. The new law made it possible for teenagers to drive.

02 '게시된' 결과이므로 현재분사가 아니라 과거분사가 되어야 한다.

03 첫 번째 빈칸에는 노래를 하는 것이므로 진행의 뜻을 갖는 현재분사가 적절하다. 두 번째 빈칸에는 가목적어 역할을 하는 it이 적절하다.

04 (1) 전체 문장과 to부정사구의 행위의 주체가 다르므로 의미상의 주어로 to부정사구의 주체를 나타내야 하며, 주로 'for+목적격'의 형태로 to부정사 앞에 쓴다. (2) 가목적어이므로 it이 적절하다. (3) 진목적어이므로 to부정사가 적절하다. (4) '말을 하는' 것이므로 능동의 뜻을 갖는 현재분사가 적절하다. (5) 아이가 '놀라게 된' 것이므로 수동의 뜻을 갖는 과거분사가 적절하다. (6) 고객이 '불평하는' 것이므로 능동의 뜻을 갖는 현재분사가 적절하다. 현재분사가 앞에서 수식하는 경우이다.

05 ⑤번은 현재완료에 쓰였고 나머지는 모두 앞에 나오는 명사를 수식하는 형용사적 용법이다.

06 앞에 의미상의 주어로 'for+목적격'이 나왔으므로 'to sing'이 적절하다.

07 '어린 왕자'가 쓰여진 것이므로 수동의 뜻을 갖는 과거분사가 적절하다.

08 ④번은 가목적어로 쓰였지만 나머지는 모두 시간이나 날씨, 거리 등을 나타내는 비인칭 주어이다.

09 분사에 다른 어구(여기서는 a letter)가 함께 있을 때는 뒤에서 명사를 수식한다.

10 think 동사의 경우 to부정사구가 목적어로 나올 때 가목적어 it을 쓰고 to부정사구를 진목적어로 문장의 뒷부분에 쓴다.

11 노래가 불리어지고 사랑받는 것이므로 수동의 의미를 나타내는 과거분사가 적절하며 이것은 '주격 관계대명사+be동사'가 생략된 것으로 볼 수 있다.

12 ① 가주어 ② 대명사 ③ 가목적어 ④ 비인칭 주어 ⑤ 인칭대명사 *goose bumps: 소름

13 책을 읽고 있는 것이므로 진행의 의미를 가지는 현재분사 reading이 되어야 한다. 접속사 없이 동사 reads와 is 두 개가 나올 수 없음에 유의한다.

14 ① 접속사 that ② It was ~ that 강조 구문 ③, ⑤ 가목적어 it ④ 가주어 It

15 첫 번째 빈칸에는 회의가 개최한 것이 아니라 '개최된' 것이므로 수동의 뜻을 갖는 과거분사가 적절하다. 두 번째 빈칸에는 음식이 무엇을 제공하는 것이 아니라 '제공되는' 것이므로 수동의 뜻을 갖는 과거분사가 적절하다.

16 지각동사 see의 목적격보어로 동사원형이나 현재분사가 적절하다. 또 쓰레기로 가득 차 있는 것이므로 수동의 의미를 갖는 과거분사가 적절하며 분사가 명사를 뒤에서 수식하는 경우에는 그 앞에 '주격 관계대명사+be동사'가 생략된 것으로 생각할 수 있다.

17 분사가 명사를 뒤에서 수식하는 경우에는 그 앞에 '주격 관계대명사+be동사'가 생략된 것으로 생각할 수 있다.

18 ② 가목적어로 that이 아니라 it을 쓴다. ③ 누워 있는 것이므로 능동의 의미를 갖는 현재분사 lying이 적절하다.

서술형 시험대비

p.192~193

01 (1) it (2) for (3) to
02 (1) I want people to know that even something worthless can make inspiring music.
(2) The teacher made it clear for the students to do their homework.
(3) Stravinsky considered it helpful to stand on his head for 15 minutes every morning.
03 (1) There is an old family photo which[that] is hanging on the wall.
(2) Only the people who[that] are invited to the meeting can attend the meeting.

04 (1) to draw pictures using his imagination
(2) to do experiments at a science lab
(3) to memorize all the poems in the book
05 (1) painting (2) painted (3) wearing (4) written
06 (1) playing (2) satisfied, written (3) playing
07 (1) it, to play
(2) it, to listen
08 (1) walked → walking (2) lain → lying
(3) calling → called (4) that → it
(5) of → for (6) visiting → to visit
(7) to carry out our design at once necessary → it necessary to carry out our design at once
09 (1) to support (2) for you to do it

01 (1) 가목적어이므로 it을 쓴다. (2) 의미상의 주어로 for를 쓴다. (3) 의미상의 주어로 'for+목적격'이 나와 있으므로 진목적어로 to부정사를 쓴다.

02 (1) 영감을 주는 것이므로 능동의 뜻을 갖는 현재분사를 이용한다. (2), (3) '가목적어(it)+의미상의 주어(for목적격)+진목적어(to부정사)' 구문을 이용한다.

03 분사가 명사를 뒤에서 수식하는 경우에는 그 앞에 '주격 관계대명사+be동사'가 생략된 것으로 생각할 수 있다.

04 가목적어 it은 긴 to부정사구가 목적어로 쓰일 때 to부정사구를 문장의 맨 뒤로 보내고 그 목적어 자리에 it을 쓴 것이고, 가주어 It은 주어 역할을 하는 to부정사구를 뒤로 보내고 가짜 주어인 it을 그 자리에 쓴 것이다.

05 (1) 그녀의 모습을 그리는 것이므로 현재분사를 이용한다. (2) 초콜릿 꽃이 그려진 것이므로 과거분사를 이용한다. (3) 모자를 쓰고 있는 것이므로 현재분사를 이용한다. (4) 편지가 씌여진 것이므로 과거분사를 이용한다.

06 (1) 학생들이 축구를 하는 것이므로 진행의 뜻을 갖는 현재분사를 이용한다. (2) 선생님이 만족해하고, 편지가 쓰여지는 것이므로 수동의 뜻을 갖는 과거분사를 이용한다. (3) 기타를 치고 있는 것이므로 진행의 뜻을 갖는 현재분사를 이용한다.

07 '가목적어(it)+목적격보어+진목적어(to부정사)' 구문을 이용한다.

08 (1) 진행의 의미를 나타내므로 현재분사로 고친다. (2) 남자가 누워 있는 것이므로 현재분사로 고친다. lie-lay-lain, lying (3) 음악 그룹이 "The Junk Orchestra"라고 불리는 것이므로 과거분사로 고친다. (4) 가목적어로는 that이 아니라 it을 쓴다. (5) 의미상의 주어로 for를 쓴다. (6) 의미상의 주어로 'for us'가 나와 있으므로 to부정사가 진목적어가 되어야 한다. (7) think, find, believe 등의 동사는 to부정사구가 목적어로 나오면 반드시 가목적어 it을 써야 한다.

09 '가목적어(it)+목적격보어+진목적어(to부정사)' 구문을 이용하여 같은 뜻의 문장으로 고쳐 쓸 수 있다.

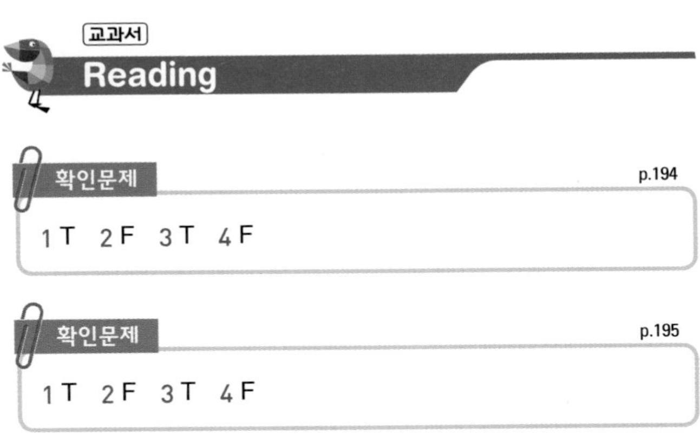
교과서
Reading

확인문제 p.194
1 T 2 F 3 T 4 F

확인문제 p.195
1 T 2 F 3 T 4 F

교과서 확인학습 A p.196~197

01 Junk 02 written by
03 garbage, music
04 on the back of
05 was called 06 made entirely out of
07 was eager to find out
08 sound strange
09 After a few minutes
10 The first thing I noticed
11 with a girl playing, on
12 was shocked by
13 was, into, made from recycled materials
14 was eager to write
15 the conductor
16 Why did you start
17 to work on, was mostly filled with
18 something positive, share, with
19 to make instruments
20 garbage, treasure
21 a local garbage picker
22 out of garbage
23 The wonderful thing, didn't have to worry about
24 through 25 worthless, inspiring music
26 as long as, into
27 not by instruments
29 how 30 endless
31 played with
32 Not only do, bring, to our attention

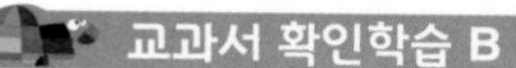

교과서 확인학습 B

p.198~199

1 The Junk Orchestra
2 written by a music blogger, Lucy White
3 "The world sends us garbage, we send back music."
4 This was written on the back of a concert ticket I was given.
5 The musical group was called "The Junk Orchestra."
6 They played instruments made entirely out of garbage.
7 I could not imagine what kind of sound these instruments would make, so I was eager to find out.
8 Before the concert, I thought that the instruments might sound strange.
9 After a few minutes, a group of young people began to walk on the stage.
10 The first thing I noticed was their instruments: a cello made out of a shiny oil tank, a violin made with forks, and a flute made with a water pipe and buttons.
11 The concert began with a girl playing Bach's *Cello Suite No. 1* on her shiny cello.
12 I was shocked by the deep sound.
13 I was so into the music that I forgot that they were playing with instruments made from recycled materials.
14 After the concert, I was eager to write a story about the orchestra.
15 I met Favio Chávez, the conductor, and asked him about the orchestra.
16 Lucy White: Why did you start The Junk Orchestra?
17 Favio Chávez: When I went to a small town called Cateura in Paraguay to work on a recycling program in 2005, I saw children living in a town that was mostly filled with garbage.
18 I wanted to add something positive to their lives, so I decided to share my love of music with them.
19 Lucy White: Why did you use garbage to make instruments?
20 Favio Chávez: One person's garbage is another person's treasure.
21 Nicolás Gómez, a local garbage picker, helped me a lot.
22 He made it possible for children to play music by making instruments out of garbage.
23 The wonderful thing about these instruments was that the children didn't have to worry about spending a lot of money on them.
24 Lucy White: What do you want people to learn through your music?
25 Favio Chávez: I want people to know that even something worthless can make inspiring music.
26 After interviewing Chávez, I realized that it really doesn't matter what instrument you play with as long as you put your heart into playing it.
27 The children of Cateura showed me that an orchestra is formed by people, not by instruments.
28 Comments
29 Annie: (23 seconds ago) So moving to see how music can change lives.
30 The power of music is endless!
31 Thomas: (1 minute ago) After the concert, I found it possible to inspire people by music played with recycled instruments.
32 Kate: (5 days ago) Not only do these talented young people deliver great music, but they also bring serious environmental problems to our attention.

시험대비 실력평가

p.200~203

01 into → out of　02 ②, ⑤
03 ③　04 ⑤　05 ③　06 ②
07 ③　08 ①, ④　09 have　10 ②
11 with a girl playing Bach's *Cello Suite No. 1*
12 ④　13 ②　14 children
15 the orchestra　16 ① of → for
17 ⑤　18 ③　19 important
20 ①, ⑤　21 touching　22 recycling → recycled
23 Not only do these talented young people deliver great music

01 '쓰레기로만 만들어진' 악기라고 해야 하므로 into를 out of로 고치는 것이 적절하다. 재료 be made into 제품, 제품 be made out of 재료, (made 앞에 which were가 생략됨.)

02 be eager to=be anxious to = long to: ~하기를 갈망하다 ③ be likely to: ~할 것 같다, ④ pay attention to: ~에 유의하다

03 '나는 이런 악기들이 어떤 종류의 소리를 낼지 상상할 수 없었고, 그래서 나는 알아보고 싶어졌다.'라고 했으므로 뒤에 올 내용으로

는 '이런 악기들의 소리를 알아보기'가 적절하다.

04 ⓐ begin with: ~으로 시작하다, ⓑ on: ('수단'을 나타내어) ~으로[~에]

05 이 글은 '재활용된 재료들로 만들어진 악기로 멋진 연주를 한 음악회에 관한' 내용의 글이므로, 제목으로는 ③번 '믿을 수 없어! 재활용된 재료들로 만들어진 악기에서 이런 깊은 소리가 난다고?'가 적절하다.

06 전반부의 'I thought that the instruments might sound strange.'를 통해 'anxious'를, 후반부의 'I was shocked by the deep sound.'를 통해 'satisfied'를 찾을 수 있다. anxious: 불안해하는, 염려하는, ① nervous: 초조한, disappointed: 실망한

07 Favio Chávez는 파라과이의 카테우라라고 불리는 작은 마을 어린이들의 삶에 긍정적인 무엇인가를 더해 주고 싶어서, 음악에 대한 그의 사랑을 그들과 나누기로 결정했다고 했으므로, 빈칸에 들어갈 질문으로는 ③번 '왜 당신은 정크 오케스트라를 시작하셨나요?'가 적절하다.

08 ⓑ와 ①, ④: 부사적 용법, ②, ⑤: 명사적 용법, ③: 형용사적 용법

09 have something in common (with somebody): (관심사·생각 등을) 공통적으로 지니다

10 악기의 재료에 '숟가락'은 속하지 않는다.

11 begin with+명사: ~로 시작하다, 소녀가 첼로를 연주하고 있는 주체이므로 능동이나 진행의 의미를 가지는 현재분사구를 써서 a girl을 후치 수식하도록 하는 것이 적절하다.

12 음악회의 첫 번째 음악은 '첼로'곡이었다.

13 쓰레기로 가득 차 있는 마을에 살고 있는 어린이들의 삶에 '긍정적인' 무엇인가를 더해 주고 싶었다고 하는 것이 적절하다. ① 수동적인, ③ 일시적인, 임시의, ④ 일반[보편/전반]적인, ⑤ 영구[영속]적인

14 '어린이들'을 가리킨다.

15 '그 오케스트라'에 대한 이야기를 몹시 쓰고 싶었기 때문이다.

16 진목적어인 to play의 의미상의 주어이므로 for children으로 쓰는 것이 적절하다.

17 ⓐ와 ⑤: 가목적어, ① 비인칭 주어, ② [3인칭 단수 중성 목적격](인칭대명사), ③ 가주어, ④ It is[was] ~ who[that] … 강조 구문에 쓰이는 It

18 Nicolás Gómez가 왜 Favio Chávez를 많이 도왔는지는 알 수 없다. ① Because one person's garbage is another person's treasure. ② He was a local garbage picker. ④ The children didn't have to worry about spending a lot of money on them. ⑤ He wants people to know that even something worthless can make inspiring music.

19 matter = be important: 중요하다

20 as long as = as far as = so long as: ~하는 한, ② ~에 더하여, 게다가, ③ ~만큼, ~ 못지 않게, ④ ~하자마자

21 moving = touching: 감동적인

22 재활용되어진 악기이므로, recycling을 과거분사 recycled로 고치는 것이 적절하다.

23 'do'를 보충하면 된다. not only라는 부사가 문장 맨 앞에 쓰였기 때문에, 조동사 do가 주어 these talented young people보다 앞에 쓰여 도치가 되도록 쓰는 것이 적절하다.

서술형 시험대비 p.204~205

01 was given
02 (a) garbage (b) music
03 I could not imagine what kind of sound these instruments would make
04 (A) strange (B) shocked (C) recycled
05 instruments
06 a shiny oil tank
07 the instrument
08 not, but
09 called
10 I saw children living in a town mostly filled with garbage.
11 (A) his love of music (B) something positive
12 need
13 priceless → worthless 또는 valueless

01 나에게 '주어진'(내가 받은) 음악회 입장권이라고 해야 하므로, 수동태로 쓰는 것이 적절하다.

02 우리는 '쓰레기'를 재활용해서 악기를 만들고, 그 악기를 연주해서 '음악'을 공연한다.

03 동사 imagine의 목적어 역할을 하는 간접의문문이 되도록, '의문사+주어+동사'의 순서로 쓰는 것이 적절하다.

04 (A) 감각동사 sound 뒤에 형용사 보어를 써야 하므로 strange가 적절하다. (B) 감정을 나타내는 동사는 감정을 느끼게 되는 대상과 함께 쓰일 경우에는 과거분사를 써야 하므로 shocked가 적절하다. (C) '재활용된' 재료들이라고 해야 하므로 recycled가 적절하다.

05 글쓴이가 처음으로 알아차린 것은 그들의 '악기'였다.

06 음악회는 한 소녀가 '반짝이는 기름통'으로 만들어진 자신의 첼로로 바흐의 <첼로 모음곡 1번>을 연주하는 것으로 시작되었다.

07 '악기'를 가리킨다.

08 not A but B = B, not A: A가 아니라 B

09 카테우라라고 '불리는' 작은 마을이라고 해야 하므로 과거분사로 쓰는 것이 적절하다.

10 'that was(주격 관계대명사+be동사)'를 생략할 수 있다.

11 Favio Chávez가 2005년에 재활용 프로그램에서 일을 하기 위해서 파라과이의 카테우라에 갔을 때, 그는 대부분이 쓰레기로 가득 차 있는 마을에 살고 있는 어린이들의 삶에 '긍정적인 무엇인가'를 더해 주고 싶어서, '음악에 대한 그의 사랑'을 그들과 나누기로 결정했다.

12 didn't have to = didn't need to

13 '가치 없는' 것도 영감을 주는 음악을 만들어 낼 수 있다는 것을 사람들이 알게 되기를 원한다고 해야 하므로 priceless를 worthless 또는 valueless로 고치는 것이 적절하다. priceless: 값을 매길 수 없는, 대단히 귀중한, worthless = valueless: 가치 없는, 무가치한

영역별 핵심문제 p.207~211

01 survival　02 ③

03 (1) stand on your head　(2) keep, awake
(3) sign up for　(4) work out

04 ⑤　05 ⑤　06 ⑤　07 ③

08 ③　09 ③　10 ①　11 ⑤

12 ⓐ → I should　13 ⑤　14 ①, ③

15 ⑤　16 it, to sew

17 (1) who[that] were　(2) who[that] was, which[that] was

18 ②　19 ⓐ, ⓒ, ⓔ

20 The deep sound shocked me.

21 a group of young people

22 two thousand (and) five　23 ③

24 It was that the children didn't have to worry about spending a lot of money on them.

25 ⑤

26 even something worthless can make inspiring music

27 be cheered up　28 up me → me up

01 주어진 단어는 동사와 명사의 관계를 나타낸다. survive: 살아남다, survival: 생존

02 '다른 목적으로 무언가를 다시 사용하다'를 가리키는 말은 'recycle(재활용하다)'이다.

04 mostly 주로, 대부분

05 notice는 동사로 '알아차리다', 명사로는 '공지, 알림, 통지'를 뜻한다.

06 주어진 문장에서 touch는 '감동시키다'를 나타내며 이와 같은 의미로 쓰인 것은 ⑤번이다. 나머지는 모두 '만지다'를 뜻한다.

07 이어지는 대답에서 Jake가 음악의 장점을 설명하고 있으므로 도움이 되는지 여부를 묻는 질문이 적절하다.

08 (A) be off to: ~로 떠나다, (B) 목적어를 이끄는 접속사 that이 적절하다. (C) '흥미로운'을 뜻하는 interesting이 적절하다.

09 주어진 문장은 곡을 쓰는 것이 쉬운지 묻는 질문에 대한 대답으로 적절하므로 (C)가 적합하다.

10 위 대화를 통해 수진과 Jason은 인터뷰 진행자와 래퍼임을 알 수 있다.

11 위 대화를 통해 수진이 Jason의 새 랩 노래를 몇 번이나 들었는지는 알 수 없다.

12 간접의문문으로 '의문사+주어+동사'의 어순이 되어야 하므로 'I should' 형태가 알맞다.

13 위 대화에는 Anthony가 공연을 보았다는 내용은 나오지 않고 있다.

14 ① Fallen leaves are under the trees. ③ This is the newest smartphone made in Korea.

15 to부정사(구)가 목적어로 쓰인 경우 가주어로 it을 쓰고 to부정사(구)는 문장의 뒤로 보낸다.

16 빈칸에 맞추어 가목적어 it과 to부정사를 쓴다.

17 분사가 명사를 뒤에서 수식하는 경우에는 그 앞에 '주격 관계대명사+be동사'가 생략된 것으로 생각할 수 있다.

18 ②번의 it은 가주어로 사용되었고, 나머지는 모두 가목적어로 사용되었다.

19 ⓑ stealing → stolen ⓓ run → running ⓕ to exercise every Sunday a rule → it a rule to exercise every Sunday

20 The deep sound를 주어로 해서 능동태로 고치는 것이 적절하다.

21 '한 무리의 젊은이들'을 가리킨다.

22 2005년을 두 부분으로 나눠 twenty five로 읽으면 25처럼 들리기 때문에, 2001년부터 2009년까지는 two thousand (and) ~로 읽는 것이 적절하다.

23 '파라과이의 카테우라라고 불리는 작은 마을의 어린이들이' 대부분이 쓰레기로 가득 차 있는 마을에 살고 있었다.

24 이 악기들의 멋진 점은 '어린이들이 악기에 많은 돈을 쓸 것을

걱정하지 않아도 된다'는 점이었다.

25 이 글은 Favio Chávez가 악기를 만들기 위해 쓰레기를 이용한 이유와 자신의 음악을 통해서 사람들이 배우기를 원하는 것에 관한 내용의 글이므로, 주제로는 ⑤번 '쓰레기를 사용하여 악기를 만드는 이유와 목표'가 적절하다.

26 현재분사 inspiring이 music을 앞에서 꾸며주게 하는 것이 적절하다.

27 '힘을 얻을' 필요가 있는 사람들이라고 해야 하므로 be cheered up으로 쓰는 것이 적절하다. be cheered up: 힘을 얻다

28 'cheer up이 '동사+부사'로 이루어졌으므로, 목적어가 인칭대명사일 경우, 동사와 부사 사이에 목적어를 쓰는 것이 적절하다.

단원별 예상문제 p.212~215

01 do you find it better to hear the performance from the second floor? 02 ⑤

03 (A) seat (B) the second floor
(C) hear the performance from the second floor
(D) the beautiful sounds of various musical instruments

04 He won the swimming competition.

05 He always listens to music before he competes.

06 It keeps him awake and it helps him focus.

07 Do you have a plan to learn a musical instrument?

08 thumb nails 09 ⑤

10 (C) → (D) → (A) → (B) 11 ③

12 (1) Can you tell me a name beginning with M?
(2) There was a small boy called "Mr. Big" in my school.
(3) The dog lying under the table is Mike's.

13 (1) to have breakfast every day
(2) to write lyrics (3) to exercise every day

14 (1) The man beating the drums is a famous musician.
(2) I went to a small town called Cateura.
(3) My mom made it possible for me to play the violin.
(4) The girl thinks it hard to learn foreign languages.

15 The world sends us garbage, we send back music.

16 as → so 17 with 18 a recycling program

19 ④ 20 ② 21 ③

22 as long as you put your heart into playing it

23 is → isn't

02 Emma가 오케스트라 콘서트를 누구와 보러 가는지는 대화를 통해 알 수 없다.

03 나는 오케스트라 콘서트를 보러 갈 계획이었다. 그러나 나는 어떤 좌석을 선택해야 할지 혼란스러웠다. 나는 Anthony에게 자리를 선택하는 데 도움을 요청했다. Anthony는 2층 좌석을 추천했다, 왜냐하면 그는 2층에서 공연을 듣는 것이 더 낫다고 생각하기 때문이었다. 그는 내가 다양한 악기 소리를 더 잘 들을 수 있다고 말했다. 그것은 내게 매우 유용한 정보였다. 나는 곧 콘서트를 보는 것이 기대된다.

04 Jake는 어제 수영대회에서 우승했다.

05 Jake는 경기 전에 항상 음악을 듣는다.

06 음악을 듣는 것은 Jake를 깨어 있게 하고 집중하는 데 도움을 준다.

07 Are you planning to ~? = Are you going to ~? = Do you have a plan to ~?

09 ⑤ 단 한 번의 lesson으로 배울 수 있다고 언급되어 있다.

10 (C) 수영대회의 우승을 축하 → (D) 감사 표현 → (A) 상대방의 의견 묻기 → (B) 대답 및 설명

11 ① The book borrowed from the library is heavy. ② These talented young people deliver great music and bring serious environmental problems to our attention. ④ She made it possible for us to sing in the talent show. ⑤ She thinks it more relaxing to sleep.

12 분사에 다른 어구(목적어, 수식어구 등)가 함께 있을 때는 뒤에서 명사를 수식한다. (1) M으로 '시작하는' 능동의 의미이므로 현재분사를 이용한다. (2) "Mr. Big"으로 '불리는' 수동의 의미이므로 과거분사를 이용한다. (3) '누워 있는'으로 진행의 의미로 현재분사를 이용한다.

13 (1), (2) 가목적어 it은 진목적어인 to부정사(구) 대신 쓰인 것이다. (3) 가주어 it은 진주어인 to부정사(구) 대신 쓰인 것이다.

14 (1) '드럼을 치고 있는' 능동의 의미로 현재분사를 이용한다. (2) Cateura라고 '불리는' 수동의 의미로 과거분사를 이용한다. (3) make 동사는 to부정사(구)가 목적어로 나올 때 it을 가목적어로 써야 한다. (4) think 동사는 to부정사(구)가 목적어로 나올 때 it을 가목적어로 써야 한다.

15 앞 문장의 내용을 가리킨다.

16 '나는 그런 악기들이 어떤 종류의 소리를 낼지 상상할 수 없었고, 그래서 나는 알아보고 싶어졌다.'고 해야 하므로, as를 so로 고치는 것이 적절하다.

17 ⓐ be filled with: ~로 가득 차다, ⓑ share A with B: A를 B와 공유하다

18 '재활용 프로그램'에서 일을 하기 위해서 갔다.

19 Favio Chávez가 쓰레기를 이용해 악기를 만든 이유를 설명하

고 있으므로, 빈칸에 들어갈 질문으로는 ④번 '왜 당신은 악기를 만들기 위해 쓰레기를 이용했나요?'가 적절하다.

20 ⓑ와 ②: 가치 없는, ① 값을 헤아릴 수 없는, 평가 못할 만큼의, 매우 귀중한, ③, ④ 가치가 있는, ⑤ 값을 매길 수 없는, 대단히 귀중한

21 Nicolás Gómez helped Favio Chávez a lot.

22 as long as+주어+동사: '~하는 한'

23 사람들이 악기를 연주하는 데 마음을 쏟아 붓는 한, 그 사람이 연주하는 악기가 무엇인지는 별로 '중요하지 않다.'

서술형 실전문제 p.216~217

01 She thinks that it is really cool.
02 He draws on his experiences and keeps a journal.
03 She uses the proverb 'No pain, no gain.'
04 (1) Einstein considered it fun to solve math problems.
(2) We found it enjoyable to sing the song written by children.
(3) The woman making a cake is my mother.
(4) We studied at desks made out of trees from the nearby mountain.
05 (1) The girl playing the piano on the stage is my sister.
(2) The box carried into the building is very big.
(3) I found it possible to inspire people by music played with recycled instruments.
(4) Rebecca thought it difficult to sing in front of others even though she is a great singer.
06 interested
07 It was made with forks.
08 (A) strange (B) deep sound
09 One person's garbage is another person's treasure.
10 these instruments
11 (A) worthless (B) inspiring

01 수진은 Jason이 녹음한 새로운 랩 노래가 정말로 멋지다고 생각한다.

02 Jason은 그의 경험을 활용해서 일기를 쓰고 있다.

03 수진은 Jason의 노력을 묘사하기 위해 '고통이 없이는 얻는 것도 없다.'는 속담을 사용했다.

04 (1) 보통 5형식 문장에서 to부정사(구)가 목적어로 나올 때 it을 가목적어로 쓴다. (2) find 동사는 to부정사(구)가 목적어로 나올 때 it을 가목적어로 써야 한다. 또한 노래가 '쓰여지는' 것이므로 수동의 의미로 과거분사로 써야 한다. (3) 케이크를 '만드는' 것이므로 진행의 의미를 갖는 현재분사 making이 되어야 한다. (4) 책상이 '만들어진' 것이므로 수동의 의미를 갖는 과거분사 made가 되어야 한다.

05 (1) 분사에 다른 어구가 함께 있을 때는 뒤에서 명사를 수식하며 피아노를 치는 것이므로 현재분사가 적절하다. (2) 상자가 '옮겨지는' 수동의 의미이므로 과거분사가 적절하다. (3) 가목적어로는 that을 사용하지 않고 it을 사용한다. (4) think 동사는 to부정사(구)가 목적어로 나올 때 it을 가목적어로 쓴다.

06 be into+명사 : ~에 관심이 많다, ~을 매우 좋아하다'

07 바이올린은 '포크'로 만들어졌다.

08 음악회가 시작되기 전에 글쓴이는 그 악기들의 소리가 '이상하게' 들릴지도 모른다고 생각했지만, 음악회가 한 소녀가 자신의 반짝이는 첼로로 바흐의 <첼로 모음곡 1번>을 연주하는 것으로 시작되었을 때 그 '깊은 소리'에 충격을 받았다.

09 주격보어 another person's treasure가 주어 One person's garbage의 의미를 보충해 주도록 쓰는 것이 적절하다.

10 '(쓰레기로 만든) 악기들'을 가리킨다.

11 자신의 음악을 통해서, Favio Chávez는 '가치 없는' 것도 '영감을 주는' 음악을 만들어 낼 수 있다는 것을 사람들이 알게 되기를 원한다.

창의사고력 서술형 문제 p.218

|모범답안|
01 (A) hard (B) easier (C) experiences
(D) keeps a journal
02 (A) be cheered up (B) Allan Hamilton
(C) bright side (D) in the hospital
(E) gave me hope

01 래퍼 Jason은 새로운 곡, 'Young and Wild'를 발매했다. 그의 노래는 너무 좋았다. 그는 곡을 쓰는 것은 처음에는 어렵지만 점점 쉬워지고 있다고 말했다. 곡을 쓰기 위해, 그는 경험을 활용하며 일기를 쓴다. 나는 그에게 행운을 빌었다.

단원별 모의고사 p.219~223

01 ⑤ 02 ①
03 (1) in harmony with (2) in the beginning
(3) sent back (4) keep a journal
04 (1) His room is filled with books and documents.
(2) My bag is similar to yours, but mine is bigger.
05 It's because she has choir practice.
06 She thinks that it's great to sing in harmony with

others.

07 ⑤ 08 ⑤ 09 (D) → (B) → (A) → (C)

10 She is planning to sign up for a drum class.

11 She is going to take it at 6 o'clock on Tuesdays.

12 ③

13 (1) to play the guitar (2) for everybody to come
(3) to clarify the objectives of the listening task

14 ⑤

15 (1) made (2) making

16 (1) Sally finds it boring to sing in the choir.
(2) She thinks it a key factor to success to make good friends.
(3) He made it possible for children to play music by making instruments out of garbage.
(4) The singer wore a T-shirt designed by an artist. 또는 The singer wore a T-shirt which [that] was designed by an artist.
(5) The man is taking pictures of people posing in front of the monuments.

17 ⑤

18 It was made with a water pipe and buttons.

19 making → made 20 ⑤

21 bring serious environmental problems to our attention, deliver great music 22 writing

23 I saw children living in a town that was mostly filled with garbage. 24 ④

25 to, could

26 ②번 played → playing 27 ⑤

01 '더 이상 쓸모가 없어 버려지는 것들'을 가리키는 말은 'garbage(쓰레기)'이다.

02 nail: 손톱, 못

05 Sally는 합창단 연습을 하러 음악실에 가는 중이다.

06 Sally는 다른 사람들과 조화를 이루어 노래하는 것이 좋다고 생각한다.

07 ⑤번을 제외한 나머지는 모두 계획을 묻는 표현이다.

08 Megan은 바이올린과 첼로로 케이팝을 연주할 것이다.

09 (D) 노래 칭찬에 대한 감사 표현 → (B) 곡을 쓰는 것에 대해 의견 질문 → (A) 대답 및 노력 설명 → (C) 대답 및 행운을 기원함

10 Sue는 드럼 수업에 등록할 계획이다.

11 Sue는 화요일 6시 수업을 들을 것이다.

12 계획을 묻는 질문에 네가 노래 대회에 참가할 것이라는 대답은 어색하다.

13 (1), (2) 가목적어 it은 진목적어인 to부정사구 대신 형식상 쓰인 것이다. 의미상의 주어가 있는 경우 빠뜨리지 않도록 주의한다. (3) 가주어 it은 진주어인 to부정사구 대신 형식상 쓰인 것이다.

14 두 문장을 관계대명사를 이용하여 한 문장으로 쓰면 'I received a letter which was written by the student.'이고 여기서 '관계대명사+be동사'를 생략하면 분사가 뒤에서 수식하는 문장이 된다.

15 (1) 포도주가 '만들어진' 것이므로 수동의 뜻을 갖는 과거분사를 이용한다. (2) 치즈를 '만드는' 것이므로 능동의 뜻을 갖는 현재분사를 이용한다.

16 (1) 가목적어로는 that을 사용하지 않고 it을 사용하며, '노래하는 것(to sing)'이 '지루하게 하는 것'이므로 현재분사를 써야 한다. (2) think 동사는 to부정사(구)가 목적어로 나올 때 it을 가목적어로 쓴다. (3) 'for children'이라는 의미상의 주어가 있으므로 playing을 to play로 고쳐야 하며, think 동사는 to부정사(구)가 목적어로 나올 때 it을 가목적어로 쓴다. (4) 현재분사가 뒤에서 명사를 수식하도록 하거나 '주격 관계대명사+be동사'가 되도록 해야 한다. (5) 사람들이 '자세를 취하는' 것이므로 능동의 의미인 현재분사가 적절하다.

17 첫 번째 빈칸에는 여자가 '서 있는' 것이므로 현재분사가 적절하고 두 번째 빈칸에는 꽃으로 '덮인' 것이므로 과거분사가 적절하다.

18 플루트는 '수도관과 단추'로 만들어졌다.

19 수동의 의미이므로 made가 적절하다.

20 ⓐ와 ⑤: 감동적인, 가슴[마음]을 뭉클하게[아프게] 하는, ①, ②, ③: 움직이는, ④ 이사하는[용의]

21 not only A but also B = B as well as A: 'A뿐만 아니라 B도'

22 be eager to부정사 = be eager for ~ing: ~하기를 갈망하다

23 living 이하가 앞의 children을 수식하고, 주격 관계대명사 that 이하가 선행사인 a town을 수식하도록 쓰는 것이 적절하다.

24 ⓐ와 ②: 부사적 용법, ①, ④: 명사적 용법, ③, ⑤: 형용사적 용법

26 '첼로 연주를 하는' 소녀라고 해야 하므로, played를 playing으로 고치는 것이 적절하다.

27 '그 지역의 쓰레기 줍는 사람의 이름이 무엇인지'는 대답할 수 없다. ① It was made out of a shiny oil tank. ② It made the deep sound. ③ To work on a recycling program. ④ He decided to share his love of music with the children.

교과서 파헤치기

Lesson 1

단어 TEST Step 1 p.02

01 막다, 예방하다 02 요구
03 구체적 내용, 자세한 내용 04 주장, 논쟁
05 부주의한, 조심성 없는 06 집중하다
07 사실은 08 딱 부러지는, 단도직입적인
09 불편한 10 효과적으로
11 말다툼하다, 언쟁하다 12 표현하다, 나타내다
13 준비하다 14 숨기다, 감추다 15 해결하다
16 화난 17 못된, 심술궂은; 의미하다
18 배려하다, 고려하다 19 아마도
20 요청 21 실망한, 낙담한 22 이유
23 관계 24 단순히 25 고민, 문제
26 그 대신에 27 우울한 얼굴 28 화난, 기분 나쁜
29 어딘가에 30 도움이 되는, 유용한
31 선택하다, 고르다 32 (~처럼) 보이다, ~인 듯하다
33 집중하다 34 크게, 큰 소리로 35 해결하다
36 ~을 중단시키다, ~을 잘라내다
37 ~을 명심하다, 마음에 담아 두다
38 ~할 준비가 되다 39 긴장하다, 겁을 먹다
40 ~이 없는 41 ~에 대해서 화가 나다
42 비밀을 누설하다 43 ~을 비난하다

단어 TEST Step 2 p.03

01 argument 02 careless 03 direct
04 somewhere 05 probably
06 focus[concentrate] 07 helpful
08 upset 09 hide 10 instead
11 argue 12 uncomfortable 13 exam
14 mean 15 consider 16 disappointed
17 solve 18 effectively 19 long face
20 pick 21 prepare 22 simply
23 actually 24 prevent 25 demand
26 request 27 detail 28 reason
29 relationship 30 scared 31 express
32 feeling 33 seem 34 trouble
35 order+사람+around
36 make a demand 37 first of all
38 be ready to 동사원형 39 keep ~ in mind
40 on time 41 in the middle of
42 end up 동사ing 43 cut ~ off

단어 TEST Step 3 p.04

1 mean, 못된, 심술궂은 2 scared, 두려워하는, 겁먹은
3 unhappy, 불만스러운, 불행한
4 helpful, 도움이 되는, 유용한
5 argument, 주장, 논쟁 6 upset, 화난, 기분 나쁜
7 concentrate, 집중하다 8 long face, 우울한 얼굴
9 consider, 배려하다, 고려하다 10 hide, 숨기다, 감추다
11 solve, 해결하다 12 prevent, 막다, 예방하다
13 express, 표현하다, 나타내다
14 detail, 구체적 내용, 자세한 내용
15 disappointed, 실망한, 낙담한 16 reason, 이유

대화문 TEST Step 1 p.05~07

Listen & Talk 1 Get Ready

Why, look, unhappy / about, copies / take it, hard

Listen & Talk 1 A-1

how come, with, these days / upset about an argument / Why, upset / cutting me off in / mad, stopped talking to / sorry to hear

Listen & Talk 1 A-2

How, going / I'm upset about / wrong / I don't think that, on time / too bad

Listen & Talk 1 B

Why, long face / angry at, said some mean / why, angry / to sleep, But, talking loudly on the phone / upset / haven't worked it out / that, mean, but I don't know how / Why don't, send

Listen & Talk 2 Get Ready

let the cat out of the bag, surprise party / That's not what, Keep, a secret

Listen & Talk 2 A-1

get, grade in, What should / concentrate, first of all, have your head in the clouds / see the sky / That's not what I meant, meant, focus

Listen & Talk 2 A-2

go diving / Actually, got cold feet / get a cold / what, I meant that, scared

Listen & Talk 2 B

stressed out about / two more to go / finishing, go on a, hair down / hair style / what I meant, feel free from, troubles

Communication

seem, wrong / keep telling me that, direct, upset / what they're talking about / What, mean / tend to say what's on, strongly / Should, keep quiet / That's not what I meant, try to consider, feelings / try

대화문 TEST Step 2 p.08~10

Listen & Talk 1 Get Ready

A: Why do you look so unhappy?

B: I'm upset about Roy. He always copies me.

A: Don't take it so hard.

Listen & Talk 1 A-1

M: Sally, how come you don't talk much with Anna these days?

W: Well, I'm upset about an argument we had.

M: Why are you upset?

W: She kept cutting me off in the middle of my sentences, so I got mad. We argued and I stopped talking to her.

M: Oh, I'm sorry to hear that.

Listen & Talk 1 A-2

W: How is your science homework going?

M: Not good. I'm upset about my science group.

W: What's wrong?

M: The group members only speak and never listen. I don't think that we can finish the homework on time.

W: That's too bad.

Listen & Talk 1 B

M: Why the long face, Julie?

W: I got angry at my sister yesterday and said some mean things to her.

M: Oh, why were you angry?

W: I was really tired and I wanted to sleep. But she was talking loudly on the phone. I was really upset about that.

M: I see. And you two haven't worked it out yet?

W: No, not yet. I want to say I'm sorry that I was mean to her, but I don't know how.

M: Why don't you write her a note or send her a text message?

W: Hmm, that's a good idea. Thanks.

Listen & Talk 2 Get Ready

A: Don't let the cat out of the bag about Clara's surprise party.

B: A cat? I don't have a cat.

A: That's not what I meant. Keep her party a secret.

Listen & Talk 2 A-1

W: Mr. Brown, I want to get a good grade in English. What should I do?

M: Well, Sujin, you should concentrate in class, first of all. I see you often have your head in the clouds.

W: Clouds? I can't see the sky from inside the classroom.

M: That's not what I meant. I meant you don't focus in class.

Listen & Talk 2 A-2

W: Did you finally go diving yesterday, Nick?

M: Actually, I got cold feet, Mina.

W: That's too bad. How did you get a cold?

M: No, Mina. That's not what I meant. I meant that I got scared, so I didn't dive.

Listen & Talk 2 B

W: I'm so stressed out about my exams, Jinsu.

M: Yeah, me, too. We have two more to go.

W: After finishing my exams, I want to go on a trip and just let my hair down.

M: You want to change your hair style?

W: No, that's not what I meant. I want to go somewhere and feel free from all my troubles.

Communication

W: Hey, Jason. You seem upset. Anything wrong?

M: People keep telling me that I'm too direct. I'm upset about that.

W: Hmm.... I kind of know what they're talking about.

M: What do you mean?

W: Well, somet imes you tend to say what's on your mind too strongly.

M: Should I just keep quiet, then?

W: That's not what I meant. You can try to consider others' feelings.

M: I see. I'll try that.

본문 TEST Step 1 p.11~12

01 Speak, Mind Effectively

02 Welcome to, Teens

03 Dr. Carter

04 using, skills, express, effectively

05 Let's, with, clip

06 tries, ends up arguing

07 find out, reason why

08 *lost, Why, so careless*

09 sentence with, express, feelings

10 Instead, use, I-message

11 focus on, rather than

12 *upset because, favorite, lost*

13 Next, Calli

14 trying, busy preparing, work

15 have a look

16 *Could, talk, something*

17 needs, find, right time

18 wanted, to what, going

19 enough time to, with

20 pick, ready to listen

21 *Could, about something*

22 *Mom, Sure*

23 take, look at 24 often hurts, feelings
25 *Don't put, on*
26 felt uncomfortable, demand using
27 simply, taking orders 28 try to, such as
29 what, like, request, demand
30 *Could, put, on*
31 change, express, solve, prevent
32 keep, in mind

본문 TEST Step 2 p.13~14

01 Mind Effectively
02 Welcome to, Teens 03 I'm
04 using good communication skills, ourselves, effectively
05 Let's, our first clip
06 tries to, ends up arguing
07 find out the reason why 08 *lost, careless*
09 sentence with, to express his feelings
10 Instead, I-message
11 focus on, rather than point the finger at
12 *I'm, upset, are lost* 13 Next
14 is busy preparing
15 have a look
16 *Could I*
17 needs to, the right time
18 what, going to say
19 enough time to talk
20 pick a time, is ready to listen
21 *Could I* 22 *Sure*
23 take a look at 24 hurts, feelings 25 *Don't put*
26 felt uncomfortable, made a demand
27 simply, taking orders
28 should try, such as
29 what, sound like, request, demand
30 *Could you*
31 a small change, express ourselves, prevent communication problems
32 keep, in mind

본문 TEST Step 3 p.15~16

1 당신의 마음을 효과적으로 말하라
2 '십 대들의 모든 것'에 오신 걸 환영합니다.
3 저는 Carter 박사입니다.
4 오늘 우리는 자신을 더 효과적으로 표현하기 위해 적절한 의사소통 기술을 사용하는 것에 대해 이야기해 보겠습니다.
5 Brian에 대한 첫 번째 동영상으로 시작해 보죠.
6 Brian이 남동생과 이야기하려고 할 때, 그는 결국 동생과 항상 말다툼을 하게 돼요.
7 그에게 이런 문제가 있는 이유를 알아봅시다.
8 Brian: "너 또 내 이어폰 잃어버렸지. 너는 왜 그렇게 조심성이 없니?"
9 Brian은 그의 감정을 표현하기 위해 '너'로 문장을 시작하고 있군요.
10 대신에 그는 '나 메시지'를 써야 해요.
11 '나'로 시작하는 것은 그가 남동생을 비난하기보다는 자신이 느끼거나 생각하는 것에 집중하도록 도울 수 있답니다.
12 Brian: "내가 가장 좋아하는 이어폰이 없어져서 난 정말 속상해."
13 다음은 Calli입니다.
14 그녀는 어머니와 이야기하려고 하지만, 어머니는 출근 준비로 바쁘시군요.
15 한번 보시죠.
16 Calli: "저기, 엄마. 엄마랑 뭔가에 대해 이야기 좀 할 수 있을까요?"
17 Calli는 어머니와 이야기를 나눌 적절한 때를 찾아야 해요.
18 Calli의 어머니도 아마 Calli가 말하려고 했던 것을 듣고 싶어 하셨을 거예요.
19 그러나 어머니에게는 딸과 이야기할 시간이 충분하지 않았어요.
20 Calli는 어머니가 들으실 준비가 된 때를 골라야 해요.
21 Calli: "저기, 엄마. 엄마랑 뭔가에 대해 이야기 좀 할 수 있을까요?"
22 Mom: "물론이지."
23 이제 마지막 동영상을 봅시다.
24 Anna와 Julie는 가장 친한 친구 사이이지만, Anna가 종종 Julie의 마음을 상하게 합니다.
25 Anna: "네 가방을 내 책상에 놓지 마!"
26 Anna가 don't라는 단어를 써서 요구했기 때문에 Julie는 아마 불편하게 느꼈을 거예요.
27 사람들은 명령 받는 것을 전혀 좋아하지 않아요.
28 Anna는 can, could 또는 please와 같은 말을 사용하도록 노력해야 해요.
29 그러면 그녀가 하는 말이 요구보다는 요청처럼 들릴 거예요.
30 Anna: "네 가방은 네 책상에 놔두겠니?"
31 우리가 동영상에서 본 것처럼, 우리 자신을 표현하는 방식을 조금만 바꾸어도 의사소통의 문제를 해결하거나 심지어 막을 수도 있답니다.
32 이 조언들을 명심합시다!

본문 TEST Step 4-Step 5 p.17~20

1 Speak Your Mind Effectively
2 Welcome to "All about Teens."
3 I'm Dr. Carter.

4 Today, we're going to talk about using good communication skills to express ourselves more effectively.
5 Let's start with our first clip about Brian.
6 When he tries to talk to his brother, he always ends up arguing with his brother.
7 Let's find out the reason why he has this problem.
8 Brian: You lost my earphones again. Why are you so careless?
9 Brian is starting a sentence with "you" to express his feelings..
10 Instead, he should use the "I-message."
11 Starting with "I" can help him focus on what he feels or thinks rather than point the finger at his brother.
12 Brian: I'm really upset because my favorite earphones are lost.
13 Next is Calli.
14 She is trying to talk to her mother, but she is busy preparing to go to work.
15 Let's have a look.
16 Calli: Hey, Mom. Could I talk to you about something?
17 Calli needs to find the right time to talk to her mom.
18 Maybe Calli's mom wanted to listen to what Calli was going to say.
19 But she didn't have enough time to talk with her daughter.
20 Calli should pick a time when her mom is ready to listen.
21 Calli: Hey, Mom. Could I talk to you about something?
22 Mom: Sure.
23 Now, let's take a look at our last clip.
24 Anna and Julie are best friends, but Anna often hurts Julie's feelings.
25 Anna: Don't put your bag on my desk!
26 Julie probably felt uncomfortable because Anna made a demand using the word "don't."
27 People simply don't like taking orders.
28 Anna should try to use words such as "can," "could," or "please."
29 Then, what she says will sound like a request rather than a demand.
30 Anna: Could you put your bag on your desk?
31 As we saw in the video clips, a small change in the way we express ourselves can solve or even prevent communication problems.
32 Let's keep these tips in mind!

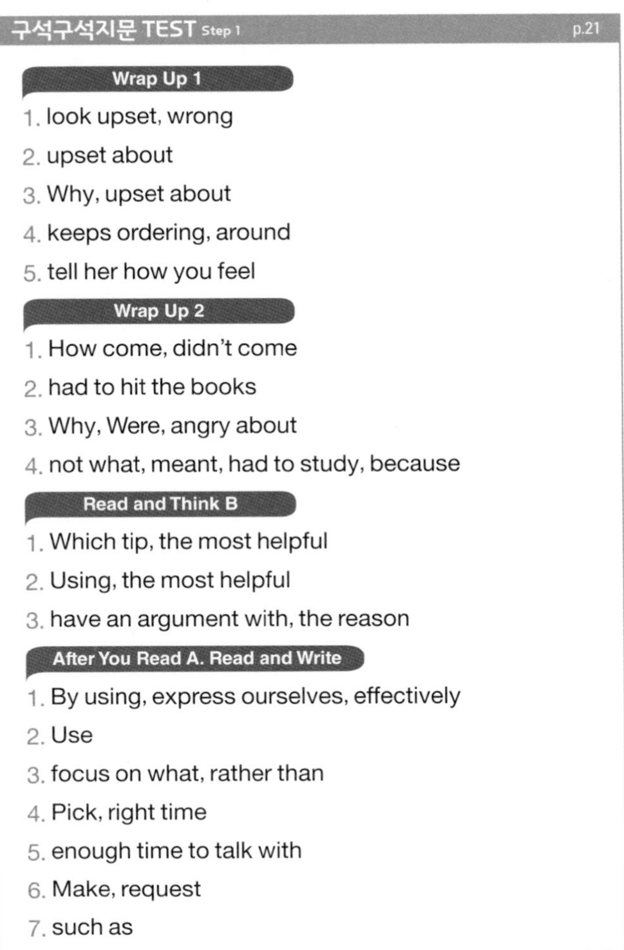

구석구석지문 TEST Step 1 p.21

Wrap Up 1

1. look upset, wrong
2. upset about
3. Why, upset about
4. keeps ordering, around
5. tell her how you feel

Wrap Up 2

1. How come, didn't come
2. had to hit the books
3. Why, Were, angry about
4. not what, meant, had to study, because

Read and Think B

1. Which tip, the most helpful
2. Using, the most helpful
3. have an argument with, the reason

After You Read A. Read and Write

1. By using, express ourselves, effectively
2. Use
3. focus on what, rather than
4. Pick, right time
5. enough time to talk with
6. Make, request
7. such as

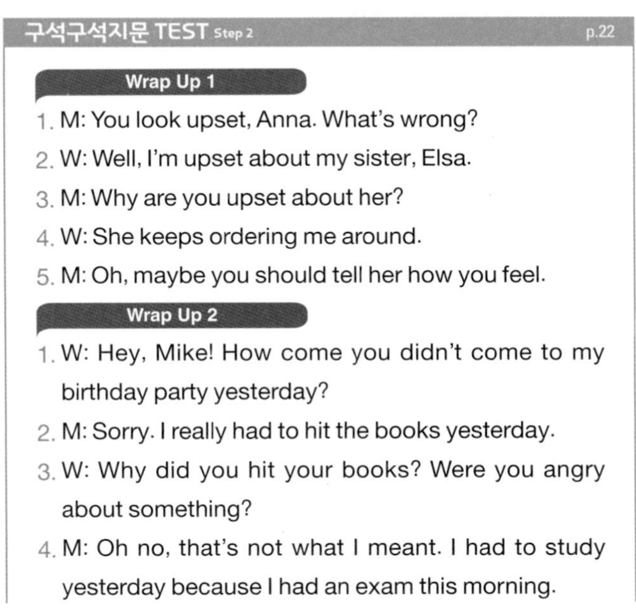

구석구석지문 TEST Step 2 p.22

Wrap Up 1

1. M: You look upset, Anna. What's wrong?
2. W: Well, I'm upset about my sister, Elsa.
3. M: Why are you upset about her?
4. W: She keeps ordering me around.
5. M: Oh, maybe you should tell her how you feel.

Wrap Up 2

1. W: Hey, Mike! How come you didn't come to my birthday party yesterday?
2. M: Sorry. I really had to hit the books yesterday.
3. W: Why did you hit your books? Were you angry about something?
4. M: Oh no, that's not what I meant. I had to study yesterday because I had an exam this morning.

Read and Think B

1. Which tip was the most helpful to you, and why?
2. Using the "I-message" was the most helpful.
3. I often have an argument with my sister, and now I understand the reason.

After You Read A. Read and Write

1. By using good communication skills, we can express ourselves more effectively.
2. ⓐ Use the "I-message."
3. You can focus on what you feel or think rather than point the finger at others.
4. ⓑ Pick the right time.
5. Others will listen to you when they have enough time to talk with you.
6. ⓒ Make a request.
7. Use words such as "can," "could," or "please."

Lesson 2

단어 TEST Step 1 p.23

01 모양, 형태　02 독특한, 특별한　03 끝이 뾰족한
04 특이한, 흔치 않은　05 황사　06 조사하다
07 풍경, 전망　08 끈적거리는, 달라붙는
09 조합　10 절정[최대한도]에 이르다
11 촬영하다　12 유성, 별똥별　13 위치, 장소
14 기간　15 살아남다, 생존하다
16 강우　17 빙하　18 대회
19 많은, 셀 수 없는　20 만들다, 발전하다
21 생기 넘치는, 살아 있는　22 생태학자
23 절벽　24 개선하다, 향상시키다
25 통찰력　26 개인적인
27 놀라운 일, 기적　28 조사하다, 연구하다
29 빛나다　30 (날씨 · 생활 환경이) 혹독한, 가혹한
31 영광으로 생각하다
32 영감을 주다, 고무하다, 격려하다　33 의류, 옷
34 색채화가　35 ~을 대신하다
36 ~에 의해 영감을 받다
37 실현되다, 사실이 되다　38 ~로 가득 차다
39 좋은 몸 상태를 유지하다
40 ~에게 정신을 바짝 차리게 하다　41 ~ 때문에
42 ~에 의해 만들어지다　43 산책하다

단어 TEST Step 2 p.24

01 insight　02 cliff　03 countless
04 peak　05 clothing　06 improve
07 colorist　08 location　09 combination
10 miracle　11 shape　12 develop
13 ecologist　14 glow　15 reef
16 harsh　17 shoot　18 inspire
19 glacier　20 investigate　21 spiky
22 survive　23 research　24 honor
25 rainfall　26 sticky　27 alive
28 unusual　29 view　30 adventure
31 personal　32 yellow dust　33 actually
34 recent　35 millions of　36 find out
37 be caused by ~　38 stand in for
39 be[get] inspired by　40 be filled with
41 get in shape　42 due to 명사　43 cut down

단어 TEST Step 3

p.25

1 glow, 빛나다 2 cliff, 절벽 3 unique, 독특한, 특별한
4 peak, 절정[최대한도]에 이르다 5 cave, 동굴
6 harsh, (날씨·생활 환경이) 혹독한 7 combination, 조합
8 period, 기간 9 glacier, 빙하 10 mixed, 섞인, 혼합한
11 adventure, 모험 12 countless, 많은, 셀 수 없는
13 ecologist, 생태학자
14 inspire, 영감을 주다, 고무하다, 격려하다
15 research, 조사하다, 연구하다
16 shooting star, 유성, 별똥별

대화문 TEST Step 1

p.26~28

Listen & Talk 1 Get Ready

view, top, amazing / can't wait to, run up

Listen & Talk 1 A-1

what's, plan / going to, wait to visit / are, that look canvases / sounds, Take lots of

Listen & Talk 1 A-2

want to watch / Which / about adventures under, was shot / heard of, has, sea life / can't wait to watch, go and get

Listen & Talk 1 B

is going to go, in / What, plan to / going to study, caves, go, watching / like, interesting trip / I've only read about, wait to actually visit / hope, enjoy, trip

Listen & Talk 2 Get Ready

is, high / I've heard that, travels from, to

Listen & Talk 2 A-1

weather report, able, hundreds of shooting stars, When, to see them / heard that, shooting stars, between, and / special night

Listen & Talk 2 A-2

are / They are, I've heard that, made by, sticky / look like / like, actually, someday

Listen & Talk 2 B

that, sets, during summer / that, How interesting / heard that, even cycling, because / love, in the middle of / too, get, chance to try, someday

Communication

winner, competition / for inviting, honored to receive / talk, heard that, was taken, true / glowing beach, caused by / amazing / can't wait to take, amazing beaches / wish, best

대화문 TEST Step 2

p.29~31

Listen & Talk 1 Get Ready

A: The view of the top of the mountain is going to be amazing.

B: Yeah, I can't wait to see the view. Let's run up there!

Listen & Talk 1 A-1

W: David, what's your summer plan?

M: My family is going to China. I can't wait to visit the Rainbow Mountains.

W: The Rainbow Mountains?

M: They are some mountains that look like canvases in rainbow colors.

W: That sounds amazing! Take lots of pictures!

Listen & Talk 1 A-2

M: Do you want to watch the new 3D movie?

W: Which one?

M: The one about adventures under the sea. It was shot near Australia's Great Barrier Reef.

W: Oh, I've heard of it. It has the most beautiful sea life.

M: Right. I can't wait to watch the movie. Let's go and get the ticket.

Listen & Talk 1 B

W: Dad, my science club is going to go to Dokdo in July.

M: Oh, really? What do you plan to do there?

W: We are going to study the caves on the island and go bird watching.

M: Sounds like it will be an interesting trip.

W: Yeah. I've only read about Dokdo in books. I can't wait to actually visit there.

M: I hope you enjoy your trip!

Listen & Talk 2 Get Ready

A: The level of yellow dust is really high today.

B: Yeah. I've heard that the yellow dust travels from the deserts of Mongolia to Korea.

Listen & Talk 2 A-1

M: Mom, did you watch the weather report today? We will be able to see hundreds of shooting stars tonight!

W: Wow, fantastic! When is the best time to see them?

M: I've heard that the shooting stars will peak between 12 a.m. and 2 a.m.

W: Wow, it will be a special night!

Listen & Talk 2 A-2

M: Erica, what are the white things in the picture?

W: They are snow rollers. I've heard that they are made by strong wind and sticky snow.

M: Interesting! They look like snow rings.

W: Yeah, I'd like to actually see them someday.

Listen & Talk 2 B

M: Jisu, did you know that the sun never sets in Norway during summer?

W: No, I didn't know that. How interesting!

M: Yeah, and I've heard that people go hiking and even cycling at night because it isn't dark.

W: I'd love to go hiking and cycling in the middle of the night!

M: Me, too. I hope we get thechance to try it someday.

Communication

M: Let's welcome Ms. Scarlett Lee, the winner of this year's photo competition.

W: Hello, thank you for inviting me. I've honored to receive the award.

M: Let's talk about your photo. I've heard that this photo was taken in the Maldives. Is that true?

W: Yes, this glowing beach is caused by plankton.

M: Wow, it truly is amazing!

W: Yes, it is. I can't wait to take more pictures of amazing beaches.

M: I wish you the best of luck!

본문 TEST Step 1 p.32~33

01 World Through, Eyes
02 beauty, nature inspires
03 find out, fields, inspired
04 Lin, Ecologist 05 Stone Forest
06 been visiting, for over
07 spiky, true miracles
08 amazing, has been created
09 down, sharp, spiky over
10 environment, harsh, animals, survive
11 which, frog-like, that, another
12 For, is like 13 surprises, keeps, on, toes
14 Fashion Colorist
15 River of Five Colors
16 filled with, different
17 mix, develop, create, clothing
18 Over, been gaining, insights
19 mixed, anywhere else, world
20 combination, colorful, alive, bright
21 Whenever, countless, waiting, created
22 Location Scout
23 National, Frozen Beauty
24 location, perfect, shoot
25 for, due to, beauty
26 My personal favorite
27 glacier, ranges, stand, place
28 recent, shot, without using
29 help make, come true

본문 TEST Step 2 p.34~35

01 World Through
02 beauty, inspires us all
03 Let's find out, fields of work get inspired
04 Ecologist 05 Stone Forest
06 I've been visiting, stone forest, for over
07 spiky stones, true miracles
08 amazing, has been created buy rainfall
09 cut down, sharp, spiky over
10 harsh for animals to live in, to survive
11 which, frog-like, that help, jump from, to another
12 is like, jack-in-the-box
13 surprises, keeps me on my toes
14 Fashion Colorist
15 River of Five Colors
16 is filled with millions of
17 mix, develop, create colors
18 I've been gaining, beautiful colors
19 wonderful mixed colors, anywhere else
20 combination, colorful plants, makes, more alive, bright
21 Whenever, makes, think, countless, waiting to be created
22 Location Scout
23 Frozen Beauty
24 perfect places to shoot movies
25 for many location scouts, due to, unusual beauty
26 My personal favorite
27 cliffs, glacier caves, stand in for any place
28 In fact, we shot here, produced without using
29 help make, come true

본문 TEST Step 3 p.36~37

1 내 눈에 비친 세계
2 "자연의 아름다움은 우리 모두에게 영감을 준다.
3 서로 다른 직업 분야의 사람들이 자연에 의해 어떻게 영감을 받는지 알아보자."
4 Lin Wang, 생태학자
5 Tsingy, 마다가스카르의 석림

6 나는 20년 이상 동안 식물과 동물을 연구하기 위해서 마다가스카르의 석림을 방문하고 있다.
7 이 지역의 뾰족한 돌들은 진정한 자연의 놀라움이다.
8 이 놀라운 모양은 비에 의해서 만들어졌다.
9 비가 오랜 기간 동안 돌을 침식해서 날카롭고 뾰족하게 만들었다.
10 이런 환경은 동물들이 살기에 험난하지만, 동물들은 생존할 방법들을 찾아냈다.
11 예를 들어, 마다가스카르에서만 사는 여우원숭이는 한 개의 돌탑에서 다른 돌탑으로 뛸 수 있도록 도와주는 개구리와 같은 다리를 가지고 있다.
12 나에게 석림은 '잭인더박스(열면 인형이 튀어나오는 상자)'와 같다.
13 그것은 늘 나를 놀라게 하고 정신을 바짝 차리게 한다!
14 Amber Smith, 패션 색채 전문가
15 Caño Cristales, 콜롬비아의 다섯 색깔의 강
16 세계는 수백만의 다양한 색깔로 가득 차 있다.
17 의류를 위해서 색을 섞고, 발전시키고, 만들어 내는 것이 나의 일이다.
18 수년 동안, 나는 카뇨 크리스탈레스의 아름다운 색으로부터 영감을 얻어 오고 있다.
19 이 강의 아름답게 혼합된 색깔은 세상 어느 다른 곳에서도 볼 수 없다.
20 물속의 화려한 식물들과 햇빛의 결합은 그 색깔을 더 생생하고 밝게 만든다.
21 내가 카뇨 크리스탈레스를 방문할 때마다 그 강은 나로 하여금 아마도 여전히 만들어지기를 기다리고 있는 셀 수 없이 많은 색깔이 있음을 생각하게 한다.
22 Danny Mehta, 장소 섭외가
23 Vatnajökull 국립 공원, 아이슬란드의 얼음으로 덮인 아름다움
24 나는 장소 섭외가이고 나의 일은 영화를 찍기에 완벽한 장소를 찾는 것이다.
25 아이슬란드는 비범한 아름다움 때문에 많은 장소 섭외가들이 방문하기에 최고의 장소이다.
26 내가 개인적으로 가장 선호하는 곳은 바트나이외쿠틀 국립 공원이다.
27 가파른 절벽, 푸른 빙하 동굴, 그리고 긴 산맥들은 세계나 혹은 우주의 어느 장소도 대신할 수 있다.
28 사실상, 우리가 여기서 찍은 최근의 공상 과학 영화는 컴퓨터 그래픽 없이 만들어졌다!
29 아이슬란드는 우리의 가장 무모한 꿈을 영화 스크린에서 실현할 수 있게 해 준다.

본문 TEST Step 4-Step 5

p.38~41

1 The World Through My Eyes
2 "The beauty of nature inspires us all.
3 Let's find out how people from different fields of work get inspired by nature."
4 Lin Wang, Ecologist
5 Tsingy, the Stone Forest of Madagascar
6 I've been visiting the stone forest of Madagascar to study plants and animals for over 20 years.
7 The spiky stones of this place are true miracles of nature.
8 This amazing shape has been created by rainfall.
9 Rain has cut down the stones and made them sharp and spiky over a long period of time.
10 The environment is harsh for animals to live in, but they have found ways to survive.
11 For example, lemurs, which only live in Madagascar, have frog-like legs that help them jump from one stone tower to another.
12 For me, the stone forest is like a jack-in-the-box.
13 It always surprises me and keeps me on my toes!
14 Amber Smith, Fashion Colorist
15 Caño Cristales, the River of Five Colors of Colombia
16 The world is filled with millions of different colors.
17 It is my job to mix, develop, and create colors for clothing.
18 Over the years, I've been gaining insights from the beautiful colors of Caño Cristales.
19 You cannot see the wonderful mixed colors of this river anywhere else in the world.
20 The combination of colorful plants under the water and sunlight makes the colors more alive and bright.
21 Whenever I visit the Caño Cristales, it makes me think that maybe there are still countless colors that are waiting to be created.
22 Danny Mehta, Location Scout
23 Vatnajökull National Park, Frozen Beauty of Iceland
24 I'm a location scout and my job is finding perfect places to shoot movies.
25 Iceland is the best place for many location scouts to visit due to its unusual beauty.
26 My personal favorite is the Vatnajökull National Park.
27 The sharp cliffs, blue glacier caves, and long mountain ranges can stand in for any place in the world or the universe.
28 In fact, the recent sci-fi movie we shot here was produced without using computer graphics!
29 Iceland can help make our wildest dreams come true on the movie screen.

구석구석지문 TEST Step 1 p.42

Communication Step

1. on receiving, I've heard, was taken, true
2. is caused by, drops
3. truly is amazing
4. can't wait to take, amazing clouds
5. wish, the best of luck

Wrap Up 1

1. coming back from
2. has been away, right
3. most of the time to research
4. can't wait to see, listen to
5. having dinner, don't make other plans
6. won't

Think & Write Step A

1. Mt.
2. Trip, Hiking
3. walk along, routes
4. in shape, keep fit
5. Trip, Soccer
6. Manchester
7. famous players
8. how to improve
9. Paris
10. Trip for Art
11. famous art museums
12. how to draw, creatively

구석구석지문 TEST Step 2 p.43

Communication Step

1. A: Congratulations on receiving the award. I've heard that this photo was taken in India. Is that true?
2. B: Yes, this rainbow cloud is caused by thin clouds and water drops.
3. A: Wow, it truly is amazing!
4. B: Yes, it is. I can't wait to take more photos of amazing clouds.
5. A: I wish you the best of luck!

Wrap Up 1

1. W: Your uncle, John, is coming back from South America this weekend.
2. M: That's great. He has been away for almost 2 years, right?
3. W: Yeah, he's been in the jungle most of the time to research.
4. M: Wow, that's amazing. I can't wait to see him and listen to his stories.
5. W: Me, too. We're having dinner with him this Saturday, so don't make other plans.
6. M: Okay, I won't, Mom.

Think & Write Step A

1. Mt. Jiri and Mt. Seorak
2. Trip for Hiking Fans
3. • walk along beautiful hiking routes
4. • learn how to get in shape and keep fit
5. Trip for Soccer Fans
6. Madrid and Manchester
7. • meet famous players
8. • learn how to improve your soccer skills
9. Paris and London
10. Trip for Art Fans
11. • visit famous art museums
12. • learn how to draw pictures creatively

Lesson 3

단어 TEST Step 1 p.44

01 끔찍한 02 기사 03 자서전, 전기
04 망치다, 파산시키다 05 남편
06 형사, 탐정 07 요새
08 도박하다, ~을 도박으로 잃다 09 실망시키는
10 나중에, 그 뒤에 11 재산, 행운 12 장군
13 ~을 포함하다 14 사물함
15 ~할 때마다, ~하면 16 독립, 광복
17 (정치적 · 사회적) 운동 18 나무로 된, 목재의
19 이상한 20 경찰관, 장교 21 진짜 같은, 사실적인
22 발명품, 발명 23 부끄러운, 당황스러운
24 낯선, 모르는 25 여자; 여자의, 여성의
26 속삭이다, (사람 · 일에 대하여) 소곤소곤 이야기하다
27 결혼, 혼인 28 서랍장, 큰 상자, 장롱
29 ~이기 때문에, ~ 이래로 30 상인
31 병원, 진료소 32 해결하다, 풀다 33 진실, 사실
34 학자 35 ~ 대신에 36 ~에게 고함치다
37 ~하는 데 익숙하다 38 ~에 일생을 바치다
39 그 순간에 40 ~을 결정하다 41 비밀을 지키다
42 ~ 몰래, ~의 등 뒤에서
43 (사람들이) ~라고 한다

단어 TEST Step 2 p.45

01 afterwards 02 merchant 03 biography
04 chest 05 movement 06 ruin
07 disappointing 08 embarrassing 09 independence
10 odd 11 fortune 12 gamble
13 social studies 14 general 15 whisper
16 include 17 machine 18 scholar
19 invention 20 horrible 21 article
22 marriage 23 female 24 wonder
25 object 26 fortress 27 clinic
28 realistic 29 detective 30 save
31 husband 32 wooden 33 locker
34 strange 35 keep a secret 36 yell at
37 take a look at ~ 38 ask for
39 at that moment 40 instead of
41 try on 42 make an arrangement
43 be used to 동(명사)

단어 TEST Step 3 p.46

1 female, 여자의, 여성의 2 fortune, 재산
3 husband, 남편 4 chest, 서랍장, 큰 상자, 장롱
5 ruin, 망치다, 파산시키다 6 general, 장군
7 include, ~을 포함하다 8 biography, 자서전, 전기
9 merchant, 상인 10 save, 구하다 11 fortress, 요새
12 independence, 독립 13 article, 기사
14 movement, (정치적·사회적) 운동 15 locker, 사물함
16 scholar, 학자

대화문 TEST Step 1 p.47~49

Listen & Talk 1 Get Ready

was a painter / read, it is said, scholar / fight, both right

Listen & Talk 1 A-1

what, reading / reading, biography / haven't heard / the first female, It is said that, over, flying time

Listen & Talk 1 A-2

interesting, detective / scholar / but it is said that he was also, solved, cases / didn't know that, detective

Listen & Talk 1 B

know about / heard / Take a look at, to be included, social studies / helped, by building a clinic, that such stories, be included in / It, to, that, such

Listen & Talk 2 A-1

can't take, museum / Is it okay, water bottle / leave, in

Listen & Talk 2 A-2

welcome to, How / is it okay if I take pictures in / don't use

Listen & Talk 2 B

How was / were / get the chance to, okay if I / remember that, closes at / on, 5th floor / Let me know if

Communication Step A

are moving onto, As you can see, many, inventions, is called / musical instrument / water clock, It is said that it is, oldest, the largest / How, Is it okay if, picture of

Wrap Up 1

what, watching / watching / Isn't he, saved / It is said that he won, wooden ships / how, possible / wise general who made creative

Wrap Up 2

Would you like to / I'd like to / Here / is it okay if, bathroom / if, on, stay, your seat

대화문 TEST Step 2 p.50~52

Listen & Talk 1 Get Ready

A: Kim Deuksin was a painter.

B: No! I read a book and it is said that he was a scholar.

C: Don't fight. You are both right.

Listen & Talk 1 A-1

M: Lisa, what are you reading?

W: I'm reading a biography of Gwon Giok.

M: I haven't heard about her. Who is she?

W: She was the first female pilot in Korea. It is said that she had over 7,000 hours of flying time.

M: Wow, I didn't know that.

Listen & Talk 1 A-2

M: I watched an interesting movie yesterday. Jeong Yakyong was a detective in it.

W: Jeong Yakyong? Wasn't he a scholar in the Joseon Dynasty?

M: Yeah, but it is said that he was also a detective. He solved about 90 cases.

W: Oh, I didn't know that he was also a detective.

Listen & Talk 1 B

W: Hey, Mark, do you know about Father Lee Taeseok?

M: Yeah, I've heard of him. Why?

W: Take a look at this article. He is going to be included in the social studies textbook in South Sudan.

M: Wow, that's great.

W: Yeah, he helped the children by building a clinic and a school. It is said that such stories will be included in the textbook.

M: It is good to hear that students will learn about such a great person.

Listen & Talk 2 A-1

W: Excuse me, you can't take your backpack inside the museum.

M: Oh, I didn't know that. Is it okay if I bring in my water bottle?

W: Yes, that's fine. You can leave your bag in the locker.

M: Okay, thank you.

Listen & Talk 2 A-2

W: Hi, welcome to the National Museum. How can I help you?

M: Hi, is it okay if I take pictures in the museum?

W: Yes, but please don't use a flash.

M: Oh, I see. Thank you.

Listen & Talk 2 B

M: Hello, Ms. Jackson. How was your tour of the Hanok Village?

W: It was wonderful. The houses were really beautiful.

M: That's great.

W: Actually, I didn't get the chance to have dinner. Is it okay if I cook in the kitchen at this hour?

M: Yes, but please remember that the kitchen closes at 10 p.m.

W: Okay. The kitchen is on the 5th floor, right?

M: Yes, it is. Let me know if you need anything.

Communication Step A

M: All right, everyone! This way, please. Now, we are moving onto the Joseon Dynasty. As you can see, there were many interesting inventions. This one is called the *Jagyeongnu*.

W: Is it a musical instrument?

M: Actually, this is a water clock. It is said that it is the oldest and the largest water clock in Korea.

W: How amazing! Is it okay if I take a picture of it?

M: Sure.

Wrap Up 1

W: James, what are you watching?

M: Oh, I'm watching a video about Yi Sunsin.

W: Isn't he the one that saved Joseon from Japan?

M: Right. It is said that he won the war only with twelve wooden ships.

W: Wow, how can that be possible?

M: He was a wise general who made creative plans.

Wrap Up 2

W: Excuse me, sir. Would you like to have curry or *bibimbap*?

M: I'd like to have *bibimbap*, please

W: Here you are.

M: Thank you. Oh, is it okay if I use the bathroom now?

W: Sure, but if the seat light is on, you should stay in your seat.

M: Okay, thank you.

본문 TEST Step 1 p.53~54

01 Secret, My Father

02 strange, visited, asked, daughter

03 odd, used to being

04 your father's friend

05 wonder if, true

06 moment, expecting disappointing, memories
07 Back, whenever, There goes
08 from, rich family
09 Instead, living, always, gambling
10 why, which, ruins, fortune
11 gambled away, asking for
12 have, left, would, whenever
13 yell at, angrily, empty-handed
14 Bring, more
15 had already made, arrangement
16 part, tradition, chest, clothes
17 Right before, taken, money
18 angrily, such, horrible thing
19 What should, do
20 have no choice
21 have to take, chest
22 How embarrassing, behind, back
23 Since, marriage, been difficult
24 dear, continued, story
25 was not, gambler
26 family money, independence fighters
27 made himself, keep, secret
28 sure if, telling, truth
29 afterwards, out, realized, wrong
30 since, proud, devoted, movement

본문 TEST Step 2 p.55~56

01 Secret, Father
02 a strange man visited, asked
03 an odd question, was more used to being called
04 your father's friend
05 wonder if, true
06 expecting disappointing, since, good memories
07 Back, whenever, There goes
08 from, rich family
09 Instead of living, gambling house
10 That is why, was called, which, ruins
11 has gambled away, asking for
12 have no more money left, would, whenever, sent
13 would yell at, angrily, empty-handed
14 Bring me, money
15 had already made an arrangement, marry
16 As part of, a new chest for clothes
17 Right before, came into, has taken the money
18 angrily, such a horrible thing
19 What 20 no choice
21 You'll have to take
22 How embarrassing, whisper behind my back
23 marriage, had been difficult for me
24 continued his story
25 a gambler 26 independence fighters
27 made himself, keep this a secret from, Japanese officers
28 if, telling, truth
29 afterwards, had been wrong
30 had devoted his life to, independence movement

본문 TEST Step 3 p.57~58

1 아버지의 비밀
2 1946년에, 낯선 남자가 나를 찾아와 물었다. "당신이 김용환 씨의 딸입니까?
3 나는 파락호의 딸이라고 불리는 것이 더 익숙했으므로 나에게 이것은 이상한 질문이었다.
4 "나는 당신 아버지의 친구입니다.
5 당신은 이것이 사실인지 의아하겠지만, 당신의 아버지는…," 이라고 그 남자는 말했다.
6 나는 내 아버지에 대해 좋은 기억을 가지고 있지 않았으므로 그 순간에 실망스러운 소식을 예상하고 있었다.
7 1920년대에 마을에서 사람들이 나를 볼 때마다 그들은 "저기에 파락호의 딸이 가네."라고 말하곤 했다.
8 나의 아버지는 매우 부유한 집안의 아들이었다.
9 선비의 삶을 사는 대신, 아버지는 항상 도박장에 계셨다.
10 그것이 그가 집안의 재산을 탕진하는 사람이라는 뜻의 파락호로 불린 이유이다.
11 "네 아버지는 도박으로 모든 돈을 써 버리고 지금 더 요구하고 계신다.
12 가서 더 이상 남아 있는 돈이 없다고 말씀드려라."라고 나의 어머니는 나를 도박장으로 보낼 때마다 말씀하시곤 했다.
13 그러면, 아버지는 나에게 화를 내시며 소리치셨다. "왜 빈손으로 왔니?
14 돈을 더 가져와!"
15 내가 16살이 되었을 때, 나의 가족은 나를 서 씨와 결혼시키기로 이미 결정을 했었다.
16 결혼 풍습의 일부로, 서 씨네 가족은 새 장롱을 사라고 우리 가족에게 돈을 보냈다.
17 결혼식 바로 전날, 나의 어머니는 내 방에 들어오셔서 말씀하셨다. "네 아버지가 장롱을 살 돈을 가져가 버렸다."
18 나는 화가 나서 물었다 "어떻게 그리 끔찍한 일을 하실 수 있나요?
19 우린 이제 어떡해요?"
20 "우리에게 선택권은 없구나.
21 큰어머니의 옛 장롱을 가져가야겠구나."라고 어머니가 말씀하셨다.

22 "가문에 부끄러운 일이야."라고 사람들이 내 뒤에서 속삭이곤 했다.
23 결혼 첫날부터, 남편의 집에서의 생활은 나에게 힘겨웠다.
24 "당신의 아버지, 나의 친애하는 친구…," 나의 아버지의 친구분은 그의 이야기를 이어가셨다.
25 "그는 도박꾼이 아니었어요.
26 당신의 아버지는 가족의 돈을 만주에 있는 독립운동가들에게 보냈답니다.
27 그는 이것을 일본 순사들에게 비밀로 하기 위해 그 자신을 도박꾼처럼 보이게 했어요."
28 처음엔, 나는 그분이 사실을 얘기하시는 건지 확신할 수 없었다.
29 그러나 나중에, 나는 나의 아버지에 대한 진실을 알게 되었고 내가 아버지에 관해 오해하고 있었다는 것을 깨달았다.
30 그 순간부터, 나는 독립운동에 그의 인생을 헌신하신 파락호의 딸인 것이 자랑스러웠다.

본문 TEST Step 4-Step 5 p.59~62

1 The Secret of My Father
2 In 1946, a strange man visited me and asked, "Are you Mr. Kim Yonghwan's daughter?"
3 For me, this was an odd question because I was more used to being called the daughter of a *parakho*.
4 "I'm your father's friend.
5 You may wonder if it is true, but your father...," the man said.
6 At that moment, I was expecting disappointing news since I did not have good memories of my father.
7 Back in the 1920's, whenever people saw me in the village, they would say, "There goes the *parakho*'s daughter."
8 My father was a son from a very rich family.
9 Instead of living the life of a seonbi, he was always at the gambling house.
10 That is why he was called a *parakho*, which means someone who ruins his family's fortune.
11 "Your father has gambled away all of the money, and now he's asking for more.
12 Go and tell him that we have no more money left," my mother would tell me whenever she sent me to the gambling house.
13 Then, my father would yell at me angrily, "Why did you come empty-handed?
14 Bring me more money!"
15 When I was sixteen years old, my family had already made an arrangement for me to marry Mr. Seo.
16 As part of the wedding tradition, Mr. Seo's family sent my family some money to buy a new chest for clothes.
17 Right before the wedding day, my mother came into my room and said, "Your father has taken the money for the chest."
18 I asked angrily, "How could he do such a horrible thing?
19 What should we do now?"
20 "We have no choice.
21 You'll have to take your aunt's old chest," my mother said.
22 "How embarrassing for the family," people would whisper behind my back.
23 Since the first day of marriage, life at my husband's house had been difficult for me.
24 "Your father, my dear friend...," my father's friend continued his story.
25 "He was not a gambler.
26 Your father sent the family money to the independence fighters in Manchuria.
27 He made himself look like a gambler to keep this a secret from the Japanese officers."
28 At first, I was not sure if he was telling the truth.
29 But afterwards, I found out the truth about my father and I realized that I had been wrong about him.
30 Ever since that moment, I have been proud to be the daughter of a *parakho* who had devoted his life to the independence movement.

구석구석지문 TEST Step 1 p.63

Grammar in Real Life A

1. have many questions, your plans
2. Are, going to release
3. interested in various, genres
4. plans to work with other artists
5. going to go on, would tour

Grammar in Real Life B

1. got back home, had gone
2. seemed a little bit strange
3. remembered, had left
4. saw, had broken
5. found out, had eaten
6. At last, who did it
7. found small footprints

After You Read: Read and Write A

1. Secret
2. thought
3. was known as
4. was born into, gambled away
5. even took, a new chest for clothes
6. Actually
8. sent, independence fighters
9. made himself look like, keep this a secret

구석구석지문 TEST Step 2 p.64

Grammar in Real Life A

1. Mary Jane, your fans have many questions about your plans.
2. 1. Are you going to release a new song this month?
3. 2. Are you interested in various music genres?
4. 3. Do you have any plans to work with other artists?
5. 4. Are you going to go on a would tour this year?

Grammar in Real Life B

1. When I got back home, my parents had gone out for a walk.
2. The house was dark and quiet, but it seemed a little bit strange.
3. I remembered that I had left the door in my room open.
4. I saw that someone had broken the lamp.
5. I found out that someone had eaten my cookies on the table.
6. At last I knew who did it!
7. I found small footprints of my dog, Lucy, and the cat next door

After You Read: Read and Write A

1. The Secret of My Father
2. I thought my father was ...
3. My father was known as a *parakho*.
4. He was born into a rich family but he gambled away all of the money.
5. He even took the money for a new chest for clothes.
6. Actually my father was ...
7. My father was not a gambler.
8. He sent the family money to the independence fighters in Manchuria.
9. He made himself look like a gambler to keep this a secret from the Japanese officers.

단어 TEST Step 1 p.65

01 배경 02 (뉴스 등의) 진행자 03 지휘자
04 전하다 05 엄지손가락 06 상상하다
07 울림, 맥박; 때리다, 두드리다 08 추천하다
09 재능이 있는 10 악기 11 방송하다
12 합창단 13 현지의, 지역의 14 고통, 아픔
15 주로, 대부분 16 끝없는, 무한한 17 감동시키다
18 관심, 주목 19 집중하다 20 보물, 보물 같은 것
21 ~이라고 여기다, 생각하다
22 (경기 등에) 출전하다 23 긍정적인
24 완전히, 전부 25 쓸모없는, 가치 없는
26 쓰레기 27 재검토하다, 복습하다
28 환경의, 환경과 관련된 29 재활용하다
30 오케스트라, 관현악단 31 ~을 알아차리다
32 빛나는, 반짝거리는
33 공연하다, 수행하다 34 깨끗한, 순수한
35 처음에, 초반에 36 진정하다
37 ~와 조화를 이루어 38 ~와 비슷하다
39 ~을 돌려주다 40 ~을 신청하다, ~에 가입하다
41 ~로 가득 차다 42 ~하는 한
43 ~을 하고 싶어 하다

단어 TEST Step 2 p.66

01 broadcast 02 choir 03 entirely
04 anchor 05 touch 06 attention
07 mostly 08 positive 09 background
10 imagine 11 index finger 12 instrument
13 local 14 compete 15 talented
16 garbage 17 concentrate 18 beat
19 consider 20 worthless 21 review
22 endless 23 perform 24 recycle
25 pain 26 thumb 27 conductor
28 deliver 29 recommend 30 treasure
31 notice 32 pure 33 serious
34 environmental 35 as long as 36 calm down
37 send back 38 be filled with 39 sign up for
40 be eager to 41 in the beginning
42 be similar to 43 in harmony with

단어 TEST Step 3 p.67

1 endless, 끝없는, 무한한 2 instrument, 악기
3 positive, 긍정적인 4 treasure, 보물, 보물 같은 것
5 musician, 음악가 6 worthless, 쓸모없는, 가치 없는
7 talented, 재능 있는 8 picker, 줍는 사람, 채집자
9 recycle, 재활용하다 10 shiny, 빛나는, 반짝거리는
11 tank, (물, 기름 등의) 저장 통 12 perform, 공연하다
13 concentrate, 집중하다 14 conductor, 지휘자
15 garbage, 쓰레기 16 recommend, 추천하다

대화문 TEST Step 1 p.68~69

Listen & Talk 1 A-1

won, swimming competition, Congratulations / compete, find it helpful / keeps, awake, helps, focus

Listen & Talk 1 A-2

off to / going, choir practice / forgot, choir, find, interesting to sing / in harmony with others

Listen & Talk 1-B

heard, you recorded / find it easy to write them / beginning, draw on, keep a journal / No pain, no gain, with

Listen & Talk 2 A-1

sign up for / Are you planning to sign up for / to perform with / are, going to / with, violin, cello

Listen & Talk 2 A-2

sign up for / planning to take the class, during / planning, weekday class, offer / another one, Both / sign up

Listen & Talk 2-B

musical instrument, recommend, is similar to, Playing, to use, thumb nails to play

Communication

help, with something / up / which seat I should choose / planning to, orchestra / orchestra / get the seats, second floor, various musical instruments / better to hear, from the second floor / find it better, other seats

Wrap Up

have, been / I've read / have you, for visiting / find, post, latest / spread news

대화문 TEST Step 2 p.70~71

Listen & Talk 1 A-1

W: Hey, Jake. I saw you won the swimming competition yesterday. Congratulations!
M: Thanks, Anna.
W: You always seem to listen to music before you compete. Do you find it helpfu to listen to music before you swim?
M: Yes, it keeps me awake and it helps me focus.

Listen & Talk 1 A-2

M: Hi, Sally. Where are you off to?
W: I'm going to the music room. I have choir practice.
M: Oh, yeah. I forgot that you've joined the choir. Do you find it interesting to sing in the choir?
W: Yeah, it's great to sing in harmony with others.

Listen & Talk 1-B

W: Hi, Jason. Great to see you again. I've heard the new rap song, *Young and Wild*, that you recorded. It's really cool.
M: Oh, thanks.
W: I really like your songs. Do you find it easy to write them?
M: Well, it was hard in the beginning, but now it's getting easier. I draw on my experiences and keep a journal.
W: Wow! As they say, "No pain, no gain." Best of luck with your new song!
M: Thank you.

Listen & Talk 2 A-1

W: Hey, Tommy. When is the last day to sign up for the talent show?
M: This Friday. Are you planning to sign up for it, Megan?
W: Yeah, I'm going to perform with a couple of people.
M: How cool! What are you going to do?
W: We will play K-pop music with the violin and cello.

Listen & Talk 2 A-2

W: Hello, I'd like to sign up for a drum class.
M: Okay. Are you planning to take the class during the week or during the weekend?
W: I'm planning to take a weekday class. When do you offer them?
M: There is a class on Tuesday and another one on Thursday. Both classes start at 6 o'clock.
W: Great. I'd like to sign up for the Tuesday class.

Listen & Talk 2-B

W: Are you planning to learn a musical instrument? I'd like to recommend the *kalimba*, a small African musical instrument. The sound it makes is similar to that of a music box. Playing the *kalimba* is very easy. You can learn to use your thumb nails to play beautiful music in just one lesson!

Communication

W: Hey, Anthony. Can you help me with something?
M: Sure, what's up?
W: I'm going to a concert at the Arts Center, but I don't know which seat I should choose.
M: Are you planning to go to the orchestra concert?
W: Yes. I'm going to watch the orchestra concert.
M: Then, you should get the seats on the second floor. You can hear the beautiful sounds of various musical instruments better.
W: Oh, do you find it better to hear the performance from the second floor?
M: Yes. I find it better than from other seats.

Wrap Up

M: Hey, Alice.
W: Hi, Sam. How have you been?
M: Great. Actually, I've read a lot of pop news from your blog.
W: Oh, have you? Thanks for visiting my blog!
M: Do you find it interesting to post the latest pop news?
W: Yes, I love to spread news to people.

본문 TEST Step 1 p.72~73

01 Junk Orchestra
02 written by, blogger
03 sends, garbage, back music
04 write on, back, given
05 musical, was called
06 made entirely out of
07 imagine, kind, eager, out
08 thought, might, sound strange
09 few minutes, walk, stage
10 thing, noticed, made, with
11 with, playing, on, shiny
12 was shocked by, deep
13 into, with, made, recycled
14 After, eager, write, about
15 met, conductor, asked, orchestra
16 Why did you start
17 work on, filled with
18 something positive, share, with
19 use, to make instruments
20 garbage, another, treasure
21 local garbage picker, lot
22 possible, making, out, garbage
23 thing, instruments, worry, spending
24 want, to learn through
25 even, worthless, inspiring music
26 matter, as long, into
27 formed, not by instruments
29 seconds, moving, how, lives
30 power, music, endless
31 found, possible, played, recycled
32 talented, deliver, serious, attention

본문 TEST Step 2 p.74~75

01 Junk 02 written by, music blogger
03 garbage, send back music
04 written on the back of, was given
05 was called 06 made entirely out of garbage
07 was eager to find out
08 thought, might sound strange
09 After a few minutes, began to walk
10 The first thing I noticed, made out of
11 with a girl playing, on, shiny cello
12 was shocked by, deep sound
13 was, into, made from recycled materials
14 was eager to write
15 the conductor, asked
16 Why did you start
17 to work on, saw, living, was mostly filled with garbage
18 something positive, so, share, with
19 to make instruments
20 garbage, another person's treasure
21 a local garbage picker, a lot
22 it, for children, out of garbage
23 The wonderful thing, didn't have to worry about, spending
24 to learn through
25 even something worthless, inspiring music
26 interviewing, doesn't matter, as long as, into
27 formed by, not by instruments 28 Comments
29 seconds, how, lives 30 endless
31 played with
32 Not only do, talented young, deliver, bring, to our attention

본문 TEST Step 3 p.76~77

1 정크 오케스트라

2 음악 블로거 Lucy White 씀

3 “세상이 우리에게 쓰레기를 보내면, 우리는 음악을 돌려준다.”

4 이것은 내가 받은 음악회 입장권의 뒷면에 쓰여 있었다.

5 그 음악 그룹은 ‘정크 오케스트라’라고 불렸다.

6 그들은 완전히 쓰레기로만 만들어진 악기를 연주했다.

7 나는 그런 악기들이 어떤 종류의 소리를 낼지 상상할 수 없었고, 그래서 나는 알아보고 싶어졌다.

8 음악회가 시작되기 전에 나는 그 악기들이 이상한 소리를 낼지도 모른다고 생각했다.

9 몇 분 후에 한 무리의 젊은이들이 무대 위로 걸어 올라오기 시작했다.

10 내가 처음으로 알아차린 것은 그들의 악기였는데, 그것들은 반짝이는 기름통으로 만들어진 첼로, 포크로 만들어진 바이올린, 수도관과 단추로 만들어진 플루트였다.

11 음악회는 한 소녀가 자신의 반짝이는 첼로로 바흐의 〈첼로 모음곡 1번〉을 연주하는 것으로 시작되었다.

12 나는 그 깊은 소리에 충격을 받았다.

13 나는 음악에 너무 심취해서 그들이 재활용된 재료들로 만들어진 악기를 연주하고 있다는 것을 잊었다.

14 음악회가 끝나고, 나는 그 오케스트라에 대한 이야기를 몹시 쓰고 싶었다.

15 나는 지휘자인 Favio Chávez를 만나서 그에게 오케스트라에 대해 물었다.

16 Lucy White: 왜 당신은 정크 오케스트라를 시작하셨나요?

17 Favio Chávez: 2005년에 재활용 프로그램에서 일을 하기 위해서 내가 파라과이의 카테우라라고 불리는 작은 마을에 갔을 때, 나는 대부분이 쓰레기로 가득 차 있는 마을에 살고 있는 어린이들을 보았습니다.

18 나는 그들의 삶에 긍정적인 무엇인가를 더해 주고 싶어서, 음악에 대한 나의 사랑을 그들과 나누기로 결정했습니다.

19 Lucy White: 왜 당신은 악기를 만들기 위해 쓰레기를 이용했나요?

20 Favio Chávez: 한 사람의 쓰레기는 다른 사람의 보물입니다.

21 그 지역의 쓰레기 줍는 사람인 Nicolás Gámez가 나를 많이 도와주었습니다.

22 그는 쓰레기로 악기를 만들어 줌으로써 어린이들이 음악을 연주하는 것이 가능하도록 만들었습니다.

23 이 악기들의 멋진 점은 어린이들이 악기에 많은 돈을 쓸 것을 걱정하지 않아도 된다는 점이었죠.

24 Lucy White: 당신의 음악을 통해서 사람들이 무엇을 배우기를 원하십니까?

25 Favio Chávez: 나는 가치 없는 것도 영감을 주는 음악을 만들어 낼 수 있다는 것을 사람들이 알게 되기를 원합니다.

26 Chávez를 인터뷰한 후에 나는 사람들이 악기를 연주하는 데 마음을 쏟아붓는 한, 그 사람이 연주하는 악기가 무엇인지는 별로 중요하지 않다는 것을 깨달았다.

27 카테우라의 어린이들은 나에게 오케스트라는 악기에 의해서가 아니라 사람에 의해 이루어지는 것이라는 것을 보여 주었다.

28 감상평

29 Annie: (23초 전) 음악이 삶을 바꿀 수 있다는 것을 보아서 너무 가슴이 뭉클하다.

30 음악의 힘은 끝이 없다!

31 Thomas: (1분 전) 음악회가 끝난 후, 나는 재활용 악기로 연주되는 음악으로 사람들에게 영감을 주는 것이 가능하다는 것을 알았다.

32 Kate: (5일 전) 이 재능 있는 젊은이들은 훌륭한 음악을 전할 뿐만 아니라, 또한 심각한 환경 문제에 우리가 주목하게 한다.

본문 TEST Step 4~Step 5 p.78~81

1 The Junk Orchestra

2 written by a music blogger, Lucy White

3 “The world sends us garbage, we send back music.”

4 This was written on the back of a concert ticket I was given.

5 The musical group was called “The Junk Orchestra.”

6 They played instruments made entirely out of garbage.

7 I could not imagine what kind of sound these instruments would make, so I was eager to find out.

8 Before the concert, I thought that the instruments might sound strange.

9 After a few minutes, a group of young people began to walk on the stage.

10 The first thing I noticed was their instruments: a cello made out of a shiny oil tank, a violin made with forks, and a flute made with a water pipe and buttons.

11 The concert began with a girl playing Bach's *Cello Suite No. 1* on her shiny cello.

12 I was shocked by the deep sound.

13 I was so into the music that I forgot that they were playing with instruments made from recycled materials.

14 After the concert, I was eager to write a story about the orchestra.

15 I met Favio Chávez, the conductor, and asked him about the orchestra.

16 Lucy White: Why did you start The Junk Orchestra?

17 Favio Chávez: When I went to a small town called Cateura in Paraguay to work on a recycling program in 2005, I saw children living in a town that was mostly filled with garbage.

18 I wanted to add something positive to their lives, so I decided to share my love of music with them.

19 Lucy White: Why did you use garbage to make instruments?

20 Favio Chávez: One person's garbage is another person's treasure.

21 Nicolás Gómez, a local garbage picker, helped me a lot.

22 He made it possible for children to play music by making instruments out of garbage.

23 The wonderful thing about these instruments was that the children didn't have to worry about spending a lot of money on them.

24 Lucy White: What do you want people to learn through your music?

25 Favio Chávez: I want people to know that even something worthless can make inspiring music.

26 After interviewing Chávez, I realized that it really doesn't matter what instrument you play with as long as you put your heart into playing it.

27 The children of Cateura showed me that an orchestra is formed by people, not by instruments.

28 Comments

29 Annie: (23 seconds ago) So moving to see how music can change lives.

30 The power of music is endless!

31 Thomas: (1 minute ago) After the concert, I found it possible to inspire people by music played with recycled instruments.

32 Kate: (5 days ago) Not only do these talented young people deliver great music, but they also bring serious environmental problems to our attention.

구석구석지문 TEST Step 1 p.82

After You Read A

1. Junk Orchestra
2. sends us garbage, send back
3. About, concert
4. played instruments made out of garbage
5. with a girl playing the cello, a shiny oil tank
6. was shocked by
7. The Interview with
8. to work. on a recycling program
9. decided to share, with
10. local garbage picker
11. by people, not by instruments

Grammar in Real Life

1. visited, broadcasting company
2. sat at, where
3. There were, hanging on the wall
4. read aloud sentences moving across
5. came out of, myself recorded
6. liked the background created with

Wrap Up 2

1. Where are, going
2. going, this Sunday
3. Are, planning to perform
4. How, know about
5. is going to play the piano, going to, too
6. Come, watch, performance

구석구석지문 TEST Step 2 p.83

After You Read A

1. The Junk Orchestra
2. The world sends us garbage, we send back music.
3. About the concert.
4. The young people played instruments made out of garbage.
5. It started with a girl playing the cello made out of a shiny oil tank.
6. I was shocked by the deep sound.
7. The Interview with Mr. Chávez
8. He went to Cateura in Paraguay to work. on a recycling program.
9. He decided to share his love of music with the children.
10. A local garbage picker helped him.
11. An orchestra is formed by people, not by instruments.

Grammar in Real Life

1. I visited a broadcasting company.
2. In the news room, I sat at the desk where anchors give the news.
3. There were two screens hanging on the wall.
4. I could read aloud sentences moving across the screen.
5. After I came out of the room, I could see myself recorded on the TV screen.

6. I really liked the background created with computer graphics.

Wrap Up 2

1. M: Hi, Julie. Where are you going?
2. W: Hi, Chris. I'm going to my guitar lesson. Our band has a concert at the hospital this Sunday.
3. M: This Sunday? Are you planning to perform at the Happy Children's Hospital?
4. W: Yes. How do you know about the concert?
5. M: Oh, my sister is going to play the piano there, so I'm going to the concert, too.
6. W: Great. Come and watch our performance!

MEMO

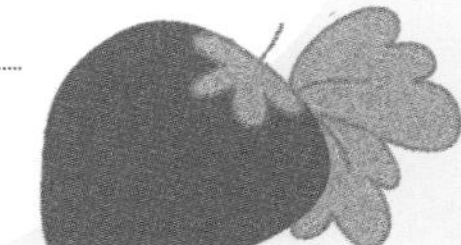

정답 및 해설

비상 | 김진완

적중 100 + 특별부록

Plan B

우리학교 최신기출

비상 · 김진완 교과서를 배우는

학교 시험문제 분석 · 모음 · 해설집

전국단위 학교 시험문제 수집 및 분석
출제 빈도가 높은 문제 위주로 선별
문제 풀이에 필요한 상세한 해설

비상 · 김진완

3학년 영어 1학기 중간고사(1과) 1회

문항수 : 선택형(22문항) 서술형(1문항)	20 . . .	반		점수
		이름		

◎ 선택형 문항의 답안은 컴퓨터용 수정 싸인펜을 사용하여 OMR 답안지에 바르게 표기하시오.
◎ 서술형 문제는 답을 답안지에 반드시 검정 볼펜으로 쓰시오.
◎ 총 23문항 100점 만점입니다. 문항별 배점은 각 문항에 표시되어 있습니다.

[종로구 ㅇㅇ중]

1. 다음 중 반의어를 만드는 방법이 나머지와 다른 하나는? (4점)

① usual
② expensive
③ healthy
④ certain
⑤ friendly

[서초구 ㅇㅇ중]

2. 다음 밑줄 친 ⓐ~ⓔ 중, 내용의 흐름상 단어의 쓰임이 가장 적절한 것은? (5점)

Now, let's take a look at our last clip. Anna and Julie are best friends, but Anna often hurts Julie's feelings.

Anna: Don't put your bag on my desk!
Julie: …(silence)

Julie probably ⓐfelt comfortable because Anna ⓑkindly asked her using the word "don't." In such situation, listeners like Julie simply don't like ⓒgiving orders. So, Anna should try to use more polite ways to express herself, such as ⓓ"can," "could," or "please." Then, what she says will ⓔsound like a demand.

Anna: Can you put your bag on your desk?
Julie: Of course!

① ⓐ
② ⓑ
③ ⓒ
④ ⓓ
⑤ ⓔ

[경북 ㅇㅇ중]

3. 다음 대화의 빈칸 (A)에 들어갈 말로 가장 알맞은 것은? (4점)

W: I'm so stressed out about my exams, Jinsu.
M: Yeah, me, too. We have two more to go.
W: After finishing my exams, I want to go on a trip and just let my hair down.
M: You want to change your hair style?
W: No, that's not what I mean. I want to go somewhere and (A)__________.

① feel free and uneasy
② feel free from housework
③ feel free to share good ideas
④ feel free from all my troubles
⑤ feel free from doing simple things

[경기 ㅇㅇ중]

4. 다음 밑줄 친 부분의 쓰임이 나머지와 다른 하나는? (4점)

① What my dad planted is this tree.
② This job is not what I want to do.
③ I don't know what food you want to eat.
④ I was surprised at what she said yesterday.
⑤ You can put on what you want to wear on No Uniform Day.

[충북 ㅇㅇ중]

5. 다음 중 짝지어진 대화가 가장 어색한 것은? (5점)

① A: David, what's your summer plan?
B: I am going to go to China. I can't wait to visit the Rainbow Mountains.

② A: Do you want to watch the new 3D movie?
B: Which one?

③ A: Dad, my science club is going to go to Dokdo in July.
B: Oh, really? What do you plan to do there?

④ A: Sally, how come you don't talk much with Anna these days?
B: Well, I'm upset about an argument we had.

⑤ A: How is your science homework going?
B: It's going well. I'm upset about my science group.

[종로구 ㅇㅇ중]

6. Complete the dialogue by filling in the blanks. (4 words) (5점)

A: I'm so stressed about my exams, Jinsu.
B: Yeah, me, too. We have two more to go.
A: After finishing my exams, I want to go on a trip and just ________________.
B: You want to change your hair style?
A: No, I meant that I want to go somewhere and feel free from all my troubles.

→ ________________________________

[종로구 ㅇㅇ중]

7. 다음 괄호 안에서 알맞은 단어를 고를 때, 올바르게 고른 것은? (4점)

① Can you tell me the reason [why / how] you are upset?

② I can't forget the moment [when / why] I rode my bike for the first time.

③ Is this the restaurant [when / where] Jack is working?

④ Is there a shop [where / when] I can buy pencils?

⑤ This is the day [when / where] my parents got married.

[경기 ㅇㅇ중]

8. 다음 대화를 완성할 때 빈칸에 들어가기에 알맞은 것만을 〈보기〉에서 있는 대로 고른 것은? (5점)

A: Why do you look so unhappy?
B: I'm upset about Roy.
He ________________________.
A: That's too bad.

<보기>
ⓐ always copies me
ⓑ makes me let my hair down
ⓒ talks about me behind my back
ⓓ talks too loudly on the phone at night
ⓔ keeps cutting me off in the middle of my sentences

① ⓐ, ⓑ
② ⓐ, ⓒ, ⓓ
③ ⓑ, ⓒ, ⓔ
④ ⓐ, ⓒ, ⓓ, ⓔ
⑤ ⓑ, ⓒ, ⓓ, ⓔ

[경기 ○○중]

9. 다음 대화의 각 빈칸 ⓐ~ⓔ에 들어갈 표현으로 알맞은 것은? (5점)

(A)

W: Don't let the cat out of the bag about Clara's surprise party.

M: A cat? I don't have a cat.

W: That's not what I meant. I meant ⓐ____________________.

(B)

W: Did you finally go diving yesterday, Nick?

M: Actually, I got cold feet, Mina.

W: That's too bad. How did you get a cold?

M: No, Mina. That's not what I meant. I meant ⓑ____________________.

(C)

W: Mr. Brown, I want to get a good grade in English. What should I do?

M: Well, Sujin, you should concentrate in class, first of all. I see you often have your head in the clouds.

W: Clouds? I can't see the sky from inside the classroom.

M: That's not what I meant. I meant ⓒ____________________.

(D)

W: I'm so stressed out about my exams, Jinsu.

M: Yeah, me, too. We have two more to go.

W: After finishing my exams, I want to go on a trip and just let my hair down.

M: You want to change your hair style?

W: No, that's not what I meant. I meant ⓓ____________________.

(E)

W: Hey, Minho! Do you want to watch a movie tonight?

M: I'm sorry, but I can't go out tonight. I need to hit the books.

W: What did you say? Is there anything wrong with your books?

M: No, that's not what I meant. I meant ⓔ____________________.

① ⓐ you cut me off again
② ⓑ it was too cold outside
③ ⓒ you don't focus in class
④ ⓓ I want to change my hair shop
⑤ ⓔ I need to get new books for myself

[경북 ○○중]

10. 다음 두 사람의 대화에서 밑줄 친 (A)~(D)의 순서가 가장 적절한 것은? (4점)

M: Why the long face, Julie?

W: I got angry at my sister yesterday and said some mean things to her.

M: Oh, why were you angry?

(A) I see. And you two haven't worked it out yet?

(B) I was really tired and I wanted to sleep. But she was talking loudly on the phone. I was really upset about that.

(C) Why don't you write her a note or send her a text message?

(D) No, not yet. I want to say I'm sorry that I was mean to her, but I don't know how.

W: Hmm, that's a good idea. Thanks.

① (A)-(B)-(C)-(D) ② (A)-(C)-(B)-(D)
③ (B)-(A)-(D)-(C) ④ (B)-(C)-(D)-(A)
⑤ (C)-(D)-(A)-(B)

[경북 ㅇㅇ중]

11. 다음 두 사람의 대화에서 빈칸 (A), (B), (C)에 들어갈 것이 순서대로 맞게 된 것은? (5점)

M: Sally, how come you don't talk much with Anna these days?
W: Well, I'm upset about an argument we had.
M: Why are you upset?
W: She kept (A)________ me off in the middle of my sentences, so I (B)________ mad. We argued and I (C)________ talking to her.
M: Oh, I'm sorry to hear that.

	(A)	(B)	(C)
①	cutting	get	stopped
②	cutting	got	stopped
③	to cut	got	stopped
④	to cut	got	stop
⑤	cutting	get	stop

[경북 ㅇㅇ중]

[12~14] 다음 글을 읽고 물음에 답하시오.

Welcome to "All about Teens." I'm Dr. Carter. Today, we're going to talk about using good communication skills to express ourselves more (A)___________.
Let's start with our first clip about Brian. When he tries to talk to his brother, he always ends up arguing with his brother. Let's find out the reason (B)___________ he has this problem.
Brian: You lost my earphones again. Why are you so (C)___________?
Brian is starting a sentence with "you" to express his feelings. Instead, he should use the "I-message." Starting with "I" can help him focus on (D)___________ he feels or thinks rather than point the finger at his brother.
Brian: I'm really upset because my favorite earphones are (E)___________.

12. 위 글의 빈칸 (A), (C), (E)에 가장 적절한 것은? (4점)

	(A)	(C)	(E)
①	effectively	carelessly	lost
②	effective	careless	lost
③	effective	carelessly	lose
④	effectively	careless	lost
⑤	effectively	careless	lose

13. 위 글의 빈칸 (B), (D)에 가장 적절한 것은? (4점)

	(B)	(D)
①	why	what
②	why	that
③	why	which
④	when	what
⑤	when	that

14. 다음 중에서 위 글의 내용과 가장 일치하지 않는 것은? (4점)

① The above paragraph is talking about using good communication skills.
② Brian always gets into an argument with his brother when he tries to talk to him.
③ The sentence starting with 'I' can express your feelings better than the sentence starting with 'you'.
④ Brian has some problems in communicating with his brother.
⑤ The problem with Brian's communication is to focus on his feelings and thoughts.

[경북 ㅇㅇ중]

[15~17] 다음 글을 읽고 물음에 답하시오.

Now, let's take a look at our last clip. Anna and Julie are best friends, but Anna often hurts Julie's feelings.
Anna: Don't put your bag on my desk!
Julie probably felt uncomfortable because Anna (A)________ using the word "don't." People ⓐsimply don't like taking orders. Anna should try to use words ⓑlike "can," "could," or "please." Then, what she says will sound like a request ⓒrather than a demand.
Anna: Could you put your bag on your desk?
As we saw in the video clips, a small change ⓓin the way we express ourselves can solve or even ⓔprevent from communication problems. Let's keep these tips in mind!

15. 위 글의 밑줄 친 부분 중, 쓰임이 어색한 것은? (5점)

① ⓐ ② ⓑ ③ ⓒ
④ ⓓ ⑤ ⓔ

16. 위 글의 흐름으로 보아 빈칸 (A)에 가장 적절한 것은? (4점)

① makes a demand
② made a demand
③ makes a request
④ made a request
⑤ made a mistake

17. 위 글을 읽고 답할 수 없는 질문은? (5점)

① Who is Anna's best friend?
② What tips do we have to keep in mind?
③ What words does Julie use when she asks Anna?
④ Why does Anna hurt Julie's feelings when she talks?
⑤ What words should Anna try to use when she asks Julie?

[경북 ㅇㅇ중]

[18~19] 다음 글을 읽고 물음에 답하시오.

Next is Calli. She is ⓐtrying to talk to her mother, but she ⓑis busy preparing go to work. (A) Let's have a look.
(B) Calli: Hey, Mom. Could I talk to you about something?
(C) Maybe Calli's mom wanted to ⓒlisten to Calli was going to say. (D) But she didn't have ⓓenough time to talk with her daughter. (E) Calli should ⓔpick a time her mom is ready to listen.
Calli: "Hey, Mom. Could I talk to you about something?"
Mom: "Sure."

18. 위 글의 흐름으로 보아 주어진 문장이 들어가기에 가장 적절한 곳은? (4점)

Calli needs to find the right time to talk to her mom.

① (A) ② (B) ③ (C)
④ (D) ⑤ (E)

19. 위 글의 밑줄 친 ⓐ~ⓔ 중에서, 어법상 어색한 것을 모두 고른 것은? (4점)

① ⓐ, ⓑ ② ⓑ, ⓒ
③ ⓒ ④ ⓓ, ⓔ
⑤ ⓐ, ⓓ, ⓔ

[서초구 ㅇㅇ중]

[20~23] 다음 글을 읽고 물음에 답하시오.

Welcome to "All about Teens." I'm Dr. Carter. Today, we're going to talk about (A)____________________. Let's start with our first clip about Brian. When he tries to talk to his brother, ⓐhe always ends up to argue with his brother. ⓑLet's find out the reason how he has this problem.

Brian: You lost my earphones again. Why are you so careless?

Brian is starting a sentence with "you" to express his feelings. Instead, he should use the "I-message." ⓒStarting with "I" can help him to focus on what he feels it rather than pointing the finger at his brother.

Brian: ⓓI'm really upset because my favorite earphones lost.

Next is Calli. She is trying to talk to her mother, but she is busy preparing to go to work. Let's have a look.

Callie: "Hey, Mom. Could I talk to you about something?"
Mom: ...(silence)

Calli needs to find the right time to talk to her mom. ⓔIn fact, Calli's mom wanted to listen to what Calli was going to say, but she didn't have enough time to talk with her daughter. Calli should pick a time (B)when her mom is ready to listen.

Callie: "Hey, Mom. Could I talk to you about something?"
Mom: "Sure."

20. 위 글의 (A)에 들어갈 위 글 전체의 주제로 가장 적절한 것은? (4점)

① why we argue with others
② the effects of active listening skills
③ the importance of using the "I-message"
④ why finding the right time to talk is important
⑤ problems in communication and tips for better communication

21. 위 글의 ⓐ~ⓔ 중 문법적으로 올바른 문장은? (4점)

① ⓐ ② ⓑ ③ ⓒ
④ ⓓ ⑤ ⓔ

22. 위 글의 내용을 잘못 이해한 사람은? (4점)

① 재은: Well, Brian made a mistake when communicating with his brother by starting his sentence with "you", as in "Why are you so careless?"
② 은주: Right. Instead of pointing the finger at his brother, he should start the sentence with "I", as in "I'm really upset."
③ 효진: In fact, the effect of the "I-message" is that he can focus on his feelings.
④ 현덕: In Callie's case, at first, her mom did not feel like listening to what Calli was going to say.
⑤ 할리: From Calli's case, we can see that it is important to communicate with others when they are ready to listen to us.

23. 위 글의 (B)when과 밑줄 친 부분의 역할이 다른 것은? (4점)

① I remember the day when we went to the beach.
② You are going to miss me when I'm gone.
③ She sometimes thinks about the time when she was healthy.
④ I miss the summers when we used to go to the beach.
⑤ Jane will never forget the day when her dog joined her family.

3학년 영어 1학기 중간고사(1과) 2회

반		점수
이름		

문항수 : 선택형(27문항) 서술형(1문항) | 20 . . .

◎ 선택형 문항의 답안은 컴퓨터용 수정 싸인펜을 사용하여 OMR 답안지에 바르게 표기하시오.
◎ 서술형 문제는 답을 답안지에 반드시 검정 볼펜으로 쓰시오.
◎ 총 28문항 100점 만점입니다. 문항별 배점은 각 문항에 표시되어 있습니다.

[서초구 ㅇㅇ중]

1. 다음 밑줄 친 단어들의 의미를 영어로 풀이한 것들 중 옳은 것을 고르면? (4점)

① <u>have one's head in the clouds:</u> to be aware of what is going on
② <u>point the finger at</u>: to say that someone should not be blamed
③ <u>make an arrangement</u>: to make a plan for how something will happen
④ <u>get cold feet</u>: to feel too relaxed to do something that you have planned to do
⑤ <u>devote one's life to</u>: to waste your time and effort not doing something you believe in or to a person

[경기 ㅇㅇ중]

2. 다음 밑줄 친 (A)와 (B)에 들어갈 단어를 순서대로 바르게 짝지은 것은? (3점)

• I can't forget (A)______________ when I rode my bike for the first time.
• This is (B)______________ where my first birthday party was held.

	(A)	(B)
①	the day	the time
②	the way	the house
③	the time	the reason
④	the place	the special day
⑤	the moment	the restaurant

[종로구 ㅇㅇ중]

3. In the following dialogue, please choose the answer that is correct. (3점)

A: I went diving yesterday but I got cold feet.
B: That's too bad. How did you get a cold?
A: ⓐ______________. I meant that I got scared, so I didn't dive.

① That was mean.
② That's what I meant.
③ You meant it like that
④ You didn't mean that.
⑤ That's not what I meant.

[경기 ㅇㅇ중]

4. According to the passage below, what should Anna say to Julie instead of (A)? (4점)

Now, let's take a look at our last clip. Anna and Julie are best friends, but Anna often hurts Julie's feelings.

Anna: (A)<u>Don't put your bag on my desk!</u>

Julie probably felt uncomfortable because Anna made a demand using the word "don't." People simply don't like taking orders. Anna should try to use words such as "can," "could," or "please." Then, what she says will sound like a request rather than a demand.

① Don't use my desk again.
② I don't want you to use my desk.
③ Could you put your bag on your desk?
④ Why did you put your bag on my desk?
⑤ Can I throw your bag away somewhere?

[충북 ㅇㅇ중]

5. 다음 밑줄 친 ⓐ~ⓔ 중 어법상 어색한 것을 고르면? (4점)

ⓐJulie probably felt uncomfortable because ⓑAnna made a demand using the word "don't." ⓒPeople simply don't like taking orders. ⓓAnna should try to use words such as "can," "could," or "please." Then, ⓔthat she says will sound like a request rather than a demand.

① ⓐ ② ⓑ ③ ⓒ
④ ⓓ ⑤ ⓔ

[서초구 ㅇㅇ중]

6. 다음 대화에서 (A)의 주어진 상황에서 쓸 수 있는 올바른 영어 표현이 아닌 것은? (4점)

M: Why the long face, Julie?
W: I got angry at my sister yesterday and said some mean things to her.
M: Oh, what happened?
W: I was really tired and I wanted to sleep. But she was talking loudly on the phone. (A)여동생의 행동으로 인해 느낀 불편한 감정을 표현
M: I see. And you two haven't worked it out yet?
W: No, not yet. I want to say that I'm sorry I was mean to her, but I don't know how.
M: Why don't you write her a note or send her a text message?
W: Hmm, that's a good idea. Thanks.

① I was really angry about that.
② I was really unhappy about that.
③ I felt uneasy because she did that.
④ I let my hair down because she did that.
⑤ My feelings were hurt because she did that.

[충북 ㅇㅇ중]

[7~8] 다음 대화를 읽고 물음에 답하시오.

Woman: Hey, Jason. You seem upset. Anything wrong?
Man: People keep telling me that I'm too direct. I'm upset about that.
Woman: Hmm... I kind of know what they're talking about.
Man: ______________________________
Woman: Well, sometimes you tend to say what's on your mind too strongly.
Man: Should I just keep quiet, then?
Woman: That's not what I meant. You can try to consider others' feelings.
Man: I see. I'll try that.

7. 위 대화의 내용에 대한 설명으로 다음 중 가장 일치하는 것은? (3점)

① 여자는 화가 나 있다.
② 여자는 직설적으로 말을 한다.
③ 여자는 남자에게 충고하고 있다.
④ 남자는 여자의 말이 마음에 들지 않는다.
⑤ 남자는 여자의 충고대로 직설적으로 말을 하려고 한다.

8. 위 대화의 빈칸에 들어갈 말로 가장 알맞은 것은? (4점)

① Why do you say so?
② What do you mean?
③ Sounds interesting!
④ I'll show you the way to talk to people.
⑤ That's too bad.

[종로구 ㅇㅇ중]

9. 다음 중 밑줄 친 부분의 쓰임이 나머지와 다른 것은? (3점)

① I can't believe what you're saying.
② This computer is what I want to have.
③ What I am looking for is a pink letter.
④ What do you want to wear on No Uniform Day?
⑤ The story is different from what I thought.

[서초구 ㅇㅇ중]

10. 다음 중 주어진 의미에 맞도록 문장의 어법이 올바르게 쓰이지 않은 것은? (4점)

① 내가 지금 당장 하고 싶은 것은 샤워를 하는 것이다.
That I want to do right now is to take a shower.
② 선생님은 그녀가 모르는 것을 안다.
The teacher knows what she doesn't know.
③ 그녀가 말할 것을 주의 깊게 들으세요.
Listen carefully to what she will say.
④ 진실인 것은 그녀가 그것을 모른다는 것이다.
What is true is that she doesn't know it.
⑤ 이 시계는 조가 지난주에 샀던 것이다.
This watch is what Joe bought last week.

[경기 ㅇㅇ중]

[11~12] 다음 글을 읽고 물음에 답하시오.

Speak Your Mind Effectively!

Welcome to "All about Teens." I'm Dr. Carter. Today, we're going to talk about ⓐuse good communication skills to ⓑexpressing ourselves more effectively.

Let's start with our first clip about Brian. When he tries to talk to his brother, he always ends up ⓒarguing with his brother. Let's find out the reason why he has this problem.

Brian: "You lost my earphones again. Why are you so careless?"

Brian is starting a sentence with "you" to express his feelings. Instead, he should use the "I-message." ⓓStart with "I" can help him focus on what he feels or thinks rather than ⓔpointed the finger at his brother.

Brain: I'm really upset because my favorite earphones are lost.

11. 위 글의 밑줄 친 ⓐ~ⓔ 중, 어법상 알맞은 것은? (4점)

① ⓐ ② ⓑ ③ ⓒ
④ ⓓ ⑤ ⓔ

12. 위 글의 내용으로 보았을 때, 다음 질문에 대한 대답으로 가장 알맞은 것은? (3점)

Q: Why should Brian use the "I-message"?
A: Because ______________________.

① his brother is so careless
② Dr. Carter likes this kind of communication skill
③ he can point the finger at his brother effectively
④ it's the way he can get new earphones from his brother
⑤ it can help him express his feelings without blaming his brother

[충북 ㅇㅇ중]

[13~14] 다음 글을 읽고 물음에 답하시오.

> Brian is starting a sentence with "you" to express his feelings. Instead, he should use the "I-message." Starting with "I" can help him focus on ⓐwhat he feels or thinks rather than point the finger at his brother.
>
> Brian: "I'm really ⓑ________ because my favorite earphones are lost."

13. 다음 중 위 글의 밑줄 친 ⓐwhat과 쓰임이 다른 하나를 고르면? (3점)

① What are you going to do?
② I can't believe what you're saying.
③ You can eat what you like to eat on World Food Day.
④ You can put on what you want to wear on No Uniform Day.
⑤ You may bring what you want to sell on Sale Day.

14. 위 글의 빈칸 ⓑ에 들어갈 가장 알맞은 것을 고르시오. (4점)

① upset ② curious
③ lonely ④ excited
⑤ interested

[경기 ㅇㅇ중]

[15~16] 다음 글을 읽고 물음에 답하시오.

> Next is Calli. She is trying to talk to ⓐher mother, but ⓑshe is busy preparing to go to work. Let's have a look.
>
> Calli: "Hey, Mom. Could I talk to ⓒyou about something?"
>
> Calli needs to find the right time to talk to her mom. Maybe Calli's mom wanted to listen to what Calli was going to say. But ⓓshe didn't have enough time to talk with ⓔher daughter. Calli should pick a time when her mom is ready to listen.

15. 위 글의 ⓐ~ⓔ 중, Calli를 가리키는 것은? (3점)

① ⓐ ② ⓑ ③ ⓒ
④ ⓓ ⑤ ⓔ

16. 위 글을 바탕으로 Calli의 일기를 완성하였을 때, 밑줄 친 부분에 들어갈 표현으로 가장 알맞은 것은? (4점)

> March 19th
> I sent my story to "All about Teens," and Dr. Carter advised me to ________________ to talk to my mom. So after my mom came back home after work, I asked her to walk our dog with me. Then I could talk to my mom because she was ready to listen. I felt better after talking with her about my problem.

① call my mom
② find the right time
③ send a text message
④ prepare to go to work
⑤ help her do the housework

[충북 ㅇㅇ중]

[17~18] 다음 글을 읽고 물음에 답하시오.

Next is Calli. She is trying to talk to her mother, but she is busy preparing to go to work. Let's have a look.
Calli: "Hey, Mom. Could I talk to you about something?"
Calli needs to find the right time to talk to her mom. Maybe Calli's mom wanted to listen to what Calli was going to say. But she didn't have enough time to talk with her daughter. Calli should pick a time ⓐ __________ her mom is ready to listen.
Calli: "Hey, Mom. Could I talk to you about something?"
Mom: "Sure."

17. 위 글의 목적은? (3점)

① 부탁 ② 조언 ③ 광고
④ 사과 ⑤ 칭찬

18. 위 글의 빈칸 ⓐ에 알맞은 말을 쓰시오. (4점)

→ __________

[구로구 ㅇㅇ중]

[19~22] 다음 글을 읽고 물음에 답하시오.

Welcome to "All about Teens." Ⓐ<u>I'm Dr. Carter</u>. Today, we're going to talk about using good communication skills ⓐ<u>to express</u> ourselves more effectively.
Ⓑ<u>Let's start with our first clip about Brian.</u> When he tries to talk to his brother, he always ends up ⓑ<u>arguing with</u> his brother. Let's find out the reason ⓒ<u>why</u> he has this problem.
Brian: (A)______________________
Ⓒ<u>Brian is starting a sentence with "you" to express his feelings</u>. Instead, he should use the "I-message." Ⓓ<u>It is a kind of messenger you can get in contact with someone quickly</u>. Starting with "I" can help him focus on ⓓ<u>that</u> he feels or thinks rather than ⓔ<u>point</u> the finger at his brother.
Brian: Ⓔ<u>I'm really upset because my favorite earphones are lost</u>.

19. 위 글의 내용을 올바르게 이해한 것은? (3점)

① Brian found his earphones.
② Dr. Carter lost Brian's earphones.
③ Brian is a character in the first clip.
④ Brian's brother apologized to Brian.
⑤ Pointing the finger at somebody is a good communication skill.

20. 위 글의 밑줄 친 Ⓐ~Ⓔ 중에서 글의 논리적인 흐름에 맞지 <u>않는</u> 것은? (3점)

① Ⓐ ② Ⓑ ③ Ⓒ
④ Ⓓ ⑤ Ⓔ

21. 위 글의 빈칸 (A)에 들어갈 Brian의 말로 적절한 것은? (4점)

① Someone has stolen my earphones.
② I can't believe my earphones are gone.
③ It's so sad that you lost my earphones.
④ You lost my earphones! Why are you so careless?
⑤ Could you please explain why you took my earphones and lost them?

22. 위 글의 밑줄 친 ⓐ~ⓔ 중에서 어법상 <u>어색한</u> 것은? (4점)

① ⓐ ② ⓑ ③ ⓒ
④ ⓓ ⑤ ⓔ

[구로구 ㅇㅇ중]

[23~25] 다음 글을 읽고 물음에 답하시오.

Next is Calli. (A) She is ⓐtrying to talk to her mother, but she is busy ⓑpreparing to go to work. (B) Let's have a look. (C) Calli ⓒneeds to find the right time to talk to her mom. Maybe Calli's mom wanted to listen to ⓓthat Calli was going to say. (D) Calli should pick a time ⓔwhich her mom is ready to listen. (E)

23. 위 글의 교훈으로 옳은 것은? (3점)

① Time waits for no people.
② Everything has its own time.
③ Time is the most wisest counselor of all.
④ The way we spend our time says who we are.
⑤ Time is the most valuable thing people can spend.

24. 위 글의 흐름으로 보아, 아래의 문장이 들어갈 곳으로 옳은 것은? (4점)

But she didn't have enough time to talk with her daughter.

① (A) ② (B) ③ (C)
④ (D) ⑤ (E)

25. 위 글의 밑줄 친 ⓐ~ⓔ 중 어색한 부분을 바르게 수정한 것은? (4점)

① ⓐ → tried
② ⓑ → prepared
③ ⓒ → need
④ ⓓ → the thing what
⑤ ⓔ → when

[구로구 ㅇㅇ중]

[26~28] 다음 글을 읽고 물음에 답하시오.

Now, let's take a look at our last clip. (A) Anna and Julie are best friends, but Anna often hurts Julie's feelings. (B)

Anna: Don't put your bag on my desk!

Julie felt uncomfortable because Anna made a demand using the word "don't" (C) People simply don't like taking orders. Anna should try to use words ⓐ________ "can," "could," or "please." (D)

Anna: Could you put your bag on your desk?

As we saw in the video clips, a small change in the way we express ourselves can solve or even prevent communication problems. (E)

26. 위 글을 읽고 답할 수 있는 질문은? (4점)

① Why did Julie feel uncomfortable?
② What kind of a bag does Julie have?
③ Why do people dislike taking orders?
④ How many times did Anna hurt Julie's feeling?
⑤ How long has Julie been keeping her friendship with Anna?

27. 아래의 문장이 들어갈 곳으로 옳은 것은? (4점)

Then, what she says will sound like a request rather than a demand.

① (A) ② (B) ③ (C)
④ (D) ⑤ (E)

28. 위 글의 빈칸 ⓐ에 들어갈 말로 옳은 것은? (3점)

① such as ② in order to
③ as long as ④ rather than
⑤ as soon as

3학년 영어 1학기 중간고사(2과) 1회

문항수 : 선택형(22문항) 서술형(2문항)	20 . . .	반		점수
		이름		

◎ 선택형 문항의 답안은 컴퓨터용 수정 싸인펜을 사용하여 OMR 답안지에 바르게 표기하시오.
◎ 서술형 문제는 답을 답안지에 반드시 검정 볼펜으로 쓰시오.
◎ 총 24문항 100점 만점입니다. 문항별 배점은 각 문항에 표시되어 있습니다.

[서초구 ㅇㅇ중]

1. 다음 밑줄 친 단어들의 의미를 영어로 풀이한 것 중 옳은 것을 고르면? (4점)

① endless: difficult to survive in
② wild: natural and not used by people
③ accident: a wonderful and surprising event that is believed to be caused by God
④ insight: an exciting and possibly dangerous activity
⑤ entirely: remarkable or interesting because it is different from or better than others

[대전 ㅇㅇ중]

2. 다음 중 단어의 영영풀이가 옳은 것끼리 나열한 것은? (4점)

(A) peak: the lowest point of something
(B) desert: an area where there is very little rain and not many plants
(C) hide: to put something in a place where it can't be seen or found
(D) communication: exchanging information through talking or body language, etc
(E) plankton: very huge animals which float on the surface of the sea where many sea animals feed on them

① (A), (D) ② (B), (E)
③ (A), (B), (C) ④ (B), (C), (D)
⑤ (B), (C), (D), (E)

[구로구 ㅇㅇ중]

3. 다음 영어 회화 동아리 회원간의 대화 중 빈칸 (A)~(C)에 들어갈 말로 옳은 것은? (5점)

Jisu: Noodles are easy to cook.
Rose: I don't agree with you. It's hard for me to cook noodles. It's impossible that everyone's good at cooking noodles.
Jisu: Oh, that's not what I meant. I mean I can cook noodles easily. I don't think that everyone's a good cook.
Rose: Then, you should say like this, "Noodles are easy (A)_______ to cook."
Jisu: Oh, I see. Then, would you let me for me cook noodles for you? It's my special dish.
Rose: It's nice (B)_______ to give me a chance for tasting your dish. However, there is a grammar mistake. You should say like this, "Would you let (C)_______ cook noodles for you?"
Jisu: You're right. You're a good teacher. Thanks!

	(A)	(B)	(C)
①	of me	of you	me
②	me	for you	for me
③	for me	of you	me
④	for me	for you	for me
⑤	of me	of you	for me

[경북 ㅇㅇ중]

4. 다음 주어진 단어를 이용하여 문장을 완성할 때, 10번째 오는 어휘로 가장 적절한 것은? (5점)

• find / how / from / get / fields / work / by /of / people / nature / inspired / Let's / out / different

① get ② field ③ inspired
④ of ⑤ work

[대전 ㅇㅇ중]

5. 다음 안내문의 내용과 일치하는 것은? (3점)

Indoor Rock Climbing Course
Come and join the indoor rock climbing at the community center on Mondays in June. We have different levels of courses. You can start to learn today!
Free Snacks for Everyone! Burgers and hot dogs will be on sale.

① 강좌는 6월에 월요일에 열린다.
② 6월 월요일마다 암벽등반 경기가 있다.
③ 다양한 난이도의 실외 등반 코스가 있다.
④ 버거와 핫도그가 무료로 제공된다.
⑤ 학교에서 주최하는 행사이다.

[경북 ㅇㅇ중]

6. 다음 주어진 문장을 영문으로 완성할 때, 가장 적절한 것은? (4점)

• 내 여동생은 어제 오후 이후로 수학 과제를 하고 있다.

① My younger sister has been done math assignments since yesterday afternoon.
② My younger sister has been doing math assignments since yesterday afternoon.
③ My younger sister has been doing math assignments from yesterday afternoon.
④ My younger sister has been doing with assignments after yesterday afternoon.
⑤ My younger sister has been working math assignments after yesterday afternoon.

[충북 ㅇㅇ중]

7. 다음 중 어법상 올바른 문장끼리 묶인 것은? (4점)

㉠ Mr. John Baker has been knowing Minsu nine years ago.
㉡ I have been living in Busan for five years.
㉢ What have you been doing?
㉣ Sam and Julie has been played soccer for an hour.

① ㉠, ㉡
② ㉠, ㉢
③ ㉡, ㉢
④ ㉡, ㉣
⑤ ㉢, ㉣

[종로구 ㅇㅇ중]

8. 다음 중 어법상 <u>어색한</u> 문장은? (4점)

① It is impossible to live without water.
② The table is too heavy for him to move.
③ I bought a chair for my mom to sit on.
④ It was careless of him to open the door.
⑤ John allowed of his daughter to go to the concert.

[충북 ㅇㅇ중]

9. 다음 〈보기〉에 있는 단어들을 배열하여 해석에 맞게 문장을 완성했을 때, ⓐ에 들어갈 것은? (5점)

<보기>
[for / difficult / to / is / her]
• 해석: 이 책은 그녀가 읽기에는 어렵다.
→ This book ________ ________ ________ ___ⓐ___ ________ read.

① for
② difficult
③ to
④ is
⑤ her

[구로구 ㅇㅇ중]

10. 다음 괄호 안에 주어진 단어를 모두 사용하여 A의 질문을 영어로 쓰시오. (4점)

A: 그는 드럼을 연주해 오고 있는 중인가요? (playing, been, the drum, 6 단어) B: Yes, he has.

답: ______________________________?

[서초구 ㅇㅇ중]

11. 다음 중 주어진 의미에 맞도록 문장의 어법이 올바르게 쓰인 것은? (5점)

① 나무에서 노래를 부르고 있는 새를 봐라.
Look at the bird sung in the tree.

② 내 가족은 1970년대에 지어진 집을 샀다.
My family bought a house built in the 1970s.

③ 너는 빨간 셔츠를 입고 있는 여자를 알고 있니?
Do you know the woman worn a red shirt?

④ 케이크를 만들고 있는 여자는 나의 엄마다.
The woman made a cake is my mother.

⑤ 선생님은 게임 결과에 만족해하는 학생들을 보았다.
The teacher saw the students satisfying with the game result.

[경북 ㅇㅇ중]

12. 다음 빈칸 (A), (B)에 가장 적절한 것은? (4점)

• It is very generous (A)________ you to help the poor and the sick. • Let me know (B)________ you reached the palace.

	(A)	(B)
①	for	why
②	of	where
③	for	what
④	of	how
⑤	for	when

[종로구 ㅇㅇ중]

13. Choose the dialogue that is unnatural. (4점)

① A: Did you know that the yellow dust travels from the deserts of Mongolia to Korea?
B: No. I've said that yellow dust is bad for our health.

② A: During my trip to Dokdo, I studied about the caves on the island and went bird watching.
B: Wow! Sounds like it was an interesting trip.

③ A: Someone told me that you can see beautiful white buildings with blue roofs in Santorini, Greece.
B: Sounds awesome! I'd like to go there someday.

④ A: Have you made plans for this vacation?
B: My family is going to China. I can't wait to visit the Rainbow Mountains.

⑤ A: We will be able to see hundreds of shooting stars tonight!
B: How wonderful! When is the best time to see them?

[종로구 ㅇㅇ중]

14. 다음 문장에 이어지는 대화의 순서로 가장 알맞은 것은? (4점)

Jisu, did you know that the sun never sets in Norway during summer?

(A) Yeah, and I've heard that people go hiking and even cycling at night because it isn't dark.
(B) Me, too. I hope we get the chance to try it someday.
(C) I'd love to go hiking and cycling in the middle of the night!
(D) No, I didn't know that. How interesting!

① (A) - (B) - (C) - (D)
② (A) - (C) - (B) - (D)
③ (C) - (B) - (D) - (A)
④ (D) - (A) - (C) - (B)
⑤ (D) - (B) - (A) - (C)

[종로구 ㅇㅇ중]

15. 다음 대화의 밑줄 친 표현을 통해 알 수 있는 David의 심정으로 가장 알맞은 것은? (4점)

W: David, what's your summer plan?
M: My family is going to China. <u>I can't wait to visit the Rainbow Mountains</u>.
W: The Rainbow Mountains?
M: They are some mountains that look like canvases in rainbow colors.
W: That sounds amazing! Take lots of pictures!

① tired ② excited
③ worried ④ unhappy
⑤ disappointed

[종로구 ㅇㅇ중]

[16~17] 다음 대화를 읽고 물음에 답하시오.

M: Hello, Ms. Lee. Welcome back to the guest house. How was your tour of the Hanok Village?
W: Hi, Jason! It was wonderful. The houses were really beautiful.
M: That's great.
W: Actually, I didn't get the chance to have dinner. (A)____________ in the kitchen at this hour?
M: Yes, but please remember that the kitchen closes at 10 p.m.
W: Okay. The kitchen is on the 5th floor, right?
M: Yes, it is. Let me know if you need anything.

16. 위 대화에 주어진 기능에 맞게 빈칸 (A)를 작성할 때, 들어갈 말로 가장 <u>어색한</u> 것은? (4점)

① May I cook
② Could I cook
③ Is it okay if I cook
④ Why don't you cook
⑤ Can you let me cook

17. Which is true according to the above dialogue? (4점)

① The kitchen closes at eight o'clock.
② Jason is going to cook for Ms. Lee.
③ Jason is full because he already had dinner.
④ The dialogue is taking place at the guest house.
⑤ Ms. Lee thinks the houses at the Hanok Village are terrible.

[구로구 ㅇㅇ중]

[18~19] 다음 대화를 읽고 물음에 답하시오.

M: Hello, everyone. This is "Tonight" talk show. Let's welcome Ms. Scarlett Lee, the winner of this year's photo competition.
W: Hello, thank you for inviting me. I'm honored to receive the award.
M: Let's talk about your photo. I've heard that this photo was taken in the Maldives. Is that true?
W: Yes, this glowing beach is caused by plankton.
M: Wow, it truly is amazing.
W: Yes, it is. (A)<u>I can't wait to take more pictures of amazing beaches.</u>
M: I wish you the best of luck!

(M: Man / W: Woman)

18. 위 대화의 밑줄 친 (A)와 바꾸어 쓰기에 가장 <u>어색한</u> 것은? (4점)

① It will be really exciting to take more pictures of amazing beaches.
② It will take some time to get more pictures of amazing beaches.
③ I'm really expecting to take more pictures of amazing beaches.
④ I really hope to take more pictures of amazing beaches.
⑤ I'm looking forward to taking more pictures of amazing beaches.

19. 위 대화를 읽고 추측할 수 있는 것이 <u>아닌</u> 것은? (4점)

① The woman is the guest at the talk show.
② The woman enjoys taking pictures of wonderful nature.
③ The woman uses the special effects to take pictures.
④ The man hopes the woman will take amazing pictures.
⑤ The woman will continue to take pictures of surprising beaches.

[부산 ㅇㅇ중]

[20~21] 다음 글을 읽고 물음에 답하시오.

I'm at the Cinema Awards. I have been interviewing actors and actresses for one hour. (A)<u>It has been raining for three hours.</u> Actors and actresses (B)<u>arrive</u> since 5 o'clock. Fans have been waiting for a very long time, but they still look very happy to see their favorite stars in person!

20. 위 글의 밑줄 친 (A)와 가장 의미가 같은 것은? (4점)

① It was raining three hours ago,
② It will be raining three hours later again.
③ It has rained before three hours and it stopped raining.
④ It rained three hours ago. but it is not sure that it is raining now.
⑤ It started raining three hours ago, and it is still raining now.

21. 위 글의 밑줄 친 (B)를 '지금도 계속 도착하고 있는 중이다'를 뜻하도록 고쳐 쓰시오. (5점)

→ h________ ________ ________

[경기 ㅇㅇ중]

22. 다음 글을 읽고 답할 수 없는 질문은? (4점)

Danny Mehta, Location Scout
Vatnajökull National Park, Frozen Beauty of Iceland

I'm a location scout and my job is finding perfect places to shoot movies. Iceland is the best place for many location scouts to visit due to its unusual beauty. My personal favorite is the Vatnajökull National Park. The sharp cliffs, blue glacier caves, and long mountain ranges can stand in for any place in the world or the universe. In fact, the recent sci-fi movie we shot here was produced without using computer graphics! Iceland can help make our wildest dreams come true on the movie screen.

① What does Danny Mehta do for a living?
② How often does Danny visit Iceland?
③ Why is Iceland the best place for many location scouts?
④ What makes the Vatnajökull Park Danny's personal favorite place?
⑤ Did they use computer graphic when they shot the recent sci-fi movie in the Vatnajökull National Park?

[종로구 ㅇㅇ중]

[23~24] 다음 글을 읽고 물음에 답하시오.

Lin Wang, Ecologist
Tsingy, the Stone Forest of Madagascar

I ⓐ________ the stone forest of Madagascar to study plants and animals for over 20 years. The spiky stones of this place are true miracles of nature. This amazing shape has been created by rainfall. Rain has cut down the stones and made them sharp and spiky over a long period of time. The environment is harsh for animals to live in, but they have found ways to survive. For example, lemurs, which only live in Madagascar, have frog-like legs that help them jump from one stone tower to another. For me, the stone forest is like a jack-in-the-box. It always surprises me and keeps me on my toes!

23. 위 글의 빈칸 ⓐ에 들어갈 말로 가장 적절한 것은? (조건: (A), (B)의 내용을 모두 포함할 것.) (3점)

(A) I started visiting the stone forest of Madagascar over 20 years ago.
(B) I'm still visiting now.
→ I ⓐ____________ the stone forest of Madagascar to study plants and animals for over 20 years.

① visited ② am visiting
③ had visited ④ will have visited
⑤ have been visiting

24. 위 글을 읽고 다음 빈칸에 들어갈 질문으로 가장 알맞은 것은? (5점)

Question: ______________________________
Answer: Rain has cut down the stones and made them sharp and spiky over a long period of time.

① How have the spiky stones of Tsingy been created?
② What is the stone forest of Madagascar like to Lin Wang?
③ What helps lemurs jump from one stone tower to another?
④ How did animals of Madagascar find the ways to survive?
⑤ Why did Lin Wang visit the stone forest of Madagascar?

3학년 영어 1학기 중간고사(2과) 2회

문항수 : 선택형(25문항) 서술형(1문항)	20 . . .	반		점수
		이름		

◎ 선택형 문항의 답안은 컴퓨터용 수정 싸인펜을 사용하여 OMR 답안지에 바르게 표기하시오.
◎ 서술형 문제는 답을 답안지에 반드시 검정 볼펜으로 쓰시오.
◎ 총 26문항 100점 만점입니다. 문항별 배점은 각 문항에 표시되어 있습니다.

[대전 ㅇㅇ중]

1. 다음 중 밑줄 친 부분의 의미가 〈보기〉와 같은 것은? (4점)

<보기>
independent

① ineffective ②insight ③include
④ indoor ⑤inside

[경북 ㅇㅇ중]

2. 다음 어휘의 뜻이 가장 어색한 것은? (3점)

① be honored: 영광스럽다
② focus on: ~에 초점을 맞추다
③ cut ~ off: ~의 말을 중단시키다
④ get in the way of ~: ~의 방해를 받다
⑤ keep ~ on one's toes: ~의 정신을 바짝 차리게 하다

[경북 ㅇㅇ중]

3. 다음 밑줄 친 (A), (B)에 들어갈 가장 적절한 것은? (4점)

• We only have seven days (A)_______ summer vacation.
• Don't let the cat out of the bag (B)_______ Sumi's surprise party.

	(A)	(B)
①	until	about
②	during	for
③	till	to
④	until	with
⑤	during	on

[대전 ㅇㅇ중]

4. 다음 빈칸에 들어갈 말로 옳지 않은 것은? (4점)

• When you inform the listener that he or she has misunderstood what you've just said, you can try to clear things out by saying "_______________"

① You've misunderstood what I said.
② That's exactly what I meant.
③ Let me explain that again.
④ You took the wrong way.
⑤ I didn't mean by that.

[충북 ㅇㅇ중]

5. 다음 빈칸에 들어갈 알맞은 단어는? (4점)

• I received a large ________ from my aunt in Boston.

① marriage ② package ③ delight
④ insight ⑤ usage

[부산 ㅇㅇ중]

6. 다음 빈칸에 들어갈 말은? (3점)

Q: ______________________________?
A: I have been preparing dinner for them.

① What are you doing?
② How are you doing?
③ What is your favorite food?
④ What have you been doing?
⑤ How long have you known each other?

[충북 ○○중]

7. 다음 대화의 빈칸 ⓐ~ⓔ에 들어갈 것으로 어색한 것은? (3점)

M: Let's welcome Ms. Scarlett Lee, the winner of this year's photo competition.
W: Hello, thank you for inviting me. I'm honored to ⓐ______ the award.
M: Let's talk about your photo. I've ⓑ______ that this photo was taken in the Maldives. Is that true?
W: Yes, this glowing beach is caused by plankton.
M: Wow, it truly is ⓒ______!
W: Yes, it is. I can't wait to ⓓ______ more pictures of amazing beaches.
M: I wish you the best of ⓔ_______!

① ⓐ-receiving
② ⓑ-heard
③ ⓒ-amazing
④ ⓓ-take
⑤ ⓔ-luck

[서초구 ○○중]

8. 다음 주어진 우리말을 영어로 가장 바르게 옮긴 것은? (4점)

• 엄마는 내가 바이올린을 켤 수 있도록 했다.

① My mom made it possible me to play the violin.
② My mom made me possible it to play the violin.
③ My mom made it possible of me to play the violin.
④ My mom made me possible for it to play the violin.
⑤ My mom made it possible for me to play the violin.

[부산 ○○중]

9. 다음 중 밑줄 친 부분이 어법상 어색한 것은? (3점)

① He pushed the door open for her to enter.
② It is kind for you to help your classmates.
③ It is easy for us to take photos of animals.
④ This is the best place for many scouts to visit.
⑤ The greenhouse is warm enough for Matthew to grow fresh vegetables in.

[경기 ○○중]

10. 다음 중 어법상 어색한 것은? (4점)

① It was smart of Mr. Smith to solve the puzzle.
② It is necessary for students to bring their ID cards.
③ The box was light enough for us to lift.
④ The boy isn't tall enough for candles to grab.
⑤ It was careless of him to leave the key at home.

[경기 ○○중]

11. 다음 중 어법상 옳은 것은? (5점)

① I had read the novel that she wrote.
② If the school lunch is delicious is not important.
③ Tell me the way how I can make a delicious pizza.
④ My dad has been working in New York a year ago.
⑤ I saw many people dance to music.

[종로구 ㅇㅇ중]

12. Put the following sentences (A)~(E) in the correct order. (4점)

(A) I'd love to go hiking and cycling in the middle of the night.
(B) No, I didn't know that. How interesting!
(C) Jisu, did you know that the sun never sets in Norway during summer?
(D) Yeah, and people told me that you can go hiking and even cycling at night because it isn't dark.
(E) Me, too. I hope we get the chance to try it someday.

① (C) - (B) - (E) - (D) - (A)
② (C) - (B) - (D) - (A) - (E)
③ (C) - (D) - (B) - (A) - (E)
④ (C) - (B) - (A) - (D) - (E)
⑤ (C) - (B) - (D) - (E) - (A)

[서초구 ㅇㅇ중]

13. 다음 두 개의 대화문에서 문맥과 어법을 고려할 때, 아래의 빈칸 (A)와 (B)에 각각 들어갈 표현으로 가장 자연스럽게 짝지어진 것은? (4점)

W: David what's your summer plan?
M: My family is going to China. (A)________________ visit the Rainbow Mountains.
W: The Rainbow Mountains?
M: They are some mountains that look like canvases in rainbow colors.
W: That sounds amazing! Take lots of pictures!

B: Mom, did you watch the weather report today? We will be able to see hundreds of shooting stars tonight!
W: Wow, fantastic! When is the best time to see them?
B: (B)________________ the shooting stars will peak between 12 a.m. and 2 a.m.
W: Wow, it will be a special night!

① (A) I can't wait to
 (B) I've heard that
② (A) I've heard that
 (B) I'm pretty sure that
③ (A) I'm pretty sure that
 (B) I have to wait
④ (A) I'm so excited about
 (B) Someone told me that
⑤ (A) I can't wait any longer
 (B) I don't want to wait

[경기 ㅇㅇ중]

14. 다음 짝지은 두 사람의 대화들 중 흐름상 가장 <u>어색한</u> 것은? (4점)

① A: The view at the top of the mountain is going to be amazing.
 B: Really? Let's run up there!
② A: Do you want to watch the new 3D movie?
 B: We shot it near Australia's Great Barrier Reef.
③ A: My science club is going to go to Dokdo in July.
 B: Have a good trip!
④ A: It's been almost a year since the last series was released.
 B: Right, it's been too long. I'm looking forward to reading it.
⑤ A: We only have five more days until summer vacation.
 B: Yes, I can't wait to go to the beach!

[서초구 ㅇㅇ중]

15. 다음 글의 내용과 일치하지 않는 것은? (3점)

Danny Mehta, Location Scout
Vatnajökull National Park, Frozen Beauty of Iceland

I'm a location scout and my job is to find perfect places to shoot movies. Iceland is the best place to visit due to its unusual beauty. My personal favorite is the Vatnajökull National Park. The sharp cliffs, blue glacier caves, and long mountain ranges can stand in for any place in the world or the universe. In fact, the recent sci-fi movie we shot here was produced without using computer graphics!

① Iceland has its own unusual beauty.
② Danny Mehta's favorite place is located in Iceland.
③ Danny Mehta's job is finding locations to shoot movies.
④ Vatnajökull National Park is famous for its cliffs, glacier caves and mountain ranges.
⑤ Computer graphics were used for the recent sci-fi movie that was produced in Vatnajökull National Park.

[충북 ㅇㅇ중]

16. 다음 글에서 흐름상 가장 어색한 문장은? (5점)

Lin Wang, Ecologist
Tsingy, the Stone Forest of Madagascar

I've been visiting the stone forest of Madagascar to study plants and animals for over 20 years. ⓐThe spiky stones of this place are true miracles of nature. This amazing shape has been created by rainfall. ⓑRain has cut down the stones and made them sharp and spiky over a long period of time. ⓒThe environment is good for animals to live in, but they have found ways to survive. For example, ⓓlemurs, which only live in Madagascar, have frog-like legs that help them jump from one stone tower to another. For me, the stone forest is like a jack-in-the-box. ⓔIt always surprises me and keeps me on my toes!

① ⓐ ② ⓑ ③ ⓒ ④ ⓓ ⑤ ⓔ

[대전 ㅇㅇ중]

[17~18] 다음 대화를 읽고 물음에 답하시오.

Son: Dad, my science club is going to go to Dokdo in July.
Dad: Oh, really? ⓐWhat do you plan to do there?
Son: ⓑWe are going to study the caves on the island and go bird watching.
Dad: ⓒSounds like it will be an exciting trip.
Son: Yeah. I've read most books about Dokdo and studied hard. ⓓI should have hit the books about Dokdo.
Dad: ⓔI hope you enjoy your trip!

17. 위 대화의 밑줄 친 ⓐ~ⓔ 중 글의 흐름과 어울리지 않는 문장은? (3점)

① ⓐ ② ⓑ ③ ⓒ ④ ⓓ ⑤ ⓔ

18. 위 대화를 읽고 대답할 수 있는 질문은? (4점)

① What is the son asking his dad to prepare for his trip to Dokdo?
② What is the most difficult problem of studying the caves?
③ How many times has the son been to Dokdo?
④ Does the dad want to go to Dokdo?
⑤ What is the son looking forward to?

[대전 ㅇㅇ중]

[19～20] 다음 글을 읽고 물음에 답하시오.

Danny Mehta. Location Scout
Vantnajokull National Park, Iceland

I'm a location scout and my job is (A)____.
Iceland is the best place for many location scouts to visit ⓐdue to its unusual beauty. My personal favorite is the Vatanajolull National Park.
The sharp cliff, ⓑblue glacier caves, and long mountain ranges can ⓒstand in for any place in the world or the universe. In fact, the recent sci-fi movie we shot here was produced without using computur graphics! Iceland can help make our ⓓwildest dreams ⓔcome true on the movie screen.

19. 위 글의 (A)에 알맞은 표현은? (3점)

① acting in plays or movies
② finding perfect places to shoot movies
③ operating the technical devices to record sound
④ training the players and organizing activities they need to do
⑤ visiting places for pleasure and interest, especially when I am on holiday

20. 위 글의 밑줄 친 ⓐ～ⓔ의 표현에 대한 우리말 설명으로 알맞지 않은 것은? (4점)

① ⓐ: 그것의 특이한 아름다움 때문에
② ⓑ: 푸른 빙하 동굴들
③ ⓒ: ~을 대신하다
④ ⓓ: 아주 터무니없는 꿈들
⑤ ⓔ: 사실임이 밝혀지다

[대전 ㅇㅇ중]

[21～22] 다음 글을 읽고 물음에 답하시오.

(A) There are many natural wonders all over the world. Let's find out more about these beautiful places. First, let's go to Turkey.
Do you see the rocks ⓐwhere look like chimneys? (B) Two million years ago, Cappadocia ⓑwill be formed by volcanic activity. ⓒAfterward volcanic eruptions, the area around the mountain was covered with lava and ash. (C) Over a long period of time, rain and strong wind gave these rocks their chimney shape. Let's look at the next place. Do you know ⓓwhere this place is? It's not another planet. (D) This is Sala de Uyuni, a salt flat in Bolivia. Long ago, Salar de Uyuni and its surrounding areas were once part of the ocean.
ⓔDuring the slow rise of the Andes Mountains, this area became a lake. (E) Over time, the lake dried up. When the seawater dried up, the salt was left over! So now it is ⓕthe largest salt flat in the world.

21. 위 글의 밑줄 친 ⓐ～ⓕ 중 어법상 옳은 표현만을 골라 나열한 것은? (5점)

① ⓐ, ⓑ
② ⓐ, ⓒ
③ ⓑ, ⓒ, ⓓ
④ ⓒ, ⓓ, ⓔ
⑤ ⓓ, ⓔ, ⓕ

22. 위 글의 흐름상 다음 문장이 들어갈 가장 적절한 위치는? (4점)

This is Cappadocia in Turkey.

① (A) ② (B) ③ (C) ④ (D) ⑤ (E)

[충북 ㅇㅇ중]

[23~24] 다음 글을 읽고, 물음에 답하시오.

The world ⓐis full of millions of different colors. It is my job to mix, develop, and create colors for clothing. Over the years, I ⓑhave been gaining insights from the beautiful colors of Caño Cristales. You cannot see the wonderful ⓒmixed colors of this river anywhere else in the world. The combination of colorful plants under the water and sunlight ⓓmakes the colors more alive and bright. Whenever I visit the Caño Cristales, it makes me think that maybe there are still countless colors that ⓔis waiting to be created.

23. 위 글의 밑줄 친 ⓐ~ⓔ에서 어법상 어색한 것을 골라 올바르게 고치시오. (4점)

→ ____________

24. 위 글을 읽고, 다음 빈칸 Ⓐ, Ⓑ에 들어갈 단어로 알맞게 짝지어진 것은? (4점)

Q: What makes the colors of Caño Cristales more alive and bright?
A: It is the combination of Ⓐ__________ under the water and Ⓑ__________.

	Ⓐ	Ⓑ
①	colorful plants	sunlight
②	colorful plants	water
③	beautiful colors	sunlight
④	beautiful colors	countless colors
⑤	sunlight	countless colors

[서초구 ㅇㅇ중]

[25~26] 다음 글을 읽고 물음에 답하시오.

Lin Wang, Ecologist

Tsingy, the Stone Forest of Madagascar

I've visited the stone forest of Madagascar to study plants and animals for over 20 years. The spiky stones of this place are true miracles of nature. This amazing shape ⓐhas created by rainfall. Rain has cut down the stones and ⓑmakes them sharp and spiky over a long period of time. The environment is harsh ⓒof animals to live in, but they have found ways to survive. For example, lemurs, ⓓthat only live in Madagascar, have frog-like legs that help them ⓔjumped from one stone tower to another. For me, the stone forest is like a jack-in-the-box. It always surprises me and keeps me on my toes!

25. 위 글을 읽고 답할 수 없는 질문은? (3점)

① What is the stone forest of Madagascar like to Lin Wang?
② How long has Lin Wang visited the stone forest of Madagascar?
③ What has created the shape of the stones in the stone forest of Madagascar?
④ How many different kinds of animals are there in the stone forest of Madagascar?
⑤ Why has Lin Wang visited the stone forest of Madagascar?

26. 위 글의 밑줄 친 ⓐ~ⓔ를 어법상 바르게 고친 것은? (5점)

① ⓐhas created → has been creating
② ⓑmakes → make
③ ⓒof animals → of animals
④ ⓓthat → who
⑤ ⓔjumped → jump

3학년 영어 1학기 기말고사(3과) 1회

문항수 : 선택형(25문항) 서술형(1문항)	20 . . .	반		점수
		이름		

◎ 선택형 문항의 답안은 컴퓨터용 수정 싸인펜을 사용하여 OMR 답안지에 바르게 표기하시오.
◎ 서술형 문제는 답을 답안지에 반드시 검정 볼펜으로 쓰시오.
◎ 총 26문항 100점 만점입니다. 문항별 배점은 각 문항에 표시되어 있습니다.

[경북 ㅇㅇ중]

1. 다음 〈보기〉의 영영풀이에 해당하지 않는 단어는? (4점)

<보기>
- to let a prisoner or animal go free
- freedom from political control by other countries
- the story of someone's life written by another person
- police officer whose job is to get information about crimes and catch criminals

① ruin ② release
③ detective ④ biography
⑤ independence

[경북 ㅇㅇ중]

2. 다음 중 짝지어진 대화가 어색한 것은? (3점)

① A: Is it okay if I cook in the kitchen now?
B: Sure. Go ahead.
② A: Would it be possible if I bring in this juice?
B: I'm afraid you can't.
③ A: It is said that he climbed Mt. Baekdu over 8 times.
B: Oh, I didn't know that.
④ A: Do you mind me sitting next to you?
B: Of course not, all these seats are taken.
⑤ A: People say that men and women have different opinions on this issue.
B: Could you explain it to me more?

[경북 ㅇㅇ중]

3. 다음 밑줄 친 부분의 의미가 어색한 것은? (4점)

① Can you promise me to keep a secret? (비밀을 지키다)
② I'm used to getting up early in the morning. (일찍 일어나는 것에 익숙하다)
③ Mother Teresa devoted her life to helping children. (그녀의 일생을 바쳤다)
④ You should not play games behind your mom's back. (엄마 몰래)
⑤ The president always makes arrangements with his advisers. (열정을 쏟다)

[경북 ㅇㅇ중]

4. 다음 빈칸에 들어갈 가장 적절한 표현은? (3점)

A: Is it okay if I ______________________?
B: Sure, but please never use a flash.

① know your sister's phone number
② take a picture in the museum
③ borrow your English dictionary
④ bring in my water bottle
⑤ use the men's bathroom

[구로구 ㅇㅇ중]

5. 다음 빈칸에 들어갈 말이 다른 것은? (4점)

① I believe ______ he is honest.
② I wonder ______ he has a passport.
③ ______ it is too far, I will go with you.
④ I asked him ______ he could join the club.
⑤ ______ you have a pen, lend it to me, please.

[경기 ㅇㅇ중]

6. 다음 대화를 바르게 배열한 것은? (3점)

Mike: Jane, what did you do during the weekend?
(A): Oh, is the book interesting?
(B): I finally finished the world history book I started to read a month ago.
(C): Really? I should also read the book and find out.
(D): Yeah, it is said that a lot of historical information we know is actually wrong.

① (B) - (A) - (D) - (C)
② (B) - (D) - (C) - (A)
③ (C) - (A) - (D) - (B)
④ (C) - (B) - (A) - (D)
⑤ (D) - (A) - (B) - (C)

[경북 ㅇㅇ중]

7. 다음 두 문장을 한 문장으로 알맞게 연결한 것은? (4점)

• I missed the subway. So I was late for the meeting.

① I had been late for the meeting because I missed the subway.
② I was late for the meeting because I had missed the subway.
③ I was late for the meeting because I have missed the subway.
④ I have been late for the meeting because I have missed the subway.
⑤ I was late for the meeting because I have been missing the subway.

[경기 ㅇㅇ중]

8. 다음 대화의 내용과 일치하는 것은? (3점)

W: Hey, Mark, do you know about Father Lee Taeseok?
M: Yeah, I've heard of him. Why?
W: Take a look at this article. He is going to be included in the social studies textbook in South Sudan.
M: Wow, that's great.
W: Yeah, he helped the children by building a clinic and a school. It is said that such stories will be included in the textbook.
M: It is good to hear that students will learn about such a great person.
(M: Mark, W: Wendy)

① Mark hasn't heard of Father Lee Taeseok.
② Father Lee Taeseok was born in South Sudan.
③ Mark has been told that students in Korea will learn about such a great person.
④ Someone told Wendy that Father Lee Taeseok was going to help the old in South Sudan.
⑤ The stories about Father Lee Taeseok will be included in the social studies textbook in South Sudan.

[경북 ㅇㅇ중]

9. 다음 중 어법상 옳은 것끼리 짝지어진 것은? (5점)

ⓐ I will go out if it rains tomorrow.
ⓑ I'm not sure if he will come or not.
ⓒ If he knows the secret doesn't matter.
ⓓ Please tell me if or not you will visit Tony.
ⓔ The problem is if I can finish the report on time.

① ⓐ, ⓑ
② ⓒ, ⓓ
③ ⓐ, ⓑ, ⓒ
④ ⓒ, ⓓ, ⓔ
⑤ ⓐ, ⓑ, ⓓ, ⓔ

[종로구 ㅇㅇ중]

10. 어법상 올바른 것끼리 짝지어진 것은? (4점)

(A) The man given the speech on the stage is a photographer.
(B) When I got back home, my parents had gone out for a walk.
(C) It has been snowing heavily for over three hours.
(D) The world is filled of millions of different colors.
(E) It is easy for us to take photos of different animals.

① (B), (C), (E) ② (A), (C), (E)
③ (B), (C), (D) ④ (A), (B), (C)
⑤ (C), (D), (E)

[경기 ㅇㅇ중]

11. 다음 글의 흐름으로 보아 주어진 문장이 들어가기에 가장 적절한 곳은? (5점)

I asked angrily, "How could he do such a horrible thing? What should we do now?"

When I was sixteen years old, my family had already made an arrangement for me to marry Mr. Seo. (A) As part of the wedding tradition, Mr. Seo's family sent my family some money to buy a new chest for clothes. (B) Right before the wedding day, my mother came into my room and said, "Your father has taken the money for the chest." (C) "We have no choice. You'll have to take your aunt's old chest," my mother said. (D) "How embarrassing for the family," people would whisper behind my back. (E) Since the first day of marriage, life at my husband's house had been difficult for me.

① (A) ② (B) ③ (C)
④ (D) ⑤ (E)

[서초구 ㅇㅇ중]

12. 다음은 의미가 자연스럽도록 주어진 두 문장을 한 문장으로 합친 것이다. 그 결과물 중 문법의 관점에서 올바르지 않은 것은? (5점)

① You may wonder. + Is it true?
= You may wonder whether it is true.
② I asked her. + Was the book difficult?
= I asked her if the book was difficult.
③ He sent me the letter. + I lost the letter.
= I lost the letter that he had sent me.
④ The train already left. + I reached the station.
= When I reached the station, the train had already left.
⑤ Does he know the secret? + That doesn't matter.
= If he knows the secret doesn't matter.

[구로구 ㅇㅇ중]

13. 다음 그림을 보고, 주어진 말을 이용하여 과거완료시제를 사용한 문장을 완성하시오. (3점)

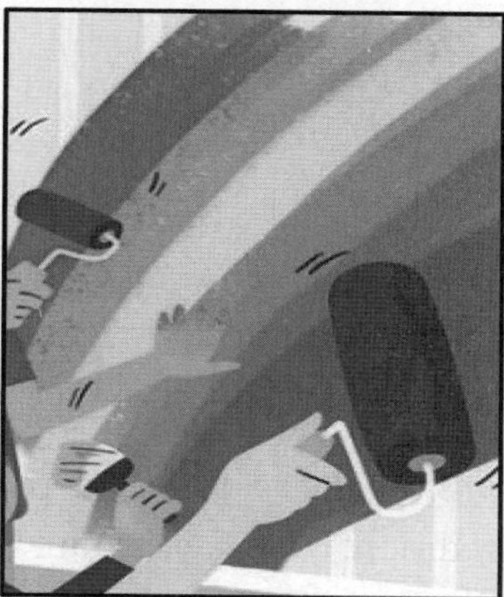

• I could smell something.
• Somebody ____________ the wall. (paint)

답: ____________

[서초구 ㅇㅇ중]

14. 다음 글에서 대답을 찾을 수 있는 질문이 <u>아닌</u> 것을 고르면? (3점)

Back in the 1920's, whenever people saw me in the village, they would say, "There goes the *parakho's* daughter."
My father was a son from a very rich family. Instead of living the life of a *seonbi,* he was always at the gambling house. That is why he was called a *parakho,* and it means someone who ruins his family's fortune.
"Your father has gambled away all of the money, and now he's asking for more. Go and tell him that we have no more money left," my mother would tell me whenever she sent me to the gambling house.
Then, my father would yell at me angrily, "Why did you come empty-handed? Bring me more money!"

① What was the daily life of a rich family in the 1920s?
② What was the writer called by people in the village?
③ What does a *parakho* mean?
④ What did the mother ask the writer to do?
⑤ Why did the father yell at her angrily?

[경북 ㅇㅇ중]

[15~17] 다음 글을 읽고 물음에 답하시오.

When I was sixteen years old, my family ⓐ<u>had already made</u> an arrangement for me to ⓑ<u>marry with</u> Mr. Seo. As part of the wedding tradition, Mr. Seo's family sent my family ⓒ<u>some money</u> to buy a new chest for clothes.
Right before the wedding day, my mother came into my room and said, "Your father has taken the money for the chest."
I asked angrily, "How could he do such a horrible thing? What should we do now?"
"We have no choice. You'll have to take your aunt's old chest," my mother said.
"ⓓ<u>How embarrassing</u> for the family," people would whisper behind my back.
Since the first day of marriage, life at my husband's house ⓔ<u>had been</u> difficult for me.

15. 위 글을 읽고 사건이 일어난 순서대로 바르게 배열한 것은? (4점)

(A) My marriage to Mr. Seo was arranged.
(B) My father took the money for the chest.
(C) I took my aunt's old chest on the wedding day.
(D) My family received some money from Mr. Seo's family.

① (A) - (D) - (B) - (C)
② (A) - (C) - (D) - (B)
③ (B) - (A) - (D) - (C)
④ (B) - (D) - (A) - (C)
⑤ (D) - (C) - (B) - (A)

16. 위 글의 밑줄 친 부분 중, 어법상 <u>어색한</u> 것은? (4점)

① ⓐ ② ⓑ ③ ⓒ
④ ⓓ ⑤ ⓔ

17. 위 글의 마지막에서 느낄 수 있는 글쓴이의 심경으로 알맞은 것은? (4점)

① bored ② hopeful ③ upset
④ proud ⑤ satisfied

[경북 ㅇㅇ중]

[18~19] 다음 글을 읽고 물음에 답하시오.

"Your father, my dear friend...," my father's friend continued his story. "ⓐHe was not a gambler. Your father sent the family money to the independence fighters in Manchuria. He made himself look like a gambler to keep this a secret from the Japanese officers."
At first, I was not sure if ⓑhe was telling the truth. But afterwards. I found out the truth about ⓒmy father and I realized that I had been wrong about ⓓhim. Ever since that moment, I have been proud to be the daughter of ⓔa *parakho* who had devoted his life to the independence movement.

18. 위 글의 밑줄 친 ⓐ~ⓔ 중, 가리키는 바가 나머지와 다른 것은? (4점)
① ⓐ ② ⓑ ③ ⓒ ④ ⓓ ⑤ ⓔ

19. 위 글을 읽고 질문에 답할 수 없는 것은? (4점)
① Was the father really a gambler?
② Who told the truth about the writer's father to her?
③ Why did the writer's father make himself look like a gambler?
④ After the writer found out the truth about her father, how did her feelings toward her father change?
⑤ How much family money did the father send to the independence fighters in Manchuria?

[구로구 ㅇㅇ중]

[20~22] 다음 글을 읽고 물음에 답하시오.

The Secret of My Father
In 1946, a strange man visited me and asked, "Are you Mr. Kim Yonghwan's daughter?"
(A) My father was a son from a very rich family. Instead of living the life of a *seonbi*, he was always at the gambling house. ⓐThat is why he was calling a *parakho*, which means someone who ruins his family's fortune.
(B) At that moment, ⓑI was expecting disappointing news since I did not have good memories of my father. ⓒBack in the 1920's, whenever people have seen me in the village, they would say, "There goes the *parakho*'s daughter."
(C) Then, my father would yell at me angrily, "Why did you come empty-handed? Bring me more money!"
(D) For me, this was an odd question because ⓓI was more used to be called the daughter of a *parakho*. "I'm your father's friend. You may wonder if it is true, but your father...," the man said.
(E) "Your father has gambled away all of the money, and now he's asking for more. ⓔGo and tell him what we have no more money left," my mother would tell me whenever she sent me to the gambling house.

20. 위 글의 내용과 일치하는 것은? (3점)
① The writer didn't take money to her father.
② The writer had good memories of her father.
③ The writer's father was an independence fighter.
④ The writer was rich enough to enjoy gambling in the 1920's.
⑤ The writer helped her father to devote his life to the independence movement.

21. 위 글의 흐름으로 보아 ⓐ~ⓔ 중에서 어법상 맞는 것은? (5점)
① ⓐ ② ⓑ ③ ⓒ ④ ⓓ ⑤ ⓔ

22. 위 글의 (A)~(E)를 자연스러운 흐름으로 잘 배열한 것은? (4점)
① (A)-(C)-(D)-(E)-(B) ② (A)-(D)-(E)-(B)-(C)
③ (A)-(E)-(C)-(B)-(D) ④ (D)-(A)-(B)-(C)-(E)
⑤ (D)-(B)-(A)-(E)-(C)

[충북 ㅇㅇ중]

[23~24] 다음 글을 읽고, 물음에 답하시오.

In 1946, a strange man visited me and asked, "Are you ⓐ<u>Mr. Kim Yonghwan's daughter?</u>" For me, this was an ⓑ<u>odd question</u> because I was more used to being called the ⓒ <u>daughter of a *parakho*</u>.
"I'm your father's friend. You may wonder (A)<u>if</u> it is true, but your father...," the man said.
At that moment, I was expecting ⓓ <u>disappointing news</u> since I did not have ⓔ <u>good memories of my father</u>.

23. 위 글의 밑줄 친 ⓐ~ⓔ에서 아래 〈보기〉 질문의 답이 될 수 있는 것은? (4점)

<보기>
• When the strange man told the writer about her father, what was she expecting?

① ⓐ ② ⓑ ③ ⓒ ④ ⓓ ⑤ ⓔ

24. 위 글의 밑줄 친 (A)<u>if</u>와 <u>다른</u> 의미로 쓰인 것은? (3점)

① I wonder <u>if</u> he is smart.
② Do you know <u>if</u> she is married?
③ She does not know <u>if</u> Mike is coming here.
④ Give him this book <u>if</u> you see him.
⑤ I am not sure <u>if</u> Jane will come to the party.

[충북 ㅇㅇ중]

[25~26] 다음을 읽고, 물음에 답하시오.

Back in the 1920's, whenever people saw me in the village, they would say, "There goes the *parakho*'s daughter." (A)
My father was a son from a very rich family. Instead of living the life of a *seonbi,* he was always at the gambling house. That is why he was called a *parakho,* which means someone who ruins his family's fortune. (B)
"Your father has gambled away all of the money, and now he's asking for more. Go and tell him that we have no more money left," my mother would tell me whenever she sent me to the gambling house. (C)
When I was sixteen years old, my family Ⓐ ________________ for me to marry Mr. Seo.
As part of the wedding tradition, Mr. Seo's family sent my family some money to buy a new chest for clothes.
Right before the wedding day, my mother came into my room and said, "Your father has taken the money for the chest." (D)
I asked angrily, "How could he do such a horrible thing? What should we do now?"
"We have no choice. You'll have to take your aunt's old chest," my mother said.
"How embarrassing for the family," people would whisper behind my back. (E)
Since the first day of marriage, life at my husband's house had been difficult for me.

25. 위 글에서 흐름상 〈보기〉가 들어갈 가장 적합한 곳은? (4점)

<보기>
Then, my father would yell at me angrily, "Why did you come empty-handed? Bring me more money!"

① (A) ② (B) ③ (C) ④ (D) ⑤ (E)

26. 위 글의 흐름상 빈칸 Ⓐ에 들어갈 가장 알맞은 것은? (4점)

① had already made an arrangement
② had bought some clothes
③ had already bought a chest
④ had given some money
⑤ had already sent a letter

3학년 영어 1학기 기말고사(3과) 2회

반		점수
이름		

문항수 : 선택형(27문항) 서술형(1문항) 20 . . .

◎ 선택형 문항의 답안은 컴퓨터용 수정 싸인펜을 사용하여 OMR 답안지에 바르게 표기하시오.
◎ 서술형 문제는 답을 답안지에 반드시 검정 볼펜으로 쓰시오.
◎ 총 28문항 100점 만점입니다. 문항별 배점은 각 문항에 표시되어 있습니다.

[종로구 ㅇㅇ중]

1. 다음 〈보기〉와 같은 방법으로 명사를 만들 수 없는 것은? (3점)

<보 기>
v. pass → n. passage

① use ② pack ③ bond
④ marry ⑤ inspire

[경북 ㅇㅇ중]

2. 다음 문장의 빈칸에 들어갈 어휘로 가장 적절한 것은? (3점)

• When the nation doesn't have __________, it may be ruled by other nations.

① poverty ② detective
③ fighter ④ independence
⑤ passage

[충북 ㅇㅇ중]

3. 다음 대화를 읽고 답변할 수 없는 질문은? (3점)

W: Hey, Mark, do you know about Father Lee Taeseok?
M: Yeah, I've heard of him. Why?
W: Take a look at this article. He is going to be included in the social studies textbook in South Sudan.
M: Wow, that's great.
W: Yeah, he helped the children by building a clinic and a school. It is said that such stories will be included in the textbook.
M: It is good to hear that students will learn about such a great person.

*W = 여자, M = 남자

① 남자는 Father Lee Taeseok에 대해 들어 본 적 있는가?
② 여자와 남자가 보고 있는 기사는 무엇에 관한 것인가?
③ Father Lee Taeseok은 누구를 도왔는가?
④ Father Lee Taeseok은 어느 과목 교과서에 실릴 예정인가?
⑤ Father Lee Taeseok은 어느 나라에서 공부를 했는가?

[경북 ㅇㅇ중]

4. 다음 중 단어의 관계가 나머지와 다른 것은? (3점)

① marry : marriage
② move : movement
③ realize : realization
④ educate : education
⑤ independent : independence

[종로구 ㅇㅇ중]

5. 다음 두 문장을 현재완료진행 또는 과거완료시제를 활용하여 한 문장으로 연결하시오. (5점)

(1) I started to learn to play the flute five months ago. I am still learning it.
(2) I left the key at school. So I couldn't open the door. (because를 활용할 것)

(1)______________________________
(2)______________________________

[경기 ㅇㅇ중]

6. 다음 대화에서 빈칸에 들어갈 수 없는 것은? (3점)

W: Excuse me, you can't take your backpack inside the museum. M: Oh, I didn't know that. ______________ W: Yes, that's fine. You can leave your bag in the locker. M: Okay, thank you.

① Can I bring in my water bottle?
② Can you let me bring in my water bottle?
③ Do you mind if I bring in my water bottle?
④ Is it okay if I take some pictures without a flash?
⑤ Could you let me take some pictures without a flash?

[구로구 ㅇㅇ중]

7. 다음 (A)~(F) 중 어법상 맞는 것을 모두 고른 것은? (4점)

(A) July is the month which I enjoy summer. (B) London is the city which I'd love to visit. (C) I found my watch, that I had lost in the theater. (D) When I got to the theater, he has already gone. (E) I had not eaten kimchi before, so I want to try it now. (F) All the tickets have been sold out when I went to the store.

① (B), (E) ② (A), (C)
③ (B), (C), (F) ④ (A), (B), (D), (F)
⑤ (A), (B), (C), (D), (E), (F)

[경북 ㅇㅇ중]

8. 다음 대화의 밑줄 친 부분과 바꾸어 쓸 수 있는 표현은? (4점)

A: Jane, what did you do during the weekend? B: I finally finished the world history book I started to read a month ago. A: Oh, is the book interesting? B: Yeah, it is said that a lot of historical information we know is actually wrong. A: Really? I should also read the book and find out.

① I'v heard that
② it is certain that
③ I'm not sure that
④ it is important that
⑤ it is recommended that

[경북 ㅇㅇ중]

9. 다음에 이어질 대화를 순서대로 바르게 배열한 것은? (4점)

Hey, Mark, do you know about Father Lee Taeseok? (A) It is good to hear that students will learn about such great person. (B) Yeah, I've heard of him. Why? (C) Wow, that's great. (D) Take a look at this article. He is going to be included in the social studies textbook in South Sudan. (E) Yeah, he helped the children by building a clinic and a school. It is said that such stories will be included in the textbook.

① (A) - (E) - (C) - (D) - (B)
② (B) - (D) - (C) - (E) - (A)
③ (B) - (A) - (C) - (E) - (D)
④ (E) - (B) - (D) - (A) - (C)
⑤ (E) - (D) - (C) - (A) - (B)

[종로구 ㅇㅇ중]

10. 다음 중 어법상 적절하지 않은 것은? (3점)

① Lucy wants to know whether Tom is going to release a new song this month.

② If you are tired, you may rest for a while.

③ I want to know if or not the school lunch is delicious.

④ I want to ask whether or not Mina can join the picnic.

⑤ I am not sure if you like a potato pizza or not.

[종로구 ㅇㅇ중]

11. 다음 중 어법상 올바른 것끼리 짝지어진 것은? (4점)

(A) Tom never shows the way how he solves a puzzle.
(B) It was nice of you to give food to the children.
(C) That my dad planted is this tree.
(D) I wonder if you can help me.
(E) Some people think it's important follow tradition.

① (A), (B)
② (A), (D)
③ (B), (D)
④ (B), (E)
⑤ (C), (E)

[경북 ㅇㅇ중]

12. 다음 글의 밑줄 친 ⓐ~ⓔ 중, 흐름상 어색한 것은? (3점)

In 1946, a strange man visited me and asked, "Are you Mr. Kim Yonghwan's daughter?"
For me, this was an odd question because I was more used to being called the daughter of ⓐa *parakho*.
"I'm your father's friend. You may wonder if it is true, but your father...," the man said. At that moment, I was expecting ⓑhappy news since I did not have good memories of my father.
In 1946, I thought my father was known as a *parakho*. He was born into a ⓒrich family but he gambled away all of the money.
But actually my father was not ⓓa gambler. He sent the family money to the ⓔ independence fighters in Manchuria. He made himself look like a gambler to keep this a secret from the Japanese officers.

① ⓐ
② ⓑ
③ ⓒ
④ ⓓ
⑤ ⓔ

[충북 ㅇㅇ중]

13. 다음 글을 읽고 (A)~(C)를 흐름에 맞게 배열한 것은? (4점)

"Your father, my dear friend...," my father's friend continued his story. "He was not a gambler. Your father sent the family money to the independence fighters in Manchuria. He made himself look like a gambler to keep this a secret from the Japanese officers."

(A) Ever since that moment, I have been proud to be the daughter of a *parakho* who had devoted his life to the independence movement.
(B) At first, I was not sure if he was telling the truth.
(C) But afterwards, I found out the truth about my father and I realized that I had been wrong about him.

① (A) - (B) - (C)
② (B) - (A) - (C)
③ (B) - (C) - (A)
④ (C) - (A) - (B)
⑤ (C) - (B) - (A)

[경북 ㅇㅇ중]

[14~15] 다음 글을 읽고 물음에 답하시오.

In 1946, a strange man visited me and asked, "Are you Mr. Kim Yonghwan's daughter?"
For me, this was an odd question because I was more used to (A)________ the daughter of a *parakho*.
"I'm your father's friend. You may wonder (B)________ it is true or not, but your father...," the man said.
At that moment, I was expecting disappointing news since I did not have good memories of my father.

14. 위 글의 빈칸 (A)에 들어갈 가장 적절한 것은? (3점)

① called ② being called
③ calling ④ call
⑤ be called

15. 위 글의 빈칸 (B)에 들어갈 가장 적절한 것은? (3점)

① if ② even if
③ though ④ that
⑤ while

[구로구 ㅇㅇ중]

[16~18] 다음 글을 읽고 물음에 답하시오.

When I was sixteen years old, my family had already made an arrangement ⓐ______ me to marry Mr. Seo. As part of the wedding tradition, Mr. Seo's family sent my family some money to buy a new chest for clothes.
(A) Right before the wedding day, my mother came into my room and said, "Your father has taken the money for the chest."
(B) I asked angrily, "How could he do ⓑ______ a horrible thing? What should we do now?" "We have no choice. You'll have to take your aunt's old chest," my mother said.
"How embarrassing for the family," people would whisper ⓒ______ my back.
(C) Since the first day of marriage, life at my husband's house had been difficult for me.
(D) "Your father, my dear friend...," my father's friend continued his story. "He was not a gambler. Your father sent the family money to the independence fighters in Manchuria. He made himself look like a gambler to keep this a secret from the Japanese officers." (E) But afterwards, I found out the truth about my father and I realized that I had been wrong about him. Ever since that moment, I have been proud to be the daughter of a *parakho* who had devoted his life ⓓ______ the independence movement.

16. 위 글을 읽고 답할 수 있는 것을 <u>모두</u> 고르면? (4점)

① What did the writer do for the country?
② Why did Mr. Seo's family send the money?
③ What did people call the writer after her marriage?
④ Why did the Japanese officers take the father?
⑤ What did the father do for the independence movement?

17. 위 글의 ⓐ~ⓓ에 들어갈 말이 <u>아닌</u> 것은? (4점)

① to ② for ③ from
④ such ⑤ behind

18. 위 글의 흐름으로 보아, (A)~(E) 중 아래의 문장이 들어갈 곳은? (4점)

At first, I was not sure if he was telling the truth.

① (A) ② (B) ③ (C) ④ (D) ⑤ (E)

[경북 ㅇㅇ중]

[19~21] 다음 글을 읽고 물음에 답하시오.

> Back in the 1920's (A)______ people saw me in the village, they would say, "There goes the *parakho*'s daughter."
> My father was a son from a very rich family. In place of living the life of a *seonbi*, he was always at the gambling house. That is why he was called a *parakho*, which means someone who ruins his family's fortune.
> "Your father has gambled (B)______ all of the money, and now he's asking (C)______ more. Go and tell him we have no more money left," my mother would tell me (D)______ she sent me to the gambling house.
> Then, my father would yell (E)_______ me angrily, "Why did you come empty-handed? Bring me more money!"

19. 위 글의 빈칸 (A), (D)에 공통으로 들어갈 가장 적절한 것은? (3점)

① since ② therefore
③ whenever ④ ever since
⑤ from then on

20. 위 글의 빈칸 (B), (C), (E)에 들어갈 것으로 가장 적절한 것은? (4점)

	(B)	(C)	(E)
①	away	at	to
②	from	for	at
③	from	for	to
④	away	of	at
⑤	away	for	at

21. 위 글을 읽고 답할 수 없는 것은? (3점)

① What does a *parakho* mean?
② Where was the father all the time?
③ Was the father a son from a poor family?
④ Why did the father yell at the writer angrily?
⑤ When did the strange man tell the writer about the writer's father?

[경북 ㅇㅇ중]

[22~24] 다음 글을 읽고 물음에 답하시오.

> My family (A)_______ an arrangement for me to marry Mr. Seo before I was sixteen years old. As part of the wedding tradition, Mr. Seo's family sent my family some money to buy a new chest for clothes.
> (B)_______ the wedding day, my mother came into my room and said, "Your father has taken the money for the chest."
> I asked angrily, "How could he do (C)_______? What should we do now?"
> "We have no choice. You'll have to take your aunt's old chest," my mother said.
> "How (D)_______ for the family," people would whisper behind my back.
> Since the first day of marriage, life at my husband's house (E)_______ difficult for me.

22. 빈칸 (A), (E)에 가장 적절한 동사형은? (4점)

	(A)	(E)
①	had made	had been
②	has made	had been
③	had made	has been
④	had been made	had been
⑤	has been made	was

23. 빈칸 (C)에 가장 알맞은 표현은? (3점)

① such a boring thing
② such a great thing
③ such a horrible thing
④ such an amazing thing
⑤ such an untruthful thing

24. 빈칸 (B), (D)에 가장 적절한 것은? (4점)

	(B)	(D)
①	After	complicated
②	Before	embarrassingly
③	Since	embarrassed
④	Before	embarrassing
⑤	After	complicating

[경북 ㅇㅇ중]

[25~26] 다음 글을 읽고 물음에 답하시오.

"Your father, my dear friend...," my father's friend continued his story. "He was not a gambler. Your father sent the family money to the independence fighters in Manchuria. ⓐ He made himself look like a gambler to keep this a secret from the Japanese officers." ⓑAt first, I was sure whether he was telling the truth.
ⓒBut afterwards, I had found out the truth about my father. ⓓAnd I realized that I had been wrong about him. ⓔEver since that moment, I have been proud to be the daughter of a *parakho* who had devoted his life to the independence movement.

25. 위 글의 밑줄 친 ⓐ~ⓔ 중에서 글의 흐름상 가장 어색한 것은? (3점)

① ⓐ ② ⓑ ③ ⓒ
④ ⓓ ⑤ ⓔ

26. 위 글의 내용으로 볼 때, 다음 중 가장 일치하지 않는 것은? (4점)

① In fact, the writer's father was not a gambler.
② The writer's father was an independent fighter.
③ There were independence fighters in Manchuria.
④ The writer's father looked like a gambler to others.
⑤ The writer had ever met her father's friend before.

[서초구 ㅇㅇ중]

[27~28] 다음 글을 읽고 아래 물음에 답하시오.

When I was sixteen years old, ⓐmy family had already made an arrangement for me to marry Mr. Seo. (A) Right before the wedding day, ⓑmy mother came into my room and said that my father had taken the money for the chest. (B) I asked angrily, "ⓒHow could he do such a horrible thing? What should we do now?" (C) "We have no choice. You'll have to take your aunt's old chest," my mother said. (D) "ⓓWhat embarrassing for the family," people would whisper behind my back. (E) ⓔSince the first day of marriage, life at my husband's house had been difficult for me.

27. 위 글의 (A)~(E) 중, 아래 주어진 문장이 들어갈 위치로 문맥상 가장 적절한 곳을 고르면? (4점)

As part of the wedding tradition, his family sent my family some money to buy a new chest for clothes.

① (A) ② (B) ③ (C)
④ (D) ⑤ (E)

28. 위 글의 ⓐ~ⓔ 중, 어법상 올바르지 못한 문장을 고르면? (4점)

① ⓐ ② ⓑ ③ ⓒ
④ ⓓ ⑤ ⓔ

3학년 영어 1학기 기말고사(4과) 1회

문항수 : 선택형(24문항) 서술형(3문항)	20 . . .	반		점수
		이름		

◎ 선택형 문항의 답안은 컴퓨터용 수정 싸인펜을 사용하여 OMR 답안지에 바르게 표기하시오.
◎ 서술형 문제는 답을 답안지에 반드시 검정 볼펜으로 쓰시오.
◎ 총 27문항 100점 만점입니다. 문항별 배점은 각 문항에 표시되어 있습니다.

[종로구 ㅇㅇ중]

1. 다음 중 밑줄 친 부분의 쓰임이 <u>다른</u> 것은? (2점)

① arriv<u>al</u> ② nation<u>al</u>
③ music<u>al</u> ④ critic<u>al</u>
⑤ environment<u>al</u>

[종로구 ㅇㅇ중]

2. 다음 빈칸에 들어갈 말로 가장 적절한 것은? (3점)

• Please ________ your message before you send it so you don't make a mistake.

① relax ② review
③ return ④ repeat
⑤ recycle

[구로구 ㅇㅇ중]

3. 다음 대화의 ⓐ~ⓒ의 단어를 어법에 맞게 수정하여 대화를 완성하시오. (6점)

A: I'm going to see *Cats* the musical ⓐ<u>play</u> by the original casts tonight. I've been looking forward to meeting them.
B: Really? I've heard that it is not that easy to buy a ticket for it.
A: How about going to the theater with me if you have time? I have one more ticket ⓑ<u>leave</u>. It will be ⓒ<u>excite</u> to watch their performance.
B: That sounds lovely. Thanks.

ⓐ play → ____________
ⓑ leave → ____________
ⓒ excite → ____________

[종로구 ㅇㅇ중]

4. 다음 빈칸에 들어갈 가장 알맞은 말을 고른 것은? (3점)

A: Are you planning to take the class during the week or during the weekend?
B: ________________________________

① I took a weekend class.
② No, I don't like planning.
③ Yes, I already made a plan.
④ Well, I'm still thinking about it.
⑤ Yes, I'm planning to take it today.

[경북 ㅇㅇ중]

5. 다음 대화의 빈칸에 들어갈 표현이 순서대로 맞게 된 것은? (4점)

Sumi: Hi! ____________________
Youngmi: Hi! I am looking at the music festival program.
Sumi: ____________________
Youngmi: Yes, this year is very special because many famous bands will be performing.
Sumi: Then it would be very popular. ____________________
Youngmi: It begins this weekend.

(A) When does it start?
(B) What are you doing?
(C) Will you go to the festival?

① (A) - (B) - (C) ② (B) - (C) - (A)
③ (C) - (A) - (B) ④ (A) - (C) - (B)
⑤ (B) - (A) - (C)

[구로구 ㅇㅇ중]

6. 다음 중 어법상 맞는 문장은? (4점)

① Do you know the girl interesting in classical music?
② The baby woke up by the bell rung in the room.
③ The movie shot in Vietnam was released last week.
④ Are you looking at the bird sung on the tree?
⑤ Cookies making by you always make me happy.

[경북 ㅇㅇ중]

7. 다음 밑줄 친 ⓐ~ⓔ 중, 어법상 어색한 것은? (3점)

I visited a broadcasting company. There were many people ⓐpreparing for the news. In the news room, I sat at the desk where anchors give the news. There were two screens ⓑhanging on the wall. I could read aloud sentences ⓒmoving across the screen. After I came out of the room, I could see myself ⓓrecording on the TV screen. I really liked the background ⓔcreated with computer graphics.

① ⓐ ② ⓑ ③ ⓒ
④ ⓓ ⑤ ⓔ

[종로구 ㅇㅇ중]

8. 다음 빈칸 (A), (B)에 들어갈 말이 바르게 짝지어진 것은? (3점)

• The man (A)_________ the drums is a famous musician.
• I really liked the pictures (B)_________ by the famous photographer.

	(A)	(B)
①	beat	taking
②	beat	taken
③	beat	took
④	beating	taken
⑤	beating	took

[종로구 ㅇㅇ중]

9. 다음 중 어색한 부분을 찾아, 수정하여 문장을 다시 쓰시오. (7점)

(1) That they say is hard to believe.
(2) I like his drum making out of garbage.
(3) Einstein considered it fun solve math problems.
(4) The jungle is a wonderful place of animals to live in.

(1) ________________________________
(2) ________________________________
(3) ________________________________
(4) ________________________________

[경북 ㅇㅇ중]

10. 다음 밑줄 친 (A), (B)를 맞게 고친 것은? (4점)

After the concert, I wanted to write a story about the orchestra. I met Favio Chávez, the conductor, and asked him about the orchestra.
Lucy White: Why did you start The Junk Orchestra?
Favio Chávez: When I went to a small town (A)(call) Cateura in Paraguay to work on a recycling program in 2005, I saw children (B)(live) in a town that was mostly filled with garbage.

	(A)	(B)
①	call	lived
②	calling	living
③	called	living
④	called	lived
⑤	calling	lived

[종로구 ㅇㅇ중]

11. 다음 표에 대한 설명으로 바르지 않은 것은? (3점)

Performance	Best Seats	Why?
Musical	near the stage	see the actor and actress up close
Piano Solo	on the left side	watch the hand movements of the person playing the piano
Orchestra Concert	on the second floor	hear the beautiful sounds of various musical instruments

① 오케스트라 공연 관람 시 최적의 자리는 2층 좌석이다.
② 피아노 독주회 관람 시 피아니스트의 손동작을 볼 수 있는 곳이 가장 좋은 좌석이다.
③ 피아노 독주회에서 연주자의 피아노 실력을 잘 볼 수 있도록 무대의 중앙에 앉는 것이 좋다.
④ 오케스트라 공연 관람 시 악기들의 아름다운 소리를 들을 수 있는 가장 좋은 좌석을 알려주고 있다.
⑤ 뮤지컬 관람 시 좌석이 무대에서 멀어지면 배우들을 가까이 볼 수 없어 무대 근처의 좌석을 골라야 한다.

[서초구 ㅇㅇ중]

[12~14] 다음 글을 읽고 물음에 답하시오.

After the concert, I was eager to write a story about the orchestra. I met Favio Chávez, the conductor, and asked him about the orchestra.

Lucy White: Why did you start The Junk Orchestra?

Favio Chávez: When I went to a small town which was called Cateura in Paraguay to work (A)_______ a recycling program in 2005, I saw children there. The town was mostly filled with garbage. I wanted to add something positive (B)_______ their lives, so I decided to share my love of music with them.

Lucy White: What do you want people to learn through your music?

Favio Chávez: I want people to know that even something worthless can make inspiring music.

After interviewing Chávez, I realized that it really doesn't matter what instrument you play with as long as you put your heart (C)_______ playing it. The children of Cateura showed me that an orchestra is formed by people, not by instruments.

Comments

Annie: *So moving to see how music can change lives.*

Kate: *Not only* (D)________________, *but they also bring serious environmental problems to our attention.*

12. 위 (A)~(C)에 들어갈 가장 적절한 것은? (4점)

	(A)	(B)	(C)
①	on	to	into
②	of	for	for
③	on	to	for
④	of	for	into
⑤	on	for	for

13. 위 글의 (D) 부분에 들어갈 표현을 바르게 쓴 것은? (4점)

① deliver these young people great music
② do deliver these young people great music
③ do these young people deliver great music
④ these young people deliver great music
⑤ these young people do deliver great music

14. 위 글을 읽고 가장 적절한 반응을 보인 학생을 고르면? (3점)

① Emma: Favio Chávez went to Cateura in 2005 to make instruments.
② Bob: Lucy White thinks that instruments we play with are the most important.
③ Jane: Favio Chávez has never believed that something worthless can make inspiring music.
④ Tom: The children Favio Chávez saw were living in a town which was filled with garbage.
⑤ Kevin: Kate thinks that the young people in the Junk Orchestra create serious environmental problems.

[종로구 ㅇㅇ중]

[15~17] 다음 글을 읽고 물음에 답하시오.

After the concert, I met Favio Chávez, the conductor, and asked him about the orchestra.
Lucy White: Why did you start The Junk Orchestra?
Favio Chávez: When I went to a small town called Cateura in Paraguay to work on a recycling program in 2005, I saw children living in a town that was mostly filled with garbage. ⓐI wanted to add something positive to their lives, so I decided to share my love of music with them.
Lucy White: Why did you use garbage to make instruments?
Favio Chávez: (A)One person's garbage is another person's treasure. Nicolás Gómez, a local garbage picker, helped me a lot. ⓑHe made it possible for children to play music by making instruments out of garbage. ⓒThe wonderful thing about these instruments was that the children didn't have to worry about spending a lot of money on them.
Lucy White: What do you want people to learn through your music?
Favio Chávez: ⓓI want people to know that even something useful can make inspiring music.
After interviewing Chávez, ⓔI realized that it really matters what instrument you play with as long as you put your heart into playing it. The children of Cateura showed me that an orchestra is formed by people, not by instruments.

(B)<Comments for Lucy's Post>

Thomas: I found it possible to inspire people by music playing with recycled instruments.
Kate: Not only do these talented young people deliver great music, but they also take serious environmental problems to our attention.

15. **위 글의 밑줄 친 ⓐ~ⓔ 중 글의 흐름상 어색한 문장 둘을 고르면?** **(4점)**

① ⓐ ② ⓑ ③ ⓒ ④ ⓓ ⑤ ⓔ

16. **위 글의 밑줄 친 문장 (A)의 의미를 가장 잘 설명한 것은?** **(4점)**

① 버려진 물건을 재활용해야 한다.
② 쓰레기 더미에 보물이 숨겨져 있다.
③ 아름다운 음악은 무엇으로도 창조해 낼 수 있다.
④ 버려진 물건으로도 악기처럼 정교한 물건을 만들 수 있다.
⑤ 쓸모없는 것도 누군가에게는 의미 있게 쓰일 수 있다.

17. **위 글의 흐름에 맞게 (B)의 밑줄 친 부분을 알맞게 바꾸시오. (답만 순서대로 쓰시오)** **(5점)**

정답: playing → ______________
take → ______________

[경북 ㅇㅇ중]

[18~19] 다음 글을 읽고 물음에 답하시오.

I want to ⓐrecommend a song to ⓑthose who need to ⓒbe cheered up. The title of the song is *Happy*, and the singer is Allan Hamilton. This song is about looking on ⓓthe bright side of life and staying happy. I want to recommend this song because I found (A)__________ helpful to listen to it when I was in the hospital. It cheered me up and gave me hope. So I think the song ⓔsung by Allan Hamilton is about happy moments in life.

18. **위 글의 밑줄 친 ⓐ~ⓔ의 뜻 중에서 어색한 것은?** **(3점)**

① ⓐ ~을 추천하다
② ⓑ ~한 사람들
③ ⓒ 격려를 받다
④ ⓓ ~의 불안한 측면
⑤ ⓔ ~에 의해 불려진

19. **위 글의 빈칸 (A)에 들어갈 것으로 가장 적절한 것은?** **(3점)**

① them ② what ③ this
④ that ⑤ it

[경북 ㅇㅇ중]

[20~23] 다음 글을 읽고 물음에 답하시오.

Lucy White: Why did you use garbage to make instruments?

Favio Chávez: One person's garbage is another person's treasure. Nicolás Gómez, a local garbage picker, helped me a lot. He made it possible for children to play music by making instruments out of garbage. The wonderful thing about these instruments (A)_______ that the children didn't have to worry about spending a lot of money (B)_______ them.

Lucy White: What do you want people to learn (C)_______ your music?

Favio Chávez: I ⓐwant people to know that even ⓑworthless something can make ⓒinspiring music.

After interviewing Chavez, I realized that it really doesn't matter what instrument you play with (D)_______ you put your heart into playing it. The children of Cateura showed me that an orchestra ⓓis formed by people, ⓔnot by instruments.

20. 위 글의 빈칸 (A), (B), (C)에 들어갈 말로 가장 적절한 것은? (3점)

	(A)	(B)	(C)
①	was	on	through
②	were	on	through
③	was	in	through
④	were	in	though
⑤	was	on	though

21. 위 글에 관한 두 사람의 대화에서, 아래 빈칸에 들어갈 말로 가장 적절한 것은? (4점)

Mihyun: How did Gómez help the children to play music?
Hyunil: ______________________________

① He helped make it is worthless for children to play music with instruments made out of garbage.
② He helped make it worthless for children to play music with instruments made out of garbage.
③ He helped make it is possible for children to play music with instruments made out of garbage.
④ He helped make it possible for children to play music with instruments made out of garbage.
⑤ He helped make it is positive for children to play music with instruments made out of garbage.

22. 위 글의 빈칸 (D)에 들어갈 가장 적절한 표현은? (4점)

① as far as
② as good as
③ as long as
④ as well as
⑤ as possible as

23. 위 글의 밑줄 친 ⓐ~ⓔ 중에서 쓰임이 <u>어색한</u> 것은? (3점)

① ⓐ ② ⓑ ③ ⓒ
④ ⓓ ⑤ ⓔ

[종로구 ㅇㅇ중]

24. 다음 글을 읽고 알 수 없는 것을 고르면? (3점)

"The world sends us garbage, we send back music." This was written on the back of a concert ticket I was given. The musical group was called "The Junk Orchestra." They played instruments made entirely out of garbage. I could not imagine what kind of sound these instruments would make, so I was eager to find out.
Before the concert, I thought that the instruments might sound strange. After a few minutes, a group of young people began to walk on the stage. The first thing I noticed was their instruments: a cello made out of a shiny oil tank, a violin made with forks, and a flute made with a water pipe and buttons. The concert began with a girl playing Bach's *Cello Suite No. 1* on her shiny cello. I was shocked by the deep sound. I was so into the music that I forgot that they were playing with instruments made from recycled materials.

① 콘서트에서 연주된 곡명
② 콘서트에서 연주된 악기의 소리
③ 콘서트 티켓 앞면에 쓰여진 문구
④ 콘서트에서 연주된 악기를 만든 재료
⑤ The Junk Orchestra라고 불리는 이유

[종로구 ㅇㅇ중]

25. 다음 글의 빈칸 (A)에 들어갈 말로 가장 적절한 것은? (4점)

After the concert, I was eager to write a story about the orchestra. I met Favio Chávez, the conductor, and asked him about the orchestra.
Lucy White: (A)______________________
Favio Chávez: When I went to a small town called Cateura in Paraguay to work on a recycling program in 2005, I saw children living in a town that was mostly filled with garbage. I wanted to add something positive to their lives, so I decided to share my love of music with them.

① Why did you start The Junk Orchestra?
② Why did you use garbage to make instruments?
③ What do you want people to learn through your music?
④ What was the wonderful thing about the instruments?
⑤ How did you teach the children to play the musical instruments?

[종로구 ㅇㅇ중]

[26~27] 다음 글을 읽고 물음에 답하시오.

"The world sends us garbage, we send back music." This was written on the back of a concert ticket I was given. The musical group ⓐwas called "The Junk Orchestra." They played instruments made of garbage only. I could not imagine what kind of sound these instruments would make, so I was eager to find out. Before the concert, I thought that the instruments might ⓑsound strange. After a few minutes, a group of young people began to walk on the stage. The first thing ⓒthat I noticed was their instruments: a cello made out of a shiny oil tank, a violin made with forks, and a flute made with a water pipe and buttons. The concert began with a girl ⓓplaying Bach's *Cello Suite No. 1* on her shiny cello. I ⓔshocked by the deep sound. I was so into the music that I forgot that they were playing with instruments made from recycled materials.

26. 밑줄 친 ⓐ~ⓔ 중 어법상 어색한 것은? (4점)

① ⓐ ② ⓑ ③ ⓒ ④ ⓓ ⑤ ⓔ

27. 위 글의 글쓴이의 심경의 변화로 가장 적절한 것은? (3점)

	Before the concert	After the concert
①	sad	surprised
②	happy	worried
③	curious	touched
④	moved	bored
⑤	excited	disappointed

3학년 영어 1학기 기말고사(4과) 2회

반		점수
이름		

문항수 : 선택형(28문항) 서술형(1문항) | 20 . . .

◎ 선택형 문항의 답안은 컴퓨터용 수정 싸인펜을 사용하여 OMR 답안지에 바르게 표기하시오.
◎ 서술형 문제는 답을 답안지에 반드시 검정 볼펜으로 쓰시오.
◎ 총 29문항 100점 만점입니다. 문항별 배점은 각 문항에 표시되어 있습니다.

[구로구 ㅇㅇ중]

1. 다음 빈칸에 들어갈 말로 바르지 않은 것은? (3점)

- How should I (A)________ for my exam?
- Is there a (B)________ museum near here?
- The book offers a new (C)________ on science.
- He began to count (D)________, "Ten, nine, eight..."
- I answered my phone when I was still half (E)________.

① (A) prepare ② (B) national
③ (C) insight ④ (D) backwards
⑤ (E) careless

[종로구 ㅇㅇ중]

2. 다음 빈칸에 공통으로 들어갈 말은? (3점)

- ________ is hard to memorize all the poems in the book.
- Anthony considers ________ hard to listen to her playing the piano.

① It[it] ② Why[why]
③ That[that] ④ What[what]
⑤ Which[which]

[구로구 ㅇㅇ중]

3. 다음 대화의 내용과 일치하는 것은? (3점)

W: Hey, Anthony. Can you help me with something?
M: Sure, what's up?
W: I'm going to a concert at the Arts Center, but I don't know which seat I should choose.
M: Are you planning to go to the orchestra concert?
W: Yes. I'm going to watch the orchestra concert.
M: Then, you should get the seats on the second floor. You can hear the beautiful sounds of various musical instruments better.
W Oh, do you think it's better to hear the performance from the second floor?
M: Yes. I think so. (M: Man / W: Woman)

① The woman disagrees with the man's opinion.
② The woman will possibly watch the concert on the second floor.
③ The man and the woman are in the concert hall now.
④ The man and the woman will go to the concert together.
⑤ The first floor is the best place to watch the orchestra concert.

[종로구 ㅇㅇ중]

4. 다음 빈칸 (A)에 들어갈 가장 적절한 것은? (2점)

M: Hi, Sally. Where are you off to?
W: I'm going to the music room. I have choir practice.
M: Oh, yeah. I forgot that you've joined the choir. Do you find it (A)____________?
W: Yeah, it's great to sing in harmony with others.

① boring to sing in the choir
② interesting to sing in the choir
③ helpful to practice in the music room
④ hard to learn how to sing with other people
⑤ possible to inspire people by holding a concert

[종로구 ㅇㅇ중]

5. 다음 중 의미나 어법상 어색한 것은? (4점)

① The local time is 11:20 in the morning.
② You can add some sugar to the mixture.
③ Environmental changes can affect all of our lives.
④ The world-famous singer sings entire in Korean.
⑤ The musician wants to deliver hope through music.

[경북 ㅇㅇ중]

6. 다음 대화를 읽고, 대답할 수 있는 질문은? (3점)

W: Hey, Tommy. What day is it today?
M: It's Wednesday.
W: When is the last day to sign up for the talent show?
M: The day after tomorrow. Are you planning to sign up for it, Megan?
W: Yeah, I'm going to perform the music of string instrument.
M: How cool! What are you going to do?
W: I will play K-pop music with the violin.

① What date is the deadline to apply for the talent show?
② Whom is Megan planning to perform with?
③ Why would Megan like to sing a K-pop song?
④ What is Tommy going to do for the talent show?
⑤ What musical instrument will be used for Megan's show?

[종로구 ㅇㅇ중]

7. Choose the dialogue that is grammatically correct. (4점)

① A: Do you find it more help to listen to music before you swim?
B: Yes, it keeps me awake and helps me focus.
② A: Do you think it's hardly to play the guitar?
B: Yes, I think so.
③ A: Do you think it's interesting to sing in the choir?
B: Yeah, it's great to sing in harmony with others.
④ A: Do you find it exciting to watch scary movies?
B: Of course. I think it's really excited.
⑤ A: Do you find it easily to write songs?
B: Well, it was hard in the beginning, but now it's getting easier.

[충북 ㅇㅇ중]

8. 다음 대화의 밑줄 친 우리말에 해당하는 문장은? (4점)

W: Hi, Jason. Great to see you again. I've heard the new rap song, *Young and Wild*, that you recorded. It's really cool.
M: Oh, thanks.
W: I really like your songs. Do you find it easy to write them?
M: Well, it was hard in the beginning, but now it's getting easier. I draw on my experiences and keep a journal.
W: Wow! As they say, "<u>고통 없이는 얻는 게 없다</u>." Best of luck with your new song!
M: Thank you.

① No pain, no gain.
② Piece of cake.
③ Practice makes perfect.
④ The early bird catches the worm.
⑤ Two heads are better than one.

[경북 ㅇㅇ중]

9. 다음 중 어법상 <u>어색한</u> 것은? (3점)

① It was hard for me to move the piano.
② Anne considered it natural that John kept quiet in class.
③ The girls found it easy to solve the problem.
④ Sara made it a habit write a diary every day.
⑤ It was a good idea to rest on the bench.

[종로구 ㅇㅇ중]

10. 밑줄 친 부분과 쓰임이 같은 것은? (두 개) (4점)

• The boy <u>making</u> cheese is my brother.

① I saw a man <u>beating</u> the drums.
② <u>Solving</u> math problems is fun.
③ I recommend the hotel where there is a <u>swimming</u> pool.
④ There isn't a <u>smoking</u> room in this building.
⑤ There is a photo <u>hanging</u> on the wall.

[경북 ㅇㅇ중]

[11~12] 다음 대화를 읽고 물음에 답하시오.

W: Hi, Jason. Great to see you again. I've heard the new rap song, *Young and Wild*, that you recorded. It's really cool.
M: Oh, thanks, Lisa.
W: I really like your songs. Do you think it's easy to write them?
M: Well, it was hard in the beginning, but now it's getting easier. I draw on my experiences and keep a journal.
W: Wow! As they say, "ⓐ<u>No pain, no gain</u>." Best of luck with your new song!
M: Thank you.

11. 위 대화를 읽고, 대답할 수 <u>없는</u> 질문은? (3점)

① What does Lisa think of *Young and Wild*?
② Has Lisa heard Jason's new rap song?
③ What genre does Lisa usually listen to?
④ How has Jason felt while he writes his new songs?
⑤ What does Jason make use of when he tries to make songs?

*make use of ~을 활용하다

12. 위 대화의 밑줄 친 ⓐ의 의미로 가장 적절한 것은? (4점)

① We will never know the result until you try.
② Health is the most valuable thing in the world.
③ We should hang out until the winter ends.
④ At the end of hard work comes pleasure or reward.
⑤ Different roads sometimes lead to the same castle.

[경북 ㅇㅇ중]

[13~14] 다음 대화를 읽고 물음에 답하시오.

W: Anthony, can you help me with something?
M: Sure. What's up, Jisu?
W: I'm going to a concert at the Arts Center, but I don't know which seat I should choose.
M: (A)<u>Are you planning to go to the orchestra concert</u>?
W: Yes. I'm going to watch the orchestra concert.
M: Then, you should get the seats on the second floor. You can hear the beautiful sounds of various musical instruments better.
W: Oh, do you find it better to hear the performance from the second floor?
M: Yes. I find it better than from other seats.

13. 위 대화를 다음과 같이 요약할 때, 빈칸 ⓐ, ⓑ, ⓒ에 들어갈 말로 알맞은 것은? (4점)

• Anthony ⓐ__________ that Jisu get the seats on the 2nd floor since he thinks it ⓑ__________ to hear the sound of musical instruments ⓒ__________ other seats.

	ⓐ	ⓑ	ⓒ
①	suggests	better	than
②	orders	worse	than
③	suggests	better	through
④	orders	better	as
⑤	suggests	worse	as

14. 위 대화의 (A)와 바꿔 쓸 수 <u>없는</u> 표현은? (3점)

① Are you going to go to the orchestra concert?
② Would you help me go to the orchestra concert?
③ Do you intend to go to the orchestra concert?
④ Are you thinking of going to the orchestra concert?
⑤ Do you have a plan to go to the orchestra concert?

[경북 ○○중]

[15~17] 다음 글을 읽고 물음에 답하시오.

Before the concert, I thought that the instruments might sound ⓐ[strange / strangely]. After a few minutes, a group of young people began to walk on the stage with their instruments.

(A) The concert began with a girl ⓑ[played / playing] Bach's *Cello Suite No. 1* on her shiny cello. I was shocked by the deep sound.
(B) The first thing I noticed was that they had very unique instruments: a cello made out of a shiny oil tank, a violin made with forks, and a flute made with a water pipe and buttons. I was curious that what sound the instruments made.
(C) I was so into the music that I forgot ⓒ[that / what] they were playing with instruments made from recycled materials.

After the concert. I felt that I was deeply touched by the music.

15. 위 글의 괄호 ⓐ, ⓑ, ⓒ에 들어갈 말로 알맞게 짝지어진 것은? (4점)

	ⓐ	ⓑ	ⓒ
①	strange	played	that
②	strangely	played	what
③	strange	playing	that
④	strangely	playing	that
⑤	strange	playing	what

16. 위 글의 흐름상, 문장 (A)~(C)를 가장 적절하게 배열한 것은? (4점)

① (A) - (B) - (C) ② (A) - (C) - (B)
③ (B) - (A) - (C) ④ (B) - (C) - (A)
⑤ (C) - (B) - (A)

17. 위 글에서 콘서트 관람 후, 글쓴이가 느낀 감정은? (3점)

① indifferent ② disappointed ③ bored
④ moved ⑤ worried

[경북 ○○중]

[18~19] 다음 대화를 읽고 물음에 답하시오.

Lucy: Why did you use garbage to make instruments?
Favio: (A)____________________ Nicolás Gómez, a local garbage picker, helped me a lot. He made it ⓐpossible for children to play music by making instruments out of garbage. The wonderful thing about these instruments was that the children didn't have to worry about ⓑspending lots of money on them.
Lucy: What do you want people to learn through your music?
Favio: I want people to know that ⓒonly something precious can make inspiring music.

<Comments for Lucys Post>

Annie: The power of music is ⓓinfinite.
Kate: Not only do these talented young people deliver great music, but they also bring ⓔserious environmental issues to our attention.

18. 빈칸 (A)에 들어갈 말로 알맞은 것은? (3점)

① Never throw garbage into a pond or lake.
② Recycled instruments will make better sound.
③ As the world sends us garbage, we will send money back.
④ We should use eco-friendly products to protect the environment.
⑤ One person's garbage can be useful to someone else.

19. 위 대화의 밑줄 친 ⓐ~ⓔ 중, 흐름상 어색한 것은? (4점)

① ⓐ ② ⓑ ③ ⓒ ④ ⓓ ⑤ ⓔ

[경북 ㅇㅇ중]

[20~21] 다음 글을 읽고 물음에 답하시오.

After the concert, I was eager to write a story about the orchestra. I met Favio Chávez, ⓐ________, and asked him about the orchestra that he leads.

Lucy White: Why did you start The Junk Orchestra?

Favio Chávez: When I went to a small town called Cateura in Paraguay to work on a recycling program in 2005, I saw children living in a town that was mostly filled with garbage. <u>나는 그들의 삶에 긍정적인 무엇인가를 더해 주고 싶습니다</u>. So I decided to share my love of music with them.

20. 위 글의 밑줄 친 우리말을 〈보기〉의 단어들을 사용하여 영작할 때 7번째로 올 단어는? (필요한 경우 단어를 변형해야 함.) (4점)

<보기>
to / positive / be / their / something / eager / to / I / add / lives

① add ② positive
③ something ④ their
⑤ to

21. 위 글의 문맥상 빈칸 ⓐ에 들어갈 단어에 대한 영영풀이로 옳은 것은? (3점)

① someone who is ready to defend his nation against an enemy
② someone who writes novels, especially fantasy novels as a job
③ someone who reads the news or introduces news reports
④ someone who stands before a choir or an orchestra and directs the performance
⑤ someone who operates the equipment of a plane, as a job

[충북 ㅇㅇ중]

[22~23] 다음을 읽고, 물음에 답하시오.

Ⓐ________________

"The world sends us garbage, we send back music."

This was written on the back of a concert ticket I was given. The musical group was called "Ⓐ________________." They played instruments made entirely out of garbage. I could not imagine what kind of sound these instruments would make, so I was eager to find out.

Before the concert, I thought that the instruments might sound strange. After a few minutes, a group of young people began to walk on the stage. The first thing I noticed was their instruments: a cello made out of a shiny oil tank, a violin made with forks, and a flute made with a water pipe and buttons. The concert began with a girl playing Bach's *Cello Suite No. 1* on her shiny cello. I was shocked by the deep sound. I was so into the music that I forgot that they were playing with instruments made from recycled materials.

22. 위 글의 빈칸 Ⓐ에 공통으로 들어갈 가장 알맞은 것은? (3점)

① The Art Museum
② The Junk Orchestra
③ The Great Musical Talent
④ The Dream of Elderly People
⑤ The First American Orchestra

23. 위 글의 내용과 일치하는 것은? (4점)

① 음악회에서 글쓴이의 친구들이 연주했다.
② 글쓴이는 음악회 콘서트 티켓을 직접 샀다.
③ 연주자는 기름통으로 만들어진 바이올린을 연주했다.
④ 플루트를 연주하는 것으로 음악회가 시작되었다.
⑤ 글쓴이는 음악회에 푹 빠져 심취해 있었다.

[경북 ㅇㅇ중]

[24~29] 다음 글을 읽고 물음에 답하시오.

"The world sends us garbage, we ⓐsend back music."
This was written on the back of a concert ticket ⓑI was given. The musical group was called "The Junk Orchestra." They played instruments ⓒmade entirely out of garbage. I could not imagine (A)이 악기들이 어떤 종류의 소리를 낼지. So I ⓓwas eager to find out.
Before the concert, I thought that the instruments might ⓔsound strange. After a few minutes, a group of young people began to walk on the stage. The first thing I noticed was their instruments: a cello made out of a shiny oil tank, a violin made with forks, and a flute made with a water pipe and buttons. The concert began with a girl playing Bach's *Cello suite No. 1* on her shiny cello. I was (B)________ by the deep sound. I was (C)________ into the music (D)________ I forgot they were playing with instrument made from (E)________ materials.

24. 위 글의 밑줄 친 ⓐ~ⓔ의 의미로 어색한 것은? (3점)

① ⓐ 돌려준다
② ⓑ 내가 주었다
③ ⓒ 완전히 쓰레기로 만들어진
④ ⓓ ~을 몹시 하고 싶어했다
⑤ ⓔ 이상하게 들리다

25. 위 글의 제목으로 가장 적절한 것은? (3점)

① The Junk Orchestra
② The World Garbage
③ The Instruments Made with Garbage
④ The Young People Playing the Concert
⑤ The Musical Group Made by the Young

26. 위 글의 밑줄 친 (A)를 가장 적절하게 영작한 것은? (3점)

① this instrument would make what kind of sound
② this instrument would make what kinds of sound
③ these instruments would make what kind of sound
④ what kind of sound these instruments would make
⑤ what kinds of sound these instrument would make

27. 위 글의 빈칸 (B), (E)에 들어갈 가장 적절한 것은? (4점)

	(B)	(E)
①	disappointed	built
②	anxious	scattered
③	shocked	recycled
④	hopeful	disappeared
⑤	annoyed	broken

28. 위 글의 빈칸 (C), (D)에 들어갈 적절한 말을 쓰시오. (5점)

(C) ____________ (D) ____________

29. 위 글의 마지막에서, 글쓴이의 심경으로 가장 적절한 것은? (3점)

① moved ② bored
③ worried ④ interested
⑤ satisfied

정답 및 해설

Lesson 1 (중간) 1회

01 ②	02 ④	03 ④	04 ③	05 ⑤		
06 let my hair down		07 ①	08 ④	09 ③	10 ③	
11 ②	12 ④	13 ①	14 ⑤	15 ⑤	16 ②	17 ③
18 ③	19 ②	20 ⑤	21 ⑤	22 ④	23 ②	

01 ②의 반의어는 inexpensive처럼 앞에 in-을 붙인다. 나머지는 모두 앞에 un-을 써서 반의어를 만든다.

02 ⓐ comfortable → uncomfortable ⓑ kindly → unkindly ⓒ giving → taking ⓔ demand → request

03 'let one's hair down'의 뜻은 '자유롭게 근심 걱정없이 지내다'라는 뜻이다.

04 ①, ②, ④, ⑤는 모두 관계대명사인데, ③은 '의문형용사'로서 '무슨' 음식이라는 뜻으로 사용되었다.

05 ⑤ 과학 숙제가 어떻게 진행되고 있는지 물었는데, 잘 되고 있다고 답한 후에, 자신이 속한 과학 그룹에 화가 난다고 하는 것은 어색하다.

06 'feel free from all my troubles'와 같은 의미의 문장을 만드는 문제이다. 'let one's hair down'이 바로 그 뜻에 해당하며, 주어인 I에 맞게 my를 쓰는 것에 유의한다.

07 선행사가 the reason이고, 뒤에 완전한 문장이 올 때, 관계부사는 why를 쓴다. ② why → when ③ when → where ④ when → where ⑤ where → when

08 빈칸에는 'Roy에게 화가 난 이유'가 되는 행동이 나와야 한다. ⓑ의 'let my hair down'은 나를 편하게 해준다는 뜻이므로, 답이 되지 않는다. ⓐ 항상 나를 따라해. ⓒ 뒤에서 내 말을 해. ⓓ 밤에 전화로 너무 크게 말해. ⓔ 내 말을 계속 끊어.

09 'have one's head in the clouds'는 '엉뚱한 생각을 하고 있다'는 뜻이므로, ⓒ '수업시간에 집중을 안 해'가 알맞은 표현이다. 나머지 각 빈칸엔 ⓐ keep her party a secret ⓑ I got so scared that I didn't dive ⓓ I want to go somewhere and feel free from all my troubles. ⓔ I have to study.

10 여동생에게 왜 화가 났는지 물어보니 [(B) 피곤해서 졸린데 시끄럽게 통화해서 화가 났어. (A) 그렇구나. 둘이 아직 해결 못했니? (D) 아직. 못되게 굴어 미안하다고 말하고 싶은데, 어떻게 할지. (C) 쪽지나 문자를 보내봐]의 순이다.

11 (A) keep V-ing 계속 ~하다
(B), (C) 과거시제 동사 병렬 구조

12 (A) 동사 express를 꾸며주는 부사 (C) be동사 뒤 주격보어 자리의 형용사 (E) be lost: 없어지다, 분실되다

13 (B) 선행사 the reason 뒤의 관계부사 자리에는 why (D) 선행사를 포함하는 관계대명사는 what이다.

14 ⑤ 'Brian의 소통의 문제는 자신의 느낌과 생각에 집중하는 것이다.'라고 되어 있는데, '자신의 느낌과 생각에 집중하는 것'은 '문제'가 아닌 '해결책'이다. 그러므로 ⑤가 글의 내용과 일치하지 않는다.

15 prevent는 타동사이므로 전치사 from과 같이 써서 타동사구를 만들 필요가 없다.

16 make a demand: 요구하다, make a request: 부탁하다, 요청하다. make a mistake: 실수하다. 주어가 3인칭 단수이고, 내용상 과거시제 동사를 쓴다.

17 위 글은 Anna가 평소 Julie에게 어떻게 말하는지 나왔지만, Julie가 Anna에게 말하는 것과 관련된 내용은 없다.

18 Calli가 엄마에게 대화를 요청한 문장 바로 뒤에, '대화의 적절한 시간을 찾을 필요가 있다'는 문장이 들어가는 것이 가장 좋다.

19 ⓑ preparing go → preparing to go, ⓒ listen to Calli → listen to what Calli로 고치는 것이 적절하다.

20 위 글의 주제는 '소통의 문제와 그 해결책'에 대한 것이다.

21 ⓐ to argue → arguing ⓑ how → why ⓒ it → 삭제, pointing → point ⓓ lost → are lost

22 'Calli의 엄마가 처음에 대화하고 싶지 않았다.'는 현덕의 말은 글의 내용을 잘못 이해하고 있다.

23 (B) when과 나머지는 모두 시간을 나타내는 선행사 뒤의 '관계부사'로서 쓰였는데, ②만 '~일 때'의 뜻으로 시간의 부사절을 이끄는 접속사로 쓰였다.

Lesson 1 (중간) 2회

01 ③	02 ⑤	03 ⑤	04 ③	05 ⑤	06 ④	07 ③
08 ②	09 ④	10 ①	11 ③	12 ⑤	13 ①	14 ①
15 ①	16 ②	17 ②	18 when		19 ③	20 ④
21 ④	22 ④	23 ②	24 ④	25 ⑤	26 ①	27 ④
28 ①						

01 ③ make an arrangement: 준비하다, 합의하다 ①

have one's head in the clouds: 엉뚱한 생각을 하다 ② point the finger at: 비난하다 ④ get cold feet: 겁이 나다 ⑤ devote one's life to ~: ~에 삶을 헌신하다

02 관계부사 when과 where의 앞에 적절한 선행사를 찾는 문제이다. (A)에는 시간, (B)에는 장소를 의미하는 단어가 적절하다.

03 나의 말을 친구가 오해할 때, '내 말은 그런 뜻이 아니야.'라고 하는 표현은 That's not what I meant.를 쓴다.

04 '요구'나 '명령'의 방식으로 말하는 것보다는 '요청', '부탁'이 좋다고 했으므로, 부탁을 하는 표현인 ③이 적절하다.

05 ⓔ ''그녀가 말하는 것'이 요구보다는 요청으로 들릴 것이다'라는 문장이므로, that을 what으로 고치는 것이 적절하다.

06 ④의 'let one's hair down'은 '자유로운 기분을 누리다'라는 뜻이다. 불편한 감정을 표현할 때 쓸 수 없다.

07 평소 직설적으로 말하는 남자가 사람들에게 화가 나 있어서, 여자가 타인의 감정을 배려하며 말하라고 충고하는 장면이다. 남자도 조언대로 하겠다고 말한다.

08 '사람들이 그러는데, 내가 너무 직설적이래'라는 말에 여자가 '음, 무슨 말인지 알 것 같아'라고 답하자, 남자가 '그 말이 무슨 뜻이야?'라고 되묻는 것이 가장 자연스럽다.

09 ①, ②, ③, ⑤의 what은 모두 관계대명사인데, ④는 '의문대명사'로 쓰여 의문문을 이끌고 있다.

10 '내가 지금 당장 하고 싶은 것'은 That이 아니라, The thing that[which] 또는 What을 쓰는 것이 적절하다.

11 ⓐ use → using ⓑ expressing → express ⓓ Start → Starting 또는 To start ⓔ pointed → point

12 본문의 'Starting with "I" can help him focus on what he feels rather than point the finger at his brother.'가 바로 대답이 될 수 있다. 같은 내용의 ⑤가 가장 적절하다.

13 ①은 '의문대명사'로 쓰여서, '무엇을 할 계획이니?'라는 의문문을 이끌고 있는 반면, ⓐ와 나머지 what은 모두 '관계대명사'로 사용되었다.

14 본문 내용은, 상대에 대한 비난보다 자신의 감정에 집중해서 말하라는 것으로서, 일반적으로 '가장 아끼는 이어폰이 사라졌을 때' ① '속상하다'고 표현하는 것이 적절하다.

15 ①은 Calli를 지칭하고 있지만, ②, ③, ④, ⑤는 모두 그녀의 엄마를 가리킨다.

16 본문 내용은 출근 준비로 바쁜 상황의 엄마에게 대화를 청하는 것보다 '소통하기에 적절한 시간을 찾는 것이 중요하다'고 조언하고 있다.

17 이 글은 '지혜로운 소통의 기술을 조언'하고 있다.

18 '엄마가 대화할 준비가 된 시간'이라는 뜻이므로, 선행사 a time 뒤에 관계부사 when이 적절하다.

19 Brian은 Dr. Carter의 쇼에서 보여주는 동영상 클립의 '등장 인물'로서 동생과의 소통에 어려움을 겪고 있다.

20 'I-message'는 '개인 간의 신속한 연락을 위한 메신저 서비스'가 아니다. Ⓓ는 글의 흐름과 무관한 문장이다.

21 빈칸 뒤의 조언에서 'You' 메시지를 사용하지 않는 게 좋다고 했으므로, You로 시작하는 직설적인 문장이 적절하다.

22 ⓓ에는 that이 아니라, 관계대명사 'what'이 적절하다. 'what he feels'(그가 느끼는 것)이 문맥상 알맞다.

23 '소통'은 상대가 준비되었을 때, 청하는 것이라는 내용이므로, '모든 것은 알맞은 때가 있다.'의 ②가 적절하다.

24 But으로 보아, '엄마는 Calli의 말을 듣고 싶었을지도 모른다', '그렇지만 시간이 없었다'의 연결이 가장 자연스럽다.

25 ⓐ, ⓑ, ⓒ는 어색한 부분이 없는데 고쳤다. ⓓ what 하나면 충분한데, the thing을 쓰려면 뒤에 which나 that을 쓴다. ⓔ시간의 선행사 뒤에 관계부사 when을 쓰는 것이 적절하다.

26 ① 'Julie가 불편한 이유' 외 나머지는 답할 수 없는 질문이다.

27 '요구'보다 '요청'의 말을 써야 한다는 조언 뒤인 (D)에 들어가는 것이 가장 적절하다.

28 '~와 같은'이라는 뜻으로 뒤에 구체적인 사례를 들 때, such as 또는 like와 같은 표현을 사용하는 것이 적절하다.

Lesson 2 (중간) 1회

01 ② **02** ④ **03** ③ **04** ⑤ **05** ① **06** ② **07** ③
08 ⑤ **09** ⑤ **10** Has he been playing the drum?
11 ② **12** ④ **13** ① **14** ④ **15** ② **16** ④ **17** ④
18 ② **19** ③ **20** ⑤ **21** have been arriving
22 ② **23** ⑤ **24** ①

01 ① endless → harsh ③ accident → miracle ④ insight → adventure ⑤ entirely → unusual

02 (A) lowest → highest (E) huge → small

03 'to부정사'의 '의미상 주어'는 for를 쓰며, '사람의 성격이나 성질'은 of를 사용한다. (C)에는 let의 목적어가 필

요하다.

04 주어진 단어들로 영작하면, "Let's find out how people from different fields of work get inspired by nature."이다.

05 ② 경기 → 강좌 ③ 실외 → 실내 ④ 무료로 제공 → 판매 ⑤ 학교 → 지역 문화센터

06 현재완료진행시제를 활용하는 문제이다. '어제 오후 이후로'는 'since yesterday afternoon'이고, 3인칭 단수 현재시제이므로 has been doing을 활용하되, 'doing' 또는 'working with'를 쓸 수 있다.

07 ㉠ 내용상 9년 전부터 알아왔다는 것이므로, since가 필요하고, know는 동작동사가 아니므로 진행시제로 표현하지 않는다. → Mr. John Baker has known Minsu since 9 years ago. ㉣ has been played → have been playing

08 ⑤ his daughter는 동사 allowed의 목적어이므로, 전치사 of를 앞에 쓸 필요가 없다.

09 빈칸에 알맞은 단어는 순서대로 'is difficult for her to'이다.

10 질문에 대한 B의 답변이 he has이므로, 현재완료진행시제로 묻는 것이 적절하며, 단어를 모두 활용한다.

11 ① sung → singing ③ worn → wearing ④ made → making ⑤ satisfying → satisfied

12 (A)에는 to부정사의 의미상 주어로서 generous(관대한), 즉 사람의 성격에 맞는 전치사 of가 필요하며, (B)는 의문부사 자리인데, the palace가 나왔으므로, where가 아닌 when 또는 how가 적절하다.

13 A가 황사가 몽골 사막에서 한국으로 오는 것을 알았느냐고 물었는데, B가 몰랐다고 하고서는 황사가 건강에 안 좋다고 말했다는 내용이 이어지는 것은 부자연스럽다.

14 지수야, Norway에서는 여름에 태양이 지지 않는다는 것을 알고 있었니? [(D) 아니, 몰랐어. 흥미롭네. (A) 응. 어둡지 않아서 밤에도 하이킹 가거나 자전거도 탄대. (C) 나도 한밤중에 하이킹 가거나 자전거를 타고 싶어. (B) 나도. 언젠가 우리도 그러면 좋겠다.]의 순이다.

15 'can't wait to V'는 '~하는 것이 너무나 기대된다'는 뜻이므로, '강한 기대'를 표현한다. 그러므로 David의 심경으로는 ② excited(흥분된)가 가장 적절하다.

16 (A)에는 문맥상 상대방에게 '허락'을 구하는 말이 필요하다. 그런데, ④는 '~하는 게 어때?'라는 권유의 표현이므로 어색하다.

17 위 대화의 첫 문장 'Welcome back to the quest house.'로 보아, 이 대화는 guest house에서 일어나고 있음을 알 수 있다. 그러므로 대화 내용과 일치하는 것은 ④이다.

18 밑줄 친 (A)는 '멋진 해변 사진을 더 많이 찍는 게 너무 기대된다'는 뜻이다. 그런데, ②는 '더 많은 사진을 찍는 것은 시간이 좀 걸릴 것이다'라는 뜻이므로, 바꿔 쓰기에 부적절하다.

19 '올해의 사진대회' 우승자인 여성이 몰디브의 빛나는 해변 사진을 찍었는데, 이것은 해변의 플랑크톤으로 인해 생긴 것이지, ③에서 언급한 '특수효과' 같은 것이 아니다.

20 (A) '3시간 동안 비가 오고 있는 중이다.'라는 '현재완료진행시제'이므로, ⑤ '3시간 전에 비가 내리기 시작했고, 지금도 비가 오고 있다.'가 적절하다.

21 주어가 복수이므로 have를 쓰고, 5시 이후로 지금도 계속해서 도착하고 있는 중이므로 '현재완료진행시제'를 쓴다.

22 이 글은 영화 촬영을 위한 장소 섭외가인 Danny Mehta가 아이슬란드의 국립공원을 소개하고 있다. 이 글로는 ② 'Danny가 얼마나 자주 아이슬란드를 방문하는지'에 답할 수 없다.

23 글의 내용상으로도 또한 (A), (B)의 조건으로도 ⓐ에는 '현재완료진행시제'가 들어가는 것이 적절하다.

24 답변으로 보아, 질문은 'Tsingy의 뾰족한 돌들과 같은 지형이 어떻게 생겨났는지'와 관련된다.

Lesson 2 (중간)

2회

01 ①	02 ④	03 ①	04 ②	05 ②	06 ④	07 ①
08 ⑤	09 ②	10 ④	11 ⑤	12 ②	13 ①	14 ②
15 ⑤	16 ③	17 ④	18 ⑤	19 ②	20 ⑤	21 ⑤
22 ②	23 ⓔis → are	24 ①	25 ④	26 ⑤		

01 independent와 ① ineffective의 in은 '부정'의 접두사이다.

02 get in the way of ~는 '~를 방해하다'라는 뜻이다.

03 (A) 여름방학까지 겨우 7일 남았다. (B) Sumi를 위한 깜짝 파티에 대해 무심코 밝히면 안 돼.

04 빈칸에는 '당신이 내 말을 오해했다'거나 '내 말은 그게 아니다' 또는 '내가 다시 설명하겠다' 등이 들어가야 하는데 ②'그게 바로 내 말이야'는 어색하다.

05 receive의 목적어로서, 형용사 large 뒤에 올 단어로 적합한 것은 ② package이다.

06 대답이 'I have been ~ing'이므로 질문도 'What have you been doing?'으로 물어보는 것이 적절하다.

07 be honored(영광이다)라는 표현 뒤에는 '이유, 원인'을

나타내는 '부사적 용법'의 to부정사가 와야 한다.

08 '내가 바이올린을 켜는 것'은 'for me to play the violin'이고, 이 '준동사구'를 목적어로 목적보어 possible을 쓸 때는 '가목적어 it'을 이용한 5형식 문장이 가장 적절하다.

09 사람의 성격을 나타내는 형용사가 오면 의미상의 주어 앞에 of를 쓴다.

10 양초가 소년을 잡는 것이 아니라, 소년이 양초를 잡는 것이므로, ④는 The boy isn't tall enough to grab the candles.로 고쳐야 한다.

11 ①→ I read the novel that she had written. ② If → Whether ③ the way와 how는 함께 쓸 수 없다. ④ 현재완료진행시제로 표현하려면 a year ago 앞에 since를 쓴다.

12 [(C) 지수야, 노르웨이에서는 여름에 해가 절대 지지 않는 거 알았어? (B) 아니, 흥미롭네 (D) 응, 어둡지 않아서 밤에 하이킹도 가고, 자전거도 타. (A) 나도 한밤중에 그러고 싶다. (E) 나도. 우리 언젠가 기회가 있기를 희망해.]의 순이다.

13 (A)에는 '기대하는 일에 대한 표현'이, (B)에는 '자신이 알고 있는 정보를 말하는 표현'이 들어가는 것이 적절하다.

14 ② A가 '새로 나온 3D 영화를 보고 싶니?'라고 말했는데, B는 '우리가 오스트레일리아의 Great Barrier Reef 부근에서 그것을 촬영했어.'라고 답하는 것은 흐름상 어색하다.

15 마지막 문장에, '실제로 컴퓨터 그래픽을 쓰지 않고 촬영했다'라고 했는데 ⑤는 'CG가 사용되었다'라고 쓰여 있다.

16 글의 흐름상 ⓒ good → harsh가 되어야 한다.

17 아들이 '열심히 공부해 왔다'고 했으므로, ⓓ '독도에 관해 공부를 열심히 했어야 했다'는 말은 어색하다.

18 이 글은 독도 여행을 앞둔 아들과 아버지의 대화로서, 아들의 독도 방문에 대한 부푼 기대감이 드러나 있으므로, ⑤가 가장 적절하다.

19 직업이 '장소 섭외가'이므로 ② '영화를 찍을 완벽한 장소들을 찾는 것'이 가장 적절하다.

20 ⓔ come true는 '실현되다'라는 뜻이다.

21 ⓐ → which 또는 that ⓑ will be → was ⓒ → After (Afterward는 부사이므로, 전치사 after를 써야 한다.)

22 Cappadocia를 소개하는 문장이므로, '굴뚝같이 생긴 바위들이 보이는지'를 묻는 질문에 대한 답변으로서 (B)에 위치하는 것이 가장 적절하다.

23 선행사가 colors로 복수이므로, ⓔis를 are로 고쳐야 한다.

24 '물 속의 화려한 식물들과 햇빛의 결합'이 강의 아름답게 혼합된 색깔을 더욱 생생하고 밝게 만든다고 했으므로, ①이 빈칸에 가장 적절하다.

25 ④ Madagascar 석림에 얼마나 많은 다른 종류의 동물들이 있는지는 본문에 나와 있지 않다.

26 각각을 어법에 맞게 고치면 ① → has been created ② → made ③ → for animals ④ → which이다. ⑤는 help의 목적보어 자리로서 jump 또는 to jump 둘 다 가능하다.

Lesson 3 (기말)

01 ①	02 ④	03 ⑤	04 ②	05 ①	06 ①	07 ②
08 ⑤	09 ①	10 ①	11 ③	12 ⑤		
13 had painted			14 ①	15 ①	16 ②	17 ③
18 ②	19 ⑤	20 ①	21 ②	22 ⑤	23 ④	24 ④
25 ③	26 ①					

01 <보기>의 단어들은 순서대로 release, independence, biography, detective이다. ① ruin의 뜻은 나와 있지 않다.

02 ④ 'Do you mind ~?'로 질문할 때, 'Of course not'은 '허락'의 의미이다. '앉아도 되나요?'라고 물었는데, 허락하는 대답과 함께 '모든 좌석이 다 찼다'고 말하는 것은 어색하다.

03 ⑤ 'make arrangement'는 '준비하다, 상의하다, 합의하다'라는 뜻이다.

04 'never use a flash'라는 표현으로 보아, '사진 촬영에 대한 허가'를 구하는 내용이다.

05 ①에는 that, 나머지에는 모두 if[If]가 들어가는 것이 적절하다.

06 주말에 뭐 했니? [(B) 한 달 전에 시작했던 세계사 책을 드디어 끝냈어. (A) 오, 재밌어? (D) 응, 우리가 아는 많은 역사 정보가 실제로는 틀린 것이래. (C) 정말? 나도 읽어봐야겠다.]의 순이다.

07 '지하철을 놓쳐서 회의에 늦었다'는 문장이므로, 지하철을 놓쳤다는 원인을 과거완료시제로, 그 결과 지각했다는 결과를 과거시제로 표현한 ②가 적절하다.

08 위 대화를 통해 '이태석 신부의 이야기가 남수단의 사회과목 교과서에 실릴 예정'이라는 것을 알 수 있다.

09 'if가 이끄는 명사절'은 '주어', '보어'로 사용될 수 없으며, if뒤에 or not이 바로 올 수 없다. ⓒ If → Whether

ⓓ if or not → whether or not ⓔ if → whether

10 (A) given → giving (D) filled of → filled with

11 '화가 나서 엄마에게 물어보는 내용'이므로, '엄마의 답변'이 나온 (C)에 들어가는 것이 가장 적절하다.

12 'If로 시작하는 명사절'이 '주어 자리'에 올 수 없다. ⑤ If를 Whether로 고쳐야 한다.

13 '누군가가 벽을 칠해서 냄새를 맡을 수 있었다'는 문장이며, 과거완료시제를 사용하는 것이므로 had painted가 적절하다.

14 위 글에서는 '1920년대 부유한 가정의 일상 생활이 무엇이었는지' 알 수 없다.

15 [(A) 서 씨와 결혼하기로 함 (D) 서 씨 가족이 돈을 좀 보내줌 (B) 아버지가 장롱 살 돈을 가져가 버림 (C) 큰어머니의 낡은 장롱을 결혼식 날 가져감]의 순이다.

16 marry는 '타동사'로서, 전치사 없이 바로 뒤에 목적어를 쓴다. ② marry with → marry로 고쳐야 한다.

17 '결혼 첫날부터 남편 집에서의 삶이 힘겨웠다'는 내용으로 미뤄 '속상하고, 화가 났을 것(upset)'이다.

18 ②는 나의 아버지에 대한 진실을 알려준 '아버지 친구'이다. 나머지는 모두 '나의 아버지'를 가리킨다.

19 '아버지가 만주의 독립 운동가들에게 얼마나 많은 가족의 돈을 보냈는지'는 답할 수 없다.

20 '빈손으로 간 나에게 아버지가 소리를 질렀다'는 내용으로 ① '필자가 아버지에게 돈을 가져다주지 않았다'가 일치한다.

21 ⓐ calling → called ⓒ have seen → saw
ⓓ be → being ⓔ what → that

22 [(D) 아버지 친구가 찾아옴 (B) 아버지에 대한 안 좋은 기억 떠오름 (A) 부유했으나 도박으로 탕진 (E) 엄마가 나를 도박장에 보내며 돈 없다 함 (C) 빈손인 내게 소리지름]의 순이다.

23 아버지에 대한 좋은 기억이 없었기 때문에, 낯선 남자가 아버지에 관해 말하며 찾아왔을 때, '실망스런 소식'을 예상했다.

24 ④의 if는 조건의 '부사절 접속사'이다. 다른 문장들과 (A)에 쓰인 if는 모두 '명사절'을 이끄는 접속사이다.

25 <보기>는 아버지가 나에게 왜 빈손으로 왔냐고 소리지르는 것이므로, 엄마가 도박장으로 나를 보내며, 돈이 없다고 말씀드리라는 내용 바로 뒤 (C)에 들어가는 것이 가장 적절하다.

26 '결혼시키기로 결정했다(make an arrangement)'는 내용이다.

Lesson 3 (기말)

2회

01 ⑤ **02** ④ **03** ⑤ **04** ⑤
05 (1) I have been learning to play the flute for five months. (2) I couldn't open the door because I had left the key at school.
06 ③ **07** ① **08** ① **09** ② **10** ③ **11** ③ **12** ②
13 ③ **14** ② **15** ① **16** ②, ⑤ **17** ③ **18** ⑤
19 ③ **20** ⑤ **21** ⑤ **22** ① **23** ③ **24** ④ **25** ②
26 ⑤ **27** ① **28** ④

01 ① usage ② package ③ bondage ④ marriage 등으로 명사를 만들 수 있는데, ⑤ inspire의 명사형은 inspiration이다.

02 '국가가 자주성(independence)이 없다면, 타국에 의해 지배될 수 있다'는 내용이다.

03 이 글은 '이태석 신부가 남수단의 어린이들을 도운 내용이 수단의 사회 교과서에 실릴 것'이라는 내용이며, '그가 어느 나라에서 공부했는지'는 알 수 없다.

04 ①~④는 '동사:명사' 관계이지만, ⑤는 '형용사:명사' 관계이다.

05 (1) '5개월 전에 플루트 연주를 배우기 시작해서, 지금도 하는 것'이므로 '현재완료진행시제'를 쓴다. (2) '문을 열 수 없었는데, 학교에 열쇠를 두고 왔기 때문'이므로, because절에 과거완료시제를 활용하는 것이 적절하다.

06 박물관에 가방을 들고 들어갈 수 없다고 하자 '물병은 가져갈 수 있는지'(①, ②) 또는 '사진을 찍어도 되는지'(④, ⑤) 허가를 구하는 내용이 빈칸에 들어간다. 대답이 Yes이고, 내용상 허가하는 것이므로, ③은 안 된다. 'Do you mind'로 묻는 질문은 '허가'할 때, No라고 해야 하기 때문이다.

07 (A) which → in which 또는 when (C) that → which (D) has → had (F) have → had

08 'It is said that'은 'People[They] say that', 'I've heard that' 등으로 바꿀 수 있다.

09 Mark, 이태석 신부 알아? [(B) 응, 왜? (D) 이 기사 봐. 수단 사회 교과서에 그가 실릴 거래. (C) 와, 잘됐다. (E) 응. 아이들을 돕고 병원과 학교 설립한 이야기가 들어간대. (A) 학생들이 그런 훌륭한 인물을 배우게 된다니 좋아.]의 순이다.

10 ③ '명사절'을 이끄는 '접속사' if는 바로 뒤에 or not을 쓰지 않는다. if or not을 whether or not으로 고쳐야 한다.

11 (A) the way와 how는 둘 중 하나만 쓴다. (C) That →

What (E) follow → to follow

12 아버지에 대한 안 좋은 기억 때문에 '행복한' 소식을 기대한다는 것은 어색하다. '불행한' 또는 '실망스러운'이 적절하다.

13 아버지가 도박꾼 행세를 하며, 만주의 독립 운동가들을 비밀리에 지원하셨음 [(B) 처음엔 믿을 수 없었음 (C) 그러나 진실을 알고 내가 그를 오해했다고 깨닫게 됨 (A) 그 이후, 독립 운동에 생을 바친 파락호의 딸인 것에 대해 자부심을 갖게 됨]의 순이다.

14 내용상 '~에 익숙하다'는 것이며, '~로 불리는 것'에 익숙한 것이므로, 전치사 to 뒤에 동명사 'being called'가 적절하다.

15 '~인지'를 뜻하는 명사절 접속사 if 또는 whether가 적절하다. if or not은 쓸 수 없으며, whether or not은 가능하다.

16 ② 서 씨네 집에서 장롱을 사라고 돈을 보냈다. ⑤ 필자의 아버지는 만주의 독립 운동가들에게 돈을 보냈다.

17 각각 ⓐ for ⓑ such ⓒ behind ⓓ to가 들어간다.

18 '처음에는 그가 진실을 말하는지 확신할 수 없었다'는 문장이므로, '아버지가 비밀리에 독립 운동가들을 지원하고 있었다는 내용'의 뒤, '나중에 진실을 알고 아버지에 대해 오해하고 있었음을 깨닫는 내용'의 앞에 위치하는 것이 적절하다.

19 '~할 때마다'의 뜻을 가진 단어가 적절하다.

20 gamble away money: 도박으로 돈을 날리다
ask for: 요구하다
yell at: ~에게 소리지르다, 호통치다

21 이 글로는 '낯선 남자가 언제 필자에게 필자의 아버지에 대한 이야기를 했는지' 알 수 없다.

22 (A)와 (B) 모두 과거완료시제 '능동'이 들어간다. 특히 (B)는 힘들었던 과거를 기준으로 그 이전인 결혼 첫날 이후부터를 가리키는 '기간'을 뜻하기 때문에 과거완료시제를 써야 한다.

23 (C)는 아버지가 저지른 '끔찍한(horrible)' 일을 가리킨다.

24 (B) 결혼 전 날
(D) 부끄러운 '사건'이므로 embarrassing

25 아버지가 비밀리에 스스로를 도박꾼으로 위장하고, 돈을 만주의 독립 운동가들에게 보냈다는 말을 듣고, 처음에는 믿을 수 없었지만 나중에 진실을 알고, 그에 대해 오해했다는 내용이다. ② '처음엔 확신했다'라는 표현은 흐름상 어색하다.

26 사실, 필자의 아버지는 남들의 눈에 비친 것과 같은 도박꾼이 아니라, 만주에 있는 많은 독립투사들과 다름없는 독립투사였다. ⑤ 필자가 아버지의 친구를 전에 만난 적은 없다.

27 '결혼 풍습의 일부로, 시대에서 장롱 살 돈을 보냈다'는 문장이므로, '결혼하기로 약속이 되었다는 내용'과 '결혼 전날 엄마가 아버지가 장롱 살 돈을 가져가 버린 것을 말하는 내용'의 사이인 (A)에 들어가는 것이 가장 적절하다.

28 ④ What → How로 고쳐야 한다. '아버지가 딸의 장롱 살 돈까지 가져가서 큰어머니네 낡은 장롱을 혼수로 해 간 일'은 'How embarrassing (the event was) for the family.' 또는, 'What an embarrassing event (it was) for the family.'로 표현할 수 있다.

Lesson 4 (기말) 1회

01 ① **02** ② **03** ⓐ played ⓑ left ⓒ exciting
04 ④ **05** ② **06** ③ **07** ④ **08** ④
09 (1) What they say is hard to believe.
(2) I like his drum made out of garbage.
(3) Einstein considered it fun to solve math problems.
(4) The jungle is a wonderful place for animals to live in.
10 ③ **11** ③ **12** ① **13** ③ **14** ④ **15** ④, ⑤
16 ⑤ **17** played, bring **18** ④ **19** ⑤ **20** ①
21 ④ **22** ③ **23** ② **24** ③ **25** ① **26** ⑤ **27** ③

01 ①은 동사 뒤에 -al을 붙여서 명사로 만들었다. ②~⑤는 명사 뒤에 -al을 붙여서 형용사로 만들었다. ③ musical은 명사, 형용사 둘 다 쓸 수 있다.

02 메시지를 보내기 전에 실수하지 않으려면, ② 검토(review)해야 한다.

03 ⓐ ~에 의해 연기되는(played by) ⓑ 한 장 더 남은(have one more ticket left) ⓒ 흥미진진한(exciting)

04 계획을 물어본 것이므로 그에 맞게 답해야 한다. ④ '아직 그것에 대해 생각 중이야'가 가장 적절하다.

05 (B) 뭐 하고 있어? - 음악 축제 프로그램 보는 중이야. (C) 축제에 갈 거야? - 응. 올해는 매우 특별해. (A) 언제 시작하는데? - 이번 주말에 시작이야.

06 ① interesting → interested ② rung → ringing
④ sung → singing ⑤ making → made

07 'TV 화면에 녹화된 내 자신의 모습을 볼 수 있었다는 것'이므로, ④ recording → recorded로 고치는 것이 적절하다.

08 (A) 드럼을 연주하는(beating) 남자 (B) 유명 사진작가

에 의해 촬영된(taken) 사진들

09 (1) That → What (2) making → made
(3) solve → to solve (4) of animals → for animals

10 (A) ~라고 불리는(called) (B) ~에 살고 있는(living)

11 피아노 독주회를 관람할 때는 연주자의 손동작을 볼 수 있는 왼쪽 좌석이 가장 좋다.

12 (A) work on ~: ~의 일을 하다
(B) add A to ~: ~에 A를 더하다
(C) put one's heart into ~: ~에 정열을 쏟다

13 부정부사 Not only가 문두에 나왔으므로, 의문문 형식의 '도치 표현'이 적절하다.

14 Favio Chávez가 본 아이들은 쓰레기로 가득 차 있는 마을에 살고 있었다.

15 ⓓ useful → worthless
ⓔ matters → doesn't matter

16 (A)는 버려진 물건을 악기로 '활용'할 수 있다는 것이므로, ⑤ '의미있게 쓰일 수 있다'이다. ④로 착각해서는 안 된다.

17 재활용된 악기들로 연주된(played) 음악, bring A to one's attention: A를 사람이 주목하게 하다

18 ⓓ bright side: 밝은[긍정적인] 측면

19 내용상 '그 곡을 듣는 것'이 도움이 된다는 것을 알았다는 것이므로 'to부정사구가 진목적어'인 가목적어 it이 와야 한다.

20 (A) 주어가 thing이므로 단수 동사가 와야 한다. (B) 'spend money on ~': ~에 돈을 쓰다 (C) '~을 통해'는 전치사 through로 표현하는 것이 적절하다.

21 문장의 구조상 ①, ③, ⑤의 it은 가목적어이므로, 'it is'에서 is는 삭제해야 한다. ② worthless → possible

22 내용상 '악기를 연주하는 데 마음을 쏟아붓는 한'의 의미가 되므로, 'as long as(~하는 한)'가 적절하다.

23 -thing으로 끝나는 부정대명사는 형용사가 뒤에서 수식한다. ② worthless something → something worthless가 적절하다.

24 콘서트 티켓 앞면이 아니라 뒷면에 쓰여진 문구를 알 수 있다.

25 Favio의 답변 내용으로 미루어 보아, Lucy의 질문은 ① '왜 정크 오케스트라를 시작했나요?'가 적절하다.

26 ⓔ shocked → was shocked

27 'I was eager to find out'으로 보아, 처음엔 호기심(curious)이었으나, 연주가 시작된 후 '음악에 심취하게 되었다'는 내용을 통해 감동을 받은(touched) 것을 알 수 있다.

Lesson 4 (기말)

2회

01 ⑤	02 ①	03 ②	04 ②	05 ④	06 ⑤	07 ③
08 ①	09 ④	10 ①, ⑤		11 ③	12 ④	13 ①
14 ②	15 ③	16 ③	17 ④	18 ⑤	19 ③	20 ②
21 ④	22 ②	23 ⑤	24 ②	25 ①	26 ④	27 ③
28 (C) so (D) that		29 ①				

01 빈칸 (E)에 careless를 넣으면 내용이 이상해진다. 내용상 asleep 또는 awake 등으로 '반쯤 잠든[깬]'이 적절하다.

02 첫 번째 문장의 빈칸에는 가주어 It이, 두 번째 문장의 빈칸에는 가목적어 it이 들어가는 것이 적절하다.

03 ② 여자는 아마 2층에서 콘서트를 볼 것이다.

04 W의 답변 내용으로 보아 (A)에는 '합창단에서 노래하는 것이 좋은지'를 묻는 내용이 들어가는 것이 가장 적절하다.

05 '세계적으로 유명한 그 가수는 전적으로 한국어로 노래한다.'는 말이다. 형용사 entire를 부사 entirely로 고쳐야 한다.

06 장기자랑에서 Megan이 바이올린으로 K-pop을 연주하겠다고 했으므로 ⑤ '무슨 악기가 쓰일 것인가?'에 대답할 수 있다.

07 ① more help → more helpful ② hardly → hard
④ excited → exciting ⑤ easily → easy

08 ② '몹시 쉬운 일이다.' ③ '연습이 완벽을 만든다.' ④ '부지런한 새가 벌레를 잡는다.' ⑤ '백짓장도 맞들면 낫다.'

09 ④는 '가목적어' it과 '진목적어'인 to부정사구가 쓰이는 문장이다. write를 to write로 고치는 것이 적절하다.

10 명사의 뒤에서 수식하는 현재분사를 찾는 문제이다. ②, ③, ④는 동명사이다.

11 위 글로는 ③ '평소 Lisa가 어떤 장르의 음악을 듣는지'에 대해 대답할 수 없다.

12 '고통 없이는 얻는 것도 없다.'라는 속담은 ④ '힘든 수고의 끝에 기쁨 또는 보상이 찾아온다.'라는 의미이다.

13 Anthony는 Jisu가 2층의 좌석을 구입하도록 제안(suggest)하는데, 다른 좌석들보다(than) 악기들의 소리를 더 잘(better) 들을 수 있기 때문이다.

14 다른 표현들은 모두 '콘서트에 갈 예정인지'를 묻는데, ②는 '콘서트에 갈 수 있게 도와줄 것인지'를 정중하게 부탁한다.

15 ⓐ 2형식 동사 sound 뒤에 형용사 보어를 쓴다. ⓑ '연주하는'은 playing이다. ⓒ 명사절을 이끄는 접속사 자

리이다.

16 [(B) 악기 소리가 궁금했다. (A) 연주가 시작되고, 깊은 소리에 충격을 받았다. (C) 음악에 심취하게 되었다.]의 순이다.

17 '감동받았다'는 뜻의 touched라는 표현으로 보아, 같은 의미인 moved가 적절하다.

18 쓰레기로 악기를 만든 이유를 물었으므로, '한 사람의 쓰레기는 다른 누군가에게 유용할 수 있다'가 가장 적절하다.

19 흐름상 '가치 없는 것'도 좋은 음악을 만들 수 있다는 내용이므로 ③을 'even something worthless'로 고쳐야 한다.

20 <보기>의 단어들을 알맞게 배열하면, 'I was eager to add something positive to their lives.'가 된다.

21 ⓐ에는 conductor(지휘자)가 들어가며, 알맞은 영영풀이는 ④ '합창단이나 오케스트라 앞에서 연주를 지휘하는 사람'이다.

22 글의 내용으로 보아 재활용품으로 만든 악기들을 사용하는 오케스트라이므로, ② '정크 오케스트라'가 가장 적절하다.

23 처음에는 호기심으로 공연을 관람하기 시작했으나, 이내 음악에 심취하게 되었다는 내용으로 보아 ⑤가 일치한다.

24 ⓑ 'was given'은 '받았다'는 의미이므로, ②가 어색하다.

25 위 글은 쓰레기를 악기로 재활용하여 가난한 마을의 어린이들이 오케스트라를 통해 감동을 주는 음악을 연주할 수 있게 되었다는 내용이므로, 'The Junk Orchestra'가 제목으로 가장 적절하다.

26 간접의문문이고, sound를 받고 있으므로, what kinds가 아닌 what kind of sound가 문두에 오는 ④가 적절하다.

27 (B) 소리에 충격받은(shocked)
(E) 재활용된(recycled) 재료들

28 '너무 ~해서, 그 결과 ~하다'를 표현할 때, so ~ that을 쓴다.

29 처음에는 쓰레기로 만들어진 악기 소리가 이상할 것이라고 생각했지만, 연주가 시작되고 깊은 소리에 놀란 후 음악에 심취해서 재활용된 재료들로 만들어진 악기로 연주 중인 것조차 잊었다고 했으므로, 'moved'(감동받은)가 가장 적절하다.